A N

MARK HUSSEY, Distinguished Professor of English Emeritus at Pace University in New York City, is best known for his decades of work on Virginia Woolf and Bloomsbury. Born in London, he moved to the US in 1982 and worked at the Association of American Publishers and the Sander Gallery in Soho.

Mark is General Editor of the Harcourt Annotated Editions of the works of Virginia Woolf, an editorial board member of the Cambridge Edition of Woolf, co-editor of *Virginia Woolf Miscellany* and founding editor of *Woolf Studies Annual*. His most recent book is *Modernism's Print Cultures*, with Faye Hammill. He is the recipient of a National Endowment for the Humanities Faculty Fellowship for his work on this biography of Clive Bell. Mark lives in Nyack, New York.

CLIVE BELL AND THE MAKING OF MODERNISM

A Biography

Mark Hussey

BLOOMSBURY PUBLISHING

LONDON • OXFORD • NEW YORK • NEW DELHI • SYDNEY

BLOOMSBURY PUBLISHING
Bloomsbury Publishing Plc
50 Bedford Square, London, WC1B 3DP, UK
29 Earlsfort Terrace, Dublin 2, Ireland

BLOOMSBURY, BLOOMSBURY PUBLISHING and the Diana logo are trademarks
of Bloomsbury Publishing Plc

First published in Great Britain 2021
This edition published 2022

A catalogue record for this book is available from the British Library

Library of Congress Cataloguing-in-Publication data has been applied for

ISBN: HB: 978-1-4088-9444-6; PB: 978-1-4088-9441-5; EPDF: 978-1-5266-4285-1;
EBOOK: 978-1-4088-9443-9

2 4 6 8 10 9 7 5 3 1

Typeset by Newgen KnowledgeWorks Pvt. Ltd., Chennai, India
Printed and bound in Great Britain by CPI Group (UK) Ltd, Croydon CR0 4YY

To find out more about our authors and books visit www.bloomsbury.com
and sign up for our newsletters

Contents

Preface

Millions of people every year walk through the main entrance and up the grand staircase of London's National Gallery, just off Trafalgar Square, but few pause to identify the figures in the floor mosaics that decorate the vestibules and halfway landing. If they did, some might recognise the ballerina Margot Fonteyn, portraying 'Delectation', many might see that Winston Churchill represents 'Defiance' and some would know that it is Virginia Woolf on whom the mosaicist, Boris Anrep, modelled Clio, the Muse of History. But how many could identify the figure of Bacchus as Clive Bell, Woolf's brother-in-law, and, in his lifetime, an internationally known and respected writer on art? Even an avid reader of the hundreds of articles and biographies about the 'Bloomsbury Group' knows Bell only as a sort of stock character, a red-faced *bon vivant* who escaped his provincial huntin', shootin' and fishin' upbringing in a nouveau-riche Wiltshire mansion by going up to Trinity College, Cambridge, where he met Thoby Stephen, Leonard Woolf and Lytton Strachey. Such a reader might also know that he later discovered the café life of artists and writers in Paris at the turn of the century, which prepared him to respond positively when Roger Fry invited him to assist in mounting an exhibition of 'post-Impressionist' painting in London in 1910.

For decades, Clive Bell has been refracted through the voluminous commentary on Bloomsbury, leaving a distorted and incomplete image of him that this biography replaces with a more accurate view. Clearing away the accumulated layers of received opinion, this is a work of archaeology, digging down to reveal the tesserae that constitute the mosaic of a life more complex, more nuanced and more sympathetic than that ossified in Lytton Strachey's witty barbs or Woolf's arch mockery. Although I do not avoid those aspects of Bell's character and behaviour that might cause a reader to cringe, I also correct inaccuracies, such as the claim by a recent biographer that Woolf 'always disliked and distrusted' Bell.

Clive Bell's groundbreaking book *Art* remained in print for fifty years. Brazenly bending the narratives of art history to his purpose, Bell offered baffled English viewers of works by Gauguin, Van Gogh, Picasso and Matisse a way to place them in the tradition which those artists were mistakenly thought to have rejected. When the painters were called 'insane', 'bolsheviks' or 'charlatans', Bell was on the barricades defending them, thereby earning grateful letters throughout his life from young artists and writers for the courage his words had given them to follow their own vision of what art could be. His credo was individual freedom, whether that meant the freedom to make art as one saw fit, to make love to whom one wanted or to say no when the government demanded that one sacrifice one's life for a cause that seemed to be a lie. Before and during the First World War, Bell was a bravely outspoken pacifist, a conviction he grimly held on to despite the tyrannies of the 1930s and a very different global conflict.

For Bell, a society's response to unfamiliar art offered eloquent testimony of its broader views on liberty. In addition to his writings on art, Bell spent his life resisting what he characterised as 'the steady transformation of Puritan prejudice into middle-class opinion'. A schoolboy when the British establishment crushed the rebellious spirit of Oscar Wilde in 1895, Bell lived his life in the service of a Wildean creed of sexual and personal freedom and disdained the notion that art must serve any purpose other than an aesthetic one. Bell was a faithful evangelist for modern art, prescient in his emphasis on the collaborative nature of perception and scathing about the habit of the wealthy to acquire works of art not because they like them but because they bestow prestige. He was thoroughly cosmopolitan and therefore suspect in the opinion of those who adhere to that persistent deep strain of antipathy in England towards anything from across the Channel.

His friends often remarked that what was most memorable about being in Bell's company was his conversation, but any traces of it which remain in letters or diaries are now so faded as to be hardly visible. As Virginia Woolf wrote, even the most interesting and important talk 'is as elusive as smoke'. This biography depends entirely upon an incomplete written record, and who can say what has been lost in the course of more than a century, a century that witnessed the two most destructive wars in all of human history? Bell seems to have kept every note, card or letter he ever received, but those he sent to others have not often found such dogged hoarders. I have refrained from speculation or invention and tried to strike a reasonable balance between Hilary Spurling's admonition to biographers 'to leave no stone unturned, and above all to turn stones over where no one has looked before', and Henry James' acknowledgement that 'relations stop nowhere, and the exquisite problem of the artist is eternally but to draw . . . the circle within which they shall happily appear to do so.'

Unlike so many of his celebrated peers, Clive Bell left no reflections on his own life. Even in *Old Friends*, the memoir he created largely by reprinting articles he had written about other people, he is most visible as an expansive host, a gregarious pleasure-seeker whose greatest enjoyment derived from sharing with others his loves, his company, his table, his tastes and, above all, what he felt when he looked at a Cézanne, a Picasso, an early Derain, a Pasmore, a Hitchens or a Grant. A year after Bell's death, the critic Herbert Read wrote a suitable epitaph: 'I prefer to remember him as an officer in the kingdom of the mind, not caring too much for discipline, encouraging insubordination, eager to share his riches with anyone who would knock at his door.'

Like Kant, Bell believed that the potential for responding to art with a 'peculiar' emotion is an important aspect of what makes us human. He was 'the right man in the right place' at a momentous time in the history of art. This biography allows Bell to step out of the shadow cast by Bloomsbury, although it also acknowledges that, as Christopher Reed has explained, 'the group continues to stand for something that threatens established beliefs', and Clive Bell was very much part of that.

I
BECOMING CLIVE
(1881–1907)

1. Beginnings

Arthur Clive Heward Bell ended a letter to his eight-year-old sister Dorothy with a cartoon of a man holding a whip, towards whom a fox is running. 'Mr. R B – – S in trouble again,' the fourteen-year-old Marlborough schoolboy captioned his drawing: 'Mr. B having been unhorsed early in the run tries to get home by a short cut trusting that his horse will turn up sometime. On his way home he has a somewhat embarrassing meeting with the hunted fox.'

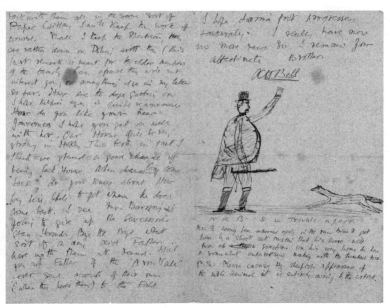

Letter to Dorothy Bell from Clive, 1 February 1895

Bell was introduced early to a world of guns, hunting, dogs and game. The third child in his family, he was born on 16 September 1881 in East Shefford, Berkshire. Two years later, his father, William Heward Bell, bought a property in the village of Seend in Wiltshire but promptly had much of the house pulled down to rebuild it on a grander scale over the next decade. Cleeve House was strewn with copies of *The Field*, the *Live Stock Journal* and *Punch*. Snapshots of ponies and dogs filled entire albums and, overlooking the great hall, a gigantic moosehead, bagged by Mr Bell in Canada, complemented the smaller trophies of English bloodsports which lined the walls beneath the minstrels' gallery. The Bell family crest adorned a rather baronial entranceway.

In marrying Hannah Taylor Cory in 1874, William Heward Bell cemented his relations with the firm of Nixon, Taylor, and Cory, a large coal-shipping concern and colliery owner based in Cardiff, where Hannah's father was a partner; William Bell's uncle, John Nixon, founded the company. William's paternal grandfather had been awarded patents in 1846 and 1852 for 'improvements in working in coal mines', but by 1857 he was in the Durham debtors' prison. The Bells seem to have started as small farmers in the Cheviots, struggling until they eventually found success and wealth in coal. Both of Bell's parents, William and Hannah, could trace their families' roots to at least the early 1600s, but the story that 'Heward' – borne as a middle name by several generations of Bell men – was a variant indicating their descent from Hereward the Wake, the eleventh-century leader of English resistance to the Norman conqueror, is almost certainly apocryphal. The nearest the family had come to any kind of fame by the end of the nineteenth century was through Hannah's sister Minnie's marriage in 1876 to Harry Liddell, whose sister Alice inspired Lewis Carroll.

There was little life of the imagination at Cleeve House, however. William Bell became a director of Nixon, Taylor, and Cory in 1901 and the family grew rich through owning coalmines throughout South Wales, in Mountain Ash and Merthyr Vale. By the time Arthur Clive Heward was born, William and Hannah had a son, Cory Heward (b. 1875), and daughter, Lorna (b. 1877), and were successfully established in their provincial world, where William dispensed charity and dabbled as an antiquary. He rode with the Avon Vale hunt, followed the Savernake Stag Hounds and was a first-class shot who regularly took a comfortable lodge in the Scottish Highlands for the season. His grandson Quentin

Clive's parents, William Heward Bell and Hannah Taylor Cory

recalled him as 'an angry little man who shouted at people, and a hypocrite who kept up a pretence of religion'. Of his four children, only Arthur – as he was known to family and friends – would seek to expand his horizons beyond the rather Trollopesque life maintained by his father at Cleeve House.

After prep school at Waynflete, about forty miles from Seend, Bell entered Marlborough College in January 1895. Like many of his and later generations who went on to be writers, he hated his public school. The surviving notebooks of his juvenilia are filled with sentimental love poetry and mockery of athletes and 'swells' (rich boys who disdained both learning and sports). Speaking on the BBC in 1945, Bell described his earliest aesthetic experience at school as occurring not in the classroom but while out fishing. Reading Keats' sonnet 'Bright Star!' had suddenly taken him out of himself in what he recognised was an 'aesthetic' experience. He had had no such response when his parents took him to the National Gallery, although they remarked on his 'peculiar interest' in its contents. Keats' 'moving waters at their priest-like task' had awakened in the schoolboy Bell a sense that his unique sensibility afforded him moments of transcendence.

One summer afternoon, a few weeks before he went up to Cambridge in 1899, Bell was playing tennis on the courts his father had built at Cleeve House, observed by his neighbour Mrs Raven-Hill, wife of the *Punch* cartoonist Leonard Raven-Hill. Raven-Hill had trained as a painter in Paris, had even shown some pictures at the Salon des Beaux Arts, but returned to England to become the art editor of *Pick-me-up*. In 1901, he was appointed junior political cartoonist at *Punch*, to whose editorial meeting in London he would travel every Wednesday. His pretty wife was the belle of the county balls but, for all her allure, Annie was thought by her many admirers to be unassailable.

When he went to the fence at the side of the court to retrieve some balls, Annie quietly complimented Arthur on his curls, making clear that she would not be averse to a visit from him. He soon rode over to the Raven-Hills' house at Bromham, where Annie did not resist his clumsy attempts to kiss her, nor his hurried unbuttoning and loosening of their clothes. The encounter lasted seconds, but the young man rode home in a state of glorious happiness, thrilled to feel the dampness of his shirt against his skin. He would turn eighteen that September, Annie

The Bell Family at Cleeve House (left to right. Lorna, Hannah Taylor Cory, Cory, Clive (seated), Dorothy, W. H. Bell)

was thirty-five; the affair would continue, with some interruptions, until 1914. Mrs Raven-Hill illuminated the dullness of Cleeve House, but in addition to sexual initiation, it seems likely that she gave Bell his first inkling of the world that existed across the Channel, in Paris.

Bell's son Quentin thought that the reproduction of a Degas – an artist almost unknown in England at the time – that his father took with him to Cambridge might have been a gift from his mistress.

The Hall, Cleeve House

2. Cambridge

It was inevitable that Bell and Julian Thoby Stephen would become friends when they went up to Trinity College, Cambridge, in autumn 1899. Thoby was a countryman at heart, despite having been brought up in London in the midst of England's intellectual aristocracy.

He was the eldest son of Leslie Stephen, a celebrated Victorian man of letters whose first wife had been Thackeray's daughter and who counted among his closest friends some of the most prominent novelists and intellectuals of the later nineteenth century, such as George Meredith and Henry James. Thoby's mother was descended from a family of famously beautiful sisters; she herself had modelled for paintings by Edward Burne-Jones and George Frederic Watts. Photographs of his elegantly attractive sisters, Vanessa and Virginia, adorned Thoby's mantelpiece. But he also loved to hunt and to walk among the hedgerows. A keen ornithologist, he decorated the endpapers of his Pindar with myriad deft sketches of birds; his letters were filled with anecdotes about fox hunts and beagling, badgers and horses. Virginia observed that the atmosphere of the countryside hung about her brother always, 'like the dew that collects in beads on a rough coat'. Although their families could hardly have been more different, Bell and Thoby Stephen were drawn together at once by their love of riding and of animals. As their friendship at Cambridge deepened, they discovered they also shared values of tolerance and a disdain for religion, as well as an interest in art. Thoby wrote home to Virginia about his 'astonishing' new friend: 'He's a sort of mixture between Shelley and a sporting country squire,' he told her – someone who continually spouted poetry yet also kept a couple of hunters in the stables.

Bell entered Trinity, one of the largest Cambridge colleges, with an 'exhibition' (scholarship) to read history, a subject which had only recently been deemed worthy of academic study at the university. We can glimpse something of Bell's outlook as a student from the marginalia in his textbooks. In H. Morse Stephens' *Revolutionary Europe, 1789–1815* (1900), for example, his notes praised Danton's efforts in the famous insurrection of 10 August 1792. He agreed with Stephens that the French were 'ready to strike a blow for political liberty' because 'Frenchmen had been in possession of a great measure of personal freedom', in comparison to a country like Germany, but took issue with Stephens' assertions about the French Revolution because they were based only on 'his own unbounded opinion of his own judgments'. Bell applauded Pitt's support of the American colonies in their resistance to British attempts to justify taxing them: Pitt today, he scribbled, 'would be called "A pro-American", "a little Englander", "an enemy of the country" and anti-English, and would probably be stoned in the streets of our great cities'.

Bell achieved a second class in Part I of the history tripos (course of study) in 1901, but his prose led one of the examiners, George Macaulay Trevelyan (great-nephew of the historian Thomas Babington Macaulay), to write to him several weeks before Part II. After praising Bell for his thinking 'and feeling' about religious toleration, Trevelyan took issue with his style:

> you must manage in the tripos to curb your <u>language</u> which often runs horrid riot . . . surely Macaulay's style is not characterized by 'voluptuous beauty' (that is Pater's or Rossetti's) – picturesque beauty is what you mean.
>
> Also your attack on America should be in a more chastened language and I think more <u>reasoned</u>. To say that their 'institutions are not worth 5 years purchase' is absurd; even if you take the worst possible view of their desirability – their <u>stability</u> is another thing. Also to say that 'American & English are not the same language' is just as absurd as to say that Cockney and English are not the same language.

While Trevelyan sympathised with Bell's views of Macaulay and of American institutions, he warned him that the 'violence' of his language had damaged his chances with the examiners even as they admired the 'force and vigour' of his feelings: 'Never use slang or colloquialisms in an exam.' In his subsequent career as a journalist and art critic, Bell would gleefully deploy just the kind of language his tutor warned against.

In his unofficial guide for new students, *The Freshman at Cambridge*, Evans Hugh cautioned against working too hard, disparaging the notion that getting a first-class in the tripos was the sole purpose of a student's time at the university: 'The all-round man who has many irons in the fire' will have many more opportunities than the 'smug' ('a quiet hard-working student' (OED)), he advised. None among those with whom Bell began to form his circle of friends were 'smugs', though several were quite brilliant. In the 1900 Lent term, a 'Midnight Society' including Lytton Strachey, Leonard Woolf, Saxon Sydney-Turner and A. J. Robertson began to meet on Saturdays in Bell's rooms to read and discuss plays. In time, the Midnight gave way to the 'X' Society, which met earlier in the day, with Thoby Stephen, Walter Lamb and D. S. Robertson joining in. By the end of their first year at Cambridge, several of the young men who would later be associated with that much-maligned and misunderstood assemblage, the Bloomsbury Group, had formed lifelong friendships.

For May Week in 1900, Thoby's sisters came up for the Trinity Ball where they met some of their brother's friends for the first time. Virginia wrote to her cousin Emma Vaughan that because they arrived late and Thoby did not know many people, they had not danced much; nevertheless, she had experienced her first ball. Leonard Woolf likened seeing Vanessa and Virginia Stephen for the first time to suddenly coming face to face 'with a great Rembrandt or Velasquez': they took one's breath away.

Their exclusion from the secret society at Cambridge known as the Apostles was another bond between Thoby Stephen and Bell. Belonging to the elite Conversazione Society, as the Apostles were formally known, created a homosocial family within the larger world of Cambridge, one which widened in the years after graduation as older members advocated for and selected new ones. Their relations were strengthened in secret meetings characterised by an exclusive and eccentric vocabulary, as well as by long discussions of friendship and love. Friends and relatives from the 'Phenomenal' world – as the brethren referred to the non-Apostolic realm – might often ask about the society, but 'against these intrusions, Lytton Strachey, Rupert Brooke, and Sydney-Turner remained firm'.

Leonard Woolf told his fellow Apostle Strachey early in 1903 that Thoby – whose solid appearance had earned from them the nickname 'The Goth' – should have been elected the previous year, but Thoby's lack of interest in the society had probably worked against him. Bell, however, was apparently not ever seriously considered. Ironically, despite his rejection, Bell's academic performance was very respectable in comparison to that of Woolf or Strachey. On the other hand, as W. C. Lubenow makes clear in his study of the society, Apostles 'were not supposed to conform to any single type; the Apostles wanted difference and variety in the Society'. Strachey, for example, was highly rated for his conversation, but although Bell was described by Thoby's sister Virginia as 'always ready to sacrifice himself in the cause of talk', it seems he was overlooked by the Apostles simply because he did not fit some secretly held, obscure criteria. During this time, the society was undergoing an Edwardian rebellion against Victorian mores under the influence of new 'Brethren' such as Strachey and John Maynard Keynes (who entered King's College in 1902). Every Easter, the philosopher G. E. Moore – whose book *Principia Ethica* marked for Lytton Strachey 'the beginning of the Age of Reason' in 1903 – hosted a reading party to which only Apostles were invited, further emphasising the boundary between them and those friends who did not belong. Some historians of Bloomsbury have maintained that Bell was 'wounded and bitter' about his exclusion from the Apostles, but there is nothing in the extant record to support this notion.

In the new year of 1905, Thoby Stephen walked from the New Forest to Hindhead in Surrey to see some Cambridge friends: 'There were there J. Pollock . . . Waterlow . . . Meredith . . . and old Bell,' he told Leonard Woolf. Most of the party were content to indulge in 'the old round' of talk about ' "what you mean by being" and so on'; Sydney Waterlow was 'a serious cove and devilish Cambridge', but eventually they all went to bed, 'leaving Bell and me who shout simultaneously "Now let's talk about hunting" '. To Desmond MacCarthy, whom Woolf described as Moore's 'favourite Apostle', Bell 'seemed to have a foot in two communities which, in the University, and indeed in the world itself, are separated from each other by as deep a trench as divides, say, Roman Catholics from the rest of mankind. He seemed to live, half with the rich sporting-set, and half with the intellectuals.'

When he first met Bell in November 1901, MacCarthy was travelling to Cambridge to visit G. E. Moore and feeling despondent. Only one other occupant shared his first-class compartment, 'a youth with a noticeable head of wavy auburn hair, and that milk-white skin which often goes with it'. MacCarthy observed that his companion was 'dressed with careless opulence', wearing 'flung open, a dark fur coat with a deep astrakhan collar'. Within ten minutes of talking with the ebullient Bell, MacCarthy's gloom had lifted and he had accepted an invitation to lunch the next day: 'I fancied myself to be enjoying, vicariously at any rate, through him, the prospect of helping myself in a generous manner to the pleasures of life . . . I could see in imagination the enormous rich hunk he was about to cut from the cake of life.' Throughout his life, many people remarked that Bell could not enjoy himself unless his friends were happy, that his social arts were perhaps his greatest gift.

Those with whom Bell associated most at Trinity stood out for their irreverence and free thinking. Religion was a matter for particular jocularity, leading a student named Arthur Gaye to tell Leonard Woolf he could no longer be his friend owing to the offensive nature of the conversation in Woolf's rooms. Strachey, said Gaye, was the worst offender. Bell found his new friends congenial after life at Cleeve House, where family and servants were summoned each morning to the breakfast room so that William Bell could read to them a passage from the Bible, while everyone knelt on the carpet. Although he disliked his irascible father, Bell cared about his genuinely pious mother, so he dutifully attended church services during vacations, putting his friend Edwin Montagu in mind of Captain Kettle.[1] Even at Cambridge, there was no escape from religious observance, although were a student artful enough he could make a case for 'conscientious objections'.

In 1904, Thoby Stephen addressed a pamphlet against compulsory chapel to the freshmen of Cambridge University because, 'I know that with you rests our chief hope of purging our Republic of bigotry and intolerance.' Bell himself had made 'a good and clear maiden speech' at

---

[1]Popularised in a series of stories by C. J. Sutcliffe Hyne in *Pearsons Magazine*, Captain Kettle is devout and devoted on land but a profane scoundrel at sea.

the Cambridge Union in November 1899 in support of the (defeated) motion 'That Disestablishment and Disendowment of the Church of England is the obvious and only satisfactory solution of the present difficulties'.

This speech had been followed by numerous others and Bell was soon known as a witty and entertaining speaker. Debating the motion 'That in the opinion of this House the increase of Trades Unionism is conducive to the best interests of the country', Bell spoke for the Nos 'like a Pied Piper'. He 'led the House dancing after him where he would, to South Wales and Piccadilly, and even, once or twice, to the outskirts of the subject of Trade Unionism. A welcome interlude.' But wit is not sufficient for a career and, as university friends dispersed after receiving their BA in 1902, Arthur Clive Heward Bell was uncertain that his future lay in the study of history.

In 1902, Bell was awarded the Earl of Derby studentship, which provided a stipend derived from the interest on £2,000, tenable for a year. He set about writing a fellowship dissertation on the 1822 Congress of Verona (held because the French king wanted the consent of his allies to invade Spain) and accordingly began research in the Public Record Office that autumn. He may, like Thoby, have been considering a career in law because he took rooms in the Inner Temple, at 6 King's Bench Walk. Thomas Greg, a barrister and family friend, guaranteed his bond for £140, telling Bell that his father would be very happy to see him a judge or even a King's Counsel.

From time to time, Bell went to Cambridge to see a play, or to see those of his friends still there trying to establish their futures, such as Woolf and Sydney-Turner who were preparing for the civil service exams. Whenever she had the opportunity, Annie Raven-Hill came to see him at King's Bench Walk. One afternoon, Sydney-Turner and Thoby hammered on his door, hoping to find some tea and conversation. Bell and Annie had been to see an exhibition of Dutch Old Masters at the Guildhall Art Gallery and were now enjoying a long afternoon in bed, so his friends left with no answer.

As Bell began his fellowship research, he continued also to give occasional lectures at the Working Men's College on Great Ormond Street. In May 1902, G. M. Trevelyan organised a weekend visit to Cambridge of forty students from the college, for which Bell was one of the hosts.

The reporter for the *Working Men's College Journal* remarked that when Trevelyan, splitting the men into groups, said, ' "Now will you Christs go away" ', the irreverence might have caused someone 'of a religious turn of mind and a stranger to University parlance' some disquiet, but it was all taken in good part. The men 'hugely enjoyed' hearing Queen Victoria referred to as ' "a good old girl" ' and chuckled at the notion that rather than being buried ' "she should have been stuffed and used as a perpetual sovereign" '. The report concluded:

> To men of the artizan [*sic*] class, like myself, who pass their lives in cities, amid the din of factories and the atmosphere of workshops, such a visit must necessarily be something of a revelation, for it gives one a peep into one phase of the intimate life of the men who are the leaders of thought and action in the world . . . if there is one thing which the average working man hates, it is to feel that he is being patronized. But there was not even a suspicion of 'side' about our hosts; dons and undergraduates alike were as genial and hearty as one could desire, and we felt at home with them at once.

Bell was one of several Trinity students who offered to share the benefits of their privileged education with the working men and seems to have had an easy rapport with them.

Louisa Gibson Blaikie was particularly interested to hear about Bell's talks to working men. Known to the Bell family as 'Louie', she was one of five daughters of Walter Biggar Blaikie, an engineer and printer who had returned to Edinburgh from India, where Louie had been born in 1877. Louie most likely met the Bell family in Scotland during summer holidays when they went to shoot in the Highlands. She had been friendly enough with Cory Bell for her mother to warn her to cease writing to him unless they intended to marry, but she kept up a correspondence with the elder of Bell's two sisters, Lorna. Louie's friendship with Bell probably began when she wrote in 1900 or 1901 to ask if he would mind showing her and some friends around Cambridge.

Only her side of their correspondence survives, but her letters reveal a close friendship whose conversations ranged widely over religion, literature, morality and philosophy, as well as aspirations and hopes for what their lives might become. Her letters also show that her younger correspondent recognised the constraints imposed on a middle-class woman by late Victorian society and engaged seriously with her views and opinions.

Bell made clear that he believed there should be no barriers of sex or class to what one read. Liberty of mind, unfettered by religion or by social or sexual taboos, was fundamental to his 'ideal'. Louie was eager to hear about Bell's talk on Henrik Ibsen, announced in the December 1902 *WMC Journal* for the next meeting of the Literary and Historical Society. Cory had told Louie he envied his brother's ability to get on so well with working men and, apart from her interest in his thinking and in the subject matter itself, she wanted to learn more about Bell's 'purely pagan point of view'. 'The more I see, of the capacities & temptations of the poor & ill-educated,' she told Arthur (as she always addressed him), 'the more amazed I stand at Christ's comprehension & programme.

Cory Bell in the uniform of the Royal Horse Artillery

And I want to understand your method too, or rather your manner of applying your ideal; for I think you have made me realise what that ideal is.'

Louie scanned the newspaper in June 1902 for a sign of Arthur's tripos result and wondered if he would attend the coronation of Edward VII that summer. The second Boer war, in which Cory fought as an officer in the Royal Horse Artillery, had ended in May, with Britain's reputation among European nations somewhat damaged: had Arthur not suggested, she later asked, that his brother had returned from the Transvaal 'almost a pro-Boer?'

Anti-German sentiment was strong in England at the turn of the century. When Thoby Stephen went to Germany after graduating from Cambridge, he reported from Freiburg that although sometimes 'rather nice', Germans were 'lower than beasts'. The Kaiser's infamous 'Kruger telegram' of 1896 congratulating the Boers for repelling a British raid, Bismarck's comment that 'South Africa would be the grave of the British Empire' (reported in the *Spectator* of 15 February 1902) and a popular genre of invasion literature initiated by *The Battle of Dorking* in 1897 all contributed to a caricature of Germans that informed even the views of those who had visited the country. From their education system to their conscripted military, the German passion for uniformity seemed to Thoby to stifle any creativity.

Soon after he returned, Thoby invited Bell to Lyndhurst in the New Forest where the Stephen family had taken a house. He wanted to disabuse his friend of the notion that modern Germany was still the land of Goethe and Heine, a conception he told Bell was as misguided as thinking that contemporary Greece was still the country of Homer and Sophocles.

3. A Brace of Partridges

His visit to the New Forest went well enough that Bell felt confident to call on Thoby's sisters in London with the gift of a brace of partridges. In what is probably her first letter to her future husband, Vanessa wrote:

> Dear Mr Bell I hope you are able to imagine the excitement and joy that your partridges have caused here, as I am quite unable to describe it. Thank you very much indeed for them . . . I really ought to thank you too for your Collins [thank you note] which was received with great applause and which ought to be shown as a model to all other visitors. I hope you will prove its sincerity by coming here again some day, in spite of death in the pony cart and the certainty of endless discussion of one subject.

The 'one subject' was painting. In 1900, Vanessa had been taken with Thoby to Paris during the Exposition Universelle by their half-brother George Duckworth, perhaps to distract her from an ill-considered involvement with her widowed brother-in-law, Jack Hills.[1] As her biographer recounts, Vanessa 'visited the Louvre for the first time and returned home ecstatic about the food she had eaten and still more about what she had seen'. Virginia warned George not to let her sister 'see too many improper studios – The artist's temperament is such a difficult thing to manage'. When she got back, Vanessa was 'quite

[1] Stella Duckworth, Vanessa's half-sister, had died suddenly in 1897 shortly after her marriage to John Waller 'Jack' Hills. Jack visited frequently thereafter and was comforted by Vanessa, who developed strong feelings for him.

intoxicated with all the things she has done and seen'. 'We shall talk and think of Paris for months to come I am sure,' Virginia told George.

Bell was in Paris in 1903, a visit that has been eclipsed by accounts of the momentous time he spent there the following year when he discovered the path the rest of his life would take. His earlier stay is dated by a letter from Thoby inquiring what people there were saying about the suicide of Sir Hector MacDonald, a Scots military hero who shot himself in a Paris hotel on 25 March 1903 rather than face a court martial over his sexual activities with Sinhalese boys while he was commander-in-chief of British troops in Ceylon. Along one side of his letter, Thoby scribbled, 'By the way, if you go to the Louvre, by any chance, remember this truth which I have just discovered – all painters without exception are sentimental, theatrical, extravagant.' The only things worth seeing there, Thoby continued, were the Greek sculptures, though the Louvre's examples were mostly 'late Hellenistic Roman'. Bantering with his friend, Thoby quoted Thomas Love Peacock's *Crotchet Castle*: 'Where the Greeks had modesty, we have cant. Where the Greeks had anything that exalts, delights or adorns humanity we have nothing but cant cant cant.'

'Cant' for the young Cambridge men of Thoby and Bell's generation, as Leonard Woolf recalled many decades later in his *Autobiography*, was their name for the Victorian 'religious and moral code' which they entered university prepared to rebel against. Leonard's example of this hypocritical code was the unjust condemnation of Alfred Dreyfus and, in 1903, Thoby told Bell that Hector MacDonald's death was 'an eternal disgrace to our blasted race of hypocrites'. Louie Blaikie was grateful when Bell told her that Parisians had shown 'kindness and self-restraint' when discussing with him the fate of a man the Scots believed had been hounded to death by the English.

It may have been on his 1903 visit to Paris that Bell picked up *The French Impressionists* by Camille Mauclair, which he inscribed with his customary signature, 'AC Heward Bell'. His copy bears the label of the Galignani Library, a bookshop on the rue de Rivoli specialising in English and American books. The English translation of Mauclair's book was brought out in 1903 by Thoby's half-brother Gerald Duckworth's publishing company. Another who read it was Thoby's sister Vanessa, who was 'converted . . . to modern art' by Mauclair's well-informed discussion of the Impressionist painters.

In Bell's copy, his underlinings and marginalia summarise without comment what Mauclair explained about the Impressionist painters' handling of light, colour and form. He underlined Mauclair's definition of Impressionism as '*a revolution of technique together with an attempt at expressing modernity*'. In 1903, it would have been possible for Bell to see examples of the work Mauclair discussed at the Musée du Luxembourg, where part of the painter Gustave Caillebotte's bequest to the French government of his collection of Impressionist works had been on public view since 1896. However, whenever Bell described his own conversion to modern art he placed it in 1904, so it cannot be said with certainty when he first entered the small room at the Luxembourg which held eight works by Monet, three by Sisley, eleven by Pissarro, one by Manet and two by Cézanne from Caillebotte's collection.

While Thoby hoped that Bell would visit the Louvre during his 1903 stay in Paris, Louie Blaikie urged him to hear mass at Saint-Sulpice – a suggestion he appears to have followed as she wrote to say, 'I know so well what jarred on you at Mass. I've felt it, but could not describe it, as you do.' They often argued about religion. Bell had given her a better understanding of Shelley's atheism, but his challenges to the proofs of Christianity seemed inadequate in the light of her own experience. Left alone in the country, Louie told him, she found his anti-religious ideology 'lofty & inspiring', but the realities of life with her large family in the city, 'with the perpetual calls on one's patience & love', forced her to rely on a 'less artistic & more personal religion' to help her endure it. Although it unsettled her to realise how much Bell valued their relationship, she was nourished by his respectful intellectual companionship and his willingness to share the benefits of his Cambridge education without patronising her. Her mother had already 'made a fuss' about her writing to his brother, so, if necessary, Cory could explain how difficult her life was, 'how little of my own way I'm allowed'. Her discussions with Bell about art and religion, Shelley and Ibsen, were 'oxygen' to her 'asphyxiated soul'.

More riskily, they had also written to each other about temptation, both painfully aware of the double standard that governed women's lives. In clarifying something Bell had been puzzled by, Louie once wrote: 'I was answering your letter, in which you thought I would sympathise with your struggles against temptation. My meaning was that I certainly did. It seems often, to me, that we girls, whose lives & actions are hedged round can only be pure or the reverse – in spirit. In spite of Ibsen, I can't be more explicit.'

In the social upheavals of 1890s England, Ibsen's domestic dramas had been regarded either as a symptom of that degeneration against which writers such as Max Nordau thundered, or as the heralds of a new honesty about bourgeois hypocrisy. For young people of Bell's generation, Ibsen provided a conduit for arguments on behalf of profound social change. Louie read what her friend had to say about Ibsen with 'much interest', but thought he was idealistic and that he probably had not yet had to face the necessity of masking his true feelings because of society's pressure to conform: 'You speak so easily of the horror of marriage where love has died, that I'm sure you can't realise what it means. The conventional mask that love lasts makes the commonplace pair jog on comfortably enough after the fire has died out . . . If you had to face it in your life without the mask I doubt if books will help.' She had few illusions about her own prospects: 'When I'm weary of my own life, I sometimes feel tempted to run away from it, into a more exciting atmosphere, through the only door which presents itself – marriage with a man I don't really love.'

Perhaps Bell had hinted at carnal 'temptations' to Louie, because early in 1903 she wrote that she knew 'how the noblest natures are tried by the hardest struggles with temptation', exhorting him ('Oh Arthur') 'by all that is highest & holiest' to keep his 'heart & character & powers pure . . . For you can reach up to that atmosphere of goodness which you call what?, & I call Heaven – the atmosphere pervaded by God & love & Holiness.' More freedom to talk openly about sexual matters was imminent in some parts of British society, but it is inconceivable that Bell would have confided in his devout friend about Annie Raven-Hill. Forty years later, Virginia Woolf would be able to note that brothers and sisters 'talk quite freely about – oh about everything. Sex, sodomy, periods, and so on', but there were no such confidences between her and Thoby in 1903: 'As for sex, he passed from childhood to boyhood, from boyhood to manhood under our eyes, in our presence, without saying a single word that could have been taken for a sign of what he was feeling.' It is tantalising to imagine what Bell might have shared with Louie about his sexual feelings, but had he alluded to anything less vague than generic 'temptations' it would have been remarkable.

Bell was no clearer in 1903 about what he wanted to do with his life than he had been when he left Cambridge. His research on the Congress of Verona was interrupted when his father took him to Alberta to hunt. They would return in time for Cory's wedding to Violet Bowley, daughter of an officer in the Royal Engineers. While travelling to Canada, Bell missed the deadline to apply for an assistant lectureship in history and political science at University College Cardiff for which a Trinity lecturer had recommended him, but he was in any case in no frame of mind to pick a career.

Some poems he had shown to Thomas Greg appeared to the older man to be 'the agonized & passionate wail of the entirely happy young man who fancies he is lacerated beyond recognition'. Just as Bell's schoolboy poems had been lovelorn and sentimental ('An ode to my darling, when my spirit is depressed' in 1896, for example), so at Trinity he had penned lachrymose verses to imaginary women ('The distant land I saw, with thee as wife,/Has wholly disappeared').

The Congress of Verona was not a gripping topic, but Bell had no alternative but to continue with his research. Louie understood his predicament. She knew that he had a 'horror' of a businessman's life but his family expected him to decide upon a career: 'You are two men in my mind – the poet, & the hard, level headed lawyer & politician. I've always heard of you as the latter, but my own knowledge of you is of the former – Who are you really?' Her question went to the heart of what many people who came to know him well would conclude, that Bell was a man who easily inhabited disparate worlds, yet seemed not entirely at home in any one of them.

Bell returned to King's Bench Walk after his brother's marriage in November 1903 and resumed the social round with his Cambridge friends. He often accompanied the prodigiously knowledgeable but alarmingly eccentric Sydney-Turner to a play or concert. Thoby urged him to come to Cambridge for the Greek play at the end of November, for which his younger brother Adrian (who had gone up to Trinity in 1902) could get them tickets. Bell had begun to realise that if his Derby sponsorship was to produce anything that would pass muster at Cambridge, he had to consult the French Archives Nationales for more of the relevant documents. Accordingly, he set off for Paris in the spring of 1904.

4. Paris

Bell brought with him a letter of introduction to the English painter Gerald Kelly, who had lived in Paris since 1901 and had already met Monet, Rodin, Sickert, Degas and Cézanne. Two years older than Bell, Kelly was at first too busy to see him, but on a wet afternoon in March, Bell made his way from his pension on rue de Bouquet de Longchamps to Kelly's studio. That night, Kelly took him to dinner in an upstairs room reserved for British and American artists, their friends and models at the Chat Blanc on rue d'Odessa.

In a memoir titled 'Paris 1904', Bell wrote that even before he arrived in Paris he knew he was not going to continue his historical research: 'Instead of wasting my time making futile pecks at a mass of . . . almost incomprehensible diplomatic correspondence, I would set myself the simpler task of learning French and seeing the sights.' His introduction to Kelly seemingly had nothing to do with an interest in painting; it was merely the friendly gesture of an acquaintance named E. S. P. Haynes doing what he could to make Bell feel less alone in a foreign city.

Despite his waning interest in the Congress of Verona, Bell's applications to consult records relevant to the Concert of Europe that emerged from the Napoleonic Wars continued to wend their way through the Affaires Etrangères office of the French government, supported by testimonials from Stanley Leathes, lecturer in modern history at Trinity, Lord Lansdowne and the British ambassador to France, Sir Edmund Monson. In June, the French Foreign Minister, Théophile Delcassé, approved his wish to consult 1820s correspondence between Turkey and England. By then, however, the direction of Bell's life had changed for good, and his 'research' was being conducted at the Louvre.

Kelly and Bell got on well at once, Bell sensing that the painter welcomed the opportunity to discuss books and ideas. After a quick trip home to Seend for Easter, Bell made his excuses at the pension and moved to the Hotel Loire, at the junction of the boulevard Raspail and boulevard Montparnasse, where he would stay until the middle of July. He had to acquire French as quickly as he could to keep up with the conversation at the Chat Blanc: despite most of the painters who gathered there being English speakers, many of them had French girlfriends. An increasing number of women artists – among them Kathleen Bruce and Eileen Gray – were studying in the area; they often lived alone 'without outraging public opinion'. James W. Morrice, a French-Canadian from a wealthy Montreal family who had already taken a law degree, was one of the first painters in this crowd to befriend Bell.

Bell arrived in Paris just as a profound revolution in art was starting, but until 1910 his visits to that city were marked by unfortunately timed departures and overlooked opportunities. His exposure to painters and painting in the spring of 1904 was unremarkable. Montparnasse was 'still the Paris of the Impressionists and the Naturalists', of Toulouse-Lautrec and Degas. Anatole France was still alive and Zola had been dead only a couple of years.

About six miles to the north, across the Seine, lay Montmartre, where the artists who would very soon explode the Parisian art world and utterly transform people's ways of seeing crowded into a warren of studios and cafés, including the building named the 'Bateau Lavoir' because it resembled a Seine washing boat. Pablo Picasso had first come from Catalonia in 1900, when he encountered at the Louvre the paintings of David, Ingres and Delacroix, as well as ancient Egyptian and Roman artefacts. In April 1904, word quickly spread among the Montmartrois artists that he had returned to Paris for a fourth time. In the stiflingly hot summer that followed, Matisse had his first one-man show at Ambroise Vollard's gallery on rue Laffitte, where Picasso had had his first Paris exhibition in 1901. Although Bell went to Montmartre – in his memoir *Old Friends* he describes taking the Odéon-Clichy horse omnibus there to visit Arnold Bennett – it left no mark in 1904. The route there led through the Luxembourg Gardens, near where he lunched at the Café de Fleurus on the street where Gertrude and Leo Stein lived, but in 1904 Bell knew nothing of Steins, Picasso or Matisse.

While Bell was in Paris, the Stephen siblings were in Italy. At Manorbier on the Pembrokeshire coast a week after their father's death in February 1904, the four of them had planned an Easter trip to Venice and Florence. That spring, Strachey was staying in Roquebrune on the south coast of France with his sister Dorothy, who had just married a French painter named Simon Bussy, an art school friend of Matisse. From the Bussys' house, La Souco, Strachey let Leonard Woolf know that he had proposed to Thoby they should meet up with Bell in Paris: 'The meeting will indeed be wonderful if it takes place. I suppose we'll all be arrested and lodged in the Bastille if it does.'

The 'grand meeting', he told Woolf a couple of weeks later, would not come off, but in the meantime Thoby had written to Bell from Venice about the possibility of calling on him in Paris on their way home from Italy. Never, he told his friend, had one seen a painting until one had been to Venice: 'Tintoret's supremacy is completely beyond a doubt.' In three long letters – one from Venice, two from Florence – Thoby conducted a fierce argument with Bell about the superiority of Tintoretto to Titian. He teasingly disparaged Bell's lack of experience, saying his friend's understanding of art must necessarily be limited because he had not yet seen Venice: 'My opinion of your general intelligence is such that I am convinced that had you visited the Scuola San Rocco and the Academia you could not have uttered those blasphemies against Tintoret with which your letter is defiled. Until a man has been there he has no more right to speak of painting than a man who has read neither Sophocles nor Shakespeare to criticize literature.' Theirs was a thoroughly nineteenth-century argument, closely following Ruskinian contours. In *The Stones of Venice*, Ruskin described the mind of Tintoretto as 'incomparably more deep and serious than that of Titian'. The friends argued about those painters found in Ruskin's pages: Titian, Tintoretto, Velasquez, Veronese, Bellini.

Thoby extolled not only a Tintoretto Madonna in the Accademia but Bellini's famous altarpiece in San Zacaria as revealing the 'ultimate point of the Catholic faith', which he explained to Bell was more Hellenic than Hebraic, which was to say more fleshly than sacred. Bell must have taken him up on this because when he next wrote, from Florence,

Thoby wryly wondered if Bell might not have confused Giovanni Bellini with his brother Gentile, or even with his father.

During the 1900 Easter term, Strachey had attended university extension lectures on Florentine art given by Roger Fry, whose first book, *Giovanni Bellini*, had been published the previous year. 'These are very interesting and good though somewhat abstruse,' Strachey told his mother. Fry had entered King's College in 1885 and had been elected to the Apostles in 1887. Although he had begun by studying the natural sciences, by the time Strachey attended his lectures, Fry was a well-respected expert on early Renaissance painting and a painter himself. Strachey and he had both been at an Easter vacation reading party on the Isle of Wight with other Apostles in 1902, where Strachey described him as 'a sort of art-critic'. Although it is possible Fry's name came up in conversations in Bell's rooms when Thoby was there, his ideas – for example, that Bellini was Titian's forerunner – left no trace in Bell and Thoby's correspondence in 1904.

Bell's opinions on art at the time can be inferred to some extent from Thoby's Italian letters, albeit filtered through their jocular tone. Bell's 'adulation' of Velasquez cannot be ascribed 'to mere intoxication of the marvels of the Prado', Thoby wrote, as he has never been to Spain, and his ranking of Titian above Tintoretto is only excusable until he is able to go to Venice. 'But I should have thought that even the limited knowledge of painting attainable in the Louvre would have enabled you to distinguish between diabolical dexterity and the grand style of the master.' In his next letter, Thoby is 'grieved' by his friend's having found 'so much ferocity' in the 'singularly temperate, restrained and direct exposition of my opinions'. Thoby was glad to learn that Bell admired 'the incomparable Mantegna', but disagreed with his opinions (whatever they may have been in 1904) of Bartolomeo or Correggio. Looking forward to arriving in Paris, Thoby closed the correspondence by urging Bell, as soon as he had the opportunity, 'to compare Michel Angelo's Thinker in the Medici Chapel with Rodin's Penseur if you want a complete education in the possibilities and limits of sculpture'. When Strachey saw a plaster version of *Le Penseur* in London earlier that year, he remarked to Leonard Woolf that it was 'rigid banks and heaps of muscle. The imagination of Michael Angelo was "spiritual" in some way that Rodin's isn't.'

Thoby and his sisters were in Paris by the beginning of May. 'Your little friend Bell is here,' Vanessa teased her art school friend 'Snow', Margery Snowden. Vanessa and Virginia stayed at the Hôtel Quai d'Orsay but Thoby lodged with Bell, who soon introduced them all to Gerald Kelly. Virginia told Violet Dickinson how they had taken Beatrice Thynne, a family friend who happened to be in Paris, to 'a real Bohemian party . . . and we all stayed talking of Art, Sculpture and Music till 11.30. This was all in the common café, while we smoked half a dozen cigarettes a piece.'

A week later, the Stephens were back in London, where Virginia immediately collapsed, exhausted and tormented by hallucinations. Violet took her to her house to be looked after by three hired nurses. Meanwhile, the exhilarated Vanessa wrote to thank Bell for his hospitality: 'We have been horrifying George with accounts of our doings at cafés & elsewhere – you must be prepared to keep it up & add local colour when you next see him. I hope you & Mr Kelly will some day drag yourselves away from the delights of Paris & will come & see us here & continue those arguments in spite of depressing London surroundings.'

Thoby continued to correspond with Bell about painting, asking in May if he knew 'one Blanche' whose 'uncommonly good' paintings he had seen at the New Gallery on Regent Street. The National Gallery now seemed to Thoby better than the Louvre, the French collection being filled with too much that was 'nugatory'. Thoby saw 'three good pictures' at Burlington House in June but the rest he considered 'merely filth'. He singled out a Watts 'which last horror', he joked, would be beyond Bell.

By mid-July, Bell was back in London, having just missed another Trinity man, Jack Pollock, in Paris, but telling him to use his name to gain admittance to the upper room at the Chat Blanc. As usual, letters from friends spoke of hunting, country walks and books. The Stephen siblings were getting ready to move to their new house at 46 Gordon Square; Woolf was studying for the civil service exams (in which he would do poorly), while Thoby was a hard-working law student.

Bell went back to Paris in late October 1904, unaware that the world he had been introduced to by Kelly was the 'scrag end of Impressionism'. Arnold Bennett was scornful of the insularity of the Montparnasse artists whose 'contented ignorance' kept them from the 'real life of the city in which they live'. If Bell visited the second Salon d'Automne, which ran from 15 October to 15 November, no comment of his on it has survived.

The Salon had begun in 1903 as an alternative for young painters to the Salon held by the conservative Société Nationale des Beaux-Arts and that of the Académie des Beaux-Arts. At the 1904 Salon d'Automne, Cézanne had a room in the Petit Palais devoted to his work. The Salon also included a special section of photographs of paintings and works by Matisse, Kees van Dongen, Othon Friesz, Francis Picabia and several others who would flourish in the modernist period. None of these names appears in Bell's correspondence at the time, his first mention of Matisse not occurring until 1908.

Bell could have been describing himself when he said that the painters who gathered at the Chat Blanc 'were anything but young lions: they were of the tame kind who worshipped Whistler and Velasquez, Rodin and Veronese, who went to the Louvre and paid their rent and read Wilde'. When he resumed dining at the Chat Blanc and drinking at the Café de Versailles that autumn, however, he encountered Roderic O'Conor, an Irish painter recently back from Brittany, who introduced him to another side of Paris. Bell had already frequented the Closerie des Lilas, where he listened to the Symbolist Jean Moréas declaim his poems and met Paul Fort, but he now began to hear from O'Conor about Guillaume Apollinaire and Max Jacob.

In Pont-Aven on the Brittany coast, O'Conor had become close to Gauguin, whose drawings, as well as photographs of his paintings, he had in his studio. It was an unusual privilege for Bell to be admitted there and he was impressed by what the painter showed him. Since the unexpected death at thirty-four of his close friend and supporter Armand Séguin, O'Conor had felt isolated among the artists in Montparnasse. He 'bewildered his companions with his advocacy of Gauguin, Van Gogh, Cézanne, Bonnard and Vuillard', and was knowledgeable about French writers such as Claudel, Laforgue and Remy de Gourmont, whom he soon recommended to Bell. O'Conor found Bell a first edition of Prosper Mérimée's *Lettres à une inconnue*, a text that Bell would unfailingly recommend to every woman with whom he had a liaison. O'Conor also afforded Bell a much deeper appreciation of the Parisian painting scene than he could gain from the

Montparnassians, whose milieu would shortly be satirised by Somerset Maugham in *The Magician* (1908), in which he caricatured the occultist Aleister Crowley, who was married to Gerald Kelly's sister. O'Conor's belief that artists who allowed themselves to be unduly influenced by what the marketplace demanded 'lost the whole sense of art' made a deep impression on Bell. Soon, O'Conor, J. W. Morrice and the English painter George Hume Barne became Bell's most trusted guides to Paris and painting.

At Cambridge, Bell had made a group of friends who seemed to 'have got hold of the key to the riddle of the universe', concerned as they were with the nature of 'good' and 'truth'. In Paris, that universe was upended by the conservative, anti-Dreyfusard milieu which prevailed at the Chat Blanc, where truth and humanitarianism seemed to Bell to be regarded as 'simply silly'. O'Conor was 'violently contemptuous' of half of what Bell had learned at Cambridge. Many of those in his new society struck Bell as 'unrighteous and indifferent to moral values, without a social conscience or a sense of responsibility' and yet he enjoyed their company. The artists he met seemed to him to live by ideals quite different from those Bell had imbibed from G. E. Moore and his friends who were Apostles, yet their passionate adherence to their own very different ideals appealed to him. He admitted in his memoir of this time to a habit that persisted throughout his life, 'of getting the best I could out of the world in which I happen to find myself, without bothering over much about complications'. The sense that Louie Blaikie had that Bell was two quite different people, and Desmond MacCarthy's observation that he was at ease in very different worlds, were borne out by Bell's explorations in Paris of whom he might become.

5. Vanessa

Having decided not to return to the Royal Academy Schools, where she had taken classes since 1901, and dissatisfied by her trial of a few weeks at the Slade School of Art at the end of 1904, Vanessa was painting a portrait of Lady Robert ('Nelly') Cecil while she reflected on the direction in which she wanted to take her art. Virginia had published her first book reviews at the end of 1904 and, as 1905 began, was writing a note to include in Frederic Maitland's biography of their father, preparing lectures for working women at Morley College and going to dances with her brother and sister from which they would return in the wee hours of the morning.

A large exhibition of French Impressionists – 'unique of its kind in England' – opened in January 1905 at the Grafton Galleries, organised by the French art dealer and champion of Impressionism Paul Durand-Ruel. Lytton Strachey wrote to Leonard Woolf, who had sailed for Ceylon at the end of November to take up a post as a colonial administrator, that the 'general effect is one of dazzling beauty – sheer physical pleasure to the eye . . . no one knew how to do colour before'. Virginia thought some of the French pictures 'lovely, one especially of a liquid & flowing sea', but she pronounced 'pompous & dull' a lecture on Impressionism by the *Sunday Times* art critic Frank Rutter.

Vanessa thought that Mr Bell, as she still addressed him, would be pleased to hear that her sister had lost 'her last scruples of loyalty' to G. F. Watts when the sisters visited his memorial exhibition at the Royal Academy. Vanessa hoped that Bell would bring J. W. Morrice to see them when he came to London, because she was eager to continue their Parisian conversations. She was thinking deeply about her painting,

'Vanessa Stephen' in Clive's parents' photograph album

telling Snow that she believed 'all painting is worth while so long as one honestly expresses one's own ideas' – 'one always must have something of one's own to say that no one else has been able to say'. Conversations about art, books and ideas could flow freely at 46 Gordon Square, where the Stephens had escaped their elderly relatives to begin life on their own terms. The day after their housewarming party in March, Strachey and Sydney-Turner came after dinner and stayed talking until midnight. A week later, Virginia came home to find Bell in the drawing room, '& we talked the nature of good till almost one!' 'Bloomsbury' was forming.

Concerned to keep his Cambridge relationships intact while he studied for the Bar, Thoby was 'at home' on Thursday evenings, a fact recorded by Virginia on 16 March 1905 when Sydney-Turner and Gerald Duckworth were his first visitors. The distance between Cambridge and London was in any case negligible because Thoby and his friends remained closely involved with university matters, such as the great issue of the vote on whether to retain Greek as a compulsory subject in the second-year examination for all students at Cambridge known as the 'Little-Go'. Strachey kept Woolf, miserable in Ceylon, abreast of all the goings-on in both Cambridge and Gordon Square, among which was news that Sydney-Turner had revived a plan to bring out an anthology of verse: 'He seems to think that he'll be able to induce Bell to finance it.'

Sydney-Turner undertook to gather poems for what literary historian S. P. Rosenbaum has called the 'first book of Bloomsbury'. Contributors included Woolf, Walter Lamb, Sydney-Turner, Strachey, Bell and an Arthur Francis Bell from Brighton. *Euphrosyne, A Collection of Verse* was produced by the Cambridge bookseller Elijah Johnson in August 1905, but in May the manuscript was available at 46 Gordon Square for Virginia to write a sarcastic response to it. It must, she said, be a 'parental fiction' that the days spent at university are the happiest in a young man's life, for *Euphrosyne*'s contributors had come from their university 'pale, preoccupied, & silent; as though in their three years absence, some awful communication had been made them, & they went burdened with a secret too dreadful to impart'. To these fraught young men, 'success is failure & they despise success', and so they do not pass their exams. They admire minor French poets and call some English authors 'supreme' (an Apostolic term of high praise), until these authors become appreciated by the public, upon which they lose interest in them. When the rest of the university was at prayer on Sundays, these young men gathered to read 'these astoundingly brilliant

& immoral productions'. The subtext of her 'review' was clear: their expensive university educations seemed to have ill-prepared these young men for life in the real world.

Many of the poems in *Euphrosyne* echo the aesthetic movement of the 1890s or are in the tradition of Tennyson, Browning and Arnold. Bell's in particular are characterised by melancholy and a sense of the physical pains of desire. He borrows mood and imagery from the Symbolists and, at times, even sounds like Lord Alfred Douglas. In Bell's 'Pereunt et Imputantur' ('they pass away but are accounted for by age' – Martial), 'sad brain-ghosts appear' in the autumn of 'passions that were strangled when the heart was young'; the twenty-three-year-old poet dreams about 'twisted, strangled corpses'. His sonnet to 'Casanova' laments the 'vile prudery and continence' of the new century and longs to 'live a life of living ecstasy'. 'In the Days of Utter Night' recoils from 'Pain to-day and pain to-morrow'. 'The Trinity Ball' has nothing to do with dancing, being rather a savage blast against 'God and the World', cursing the 'crapulous spawn' who follow their faith.

Some of Bell's contributions reflected the influence of the time he had spent in Paris. In 'Rain at Night After a Day of Heat', the bell of Saint-Sulpice strikes eight while the speaker reflects on a quarrel with a friend that has left him alone with 'Contempt and rage and that we fear to name'. A less sentimental poem is 'After a Dance', dedicated 'à Madame de Montmartre'. The speaker contrasts the 'Good boys and simple-minded misses' who would be embarrassed 'at thoughts of ruby kisses' as he sits in a café where champagne flows and the women's shoulders are bare. A translation of de Musset's 'L'Andalouse' demonstrates the facility Bell had gained with the French language by 1905. The most striking of his contributions to *Euphrosyne* is 'A Lady Smoking a Cigarette':

Pastel-like evanescent hues,
   Watched through the drifting whites and greys,
   Subtly changed as the ripple sways;
   Floating us this way green displays,
Floating us that way hints at blues.
Shifts our boat in the moody stream,
   Hangs the smoke in a tattered cloud,
   Lovingly lifts the fragrant shroud,

> Peers at the purple eyelids proud
> Reposed in an alabaster dream.
>
> All a symphony mystic, now
>   Slate-blue, purple, now white, now mauve,
>   Mystical colours our lady wove,
>   Themes of weariness nightfall drove
> Home from an Autumn sunset's brow.
>
> What the dreams you are dreaming say –
>   Are you lost in some listless skein,
>   Golden shreds of a topaz stain,
>   Or turquoise-dust which Charles' wain
> For ever spills through the milky way?
>
> Of far adrift in moonstone rays,
>   Or swooned 'neath breathless lilac trees,
>   Like tuneful gems, melodious bees
>   Drone Aristaean epopees,
> And lyrics of long summer days?

Thoby anonymously reviewed *Euphrosyne*, pointing out that some of the poems would be familiar because they had been previously published in the *Cambridge Review* and claiming the mantle of 'decadence' for these Cambridge men. Thoby had hoped his review would elicit discussion, but the only response came from Walter Lamb, editor of the *Review*, who wrote pseudonymously as 'A Cambridge Graduate' to claim that if there was a decadent element at the university, it was confined to a 'very small . . . uninfluential group'. However, 'OXON', of Balliol College, Oxford, whom Lamb had invited to write about the volume, singled out 'A Lady Smoking a Cigarette' (among others), seeing in it the influence of Verlaine, as well as Mallarmé, and commended the author for his 'familiarity with the polychromatic visions of Renoir and Monet'. One might have thought such praise would thrill Bell but by the time this correspondence was published he had lost interest in *Euphrosyne*, cast into despair by developments in his romantic life.

Since spending time in Paris with him in 1904, Vanessa Stephen had continued to discuss art with Bell. In the summer of 1905, she enlisted his help in establishing a 'Friday Club' to afford a wider circle of friends and acquaintances the opportunity to gather for conversation, informal talks on art and the exhibition of works by its members. She and Bell agreed that if the club's discussions were to be fruitful, 'politeness' would have to be 'eradicated', which would be easier to accomplish on 'neutral ground' rather than at 46 Gordon Square. To that end, she asked him to join a committee and help her locate rooms to rent. Bell told Strachey of a Friday Club committee meeting at which he had endured 'platitudinous gibberings of opaque inanity' – the compensation for which was having a 'charming and continuous view of Vanessa's superb profile' from his corner of the room.

Strachey, who preferred the 'purely Cambridge' atmosphere of Bell's rooms on King's Bench Walk to the mixed company at Thoby's Thursday evenings at Gordon Square, found Bell puzzling. He described for Leonard Woolf how he had invited Bell to accompany him to Sarah Bernhardt's *Phèdre* at the Coronet Theatre in July, her only performance in the role that season. Thoby and Adrian Stephen were also there, who, Strachey told Woolf, 'really see the point – but Bell? he's really rather a mystery'. The trouble was that Bell seemed to be interested in the same things as Strachey and yet 'he's not under our control like [Henry] Lamb. He's even independent of the Goth [Thoby]'. The apparent contradictions in Bell's character confused Strachey. He described them at the time to Bernard Swithinbank, a Balliol undergraduate whose friendship Strachey was cultivating:

His character has several layers, but it is difficult to say which is the fond. There is the country gentleman layer, which makes him retire into the depths of Wiltshire to shoot partridges. There is the Paris decadent layer, which takes him to the quartier latin where he discusses painting and vice with American artists and French models. There is the eighteenth-century layer, which adores Thoby Stephen. There is the layer of innocence which adores Thoby's sister. There is the layer of prostitution, which shows itself in an amazing head of crimped straw-coloured hair. And there is the layer of stupidity, which runs transversely through all the other layers.

There was nothing innocent about Bell's adoration of Vanessa, as Strachey discovered when he stayed in Bell's rooms until two o'clock one morning, pressing him to reveal his true feelings. Bell was tortured by desire – 'his frightened pathetic face shows it' – and was 'wildly in love' with Vanessa. The Stephens were taking a house for several weeks in August and September on Carbis Bay in Cornwall and Bell told Strachey he intended to propose to Vanessa when he visited the family there. His frankness won Strachey's admiration but he told Woolf it was inconceivable that Vanessa would agree to marry him.

Just before she left for Cornwall, Bell invited Vanessa to King's Bench Walk for dinner, filling his rooms with 'armfuls' of red roses that, he told Strachey, enhanced the 'duskiness' of her complexion. Strachey told Woolf that when Bell confided in him about his love for Vanessa, his 'small lascivious body oozed with disappointed lust'. Bell was terrified that she would find his proposal ridiculous, telling Strachey that were she to turn him down he would leave the country. When the moment came and his worst fears were realised, it was Strachey whom Bell told; he could not face discussing his rejected proposal with Thoby, and if losing Vanessa meant that he also would have to 'surrender' Thoby, it could not make him any more unhappy than he already was.

Thoby had long suspected what was going on and Vanessa in fact told her brother about her refusal of his best friend's proposal. Thoby wrote to Bell to say that he was 'very sorry' to hear about the sad outcome and Strachey assured Bell he should have no concerns about Thoby's friendship being affected by what had happened. Vanessa seems to have told Thoby that Bell had even promised to give up hunting (of which she disapproved) in case that were an impediment to her accepting him, but her reasons had little to do with Bell himself and more to do with her resolute antagonism to the very idea of matrimony. She had enjoyed Bell's easy friendship as they worked alongside one another to set up the Friday Club, but she admitted to Snow that she should have foreseen what would happen, even though she had not flirted. Vanessa was sure that 'unless this particular man is unlike every other', he would fall in love with someone else within the year and she would think no more about it. She and her sister had determined when they left their childhood home at Hyde Park Gate in 1904 that their new lives at 46 Gordon Square would be entirely different from what was typically expected of young late Victorian ladies. Virginia and Vanessa regarded marriage as a 'horrible necessity', a fate that 'would descend and snatch us apart just as we had achieved freedom and happiness'. Vanessa recognised that for Bell the matter was tremendously serious, but, she told Snow, 'I could no more marry him than I could fly.'

After this disaster, Bell left London, not at first to go abroad but to Seend, and then on to Scotland with his family. He had done what he could to get *Euphrosyne* reviewed but was too dejected to think any more about it. Louise Blaikie wrote to thank him for her copy, received in the Transvaal where she had gone soon after her marriage to Major Henry Barnes. She identified 'After a Dance', 'Rain at Night' and 'Lady with a Cigarette' as Bell's, the latter being 'Whistler incarnate'. Bell asked Sydney-Turner to find the remaining copies in King's Bench Walk waiting to be posted. He would not be back, except in passing, for perhaps a year or more, so if any unpaid bills for *Euphrosyne* should arrive, Sydney-Turner should forward them to his bank in Cambridge.

In Scotland, his family could not understand why Arthur seemed so downcast and he did not enlighten them. In the autumn, he sailed for France, stopping briefly in Cambridge to see Thoby. His destination was St Symphorien, a village in the Tours region, but first he went to Paris. If Bell had any inkling of the volcanic year of the Fauves, he gave no sign in his correspondence.

This had begun in March 1905 with the opening of the Salon des Indépendants. 'From one end of the hall to the other you still heard intemperate laughter and sarcasms rising to open contempt,' recalled the gallerist Berthe Weill, who herself showed Matisse, Marquet, Manguin and Camoin the following month. Bell arrived in Paris while the 3rd Salon d'Automne (18 October – 25 November) was open, where Leo Stein bought Matisse's sensational *Femme au Chapeau*. Shortly thereafter, Stein met Picasso in his studio at the Bateau Lavoire, having recently seen the artist's work at Clovis Sagot's gallery. The American sisters Etta and Claribel Cone were in Paris, acquiring the modernist paintings they would eventually leave to the Baltimore Museum of Art. Bell, more concerned with affairs of the heart than with the revolution in painting in 1905, left no evidence he was aware of it that year.

He wondered if the tears Vanessa had shed when he called on her before setting sail for France were sincere. Once in Paris, however, the beauty of the city lifted his mood. By now he spoke French 'rather well', and reacquainted himself with the Closerie des Lilas, where Paul Fort asked him for names of anyone who might be interested in subscribing to *Vers et Prose*, the journal he had started with Guillaume Apollinaire. Strachey was delighted to receive a notice. But the *quartier Latin* had lost its appeal for Bell because 'all these artists and journalists are so unutterably stupid and degraded'. When Thoby arrived in Paris for Christmas, he agreed with Bell's estimation of the Montparnasse scene.

Bell spent his days in St Symphorien reading or playing chess with a 'maniac' who followed him around with a board under his arm. News from Seend arrived, where life continued unchanged. The Japanist and botanist F. Victor Dickins, like many of the Bell family's friends, took an interest in his career prospects, suggesting he undertake a study of Balzac while he was in the Tours region. Soon after Christmas, Bell became ill – '*poitrinaire*' (consumptive), according to Strachey. From Wiltshire came exhortations to exercise and maintain his health, which continued to be poor throughout the winter while Bell nursed his broken heart.

In London, the first meeting of the Friday Club took place in October. Virginia had described to Violet Dickinson how in the planning meetings earlier that summer 'one half of the committee shriek Whistler and the French impressionists, and the other stalwart British', requiring considerable diplomacy from Vanessa as the secretary. By the new year, the club was firmly established and had held its first exhibition in December (for which two drawings of birds by Bell had been accepted). Desmond MacCarthy, now married to Molly Warre-Cornish, roused a 'fiery discussion' with a talk in February 1906 that again exposed divisions between supporters of the Impressionists and those of a more conservative cast of mind. Strachey attended the club's events but gave painting short shrift. This business of 'arranging different coloured pigments' on a canvas he thought rather 'lowering to the intellect'.

Strachey's letters to Bell in early 1906 were more than usually full of ennui and self-pity. Vaguely he had heard there was an election going on but he could not rouse himself to take much interest in it. Bell did not profess to care either about what was in fact a turning-point in British politics. While the newspapers were full of the Taff Vale case, with its profoundly negative implications for trades unions (because the House of Lords had ruled they were liable for any injuries or damages arising from the actions of their members), Thoby wished Bell might stand for Parliament in Merthyr Tydfil, the coal-mining and iron-working region of South Wales from which the Bell family's money derived. But he was ill in France where 'the froggy doctor' did not inspire Thoby with much confidence in his friend's care.

The consequence of the Conservative split that had begun in 1903 over free trade and tariff reform was a Liberal landslide. Arthur Schomberg – a Seend neighbour whom Bell had cajoled into a game of correspondence chess with the St Symphorien 'maniac' – wrote from Seend to rejoice in the results, adding that he was also pleased that France had severed Church and State by its law of 9 December 1905 which codified the movement towards state secularism that had gathered force since the late nineteenth century. We can be certain Bell welcomed *laïcité* too, though he was perhaps too immersed in his lovesickness at the time to mention it.

Thoby continued to send Bell news from London about exhibitions he had seen, their epistolary discussions still running along very traditional tracks. Thoby pronounced the International Society's show 'practically nugatory, except dead or dying froggies, Rodin, Cézanne, Degas, Monet, Forain'. In March, stopping in Rome before coming back to England, Bell told Thoby he had not been impressed by Raphael's frescoes in the Vatican Palace. He was in good company, Thoby pointed out, because Joshua Reynolds had also passed them by without comment on his first visit in 1750. He reminded Bell that he had already told him he was planning an excursion to Greece that autumn, which he hoped his friend would join. While Thoby wrote to Bell about the fine watercolours by Frederick Goodall, RA, at the International, Matisse's one-man show opened on 19 March at Druet's on the Faubourg Saint-Honoré; shortly thereafter, Matisse and Picasso met at the Steins' apartment on rue de Fleurus.

Bell told Strachey he was inclined to think that France was really the only civilised country but he wondered if Gordon Square was still the centre of civilisation in London. As spring approached, he shook off his lethargy and contemplated going home. News from Cambridge – Keynes's pursuit of an undergraduate named Harry (H. T. J.) Norton, A. W. Verrall's superb new book on Euripides – piqued his interest again. Jack Pollock enjoyed the cynicism of Bell's letters but was profoundly bored by Camille Mauclair's *De Watteau à Whistler* (1905), which Bell had insisted he read. More to his taste was another of Bell's recommendations, Laclos' *Les Liaisons dangereuses*, which he told Bell was one of the cleverest books he had ever read. This book would join *Lettres à une inconnue* on Bell's list of required reading for all his lovers. In preparation for Bell's return, Pollock sent membership forms for the London Library. Strachey asked his attractive cousin Duncan Grant, who was studying painting in Paris and with whom Strachey had fallen 'in love hopelessly and ultimately', if he would be interested in seeing Bell there. Duncan agreed the rendezvous might be amusing, but did not 'feel inclined to bother about it much'.

At the end of April, Bell returned to London, just too late to hear Thoby deliver a paper on the decadence of modern art to the Friday Club. Teatime conversation resumed at the rooms on King's Bench Walk and he planned to see the *Ring* cycle with Sydney-Turner. Strachey's criticism of Bell in his letters to Woolf somewhat relented because, he admitted, 'It's a great comfort to meet someone who even *says* that he admires Gluck & despises George Meredith, and isn't ashamed of Sodom.' Bell's harsh review of G. M. Trevelyan's *The Poetry and Philosophy of George Meredith* appeared anonymously in the *Cambridge Review* at the end of May, providing some small insight into the current state of his aesthetic ideas. Trevelyan's comparison of Meredith with Balzac and Flaubert shows 'a complete ignorance of French', he wrote, and furthermore, he

> has never fully appreciated the importance of art in literature . . . he
> seems to regard language as a mere vehicle for thought . . . He knows
> nothing of that art which delights in the beauty of words, fingering
> them with delicious precaution as we finger exquisite gems; the art
> that feels for strange tones and subtle phrases, and weaves them into
> symphonies of glorious harmony.

Was Bell perhaps recalling his former teacher's criticisms of the 'violence' of his language? Vanessa would have concurred with his objection to critics writing about the 'moral message' of painters and poets: 'When we meet with an exegesis of the "message" of Browning or the "moral teaching" of Shelley, we confess that our frayed nerves are racked almost beyond endurance.' She had once complained to Snow about a 'long lecture upon Art' delivered by G. F. Watts when she and George

Duckworth had been his weekend guests, in which he had said, 'When I paint a picture I want to give a message and I care comparatively little about how good the art is.'

Bell was still in love with Vanessa but 'behaved with great self possession' when he attended a Thursday 'at home' that summer, laughing and acting as though he had put passion behind him while recuperating in France. Nevertheless, Vanessa was wary of encouraging him. Such 'affairs of the heart' perplexed Virginia, who found Bell's feelings opaque. Within the month, he proposed again to Vanessa who once more turned him down. She explained that his first proposal had taken her by surprise because she had assumed he thought her 'rather stupid and quite illiterate'. She had told Thoby about it so that he would not invite his friend to stay and thus cause him pain. This time, however, Vanessa told Bell that she valued their friendship very much, particularly because their conversations about art and the Friday Club had been so easy and natural; outside her family, she liked him 'much better than I like anyone else', but she simply did not feel for him what she supposed it was necessary to feel for the man she would marry. To Snow, she expressed herself more vehemently: 'to marry without love would be utterly degrading & horrible'. That had been the fate Louie Blaikie had told Bell she feared, but orphaned Vanessa and Virginia Stephen were unencumbered by parental expectations and the hold over them of their half-brothers had waned.

The Stephen siblings rented Blo' Norton Hall in Norfolk at the beginning of August, from where Vanessa again wrote to 'Dear Mr. Bell', absolving him of trying to 'drag' her into correspondence. It was as important to her as she presumed it was to him that he understand how she felt. Thus, despite her wish not to marry, she encouraged him to continue writing to her. She also let him know that she would forward to Athens a letter to Thoby that had been delivered to Gordon Square after her brothers had left for the planned trip to Greece, where Vanessa and Virginia, accompanied by Violet Dickinson, would later join them.

Once more frustrated in his desire to marry Vanessa, Bell made preparations to leave England after Christmas. He asked Sydney-Turner to keep an eye on his King's Bench Walk rooms in case his servant decided clandestinely to rent them out to someone in his absence and joined his family in Scotland, where they had rented Merkland Lodge in Lairg. Knowing they would be leaving him alone there in September, Bell invited Strachey to visit him. He arrived just before the Bells' departure ('abominably rich and devoid of any shred of gentility') with their guest, the *Punch* cartoonist G. D. Armour. Strachey reported with some smugness to Woolf that he at last had been able to see Bell 'in his true colours': 'He's a perfectly healthy and normal English sportsman with a tic for intellect. His fading decadence in London is affectation, and gross affectation . . . The paraphernalia of cultivation sits upon him most clumsily. He's a Monsieur Jourdain up to date.'

Although Strachey had been a sympathetic confidant when Bell first divulged his love for Vanessa, he continued to denigrate him in letters to Woolf, who followed the progress of Bell's courtship with interest from his remote colonial outpost in Ceylon. Strachey often described Bell as 'stupid' – surprisingly, given Bell's erudition and relative academic success. Bell's insecurities as a provincial who found himself among contemporaries whose well-connected families gave them easy social assurance undoubtedly made him prone to a certain degree of posing, while his hedonism and passion for women would always set him apart from the ascetic and brittle ethos of the Edwardian Apostles. Strachey's mocking comparison of Bell to Molière's *bourgeois gentilhomme* was the kind of barb that would sometimes find its way back to Bell and lead to bitter ruptures in their friendship.

Bell still believed that Vanessa would marry him, perhaps encouraged by her willingness to continue seeing him. It was a prospect that appalled Strachey: 'If by any mad chance it should occur it would be a complete amalgamation of the disgusting and the grotesque. Imagine, please, the family!' Vanessa had plenty of time to reflect on her decision, while she was in Greece. After seeing Corinth, Nauplia and Mycenae with her siblings, she fell ill and remained in Athens with Violet while the others journeyed on to Euboea. Thoby wrote to Bell from the Hotel d'Angleterre (whose letterhead boasted 'Electric Light Throughout the Building'), describing the sights and smells of the Adriatic and the Peloponnese, an environment his sister Virginia would summon up in her novel *Jacob's Room* (1922), where she also drew on their 1904 trip to Paris. As he had when in Italy in 1904, Thoby again gently mocked Bell's supposed parochialism. The Parthenon might exist in his friend's mind's eye as a kind of 'dismantled & disreputable British Museum', but it was nothing of the kind. No description could substitute for the reality of its colour. Virginia agreed, noting in her travel journal that language and paint could not capture the experience of the Parthenon seen at sunset.

In Vanessa's sick room, Virginia read Mérimée's *Lettres à une inconnue*, writing out her impressions at length. By now, Vanessa was suspected to be suffering from appendicitis so would not be able to go on with the others to Constantinople. Although the women had arrived in Olympia 'in a great first class carriage', travel through the region in 1906 was far from luxurious. The night before they met their sisters, Adrian and Thoby had been bitten so badly by bed bugs that their efforts to avoid them roused their 'filthy host & disreputable hostess' who barged into their room without knocking. Then, the presence of a huge scorpion drove them outside to try and sleep in a dry ditch but it became too cold so they dozed in chairs until dawn. Thoby set off from Athens for London, leaving his siblings to board the Austrian ship *Dalmatia* from Piraeus, bound for Constantinople. Vanessa was thought well enough to travel, despite her severe weakness, but in Constantinople her condition worsened. On the advice of a doctor from the English hospital, they would take the Orient Express back to London on 29 October. Thoby, too, arrived in London seriously ill. As soon as Bell saw him, he insisted that Thoby take to his bed.

After weeks resting in Greece, eating very little, but revived somewhat by champagne and brandy, Vanessa wrote a long letter from Constantinople to explain to her suitor what she had been thinking since she left England. She had promised Bell that she would make no major decisions without first consulting him (he may have worried that she would accept a proposal from someone else) but she felt no clearer than before about whether she would ever agree to marry him. She invited him to come and see her as soon as she was home so that she could explain in person her belief that they should not see one another again for a fixed period.

When she reached Gordon Square at the beginning of November, however, Vanessa was deemed too unwell for visitors, although she disagreed with her doctor and thought seeing Bell 'would do me a lot of good'. She thanked him for making Thoby go to bed: 'I think you just prevented him from getting really bad.' A few days later, she wrote again, explaining that were she to go on seeing him as she had in the summer, she would never make up her mind about marriage. She offered him a choice: either go away for a year and not see her at all, at the end of which she would give him a definite answer, or abandon the idea of marriage altogether and agree to go on seeing her only as a friend. If he chose the former, Vanessa hoped that he would find some employment that would use his intellect. 'I can't imagine you being a successful barrister or man of business,' she wrote, but he must find some satisfying work that would make him see how he had idealised her and the Stephen family.

As soon as he received Vanessa's letter, Bell went to Gordon Square, but she was confined to her room, while Thoby suffered in his. In the ensuing weeks, Bell provided friends with bulletins from the sick rooms while the burden of care for her siblings fell on Virginia, who welcomed the distraction that Bell provided. When he was not at Gordon Square, Virginia kept Bell informed by postcard of her brother and sister's progress, as well of the doctors' opinions. If she had to be out, Bell would come to read to Thoby. Virginia began to refer to her sickroom companion as 'Peter', after Wordsworth's Peter Bell (a sinful ruffian who renounces his past wicked ways through the beneficent influence of nature).[1] She told Violet Dickinson, who was also ill, that they discussed modern verse and the correct way to pronounce 'enema'. When she looked at 'Peter', she imagined how one day she would need to tell him he was not good enough for her sister 'and then he will kiss me, and Nessa will wipe a great tear, and say we shall always have a room for you'. Bell and Virginia bantered about 'love and marriage and what will be good for a woman who has had appendicitis, and a proposal, a woman of very scrupulous mind and unselfish nature', which made him blush. Bell more or less lived at Gordon Square, even occasionally sleeping there.

Thoby's condition had at first been misdiagnosed as malaria and it did not improve. On 17 November, realising that the problem was typhoid, his doctor advised an operation. On the morning of 20 November, Thoby died. Strachey learned the news from Desmond

---

[1] 'His later friends made much of the Peter Bell buried within Clive Bell. They nicknamed him Peter. They thought it a bit of a joke. . . Why did he read so much? Why was he so hungry for art? . . . Clive Bell never triumphed altogether over Peter Bell; but the two lived harmoniously together. Wordsworth's Peter enabled Clive to see that the emperor did not always wear clothes . . .' (Edel, *Bloomsbury* 29).

MacCarthy; he wrote to Woolf that he dreaded seeing Bell. Thoby's funeral took place at Golders Green on 22 November, attended by twenty or thirty people, among whom were Adrian and Virginia, the Duckworths, Strachey and his mother, and Thoby's aunt, Mary Fisher. G. M. Trevelyan read the part of the burial service that Leslie Stephen had chosen for his own funeral. Vanessa was too unwell to attend, so Bell stayed with her at Gordon Square. By the end of the day, she had agreed to marry him.

For the most part, news of their engagement was received as a happy ray of light amidst the gloom cast by Thoby's shattering and unexpected death. Some had misgivings, however: Strachey was reminded of lines from Thomas Beddoes' *Death's Jest-Book*:

A wedding-robe, and a winding-sheet,
A bridal bed and a bier.

He had to be the 'bringer of bad news' about the engagement to Woolf, but tried to cling to the idea of Bell's 'fundamental goodness'. A Stephen family friend, Kitty Maxse, wrote to her sister Susan that Virginia had told her about Vanessa's fiancé: he 'has no profession – & likes hunting & shooting – & writes rather good poetry & I hope is quite well off'. Bell was already well known to Vanessa's friends, several of whom wrote at once to congratulate him and at the same time console him for the loss of his closest friend. Among them was Margery Snowden, who told Bell that she had known for the last few years how much Vanessa craved the kind of unselfish affection he could give her. Snow added, teasingly, that she of course did not think him good enough for her friend. That he was 'not good enough' became a refrain within their close circle, and what had been Virginia's jest to Violet Dickinson would soon imbue her complicated feelings for her brother-in-law. When she passed by her sister's door now she heard 'not only perpetual voices but laughter'. They told her they were talking about art, but Virginia was sceptical. 'Do you believe it?' she asked Nelly Cecil. 'Well, you may mix art with many things.'

As Strachey had feared, Adrian and Virginia would now have to move out of Gordon Square. Virginia recognised that living too near the newly married couple would be 'dangerous'. When Bell took Vanessa to Seend to meet his family, Virginia reflected on her feelings about the engagement. She told Madge Vaughan that Bell had the gift of making others shine, that Vanessa was as happy as she could be (indeed, Vanessa had herself told Madge a few days earlier that she was 'happier than I ever thought people could be'). But Strachey and Virginia could not separate their feelings about Vanessa's engagement from the tragedy of Thoby's death. As Thoby was memorialised – for example by Walter Lamb in the *Cambridge Review* – the couple began to make plans for a simple wedding to take place in February 1907. It was thought that Strachey might write something about Thoby for private circulation so Bell loaned him all of Thoby's letters. Nothing would come of this 'terrible task', as Strachey described it to Woolf, but Bell carefully preserved the letters for the rest of his life.

On the day of Thoby's funeral, 'Virginia Stephen' wrote to 'Mr Strachey' that Vanessa would like to talk to him, if he could come to tea on the following Sunday. Strachey came, feeling overwhelmed and at a loss for words. His written apology to Vanessa's fiancé for his 'rigidity' that afternoon was a milestone in the history of Bloomsbury. It began: 'Dear Arthur? Clive?' 'Henceforth between friends manners were to depend on feelings rather than conventions.' 'Strachey' became Lytton and 'Bell' became Clive.

II

ART AND LETTERS

(1907–1914)

6. Virginia

Women, Leonard told Lytton, were 'absolutely the abomination of desolation'. He confessed that he thought 99 per cent of being in love was just the degraded 'desire to copulate', a pleasure he found less satisfying than riding a horse. Nevertheless, when Lytton told him of Clive's first proposal to Vanessa in 1905, Leonard sent a curious analysis from 5,000 miles away. He wondered if Clive's affection for Thoby had been a displacement of his hitherto unarticulated love for Vanessa. Leonard himself confessed to having been 'wildly in love' with Vanessa when the Stephen sisters had come up for the May Ball in 1900, but now he thought this might have been due to his love for Thoby: 'She is so superbly like the Goth. I often used to wonder whether [Clive] was in love with the Goth because he was in love with her & I was in love with her because with the Goth.' When Vanessa agreed to marry Clive, not only were they involved in a queer complex of emotional crossings that reached back to Cambridge, they also lived in a society that for some time had been restless about the institution of marriage itself.

Heterosexual relations were fraught in the Edwardian era, when the Victorian 'Woman Question' had sharpened around issues of marriage and divorce reform. The suffrage movement exacerbated 'a growing sense of moral crisis in man–woman relations', adding to the anxieties around gender that coursed through English culture and society in the years before the First World War. The Divorce Law Reform Union was consolidated in 1906 and books and periodical articles on such issues as the low birthrate and contraception poured forth. Lytton's sisters were deeply involved in what became known as the 'Mud March', when 3,000 women demonstrated for the vote from Hyde Park Corner to

Exeter Hall on 9 February 1907 (two days after the Bells' marriage). Although Pippa Strachey had enlisted the aid of several men, including Maynard Keynes, Harry Norton and her brother James, she could not win the support of Lytton, who escaped to Cambridge, unable to face the march. (Perhaps this is what Clive meant when he wrote in *Old Friends* that Lytton 'went out of his way to help the cause of Women's Suffrage'.) The first ever play to deal with the suffrage movement, Elizabeth Robins' *Votes for Women!* (1907), had moved Lytton drolly to propose 'universal buggery' as the obvious solution to the vexed issue of women's rights.

Clive's family welcomed the Stephen siblings for New Year's Eve 1906. Virginia and Adrian were greeted at Cleeve House by Vanessa and Clive standing before a great log fire in a pose Virginia found uncharacteristic but at the same time natural. Clive's parents were solicitous, his sisters laughed at Adrian's jokes, but Virginia acerbically described Cleeve as a 'rich and illiterate' house, 'gothic and barbaric'. Though she had lived so closely with Clive during the final, agonising days of Thoby's illness and death she had still not made up her mind about him. He did not seem at all a worthy husband for a Stephen: 'When I think of father and Thoby and then see that funny little creature twitching his pink skin and jerking out his little spasm of laughter I wonder what odd freak there is in Nessa's eyesight.' She could see nothing inspiring in Clive. Lytton, too, always underrated Clive's intelligence; he wondered whether Vanessa would see how ordinary his mind was and whether it would matter if she did because she was obviously happy, excited by the prospect of having her own house with Clive at 46 Gordon Square to furnish as she chose.

Their marriage took place at the St Pancras Register office on 7 February 1907. Vanessa arrived late in her sister-in-law Margaret Duckworth's motor,[1] loaned for the occasion through the intercession of George, who had assumed a quasi-paternal role when he negotiated with Clive's father a marriage settlement for Vanessa of £20,000 (in investments). As Leonard and Virginia would five years later, when they also married at St Pancras, Vanessa and Clive offended their relations

---

[1] Vanessa's half-brother George Duckworth married Lady Margaret Herbert, daughter of the fourth Earl of Carnarvon, in 1904.

Clive Bell with Julian, 1911

by not inviting them. Henry James visited Vanessa on the eve of her wedding to give her an antique silver box. He wrote ruefully to Lucy Clifford that Clive was a 'quite dreadful-looking little stoop-shouldered, long-haired, third-rate' man, comparing him unfavourably, as did Virginia, to 'poor, dear, clear, tall, shy, superior Thoby'.[2] He heard that the couple almost missed their own wedding because they were so late (the driver got lost), and indeed Mr and Mrs Clive Bell missed their train at Paddington and had to wait for another to take them to the first stop on their honeymoon, Manorbier on the Pembrokeshire coast.

In marrying Vanessa, Clive would be intruding upon a sororal relationship rooted in shared bereavements, struggles against a

[2]When the newlyweds visited him at Rye in the autumn, James's opinion had not altered: 'the handsome (and most loveable) Vanessa Clive-Bell sits on my lawn (unheeded by me)', he wrote to Sara Norton, 'along with her little incongruous and disconcerting but apparently very devoted newly acquired *sposo*' (Edel 394). Even five years later, James told Sydney Waterlow that much as it pained him to have abandoned the children of his dear friend Leslie Stephen, Clive's presence at Gordon Square made it intolerable to him (Waterlow 10 March 1912).

sometimes tyrannical though often loving father and brilliant ambitions – a relationship which employed a coded language both to reassure one another where true loyalties lay and to proffer conditional admission to outsiders such as Clive to the charmed circle. Vanessa was a romping 'dolphin', sometimes submerged in deep waters, who would burst, glistening, through the surface; Virginia was 'the Apes', a roiling simian bundle of sudden sharp attacks and profound needs. Virginia experienced her sister's marriage as a kind of second bereavement, following so closely on the death of her beloved Thoby. The day before the wedding, she wrote to Vanessa in the voice of 'the Apes'. In this intimate and strangely sad letter, Virginia gave an awkward blessing to her sister for having found what she called 'a new Red Ape' who had the advantage of being allowed to marry her, 'from which we are debarred'. Her letter presaged what would become a 'three-cornered love affair' between Clive and Vanessa, Vanessa and Virginia, Virginia and Clive, a situation that, Virginia would tell her friend Gwen Raverat many years later, 'turned more of a knife in me than anything else has ever done'.

The affair was brewed in letters, some secret, some open, that traded in a language of kisses bestowed, sought or proffered. These letters also built upon the sisters' early rivalry between writing and painting, with Vanessa often deprecating her ability to critique her sister's writing as she deferred to Clive and Virginia insisting that painting was a mystery to her. Virginia was at first unsure what tone to take with her brother-in-law. In the first letter she wrote him after the bulletins sent during Thoby's illness, she discoursed on the syllables of Vanessa's name, on art and on reading, signalling her jealousy when she called Clive a dweller in the Temple dedicated to her goddess sister, while she was but 'a worshipper without'. Virginia wrote to Clive in Manorbier of books and reading, and asked that he kiss her sister on 'her left eye, with the eyelid smoothed over the curve, and just blue on the crest'. Literature and kisses soon provided the vocabulary of a risky intimacy. When she began to show Clive drafts of her first novel, his genuinely valuable criticism became entangled with his manipulation of her feelings of exclusion from and jealousy of her sister's new life, as well as with her own provocation of Clive's insecurity about his worth.

From Manorbier the Bells went to Paris, where Virginia and Adrian joined them for a week to escape the chaos of their move from Gordon

Square to a new home at 29 Fitzroy Square. Duncan Grant, studying at Jacques-Emile Blanche's school, La Palette, was staying on the boulevard Raspail, where Clive had had rooms in 1904. Vanessa welcomed Lytton's suggestion that she look up his cousin and soon Clive had invited him to 'come and wrangle about pictures with us at the Louvre'. 'What a quartet!' Duncan reported to Lytton. 'I seem to like them all so much, after these frogs & people. I feel I should rather soon be bored with Bell & he with me, but he's been very charming. As for Virginia I think she's probably extremely witty & amazingly beautiful & then there's old Adrian' – 'old Adrian' would occasion many visits by Duncan to Fitzroy Square in the coming months. Clive showed Vanessa around the Paris he knew, reacquainting himself with 'various old bachelors who have known Whistler and play the violin, and can't paint', Virginia archly remarked.

Although Clive had seen photographs of Gauguin's work in O'Conor's studio in 1904, he, like Duncan and Vanessa, evinced little inclination in 1907 to pursue what was causing a revolution in the art world of Paris. On the same day that Clive wrote to Lytton with his favourable impressions of Duncan's good looks and good company, Picasso and his lover Fernande Olivier were visiting a Montmartre orphanage to select a child (the unfortunate Raymonde, whom Fernande and Picasso would return to the orphanage three months later). The chaotic brew of creativity and iconoclasm emanating from the Bateau Lavoir, where Picasso was working on the *Demoiselles d'Avignon*, the developing productive rivalry between Picasso and Matisse, the influence of the Steins – Leo and Gertrude, Michael and Sarah – even the shock and outrage caused by Matisse's *Nu Bleu: Souvenir de Biskra* shown at the Salon des Indépendants in spring 1907, all went unnoticed by the English couple. Given that O'Conor exhibited at the 1907 Indépendants, their lack of comment seems all the more remarkable. March 1907 had been a momentous month for Picasso because Géry Pieret, Apollinaire's 'secretary', sold him Iberian heads that he had stolen from the Louvre. At André Derain's instigation, Picasso probably also went to the rarely visited Ethnographical Museum at the Trocadéro (now the Musée de l'Homme) around this time, where he saw the African masks that would influence the 'primitivism' that marked so much modernist art. Art historian Patricia Leighten argues that the 'politically charged atmosphere' in Paris in 1905 over French colonial atrocities inspired Picasso, Derain, Maurice Vlaminck and others to '"discover" African art that had been visible in Paris since at least the 1890s'. That art had its 'first real impact' on these painters in 1906, but Clive's familiarity with the Montmartrois scene was delayed for some years because, by chance, he gained his introduction to Paris through Gerald Kelly's Montparnasse.

During their honeymoon, Vanessa and Clive could have visited Berthe Weill's gallery at 46 rue Lafitte, had they known about it, where from 30 March until 15 April she showed works by Camoin, Derain, Dufy, Friesz, Manguin, Marquet, Matisse and Puy. Duncan would not have told them about it, because, despite his interest in the Impressionists, he 'showed no inclination to learn about the latest developments in art'. The Durand-Ruel exhibition of 315 Impressionist paintings at London's Grafton Galleries in early 1905 marked a belated turning point in attention to recent French painting, but English critics at the time were 'busily occupied trying to persuade the pundits of British art to accept Manet, Monet, Degas and Renoir'.

In France that year, on the other hand, a new ferment had stirred the critics. The *Times* covered positively both the 1905 Salon d'Automne, with its *cage centrale* of 'Fauves', and the spring 1906 Indépendants, but the specialised art magazines (such as the *Burlington*, *Studio* and *Connoisseur*) were more critical. English critics for the most part railed against Gauguin's 'primitivism'. Only in 1908 would Roger Fry begin to develop a usable critical vocabulary with which to discuss modern painting and by the time English gallery-goers were exposed to work that would astonish and unsettle them, it had already been eclipsed by further developments in Paris.

Settling into married life at Gordon Square, Clive was no clearer than he had been after leaving Cambridge about how to appear to his family to be earning a living, though he now had several friends who might assist him were he to pursue writing as a profession. Clive sought advice from Wiltshire neighbours such as F. Victor Dickins and from his network of friends from Cambridge on how to get reviewing assignments. G. M. Trevelyan and Jack Pollock would see what they could do, but nothing bore fruit. Clive asked Lytton if he knew of a weekly or daily for which he could write, at least to provide evidence to his family that he was not completely idle. He showed Lytton and Walter Lamb an article he had written on Thomas Love Peacock but it remained unpublished.

Thursday evening 'at homes' were resumed, and soon a pattern of visits between the households at 46 Gordon Square and 29 Fitzroy Square was established. Vanessa invited Maynard Keynes to come for dinner and hear Clive read a paper, if he could 'face another evening at the Friday Club'. The topic of Clive's paper has not survived. Various relatives and old family friends of the Stephens paid calls on the new couple, but were soon led to understand that their visits were not appreciated. Lytton was relieved to see that Clive and Vanessa 'were somewhat less insistent on the fact that they were in love', although once, when he entered a room unexpectedly, 'There was a most violent scrimmage heard & they both appeared very red and tousled.'

Clive and Lytton shared an enthusiastic enjoyment of sex, though obviously differing in 'one important respect', as Clive noted. Both Bells were impressed by Lytton's lewd poems: Vanessa enjoyed them so much she learned them by heart and typed copies for Virginia. Lytton thought they were a 'wild sprightly couple' whose surroundings reflected the influence of both their heritage and their modern ideas about marriage: 'The drawing room has no carpet or wall-paper, curtains some blue and some white, a Louis XV bed (in which they lie side by side), two basket chairs, a pianola, and an Early Victorian mahogany table!' Clive demonstrated his aesthetic sensibility by hiding 'all the match boxes because their blue and yellow swore with the prevailing colour scheme'.

For Clive, Cambridge remained a centre; he went there often for readings, plays or meetings of an Essay Club. Weekends in rented Cornwall or Sussex cottages invariably meant reunions with Saxon, Lytton, Walter, Desmond and others. Pressing on Vanessa was the question of who might be a suitable husband for her demanding sister, with men from the Cambridge circle the most likely prospects. They made plans for an autumn holiday at Playden, near Rye in East Sussex, with Adrian and Virginia to take one cottage, Clive and Vanessa another, and several friends promised to visit. But first they had to endure summer at Cleeve House and by June, Vanessa was pregnant.

Virginia once described Clive's mother as a 'little rabbit-faced woman';[3] his sisters were 'exactly what one would have guessed'. Lorna, twenty-nine in 1907, and Dorothy, nineteen, seemed to Vanessa to have few interests beyond balls, hunting and hockey; she disdained what she felt was their simpering prurience about sex. Cory Bell, a career military officer with whom Clive always got on well, visited infrequently now that he was married; Vanessa appreciated his bluff straightforwardness. Although Clive's feelings about his family generally differed little from Vanessa's, he discriminated between the abrasive Lorna and his youngest sibling, Dorothy, with whom he maintained affectionate relations. Dorothy had spent a long time convalescing at home from an illness, attended by a doctor and three hospital nurses, and would never enjoy complete good health.[4]

The countryside to some extent redeemed Cleeve House for Clive, who never lost his enjoyment of beagling, shooting and hunting. He took pleasure in sitting until dark in the garden, watching nocturnal creatures emerge while he escaped the prevailing lethargic atmosphere of 'discussion without thought, joviality without wit, dissertation without intellect or knowledge'. He viewed sardonically his treatment at home as a 'clever young man'. For her part, Vanessa at once set about establishing boundaries at her in-laws' to allow her to work. Mr Bell added a library with bedrooms above it in 1907, completing the renovations he had begun in the 1880s. Rare for the time, the house had electric light, the harsh glare of which both Clive and Vanessa detested.

Whenever she wrote to Virginia from Seend, Vanessa worried about using her father-in-law's blotting paper lest it carry traces of her 'seditious remarks'. On the other hand, she did not worry about leaving letters lying about the house because she knew that the upright Bells would not dream of prying in the manner of Lytton, who liked wicked gossip as much as Virginia did. As far as she could, Vanessa

[3]Angelica Garnett described Hannah Bell in her seventies: 'Her skin was as soft as down, her lips pleated round the edge as though drawn by a thread. Her pale prominent eyes were very like those of Clive, and her hands so fragile they reminded me of the claws of a marmoset.' (*Deceived* 61)

[4]Her daughter Dinah Baxter thinks Dorothy might have had typhoid in the early 1900s, and noted that her mother suffered from numerous ailments throughout her life (email 1 April 2019).

avoided Clive's family, first setting up an area in Clive's dressing-room in which to paint and later in a barn, where she attempted a portrait of her husband and an almost life-size one of Virginia wearing a green and yellow dress. When she thought about her developing baby, she feared its genetic inheritance, worried that the Bells' 'conventionalities' might emerge in her own children.

The sole relief from endless discussion of the weather and illness was provided by Annie Raven-Hill, to whom Vanessa quickly warmed. Any kind of mockery was insulting to Lorna and Dorothy, but Mrs Raven-Hill delighted Vanessa not only by revealing that she concurred with her opinions of her in-laws but by sharing with her stories of their behaviour in a Scottish shooting lodge where Lorna and Dorothy 'thought of nothing but polishing their nails & showing off their innumerable pairs of shoes, for they also pride themselves greatly on their feet'. Annie was a source of bawdy humour and when they came to lunch or dinner, or when Vanessa and Clive went over to the Raven-Hills' house at Bromham, Vanessa could be more herself. Although the nature of the relationship between Clive and Annie might not have been made clear to her at first, by 1910 Vanessa was asking Clive for news of his 'Wiltshire whore' with whom he had by then resumed occasional sexual relations.

While Vanessa painted, Clive read a great deal at Seend – one summer he re-read all of Jane Austen – or continued to work on literary articles that would never be published, sharing them amongst a small group of friends that included Saxon, Walter Lamb and Lytton. Lytton was put in an awkward position when Clive asked for his comment on an essay he had written on Mérimée. Lytton tried to avoid answering, but Clive pressed him. 'I consulted with Virginia on the question,' Lytton told Duncan, '& she takes the same hopeless view. I wonder how long he'll go on being a literary gent.'

Clive wrote to Virginia on most evenings, flirtatious letters that often dwelled on literary matters. By the summer of 1907, she had advanced much farther along the path of a professional writer than either Lytton or Clive, having become a regular contributor to the *Times Literary Supplement*, with more than sixty reviews published. Once, after Vanessa had gone to bed, Clive wrote to ask his sister-in-law what French novelists she had read and made some recommendations. Had she read Edouard Estaunié (already regarded as old-fashioned at the time)? Mérimée's *Lettres à une inconnue*? Paul Bourget, René Bazin? And what about *Les Liaisons dangereuses*, 'the most indecent work of genius I know', and a favourite in Clive's repertoire, though Virginia would not read it until 1911. French literature, with its frisson in turn-of-the-century England of licentiousness and naughtiness, provided Clive with a topic for flirtation with his sister-in-law: when she told him that she was reading Flaubert's letters, Clive charged Roderic O'Conor with finding him a handsomely bound edition of Flaubert in Paris.

Clive found new opportunities for dalliance with Virginia when a play-reading society began to meet at either the Bell or Stephen household in London, with Lytton and Saxon Sydney-Turner regularly taking part. Clive could turn even this society's minutes (usually Saxon's task) into an opportunity for flattering Virginia. Lytton enjoyed the intellectual recklessness and intimacy of the readings, but complained to Leonard, 'If only Clive were a little less Clivy, it would be perfect.' Clive's 'Cliviness' often irritated Lytton, forming a significant refrain in the gossip he enjoyed with Virginia, who could be relied upon to repeat his bitingly witty remarks to their friends. The dramatic readings began just after Christmas 1907 with Vanbrugh's 1696 comedy about adultery, *The Relapse*. In the new year, for the first meeting at Fitzroy Square, the group read Milton's *Samson Agonistes* and *Comus*.

As the birth of his first child drew nearer, Clive's correspondence with Virginia became even more amorous. *Comus* left its traces in the rondeau titled 'Yellow & Green' that Clive wrote for Virginia's twenty-sixth birthday:

Yellow and green may well beseem
    Skin like rose petals washed with cream,
    Eyes where blithe fancy's sparks contest,
    With sombre moods of rich unrest,
And emerald sleeping passions gleam.

Passions that in some wakeful dream,
Forked-lightning-like, a cobalt seam
Split through those depths that we love best
    Yellow and green.

Peace! Take our treasures, nor misdeem
Their double import, but esteem
    These artless tokens, which exprest
    Like some fair time-worn palimpsest
Thoughts various as the Iris beam;
    Yellow and green.

In Milton's masque, a Lady is kidnapped by the lustful Comus, son of Bacchus and Circe; Comus attempts to seduce her, but she resists, telling him that he cannot understand 'the serious doctrine of virginity'; the Lady enlists the aid of Sabrina, goddess of the river Severn, who helps the Lady because she is also 'a Virgin pure'. Clive took the part of Comus, while Virginia read The Lady and Sabrina. The 'emerald sleeping passions' of Clive's poem recall the nymph Sabrina's chariot of 'Turkish blue and emerald green'; the 'depths' in which passions lie echo Milton's river imagery. Although Clive had not yet seen any of it, Virginia was already writing the novel eventually published as *The Voyage Out* (1915), in which Terence Hewet reads *Comus* to his fiancée, Rachel Vinrace, just as she begins to experience the symptoms of the illness that will kill her; the lines seem to Rachel to be 'laden with meaning'. To some extent, Virginia modelled Hewet (the son of a 'fox-hunting squire') on Clive, just as she modelled his friend St John Hirst on Lytton.

Vanessa and Clive's first child, Julian Heward Bell, was born at 46 Gordon Square on 4 February 1908. Visiting Julian's grandparents in April, Vanessa again felt cut off from the 'civilization' her sister's letters represented. Julian 'screams all day', Clive told Virginia, and Vanessa was depressed. She looked forward to dinner at the Raven-Hills', where Annie discussed contraceptive methods with her, suggesting that ways of limiting a family might have been on Vanessa's mind following the shock of a newborn. Clive entertained the idea of telling his family what he knew about Annie's daughter Betty – 'the pretty five-year-old mistake' who was the accidental result of an affair with an adjutant in the Wiltshire regiment – simply to outrage their morals.

Although unthinkable at Cleeve House, explicit discussion of sexual matters was common in Fitzroy and Gordon Squares, where there might be debate about the 'advantages of promiscuous copulation', with

Adrian and Vanessa tending against it, and Harry Norton in favour. As Virginia memorably recorded in her account of the pre-war years, when Lytton pointed at a stain on Vanessa's dress and asked, 'Semen?' it suddenly broke through 'all barriers of reticence and reserve': 'Sex permeated our conversation. The word bugger was never far from our lips. We discussed copulation with the same excitement and openness that we had discussed the nature of good.' Annie Raven-Hill provided a similar freedom in Wiltshire.

Clive, refusing even to hold Julian, endorsed the narrative Virginia began to promulgate that Vanessa's entire life was now consumed by her infant. In fact, nurses were always on hand, and Vanessa became more productive and disciplined about her painting after Julian's birth. But, as Vanessa later told Clive, her sister had since they were young 'made it her business to create a character for me according to her own wishes & has now so succeeded in imposing it upon the world that the preposterous stories are supposed to be certainly true because so characteristic'.

Ostensibly for Julian's benefit, Virginia sent two chapters of what she described as 'Nessa's life'. 'Reminiscences', as it is now known, limned a gloomy tale of life at Hyde Park Gate, that 'house of all the deaths' as Henry James described it. Clive and Virginia might well bond over literary endeavours – Vanessa maintaining that she was 'illiterate' – yet Vanessa shared with her sister a distinguished intellectual heritage. When the sisters heard of Clive's speechless amazement after reading *Adam Bede*, Vanessa remarked that she and Virginia surely had discovered George Eliot, whom their father knew, 'in the nursery'. But she would leave 'literary criticism' of 'Reminiscences' to Clive (which amounted only to correcting typing errors, 'deleting frequent occurrences of the word "painful" and approving its most rational, balanced bits of prose').

When she promised to send Clive one or two chapters of 'Reminiscences', Virginia told him she had just had a dream, about 'showing father the manuscript of my novel; and he snorted, and dropped it on to a table, and I was very melancholy, and read it this morning, and thought it bad'. This was the first time she mentioned the work-in-progress whose drafts she would show only to Clive. As usual, she ended her letter with an injunction to kiss her sister 'passionately' on her behalf.

In reply, Clive gave an account of their dinner at the Raven-Hills'. When the women left the men to their port and talk of 'music-halls and dancers and bullfights', they indulged in bawdy conversation that, according to what Vanessa had told him, would have made their husbands blush. He hoped Vanessa would not repeat the gist of it to Virginia, although it had done Vanessa good: 'It is just because women are so deliciously soft in some places that they are so exquisitely hard in others; and you who are as feminine as anything that wears a skirt (I forebear a more scientific classification) are too much of a genius to believe in your own sex – or in ours either.' The differences between men and women would frequently be the focus of Clive and Virginia's ensuing correspondence about her novel.

Literary banter gave way to more provocative elements when the Bells joined Virginia for a holiday in St Ives. Clive rarely took seriously the fragility of Virginia's psyche, encouraging her flights into mania with dangerous results and relishing the attention she gave him. To escape the cries of the 'terrible' baby who was 'the very devil', Clive and Virginia went on long walks where they discussed 'intimacy and the really exciting moments in life'. 'Tormented' by his 'half uttered and ambiguous sentences', Virginia was willing to kiss him, but, although he wanted this very much, he was too shy to act. She wrote a 'Dialogue upon a Hill', set in Cornwall, in which 'Charmides' and 'Eugenia' discuss how difference of sex lends points of view particular emphases: 'It seems to be true that when an equal, and a sufficiently high, level of intelligence is reached by both they have much to say to each other which neither would say to a person of the same sex.' Tellingly, the narrator remarks that 'their relationship forbids any motive of another kind to have its effect upon their words': indeed, common morals forbade Virginia and Clive's flirtation. When Clive asked if she thought they had ever 'achieve[d] the heights' he had these Cornish walks in mind. Back in London, Virginia learned from Saxon that in running after her train with a book that she had left behind, Clive had fallen on the platform, injuring his hands and knees, which led to correspondence in the language of chivalry, with Clive as a knight who had suffered wounds in her service.

Clive's rejection of the role of *père de famille* and Vanessa's self-consciousness about the encumbrances required by a baby, occasioned a rift between them that fed the 'blue devils' of depression which seized

Vanessa. Clive's letters to his sister-in-law began to sound more like a lover's: 'I can't resist writing a note to tell you that I am very happy and that I have thought a great deal about you since Friday; not more than during the black, preceding fortnight, I daresay, but how differently, with how new a delight. I want to come and see you, but I scarcely know what I should say if I did.' Clive apologised for the way he talked when Adrian was present – 'The robust, manly way, I mean. You see it's impossible to say "That's what you and I think about it, but Virginia has a view of the world which makes what she says about it worth a great deal more than all we shall ever think".' He could not take a tone of high seriousness in conversations with Virginia when her brother was present, but took 'refuge under the nonsensical and patronising tone'. Virginia told Clive that when he and Adrian talked, she plunged into 'a phantom world' of her own thoughts, though she did not 'see that these matters are very exalted, or any better than your manly talk'. She longed to find 'a kind of talk which we could all talk, without these mystic reservations'. Vanessa, too, had commented on the nature of male conversation as she experienced it in a Scottish hunting lodge with Clive that summer:

> At lunch they talked of wine – at dinner of beer – after dinner of cigars. I feel that if only I were writing a novel this would probably be an unequalled opportunity for me to hear what male conversation is really like – for one single & solitary female I think makes practically no difference to their talk. It is such undiluted male that it quite amuses me, as watching some strange beast would.

Clive agreed that the 'overpowering aroma of the well-washed natural British male' would be useful to Virginia as a novelist.

While Vanessa imagined her sister's life of 'rarefied culture' in London, she had to listen to Lorna discuss a bazaar at which the entire village of Seend was expected. Vanessa's suggestion that 'Apricot' would be a suitable name for the protagonist of her sister's novel might have been an acerbic joke prompted by Vanessa's irritation at being in Seend, but Clive felt rebuffed when Virginia rejected his sincere proposal that the character be named 'Belinda'. Vanessa wondered whether she would be allowed to see the letters Clive wrote her sister, 'or are they too private?' No doubt her husband had told Virginia in 'one of his 18th century epistles' that they were discussing her genius, a word guaranteed to excite Virginia's curiosity.

Clive had a sincere belief in Virginia's genius and took seriously his role as first critic of her fiction's drafts, telling her that she was likely to penetrate as far as Vanessa had 'into the arcana of the male mind'. Reading Virginia's prose humbled Clive. She captured 'by sheer force of imagination' a form that he could only 'enjoy through an interpreter'. She had the 'power . . . of lifting the veil & showing inanimate things in the mystery & beauty of their reality'. He consoled himself with the thought that 'the next best thing to appreciating reality is, I suppose, to appreciate genius'. If Clive could not be an artist himself, he could explain art to others, sharing his finely tuned sensibility.

The trust that developed because of their intimacy allowed Clive to respond sincerely to 'Melymbrosia' (the working title of Virginia's novel) without ever teasing or patronising her. Her willingness to show him her work gave Clive the necessary confidence to hone his critical skills as she made clear that she found his frank comments helpful. He worried that her revisions might 'splinter' the 'hard, solid, thing' he detected beneath the 'loose draperies in the first hundred pages'. The comment seems prescient now, given Virginia's later expression of an aesthetic embodying the 'light of a butterfly's wing' on a 'framework of steel'. The changing of characters' names was trivial, as far as she was concerned, but the question of whether her conception was solid was vitally important to her and therefore Clive's analysis was highly interesting, his encouragement immensely welcome. Rather pathetically, all Clive had to offer of his own writing was his letters to her, which he asked Virgina to re-read and comment on. Dutifully, she urged him not to remain content only with what he knew he could achieve easily, but to take the risk of trying 'to grasp things that you don't quite grasp'.

'Melymbrosia' deformed the traditional marriage plot as it drew upon its author's circumstances in 1908 and 1909. Clive often took advantage of his position to manipulate relations with Virginia's suitors, as Vanessa, finding herself in the role of caretaker when Virginia's health broke down, urged her to marry. After Walter Headlam, who had been a protégé of Julia Stephen, their mother, and was sixteen years older than Virginia, died suddenly in 1908, the possibilities became limited to Cambridge contemporaries of Clive's such as Hilton Young or Walter

Lamb (and later, Sydney Waterlow). Clive's confidence in his special place in his sister-in-law's life was easily shaken by any attentions she bestowed on these men he perversely saw as rivals.

Vanessa discussed her sister's marital prospects with Clive and once told Virginia that she would like Lytton as a brother-in-law better than anyone, though that could only be realised if he were to fall in love with Adrian. Walter Lamb, diffident and awkward, had no notion that Virginia was discussing his approaches to her with Clive, although he welcomed his friend's insights into her thinking, as well as his reassurance when he worried that Virginia did not like him. 'I must leave him to fight his own battles, only too happy to escape his fate,' Clive wrote mockingly of Walter to Virginia. Meanwhile, Virginia resented the pressure to marry.

By the time Virginia joined the Bells for a holiday in Tuscany in 1908, the emotions contained in letters that Vanessa might not have been allowed to read threatened to erupt in the open. In keeping with a long family tradition of life-writing, Virginia followed 'Reminiscences' with a brief biography of Clive, penned in her Italian travel diary. The sketch reveals what Clive (or maybe Vanessa) had told her about his early life: a young man at odds with a family that is untouched by the arts returns from school scornful of young ladies who do not recognise when he is quoting Shakespeare. He discovers 'that he belonged to the select race of people who are called clever'. Perhaps the tone of the sketch annoyed him, or maybe the strain of being with the married couple away from England exacerbated Virginia's tendency to mock. Whatever the cause, Quentin Bell was later told that Virginia and Clive screamed at one another in the streets of Perugia. They quarrelled again so fiercely in Siena that Virginia abruptly returned to England. (In 1935, she sent Clive a postcard from that city with an 'x' drawn on the photograph of the Via della Fortezza to mark the spot where they had argued in 1908.)

At the Duomo di Siena, with its striking black and white striped columns, inlaid marble mosaic floor and statuary by Bernini, Donatello and Michelangelo, Clive 'spent many exquisite hours entranced by the richest interior I have ever seen, lost in infinite splendour of colour and line'. As art historian Richard Shone notes, Clive's 'enthusiasm for the early Sienese was infectious and in Perugia Vanessa's main discovery seems to have been the Peruginos in the Galleria Nazionale and his frescoes in the Collegio del Cambio'. Unencumbered by Julian (who was with a nurse at Seend) or by Virginia, Clive and Vanessa continued on to Paris to sit in cafés with his artist friends. They discussed spending an entire winter there, though the thought of what Julian would need deterred Vanessa. In Italy, Clive had found Virginia too ethereal, floating through the country 'like the moon in a wind-storm'. With Virginia gone, Vanessa took on a renewed appeal for him. She was one of 'the best specimens of her sex', he told Lytton, and he should not take too seriously whatever Virginia told him about Clive's compliments. It seemed extraordinary to Lytton that the 'little canary-coloured creature' should have managed to accompany to Italy the 'two most beautiful and wittiest women in England!' He teased Leonard that he should not be surprised were he to hear that he had married Virginia.

The circles around Fitzroy and Gordon Squares began to expand. Duncan Grant now regularly visited 29 Fitzroy Square, enamoured of Adrian, and both households had also caught the attention of Lady Ottoline Morrell, who invited them to 'at home' evenings at 44 Bedford Square where they mingled with politicians, intellectuals and artists at the forefront of new ways of seeing and thinking. Ottoline had first met the Bells at Augustus John's studio. She had heard of Vanessa and Virginia as the flames to which some young Cambridge intellectuals were drawn like moths: 'They sit round the fire in a dark room and say nothing, except occasionally, after a long silence, one of them makes a very clever remark.' That day at John's studio, the Bells stood in front of a picture of a boat and a fisherman on a lake, Clive 'gesticulating in an excited way, showering speechless admiration, Vanessa, head bent, approving'.

John was the star of the New English Art Club,[5] a painter whose gifts were admired by critics but whose distortions placed him dangerously close to what was in vogue in Paris. Even Lytton, who had found the NEAC exhibition of 1907 a 'depressing spectacle', told Leonard, in Apostolic vocabulary, that John was 'a reality, though a terrific one'. Clive told O'Conor that John reminded him of Poussin. His *Childhood*

---

[5]Founded in 1886 to counter the power of the Royal Academy, by 1890 the NEAC was briefly dominated by a group led by Walter Sickert that favoured work in the manner of Degas and Monet. By 1905, although the NEAC was showing work by the most talented Slade students, such as Augustus John and William Orpen, 'it was no longer the place to hang truly radical painting' (Gruetzner Robins, *Modern* 181).

of Pyramus soon appeared on the wall of 46 Gordon Square, purchased by the Bells for 100 guineas. However, reviewing the 1908 Salon d'Automne, a *Times* critic made clear the distance between what was considered progressive in London and in Paris: 'Those who may fancy themselves shocked by occasional examples of what they take to be revolutionary painting at the New English Art Club or elsewhere in London should pay a visit to the Autumn Salon in Paris. There they will see real revolutionary painting, compared to which the most extreme works of Mr. John are as timid as the opinions of a Fabian Socialist compared with those of a bomb-throwing anarchist.' It would take some time for Clive to catch up with this estimation of John. To Lytton, the wild, hard-drinking and promiscuous John was the epitome of the 'horrid sordid' creatures that were painters; he worried that Duncan might end up becoming like that.

Clive heard often from Lytton that Gordon and Fitzroy Squares were the only sources of his happiness, to which he escaped as often as he could from the misery of various amorous disasters in Cambridge. One November evening in 1908, Lytton and Vanessa had such a long and 'remarkable' conversation that, as she prepared to go to Seend for Christmas, she told Clive 'something definite is bound to happen': Virginia would be 'practically engaged' to Lytton before long. Clive tried to regard Virginia's suitors as minor irritants but Lytton was in a different category.

Towards the end of 1908, Clive fell into a melancholy state, complaining to Virginia that he and Vanessa did not even sleep together any more because 'the baby takes up all her time'. He spent a few days alone on the Norfolk coast where, he was ashamed to admit, he had adapted his demeanour to suit the company of a young lieutenant he met at his hotel. Despondently, he told Virginia that someone like Hilton Young could never understand such complex emotions as he was experiencing, implying that Young would not be an adequate match for her. The idyll of Paris was a dim memory that Christmas at Seend, where the unvaried round of balls and meets seemed to Clive like a dull toothache. On Christmas Day, Virginia reassured Clive that she was not in love with Lytton, who had spent Christmas Eve with her at Fitzroy Square.

Just before the first play-reading of the new year, Lytton abruptly left for Cambridge, messing up the casting for *Antony and Cleopatra*, so the friends chose instead to read from whatever books they had to hand. As Walter Lamb was in attendance, Virginia's choice of Spenser's *Epithalamion* (bridal song) was provocative. Clive recorded in the minutes that her reading 'revealed beauties at which I'd never have come unaided. The poem possesses, henceforth, a new loveliness and an added association.' The Bloomsbury denizens also embarked on a new amusement, a series of pseudonymous letters they thought might result in a collectively produced epistolary novel in the manner of Laclos: Clive liked nothing better than some *liaisons dangereuses*.

Under cover of their pseudonyms in the letter-writing game – in effect, a *bal masqué* – Vanessa was able to tell her sister she felt deserted by Clive. Lytton used the game to probe Virginia's feelings about Clive, and Clive in turn complained to Virginia that Vanessa gossiped too much with Lytton. The eighteenth-century epistolary convention led Clive into even more sentimental flirtation with Virginia: 'I once saw you, sitting on a bench at Hampton Court with soft deep eyes, and in their depths the last secrets of things.' In the midst of all this, Lytton sudenly proposed to Virginia, although both of them dropped the idea of their marriage as preposterous almost at once. Clive had been worried enough by what Vanessa told him about Lytton's intentions to try to dampen his ardour, but had to 'unsay' what he had written to Lytton when Virginia made clear that she reciprocated his feelings. Although, as Adrian noted, Virginia's 'most daring sallies . . . never fail of their guffaw when Clive is present', he did not have quite the exclusive hold on her affections he imagined.

Virginia had sent a revised draft (now lost) of 'Melymbrosia' to Clive in early 1909 but it would be the last time she did so. He faulted her for having destroyed the atmosphere he had so admired in the earlier draft. More significantly, he rejected what he characterised as her didacticism: 'Our views about men & women are doubtless quite different, and the difference doesn't matter much but to draw such marked contrasts between the subtle, sensitive, tactful, gracious, delicately perceptive, & perspicacious women, & the obtuse, vulgar, blind, florid, rude, tactless, emphatic, indelicate, vain, tyrannical, stupid men, is not only rather absurd, but rather bad art, I think.' Despite these objections, he remained astonished by the poetic force of her writing, as well as her ability to convey Rachel Vinrace's impressions of other characters. The picnic scene (chapter 10 in *The Voyage Out*) he thought

Clive Bell with Julian Bell

comparable to Austen's in *Emma*: 'How on earth, by telling us what it was like at noon, do you show us what it was like at five, at sunset, and at night?'

Virginia's reply was firm: grateful for his advice, she outlined how she planned to continue, explaining that the passages Clive had found clumsy were in effect her notes on how to deepen her sense of her characters. 'Your objection that my prejudice against men makes me didactic "not to say priggish", has not quite the same force with me,' she told him. 'Possibly, for psychological reasons which seem to me very interesting, a man, in the present state of the world, is not a very good judge of his sex; and a "creation" may seem to him "didactic".' His encouragement had made all the difference but now, terrified by her 'boldness', she was ready to move past his advice. Their discussions about the difference between men and women had been useful, but Clive would receive no more drafts of 'Melymbrosia'.

Clive realised that Virginia was pulling away from him. He wrote to tell her that the night before her 'beautiful grey manuscript' arrived, he had dreamed she was reading stories to him: 'If you believe you have anything else worth reading, you must believe also that I would be at any pains to read it.' His letter closed with 'a fragment of a sonnet' purportedly found 'amongst the papers of an obscure but highly interesting poet of the early 20th century'. The fragment, he said, had a faint dedication, 'To V. S. suggested by a certain philosophic debate on the nature of genius.' His fantasy concluded with Clive's invention of an editorial annotation identifying '[V.S. The great contemporary novelist (1882–1972)?]'.

Despite his transparent motive to flatter Virginia into continuing to send him her drafts, Clive did genuinely believe in his sister-in-law's genius. Near the end of his life he maintained that among all the many clever and gifted people he had known there had been only two geniuses: Picasso and Virginia Woolf.

In 1909, Vernon Rendall took Clive on as a regular reviewer for the *Athenaeum*. Continuing to feel directionless, Clive chafed at being viewed as a professional writer rather than a man of letters. At the same time, Virginia was honing her craft under Bruce Richmond's tutelage at the *Times Literary Supplement*, although being taken to dinner by him made her feel like a 'cannibal', aware that the meal was paid for in the blood of struggling young writers such as herself. When she, Clive and Lytton (in the *Spectator*) all reviewed *The Love Letters of Thomas Carlyle and Jane Welsh*, the old Wiltshire gentlemen at Cleeve House praised Virginia as 'that remarkably clever and original young writer' in the *TLS*, while discussion of Clive's *Athenaeum* review fell flat. Having no illusions about who was the better writer, Clive made sure not only to show Virginia his publications but to seek her advice. Her innovative 'Memoirs of a Novelist' might have influenced Clive's review of Arthur Clutton-Brock's biography of Shelley, which he praised as an interesting new approach to the genre that eschewed the 'grave defect' of Victorian biography, the assumption that a life developed logically. If every life is a 'work of art', he wrote, then only an artist can create a biography from 'a heap of small and seemingly disconnected facts'. Some of the concerns of the gifted group of young writers to which Clive belonged were beginning to emerge.

Clive's contributions to the *Athenaeum* were solid, journeyman pieces which rarely showed the flair of his later writing. He had begun to realise that he wanted to write about the plastic arts but was unsure how to do so or where. He had very little, if any, interest in the material aspects of Vanessa's world of pigments and brushes, stretchers and canvas, and as yet lacked a vocabulary for articulating whatever inchoate ideas he might have had about aesthetics. As far as Roderic O'Conor was concerned, the *Athenaeum* was risible for taking seriously the work of a painter like Gerald Kelly.

Since becoming editor, Rendall had done little to alter the appearance or outlook of the Victorian flagship. The literary marketplace was rapidly changing, with what Ezra Pound would call the 'elder magazines' challenged by the emergence of myriad 'little magazines' to feed a public hungry for new reading matter. Echoing O'Conor, Arnold Bennett, writing in the *New Age* as 'Jacob Tonson', attacked the *Athenaeum* for its obsequiousness. O'Conor hoped that Clive would revitalise the 'staid and respectable and somewhat pedantic' periodical, but Clive complained about the interventions of his editor. His greater interest lay in the discussion he and O'Conor continued about art.

When he sent the painter a portfolio of drawings, O'Conor commented that English artists seemed perpetually in thrall to

Turner and Hogarth, always dragging in 'something literary', and recommended more study of 'the Egyptian, Assyrian and Cambodgian [sic]' as a corrective.[6] He also kept Clive apprised of the work of artists in Paris about whom he inquired, such as the sculptor Aristide Maillol, Matisse, Puy and Lapirade. O'Conor was pleased to hear from Clive when Gauguin was being discovered in England because he believed that Gauguin might provide a pathway for English painters to follow, but he lamented that no appropriate language for modern art other than 'new fangled jargon' existed. If a critic were to write intelligently about the work of a Cézanne or a Matisse, he would have to be 'as much of an artist as the painter he criticizes'.

Discussing art with O'Conor made Clive feel more than ever isolated in London. The many friends from Cambridge whom he continued to see, such as Harry Norton, Ralph Hawtrey and Saxon, might think more or less like him but, he told Lytton, 'we don't feel alike'. The feelings he had experienced before works of art in Italy and in Paris were what he wanted to write about. He and Vanessa even discussed not renewing their lease and moving to Paris: in London there was 'no splendour of harmonious composition such as ravished' his soul in Paris.

Both Clive and Vanessa felt 'oppressed by the family weight' at Cleeve House and on a brief holiday in Cornwall, Clive had even found the Stephen family depressing when Adrian spent the entire time berating his sisters for having suppressed him in childhood. As the Bells made plans for another trip to Italy with Virginia, she could not help asking Clive why he would want her 'bundle of tempers' with him in Florence. It was a wise question because, despite once again having wanted to kiss her in Cornwall and once again being too shy, Clive also again quarrelled with her in Italy, which led Virginia to storm home and leave Vanessa and Clive to enjoy Florence in peace.

Before the contretemps, they had visited old Hyde Park Gate friends of the Duckworths, the Corsinis, at the Villa Fontellerta, as well as the celebrated art historian Bernard Berenson and his neighbours, Janet and Henry Ross. Mrs Ross commanded Clive to take a young woman to see her rose garden, but it was cold and raining and he

[6]Elizabeth Berkowitz notes that Cambodian art was exhibited in England, Europe and America since at least the nineteenth century under various names, including Khmer and Cambogian. Gauguin owned photographs of Cambodian objects (email 29 December 2017).

had no idea where the garden was. 'Who are some awful relations of yours called Barnes?' Vanessa inquired of Lytton on her return to London. Mary Barnes and her brother James had been brought up in Florence by their grandparents, Sir John and Lady Strachey, following the premature death of their mother, Winifred Strachey; Sir John was Lytton's uncle. After schooling in India and England, Mary was visiting Florence from London, where she would marry the barrister St John Hutchinson the following year. At the villa Poggio Ghirardo, the twenty-year-old Mary left no favourable impression on the gentleman attempting to show her Mrs Ross's rose garden, but in 1914 Mary Hutchinson would become one of the most important people in Clive's life.

Vanessa found Clive a perfect companion in Florence, admiring his competent and unfussy organisation of their accommodations. With Virginia back in England, they fell into a routine of mornings spent looking at art, napping or reading after lunch (Vanessa finished *Les Liaisons dangereuses*), walking around the city after tea at 4.30 until dinner, after which they talked until bedtime. At the Galleria dell'Accademia, Vanessa particularly admired Botticelli's *Primavera* (now in the Uffizi), but was irritated by the 'fat backs' of German tourists who got in her way, making vivid, she told Lytton, the 'horrors of a German invasion'. They visited the Magi Chapel at the Riccardi Palace, where Benozzo Gozzoli's frescoes line the walls, and went to the Badia where they saw Giotto's Polyptych (also now in the Uffizi). They returned to S. Croce after Virginia left because they had missed visiting several of its magnificently frescoed chapels. Clive, Vanessa told Snow, was 'inclined to put the primitives high above everyone else – above all the great Venetians even', though Vanessa still revered Titian. When Walter Lamb visited Venice that May, he decided that Clive was right about the 'primitives'. Before long, Clive would discover in Roger Fry the interlocutor he needed to help him articulate the ideas that had been forming about the art he had seen in Italy in 1908 and 1909. For now, though, returning to England meant a return to malaise and to his infatuation with Virginia.

By the end of 1909, Clive had also resumed his affair with Annie Raven-Hill, who looked 'delicious' in a fur coat when he met her at Paddington one morning. If life were a play, he told Virginia, he had no idea whether he was in the audience or on the stage. Clive's letters made Virginia feel uncomfortably self-conscious, so on Christmas Eve she impulsively decided to go by herself to Lelant in Cornwall. Despite their quarrel, Clive recalled their time in Florence with a romantic glow in a poem that at first Virginia was too shy to admit had greatly pleased her. 'To V. S. with a Book' also alluded to the 'heights' of their flirtation in Cornwall:

> The cypress shadows creeping gnomonwise
> Still stretch their purple fingers down the hill
> That hangs above Fiesole: and still
> Your English fireside glows. Do you most dear –
> Sometimes just guessed at, sometimes very near –
> Yet always dear and fairest friend, do you
> Recall the sunlight and the firelight too?
> Recall the pregnant hours, the gay delights,
> The pain, the tears maybe, the ravished heights,
> The golden moments my cold lines commend,
> The days, in memory of which I send
> A book?

Clive would remain proud of this poem, including it in both a privately published collection made for his friends in 1917, and for a wider audience in his *Poems* of 1921.

As the momentous year 1910 began, Vanessa increasingly worried about her unstable sister. Avoiding 'excitement' became a refrain in Vanessa's letters to Virginia, and perhaps, for once, Clive showed concern for her mental state when he grumpily disapproved of her participation in the Dreadnought Hoax, infuriating Virginia.[7] In March, the Bells took Virginia to rest in Studland on the Dorset coast. In what might be the very first use of the term, Lytton asked Duncan if he had heard that 'the Bloomsbury set' had gone to the coast because Virginia had had a breakdown: 'They're all still there – quarrelling I gather from morning till night in their lodging house.'

---

[7]Virginia, Duncan, Adrian and others dressed up to convince the Navy that they were the retinue of the Emperor of Abyssinia and gained access to Britain's newest warship, causing a scandal when word of the hoax was leaked to the newspapers.

Virginia and Clive at Studland, 1910

Hoping to avoid the sorts of people who might excite Virginia, Clive asked Lytton what he knew about a reading party gathering at Studland at Easter. As G. E. Moore that year had not organised his usual gathering, Bertrand Russell (whom Moore never invited and whom Clive now met for the first time) was staying nearby with Ralph Hawtrey, Bob Trevelyan (G. M.'s brother), the barrister Charles Sanger and the economist Gerald Shove. The Bells saw little of the reading party, keeping Virginia on a strict regimen of quiet days and early nights, but on one social call Bob Trevelyan accidentally introduced Virginia as Clive's wife. The MacCarthys came for a weekend and when Desmond had to leave, Virginia invited Molly to stay on, establishing the foundation of an important friendship. Molly, now the mother of two very young children, had caught Clive's eye, but it would be another year before he began to pursue her. Clive tried to behave himself in Studland, reporting to friends such as Ottoline and Lytton on Virginia's progress, and assuring Lytton that if he believed his presence was exacerbating her anxiety he would leave.

Two weeks at Studland had no lasting salubrious effect on Virginia, so by June Vanessa had consulted Dr George Savage, who advised continued rest and removal from London. She and Clive, therefore, again took Virginia with them to the country, when they rented the Moat House in Blean, near Canterbury. Just before they left for Blean, Clive had gone with Virginia to the huge Japanese–British Exhibition at White City, where both had been strongly affected by recreations of Ainu and Uji villages, populated by actual villagers from Japan imported to demonstrate how traditional rural Japanese lived.

Clive thought Virginia had disliked seeing 'the savages: another proof if proof were needed of lack of sympathy I suppose. But it was queer, I think, that Formosa (was it or Ainoo land?) made us both sad and for quite different reasons. For the first, and I daresay the last time, I believe you felt something of what I often feel, and I felt something of what you are always feeling.' On the same day, Virginia wrote to tell him 'how much pleasure you give me'. Seemingly, both were united by an undefinable sadness, but neither elaborated on its cause, Clive remarking that his own 'depression had to do with something more fundamental than yours'.

When Vanessa returned to London with Julian, Clive stayed in Blean to look after Virginia. He had claimed that Vanessa, now pregnant again, should not exert herself, but she went directly to a meeting of the Friday Club where she noticed the promise of an eighteen-year-old Slade student named Mark Gertler. She also decided that Duncan Grant was going to be a great artist and bought his *Lemon Gatherers*, justifying the purchase by reminding Clive that they would receive a £1,000 gift from his parents on the birth of their child. Vanessa's letters to her husband while he was with Virginia at Blean tried to steer a difficult course between letting him know how much she missed him, and accepting his reasons for being there: 'the Goat [Virginia's childhood nickname] must be considered'. She knew that Virginia would blame her for enforcing Dr Savage's recommendation that she should take a rest cure at Burley in Twickenham – 'a kind of polite madhouse for female lunatics' run by a devout Christian named Jean Thomas.

To maintain private correspondence with Clive, Vanessa enclosed secret notes addressed to 'My Peak' (a nickname only she used for him) with the letters to him she knew that Virginia would insist upon seeing.

These notes, signed 'Dolphin', Virginia's nickname for her sister which had also been adopted by Clive, make clear that Clive's absence in Blean caused her pain, yet also that Clive disliked overt expressions of emotion from her. Vanessa told Clive she had been 'meditating on marriage! How odd it is – it seems to give me something that these other people & I before I married had no conception of. It is you who give it to me I suppose not marriage – Your nature gives it to me. It is like being always thirsty & always having some delicious clear water to drink. You do make me astonishingly & continuously happy. <u>Be quiet Dolphin.</u>'

Given her husband's 'strange virile jealousies' of Virginia's suitors, his treatment of Vanessa at this time is simply cruel. As they had in 1908, letters between the three became fraught with emotional risk. Vanessa feared 'four cold & critical literary eyes' at Blean dissecting every word she wrote and, when later that year Virginia entered Jean Thomas's nursing home, Vanessa continued to feel excluded because Clive would not show her the letters Virginia wrote him. Vanessa hoped that by the time her baby was born, Virginia might be someone else's responsibility.

When Quentin Bell was born on 19 August, Virginia was in Cornwall on a walking holiday with Jean Thomas. Vanessa had hoped for a girl, naming her baby *in utero* Clarissa; when Clarissa emerged as a boy, the child remained nameless for some time until his brother, Julian, said that Quentin would be the best name. Almost as soon as his second son was born, Clive wrote anxiously to Virginia that she seemed changed, urging her to keep him and Vanessa informed about her state of mind. Her reply did nothing to reassure him when she told him she had been thinking about the man 'to whom I shall say certain things'. As he did so often, Clive mingled his emotional possessiveness with ostensible concern for Virginia's work:

> To speculate on what exactly it is that you want to say to the man you will love is not a congenial occupation: that way ill temper and irritation lies, if not madness. You'll see what a jolly, hearty, well-feeling, affectionate, slap-you-on-the-back-with-a-tear-in-one-eye, manly, pseudo-insouciant, damme-don't-care-a-rap-have-a-cigar-old-chap attitude I shall take up about your marriage in the future. But I hope you're going to write something about women first, before your sharp edges get blunted in the bed.

His attitude to her marriage would be nothing of the sort, at first.

Some time in the autumn of 1910, Vanessa let Virginia know that Lytton was anxious to 'get on friendly terms again with us all'. The precise reasons for a severe breakdown in relations between Clive and Lytton cannot be recovered but while at Studland in April, the pent-up feelings Clive apparently had long harboured about what he heard through the Cambridge and Bloomsbury grapevines boiled over in an extraordinarily bitter letter to Lytton. Significantly, Clive told Lytton that Vanessa approved of what he had to say:

> I should be even more obtuse than you suppose had I not perceived long ago that you despised me. Your arrogant manners, your condescending attitude, the things that you are in the habit of saying to our common acquaintances, leave no doubt as to your feelings. You are painfully alive to the fact that I was trained outside the mystic circle of metropolitan culture wherein alone a young man may hope to acquire the distinguished manner. My manners you find florid and vulgar, over emphatic and underbred, whence you infer – wrongly as I think – that my appreciations are more or less blunt and that I am deficient in sensitiveness to the finer shades of thought and feeling. Your consciousness of my faults – my lack of refinement in particular – is a cause of constant irritation in you, in me a cause of sporadic bitterness. Such feelings are incompatible with anything approaching confident friendship. As you are never at the least pains to conceal your opinion of me, though diligent enough in making it manifest, I shall not hesitate for once, to speak frankly of you, though I should not care to publish my thoughts abroad.

Evidently, Lytton's complaints about his 'Cliviness' had got back to Clive, but the letter – to which no reply survives – is shot through with Clive's uncomfortable awareness that he is an interloper in a class that would never overlook his provincial origins. That he was so regarded is exemplified by a remark Rupert Brooke, with whom Lytton was staying when Clive wrote this letter, made to Lytton's brother James. After encountering Clive at the theatre, Brooke 'felt sharply and suddenly what you perhaps meant when you said he was no gentleman'. Clive reminded Lytton that at Cambridge his closest friend had had no such supercilious feelings about him: 'Do you suppose that Thoby was or Vanessa is blind to my florid ways? When one cares, such superficial things become a joke, an attraction almost, not a source of constant irritation or an excuse for studied contempt.' Lytton was no longer welcome at Clive and Vanessa's house in Gordon Square.[8]

Virginia shortly heard from Walter Lamb 'that Lytton is much broken in mind and health and is looking for lodgings for the term. Perhaps this is a result of the letter.' She could appreciate Clive's 'position under Lytton's treatment' because she thought Vanessa probably 'abused' her in private similarly to how Lytton abused Clive. Although Clive had confidence in his sensibilities and in his growing interest in aesthetic theory, a figure such as Lytton could lead him to suspect that everyone was laughing at him behind his back. Vanessa gave Clive the confidence to stand up to Lytton's mockery but the impetus to formulate his emerging ideas about art would come from a new member of the Bells' intimate circle.

[8] The letter has an interesting history. Levy's edition of Strachey's letters transcribes a typewritten 'draft' which 'Olivier Bell thinks was probably written in autumn 1911' (203). Peter Stansky also quotes from the letter, basing it on the typewritten version shown him by Anne Olivier Bell and, he says, dated to June 1911 (*On* 256n3). The draft was made on a typewriter belonging to Virginia Woolf; Levy says it was 'apparently typed by' her, but it is possible, of course, that someone else used her machine. Levy also notes that this draft was 'corrected in pencil and pen by Leonard Woolf' (203). In 2015, a group of letters from Clive Bell to Lytton Strachey was sold at auction in London. Among them was the holograph original of this letter (C-W). There are only four minor differences between the text of the original and the typescript, but the letter is clearly dated 'April 17 '10' (so if Leonard Woolf annotated the typed 'draft', it must have been much later).

7. Roger

When Vanessa and Clive met Roger Fry one January morning in 1910 waiting for the train to King's Cross from Cambridge, the eminent art scholar was at a low point in his life. Walter Headlam had once reverently drawn Vanessa's attention to Fry and his wife, Helen, as they crossed the Fellows' Garden at King's College and when, some years later, she had sat next to him at a dinner given by Desmond MacCarthy, Fry seemed to be one of the older 'terrifying figures' who 'somehow [had] the secret of the art universe within their grasp'.

Had Clive been elected to the Apostles, he might have met Roger at Cambridge before 1910. Fifteen years older than Clive, Fry was a recognised authority on Florentine art and one of the founders of the *Burlington Magazine*. In 1904, after reviewing in the *Athenaeum* D. S. MacColl's collection of articles on *The Administration of the Chantrey Bequest*, Fry had given evidence to the House of Lords' inquiry into how the Royal Academy had been spending the funds which the Regency sculptor Sir Francis Chantrey had left for the purchase of works of art for the nation, a topic that would continue to arouse controversy, ire and ridicule for at least another fifty years.

It was only around 1905 that Fry had begun to show any interest in modern painting. When Clive and Vanessa encountered him at the railway station, he had just returned from New York and was about to lose his position as curator at the Metropolitan Museum of Art there, having clashed repeatedly with the unscrupulous president of its board of trustees, J. P. Morgan. Fry hoped to be appointed the first Slade professor of art at Oxford, but the position instead went to the Arts and Crafts designer Selwyn Image. In addition to these professional frustrations, it had become clear to Fry that his wife's mental illness made it inevitable she would have to be committed to an asylum. Yet Fry's passion for art and boundless enthusiasm for all kinds of schemes to enlighten the public remained undiminished. By the time their train reached London, Clive had agreed to help Roger organise an exhibition of recent French painting, thus decisively changing the direction of his life and providing the origin story of England's encounter with post-Impressionism.

Clive thought Roger's idea was fantastical but, as he and Vanessa would quickly discover, the older man's optimism was indomitable. Looking back on that railway journey in the 1950s, Clive claimed to have 'already written in praise of Cézanne and Gauguin and other "revolutionaries"' when he met Roger, but unless he had in mind his correspondence with O'Conor and other friends in Paris, this was wishful thinking. Even so, the two men could not have met at a more fortuitous moment because Clive would be helped through Roger's writing and conversation to express his own inchoate ideas about modern art and Roger would find in Clive a relentless proselytiser of the new. Vanessa and Clive brought him into contact with the circle of young painters connected with the Friday Club (to which he lectured that February). Roger, in turn, gave the Bells access to the Bond Street art world, 'taking them to see rare primitives and Old Masters hidden away in dealers' stores'. They made several visits that summer to Durbins, the house Roger had designed for himself near Guildford, where his eight-year-old daughter, Pamela, sometimes found Clive's efforts to amuse her 'ended in too much teasing and too much tickling', although she did feel friendly towards him.

Clive soon became familiar with the trait for which Roger was both loved and teased by many of his friends: he always had a dozen schemes of varying degrees of possibility afoot. In addition to the exhibition of modern French art, Roger asked Clive's help in beginning a new periodical for which he already had £500 promised. While this came to nothing, a venture he had initiated in 1909 was bearing fruit. Pondering how to support living British artists – something the Royal Academy's administration of the Chantrey Bequest woefully failed to do – Roger had solicited Ottoline Morrell, D. S. MacColl (Keeper of the Tate Gallery) and C. J. Holmes (director of the National Portrait Gallery) to start a fund for the purpose of buying paintings. In 1910, Roger invited Clive to join the committee for what came to be named the Contemporary Art Society.

Roger's thinking about modern painting had begun to evolve when two works by Cézanne had caught his attention at the International Society exhibition in 1905. In an article in the *Athenaeum*, Roger described Cézanne's 'peculiar genius' as a solution to a problem that had long vexed him: how to integrate a modern vision with the old masters' sense of design. His ideas about Cézanne received confirmation when an English translation of the German critic Julius Meier-Graefe's *Modern Art* appeared in 1908. Its subtitle – *Being a Contribution to a New System of Aesthetics* – indicated its emphasis on formal problems rather than on art as an expression of personality or narrative.

Giorgio Vasari's influential model of a progressive development from childish 'primitivism', exemplified by artists such as Cimabue and Giotto, to the 'classical' pinnacle of Michelangelo, via the 'adolescence' of the period of Masaccio and Donatello, provided a narrative framework for art history well into the twentieth century. It was disseminated, for example, by Heinrich Wölfflin's *Classic Art* (1899 and 1903) which, like Vasari's *Lives of the Artists* (1550 and 1568), glorified 'the High Renaissance by denigrating that which came before'. 'Painters from various centres in Italy, working in the period c.1180–1400 or even later were known collectively as the "primitives" as late as the 1970s.' Meier-Graefe treated Gauguin as a 'primitive' and, like Fry, regarded Cézanne as an established 'master'. But the English public had virtually no context within which to evaluate these arguments, having seen almost none of the works.

In 1908, Fry published a long letter in the *Burlington Magazine* criticising its review of that year's International Society show for unjustifiably treating modern art with less seriousness than it gave to the Old Masters. He argued that Impressionism should be seen as analogous to the art of the Roman empire, which had been followed by what might be called 'for convenience Byzantinism'. Fry labelled Cézanne and Gauguin 'proto-Byzantines', an appellation that avoided the pejorative connotations of 'primitive' yet amounted to much the same thing.[1]

[1] Elizabeth Berkowitz explains how use of the word 'primitive' shifted within art history after Darwin's *Descent of Man* (1871) 'to connote instead the cultural productions of less advanced societies and peoples, often decidedly non-European in origin' (101).

Roger had been introduced to the work of Matisse by Matthew Prichard, adviser to the American collector Isabella Stewart Gardner, and visited the painter's studio in 1909, describing him to his wife as 'one of the neo, neo Impressionists quite interesting & lots of talent'. He had been looking at a lot of modern painting and told Helen that he had 'got rather keen on these people lately'. Just as Clive and Vanessa left for Florence in April 1909, where Clive's high esteem for the 'primitives' would be confirmed, Roger published 'An Essay in Aesthetics' in the *New Quarterly*. It did not receive wide notice at the time, but as Desmond MacCarthy was editor of the *New Quarterly* probably Vanessa and Clive would have been aware of Roger's argument. He stressed the separation between 'imaginative life' – expressed and stimulated by art – and 'actual life'. Art, Roger maintained, expressed emotions as 'ends in themselves' and required 'unity of some kind' for the restful contemplation of what he enumerated as 'emotional elements of design'.

Even had the Bells been unaware of 'An Essay in Aesthetics', its content suggests why the three would have found they had much to discuss on their way to London from Cambridge in January 1910. As further evidence of the way Roger's thinking was tending, the first part of his translation of the French painter Maurice Denis's essay on Cézanne appeared that month in the *Burlington Magazine*. Introducing it, Roger wrote that modern French painters displayed 'a new courage to attempt in painting that direct expression of imagined states of consciousness which has for long been relegated to music and poetry'.

Also that January, Roger reviewed several books on 'Oriental Art' in the *Quarterly Review*, where he asserted that any 'critic and student of applied aesthetics' must nowadays find himself 'bewildered and amazed at the multiplicity and strangeness of the new unassimilated material'. The art of the East provided a means, he declared, for Westerners to throw off the dogma that art's purpose was representation of the natural world. Roger thought that familiarity with art from the East could encourage Western artists to 'portray only the essential elements of things' and return 'to their own long forgotten tradition'. Roger's revision of what had for so long been the received wisdom of art historical tradition would profoundly influence Clive's understanding of his own sensations.

Roger was not alone in his endeavour to change English thinking about visual art. Frank Rutter, art critic of the *Sunday Times* and English correspondent for *L'Art et les artistes* in Paris, founded the

Allied Artists' Association in 1908, the 'first British exhibiting society to introduce an absolutely liberal constitution along the lines of the Salon des Indépendants'. The AAA afforded progressive British painters an opportunity to show their work, although with 3,000 entries for its first exhibition, held at the Albert Hall, standing out was a challenge. Many of the painters – including O'Conor, Walter Sickert and J. D. Fergusson – who exhibited at the AAA 'were familiar with the work of the first-generation post-Impressionists and with more recent French art long before either were seen in London'. The time was ripe for the exhibition Roger had proposed to Clive and Vanessa on the train: by chance, he was contacted in the autumn by the Grafton Galleries in Mayfair to ask if he might have anything to fill their space between two planned shows later that year.

An important contact for Roger as he set about gathering the works for the Grafton show was Robert Dell, Paris correspondent of the *Burlington Magazine*. The mayor of Brighton had suggested an art exhibition might be attractive to Continental tourists and Dell was enlisted to choose the French section for the show that opened that summer in the seaside resort. Among works by Cross, Denis, Friesz, Rouault, Sérusier, Signac, Valloton and Vlaminck, Dell hung two still-life studies by Matisse, Gauguin's *Les Boeufs* (now known as *Christmas Night*) and Derain's *Westminster Bridge, London* (sometimes known as *Charing Cross Bridge*). Dell sounded a note in his catalogue essay that would recur often in English defences of the post-Impressionists: all new movements have at first been dismissed with ridicule but eventually 'the heresy of the past . . . has become the orthodoxy of the present'.

When Fry reviewed the exhibition for *The Times*, he singled out the one Cézanne, *M. Valabrègue*: 'You may think the picture ugly, but it stays in your mind – a sign that it has been clearly conceived in the mind of the artist.' He reiterated his argument that viewers of modern painting should relinquish their adherence to representation as a sole value: Matisse, he continued, is in many ways 'more primitive than the early Sienese in his reaction against photographic realism'.

Clive was familiar enough with the painters Dell had selected to pronounce the Brighton exhibition at once interesting and disappointing when he visited it on 22 August. There were 'good men but unrepresentative pictures', he told Virginia. The next day he discussed it with Duncan, whom he knew could appreciate it. Vanessa also now enjoyed talking about painting more than anything else with Duncan. Having had relationships with both Lytton and Maynard, Duncan was now a familiar visitor to Gordon and Fitzroy squares due to his emotional involvement with Adrian. He was also beginning to make a name for himself as a painter.

When Roger made a second trip to Paris in October to choose paintings for the Grafton exhibition and to visit the Salon d'Automne, Clive joined him there with Desmond MacCarthy (who shortly travelled to Holland to secure works by Van Gogh) and Ottoline Morrell, whose connections, for example with the American heiress Emily Chadbourne, were invaluable to Roger. Vanessa envied Clive being 'in that exciting atmosphere where people really seem to realise the existence of art'; perhaps he would come back determined they should live in Paris. The idea would recur often in their correspondence.

By the time 'Manet and the Post-Impressionists' closed at the Grafton Galleries on 15 January 1911, about 25,000 people had seen it. Many of them were baffled, scornful, outraged or offended. Roger had been prepared for 'a huge campaign of British Philistinism' and he was not disappointed. It was not lost on those critics who saw post-Impressionism as 'aesthetic Bolshevism' that the private view was held on 5 November, celebrated annually in the United Kingdom as Guy Fawkes day to commemorate the thwarted plot to blow up the House of Lords in 1605. However, many of the 'revolutionary' painters featured at the Grafton Galleries were in fact figures from *fin-de-siècle* Europe: Van Gogh had died in 1890 and Seurat in 1891 – the same year Gauguin had sailed to Tahiti.[2] Even so, by 1910 only four works by Van Gogh were in private collections in England.

As is now well-known, Roger came up with the term 'post-impressionist' at the last moment, needing to answer a journalist's question;[3] the label suited those who wished either to attack or defend what in fact was a more eclectic group of artists than the

---

[2] The most thoroughly researched account of what was exhibited is Gruetzner Robins, 'Manet and the Post-Impressionists'.

[3] Or, at least, that is the generally accepted narrative. Bullen points out that 'Frank Rutter seems to have been the first writer to use the term "Post-Impressionist" in print. In a review

term suggested. Desmond MacCarthy wrote the introduction for the exhibition's catalogue, providing hostile critics with several targets, most notably his contention that a 'good rocking-horse often has more of the true horse about it than an instantaneous photograph of a Derby winner'.

Roger's efforts to explain that the post-Impressionist painters had 'stumbled upon the principles of primitive design out of a perception of the sheer necessities of the actual situation' were not enough to thwart the onslaught of articles and letters to newspapers that saw the movement as yet another manifestation of those dangers with which late nineteenth-century England had been obsessed: degeneration, foreign invasion, infection, anarchy, revolution. An especially nasty charge emerged which often singled out Van Gogh's *Wheatfield with Crows* as its principal example: the paintings were evidence of 'aesthetic insanity'. Desmond would later recall that not only did some people say that Roger was mad, they 'reminded others that his wife was in an asylum'. The reaction of the 'cultivated classes' who had tamely absorbed his lectures on Old Masters particularly incensed Roger: 'Their interest in his lectures had been a pose; art was to them merely a social asset.' The elision of monetary and aesthetic value would become a perennial object of Clive's scorn as he transformed himself over the next year from 'literary gent' (Lytton's disparaging term) into outspoken champion of modern art.

For some people, 'Manet and the Post-Impressionists' was a liberating revelation. The New Zealand writer Katherine Mansfield, living a Bohemian life in London, learned 'a kind of freedom' in her writing from seeing the Van Goghs. Vanessa experienced a breakthrough in her painting after the Grafton show: 'It was as if at last one might say things one had always felt instead of trying to say things that other people told one to feel. Freedom was given to one to be oneself.' Freedom to be oneself would become the watchword of Clive's mature critical writing, but in 1910 he was still trying to find a usable language for his ideas and made only tentative gestures towards aesthetics in the literary reviews he continued to write for the *Athenaeum*. It was left to Frank Rutter to

of the Salon d'Automne in *Art News*, 15 October 1910, he described Othon Friesz as "a post-impressionist leader", and the same issue of *Art News* carried an advertisement for "The Post-Impressionists of France"' (5).

write *Revolution in Art* that year, dedicated 'to rebels of either sex all the world over who in any way are fighting for freedom of any kind'.

Virginia's views continued to hold sway over Clive. Her wry comment to Violet Dickinson that she was hearing 'a lot about pictures' now that her brother-in-law was 'in the van of aesthetic opinion', and that she did not think the Grafton paintings 'so good as books' hints at an attitude that might have undermined Clive's confidence. Virginia continued, 'But why all the Duchesses are insulted by the post-impressionists, a modest sample set of painters, innocent even of indecency, I cant conceive. However, one mustn't say that they are like other pictures, only better, because that makes everyone angry.'

Always eager to know what she thought, Clive was still sending Virginia his articles. She might have caught in his brief notice of E. M. Forster's *Howards End* a strange echo of his admonition that she should write something about women before her 'sharp edges get blunted in the [marriage] bed'. Forster's readers had to observe Margaret Schlegel's 'fine edges grow blunt' after her marriage to Wilcox, Clive wrote. On Christmas Day 1910, he urged Virginia to stop his 'nightmares of you trembling on the threshold of a mad-house' by letting him know how she was. On her own in Lewes, shortly to rent a house in Firle she called 'Little Talland' in memory of her childhood summers, Virginia told Clive he would have to wait and see what she had made of 'Melymbrosia': she had 'given up adventuring after other people's forms'. He sent her his review of the letters of Edward John Trelawny, friend of Byron and Shelley, which, she told him, showed he was 'much sturdier' on his legs than he had been.

Clive reviewed three short books that appeared in the wake of the Grafton exhibition. He appreciated the tolerance shown in C. J. Holmes' *Notes on the Post-Impressionist Painters*, although, like Roger, Clive drew attention to Holmes' conservative notion that paintings should function as decoration for a room. Rutter's *Revolution in Art* was a more welcome response because he had understood that 'the younger French painters' were 'not trying to represent youths dancing, oak trees in a storm, or gardens on the banks of rivers, but rather to translate into line and colour such abstractions as the rhythm of the dance, the stir of trees, and the lush wetness of swampy places'. The book that came closest to Clive's emerging aesthetics was C. Lewis Hind's *The Post Impressionists* (1911). This consisted mostly of reprints of articles by the well-informed Hind, who wrote regularly for the *Art Journal* and the *Daily Chronicle*, and had seen the Matisses owned by Michael and Sarah Stein. Clive suggested that what Hind 'dimly' perceived the post-Impressionist painters were trying to get at was 'a sense of the spiritual significance of the universe'. Cézanne and those who followed him 'have restored religious sense to the plastic arts . . . They see the universal in the particular.' With the support gained from Roger's efforts to explain these new kinds of painting, Clive was developing the vocabulary he needed to express what he felt when he looked at a Cézanne.

As he ventured beyond solely literary topics into the modernist ferment that the Grafton show had inaugurated in London, Clive began to deploy a 'post-Impressionist' vocabulary in all kinds of contexts. Trelawny's letters, for example, present the picture of a man 'historically unfinished, but, from a post-impressionist point of view, final' – 'as the catalogue at the Grafton Galleries might say, the Trelawniness of Trelawny is completely expressed'. Such notes became commonplace in his reviews: the Irish playwright Synge reminded Clive of Gauguin, who 'sought among simple people to discover the significance of human life'.

In his first contribution to *The Nation*, Clive overtly, albeit tendentiously, advanced his aesthetic ideas in a review of 'Old Masters at the Grafton Galleries'. It must surely have confused readers to learn that there were few 'works of art' in this exhibition, held in aid of the National Art Collections Fund (and hung by Roger). A *Salvator Mundi* ascribed to Giotto was a picture not of God but of a 'holy man', because to an artist 'who perceives the universal in the particular' a holy man is more moving. Clive named sincerity of emotion as his main criterion of value; therefore, Rembrandt's *Catharina Hooghsaet* is worthless 'as a work of art, as an expression of emotion that is to say'. As he pronounced on Duccio, Masaccio and the other Old Masters, the iconoclasm and insouciance of Clive's attitudes to the canons of art history came through clearly. He also expressed some of the unthinking elitism for which his later work would draw criticism. Finally able to have his say in print about Thomas Love Peacock, Clive praised the writer as one 'blessed with that keen delight in his own sensations which makes a world full of beautiful and amusing things, charming people, wine, and warm sunshine seem, on the whole, a very tolerable place, and all metaphysical speculation and political passion a little unnecessary'. Clive's detractors occasionally used similar language in their descriptions of him.

Sydney Waterlow complimented Clive on his Peacock article and then, rather surprisingly, asked him how he was getting on with his book about socialism. This suggests that Clive may have briefly contemplated writing about politics but, if so, the idea was soon abandoned in favour of another work, one that he would never fully realise, but that he would plunder for material to use elsewhere in the coming years.

The portentous title 'The New Renaissance' appears in a large sketchbook dated 1912 in which Clive outlined his ambitious claim that the world was on the cusp of a renaissance heralded by painters who were exploring new worlds of emotion and, in doing so, satisfying the world's hunger for 'ultimate realities, or at least for a deeper emotional perception of the significance of things'. The painters were the discoverers while the intellectuals – like himself – were the cartographers of a new world. The fundamental idea, if not the terminology, of 'significant form' as the common element of all that Clive would define as art, as well as the argument that the post-Impressionists were the 'primitives' of a new age, were already in place. The ideas recur in many of the reviews Clive published from around 1911 to 1914 as he, in common with Roger Fry, began to prise the public away from the conviction that 'beauty' was the most important aspect of art and direct them towards an emphasis on emotion and form.

Whether writing about ancient Chinese painting or Greek sculpture, Clive used a post-Impressionist lens, indicative of the almost obsessive conversations he was now having with Roger, Duncan, Vanessa and anyone else who would listen. Sydney Waterlow might feel dizzy after interminable discussions about art that seemed to him to go round and round in circles but between them Roger and Clive were delineating the contours of a new approach to thinking about visual art. Virginia recognised the importance of this moment when she famously wrote that 'in or about December, 1910, human character changed'.

As the Grafton exhibition was closing, Roger gave a lecture, reprinted in the *Fortnightly Review*, in which he said that the painters were attempting 'to discover the visual language of the imagination. To discover, that is, what arrangements of form and colour are calculated to stir the imagination most deeply through the stimulus given to the sense of sight.' Freed from the 'incubus' of representation, the artist now created 'particular rhythms of line and particular harmonies of colour' which have 'spiritual correspondence'. Within a year, Wassily

Kandinsky would make a similar argument in *Uber das Geistige in der Kunst* ('Concerning the Spiritual in Art'). The zeitgeist was changing.

Much of the discussion of modern art in England was carried out in 'little magazines' that are now identified as one of the main wellsprings of modernism. John Middleton Murry and Katherine Mansfield brought out the first issue of *Rhythm* in June 1911. Had he been aware of it (*Rhythm*'s circulation was tiny), Clive would no doubt have appreciated Murry's 'Art & Philosophy', in which he wrote that 'Art is consciously eternal. The creation of art is the expression of the continuous and undying in the world . . . the artist's vision is a moment's lifting of the veil, a chord caught and remembered from the vast world music, less or more, yet always another bond between us and the great divinity immanent in the world.' Strongly influenced by Henri Bergson, Murry (still at the time an Oxford undergraduate) viewed modern painting as a restatement of Platonic philosophy, 'which the blind call mysticism'. The new movement, 'Modernism', was 'not the capricious outburst of intellectual dipsomania. It penetrates beneath the outward surface of the world, and disengages the rhythms that lie at the heart of things, rhythms strange to the eye, unaccustomed to the ear, primitive harmonies of the world that is and lives.'

The art critic of the *New Age*, Huntly Carter, noted that 'ideas of rhythmic expansion and vitality' were in the air and recommended that artists read Lawrence Binyon's *The Flight of the Dragon*. Clive had reviewed Binyon's essay, subtitled 'On the Theory and Practice of Art in China', a month earlier, once again taking the opportunity to proselytise for his view of art. Binyon, who worked in the department of prints and drawings at the British Museum, listed six 'canons' of ancient Chinese art, the first of which was 'Rhythmic Vitality', restated by Clive as finding the universal in the particular. Clive used the review to rehearse the arguments about primitivism he and Roger were developing. At the decadent point of a particular movement when technique has become an end rather than a means, 'men suddenly become aware that the universe has a soul' and those artists who are compelled by 'intolerable necessity' to express what they feel are called 'primitives'.

The Japanese–British exhibition of 1910 had given Clive an idea of how 'Japanese primitives could enter and express the world of reality', an insight that could be applied also to the mosaicists of the Byzantine sixth century, 'which express the earliest triumphs of another spiritual revolution over the cultured materialism of a moribund civilization'. Clive was staking out the position that post-Impressionism was the overturning of Victorian ideology, the 'cant' his generation abhorred: 'Few observant people will deny that there are signs of an awakening in Europe. The times are great with the birth of some new thing. A spiritual renaissance may be at hand' – heady stuff for a review of a little book on ancient Chinese painting.

Clive was so determined to put his ideas into a book that he declined an offer from Desmond to write about Matisse for a series commissioned by the publisher Stephen Swift (which came to nothing). As Clive's own book was so far no more than 'ein punkt' (a point), Desmond said, perhaps writing on Matisse could help Clive 'shift, elucidate, illustrate, elaborate, distinguish, test your ideas'. Since late 1910, conversation about aesthetics, form, rhythm, paintings had consumed Clive and Vanessa. It exasperated Lytton, who wrote to his brother James from a visit to the Bells at Studland in September 1911 that Clive was 'much worse – burgeoning out into inconceivable theories on art and life – a corpse puffed up with worms and gases. It all seems to be the result of Roger, who is here, in love with Vanessa.' Indeed, the next phase of Vanessa and Clive's relationship, as well as the next phase of Clive's development as a writer on art, would be deeply influenced by Roger Fry.

8. A Hornets' Nest

A linguist fluent in German, French, Arabic and Turkish, Henry Hony of the Levant Consular Service had been a frequent visitor to his neighbours at Cleeve House. In 1923, he would become Clive's brother-in-law when he married Dorothy Bell. Early in 1911, at the Embassy in Constantinople, he received a piece of correspondence which confused him. I 'had a letter signed Clive Bell the other day', Henry wrote to his mother, 'saying that he, his wife and Roger Fry . . . were coming to stay here for a bit, and he hoped to see me. I thought of course that this must be Mr. Bell of Seend, but was very bothered by the name Clive; Joan [Henry's sister] too felt certain that Mr. Bell's name was not Clive.' Henry assumed that William H. Bell must be passing through Turkey on his way to Siberia on coal-mining business, but the matter was soon cleared up, as he explained to his father: 'You will probably have discovered my silly mistake about the Bells by now: it is Arthur Bell & his wife who are coming out. But why do people whose name is Arthur and who have always been known as Arthur suddenly start calling themselves Clive without any hint that they have another name?'

Clive, Vanessa, Roger and Harry Norton went to Turkey in April 1911, intending to go on to Italy and Greece. After the Grafton show, Clive and Roger wanted to see first-hand the Byzantine art they linked to post-Impressionism's place in the art-historical narrative they were constructing. Roger was already thinking about a second exhibition. He and Norton set off for Turkey first, but when the Bells arrived at Dover, Clive insisted to Vanessa that the Channel was too rough for them to make the crossing. A delay would cause them to miss the Orient Express in Ostend, so Vanessa went straight to their cabin, and

Henry Hony

refused to move. 'Clive gave up in despair & sank down with a groan,' Vanessa wrote to Virginia from the train between Passau and Vienna. He looked after her 'like an old Granny' and she promised her sister she would take no risks with her health.

Once in Constantinople, Clive relaxed into the kind of life he most enjoyed, feeling 'superbly Byronic' as he smoked a cigar on the drive over the ridge of Pera, looking over the Bosphorus to Scutari, after dinner at the British Embassy with Henry Hony and his sister. The party got to see some mosaics in the Kariye Camii (now the Chora Church), though many had been obscured with plaster walls by the Ottomans. Roger, who spent much of his time painting or sketching alongside Vanessa, discovered a facility for communicating with the locals despite not speaking their language. To their delight, this led to an invitation into a Turkish home, but the visit ended disastrously when Vanessa lost down a well 'a very pretty old French ring' that Clive had given her on their engagement. 'It seemed to me as if something obscure but terrible had happened,' she later wrote.

All was indeed not well, for at Broussa in late April, Vanessa collapsed. Clive was very worried and wished Virginia were with them so that he could confide all the 'silly things' he was thinking. Illness frightened Clive; perhaps Vanessa's fainting fits in Turkey aroused memories of Thoby's fate. Roger, as was his wont, bustled about organising everything, doing his best to look after Vanessa. Virginia was so alarmed by Clive's bulletins that she set off by herself from London to meet them. By the time she arrived, Norton had gone on to Trieste alone, and Virginia accompanied Clive, Vanessa and Roger home on the Orient Express. Vanessa had had a miscarriage.

In 1911 there were a series of emotional rearrangements in Vanessa and Clive's marriage. On their way to stay with Sydney Waterlow just before leaving for Turkey, they had discussed 'the possibility of change, and whether we were happy, and with whom we were intimate', Clive told Virginia. While caring for Vanessa in Turkey, Roger came to realise he had fallen in love with her and in her long recuperation once home in London, Vanessa found she also loved him. This involvement had the effect of reawakening Clive's attachment to his wife, an irony not lost on her: 'If this had happened 3 years ago when Clive was thinking only of Virginia, it might all have been easy!' she exclaimed to Roger. Virginia threatened to cause mischief by needling Clive about Vanessa's love for Roger. The affair seemed to Harry Norton (himself rather enamoured of Vanessa) unlikely to result in a breakdown of the Bells' marriage, but he told Sydney Waterlow that if the lovers did run off together, Clive's body would have to be fished out of the river.

Clive would continue to love Vanessa through all the tortured permutations of their household. When he, Roger and Duncan took a touring holiday in France in October 1911, Vanessa intended to join them in Paris but her plans nearly went awry when she thought she might be pregnant again. She felt foolish for not having followed her usual contraceptive practice of douching: 'If it is a baby it can only have happened that time a week ago,' she wrote to Clive, 'when I thought I had made safe by washing. I know the stuff did go all over the place & of course I had to get upstairs – but it seems hardly possible.' Despite her affair with Roger, Clive was still her 'legitimate male', she told him two days later when her period started: 'Do you really miss your Dolph . . . ?' Even in the summer of 1913, Vanessa told Clive she was missing his 'nice firm flesh very much'.

Nevertheless, Clive did not stop sending sentimentally flattering letters to Virginia that often expressed his rivalry with one or another of her suitors. She 'looked so lovely' when he saw her one Friday night that he lost his 'nerve and head for a time', but he would not tell Walter Lamb, who had praised her, how beautiful she looked. Clive knew Virginia had, as he put it, 'managed' him skilfully since her time with Jean Thomas in Twickenham. He sent her books for her twenty-ninth birthday and told her she was 'more beautiful and more charming, and more like a genius' than she had been at twenty-eight, but in 1911 there was no poem. It was, Clive knew, only a matter of time before she was engaged. Perhaps it would be to Lytton's brother Oliver, he ventured, somewhat improbably.[1] Clive implored Virginia to see him the week he left for Constantinople because he feared she would fall in love while he was away and wanted to be reassured that he would never lose his 'little niche' in her life.

A proposal did come that summer from Walter Lamb, whom Virginia gently turned down, but Clive's interference damaged his friendship with Lamb and angered Virginia when she discovered that Clive had 'blackened [her] with bitterness'. Lamb told Virginia

[1]Oliver Strachey married Ray Costelloe, the feminist writer; her sister, Karin, married Adrian Stephen. They were daughters of Mary Berenson by her first husband.

that Sydney Waterlow (whose struggling marriage would soon end in divorce, freeing his own romantic interest in Virginia) had not passed on to him anything Clive had said about her character but that he had remarked on Clive's 'perfectly absurd' passion for his sister-in-law. Waterlow denied this to Clive but, as Lamb perceptively noted, Clive 'seemed to regard both sisters, to one of whom only was he married, as in some sense his property or preserve'. Vanessa understood this, and, by 1912, when it was clear Leonard Woolf's wooing of her sister would be successful, she kept the progress of their courtship from Clive as much as she could. As Virginia said, they lived in a 'hornets' nest'.

9. Leonard

Leonard had returned on leave from Ceylon in July 1911, encouraged by Lytton to press his suit for Virginia. As soon as he got to London, he dined at 46 Gordon Square with Clive and Vanessa, Virginia joining them afterwards with Duncan and Walter Lamb. In November, Maynard Keynes, Duncan, Adrian and Virginia moved to 38 Brunswick Square, where Leonard, having extended his leave, was shortly afterwards accepted as a lodger. While Clive was in Italy with Vanessa and Roger in May 1912, Leonard gave up his civil service post, hopeful Virginia would accept him as her husband. While Clive was away, Adrian was his most promising source of information about Leonard's efforts to win Virginia, but he told Clive that if anything were going on upstairs at Brunswick Square between 'the Goat' and Leonard, they were being very quiet about it.

Although Clive and Lytton had reconciled after their terrible row, their relations were never easy. Lytton reported to his brother James in spring 1911 that Clive was 'possibly working up for a grand Reconciliation' but his contempt for and suspicion of Clive was never far from the surface. Clive had praised Lytton's *Landmarks in French Literature* (1912) as the best book in the Home University Library series, but Lytton mistrusted the sincerity of his words. On the contrary, Clive had tried to engage Lytton in discussion of their mutual love of eighteenth-century French literature, while also assuring him that all his friends knew he would achieve something really important.

Lytton's letters had darkened Leonard's view of Clive and finding out how jealous Clive was of his courtship of Virginia did nothing to improve his opinion. In 1912, shortly before leaving for Italy, Clive initiated an amorous correspondence with Desmond MacCarthy's wife, Molly, to whom he poured out his feelings about Leonard's pursuit of Virginia. Vanessa had immediately noticed Clive's interest in Molly, teasing him not to run off with her just as Vanessa was due to return from a brief holiday on the Isle of Wight. Molly found Clive's interest confusing because she felt dowdy and insignificant at twenty-nine, depressed by what she saw as her wasted opportunities. Furthermore, she could not understand why Clive and she were friends, given that she usually yawned when looking at a painting.

Molly had had a nervous breakdown upon her engagement to Desmond over her fear and ignorance of sex, occasioning a three-month stay in a nursing home, and Vanessa sometimes found her rather too 'moral' in comparison to her other friends, the free flow of whose conversation she felt Molly somewhat inhibited. Molly certainly could be terse and told Clive more than once that she could see he was 'not nearly so clever as many of your friends', despite his being more 'vital' than they were. Clive did what he could to help the MacCarthys' usually precarious financial situation, about which Molly was perpetually worried, recommending her to Vernon Rendall as a reviewer and giving Desmond an indefinite loan of £100 in the hope it would afford him the time to write a play. Clive assured Desmond that he had 'always held it absurd that amongst friends one should want money and another have it'.

Molly believed her relations with Clive to be 'innocuous', telling Ottoline that she was 'glad to feel so fond of him, & understand him so well. He has got a very poetical & beautiful side to his character, & as I know that, I mind so much less about all the part that will for ever be unsatisfactory in him.' She saw no reason not to let Desmond know all about her friendship with Clive, especially as she was so often alone with her children while Desmond pursued his own interests, which included Violet Asquith and Irene Cooper-Willis, among other women. However, when Molly eventually did succumb to Clive's seduction, it altered the 'whole emotional pattern' of her marriage. Molly and Clive's meetings were often derailed by the illnesses or other demands of her three small children (born in 1907, 1909 and 1911), yet Clive continually flattered and cajoled her. While in Italy in May 1912, he had gone off by himself to Arezzo one day where, to the envy of Vanessa, he saw Piero della Francesca's fresco cycle based on the story of the True Cross at the Capella Maggiore in the Franciscan church. He told Molly that he wished he could have been there with someone whom he could make feel 'what it is to be in a town where Vasari's piazza seems a vulgar modernism'. When she later questioned his sincerity, Clive told her he had in mind a 'very definite woman'.

In Italy with Roger and Vanessa, Clive wrote to Molly despondently from Bologna that his wife had again fallen ill, this time with suspected measles: 'Evidently it is written that I shall never go to Ravenna, though there is no one alive more deserving to go there than I,' he moaned. Their party had made a quick detour to Paris to help Roger hang a small show at the Barbazanges Gallery, where Percy Moore Turner introduced them to the French writer Charles Vildrac, the painter Henri Doucet and the theatre director Jacques Copeau, one of the founders with André Gide of the literary magazine *Nouvelle Revue Française*. Clive offered to provide Copeau with a list of people in England who might be interested in the journal.

When they dined with the Vildracs, Vanessa felt she was surrounded by characters Virginia could use in her novel. She knew that Clive was by now convinced that Leonard's resignation from the colonial service meant that Virginia had agreed to marry him. Grumpy at Roger's solicitous care of Vanessa, at his thwarted plans to go to Ravenna and at Virginia's having slipped from his grasp, Clive lashed out wickedly to Molly that it was 'rather horrible' to think that most people would feel for any children Virginia and Leonard might have 'what none of us can help feeling for Jews'. Rather than continue on to Vienna, Clive wanted to go straight home. He asked Vanessa 'point blank' if Virginia had been shown the letters he had written to Adrian seeking information about Leonard and Virginia's relations. His suspicions confirmed, Clive claimed that he was 'not unworthily jealous'.

Despite her misgivings about his being a 'penniless Jew', Virginia had agreed to marry Leonard. Once back in London, Clive refused to see the newly engaged couple and even resented Vanessa doing so. Adrian had shown Clive's letters not only to Virginia but also to Leonard and both were angry. Clive outrageously told Virginia that he would always believe he appreciated and loved her more than her husband could. The situation was untenable. Their wedding took place on 10 August 1912. On the day of the wedding, Clive sent a note to Virginia. He now

Asheham House

understood 'what your husband has got'; 'in spite of all my craziness, I love you very much, and . . . I love your lover too'. Diplomatically, Virginia told Clive his letter 'made a great deal of difference . . . Leonard sends his love'.

Years later, Virginia got out of Molly the story of 'copulating with Clive on a hard bed on a cold night . . . and how she flared up next morning and went home'. It happened in 1913 at Asheham, a house Virginia had discovered in October 1911 while walking on the Sussex Downs with Leonard. Quentin Bell described Asheham as a 'strange and beautiful house in a lonely and romantic situation'. Supposedly haunted, Asheham began to fill with frequent visitors from London or Cambridge soon after Virginia and Vanessa took the lease. Clive, whose physical comforts were of great importance to him, found it too rustic, but Vanessa cherished the house as a place where she could paint while living the kind of simple existence she preferred, and so set about making it as attractive as possible, hoping Clive would agree to keep it. When the water pump broke, Clive announced that they should all return at once to London, but within hours Roger had mended it, Clive had hired a farm labourer to maintain it and clean the earth closet and all was well. Within a week, Clive went from being 'rather against the place' to being 'very happy', much to Vanessa's relief: 'No one wants to leave; everyone wants to visit; never was there such a good place for painters.'

It was at Asheham that Virginia would recover after attempting suicide by overdosing on veronal, a sedative. It is likely that the proximate cause of her unbearable anxiety was Gerald Duckworth's acceptance for publication in April 1913 of *The Voyage Out*. The burden of caring for Virginia in her mental instability had now fallen almost entirely on Leonard. That summer, as Clive casually remarked to Lytton, Virginia had 'retired to the mad-house': 'Some say she worried herself in, wondering what we should all say about her novel; others that co-operation was the cause.'

Leonard and Virginia's worthy expeditions early that year to research co-operative societies in the north of England had been an object of derision in Clive's prickly letters to Molly. He often treated Virginia's 'madness' with levity and his attitude towards the psychiatric profession throughout his life would range from dismissing it as quackery to a more serious questioning of the power wielded by 'alienists'. In a 1912 letter to the *Eye Witness*, Clive warned against the power of 'mad doctors' over the poor, faulting psychiatry's premise that seeing the world differently from doctors justified confining someone to an asylum. He had heard in person as well as read the denunciations of post-Impressionist painters as lunatics and knew that, along with Roger, he was regarded by some as of questionable mental hygiene himself.[1] The psychiatric profession was inherently eugenicist, he argued: 'Now the Eugenist [*sic*] reckons crazy and "feeble-minded" any one who differs greatly from the normal, and his notion of a normal man is – a Eugenist,' on which basis they 'are ready to castrate or imprison the poor'.

---

[1] In 1911, T. B. Hyslop, who would retire that year as Superintendent of the Bethlem asylum, gave a talk at the Grafton Galleries, where Roger Fry was in the audience, on 'Post-Impressionism and Art in the Insane'. It was Hyslop who referred to 'aesthetic insanity' in comparing paintings by inmates of the Bethlem asylum with those of the post-Impressionists (Trombley 225). He argued that 'Both the insane artist and the borderland critic have certain characteristics which are peculiar to them' (Trombley 226).

It was unfortunate that in March 1914 Lytton showed Leonard a box of letters he disingenuously told Clive did not seem 'too confidential'. Clive's letters to Lytton were often far more cynical, offensive, even occasionally misogynist, than those he wrote to anyone else, as if he knew that to impress Lytton he had to be as scurrilous as possible. In one, Clive wrote that he had heard Virginia 'was almost as crazy as ever at Asheham', though he hoped she would recover soon because 'I want to try to have an affair with her.' Surprisingly, when Leonard confronted Clive, Clive seemed more peeved with Leonard than with Lytton, whom he merely scolded for showing his letters 'to that bloody Jew'. Leonard angrily accused Clive of causing Virginia's breakdown, challenging him to promise either never to 'excite' her again or never to see or write to her. Clive would make no such promises. He thought that Leonard was suffering because Virginia blamed her husband for all her troubles and, in an attempt to escape her accusations, Leonard was desperately seeking another cause than the one that appeared plain to Clive: 'sheer misfortune and the act of God'.

There was some truth to Clive's brazen riposte to Leonard, for Virginia did indeed take against Leonard during the difficult years immediately following her marriage. Clive's callousness, coupled with the evidence presented by Lytton to Leonard of his past inappropriate intimacy with Virginia, meant that there would rarely be any warmth between these brothers-in-law. Lytton gave Clive flowers by way of apology for having caused the confrontation.

10. Significant Form

Within weeks of 'Manet and the Post-Impressionists' closing at the Grafton Galleries in early 1911, Roger was thinking of a second exhibition. He asked Clive to be responsible for selecting works by English artists, while he would select the French. Boris Anrep – a Russian mosaicist living in Paris who had been introduced by the painter Henry Lamb at one of Ottoline's gatherings in 1911 – would travel to Russia to obtain works there. Clive, in collaboration with Roger, chose paintings by Vanessa, Duncan, Frederick and Jessie Etchells, Henry Lamb, Percy Wyndham Lewis, Stanley Spencer, Bernard Adeney and Spencer Gore, as well as Eric Gill's sculpture *Golden Calf*, having been persuaded by Roger to overcome his misgivings about it.

Frederick Etchells, Adeney, Roger, Duncan and Gill's brother MacDonald had all participated in what was in effect the first post-Impressionist collaboration among English artists when Roger secured for them a commission to decorate the dining room of the Borough Polytechnic in London. The resulting mural explicitly demonstrated the link between modernism and Byzantinism that Roger and Clive were promulgating. As several critics pointed out, Duncan Grant's mural of swimmers in the Serpentine (*Bathing*) had particular ties to fifth-century mosaics.

Reviewing the project in the *Athenaeum*, Clive praised the artists generally for having subordinated their individuality to a common purpose: 'by unity of style, rhythm, and sentiment an astonishing sense of coherence has been obtained'. As he would do so often, Clive singled out Duncan, whose work, he wrote, was 'always beautiful' yet always 'significant'. 'Beauty' was no longer a prime consideration, displaced by the 'significance' upon which Clive's reputation would shortly come to rest. From now on, his statements about visual art would be marked by a new sense of conviction.

When the 'Second Post-Impressionist Exhibition' opened on 5 October 1912, with Leonard acting as secretary, Clive's catalogue preface for the English section allowed him to consolidate his ideas as they had progressed so far. 'The battle is won,' he announced. 'We all agree, now, that any form in which an artist can express himself is legitimate, and the more sensitive perceive that there are many things worth expressing that could never have been expressed in traditional forms.' French painters, he went on, have given English painters the gift of 'simplification', turning away from mimesis to 'something more important – the significance of form'. Thus any object – a coal scuttle, for example – could be incorporated as a 'significant form' by a post-Impressionist painter without any associations attendant on the object's function.

Clive had rehearsed these arguments a few months before the opening of the 'Second Post-Impressionist Exhibition' when he praised those artists at the 1912 Allied Artists Association exhibition who had been taught by Walter Sickert's example to not 'select the obvious, the romantic, and the pretty'. 'Significance', he wrote, could not be taught. He singled out Wyndham Lewis's large painting *Kermesse*, which was among the first works visitors encountered at the Albert Hall show. It was a solid work if viewed solely in terms of 'pure, formal expression'.[1]

The conversations Clive had been having since 1910 with Fry, Vanessa and Duncan, as well as his growing familiarity with painters in Paris, had greatly increased his confidence in articulating his ideas, and although it has become a critical commonplace to assume that Clive drew not only his ideas but also their terminology from Fry, this supposition rests on an oddly linear notion of how intellectual culture operates. Clive popularised the term 'significant form' but, like 'post-Impressionism', it

[1] Richard Cork points out that the only exhibit by Lewis listed in the AAA's catalogue is *Creation*, which was 'included in the "large paintings and decorative works" section', but as no one ever referred to this work as *Creation*, he surmises that it must have been *Kermesse*, adding that it 'should not be confused with the lost *Creation*' illustrated in the catalogue of the *Second Post-Impressionist Exhibition*, which was a wash drawing (n47). For an account of responses at the time to *Kermesse* and its context, see Tickner, 'Popular'.

served as a shorthand for concepts already in circulation.[2] Furthermore, not only Clive had evolved: Roger, for example, told Simon Bussy that he had become 'completely Matissiste. I was very suspicious at the beginning of our exhibition, but after studying all his paintings I am quite convinced of his genius.' It is difficult now to imagine the utter astonishment such well-known paintings as Matisse's *Woman with green eyes* or Edouard Manet's *A Bar at the Folies-Bergères* caused in 1910. As Virginia would write in 1940, 'The pictures are the same; it is the public that has changed.'

Roger's catalogue essay on 'The French Group' demonstrated how the term 'post-Impressionism' had outlived its usefulness as a kind of journalistic shorthand. The 1912–13 exhibition was different in several respects from 'Manet and the Post-Impressionists' of 1910, bringing developments in Cubism to a wider English audience, and focused almost exclusively on living artists, with the exception of Cézanne who, for both Roger and Clive, was the origin of the movement. If the painters in the second exhibition, which included Derain, Herbin, Marchand, Lhote, Asselin, and the first English showing of Le Douanier Rousseau, all were concerned not to imitate but to create form, Roger wrote, the 'logical extreme of such a method would undoubtedly be the attempt to give up all resemblance to natural form, and to create a purely abstract language of form'.

The 1912 show included a cubist work by Braque (*Violin:'Mozart/ Kubelick*) and several by Picasso (such as *Buffalo Bill*) that for Roger embodied this 'logical extreme', but he cautioned that it was too soon 'to be dogmatic on the point, which can only be decided when our sensibilities to such abstract form have been more practised than they are at present'. As he would shortly explain to Gertrude Stein, Roger found that his lecture audiences did not have 'the sensibility to form. They'll take one's ideas as pure ideas, but they can't fit them on to the pictures at all.' 'Post-Impressionism' and 'Cubism' came to be barely distinguished from one another in popular discourse in England, treated as just two examples of the lunatic notions Roger had imported from the Continent, similar to Diaghilev, Stravinsky and Nijinsky's ballet

---

[2]For a detailed account of how the term 'significant form' circulated in the early twentieth century, as well as its legacy in aesthetic theorising up to the present, see Hussey, 'Case Study'.

Sacre du Printemps, which would be described in *The Sketch* as a 'Post-Impressionist and Prehistoric Dance', and 'The Twitching, Bobbing, Turn-Your-Toes-In Cubist Dance'.

Despite the headway made by 'Manet and the Post-Impressionists', the characterisation of modernist art as a hoax or as the work of lunatics was still prevalent. When the *New Age* reproduced a cubist work by Picasso (now known as *La Mandoline et le Pernod*) in its November 1911 art supplement, there had been a 'massive and hostile response'. G. K. Chesterton in the *Daily News* objected to it as an example of the 'latest artistic insanities (Cubism and Post-Impressionism and Mr. Picasso)'. Clive's catalogue essay on 'The English Group' also attracted abuse, for example from the *Saturday Review*'s critic C. H. Collins Baker, who found it 'a muddle of clouded thought, loose argument, historical inaccuracy and phrases'.

Desmond MacCarthy endeavoured to explain what Clive was getting at by connecting significant form to Kant's concept of 'free or disinterested beauty' and thus put the term in the context of canonical aesthetic theory. By January 1913, Clive could expound in greater detail the ideas he had tentatively tried out in his reviews of the previous two or three years when he published 'Post-Impressionism and Aesthetics' in the *Burlington Magazine*. The article succinctly outlined the claims that would bring him wide fame when he repeated them the following year in the first chapter of *Art*.

The essential quality of a work of art, he wrote, is 'its power of raising a peculiar emotion, called aesthetic'. This emotion will differ according to each person's subjective experience: we can be certain of no one's feelings but our own. Although the emotions produced by various works differ, they are the same *kind* of emotion and can be produced by 'every kind of visual art, by pictures, sculpture, buildings, pots, carvings, textiles'. That art was not just what hung in museums would remain one of Clive's fundamental ideas. The 'essential' quality evoking the aesthetic emotion is 'significant form'. *Why* significant form evokes aesthetic emotion is irrelevant, he claimed, because that was a question for metaphysics rather than aesthetics. 'For a discussion of aesthetics it need only be agreed that forms arranged and combined according to certain mysterious laws do move us profoundly, and that it is the business of an artist so to combine and arrange them that they shall move us.'

Roderic O'Conor was painting in Cassis with George Hume Barne when he received a copy of Clive's article. Barne wrote to Clive that he was prepared to accept significant form as the quality that moves a viewer aesthetically, as long as Clive acknowledged colour as an aspect of form. He was surprised that Clive included Poussin among the examples of artists who provoked aesthetic emotion yet did not mention Rembrandt, whom he believed as good as any primitive when it came to capturing the 'great reality'. Barne's letter confirmed what Clive's article emphasised: 'The degree to which my conclusions commend themselves to others will depend upon the degree in which my experience tallies with theirs.' The subjective nature of Clive's theory, its implicit challenge to a critical discourse that still uses such terms as 'interesting' or 'significant' as if they were objective truths, would become a crux in the arguments that have persisted since he wrote. 'Post-Impressionism and Aesthetics' reflects a profound ontological shift in thinking about aesthetics between the late nineteenth and early twentieth centuries as 'new physiological theories of vision' and philosophical challenges to the Cartesian notion that experience is universal argued that perception 'is embedded in the relation between the perceiver and the thing perceived' and thus differs for every person.

The 'Second Post-Impressionist Exhibition' was supposed to close at the end of December, but was extended for what a new catalogue described as a 'Re-Arrangement' from 4 to 31 January 1913. Several of the Matisses and Picassos had been promised to the Armory Show in New York but other works were added, including thirty-three Cézannes from the Bernheim-Jeune gallery in Paris. Among the additions was Picasso's *Pots et Citron* which Clive and Vanessa had bought in 1911 in Paris from Daniel Kahnweiler for £4, the first painting by Picasso to enter a private collection in England. 'It's "cubist"', Vanessa told Virginia, 'and very beautiful colour'.

When Vanessa excitedly told Clive she had sold her *Spanish Lady* to the Contemporary Art Society in 1912, she let him know that Robbie Ross was interested in purchasing their Augustus John for a gallery in Johannesburg. She wanted to sell it because, 'I would rather possess a Cézanne or some modern French painting.' Clive encouraged his friends to buy modern paintings, which were, he told Molly just as the 'Second Post-Impressionist Exhibition' opened, 'selling like hot cakes'. He had bought Maurice Vlaminck's *Poissy-le-pont* from the

1910 exhibition for £14 (it had also been in Dell's Brighton exhibition); he would sell it in 1958 for £5,400. From the 1912–13 exhibition, he bought Jean Marchand's *Vue de Ville* and in 1914, he bought a Vlaminck landscape from Kahnweiler, as well *Les Oeufs*, an important early still life by Juan Gris.

The weekend after the Grafton show closed, Clive's *Burlington* article was fiercely debated at Asheham. Roger was staying, so 'the air is teeming with discussion on Art. They think they are getting further,' Vanessa told Virginia, but 'I don't know. Roger's views of course are more mature than ours. He is at one pole and Clive at the other and I come somewhere in between on a rather shaky foothold, but none of us really agree with Leonard.' Clive thought he had convinced Roger to mention the 'great doctrine of significant form' in lectures he would be giving the following week in Leeds and Leicester, but the article, Clive told Molly, had made Lytton 'furious. There must be something in a theory, you know, that drives Lytton into quarrelling with Duncan.' Whatever Leonard took issue with can only now be inferred from Vanessa and Clive's responses to him, but their letters indicate the terms of the debate at Asheham that weekend.

Vanessa's letter to her brother-in-law – a rare instance of her theorising about art – confirmed that when she looked at a picture, she responded to 'forms and colours' without paying any attention to whatever objects might be represented, contrary to what Leonard had insisted must be the case. As a matter of fact, she told him, 'We do first feel the emotion and then look at the picture, that is to say, look at it from the point of view of seeing its tertiary form.' In Clive's rebuttal of Leonard, he agreed that 'to eliminate three dimensional space would be to rob art of some of its most moving forms' and, further, that creating three-dimensional space was tantamount to representation, something he needed to think about more carefully before he finished writing his book. But Clive would not concede that his theory was invalid just because Leonard's experience differed: 'I insist that a theory of aesthetics must be based on the experience of the person who elaborates it. Your experience differs from mine, since you are more profoundly moved by pictures (and statues I suppose) than by buildings, pots, carpets, etc. Naturally, you explain your different experience by a different aesthetic.' Clive's 'catalogue of favourites' was vital to his argument – 'S[ancta] Sophia and the windows at Chartres, Mexican sculpture, a Persian bowl,

Chinese carpets, Giotto's frescoes at Padua, the masterpieces of Poussin, of Cézanne, and of Henri Matisse'. Clive adhered to this approach in *Art*, which was illustrated with a selection from his personal catalogue. He was appealing not to an established canon of taste, of 'great works', but to his own subjective experience, a key aspect of the radicalism of his aesthetics. The mode of criticism he would become associated with did not argue from a norm but rather tried to establish a community of feeling by sharing those objects that provoked in him an aesthetic emotion.

Clive acknowledged he and Leonard were probably 'thinking about different things. Your account of your aesthetic experiences makes me suppose that they are altogether unlike mine. It seems that you first establish the relations of the forms in a picture to the objects of life and then get your emotion. In my case the emotion comes first; afterwards I may or may not make out what the . . . forms represent: often I don't.' When Vanessa said 'we' in her letter to Leonard, the pronoun probably included Duncan; it certainly included Clive. Leonard questioned Clive's analysis of his own psychology, on which, he contended, the theory must be based: 'It is a common thing for people to think they feel something which they don't feel at all . . . This may happen either because they are not good at introspection or because they do not keep clearly before their minds the meaning of the words used by them.' If Clive explicitly founded his theory of aesthetic emotion on his subjective experience of a work of art and Leonard denied that Clive understood his own feelings, obviously there could never be a meeting of the minds. Leonard's Apostolic rationalism had no place for what was in effect Clive's mysticism, yet Clive repeatedly acknowledged that such a gap between two people's experience was a limitation of his theory. Such objections as Leonard had would only pose an insoluble problem if Clive's theory were understood as doctrinal rather than subjective.

Clive had written angrily to Molly when his article appeared, perhaps because she had repeated a critical remark of Virginia's, since his letter began, 'My dear Virginia – Molly I mean'. Molly often criticised Clive's abilities harshly but he now struck a proud rather than defensive tone. That Desmond, Leonard or Virginia thought his ideas either wrong or parroted from others did not concern him because he felt driven to write for his own 'peace of mind'. He was sorry that Molly thought him 'stupid', but perhaps it was less his writing itself that troubled her and more that he gave himself the 'airs of a writer' (which, of course, was Lytton's complaint). Clive urged Molly to discuss his ideas not only with Virginia but with those who understood better what he was trying to explain: Duncan, Sydney Waterlow, Saxon or Roger.

The image of Clive as a puffed-up and self-important parrot (or parakeet) was promulgated particularly by Lytton, often abetted by Virginia. Visiting the 'Second Post-Impressionist Exhibition' had given Lytton the vapours, as he told Ottoline Morrell:

> When last I went it was most painful. Clive was strutting round in dreadful style, without a hat, as if he owned the place. It was impossible not to talk to him, and of course he would shout his comments, so that crowds collected – all so ridiculous and unnecessary. At last, when he began to explain the merits and demerits of the Gill statue, and positively patted it with his fat little hand, I had to disown him, and become absorbed in a Matisse drawing.

However, Clive could concern himself less with Bloomsbury backbiting now because his circle of influence was widening beyond it and would continue to do so. He was developing new networks in Paris as well as in London that had nothing to do with Lytton or Virginia. After the weekend at Asheham arguing about his article, Clive joined Roger to host a lunch for Gertrude Stein who was in London with Alice B. Toklas. Gertrude and Leo Stein (who loaned Picasso's *Green bowl and black bottle*) had visited the 'Second Post-Impressionist Exhibition' and Gertrude gave Roger a photograph of her portrait by Picasso. Clive was interested in what Stein was trying to do in her writing but doubted she could pull it off. Nevertheless, when Marjorie Strachey made a sneering comment about her, Clive defended the American writer 'as if she were a misunderstood artist'. Like Roger, Clive had found purpose in trying to explain the new movement in art to the public.

11. Omega

In March 1913, Roger organised an exhibition at the Alpine Club of several artists he named the Grafton Group. Vanessa, Frederick Etchells, Duncan and Wyndham Lewis were at its heart and in his review of their first show Clive took the opportunity to continue the argument he had made in the *Burlington Magazine*. The 'central proposition of the Post-Impressionist faith' was that painting is an 'arrangement of lines and colours' in which the mimetic representation of objects is not the primary concern: 'reality is sacrificed without scruple to abstract design'. Cubism was 'an attempt to dissolve facts entirely in design' with the consequence that conventional understandings of beauty had become irrelevant in modern painting.

The exhibition included several works by the American artist Max Weber, as well as a number of drawings by Wassily Kandinsky, which Fry had seen in Leeds in the collection of Michael Sadler. In keeping with his view that the represented element in a picture should be only an aspect of design and not be associated with memory, anecdote, biography or any other non-aesthetic matter, Clive found faintly distracting the title of Weber's cubist painting, *New York*. Better, Clive thought, to follow Kandinsky's example, who simply named all his 'patches of colour and scribble' compositions.

A *Times* review also mentioned that 'no one could guess' that Weber's painting 'was the representation of a place', though its forms and colours had 'an abstract beauty'. The reviewer was open-minded, but considered the abstract works in the Grafton Group's show in terms of their potential to decorate a space, seemingly relieved that they did not 'take aim at obvious prettiness either of form or of colour'. 'Prettiness' was anathema to Vanessa, who saw it as a particularly English disease.

Staying with Clive for the weekend at Newington, the very refined home of the painters Ethel Sands and Nan Hudson, Vanessa had been given the creeps by its eighteenth-century furnishings, Japanese panels and Augustus John drawings. Decoration was much on her mind because, while he was organising the 'Second Post-Impressionist Exhibition', Roger had also been making efforts to realise his vision of an artists' collective that would provide those in it with a reliable income through selling the fabrics, pottery, furniture and housewares they designed and made. Among the artists he was considering inviting to participate in his Omega Workshops were Ethel and Nan, prompting Vanessa to worry that English artists such as Duncan might never be able to avoid the 'fatal prettiness' she observed at Newington, in contrast with what had been achieved in France by Derain, Picasso or Matisse.

Roger conceived the Omega as a realisation of post-Impressionist tenets, holding as an article of faith that 'artists express emotion through form'. But 'post-Impressionism' as a usefully descriptive term was under great strain by 1913. Introducing his 'Post-Impressionist and Futurist' exhibition at the Doré Galleries that October, Frank Rutter noted that the 'loose way' the term had been used to 'cover a number of varying, and in some respects contradictory movements, has naturally confused a public seldom inclined to push very far its analysis of modern painting'. Wyndham Lewis was more harsh when he introduced a 'Cubist Room' at an exhibition in Brighton of 'English Post-Impressionists, Cubists and Others' at the end of the year, writing that post-Impressionism was 'an insipid and pointless name invented by a journalist, which has been naturally ousted by the better word "Futurism" in public debate on modern art'.

Clive disdained Futurism as the realisation of a theory, a way to convey ideas rather than emotion. He disliked the tendency in some versions of Cubism towards geometric abstraction, but in the blizzard of '-isms' by which modern art quickly came to be characterised in the early twentieth century, Clive's 'significant form' remained his lodestar. When Clive saw Lewis's *Kermesse* at Rutter's Doré Galleries exhibition, he praised how the artist had 'altered and greatly improved' the work since he had first seen it in 1912. He dismissed Futurism as a 'negligible accident', apparently absolving Lewis of his connection to the movement because he was 'that rare thing, a real academic artist' who used a 'formula of which he is the master and not the slave'. Clive tempered his praise by pointing out that *Kermesse* showed Lewis was 'inclined to modify his forms in the interest of drama and psychology', rather than follow the impulse of pure design. His review of Rutter's show amounted to a 'sermon' to English painters not to be overly concerned with technique or to try to demonstrate how modern they were by shocking the public. They would do better, he wrote, to emulate their colleagues in France who followed their individual visions without caring what the public thought.

When he compared *Kermesse* to Robert Delaunay's *Cardiff Team*, an early version of which hung opposite Lewis's painting, this was Clive's highest form of praise. It would be some time before English painters other than Duncan would fare well against the School of Paris in Clive's estimation. When he singled out Richard Nevinson for lacking the 'artistic courage' shown by a less able Frenchman, Maurice Asselin, Clive made an enemy. Like his fellow Slade student Mark Gertler, Nevinson had been unimpressed by 'Manet and the Post-Impressionists', and was angry at the rise of Roger and Clive's reputation.

At the end of 1912, prospectuses for Roger's Omega Workshops were sent out which attracted financial support from a number of prominent people, including George Bernard Shaw and Sir Hugh Lane. Clive's father was prepared to invest until he visited the 'Second Post-Impressionist Exhibition', after which he would have no more to do with it. Clive and Vanessa came up with a scheme to give a dinner at Pagani's on Great Portland Street where aristocrats could mix with artists and go afterwards to the workshops to 'dance, kiss and drink', in the hope that these festivities would result in 'a great send off for the business'.

The workshops opened at 33 Fitzroy Street in July 1913, with three Slade students helping to run the shop – Barbara Hiles, Gladys Hines and Winifred Gill. Roger encouraged an anonymous, collaborative ethos, all products being signed only with the Omega symbol, Ω. The enterprise was generally well received by the press, although several reviewers commented on the poor craftsmanship of its housewares. Despite his argument that significant form could be found just as well in a carpet or a pot as in a painting, Clive seems not to have published anything about the Omega's wares, nor does it feature very much in his correspondence, except for complaining when Vanessa invested more money in it as Roger struggled over the next few years to keep it going. Within a few months of its successful launch, however, the Omega was plunged into controversy.

In October 1913, Omega's shareholders received a 'round robin' letter signed by Wyndham Lewis, Cuthbert Hamilton, Frederick Etchells and Edward Wadsworth accusing Roger of having appropriated for the Omega a commission from the *Daily Mail* to decorate a 'Post-Impressionist' room at the Ideal Home Exhibition. Lewis, who was the instigator of the letter, claimed that the commission had been intended to be shared between the Omega, himself and Spencer Gore. Because Roger was in France, Vanessa asked Clive and Desmond to draft a response on his behalf, although Clive wondered why Roger 'should wrangle with four grubby little ill-bred painters'. Running into Lewis on Bond Street later that week, Clive told him the whole matter was so provincial and 'suburban' it should simply be dropped. Lewis may have not wished to alienate Clive, who thought that if there were to be any alienation it would be engendered solely by Lewis. In Clive's opinion, the salient issue was character – Lewis's assumption that Roger had acted dishonestly being based on his view that Roger was a 'bad egg'. Facts, Clive argued, mattered far less than the interpretation one put on them.

The 'rumpus' over the Ideal Home commission turned out to be of greater import than Clive's breezy waving off of Lewis's concerns implied. Not only had Lewis accused Roger of tricking him and the others, he also launched a bitter attack on the post-Impressionist aesthetics of the Omega Workshops on the very grounds Vanessa had feared in 1912:

As to its tendencies in Art, they alone would be sufficient to make it very difficult for any vigorous art-instinct to long remain under that roof. The Idol is still Prettiness, with its mid-Victorian languish of the neck, and its skin is 'greenery-yallery', despite the Post-What-Not fashionableness of its draperies. This family party of strayed and Dissenting Aesthetes, however, were compelled to call in as much modern talent as they could find, to do the rough and masculine work without which they knew well their efforts would not rise above the level of a pleasant tea-party, or command more attention.

With this, Lewis laid down several lines of attack on 'Bloomsbury' that continue to flourish:[1] that it was inbred (a 'family party'), effeminate (in 1913, 'Aesthetes' would have instantly called to mind the name of Oscar Wilde) and effete ('a pleasant tea-party'). The immediate consequence of Lewis burning his bridges with the Omega was his formation of the Rebel Art Centre on Great Ormond Street, where the other signatories to his 'round robin' letter joined him in March 1914. This soon dissolved in internecine squabbles, as Richard Nevinson put out *A Futurist Manifesto: Vital English Art* with F. T. Marinetti, against which Lewis retaliated by launching 'The Great English Vortex' and his short-lived journal *BLAST*. Yet, as Spalding has argued, the defections were 'more damaging to the Omega than Fry at first admitted'. The split was symptomatic of a gulf that widened in 1913 between Fry and Bell's championing of French post-Impressionism, and the avant-garde with which Lewis associated his own work, promoted by writers such as Ezra Pound (who gave a lecture at the Rebel Art Centre) and T. E. Hulme, the Imagist poet who wrote for the *New Age*.

[1] For example, in John Richardson's biography of Picasso, where the Omega's 'painfully artsy-craftsy' aesthetic is compared to the more 'progressive' vorticism (v3 126); for Richardson, Bloomsbury's was a 'genteel' modernism (v3 234).

12. A Complete Theory of Visual Art

Although there were times when Clive's emotional entanglements and penchant for chasing inappropriately younger women would exasperate Vanessa, she was usually interested to hear about his escapades. She knew that he still saw Annie, sometimes at the Raven-Hills' London flat, sometimes at their seaside cottage near Colchester, and would have known about his dalliance with Amber Blanco-White, the former Amber Reeves who had had a child with H. G. Wells and was the model for the heroine of his 1909 novel *Ann Veronica*. Vanessa also confided in Clive, as her feelings began to turn away from Roger (to his enormous misery) towards Duncan.

Bicycling with Roger in France in 1914 ('a little hard on the cunt and on the muscles of my soft legs'), she contrasted their modesty with what she surmised was her husband's 'bachelor existence' in Paris. 'I suppose you are at this moment being fondled under the table by some whore and presently you will go off with her, thankful that I am not there to spoil things.' She joked unkindly about Roger: 'I can't give the account you wished for of the Great Man's conversation, but you can imagine our topics. Art. Gothic Art. Omeganic Art. My Art. Roger's Art. Duncan's Art. Art of the Theatre, etc.'

Roger was perhaps rather too earnest for Vanessa. She had had a more spirited time in Paris earlier that year when Clive and Molly joined her and Roger and they visited Matisse's studio, Copeau's Théâtre du Vieux-Colombier, and were taken by Gertrude Stein to see Picasso's 'wonderful studio'. Vanessa wrote delightedly to Duncan about their 'exciting time with pictures', declaring Picasso 'perfectly charming and quite easy and simple', despite being 'one of the greatest geniuses that has ever lived'. She would have loved to stay in Europe but Clive's sister Lorna was to

Quentin and Julian Bell, pages at wedding of Lorna Bell, 1914

Lorna Bell and her father on her wedding day, May 1914

be married in April to Captain William Maxwell Acton and the Bells' presence was required. Mr and Mrs Clive Bell duly attended, with their sons, Quentin and Julian, attired in silk and lace pages' suits.

While the rumpus with Lewis and the Omega Workshops was going on, Clive finished *Art*, on which he had been working diligently all year. His book would embody such an assertive version of art history that his and Roger's view of the pre-eminence of those artists shown at the two post-Impressionist exhibitions would become dominant in popular discourses about modern art for several years. *Art* left no doubt about the battle lines being drawn: 'Only artists and educated people of extraordinary sensibility and some savages and children feel the significance of form so acutely that they know how things look.'

Clive circulated the proofs of *Art* among his friends just before it was published. 'Are you waiting for Clive's book to come out to know what to think on Art and every other subject?' Lytton sniffily asked Duncan. Desmond stayed up all night to finish reading it and Sydney Waterlow offered the high Apostolic praise that he would place it on his bookshelf next to Moore's *Principia Ethica*. Waterlow most likely was the *Athenaeum*'s reviewer who acknowledged that many readers might be irritated to be lectured on art by a man who had never held a paintbrush and who dismissed most Italian Renaissance and eighteenth-century paintings as 'garbage'. But Waterlow relished the book's 'poor taste', its hitting below the belt, as an impassioned apology for art that should lead readers to revise not only their aesthetic values but those of 'life and conduct' as well.

When *Art* appeared in February 1914, the English public was eager to understand modern art and it welcomed Clive's claim to provide 'a complete theory of visual art'. Thousands heard Roger's lectures, accompanied by lantern slides. Even the mocking cartoons in *Punch* or wry headlines in *The Sketch* testified to how 'post-Impressionism' and its attendant forms had entered popular consciousness. *Art* provided not only a sweeping historical overview of the new art's place but also a vocabulary that could be deployed without much analysis: as Clive said, 'significant form' was the quality *he* found in all works *he* would call art but he could not explain what it was beyond 'a combination of lines and colours (counting black and white as colours) that moves me aesthetically'. Such form had nothing to do with *beauty*, thus rejecting a hitherto unquestioned tradition of what the proper object of visual art was. Beauty could be found in nature, of course – the wings of a butterfly or a flower – but in a painting form was paramount and content only accidental.

Art included six illustrations, minimally captioned: a fifth-century Wei sculpture, as frontispiece; an eleventh-century Persian dish; a Peruvian pot; a detail from a sixth-century San Vitale mosaic; a painting by Cézanne (in fact, *Maison devant la Sainte-Victoire près de Gardanne*, 1886–1890); a painting by Picasso (the Bells' own *Pots et Citron*). These illustrations exemplified Clive's fundamental argument that significant form was not identified with any specific kind of object, particular historical era, location or medium. Clive posed again the question he had asked in his *Burlington Magazine* article of 1913: what quality is 'common to Sta. Sophia and the windows at Chartres, Mexican sculpture, a Persian bowl, Chinese carpets, Giotto's frescoes at Padua, and the masterpieces of Poussin, Piero della Francesca, and Cézanne?'

When Roger reviewed *Art* in *The Nation*, he drew particular attention to the point that significant form was not confined to painting and sculpture. The very heterogeneity of Clive's catalogue of objects 'separated out the emotions aroused by certain formal relations from the emotions aroused by the events of life'. Yet Roger was sceptical about Clive's claim that significant form led to 'ultimate reality', and 'never quite swallowed' his 'impetuous doctrine – Significant Form first and last, alone and all the time'. As far as Roger was concerned, something had to be fused with form to make the form significant.

'Solomon Eagle' (J. C. Squire's pseudonym) in the *New Statesman* warned readers a month before *Art*'s publication that its coat-trailing was justified because 'any new movement in art has often an affinity with a general attitude of mind towards other things, morals, customs, habits'. Clive would have agreed and never felt any compunction about commenting on any subject, from politics and peace to fashion and food, from his perch as a celebrated art critic. As he saw astutely, a society's response to art eloquently indicated its overall liberty.

Virginia read *Art* 'laboriously' so that she could argue about it with Leonard. She liked the theoretical chapters more than the historical, where she thought Clive generalised too much. Leonard was staying with Lytton when *Art* came out: 'We have not discussed Clive's book very much,' he wrote grimly to Virginia, 'it is condemned.' Leonard was at work on his own book, a roman à clef that made no effort to disguise the character based on Clive: 'Arthur Woodhouse tossed his fat, round little body and his little, round, fat mind from side to side . . .

Officially he was a disciple of the few papers on Byzantine art published
. . . in obscure but learned periodicals.'

Clive had anticipated Leonard's disdain, no doubt recalling the objections
his brother-in-law had made to his theories when he first published them
in 1913: 'No Cambridge Rationalist can presume to deny that I feel a
certain emotion, but the moment I attempt to prove the existence of its
object I lay myself open to a bad four hours.' Lytton, writing the Cardinal
Manning chapter of *Eminent Victorians*, told Clive he thought it 'very
strange' that *Art* was to be published by Chatto & Windus: 'I thought
they did nothing but bring out superannuated editions of Swinburne
variegated with the Children's Theological Library and the Posthumous
Essays of Lord de Tabley.' He would, nonetheless, be grateful when Clive
recommended *Eminent Victorians* to Chatto, who published it in 1918.

Art brought Clive Bell widespread fame throughout his life and an
introduction to social circles well beyond Bloomsbury, and it eclipsed
everything else he wrote during the next fifty years. Now regarded as
solely of historical interest, it was a manifesto published in an era of
similarly sententious declarations of the new. Of the third edition,
published in 1949, Clive explained he had not revised the book because
it was the work of a young man writing when the 'battle' of post-
Impressionism raged; he let it stand as a record of 'what people like
myself were thinking and feeling in the years before the first War'.

At the time, Clive believed his egregious generalisations, his sweeping
dismissal of the Renaissance, necessary to the artistic revolution he and
Roger – the movement's English high priests – were waging. *Art* became
Clive's calling card and he received admiring and grateful letters about
it for the rest of his life. The painter Ivon Hitchens recalled the startling
effect on him in 1914, aged twenty-one, of discovering Clive Bell as
a young Royal Academy student with very traditional ideas: suddenly
'the world opened onto the great modern French masters – & perhaps
from them has never closed again.'

In 1914, thirty-two-year-old Clive really could believe that a new
renaissance was at hand as a young generation in England laughed at
the quaint beliefs of their Victorian forefathers and crossed borders both
national and psychological, aesthetic and scientific, determined to create a
cosmopolitan society where aesthetic ideas and one's personality mattered
more than where one chanced to be born. As the glorious early summer
that year seemed to confirm the optimistic mood, Clive also basked in
the thrill of a new affair that had begun with talk about paintings.

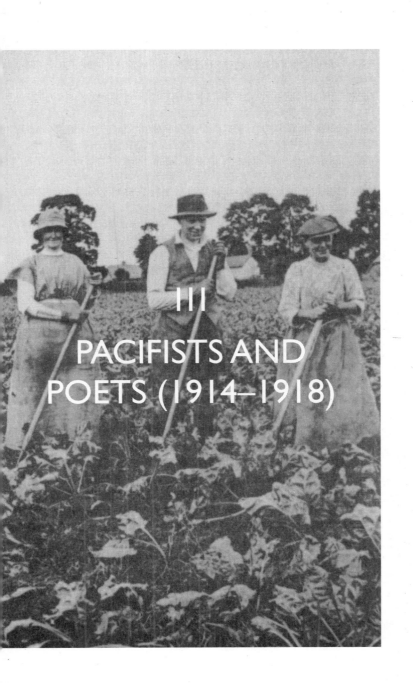

III
PACIFISTS AND
POETS (1914–1918)

13. Mary

On 4 August 1914, Clive drafted a letter to the editor of the *Daily News and Leader*: 'So we are to fight Germany to preserve the balance of power which exists only to preserve peace.' If he sent the letter, it was not published, but Clive never relinquished his conviction that war was the worst way to settle disputes between nations and invariably served the interests of a few at the expense of the many. Anti-German sentiment had grown unabated in the preceding decade, but even his pleasure at witnessing the destruction of Prussian militarism could never outweigh the misery war would bring.[1]

Late in the war, Clive recalled the months leading up to it as a time that held the promise of a new open-mindedness that might allow 'a certain receptivity to new ways of thinking and feeling'. 'For a few dizzy years it was wildly surmised that to found a civilisation might be as thrilling as to found a family, and that one could be as romantic and snobbish about Art as about bulldogs or battleships.' The international salon of like-minded people who gathered at Lady Ottoline and her husband Philip Morrell's Thursday evenings in Bedford Square regarded themselves as citizens of the 'Republic of Thought and Feeling'. These evenings were halted temporarily when Britain went to war, and within a year Clive would have to annotate some of the names he had listed among the citizens of his brave new world: Henri Doucet, 'killed in

[1] When Clive, Vanessa and Roger went to Cologne in August 1912 to see the Sonderbund's large exhibition of modern paintings, Vanessa wrote to Snow that although she admired the exhibition, the Germans were oppressive and ugly; to be invaded by them would be horrible (VB/M. Snowden 20 August 1912 TGA).

Flanders, fighting for France against Germany'; Ferenc Békássy, 'killed in Galicia, fighting for Germany against Russia'.

A few of Clive's friends were 'desperately jingo' at first, 'longing to rush into the war', mainly because of the widely held belief that the conflict would be brief, more like a sporting event than the horrific carnage it quickly revealed itself to be. Clive even told James Strachey he thought it would be boring simply to observe the war as if he were a spectator 'at a university match that's going to last three years'; he wondered if James could ask his brother Oliver to help him get a position as an interpreter in the Army Service or Medical Corps. Nelly Cecil (her 1905 portrait of whom was the first painting Vanessa exhibited) told Clive that her husband, Lord Robert, was grateful for his offer to put his ability to speak French to use for the Red Cross and that if he could teach the language to English nurses he would be doing noble work. One imagines Clive would have found such service congenial had he done it.

Life in London continued as before, at least until the first successful German air raid in May 1915. Clive saw his friends and acquaintances at concerts, at the opera and sometimes sat late into the night playing poker with Saxon, Lytton and Gerald Shove at Adrian Stephen's flat at 37 Bedford Square. A younger generation of Slade art students was a new element in the social life of Gordon and Bedford Squares, Fitzroy and Gower Streets, augmenting the 'neo-pagans' (as Virginia dubbed them) gathered around Rupert Brooke, whom the Stephens had known since their childhood. Barbara Hiles brought her friend Faith Bagenal (who married the economist Hubert Henderson in 1915) to Bloomsbury parties and Barbara would marry Faith's brother Nick at the end of the war, but for now, Clive told Ottoline, they did 'all that virgins can do to make us merry'. Amongst the newcomers was Adrian's friend David Garnett, known always by his childhood nickname, Bunny. When Bunny first met Duncan at one of Adrian's poker parties he assumed the painter did not like him, but at Christmas 1914, Bunny went with his close friend Frankie Birrell to stay with Lytton in the country. Duncan was also there and, in the course of a long walk over the Marlborough Downs, he and Bunny began an intimacy that within a week or two of returning to London became sexual.

On Twelfth Night 1915, Maynard Keynes held a dinner party at the Café Royal to celebrate his appointment to the Treasury. The Woolfs and

Mary Hutchinson

the MacCarthys were there, as were Frankie Birrell, Duncan, Clive and Vanessa. Slyly, Maynard seated Bunny between Vanessa and Duncan. Quite soon afterwards, Vanessa visited Bunny to clarify how things stood between her and Duncan. She told him she was in love with Duncan 'but couldn't feel jealous of any man', and informed him of Duncan's involvements with her brother Adrian and Maynard. Bunny told Vanessa that he 'had been much more falling in love with her than Duncan and that [he] was a womaniser', which was honest. Vanessa added 'that Clive said he would never live with anyone but her, but of course had his affairs'. The latest of these was with Mary Hutchinson, the elegant wife of the barrister and art collector St John Hutchinson, known to all as Jack. Vanessa assumed Mary would be just another of Clive's amorous adventures, expecting him to spend different months with different women, occasionally returning to say 'Poor old Dolphin & give her a pat'.

The Hutchinsons were frequent guests of the Morrells, St John was on the executive committee of the Contemporary Art Society and Mary was a frequent customer of the Omega Workshops. Since Clive had reluctantly escorted her around Janet Ross's Florentine rose garden on a wet afternoon in 1909, Mary had become a stylish and sharply intelligent woman. Their paths could have crossed many times in London after her marriage in 1910, but their flirtation began with an exchange of letters about art.

At 2 a.m. from Gordon Square in the summer of 1914, Clive wrote to 'Dear Mrs. Hutchinson' that he wished he had seen her again because he wanted her advice about a painting he might buy on behalf of an 'eminent American collector' – neither the painting nor the collector can be identified. Would she accompany him around some galleries, after coming to lunch – 'in the cause of art', of course, not to please him. Accepting, Mary asked why he wrote letters at such an odd hour of the night. 'Considering the rapidity and unexpectedness of your movements I may have felt that I hadn't a moment to lose,' Clive replied. Sensing an opportunity, he continued, 'Are you constant only in the colour of your note-paper?'

Mary was Clive's guest at Maynard's Café Royal dinner. Afterwards, the party went back to 46 Gordon Square for a recital by the D'Aranyi sisters, Jelly and Adila, followed by a performance upstairs of Racine's *Bérénice* for which Duncan and Vanessa had constructed huge puppets to be given voice by various Stracheys. (The performance would be repeated more formally in February at the Omega Workshops.) Mary had proved by then that she was not 'constant', and the arrival of her blue envelopes always gave Clive a thrill of anticipation. Someone had told him – or so he said – that Mary was like Strindberg's Baroness in *The Confession of a Fool*, which she coyly complained must mean he thought she had thick ankles; she was thinking of another baroness, Clive assured her. By the end of 1914, the 'Mrs Hutchinson' Clive wrote to about seeing a thirteenth-century painting at Chichester Cathedral had become his 'Chère Baronne' or 'Chère belle dame'. When he read the letters of John Wilkes, the eighteenth-century libertine and champion of press freedom, he bestowed on Mary the name of Wilkes' daughter, Polly.[2]

To Mary, a love affair was an excellent game played by well-matched equals with the sole object of 'mutual enjoyment'. Her brother Jim

[2]This led in turn to the pseudonym that Mary would use for most of her magazine contributions, Polly Flinders, from a nursery rhyme.

remembered how she appeared to him at the time of her marriage a 'very extraordinary woman' who 'was at this time forcing her brain to grapple with subjects that none but the most masculine intelligences succeed in mastering in the manner in which we men understand the term'. He added that it would be 'difficult to talk above her head'. Mary would have called herself 'a pagan, with a code of life based on purely aesthetic values'. She was 'smallish, Parisian, pliable like the reed that never breaks, possessed of a roguish and naïf humour'. Mary's son, Jeremy, remembered how she strode through the muddy streets of Hammersmith in an Omega dress, urchins yelling 'Here comes the Queen of Sheba!' Clive fell deeply in love with Mary, beginning an affair that would flourish over the next thirteen years. Apart from some periods of estrangement, they remained close: in the final weeks of his life, Mary was one of the old friends who visited him.

When her affair with Clive began, Mary was pregnant with Jeremy, born 28 March 1915, the day before her twenty-sixth birthday (her daughter, Barbara, had been born in 1911). A certain degree of subterfuge was necessary at first to avoid arousing the ire of Mary's husband, but friends such as Ottoline or Lytton aided the lovers by sending Mary spurious postcard invitations, thus providing 'documentary evidence that she was not going to the hotel Metropole at Brighton for the week-end'. When Mary once told Clive she had lied about him, he was relieved to discover 'an unlooked for balance in the bank of morality'.

Vanessa's cousin Florence Maitland accepted the liaisons between Vanessa and Duncan, Clive and Mary with equanimity when her daughter Fredegond told her about them but was 'most disgusted' at learning all four were great friends. Vanessa was glad that Mary was in Clive's life because, conscious that Duncan's feelings for Bunny made her own position somewhat tenuous, she could devote herself to making Duncan happy.

In April 1915, Vanessa joined Duncan at Eleanor House at West Wittering, near Chichester, which the Hutchinsons had rented the year before, and where the Slade professor Henry Tonks kept a studio. From Eleanor, Vanessa wrote to Clive that so far 'no little Grant has yet had a chance to come into existence'. When the Hutchinsons planned to take up the rent of Eleanor again in May, Vanessa found a nearby cottage

Mary Hutchinson and Clive Bell

where Clive could stay in a caravan in the garden; it seemed silly, she thought, for Clive to go back to London just as Mary arrived for the summer.

Before the depth of Mary and Clive's feelings for one another was as apparent as it would become, the Hutchinsons and Bells, with Duncan and Bunny usually in attendance, peacefully coexisted on the Sussex coast. Vanessa explained the situation to Roger:

> The Hutchinsons are at their house, I and the children are in lodgings 5 minutes off and at this moment Duncan and Bunny are in Tonks' studio. Clive has taken two rooms in the village ¼ of an hour's walk away, where he sleeps and has breakfast and spends the morning writing. It is extraordinarily nice and quiet and one hears as little of the war as possible.

But Vanessa did not care much for Jack Hutchinson. In the same letter, she told Roger she had had to move because Jack never stopped talking as he sat with Mary and Clive just outside the studio. 'His talk bores me to such an extent that I can't stand it. Last night we had to dine with them and if it weren't for my faculty of not listening I should have died, I think. He has that peculiar type of open minded tolerance which is more deadly than anything and he tells innumerable bawdy stories which even I can never succeed in listening to the whole of.'

When Jeremy was born, Clive fretted about Mary's health, anxiously appealing to Vanessa for advice which he relayed at once to Mary, who was apparently suffering from postnatal depression. He urged her to wean the baby as soon as possible (a suggestion of Vanessa's which his own sister Lorna had followed when her baby was only five weeks old). Vanessa was incredulous that Mary's doctor had not recommended a breast pump, so Clive begged her to order one. Although it seemed absurd to Clive, Vanessa insisted that continuing to nurse Quentin after her periods had resumed was the source of all her ailments. She dug out her copy of Dr Chavasse's *Advice to Young Wives & Mothers* (1868), which reassured everyone that there was nothing unusual about Mary's condition.

Clive's worries about illness were by now well established. At Eleanor there had been some trouble with the water supply, convincing Clive that they would all get typhoid (except for him, that is, as he had been inoculated against it in late 1914 when he had planned to go to Palermo 'to elaborate in peace and sunshine a complete theory of civilization'). He ranted to Mary about the dangers of maternity: 'Babies have been the ruin of half the women I know. And it's all superstition too, superstition and sentimentality. Everyone knows it would be the death of people like you and Vanessa to try and do the work of peasants but in the matter of babies you're expected to be a match for the blackest savage in Togoland. It's a mere Victorianism.' They had the right idea in the eighteenth century, when a baby was given almost at once to a wet nurse. Sheepishly, he asked Mary if she would prefer he not write to her in this peevish state of mind.

Clive's attitude to domestic work was unremarkable for his time and class: women like Vanessa and Mary should avoid it. 'You might spend your lives looking after your children and your houses,' he told Mary when she complained to him about a servant she suspected had cheated her, 'but you would be idiots and worse if you did, because you have better things to do.' The material comfort enabled by one's 'body-slaves' was worth the trouble their dishonesty might cause and whatever losses Mary had suffered should be regarded as 'a slight addition to

their wages'. Railing against Vanessa's or Mary's doing household chores
was a refrain in Clive's letters to them both, although he sometimes
included Duncan in his protests: if one were an artist and could afford
it, no time should be wasted doing anything but making art. 'It's all
very well Bunny doing menial work, but it's preposterous you should
or Duncan for that matter,' he told Vanessa.

Clive believed that state-sponsored crèches and an allowance for
mothers would be more valuable to women than the vote or divorce
law reform. He had been brought up 'in an unsympathetic middle-class
home, a private school of eighty boys, and a public of 640' and although
he had managed to hold on to his individuality, he was convinced he
would have fared better in 'a well-ordered crèche'. Those of his and
Mary's class 'make more fuss about the welfare of our babies than we
feel' because the 'most highly civilised' people did not usually have
strong parental instincts: 'There's hardly one of us that escapes some
insincerity, some conventionality in the matter.' When he discussed the
same issues with Fredegond Maitland, who married Gerald Shove in
1915, she told him he was 'like a woman' in understanding her worries.

With a new baby and a suspicious husband, Mary had few
opportunities to see Clive, which made him miserable in the summer
of 1915. His discomfort was exacerbated by Virginia's hostility. A month
before *The Voyage Out* was published, she had fallen into panic and
anxiety. She proposed acidly to Lytton that they should all subscribe
to buy a parrot for Clive: 'It must be a bold primitive bird, trained of
course to talk nothing but filth, and to indulge in obscene caresses – the
brighter coloured the better. I believe we can get them cheap and gaudy
at the Docks. The thing is for us all to persuade him that the love of
birds is the last word in Civilisation.'

A few weeks later, Clive received a 'bitter and hateful' letter, 'raking
up old quarrels', and warned Mary that she might receive a similarly
abusive one because Virginia had heard about their affair. Leonard
had promised Virginia he would send her letter to Clive but enclosed
with it a note hoping that Clive would 'know how to understand' it.
Throughout most of that spring and summer Virginia was plagued by
debilitating headaches and insomnia. Clive was disappointed by *The
Voyage Out* but recommended it to the convalescent Mary because it
was 'all about illness'. Virginia's insight into human psychology seemed
to him profound but the novel had ended up being 'all about life and

states of mind', he told Mary, 'and nothing about that other thing which you have discovered to be the essence of a work of art'. By which, presumably, he meant significant form.

The publication of *Art* brought Clive invitations to lecture around the country about 'The Essential Quality in Art'. Although he claimed that that quality transcended history, he recognised that art was often deployed for political and social purposes in wartime. An elderly gentleman in the audience in Hampstead had chastised him 'for giving myself the airs of a superman', but a suffragette and a 'territorial' had come to his defence. Nietzsche's popularity amongst young artists before the war had introduced the word 'superman' to English discourse, but it took Clive (who read some of the German philosopher's works in a French translation by Henri Albert) some time to decide that he was not a 'rubbishy romantic', as he had told Ottoline, but 'very bright' and probably a poet to those who could read German.

Clive sent his Hampstead lecture to Mary for her comments and used it as the basis for 'Art and War', which appeared as the lead article in the *International Journal of Ethics* in 1915. In this example of Clive's polemical fearlessness he addresses highly contentious wartime events that had been thoroughly exploited by the pro-war press. 'Art and War' exposes the hypocrisy of those who extol the value of art in peacetime but see it as an irrelevant luxury in times of war, or use it as a tool of propaganda: 'When the Germans sacked Louvain and shelled Reims our politicians and press discovered suddenly that art is a sacred thing and that people who disrespect it are brutes. Agreed: and how have the monied class in England respected art? . . . What institution do we starve so abjectly as we starve the National Gallery?' To put art at the service of patriotism was as meaningless as calling for a patriotic mathematics. The internationalist pacifism that drove Clive's opposition to compulsory military service was entwined in 'Art and War' with his aesthetic hypothesis. The duty of artists and philosophers is to 'tend the lamp' of civilisation, especially in times when a nation might itself become barbaric in the fight against barbarism.

Frustrated by how little he was able to see Mary, who struggled for some months with illness after Jeremy's birth, Clive grasped rather desperately at Bertrand Russell's suggestion that he go to America in the cause of peace, writing to her: 'I mayn't see you; you can't see me. In the circumstances I must turn my mind to something and stop thinking about you.' When Mary seemed to be getting better a few days later, Clive told Russell that nothing would persuade him to go away when he had the chance of seeing her.

In August, the Bells rented a house at Bosham, about ten miles from West Wittering, which enabled Clive and Mary to see one another from time to time, but the situation remained fraught. Jack made a scene when he worried that the servants at Eleanor might be scandalised by Clive's presence. Jack's mood was not improved when Clive prevailed upon Lytton and Ottoline to invite Mary to visit them at Garsington, the Morrells' country estate, without her husband. 'Jack has had to put up I think rather against his will with again not being asked,' Vanessa told Maynard; she could not imagine what her servants must think. But to Garsington Mary and Clive did go, and on from there to a weekend with Lytton at his cottage in Wiltshire, who reported to Ottoline on their visit: 'Clive was in a very good "so-happy-that-I-don't-care-whether-I-impress-you-or-not" sort of mood – which suits him better than some others.' On their way back to London, Clive and Mary stopped at Marlborough College where they 'shed tears over Clive's past: his desk, his bed, his spoon and fork. We even found an album of beautiful boys in which his career, mental and physical, could be traced year by year.'

Their affair became easier to conduct in London, where Mary had at once begun to receive postcards from Clive informing her of the part she was to prepare for meetings of the play-reading society that had resumed in Gordon Square. Duncan and Vanessa had amused Clive by treating him in the month following Jeremy Hutchinson's birth 'rather as though I were a widow – discreet sympathy' but for now, Clive planned to spend his 'widowhood' writing a brilliant pacifist pamphlet; after all, had not Milton, Swift, Voltaire and Demosthenes all been pamphleteers?

14. Peace at Once

The war was welcomed at Cleeve House. Clive's family not only supported it but stood to gain from it considerably as the British Navy's demand for coal increased. Cory and William Acton, Lorna's husband, would receive military honours for their service in France.

Two weeks after war was declared, Clive sent Mary some grouse from Scotland, where he had gone with his family to shoot. He was in a melancholy mood as he thought how his children and Mary's would probably have to spend their lives working to recoup the costs of the war instead of exploring new ideas. It was not so much the thought of armies killing each other that bothered him, it was the 'collapse of civilization'. Their lives would be 'cut in two' by the war, leaving them in its aftermath only 'lookers on', forced to retreat into a world of 'private feelings, aesthetic emotions and personal affections'. Despite this moment of Moorean gloom Clive did not retreat into a private world at all, and would never do so.

In a number of unpublished drafts, Clive accounted for his attitudes to the war. As soon as it began, it seemed to him, the 'mind of a whole nation' gave way to 'instinct and passion'. Even some non-interventionists 'seemed to lose their reason once it became clear that England would go to war over Belgium', although some, such as Bertrand Russell, Goldsworthy Lowes Dickinson and Bernard Shaw continued to speak out against the folly of war. Liberals who had all their lives denounced 'war and armaments and conscription and race-hatred and the silly provincialism that prevents the inhabitants of this wretched planet from seeing that they are all in one boat' suddenly lost their courage in August 1914: 'Their bodies were caught in the machinery they had spent their lives in trying to destroy.' Clive urgently wanted to do something to preserve what he described as a 'planetary' civilisation, deploring abstractions such as 'national honour' that were promulgated by the ruling class and their lackeys in the press to incite people to violence.

Britain had a volunteer army, setting it apart from other European powers, but naval competition between Britain and Germany, as well as Prussian militarism, had changed the national attitude towards compulsory military service. By 1914, conscription was being debated frequently in Parliament and before the end of the year Fenner Brockway's call in the *Labour Leader* for 'enrolment in a Fellowship of all men who would refuse conscription should it come' had resulted in the creation of the No Conscription Fellowship. Clive agreed with NCF co-founder Clifford Allen, who argued that conscription embodied a philosophy that 'exalts the State as an entity, distinct from its citizens'. Compulsory service in a supposedly free society offended Clive philosophically. He plunged into the debate about conscription early in 1915 with a letter to the *Nation*, inaugurating the political activism that would occupy him for the first two years of the War when he wrote: 'Before many months are passed a score of gentlemen living in the West End of London may feel it their duty to order every serviceable male in Great Britain to prepare himself to kill or to be killed.' Clive's argument rested on two main ideas: that patriotism was a fluke of national borders and that the 'freedom' for which Britain was ostensibly fighting was undermined by its own restrictions on what thoughts could be expressed within those borders.

The Defence of the Realm Act (DORA), which had been passed within days of the declaration of war and was amended several times throughout 1914 and thereafter, gave the government powers to suppress and seize writings deemed to promote 'disaffection' among His Majesty's forces. The 1857 Obscene Publications Act was still in effect and public performance of dramatic works had to be licensed by the Lord Chamberlain. Clive claimed that he had 'plays, stories, and essays that I should be free to publish in Germany but may not print in England', arguing that the price of German domination might be a loss of political liberty, but a 'moral and religious' gain. This was naive: like England, Germany had imposed censorship at the outset of the war. However, his larger point about the contradiction inherent in an ideal of freedom that is upheld by coercion would resonate through much pacifist writing of the period: if the governing class can send people to die for things in which they do not believe, 'It has over them precisely the same right that the owner has over his slave – the power of life and death.'

Clive resisted being drawn too deeply into the committee work of pacifism because while he found the people involved good and honest, they often seemed to be 'quacks'. Nevertheless, when the 'bank-clerks and shopmen' began to move against conscription, he wanted to support them. At Eleanor House, where Maynard would sometimes visit, 'full of cabinet secrets', Clive set to work on a 'seditious pamphlet', and by early summer 1915 he was ready to look for a publisher. Returning to London one evening from Cambridge, where he had debated with Russell, Lowes Dickinson and Karin Stephen whether they should spend whatever life remained to them stating a position and handing on a tradition of civilisation or just enjoying themselves, he found Vanessa and Duncan about to go to a reading in Red Lion Square. There they found Maynard and the Shoves, Alix Sargant-Florence, Frankie Birrell and Bunny (the latter two about to leave for France on a Quaker relief mission). After the reading, they all came back to Gordon Square, where Clive concluded that it was a 'little ridiculous to take life tragically': if life was to be short, it might as well be merry.

In *Peace at Once*, officially published in September 1915 by the National Labour Press, Clive posed the question of whether 'crushing' Germany was worth 'killing and maiming half the serviceable male population of Europe, starving to death a quarter of the world, and ruining the hopes of the next three generations'. The war was being fought on behalf of the 'small ruling caste' that existed in each of the countries in the conflict, which had, with the assistance of a docile press, found it necessary to invent a rationale to stir up war fever, a rationale rooted in abstractions such as 'National Honour' and 'National Interests'. This idea of a 'nation' struck him as absurd: 'It is as though a shepherd should believe that there was such a thing as *a flock of sheep* which had a real existence of its own quite apart from the sheep that composed it.' The patriotic sacrifices urged on the populace by the editor of *The Times* were tantamount to driving the flock over a cliff's edge in the interests of the sheep.

Clive thought that the Regius Professor of Greek at Oxford, Gilbert Murray, made the best pro-war case in his pamphlet *How Can War Ever be Right?*, so he addressed Murray directly in *Peace at Once*. Murray argued that death with honour is always better than life with dishonour because our 'ultimate happiness' rests in 'the power to do our duty and when we die to have done it'. In Clive's view, the ideas flitting in and out of the minds of politicians and professors had little to do with the lives of ordinary people. Could Murray honestly believe that 'the men who are dying all over Europe, in Asia, and on the high seas, are dying for their outraged feelings?' Cavalierly, Clive wrote that it would make little difference to ordinary working people to whom they paid their taxes or for whom they laboured. 'Would the average Englishman rather be dead than have a German policeman round the corner?' was a sentence soon seized upon by his antagonists as especially offensive, but as far as Clive was concerned – and he was far from eccentric in this view in 1915 – the longer the conflict continued the more the warlike elements in Germany would appeal to the nationalism that 'sensible, civilised people' abhor. H. G. Wells believed the war would be the end of war itself,[1] but Clive appealed to what surely everyone knew: the war would be ended by treaty, 'drawn up after a deal of that particular kind of lying and cheating which is called diplomacy', putting off the necessary international agreements which were the only guarantee of a permanent peace. With a prescience confirmed in 1919 by Keynes in *The Economic Consequences of the Peace*, he argued that 'the surest means to another European war would be a peace that humiliated someone'.

The terms in which Clive argued against conscription and for a quick resolution to the conflict through negotiation aligned with the pervasive internationalism of contemporary peace movements, as well as with the traditional Liberalism that would be unrecognisable by the war's end. His optimistic sense that before the war a new era was about to dawn of cultural and aesthetic experiment, of intellectual and artistic collaboration, with national borders disregarded, was dashed by the realisation that most people did not care for art and ideas nearly as much as they wished to 'smash' Germans. Clive came to understand

---

[1]Wells urged that everyone in England should be armed so that invading Germans could be massacred (*Times* 31 October 1914). In an unpublished letter to the *New Statesman*, Clive asked 'My Lord Kitchener for God's sake let this fat, pushing little fellow have an officer's uniform!' ('Flying to Arms' Trinity Bell 5/6).

that he and those who felt as he did were now exiles in their own country. 'Internationalism' had a specific connotation in this period, being tantamount to pacifism (or, in the case of those, like Leonard, who believed in the use of military force to enforce the decisions of an international body, 'pacificism'). The general outlook in Clive's milieu was internationalist in the sense of alienation from their own nation-state in favour of affiliations with like-minded artists and intellectuals, wherever they might be. Duncan's explanation to his father, Major Bartle Grant, of why he had a conscientious objection to the war perfectly expressed this outlook:

> I had become I suppose in a sense unpatriotic, as most artists must do. I began to see that one's enemies were not vague masses of foreign people, but the mass of people in one's own country and the mass of people in the enemy country, and that one's friends were people of true ideas that one might meet and did meet in every country one visited.

Clive used his relative celebrity to position himself as a spokesman for the cause of conscientious objection and pacifism. When Lytton remarked that after the age of forty-five one lives for fame and power, adding with slight bitterness that Clive already had 'enough to make age agreeable', he acknowledged that *Art* had brought its author greater public recognition than had yet been achieved by the younger members of their circle. Rather to his surprise, Lytton was impressed by *Peace at Once*, telling Leonard that Clive 'seems able to express himself, in rather an odd way; and it's difficult to see what can be said on the other side'. Lytton wished Clive's pamphlet was '40 times as long', but a brief notice in the *TLS* carped that it was not only 'statesmen and journalists' who were prone to pumping 'political and pseudo-historical nonsense' into people. G. E. Moore found *Peace at Once* 'very persuasive', but Clive wavered, telling Mary at the end of July to destroy his pamphlet because it was 'sad, journalistic stuff'.

This moment of doubt did not stop him from reiterating his view that if a few rich old men were allowed to send young men to die for views they did not share, then it could not be said that their cause was 'freedom'. Under Clive's letter in *The Nation* of 26 June 1915 was one from 'United We Stand' arguing that the division of opinion about conscription was not by class, but vertically, within all classes, on both sides of the issue.

As the first year of the war gave way to the second, tensions increased in England around how to supply the army with sufficient numbers of troops without forcing men to fight. Suppression of dissenting voices became more severe; propaganda emphasised the barbarism of the 'Hun' and characterised the invasion of Belgium as its 'rape'.

On 20 August 1915, the *Times* reported police raids in Manchester and London on the offices of the Independent Labour Party, publisher of the *Labour Leader*. Issues of the paper were seized and one that was ready for the press was not allowed to resume printing before a letter from Clive on 'Trade Unions and Conscription' had been deleted. The *Labour Leader* ran the issue with a blank space between the title and Clive's name where the letter would have appeared, accompanied by a notice describing the raid and its consequences. In court at Salford, a magistrate decided that the police had exceeded their authority under DORA in seizing and intending to destroy the newspaper but that the pamphlets seized from the ILP's office should be destroyed, among them 1,642 copies of *Peace at Once*. Three weeks later the owners of publications seized in the raid were summoned to the Mansion House in London where Alderman John Knill, over the objections of the ILP's counsel, decreed that the case would be conducted in camera; after an hour's secret discussion, the case was adjourned until 22 September. Clive attended the hearing, represented by Jack Hutchinson. Following the Manchester raid, Clive understood that his pamphlet was to be burnt by the 'common hangman', though in what manner it was actually destroyed is unknown. He joked to Mary that his main worry was that the notoriety he would now gain would make him a hero with pacifists and he would thus be forced into personal involvement with them.

Yet Clive made sure that the fate of *Peace at Once* would not go unremarked. On 4 September 1915, letters about the suppression of his pamphlet appeared over his name in both the *Nation* and the *New Statesman*. In the *Nation*, he pointed out that many people had read his pamphlet and found it neither seditious nor improper; even Gilbert Murray had sent him a 'particularly obliging letter'. If the government could not allow any questioning of its reasons for continuing the war, then could the *Nation* maintain that 'we are fighting for freedom?' In the *New Statesman*, he claimed to be speaking 'on behalf of thousands of people who share my views'. If the *New Statesman* would not defend his pamphlet, then 'it is less tolerant than the German government'.

The *New Statesman*, begun as a Fabian challenger to the *Nation* and the *New Age* in 1913, had done an about-face immediately after Britain's declaration of war in August 1914. Its editor, Clifford Sharp, appended a note beneath Clive's letter doubting the 'thousands' who shared his views, dismissing as foolish the notion that press freedom was not far greater in England than in France, Germany or Russia and expressing surprise that Clive seemed unaware of the 'reality of the sentiment called patriotism'. In the *Nation*, Hugh Massingham also responded to Clive, singling out, as did Sharp, the presumably facetious notion that it would not matter whether an English or a German policeman stood on the street of an English town. Like Sharp, Massingham did not believe *Peace at Once* should be suppressed, but he too refused to accept its argument: 'A nation does not act in that way,' he wrote.

Although in a minority, Clive was by no means isolated. His letter appeared in the *Nation* on the same page as one from Norman Angell, founder of the Union of Democratic Control (UDC), who was speaking in the United States about the war, and another from 'A.G.W.' of York, who complained that the silence of Liberals about conscription was too often taken for 'agreement with a policy which we loathe'. Bernard Shaw came to Clive's defence, arguing that Clive was surely right to expect 'all freeborn Englishmen to rally round freedom of the press' at a time when Britain was ostensibly fighting for precisely that kind of liberty. G. K. Chesterton issued a sharp rejoinder to Shaw's tacit support for the argument of *Peace at Once*, which he criticised for inculcating a 'squalid panic'. Shaw replied to his 'friendly enemy' Chesterton that Clive had said in his pamphlet 'that war is sin; that the wages of sin is death; and that the best cure for sin is to stop sinning'. By then, Clive had written to James Strachey, 'If you know anyone who could keep the correspondence in The Nation or The New Statesman going, and turn it off my pamphlet and onto free speech, would you egg him on.' He would say no more about his pamphlet in public while he waited for the court's decision.

William H. Bell had already passed his verdict, as Virginia told Margaret Llewelyn Davies: 'Old father Bell threatens complete rupture with Clive if he writes more in the style of the pamphlet.' Clive had found his family almost afraid to discuss the war with him when he went to Seend just before *Peace at Once* appeared. They seemed even more contemptible than ever, he told Ottoline: 'No beings were ever so completely pleased with themselves . . . They feel that they have the run of God's cupboard, and they help themselves judiciously to all that's not worth having. I wish it could all be expressed on a recruiting poster, and below this legend – "Is this worth dying for?" ' Clive might have worried that his antagonism to the war would lead his father to disinherit him but Vanessa told Maynard that, far from disowning them, the Bells had sent them 'a handsome present, thinking we might be hard up on account of the war'. Clive's father's help was always welcome in a crisis, such as when the authorities came to Eleanor House in May 1915 looking for spies. It was a bore, Duncan told Lytton, but 'Clive whose father turned out to be a Lord High Sherriff saved the situation.' The threat of a break over *Peace at Once* did not trouble Vanessa. Secure with her marriage settlement in trust, she was relieved by the thought that she might now not have to go any more to her in-laws for Christmas.

15. Art and War

The Bells spent Christmas 1915 at Garsington Manor, the Morrells' estate near Oxford that would become an important refuge for conscientious objectors after the passage of the Military Service Act in January 1916 that introduced conscription for all single men between the ages of eighteen and forty-one. Ottoline, who had observed her husband, MP for Burnley, being shouted down in Parliament when he spoke against Britain going to war, had been taking in refugees and hosting meetings of the UDC in her drawing room at Bedford Square, but in May 1915 she and Philip had moved full-time to Garsington. Visiting for the first time that summer, Clive told Mary Hutchinson that 'if one arrived by gondola it would not look out of place'. Charles and Dora Sanger, Harry Norton, Bertrand Russell, and the writer Gilbert Cannan with his wife, Mary, were there on this occasion, as were Maria Nys, a teenage Belgian refugee whom Ottoline had taken in. Clive at first thought Maria might be the governess of Ottoline's daughter, Julian. At the Morrells' lavish house, Clive fell into a 'scented coma' and was soon dubbed 'the autocrat of the breakfast table' by his hostess.

The train to Oxford at Christmas was so crowded that after bundling Vanessa, Quentin and Julian into a compartment, Clive sat in the first-class lavatory for the entire journey, reading the letters of Horace Walpole, ignoring hopeful taps on the door. Clive approved of Ottoline's 'real democratic instinct' as she led the villagers in festivities in the barn. Clive and Vanessa, with Julian and Quentin, Maynard, Maria Nys, and Juliette Baillot (Julian Morrell's actual governess) took part in a theatrical performance of 'The Life and Death of Lytton'. After

Christmas, Julian and Quentin were sent on with a nurse to Seend for a week.

The Morrells had a full house. D. H. Lawrence had asked Ottoline to invite his friend John Middleton Murry, who was alone while his lover, Katherine Mansfield, was in France mourning her brother Leslie's death. 'Bertie Russell, me and Clive Bell,' Murry wrote to Katherine, 'feasts of intellect, I don't think.' Lawrence was not there himself but, one evening after dinner, Ottoline read aloud a long, repetitive letter from him about his love for his coalminer 'brothers'.

When Lawrence's novel *The Rainbow* was prosecuted for obscenity in 1915, he and his wife, Frieda, met with Jack Hutchinson and Mary, Clive and Vanessa at 46 Gordon Square to see what could be done. Clive had been trying to arouse indignation in the press about the prosecution, despite his opinion that the book was 'a sentimental, romantic reaction from Edwardianism'. At Clive's urging, Jack Squire, literary editor of the *New Statesman*, used his 'Books in General' column to comment on the absurdity of the proceedings. If the magistrate had 'never seen anything more disgusting' then he was not familiar with many of the books published in England, and must be 'abysmally ignorant of the literatures of our two Allies, France and Great White Russia'. *The Rainbow* was ordered destroyed, but Clive's efforts on its behalf earned him Lawrence's gratitude: 'I rather like Clive Bell,' he told Ottoline, but 'not deeply. He says it is tragic that you can never have any *real* connection with anybody.' At this point, Lawrence exempted Clive from the homophobic disgust he had expressed to Bunny earlier that year about his 'set, Duncan Grant, and Keynes and [Frankie] Birrell' who made him 'feel I should go mad' whenever he thought about them. Lawrence would later mock 'all that significant form piffle'.

Given his attitude that significant form outweighed any other consideration in a work of art – events, places, ideas were all of secondary interest – it is not surprising that Clive wrote relatively little about art during the war. He was dubious about where Cubism might lead and had dismissed Futurism as a fad that distorted the promise of Wyndham Lewis. He saw the Vorticists' exhibition at the Doré Gallery in June 1914 (the 'most avant-garde show London had ever seen', according to Richard Shone), but no comment of his about it has survived. He had been invited to the dinner marking the publication of Lewis's *BLAST*, but disdained its point of view as that of people who wanted to smash things because they felt they had not been given their due. More to Clive's taste was Jean Marchand, whose *Still Life with Bananas* had been exhibited at both the 1910 and 1912 post-Impressionist exhibitions. In a preface Clive wrote for the catalogue of Marchand's show at the Carfax Gallery in June 1914, although he gave his opinion that the Frenchman did not display the 'delicious handling of a Duncan Grant', he thought that this inheritor of the tradition of Cézanne, who had been influenced by Picasso, Matisse and Gauguin, exemplified what was lacking in British art – a commitment to 'the emotional significance of shapes and colours', with nothing to say about 'Man's place in the universe', a topic best left to literary gentlemen.

Even though, by 1916, the Tate, the National Portrait Gallery and the Wallace Collection were closed, the Victoria and Albert Museum partly closed and much of the collection of the National Gallery removed to storage, Londoners sought solace in art. The number of visitors to museums slightly increased after war was declared, though the government regarded art as a private luxury that diverted money from the war effort. With the public's already scant tolerance for modern art further reduced, wartime economics meant that several of the artists whom Clive praised were struggling to earn a living.

In May 1916, Lytton asked Clive if anything could be done to help Mark Gertler, who was about to run out of money completely: 'I'm sure £10 would make a great difference to him, and I thought perhaps you might be able to invest some such sum in a minor picture or some drawings. Or perhaps you could whip up somebody else.' Gertler had been brought into Ottoline's milieu by Gilbert Cannan, a friend of Gertler's patron Eddie Marsh (an Apostle of G. E. Moore's generation who spent most of his career in the service of Winston Churchill). Gertler and Richard Nevinson were both in love with Dora Carrington, a young painter who, like Barbara Hiles and another 'Slade maid' named Dorothy Brett, could sometimes be found at the Morrells' soirées in Bedford Square. Lytton was a frequent visitor to Gertler's studio in early 1915, though Gertler tried to avoid him after Lytton made a pass at him.

That autumn, the Bells borrowed Asheham from the Woolfs, and invited Lytton, Barbara and Carrington to stay. Carrington was shocked by the conversation carried on by Duncan and Vanessa, Clive and Mary, bursting out in a letter to Gertler: 'What traitors all these

Carrington, Barbara Bagenal and Dorothy Brett

people are! They ridicule Ottoline! even Mary Hutchinson laughs at the Cannans with them. It surprises me. I think it's beastly of them to enjoy Ottoline's kindnesses and then laugh at her.' They were all 'poseurs', she told her friend Christine Kuhlenthal.

Gertler was amazed that Carrington had 'stayed with the Clive Bells and that crew', resenting her having shunned London 'as if it was Hell . . . and I was the Devil!' His tortured love for Carrington would become a reliable subject of gossip at Garsington, especially after Cannan's 1916 novel *Mendel* transparently depicted it. Although she would keep it from him for some time, Carrington's weekend at Asheham would bring further misery to Gertler because she had suddenly fallen in love with Lytton there.

Gertler exhibited at the Friday Club (*Jews Arguing* in 1911, for example), as well as the New English Art Club and was a member of the London Group. Richard Shone has described him as a 'Yiddish Cézanne', and Clive was not unusual in pointing out how Gertler's ethnicity informed his painting. Much of his early work drew on the harsh experience of growing up poor in London's Jewish enclave in the East End, the son of Polish immigrants. Clive regretted that Gertler seemed more interested in Spitalfields than in Piero della Francesca, but ignoring important predecessors was a trait Clive often erroneously ascribed to young writers and painters. When Gertler's *Fruit Stall* was exhibited at the third London Group show, Clive was impressed, as was Roger. 'I don't know when I saw an English picture that seemed to me so much the real thing,' Clive told Gertler. 'If I were to try and tell you why it moved me so much I should have to try to rewrite my book.'

As the war went on, Clive made a point of visiting Gertler's studio, often accompanied by Mary. He considered four paintings Gertler made at Garsington in 1917 'really very interesting and superbly conscientious'; when he told Mary that Gertler was second only to Duncan among painters in England, this was about the highest accolade he could bestow. Yet despite his high regard for Gertler's work, Clive – in common with many others – found personal interactions with the self-absorbed artist trying. It would not be until 1941 that Clive devoted an article solely to Gertler, two years after his death.

Clive preferred *Fruit Stall* to Gertler's anti-war masterpiece *Merry-Go-Round*, though he acknowledged the latter's great power. Jack Hutchinson, legal counsel to several conscientious objectors, warned Gertler that showing *Merry-Go-Round* might lead to 'a tremendous outcry' were it to be mentioned in newspapers by critics who would 'write all sorts of rubbish about German art and German artists' (someone had stuck a label reading 'Made in Germany' on Gertler's *Creation of Eve* at the 1915 London Group exhibition).

Most reviewers emphasised artists whose work could in some way be related to the war effort or patriotic feelings and gallery owners favoured such work as a means of surviving financially. Clive expressed his resistance to this nativism in 'Contemporary Art in England', an article for the *Burlington Magazine* in July 1917 that irritated Gertler because his name did not appear in a list of young English artists of note. Although Clive had worried that his excoriation of what he viewed as English artists' insularity might cause difficulties for Roger just as he had begun a 'reformation' of the magazine he had helped found and co-edited, Roger thought the article 'splendid – just what I wanted said. I hope it'll make people sit up; but I believe nothing will disturb the profound self-complacency of the English.'

Clive harshly criticised those who regarded art merely as an amenity, those with money who 'want furniture and a background, pretty things for the boudoir, handsome ones for the hall, and something jolly for the smoking-room'. He argued that artists in England suffered from lack of a 'live tradition', such as flourished in France. When Clive reprinted the article in his collection *Pot-Boilers* in 1918, he deleted the point about the absence of a live tradition and remedied the omission of Gertler from what had been a very short list of young artists of talent (Duncan Grant, Wyndham Lewis and Jacob Epstein), also adding Stanley Spencer, William Roberts, David Bomberg and Vanessa. For Clive, English artists had somehow to try to develop in an environment where the public had ignored Renoir's *Les Parapluies* when it was hung in the National Gallery as part of the Hugh Lane bequest, but raised an outcry when it was proposed to sell 'a block of unimportant water-colours' by Turner. Clive would return many times to consideration of *Les Parapluies*, writing a close analysis of it in 1945.

Conscription had moved inexorably closer since 1915 when various efforts of the government and the supportive Northcliffe press failed to result in sufficient volunteers. The outcry over the sinking of the *Lusitania* in May 1915, the propagandistic Bryce Commission report on 'atrocities' in Belgium and the shaming rhetoric deployed against 'shirkers' had all contributed to an atmosphere that made opposition to the war more dangerous to express. When the Earl of Derby's scheme requiring men to declare their availability for service was put in place, local tribunals to hear conscientious objections were established by October 1915, and by November the Central Tribunal was in place. By mid-1916, two Military Service Acts had been passed and objectors began to be treated 'as crackpots or madmen'. The view of peace campaigners as 'cranks or lunatics' echoed the discourse that had treated modern artists similarly since 1910. As feelings rose against those opposed to the war, people like Clive were targets.

'I am called a pimp in the New Age,' Clive wrote to Ottoline in January 1916. 'I am ready to be shot on the miniature rifle range in the Tower, or at Paddington station, or wherever one is shot – except in Flanders.' Under the pseudonym 'North Staffs', T. E. Hulme launched a torrent of abuse against Clive in his 'War Notes' column in the *New Age*, the first in a series of direct addresses to 'some literary men' intended to shame them into enlisting. In the course of this diatribe, Hulme called Clive a 'rich man', a 'contemptible ass', 'a wretched creature', a 'particularly foolish specimen of the aesthete', 'a pup of Mr Roger

Fry', a 'male Mrs. Humphry Ward' and a 'pimp'. Hulme's attack was distinguished by drawing together *Art* and *Peace at Once*, using one to undermine the argument of the other. He seized upon the example in *Art* of a painter who starves for his art, who would 'quite possibly' kill anyone who tried to force him to compromise with the market. Hulme treated *Peace at Once* as representative of the arguments made by most pacifists, except in its questioning of whether there is *any* cause worth dying for. Had Bell not said in *Art* that lofty aesthetic experiences were more valuable than life itself? *Peace at Once* emphasises continually 'what men lose by death', Hulme wrote, so surely, 'for the emancipated man death is too great a price to pay for anything', but that was apparently not the case for the painters in Paris in Bell's anecdote. Like any good polemicist, Hulme omitted the context of his example from *Art*, which Clive ends by likening the single-minded artist to a religious person who 'so cares for truth that he will go to prison, or death, rather than acknowledge a God in whose existence he does not believe'. In a biting conclusion, Hulme asked if the plight of soldiers in the trenches did not impose a moral demand on the comfortable to join them. 'There is a certain generosity of mind which makes such feeling unsupportable to most men. It was probably a reason of this kind that made the sculptor Gaudier Brzeska go back to France,' and it was sickening to think such a promising artist died 'while this wretched artistic pimp still survives'.

Letters from 'W. R.' and S. H. Rudd the following week deplored North Staffs' deployment of abuse as a form of argument. George P. Chapman asked if the *New Age* could not 'leave the killing of pacifists to superior papers like the "Daily Sketch" and the "Daily Mail"?' Clive made no reply, in contrast to his customary alacrity in joining aesthetic controversies, particularly when they were made personal. For much of 1916 he would be involved in serious activism around the question of conscientious objection to military service, drafting memoranda, meeting with politicians and conferring with leaders in the anti-conscription movement, such as Clifford Allen and Bertrand Russell. Apart from a tongue-in-cheek proposal that the government should establish private bull-rings in the countryside for the purpose of breeding bulls to pull artillery, his public letters were measured contributions to the debate.

For many, as the silencing of dissent increased, this debate struck at the heart of England's character as a free society. Clive heard that the police had visited Agnes Hamilton, a Labour Party worker and friend of Ramsay MacDonald, to ask about 'improper conversations she is supposed to hold concerning the war'. A Fellow of Trinity College serving as a lieutenant in the County of London Regiment had been cashiered for a mild letter to the *Times* against conscription. 'By passing a Compulsion Bill, in the middle of a war,' Clive wrote in an unpublished manuscript titled 'A Reign of Terror', 'without even appealing to the constituencies, the government has taken to itself the right of compelling its opponents to sacrifice their principles, and in some cases their homes and lives, in a cause which is not theirs.'

Exemption from military service on the grounds of conscience was decided by local tribunals who often were hostile to the very notion of such an exemption. If the exemption was granted, work 'of national importance' had to be performed. When the Military Service Act was amended to include married men, Clive became involved in discussions about how to ensure that conscientious objections were genuine, and what provisions could be made for COs. The prevailing mood was that COs were cowards who used the exemption in bad faith. When the No Conscription Fellowship gathered in London for a convention, the Northcliffe press not-so-subtly encouraged violence against its members. Gerald Shove attended an Anti-Conscription meeting in Finsbury in May where he was beaten up in a 'riot'. Clive lived in a 'world of agitation and uneasiness'. He would probably be in jail before Duncan or Bunny, he told Vanessa, but was working furiously behind the scenes to help the CO cause. If he were taken to jail, he advised her to clear Gordon Square, store 'all superfluous furniture, and protest to the landlord that in the absence of the bread-winner it was impossible to pay rent'.

In 1917, Clive penned a 'sort of fantasia' as a riposte to H. G. Wells' popular novel *Mr Britling Sees it Through*. In 'Young Mr. Britling', the conservative newspaper owner who narrates Clive's story learns that before the war Hughie Britling fell under the influence of a decadent promoter of French art and culture named Evelyn Townshend. The narrator believes that the war, in which Hughie is killed, arrived just in time to save England from the 'infection' of modernism. Clive knew that his fantasy would very likely meet the same fate as *Peace at Once* if he tried to publish it.

In the context of conscription, the discourse that mocked post-Impressionist art as the work of madmen and charlatans became indistinguishable from the rhetoric depicting conscientious objectors as unmanly lunatics. Modern art was shamefully unpatriotic, deranged, debauched, degenerate – just like those who refused to die for 'National Honour'. The association of modern art with mental instability and sexual perversity had its roots in late nineteenth-century England's fear of degeneration, which had informed the trial and conviction of Oscar Wilde. Clive's work on behalf of COs and the notoriety that had come with the publication of *Art* identified him with attitudes and ideas towards which the war had intensified public antagonism.

Reading Frank Harris's 1915 biography of Oscar Wilde confirmed Roger's feelings about 'the impossibility of art in England'. 'I don't think any other civilisation is so recalcitrant to art,' he told Vanessa. If she could have seen what happened in 1895 (when Roger was twenty-nine), she would understand what could happen to an artist if the British public 'could get its teeth into' him. Clive had no illusions about British philistinism, misogyny and homophobia. Wilde's antagonist, Sir Edward Carson, was the attorney-general in Asquith's government who led the movement for censorship when war was declared. The CO was feminised in the jingoist press, both in words and in cartoons, and the prevailing climate of the military tribunals was famously emblematised in the question of whether an objector would be man enough to defend 'his' women. Clive welcomed the works of sexologists such as Havelock Ellis and Richard von Krafft-Ebing as symptoms of a movement towards more tolerant attitudes to diverse sexual practices, but the socially regressive wartime atmosphere discouraged his optimism.

Art went on being quarrelled with, dismissed and lauded throughout the war years, with 2,500 more copies (over the initial run of 1,500) in print by 1919. Albert Barnes wrote that it had been the 'most helpful' book to him when trying to understand the paintings he had amassed for his important collection of modernist art in Philadelphia. Meanwhile, in New York, unknown to Clive, Mary Mowbray-Clarke filled an entire notebook with quotations from *Art*. In 1916, she and Madge Jenison opened their 'modern' bookshop The Sunwise Turn, where they hoped to also sell Omega Workshops wares. Jenison dedicated her memoir to Clive, 'Who, though I have never seen him, founded this bookshop because he wrote a book.'

In the last year of the war, an American writing as 'Petronius Arbiter' in *Art World* pilloried Clive's book as a plot of European art dealers intended to boost their market. Taking as his pretext Cézanne's *Bathers* ('A Degenerate Work of Art'), Arbiter excoriated as a kind of lunacy Clive's 'insolent and inartistic twaddle' that rhapsodised over the 'malformed and deformed works of Cézanne'. Clive noted that the article was accompanied by an upside-down reproduction of Picasso's *Pots et Citron*. Petronius Arbiter's heated rhetoric could be laughed off if it were isolated, but in the context of the cultural battles that would rage around modernism throughout the first half of the twentieth century, it is sinister. 'Normal' people, Arbiter wrote, do not admire the art of Matisse or Cézanne, only savages or the insane do. The article was explicit about the ramifications of this view of the proper role of art: 'The police of Europe, familiar with the purlieus and cloaca of their cities and with the portentous ravages there of sex-perversion, understand these symbols and suppressed much of this modernistic art – when it went too far. And after this war, much more will certainly be suppressed by an awakened public opinion.'

England had its own version of moral panic in the notorious 'Billings case', which confirmed Clive's worst opinions of the social effects of the war. In his *Vigilante* newsletter, the MP Pemberton Billings had linked the dancer Maud Allan's private performance of Oscar Wilde's *Salomé* to his sensational claim that a 'Black Book' had been discovered in Berlin that listed the intimate 'debauched' secrets of 47,000 British subjects, including Margot Asquith, the wife of the prime minister. The libel case over Billings' article, 'The Cult of the Clitoris', brought Wilde back into public consciousness in association with a decadence that was now also identified with resistance to military service.

The war on the home front was being fought over cultural values, and although there were glimmers of the hopefulness Clive had identified before the war – a 'new frankness' about men's lusts in novels, for example – the Billings case made him determined to leave England for good after the war. When he read the novel *Despised and Rejected* (by Rose Allatini, published in 1918 under the pseudonym A. T. Fitzroy) before it was banned under DORA, he found its treatment of what we would now call queer sexuality 'in so open and sensible a way' encouraging, despite his judgement that the novel was 'one of those terrible lower class intellectual books'. Although he could see that its ideas derived from Edward Carpenter, Clive shrewdly assumed it had been written by a woman. Jack Squire – who had told Lytton he would not write in defence of Lawrence's *Rainbow* if the reason for its prosecution was 'sapphism' – pointed out that *Despised and Rejected* joined the themes of 'moral perversion and conscientious objection'. He assumed that it was the 'evil odour' of the recent Billings trial which led the authorities to fix upon the pacifism of the novel as a reason to impose an enormous fine on its publisher.

16. Tribunals and Tribulations

In addition to meeting with politicians such as Reginald McKenna, T. E. Harvey and Lloyd George, Clive directed his energies on behalf of COs in the first half of 1916 to a memorandum which he hoped Gilbert Murray would show the prime minister to strengthen the mandate of the Pelham Committee, as well as to ensure that sincere COs were not suspected of misleading the tribunals. The Pelham Committee had been appointed by the Board of Trade to advise tribunals – who often ignored it – on alternative service for objectors.

Clive considered Murray to be the figurehead of 'the patriotic intellectuals' who had the ear of both Liberal politicians, such as Asquith and Grey, and of those Clive considered reactionaries, like Lloyd George and Walter Long. Clive breakfasted with Lloyd George in May, just before he became Secretary of State for War. Lloyd George advised Clive to produce a set of cut-and-dried proposals to present to Asquith, so Clive sent Murray a memorandum outlining how the tribunals could confirm the sincerity of a conscientious objection by working in concert with well-established peace organisations such as the Fellowship of Reconciliation, the Society of Friends and the No Conscription Fellowship. A particular cause of friction had been that tribunals were deliberately assigning men to do work at odds with their peacetime skills, or sending them far away from their families, which was clearly punitive and not in the spirit of the conscience clause. Clive hoped that Murray's intercession might get politicians to do something about the abuse of COs: the ministers with whom he met were 'all as civil as be damned. I think they honestly dislike persecution, but they dislike far more the idea of setting their faces stiffly against it.'

In two letters to the *Daily News* in May 1916, Clive explained what he and Murray had been discussing. The question of alternative service would become acute by the summer and Clive's suggestions seem to have been taken seriously by the government. Whenever Mary visited Gordon Square she found Clive closeted with an editor, telephoning Lloyd George or 'drafting some immensely practical proposal instead of writing a love letter'; whatever happened to benefit the COs would be 'a great deal due to Clive & his writing letters, interviews & string-pulling', she told Vanessa.

At Garsington, Bertrand Russell had made a moving speech about the COs in Asquith's presence and Ottoline urged the prime minister to listen to the scheme proposed by Clive and Murray. On the day that Clive's 'A "Grave Issue" and a Way Out' appeared in the *News*, a letter from Russell headed '*Adsum qui feci*' was published in the *Times*, disclosing that he was the author of a pamphlet distributed by the NCF that addressed the case of Ernest Everett, a teacher and CO who had been sentenced to two years' hard labour. The next day, eight members of the NCF executive were convicted under DORA for distributing Russell's pamphlet and fined £100 each by Sir Archibald Bodkin. Clive heard that there was laughter in the House when Russell was referred to as a 'distinguished philosopher'. Russell was fined £100 in June, and lost his teaching position at Cambridge, thus allowing him the time to go around the country speaking against the war.

Clive faced his own tribunal that summer. He had told Murray that were it not for a 'physical infirmity' he would be in France with a Quaker ambulance unit: 'I am a rather notorious pacifist and, at the same time I have always urged my friends to join ambulances and generally make themselves useful to their wretched fellow creatures.' Because his injury (most likely an unhealed hernia) already exempted him from active service, he said, his interventions on behalf of the CO cause would be seen as disinterested. Clive thought that as a moderate he had a better chance of being heard by the government than people like Clifford Allen and Russell, who had antagonised it and, in any case, he believed that 'subterranean agitation's much more effective and disquiets the government much more'.

Clive in fact appears not to have had an official medical exemption, such as Leonard Woolf obtained without any difficulty due to his persistent tremor, so in July he appeared before the tribunal in St Pancras, which sent him straight to the Pelham Committee. Being 'more and more in the councils of high liberalism' he assumed he could make his own position secure if he 'ate humble pie', but chose not to. He was rather taken by the notion of getting a letter from Murray about the strength of his conscientious objection, even though he did not lack for other witnesses. As Bernard Shaw had come to the defence of *Peace at Once*, Clive asked him for a testimonial but Shaw declined, pointing out that the pamphlet should suffice, and adding that the tribunal would not regard writing art criticism as work of national importance. Clive wondered if Ottoline's brother, Lord Henry Bentinck, chairman of the Contemporary Art Society executive committee, might attest to his being 'a writer of national importance on art'. He may have believed that there was a real chance he would be shipped to France, either to fight or serve as a non-combatant, and Clive definitely did not want to go, despite what he told Murray. He had once declared he would rather go to jail than work on the land, but in July Clive asked if he could be taken on as a volunteer on the Morrells' farm. By early August he was registered officially as a CO performing 'work of national importance' at Garsington.

Duncan and Bunny had faced the identical challenge of finding approved work when they applied for their exemptions. A recently deceased cousin of Duncan's mother had left Wissett Lodge, a house in Suffolk, to which Duncan, Vanessa and Bunny moved in the spring of 1916 so that the men could use farm work as their alternative service. After a series of denials and appeals, the Central Tribunal decreed that the men could not be self-employed but must work for a farmer. Vanessa recalled that Virginia had been urging her to see Charleston farmhouse near Firle in Sussex, not far from Asheham; Adrian Stephen was also considering it, so Virginia hoped her sister would hurry up and take a look. In September, Vanessa met with the farmer on the Firle Estate, and by October she, Duncan and Bunny had moved in to Charleston, a house that would in time become synonymous with 'Bloomsbury' as Duncan and Vanessa (and, from 1939, Clive) made it their home.

During the early period of the war, Vanessa and Clive discussed giving up Gordon Square, finding a suitable country house with space enough for the children and each keeping a room in London to use whenever necessary. Clive wondered if for sentimental reasons some of those whom Virginia would later describe as 'Old Bloomsbury' might like to save 46 Gordon Square as a 'monument historique'. By the end of 1915, Maynard was part of the discussion as Clive considered moving to one of his rooms in Gower Street. The necessity of moving to Garsington as a registered CO, however, made matters more pressing, so Clive urged Vanessa to negotiate with Maynard about a change in their living situations. He emphasised his need for rooms in which he could meet Mary, but Maynard was nervous about having Clive as a lodger were he to agree to the proposal that he take over 46 Gordon Square. 'He evidently means to be in London a good deal,' Maynard wrote to Vanessa, 'and there really isn't room for him.' Maynard could foresee that rather than becoming a leaseholder he might well become instead 'the rather insecure tenant of two rooms'.

Clive put the onus of negotiation squarely on Vanessa, with the imperative that she should not agree to anything that would prevent him and Mary spending a night together every two weeks at no. 46. Vanessa saw that Clive's plan was 'one of great convenience for him & bother & expense for me' but by September the deal was struck. Maynard moved from Gower Street into 46 Gordon Square with another Cambridge contemporary of Clive's, John Tressider Sheppard, paying the rates while the Bells paid the rent and kept four rooms. Harry Norton joined the household in March 1917. Maynard still had nine months of his lease on Gower Street to run, so it was arranged that Dorothy Brett, Carrington, Katherine Mansfield and Murry would live there. For Vanessa, this was a particularly fraught time as she was making Charleston habitable for Bunny and Duncan while they fulfilled their alternative service requirement. In the midst of all this, Clive wrote to ask if Vanessa had heard from Mary (who herself was moving from Cheyne Row to River House in Hammersmith) about staying a night or two at Gordon Square; could Vanessa also be sure that his things were not damaged in the reconstruction going on at the house during the move?

Clive's reliance on Vanessa to deal with all household matters continued once everyone was settled, despite the fact that she was hardly in London at all and had her own worries in Sussex. When a cow-hand voiced suspicions to one of the household servants after Lytton had visited, Clive reassured Vanessa they were probably just 'dreaming of German spies', but told her she should firmly remind the gossips that Lytton was the son of a general and had two brothers at the War Office. COs were especially at risk from malicious rumours and persecution by

Lytton Strachey, Duncan Grant, Clive Bell

the police; Clive told Mary that, considering who they were, Duncan and Vanessa felt the fewer local eyes on them the better. Nevertheless, Clive expected Vanessa to take care of Gordon Square. Would she 'broach the money question' with Maynard, who, Clive felt, was not paying his full share of the bills? Could she let Bunny and Duncan know that there would be no room for them in December because he would be there? He wished that Vanessa would warn all their friends that the former maid's room was no longer available: 'Obviously, it is essential to my comfort and to any chance of working that my study should not be used as a bedroom.' Duncan and Bunny were welcome, as long as Clive was guaranteed the top-floor room. And wasn't Maynard mistaken about to whom the furniture belonged?

An explosion between Clive and Maynard was inevitable, but the spark that set it off was unexpected. Through Roger, Clive had befriended Tancred Borenius, a Finnish art historian who had been appointed lecturer at the University of London in 1914. Borenius had a high opinion of Vanessa and Duncan and Clive saw him often socially. After a dinner with Borenius at which Max Beerbohm's niece Marie joined them, Clive had loaned the professor his key for an assignation at Gordon Square with her, but the 'oafish Finn' stumbled into Sheppard's room by mistake, keeping him out, and the rest of the household awake until half past three in the morning. Although Clive apologised to Sheppard and scolded Borenius, he was incensed by a high-handed letter he received from Maynard, like that 'an ill-bred millionaire might write to a defaulting office boy', Clive complained to Vanessa, adding that everything at no. 46 seemed to be arranged for Maynard's convenience even though the house was still in their name. As Maynard's biographer remarks, 'actual possession and a Treasury salary increased to £1,000 a year proved stronger than Clive's resentment', and by the end of the year the lease was renewed in Maynard's name. Clive sulkily asked both Lytton and Vanessa to try to find out if Maynard and Sheppard would be glad to see him go and wondered if he should look for rooms elsewhere.

Matters did not improve after this. Clive was usually at Garsington, so Maynard had taken his bed, substituting for it one that Clive found unacceptable. Clive swapped them back, commenting that as Maynard appeared 'to fuck less than I do it may serve well enough'. Maynard was 'a little cracked' about this, Clive explained to Mary, but had promised to invest in new sheets and blankets 'so no more holes through which you used to poke your little toes'. When it suited him (as, for example, when Mary once stayed at Gordon Square without Clive, transgressing a household rule), Clive appealed to the 'Bloomsbury-Asheham tradition of not bothering about trifles of that sort', but the difficulties of sharing a house persisted, erupting again one night near the end of the war in an angry row that Clive assumed must have surprised Mary, 'who had supposed fellows of King's to be godlike & above passion'. Just before the Armistice, Clive told Vanessa that he planned to leave Gordon Square and take rooms nearby; 'He means to have rooms in London, but he thinks life with Maynard at Gordon Sq. too uncomfortable and difficult,' Vanessa told Roger.

17. Garsington

On the day in 1916 Clive packed his clothes at Gordon Square in readiness for an indefinite stay in the bailiff's cottage at Garsington came news of the execution for treason of Roger Casement, who had arranged for armaments to be supplied by Germany to assist the Easter Rising in Dublin. 'I feel slightly sick,' Clive told Mary. 'I suppose an execution means no more to Asquith than anything else that happens out of his sight.' Ottoline and Philip had done all they could behind the scenes to help Casement, to no avail. 'God help us all,' Clive commented ruefully to Ottoline.

At Garsington, the Morrells continued the passionate activism against war they had been known for at Bedford Square. When Jacques Copeau appealed to Clive on behalf of the French actress Valentine Tessier, it was Ottoline who took her in. Soon after they moved in to Garsington Manor, the Morrells created a refuge that in many ways recreated the salon of civilisation that Clive had upheld as his ideal of the promise of the pre-war years. Their estate became a haven for writers, musicians and painters, for conscientious objectors and those poets of the Western Front, Siegfried Sassoon and Robert Graves. Politicians visited often, from the prime minister H. H. Asquith and his daughter Violet (who had a memorably violent argument about the war with Lytton in May 1916) to Ramsay MacDonald, leader of the Labour Party. It was a place of love affairs (in 1919 Aldous Huxley married Belgian refugee Maria Nys, while his brother Julian married the governess Juliette Baillot), intrigues and endless gossip, much of which usually got repeated to its subjects with predictable results.

Posthumous opinion has singled out Clive as a particularly malicious offender against the generosity of his hosts, both for his rudeness to Ottoline and his ostensibly disdainful attitude towards working on the land. Yet Dorothy Brett, who spent many months at Garsington with Clive, recalled that he was 'immensely popular with the farm hands and farmers. He was jolly, never did a lick of work, but kept them laughing and gave birthday cakes to their wives and children.' Actually, he did do *some* work and was certainly thoroughly at home in a rural setting. In addition, the police were watchful, making unannounced visits to places where COs were employed to ensure they were fulfilling the conditions of their exemption, so despite Ottoline's insistence that Clive would be 'a traitor to civilization if I didn't write all the morning', he did farm work in the afternoons: felling trees with Aldous Huxley and Gerald Shove one afternoon, he sliced off the toe of his boot with an axe.

Dorothy Brett's sister Sylvia – whose marriage made her the Ranee of Sarawak – found the atmosphere at Garsington disgusting when she came to open a fête to raise funds for the village nurse in August 1917. In a letter to her father, Oliver Brett, the Viscount Esher, she described the COs as 'awful – flabby cowards – over-sexed – never normal':

> The conversation consists of depraved and curious conditions in life so that you long for an ordinary couple to come in and say 'Well, we live an ordinary life, do ordinary things in the ordinary way and have ordinary children.'
>
> At breakfast with your bacon and eggs you get a minute and detailed description of life *à la* Oscar Wilde – by dinner time the tales become more lurid . . . Clive Bell, who [Dorothy] is always quoting as if he is Jesus Christ, is a fat greasy looking creature with long *Henna* coloured hair – he has a trick, most embarrassing, of fiddling with himself – all day and all the time – Doll wanted *me* to tell him not to – Oh, I tell you I had to have a mental bath when I got home, as well as a bodily one.

Clive had met nobody like the Ranee 'since the times of the Troubridge mixed hockey club'; she seemed to him like a nice shop assistant. More to his taste was Elizabeth Asquith, Violet's half-sister, with whom he flirted at the fête, appreciating her 'civil and civilized egoism'. Although Elizabeth turned down Desmond MacCarthy's friend Antoine Bibesco three times before marrying him in 1919, Clive correctly predicted that the Romanian prince would play a part in their lives.

The most infamous example of the vicious criticism Ottoline's eccentric appearance and passionate intensity sometimes elicited from those who accepted her hospitality is D. H. Lawrence's portrait of Hermione Roddice in *Women in Love* (Huxley's Priscilla Wimbush in *Crome Yellow* would also be in the running). Almost as soon as the manuscript was passed around at Garsington, Clive teased Ottoline about it. A misunderstanding about who had invited whom to tea prompted him to send her a note: ' "No you don't Hermione" as I dare say you remember Lawrence's hero says when he has had a smart clip with a lapis-lazuli ball over one ear and looks for no less over the other.' Clive kept Mary informed about the course of the Morrells' reaction to Lawrence's 'observations of photographic accuracy and extraordinary offensiveness', but was not impressed by his writing.

Lawrence's disdain for Clive's friends extended also to their pacifism. Shortly after the second Military Service Act, Lawrence wrote to E. M. Forster that 'Lytton, Duncan Grant, all that set, got off as "conscientious objectors". They are most of them in London as usual, I suppose. Clive Bell and Hutchinson worked for the No-Conscription league. What will they do now, God knows.'

Clive thought Lawrence's novel only fit for the servants' hall: 'Strand magazine gone smutty'. He had defended *The Rainbow* in spite of his poor opinion of it, just as Virginia and Forster would defend Radclyffe Hall's *Well of Loneliness* in 1928 despite disparaging its literary quality. As Lawrence struggled to find a publisher (*Women in Love* would not appear until 1920, in the USA), Clive told Mary it should be published 'in the interests of free speech of course, and of scandal'. When he read *Sons and Lovers* in 1918, he allowed it 'a modicum of uncouth power', but lamented, 'O these underbred, overbearing egoists! Why can't they fuck and have done with it?'

Sex was a major element in Clive's circle's sense of liberation from Victorian mores, but it was more often a topic for humour than obsessive seriousness of the kind Lawrence seemed to them to indulge in. Adrian Stephen's wife, Karin, who after the war would give the first lecture course at Cambridge on psychoanalysis, took an academic interest in sexuality. She asked Duncan if he would send her books of the kind recommended by Clive, such as *Coups de Fouet* (Whip Lashes) and 'anything interesting' about *Fessades* (Spanking). Clive did read Carpenter and Ellis, but preferred to do empirical research. Roger envied Clive's knack of having sexual liaisons and ending them without any resulting bitterness, whereas he seemed to have hardly any affairs yet be beset by women whom he could not elude. Duncan and Maynard had once teased Clive at Eleanor – stranded on a desert island with a boy scout how long would he hold out? To impotence, he assured them. But if the choice were between the scout and a female ape? Then he might choose the scout – 'general triumph' of Maynard and Duncan, Clive reported to Mary. But 'homosexuality – both buggery and Sapphism – seems to miss the last subtlety. What it lacks is the supreme adventure, the voyage into the unknown, the preposterous intimacy, the taking of an outrageous liberty . . . for most men, I know, the idea of Sapphism has an odd fascination and I daresay the idea of buggery has for most women. Has it?' he asked her.

Until he fell in love with Mary, it had not mattered to Clive with whom he went to bed, as long as it was a woman. He considered sex with Amber Blanco-White no more significant than a night at a music hall – entertaining and pleasurable, but not profound. When both of them were in love with other people, Clive and Vanessa had slept together once at Eleanor in 1915, but 'it didn't do,' according to Clive. Telling Mary this story, he at first wrote that the 'experiment' had been 'most painful', but struck out the phrase.

Clive, Vanessa, Duncan, Bunny and others with whom they were close were preoccupied with the question of what were the proper relations between sex and love, fidelity and freedom. But often, no matter how strongly these friends wanted to escape conventional morals, sex and love refused to cooperate. In January 1918, Duncan recorded in his diary a conversation at Charleston just after Bunny had left for London about whether there was an emotional difference between homosexual and heterosexual love. Clive argued that there was a difference, 'because for him the root cause of love was the complementary appeal of the different sex'. When their conversation moved to the question of sex with a person one loved but who did not reciprocate one's feelings, Clive said it would be too humiliating. Vanessa stopped contributing to the discussion after this remark and

Duncan later realised that it 'had made her bitterly aware of what she had lost through loving him'.

In November 1916, the St Pancras tribunal gave Clive permission to travel up to London whenever he could demonstrate the necessity. Dental problems that began to plague him during the war years sometimes provided an excuse to leave Garsington, as well as an opportunity to meet Mary. Although Ottoline cooperated when she could with his desire to have Mary come to Garsington, the affair was complicated not only by wartime travel restrictions but by Jack Hutchinson's anger, at which Clive usually scoffed. 'We are supposed to be lovers,' he wrote peevishly to Mary in 1916, but 'I shall not expect you before dinner time on my birthday.'

The febrile emotional atmospheres of Bloomsbury and Garsington undoubtedly exacerbated the tensions in their relations but life on the Morrells' estate suited Clive very well. He was able not only to see friends such as Lytton, Desmond and Bertrand Russell in comfortable surroundings, but also became acquainted there with a generation of writers who included Katherine Mansfield, J. Middleton Murry, Siegfried Sassoon, Robert Graves, T. S. Eliot, Aldous Huxley and the poet and critic Thomas Wade Earp, who, like Huxley, was studying at Oxford during the war. Some of these, such as Eliot, Huxley and Earp, became lifelong friends, while others faded after the war. Roger Fry thought that 'being a good deal alone in the country and doing a lot of reading' was good for Clive, who had become 'amazing in the quantity and flow of his mind'.

Mary somewhat widened Clive's literary tastes, her own sensibilities being much more sympathetic than his to contemporary experimental writing (she would be one of Samuel Beckett's earliest supporters in England). Clive might have laughed at Ottoline for acting like an eighteenth-century salonnière, but his own preferences were for literary works of the distant past. During the war he read (or re-read) Pope, Donne, Milton, Dante, Cowley and Jonson; Laforgue, Mommsen, Michelet, Voltaire, Thucydides, Carducci and Ariosto; he recommended to Mary the Renaissance Jacques Amyot translation of *Daphnis and Chloë*, read George Sand's memoirs, the Goncourts' journals, Huysmans and the letters of Flaubert, Pascal and Gibbon. When Mary did not appreciate Casanova, he suggested she read the correspondence of

Walpole, Byron, Madame de Sévigné, Pepys, St Simon, Gray, Gibbon, the Goncourts and Voltaire, and then try Casanova again. He discussed Alfieri with Mary's brother, Jim, reading the *Vita Sua* in Italian. Lytton 'was furious to hear that the wretch had mastered Italian, and was reading Ariosto', and surely was not happy when Clive told Mary that Aldous had given him a French translation of Alfieri that he would 'thrust on' her and Lytton if they continued to refuse to read the Italian. He read contemporary English fiction if he knew the author or had it recommended to him but rarely sought it out himself. When he did venture into the twentieth century, Clive often found the work thin, disappointing or meretricious. 'I'm glad I'm a modern,' he told Mary, 'but gladder I'm not modern – like Katherine for instance,' who had never read anything written before she was born, or like Gertler, whom Clive did not think would have liked to join him in fifteenth-century Florence.

Katherine Mansfield and Middleton Murry's tribulations often fed the gossip at Garsington. Clive got on well with Murry, finding his ideas about literature and art sympathetic, discussing whether there are states of mind that are inexpressible, sharing their views on the contributors to *Rhythm*, as well as about 'various London comics and Paris curiosities we had known'. He thought well of Murry's first novel, *Still Life* (1916), which drew on the author's experience living in Paris but was annoyed when his *TLS* obituary of Octave Mirbeau objected to the French writer on moral grounds. Mirbeau had been on the committee for 'Manet and the Post-Impressionists' and had treated Clive as a protégé. Clive confided his displeasure to Mary, rather than sending an objection to the *TLS*, because he did not want Murry to think he was motivated by a personal slight.

As she did with Virginia, Katherine Mansfield could elicit the worst of Clive's snobbery. She was 'definitely second-rate', 'suburban', but also could be great fun, he opined. If Mary objected to his verdict, Clive's defence was that most great letter writers occasionally indulge in such a 'pompous character sketch'. Katherine did not think much of Clive either, sometimes becoming Ottoline's ally in distaste at his habits. On her second visit to Garsington, Katherine was 'very scornful of Clive who is so superior'. She could not come as often as Murry did and wanted Ottoline to tell her what 'wretched little bones has Clive been stealing from grubby little plates & tossing to his friends now – I wonder. Let them pick them clean if they will – and snigger and crack them up as they please. He is an appalling creature – but I cannot bear to look in his direction.' Katherine was quite a gossip herself. She described to Ottoline how Mary Hutchinson had flirted with both Robert Graves and T. S. Eliot at a party in Hammersmith, while Jack Hutchinson had 'cut up, trimmed and smacked into shape the whole of America and the Americans', to Eliot's chagrin. Gossip got Virginia into hot water with Clive when she repeated to Katherine all the nasty things he and Maynard had said about her.

Katherine (and Murry) had not been impressed by 'The Mark on the Wall', the first publication of the Woolfs' Hogarth Press (bound in a pamphlet as *Two Stories*, with Leonard's 'Three Jews'). She found the thoughts 'commonplace', but her opinion convinced Clive that Katherine was a 'fraud'; no doubt she thought he was a 'fool'. Clive and Katherine did agree, however, that neither of them could bear Leonard. Clive dutifully ordered Katherine's short story *Prelude* from the Hogarth Press, which was 'pretty good', he told Virginia, very well observed, 'very well remembered, seen sharply, and interesting', but 'nothing to set the Thames on fire', an evaluation Virginia recorded in her diary, adding that the work did not 'turn his fastidious head'. He was only slightly more generous about *Prelude* to Mary, conceding that it showed an 'amusing method too, seeing the same thing from half a dozen points of view'. When Murry praised Katherine's nearly finished novel (of which *Prelude* was a part), Clive anxiously urged Mary to focus on her own writing, which he told her was better than anything Katherine could do.

Clive was thrilled when Mary's story 'War' appeared in the *Egoist* in December 1917, but Virginia described it as 'merely a piece of Omega linen surrounded by twenty looking glasses and entirely arranged for the eye of the Master'. Katherine Mansfield understood the power of the clique she had encountered. When Virginia's second novel, *Night and Day*, was announced in 1919, Katherine carped to Ottoline, 'I expect it will be acclaimed a masterpiece and she will be drawn round Gordon Square in a chariot designed by Roger after a supper given by Clive.'

Following a severe breakdown in 1915, Virginia had for a time receded from Clive's life. The Woolfs' move to Hogarth House in Richmond that year, together with Leonard's caution about his wife's fragility, meant they were rarely seen in central London. Virginia appears to have written no diary in 1916 and if she wrote at all to Clive, no letters survive.

The establishment of the Hogarth Press in 1917 marked her re-emergence. Clive hoped that Leonard would allow Virginia to visit him but was wary about what might happen if she and Mary were in the same room. Had Virginia been 'driving in any little wedges', he asked Mary after the women had tea together. He had reason to be concerned, knowing how jealous his sister-in-law could be. 'She made me quarrel with Lytton and we didn't speak to each other for a year, she embroiled me with Molly, she did her best to upset my relations with Vanessa and to break my friendship with Duncan,' he warned Mary.

Clive wrote Virginia a long letter of praise about 'The Mark on the Wall', which he thought 'extraordinary'. 'It quite took my breath away and made my head spin as your writings used to do in the days of my nonage.' Despite his occasional resistance to innovative forms of fiction, he understood that Virginia was attempting something that would challenge readers and critics: 'All that one could say would be that it wasn't something else,' but he suspected that some would assume she was merely following the example of Joyce, who he thought had spilled the contents of his mind onto the page willy-nilly in *Portrait of the Artist as a Young Man*. That would miss the essential point, that 'You have got to put down what goes on in Virginia's head and I have never doubted – you know I haven't – that what goes on in there is about as exciting as anything in the world.'

Virginia had not forgotten Clive's early encouragement of her writing, and their fruitful discussions. She wanted to talk with him about her story and find out more about *why* he thought it was good. 'Its an absorbing thing (I mean writing is) and its high time we found some new shapes, don't you think so?' Years later, when Leonard was considering publishing some of his late wife's letters, Clive hoped he would include this one. Having Virginia tell him he was the first person who thought she wrote well seemed to Clive 'the finest feather I shall ever be able to stick in my cap'.

Virginia observed Clive carefully when they began to see one another again in 1917, aware that their relationship had shifted. Unlike many other people, she was amused rather than repelled by Clive's vanity, his social gifts more than compensating for it in her opinion. 'He is so brisk & well kept mentally that I like an evening of him,' she wrote after he had forgiven her for indiscreetly repeating what he and Maynard had said about Katherine Mansfield. There he sat at tea, in his 'chestnut suit; combs his hair back to hide the bald spot, but didn't hitch his trousers so much as usual – in short he was at his best'.

If Clive had an inferiority complex about not having been an Apostle, it was not apparent to Virginia. Whenever they met, the conversation flowed easily. He might have become 'rather a raconteur', with a man-of-the-world pose, yet there was 'something of the Cambridge standard' she admired in Clive. Lytton, too, found Clive more interesting in the war years, but always preferred the familiar comfort of an Apostolic group. Tea at Gordon Square with Clive, Norton, Maynard and Sheppard was very agreeable, but improved 'after Clive had bustled off, and the solid Cambridge element was left talking'. Virginia saw through Clive's insecure boastfulness: 'He's no fool, though his manners suggest overwhelming reasons for thinking him one now & then.' When he brayed about how he had refused to join the socialist 1917 Club, but then said that now 'of course I find it's the thing to do,' Virginia confided to her diary the truth that Clive had been blackballed by Leonard.

In his seventies, Clive remembered bringing copies of Eliot's 'The Love Song of J. Alfred Prufrock' with him to Garsington in 1917, which Katherine Mansfield read aloud after he handed them round 'like so many Good Friday buns'.[1] The young American had been introduced to Garsington by Bertrand Russell (who had met Eliot at Harvard when he seemed on the path to a career in philosophy). Prevented by the outbreak of war from returning to America from a fellowship at Oxford, Eliot had set his sights on entering the literary salons of London. Of the poets championed by Ottoline during the war, Clive

[1]The editors of Mansfield's letters incorrectly state that *Prufrock and Other Observations* was published by the Hogarth Press. The title poem first appeared in *Poetry* in June 1915 and was reprinted that November in the *Catholic Anthology*. The collection was published by the Egoist Press in January 1917, so Clive's memory is probably accurate, although he allows that 'anyone with a taste for research can fix the date' (*Old* 121). Less probable is his recollection that it was Roger Fry who encouraged Eliot to add notes to *The Waste Land* (*Old* 120); he might have been recalling that in 1918 Roger told Leonard that Eliot was looking for a publisher.

agreed with Mary that Eliot 'was the best of the young', but he began to suspect Eliot of being his rival for Mary's affections when the poet and his wife, Vivien, summered at Bosham, near West Wittering, socialising with the Hutchinsons both there and in London. Eliot would come to appreciate Mary's shrewd judgement and sent her drafts of his poems, as well as discussing with her his thoughts on culture.

Eliot's idiosyncratic imagery and rhythms soon entered the correspondence between Garsington and London, often in parodic form. After the dinner at which Jack Hutchinson's attack on America had caused Eliot to blanch, Katherine Mansfield walked with him past 'rows of ugly little houses' while 'a great number of amorous cats looped across the road and high up in the sky there was a battered old moon'. Clive dined with Eliot for the first time in June 1916 and when he read the plays of Henri Becque, originator of the Theatre of Cruelty, that autumn they inspired him to quip, 'I run to seed, I run to seed, I shall make my nose and fingers bleed – as Mr Elliott [sic] might say'.

Despite – or because of – Ottoline's enthusiasm for it, contemporary poetry was sometimes made fun of at Garsington: there had been jokes about Edith Sitwell's *Wheels*, the first number of which appeared just before Christmas 1916. Hearing some of Eliot's poems read aloud for what seemed to be 'the hundredth and seventieth time' did not improve them for Clive, although he did like 'Prufrock'. They were recondite and clever, certainly, he thought, but not 'creations'. Eliot himself worried when *Prufrock and Other Observations* was published that it might 'simply appear a *réchauffée* to most of my friends – they are growing tired of waiting for something better from me'.

There had been a good literary discussion at Garsington with Huxley, Graves and W. R. Childe, the editor of the Oxford Poetry series, when Clive brought 'Prufrock' with him. Clive had just finished reading Huysmans' *À Rebours* and a work by the Italian scholar Francesco de Sanctis but Eliot was on his mind. Had Mary been kissing him? Could she get Eliot to explain how 'the footman sat on the dining room table with the second housemaid on his knee' (in his poem 'Aunt Helen')? That Mary flirted with Eliot became a theme in Clive's letters to her from late 1916, but as he got to know him better and read more of his work, Clive admitted he was fundamentally in agreement with what Eliot was trying to do.

The *TLS* said that what Eliot had written in *Prufrock* could not be called poetry, which considerably irked Clive and inspired him to toy vaguely in the following months with the idea of writing about the state of criticism for the *New Statesman*. This came to nothing at the time but as Clive's thinking about standards and values sharpened towards the end of the war, his ideas came to bear considerable similarities with tendencies in Eliot's critical writings. Clive would make some tentative moves toward articulating his critical standards in the 'Foreword' to *Pot-Boilers*, but his ideas on criticism did not take firmer shape until the 1920s.

Mary's growing friendship with the Eliots became a conduit for new writing that Clive might otherwise have overlooked, especially as he was usually removed from metropolitan currents while at Garsington. She showed him back numbers of the *Little Review* in 1918, interested to know what Clive thought of Joyce and Pound. He thought the best result of Joyce's *Portrait of the Artist as a Young Man* was that it led to conversations that 'reveal by implication the personal and domestic secrets of one's friends: Gerald [Shove], for instance, feels that twice a week is not excessive, and Aldous believes that moderate masturbation is perfectly innocuous.' On finishing the novel, Clive declared, 'Alas, I am not modern. I thought it trash.'

Reading the chapters of *Ulysses* appearing in the *Little Review* in 1918, however, led Clive to admit to Mary that she had been right about Joyce: 'He does hold one's interest and I haven't a shadow of a doubt that there's something in him.' As for Pound, though: 'Jesus Christ, what stuff! stuff! stuff!' Just as Virginia would in her 1919 *TLS* essay 'Modern Novels', Clive pronounced the Edwardian writers 'about whom everyone was talking when we were at Cambridge' – Wells, Bennett, Shaw, Galsworthy – failures. And like Virginia, he was slow to recognise Joyce's importance. When Joyce's play *Exiles* was published in 1918, Clive saw that it was rare in English literature to have a work of such psychological insight, but thought Chekhov's stories were more profound.

It is not surprising that Clive was slow to awaken to the excitement and innovative experimentation of writers such as Joyce, Pound and Mansfield, in spite of his praise of Virginia's 'Mark on the Wall'. He was more concerned at the time with having Rafaello Piccoli – a professor of Italian at Cambridge whose work Jim Barnes had recommended – confirm what he had said in *Art* about the *Lamento* of Rinaldo d'Aquino being the best of all pre-Dante Italian poems. He, Lytton and Desmond had matured in an atmosphere dominated by Leslie Stephen, he explained to Mary, therefore his tastes would appear to her old-fashioned.

Mary had fun reading aloud Eliot's new poems from the September 1918 *Little Review* at a party where she, Molly MacCarthy and the barrister and art collector Monty Shearman played a game 'comparing our friends to sauce-boats and pineapples, chandeliers and cubist pictures', but Clive's view of 'Mr Eliot's Sunday Morning Service', 'Whispers of Immortality', 'Sweeney and the Nightingales' and 'Dans le Restaurant' was dour: 'I can't say that your description of Eliot's poems encourages me to believe that there is much besides nonsense in them – of that clearly a good deal. However I will preserve as open mind as possible.' Keeping an open mind and being willing to revise one's opinions in the light of new experiences or knowledge became a hallmark of his criticism, despite the apparent dogmatism with which he could occasionally express his judgements.

Clive was not unusual in his scepticism towards the new forms of poetry pouring forth from innumerable small presses and magazines in the second decade of the twentieth century. His tastes in literature still remained far more conservative than his tastes in the plastic arts. Although he came to appreciate Graves better after the poems in the 1916–17 *Georgian Poetry* volume, neither he nor Sassoon impressed Clive at first (although he enjoyed their company). After reading a 'very, very new anthology called "Others"' at Garsington one tipsy night, Clive penned an Eliotic parody titled 'The young poet grown old' that on sober reflection he decided against submitting to the *Egoist* as he did not want to appear to be attacking Eliot. The momentum he had gained from *Art* had been suddenly arrested by the war. Without access to Paris, Clive fell back on the tradition his Cambridge education had best prepared him for.

18. Ad Familiares

At Christmas in 1917, scores of Clive's friends and acquaintances received a personally inscribed copy of *Ad Familiares* ('To Friends'), a slim pamphlet containing thirteen poems that Clive had had printed by Francis Meynell's Pelican Press. He had worried that Meynell might be disappointed that the poems were not written in the cause of pacifism, but his witty preface (beginning 'Dear – – ', with space left for him to write in a name) assumed that the recipients would understand the mild subversion it embodied, inviting them to what art historian Grace Brockington has termed 'a conspiracy of levity against a war-crazed public'. Alluding to the pessimism of the time as well as to the government's censorship, Clive pointed out that 'hoping for what we all desire is treasonable almost'. He offered his poems in lieu of more expensive gifts, because 'to be extravagant in war-time is worse than unpatriotic', or so the hoardings said.

The preface takes a hit at critics who praise 'the stuff with which schoolboys line their lockers', while they can be trusted to 'maul' any 'man of merit'. Leaving it to his intimates to discern whom he might have in mind, Clive lamented 'the amount of trash that contrives to make its way into one-man volumes, newspapers, reviews and choice anthologies'. But, above all, his poems would give his friends the opportunity of making him the butt of remarks about his 'moral, intellectual, and physical oddities' on their Christmas Day walks, and thereby he was providing a patriotic service, momentarily relieving the 'battered public laughing-stocks' of government of the criticism that would otherwise be directed at them.

Ad Familiares delighted its recipients, several of whom, such as Roger, Goldie Dickinson and the sinologist Arthur Waley, thanked Clive in verse. Sydney Waterlow came home from the Foreign Office amid bombs dropping and the sound of guns to find the poems and Clive's card waiting, leading him to compare his own broken spirits ruefully with Clive's more cheerful outlook. *Ad Familiares* is indeed a testament to Clive's incorrigible enjoyment of life, or perhaps to his refusal to face its darker aspects. Frankie Birrell lavished praise on five love poems, each named after a month, which had been published in the *New Statesman* the previous year. In Mary's copy these were marked 'M' and near the end of her life she would call 'June' one of the kindest presents she ever received. Lytton, whose *Eminent Victorians* had just been accepted by Chatto, was not sure what to say about *Ad Familiares*: 'Good gracious me!' he expostulated to Virginia. 'What – but bright comments are unnecessary, and besides, your well known indiscretion . . .', yet he thanked Clive for his 'magnificent Christmas bouquet'. Leonard was not as pleased as everyone else. Barbara Bagenal (née Hiles), who was now working at the Hogarth Press, found Virginia reading her copy when she got to Richmond one morning. Clive had 'enlivened Christmas', Virginia wrote in her diary, his verse 'very pretty & light, to my mind (by wh. I mean not altogether to L.'s mind)'. She thought Clive's efforts better than the third volume of *Georgian Poetry*, just published by Eddie Marsh, but Leonard, she told Lytton, 'is seized with a spasmodic clutch' at the sight of *Ad Familiares*. Clive had included his 1909 poem 'To V.S. with a Book', recalling the 'ravished heights' and 'gay delights' of a time in Italy when Virginia and he were emotionally entangled. Leonard made no comment.

The problem between Virginia and Clive had always been jealousy. She admitted that his praise of Vanessa would once have discomfited her but told herself this was no longer the case. Mary Hutchinson was a different matter. Word reached Clive that Virginia intended to show Mary his letters to disabuse her of any illusions she might have about her lover. After a day spent supervising the removal of furniture from Gordon Square to Charleston, Vanessa joined Mary and Clive for dinner with Virginia, whom they scolded for her mischief-making. Clive did not mind Mary seeing his letters but he would object to Virginia showing them to Ottoline. Mary and Vanessa chided Virginia for her exaggerations and manipulations of the truth, but Clive seemed to her bitter. 'Everything goes over the same rapids,' she wrote, but Clive had never forgiven her. There seemed to her always an unstated 'reserve of grievance' at the decline of their former intimacy. And now, she saw, 'he lives in dread of some alliance between Mary & me which shall threaten his position with her.'

This was probably wishful thinking on Virginia's part. Clive was pleased that Mary was 'philosophical' about Virginia; they would 'laugh at her in their sleeves'. But trouble erupted at the Café Royal one day when Gertler made Mary cry by telling her that Virginia had said Clive's friends could not stand her and tolerated her only because she was his 'concubine'. With Mary's own circle of friends, such as Monty Shearman, jealous of her defection to Bloomsbury, and Jack furious with her, Mary's emotions were in a fragile state. When Gertler demonstrated for Clive how Jack imitated him, Clive warned Mary that Gertler could not be trusted; in any case, he said, no one took Virginia seriously. Vanessa confirmed that her sister wanted to put Mary at odds with Clive and told her that Roger, Maynard and Harry Norton all agreed that Virginia was being absurd. At Hogarth House the atmosphere was sombre when Clive visited: Leonard, he told Lytton, 'makes conversation impossible and he's always there. It isn't that he's disagreeable; but he's gloomily silent, one tries to draw him in, and then the conversation's lost.' Perhaps Virginia missed Clive's effervescent gaiety, the compliments with which he once showered her now bestowed on Mary.

Mary's sensitivity to slights about her position in Clive's milieu had been heightened by another unfortunate incident. At Durbins, Roger's house near Guildford, she happened to see a letter to Roger in which Vanessa expressed her irritation at Clive and Mary's imminent visit to Charleston. As he would so often where Mary was concerned, Clive overreacted and announced to Vanessa that he would no longer come to the house. She had to understand that during the war, his free time was very limited and he wanted to spend it with Mary, but he did not 'want to lose all knowledge of the children'. Vanessa must arrange for Julian and Quentin to be sent to Gordon Square so that he could see them when he was with Mary. He was not angry, but Mary always felt that Vanessa and Duncan disliked her. Selfishly, Clive blamed Vanessa's resistance to having visitors on what he called her 'agoraphobia'; it had been 'one of the most pronounced symptoms of your bad illness' he said, presumably referring to her collapse in Turkey in 1911.

Mary took a calmer approach and had a frank exchange with Vanessa. She understood very well that she was an outsider in Vanessa's world and commented astutely that 'there is a definite limit to the kind of people you want to know; you prefer to develop minutely along particular lines rather than to explore new ones which would necessitate talking "other people's language" instead of your own.' Mary admitted this made her somewhat melancholy but she also recognised that her shyness and reticence in conversation with Vanessa and her friends made things awkward.

Mary's letter eased the tensions. Roger was glad to hear things had blown over because he knew that Clive got irrationally angry about what he perceived as slights, but he also pointed out that Vanessa's letter had not been left where Mary would have seen it. Mary was by no means innocent of the Bloomsbury habit of prying. Once at Garsington she had read Ottoline's diary while her hostess used the WC, telling Vanessa that 'unfortunately she was not constipated that morning & I couldn't go on' reading 'page after page about love & high thinking'.

For Clive, notoriety was measured by appearing in the illustrated papers, but Fredegond Shove argued that a surer sign of public recognition was to appear by name in a work of popular fiction. She pointed out that Clive was mentioned in Rose Macaulay's *Non-Combatants and Others* (1916), where an art student named Alix gets into bed to read 'Mr. Clive Bell's last book, with much of which she differed violently, so violently that she made marginal and unsympathetic notes on it in pencil as she lay.' When her cousins come upstairs, Alix puts Clive's book under her pillow, 'where, deeply as she differed from him, he seemed to lie as a protection against something'. After *Art*, Clive was not the 'somewhat obscure individual' Hulme had described him as in the *New Age*. With her habitual hyperbole, Virginia told Clive he was the 'hero' of Agnes Hamilton's anti-war novel *Dead Yesterday* (1916), though its author assured Clive her book had nothing to do with either him or Bloomsbury. In the novel, Omega Workshops curtains shade the windows in Gertrude Fenner and Chris Bampton's flat, a 'Slade School essay in Post-Impressionism' hangs over the mantelpiece and among 'a motley collection of books' are modern novels, two or three volumes of the *Yellow Book* and 'a miscellaneous collection of small shilling books, mostly on labour questions', including *Art*.

Charleston

Seeking to capitalise on his celebrity, Clive proposed that Chatto publish a selection of his *Athenaeum* reviews, which, he told Geoffrey Whitworth, 'must be amongst the earliest expressions in English of that Post-Impressionist-Unanimist-Neo-Individualist movement which the war may or may not have nipped in the bud'. Chatto's reader thought Clive was probably well-enough known to sell 1,500 copies, but only if the older reviews were made relevant. This was good advice as it gave Clive the opportunity to think about them in light of the changed circumstances of the war: a 1912 review of a translation of *Lysistrata* which Clive had cast as a commentary on the suffrage movement, for example, he now transformed into a warning against censorship.

Pot-Boilers also reprinted some of Clive's relatively scarce wartime writings on art, including 'Contemporary Art in England'. When the article had appeared in the *Burlington Magazine* in July 1917, Clive's customary elevation of the French, coupled with his accusation that English visual art was 'provincial', was made even more infuriating by the fact that he ignored those young artists, many of whom had been at the Slade before the war, who took the devastation and suffering of the conflict as their subject. He had criticised what he termed Wyndham Lewis's 'canalizing' of his talents into the 'little backwater called English vorticism', and sharpened the point in the *Pot-Boilers* version by adducing the fate of Eric Gill (as Clive saw it) as a warning to Lewis of where Futurism and Vorticism might lead. Many English artists had, of course, very successfully 'canalized' their talent into work that either drew upon their experience in the trenches, or rendered the war's effects on the home front. When Gertler was commissioned by the War Memorial Committee in 1918, he told Ottoline,

> There is a good time coming for Art yet in England, no it shan't always be French, French, French. What will Clive Bell jaw and write about then?!! This idea – I mean this War Memorial committee, has somehow excited me very much! Because I see so much, that is significant in it. I am ambitious about having a really good school of painting in this country. I am sick of it always being <u>French</u>. Yes, about painting I am <u>patriotic</u>! What's more, I have a feeling that we <u>are</u> going to have good painting after the War – there are good times coming if only we can hold out. This War is not the end.

Other painters, such as Paul Nash and Richard Nevinson, shared Gertler's anger at Clive's single-minded focus on French painters. The rejection of his war paintings by what he termed the 'Clive Bell group' irritated Nevinson; it was, he later wrote, 'my first real taste of the jealousy of artists and the nastiness of intellectuals'.

As well as taking every opportunity to laud Duncan and Vanessa, Clive never failed to flatter Virginia. The 'Foreword' to *Pot-Boilers* gave his opinion that Hardy, Conrad and Virginia Woolf were the three best living English novelists. Virginia had no wish to be so fêted by her brother-in-law, and dismissed Clive's book for wanting to 'give the impression that he sits drinking in the Café Royal with Mary, & the young poets & painters drift up, & he knows them all, & between them they settle the business'. Reviews of *Pot-Boilers* divided predictably between those that liked the book almost as much as its author seemed to and those (like the *TLS*) who complained about his slavish adherence to vague phrases such as 'significant form'. Whether hostile or complimentary, reviewers agreed that Clive's writing was entertaining – like 'listening to a really brilliant conversationalist without having the trouble to think of brilliant answers whenever there happens to be a pause in the flow of ideas', as the *Tatler*'s 'About People and Things that Matter' column put it.

In France, however, where Matisse and Picasso were already old news, Clive was regarded as outdated. To the *Mercure de France*, which found he had nearly nothing to say about young French artists, he was merely an English writer faithfully representing a narrow point of view. When the *Egoist* called Clive 'the Matthew Arnold of his time', Clive suspected that Eliot was the reviewer (though Mary assured him he was not). It would remain to be seen how accurate the *Egoist*'s prediction that Clive would 'survive not as an individual, but as the representative of a little world of 1914' turned out to be.

Writing 'Contemporary Art in England' made Clive excited to see art again; he wanted to go to 'all the galleries'. Roger arranged an 'Exhibition of Works Representative of the New Movement in Art' for the Royal Birmingham Society of Artists in summer 1917, which moved in October to the recently opened Mansard Gallery at Heal's furniture shop on the Tottenham Court Road. Clive loaned works by Othon Friesz, Duncan (including *The Lemon-Gatherers*) and Vlaminck to the exhibition. When the *Nation* delayed Clive's review until after the exhibition had closed, Clive withdrew it to include in *Pot-Boilers*, the only previously unpublished piece. He regretted that no works by Spencer, Bomberg, Lewis or William Roberts had been included, and complained about Roger's choice of French painters – why, for example, was there nothing by Picasso (who, despite being Spanish, was usually described as French by virtue of living in Paris)? Clive particularly lamented the omission of André Derain, 'because there is no man in the modern movement more readily appreciated by people who care for painting'. Even so, the works of Vlaminck and Marchand gave Clive that 'sense of being in the presence of great art' he invariably felt upon entering a gallery on the Continent.

By now it was to be expected that Clive would identify Duncan as the only English painter who could compare favourably with any Frenchman, but he also focused attention on Gertler's *Swing Boats*, which allowed a critic to 'see pretty clearly the strength and weakness of this remarkable person'. What Clive gave with one hand he often took away with the other: he praised Gertler for his industry, but Duncan was 'all over an artist'.

Clive also singled out his wife, grouping Vanessa with Marie Laurencin and Natalia Goncharova (who were not exhibited), three painters who gave the lie to the truism that women could not compete with their male contemporaries. Clive would occasionally return to the question of whether the work of female visual artists was discernibly different from that of their male peers, a subject that was of particular critical interest in postwar France. For now, he proposed that Roger should arrange an exhibition of women painters that would provide a means to explore the question.

19. Angelica

Early in the summer of 1918, Vanessa let Clive know she was pregnant. He took the news 'in the greatest good part', Duncan told Maynard; Clive surmised that a third child might qualify him and Vanessa for an abatement under new income tax regulations. He had already attempted to reduce their tax burden by formally declaring that they lived apart due to his CO status. Despite the need to be circumspect about the baby's true parentage, Clive told Mary at once. She would know that the baby could not be his because he had not had sex with Vanessa 'in ages', but did that mean that Mary's own contraceptive precautions were not 'absolutely effective', Clive worried? Vanessa reassured him that she and Duncan had taken no precautions because they had been trying to have a baby for two years.

The more pressing question was what to tell Clive's family. Their news might elicit an invitation from his mother for Quentin and Julian to visit Seend, where it would be disastrous were the boys to let slip Clive's CO status (his father sat on the Appeals Tribunal for Wiltshire, and, like the majority of Tribunals, did not look kindly on 'shirkers'). It 'would be fatal to everything – it would probably lead to a rupture with the whole family and the loss of all our prospects'. Perhaps the children could be instructed to say that their father was medically unfit: 'It's worth taking some trouble to preserve our lien on the Bell millions,' Clive wrote to Vanessa. Although he controlled some investments of his own, most of Clive's money was in trust, and his inheritance would be considerable. A visit to Seend by the Bell children, now eight and ten, might also expose the make-up of the ménage at Charleston, something that Clive assured Vanessa he would address before Cleeve House could be deemed a safe place to send them.

Questions about the paternity of Vanessa's third child had to be deflected or dismissed at the outset, setting in place a pattern of deception that would last until Angelica Bell was eighteen. Clive joked to Lytton that it might be a wise child that knew its own father, but it was 'a wiser father that knows its own child'. The baby was due in January, so Clive planned to remain at Garsington, where he was preoccupied with writing a 'little book about civilization' which he had begun to formulate in the summer, which would take as models Periclean Athens and eighteenth-century France. He would be at Charleston when the baby arrived to 'write the letters, impress the nurse & doctor, & generally make things respectable'. In early December, Clive visited Duncan and Vanessa, walking from Lewes station with Molly MacCarthy. She and Clive had quarrelled at length earlier in the war, but were now reconciled and would remain good friends.

Vanessa had been unwell during the summer and continued to be out of sorts and weak throughout the winter, with 'Claude', as the imminent child had been named, giving her trouble. Clive had urged her to take a holiday but she and Duncan, he told Mary, 'seem to have no plans but to have their babies and get on with their painting – a way of life with which I have no quarrel since it is not I who am to have the baby.' Whenever he communicated with his family, Clive remained vague about his movements, taking advantage of the fact that his persistent dental problems meant he often had to be in London.

As her due date approached, Vanessa intended to send Quentin and Julian to stay with Virginia and Leonard; they could come back to Charleston when Clive arrived in early January. But, as it turned out, Angelica was born early, at 2 a.m. on Christmas Day 1918. Duncan let Clive know, adding that Vanessa wanted an announcement placed in the *Times* so that she would receive congratulations and free samples of Nestlé milk. This duly appeared on New Year's Eve: 'On Christmas Day at Charleston, Firle, Sussex, the wife of Clive Bell, of a daughter'. As she did not know where Clive's parents thought he was, Vanessa relied on him to inform them. Virginia and Vanessa were delighted it was a girl.

The first few weeks of Angelica's life were frightening because she failed to thrive. Vanessa's chaotic household, with servants who took advantage of her bedridden state, could not sustain the presence of

Julian and Quentin, but they proved too much for Virginia to cope with and so had been sent to 46 Gordon Square to be cared for by the cook, Blanche, and maid, Jessie. Clive had seen very little of his sons during his residence at Garsington. He sent them presents by way of friends who were visiting Charleston – Saxon was asked to take butterfly nets because they could not be posted – ordered toy pistols for them from Hamley's and asked Mary if she would buy sweets for them in London. Whenever they came to Gordon Square, he made sure to spend time with his 'bantings', taking them to the cinema, or to pantomimes at the Palladium with Mary.

By the time Clive got down to Charleston in early January, Dr Marie Moralt had taken charge of improving Angelica's condition. Clive had nothing to do but read and help Duncan chop wood, until Duncan left to visit his parents. He could get no work done, Clive complained to Mary. When he visited again later that month, the atmosphere was calmer and Clive impressed the nurse by his attention to 'his' daughter. Virginia told Vanessa that Angelica's beauty had convinced their aunt Anny Ritchie that she must be Clive's child, though her knowledge of Vanessa's admirers had given her some suspicions.

No money arrived from Seend. Cory let Clive know that his parents were 'seeking a rapprochement', but Clive wanted to see 'a thousand' first. He would go in the hope of getting enough money to 'meet all difficulties', but if he did not, he would go there no more. While Vanessa may have despised her in-laws 'for their "awful rich fox-hunting self-complacency"', the Charleston household partly depended on the Bells' wealth and so she was careful to keep secret Angelica's paternity. Beyond the financial motivation, it was also necessary to avoid the scandal that would have ensued had the baby's actual parentage become known publicly.

Soon after Angelica's birth, Mary sent clothes for the baby. Her own marriage was about to enter a crisis worse than any that her affair with Clive had occasioned so far. Once Clive was resident at Garsington, his importuning of Mary had become more insistent, accompanied often by either a genuine or feigned insouciance about Jack's likely feelings in the matter. Could she not promise to see him every Friday night throughout the winter, Clive asked Mary in the summer of 1916. If she ever disliked 'the violence of my physical passion' she must tell him, though he always believed her when she said she didn't. Anticipating a momentous ten-day visit to Charleston in 1917, 'as though we were lovers', he reminded her that 'to please Jack' they had seen one another only once in six weeks. He suggested that if things did not improve between her and Jack, she should come to stay at Garsington. Disingenuously, Clive told her, 'I don't underrate feelings and the painfulness of one person being in love and the other not: but two people who like each other and keep their tempers and a little sense of humour can, I'm persuaded, live together once complete individual liberty is established.' 'If only Jack would start an affair!' he exclaimed, rather more honestly. But when Lytton did not see Clive at a party given by the Hutchinsons, he assumed 'M. le Mari had issued a non possumus.'

Perhaps it was the resumption of more normal patterns of life after the Armistice, or perhaps Jack's patience simply was tested too far, but by late January 1919, Mary had fled the Hutchinsons' River House for Durbins. Lytton had assumed Clive and Mary's affair was 'almost settled and based on such definite sympathies as to make it more or less respectable', but Jack evidently did not share this view. Clive immediately climbed up to his high horse, telling Mary that Roger had agreed with him 'that two modern civilized people could only live together on terms of absolute freedom for both'. He thought that Mary should stay away from her home until Jack gave her written assurances that nothing of this sort would happen again.

IV

A HIGHLY CIVILISED
LOAFER (1919–1929)

20. The New Ballet

On Monday 11 November the Armistice was signed. Carrington was swept along in tides of rejoicing Londoners and ended up at Monty Shearman's flat in the Adelphi to celebrate the peace. 'Everyone was there,' she told her brother Noel; 'the halt, the sick, & the lame. Even old Lytton from his deathbed in Sussex rushed up & joined in the merriment.' As the party continued, more and more people came – Augustus John, Ottoline, D. H. Lawrence and Frieda, Gertler, Maynard, Bunny, Roger and Clive. Everyone danced, even Lytton, and the flat became so hot that the rich industrialist Henry Mond 'played the pianola stripped to his vest and with champagne being poured over his head'. Osbert Sitwell brought Sergei Diaghilev and the choreographer Leonid Massine from his house in Swan Walk where they had been dining together.

Before the war, Clive had regarded such productions of Diaghilev's Ballets Russes as *Schéhérazade*, designed by Léon Bakst, as a *faux bon*. This 'pure orientalist fantasy', as dance historian Lynn Garafola describes it, was to Clive a simulacrum of art, giving the moneyed Covent Garden audience a stimulus 'subtle enough to do duty for aesthetic emotions'. This was not to say that Clive and his friends did not enjoy a night at the ballet. The pre-war shows brought by Diaghilev to London inspired many a Bloomsbury revel. At a party given by Ray Costelloe in June 1913, her sister Karin dressed up as the ballerina Tamara Karsavina to enact the *Spectre de la Rose*, with Oliver Strachey dressed as Nijinsky. Afterwards, Maynard 'as the devil, poured boils in the shape of cherries upon the writhing Roger Fry' in a version of the ballet of Job. These balletic charades were followed at Ray's party by *The Unfortunate Lover*, *or Truth Will Out*, a play by Lytton in which Duncan, 'disguised as a midwife, was suddenly seized with labour pains – doctors and midwives were summoned, and amid horrid groans he gave birth to a pillow'. Clive played Duncan's apparently homosexual lover, Marjorie Strachey was dressed as a man and Vanessa was 'attired simply, but misleadingly, as a woman'. Lytton was more likely to draw inspiration from Restoration comedy than from the Russians. Even after Diaghilev replaced Fokine with the entrancing Nijinsky, Lytton remained unimpressed by the ballet. *Sacre du Printemps*, he told Henry Lamb, was 'one of the most painful experiences of my life'.

Sacre, *Jeux* and *L'après-midi d'un faune*, the ballets choreographed by Nijinsky, had been only a very small part of the repertory before 1914, but they presaged the transformation of the company that would excite a new audience when Diaghilev brought his dancers back to London in 1918. As part of a mixed programme of entertainments at the Coliseum in September, with ticket prices that opened the ballet to a broader audience than the elite who had flocked to Drury Lane and Covent Garden before the war, the Russian dancers would soon be 'promoting modernism through the music-halls' in Diaghilev's collaborations with Mikhail Larionov, Natalia Goncharova, Picasso and Derain.

The boxes and dressing-rooms of the theatres where the Ballets Russes performed became sites of social rivalries and jealousies. When Ottoline introduced Duncan to Diaghilev, he could not understand why she was so close to the Russian, unless it was simply to 'queen the ballet'. Duncan was perceptive, for when Ottoline's throne seemed threatened by Clive she was extremely put out. Roger, enthralled by the colours and designs of the productions, gave a lunch for Diaghilev and Massine to which he invited Clive. When it had seemed to be true that peace would finally come that autumn, the Ballets Russes became the focus of Clive's social life. He told Mary he would purchase tickets well in advance if she wanted to go with him.

In October, Duncan decorated 46 Gordon Square for a grand party in honour of the Russian dancers. Ottoline came, as did all three Sitwells, Simon and Dorothy Bussy, Nina Hamnett, Adrian and Karin Stephen, Barbara Bagenal and Mark Gertler. Lytton and Carrington were expected but had to stay in Tidmarsh where they had moved at the beginning of the year because both were suffering from shingles. The party was a great success. During it, Clive inscribed a copy of *Art* to Lydia Lopokova, the *prima ballerina* who was the audience's favourite. Before long, an intense rivalry had developed between Clive and Ottoline over who was more intimate with the Russians and their entourage.

Clive often visited Lydia backstage, taking Mary with him, where both chattered with her in French. The Hutchinsons had not attended the party at Gordon Square and it soon appeared that not only Ottoline was jealous of Clive's friendliness with the Russians. At a performance of *The Good-Humoured Ladies* in September 1918, even Vanessa and Duncan noticed Jack Hutchinson's bad mood. Clive saw that he would need to restrain his ebullience when he, Mary and Jack saw each other at the ballet, telling her, 'It's hopeless to be more than just decently civil when we're all together.' Jack felt excluded by Mary and Clive's easy badinage with Lydia and soon word reached Clive that Mary was being driven 'hysterical' by 'the incessant and remorseless hammering of Jack, Gertler, and their friends', which Virginia also seemed to be egging on because she was jealous of Mary. When Clive penned a gallant verse 'To Lopokova Dancing' that delighted Lydia, charmed Lytton and inspired Roger to write 'an answer' to it, he hoped Mary would not think he was pursuing the ballerina.

There was an uncomfortable encounter with Jack in Lydia's loge in January, when Duncan and Maynard were 'determined not to let him spoil the conversation'. It was shortly after this incident that Mary sought refuge from her unhappy marriage by going to stay with Roger at Durbins. Roger's closeness to Clive only exacerbated Jack's anger, despite Roger's efforts to act as go-between for the Hutchinsons in their crisis. His assessment was that Jack could not see that his anger was not the result of indignation at Clive's 'unseemly behaviour' but was in fact rooted in a sexual jealousy he denied. Although some thought that Mary would leave her marriage, Clive was sure she would eventually return to River House. Within a few months, the crisis passed. According to Jeremy Hutchinson, his father decided to 'simply put up with it' to keep his family together.

A new front in what Clive described as Ottoline's 'open war on Bloomsbury' formed when rumours circulated that Picasso was coming to London. He had married the ballerina Olga Khokhlova in July 1918, resulting in a transition to the more bourgeois environment in which Clive would find him in Paris after the war in his well-appointed quarters on the rue la Boétie. The Ballet's success in London had led Diaghilev to plan more productions to continue the collaboration with Picasso begun in 1917 when he designed the sets and costumes for *Parade*. In

March 1919, Massine went to Paris to discuss with Picasso the décor for *Tricorne* (*The Three-Cornered Hat*) and with André Derain designs for *La Boutique Fantasque* (*The Magic Toyshop*).

Anticipating Picasso's arrival, Clive beseeched Vanessa, Duncan and Roger to help him arrange a reception at Gordon Square. He would invite Mary, because Massine and Diaghilev wanted the beau monde there as well as artists: 'It must be a great success in the half bohemian, half mondaine style,' he told Vanessa. He supposed Jack would have to be invited as well but he would not invite Ottoline. This was a 'last crushing defeat', as Vanessa described it to Maynard. Ottoline tried to enlist Osbert Sitwell to host a rival party, but to her great rage it was cancelled 'on account of some row with Diaghilev'.

As it turned out, visa problems delayed Picasso's arrival and the Gordon Square party did not take place. Vanessa had rented a small flat in Regent Square from Alix Sargant-Florence (who had moved in with James Strachey, whom she would shortly marry), and offered it to Derain while he worked on the ballet. When Picasso arrived on 25 May 1919, his first visit to London, Clive took the opportunity to act as his cicerone, showing him around the East End and taking him shopping for clothes. He lunched often with the painters, warming at once to 'le gros', as Derain was known, in comparison to 'le petit' Picasso. Clive became an avid champion of the Ballets Russes, badgering Maynard – at the time deeply involved in the government's treaty negotiations at Versailles and also suffering from the flu – to do whatever he could to put Diaghilev's company on a more stable financial footing. He thoroughly enjoyed his role as man-about-town of the ballet that summer, an apparition that amused Lytton almost as much as it repelled him:

> I went to the Russian Ballet last night, and found there Clive and Mary. Clive was an extreme mixture of real charmingness and pure horror. He insisted on taking me (he being in his usual raucous evening clothes, rather red in the face, and a top hat planted on the very back of his head) to the most conspicuous spot in the house, and standing there gesticulating and making a disgrace of himself. We also went behind the scenes to Lopokhova's dressing-room, where, as you may imagine, the noise was appalling. But he was very nice afterwards, pouring champagne down our throats at Gordon Square.

A more sympathetic perspective came from Aldous Huxley, who told
Ottoline he had glimpsed her at the Alhambra on the first night of *La
Boutique Fantasque*:

> Clive doing his round of the boxes was a superb spectacle. One could
> almost hear his voice across the whole breadth of the building. And
> Lytton drinking lemonade in the foyer; and Roger, perspiringly
> radiant; and Hutch, very man about town, with Nina [Hamnett]
> looking very gamine.

By the time *Tricorne* premiered in July, Jack was content to let Clive
escort Mary to the theatre because he had taken a box for his own
friends. All of literary and artistic London was there to see Picasso's
costumes, drop curtain and sets. Tom and Vivienne Eliot were there
and went again with Mary and Jack the next night. Vivienne later
told Mary that she had given up a great deal of herself to her husband
but observed that Mary seemed prepared to do so for no one. Jack's
acceptance of Mary's affair with Clive might have had less to do with
his well-known tolerance, and more with what Clive described as her
'deep, furious passion for liberty'.

Ottoline had Diaghilev, the Picassos and Massine to lunch at
Garsington after *Tricorne*'s opening and again at the end of July, while
Clive was able to give a farewell party for Picasso at Gordon Square.
He and Maynard invited 'some forty young or youngish painters,
writers and students'. Aldous Huxley brought the writer Pierre Drieu La
Rochelle and at one end of the table sat the conductor Ernest Ansermet,
while at the other was Lytton, 'so that their beards might wag in unison'.
Picasso told Duncan that 'this was the party he had been looking for
ever since he had been in England'. Ansermet, who had introduced
Clive to Stravinsky (whose 1910 *Firebird* was revived for the season) and
to the composer of *Tricorne*, Manuel de Falla, told Clive he had read
Art with pleasure. But he was interested to know if Clive thought there
was 'significant form' in literature and music as well as in visual art.
He was intrigued to hear if Clive's concept was absolute, applicable to
all times and all races. The American magazine *New Republic* had just
offered Clive £10 an article for a series on art and aesthetics, so amidst
the 'excitements, rumours and entertainments' of the Ballets Russes'

season, he had been formulating a serious critical analysis of the dance as a modernist form that would go some way to answering Ansermet's questions.

'The New Ballet' used Lopokova's performance in *La Boutique Fantasque* as evidence of how the Ballets Russes now brought to the stage works of art rather than mere entertainments. Tamara Karsavina might have seemed 'miraculous' in 1914 but five years later she was disappointing in comparison with Lopokova. Clive had argued that all successful works of art depend upon solving the problem of how to sustain the 'white heat' of emotion by finding a suitable form. As a dancer, Clive wrote, Lopokova was an impersonal artist, tantamount to the 'choreographer's first violin'. She did not 'express herself directly to the audience' but 'transmuted personality into something more precious'. Clive's use of the relatively new word 'choreography' exemplifies how it had come quite suddenly to imply a 'new way of looking at dance, an awareness of movement as design'. 'The New Ballet' explained that the art of Lopokova and of Massine was impersonal because it was 'detached from circumstance', even though the personality of the choreographer imprinted the work. Once again, Clive extolled the French (and Russian, in this case) at the expense of the English, arguing that the combination of dance, painting and music in this 'new ballet' had realised a dream that the English director Gordon Craig had 'fumbled' when he had made a similar effort to reform the art of theatre through innovations in set design and lighting: in collaboration with 'one of the greatest living painters, M. Derain', *La Boutique* was a 'foretaste of the new art of the theatre'.

Clive's article elicited a warm response from Lydia, who told him that she had always found it difficult to express the many thoughts and feelings she had about her art, but now his 'torrent' of ideas had unleashed her eloquence. She was sure the article would interest Massine, for whom Diaghilev would enthusiastically translate it.

Although Clive's fame rested on 'significant form', after the fallow years at Garsington his thinking turned to those questions of tradition, of individuality and of the function of criticism with which many intellectuals in postwar England were engaged. 'Impersonality' was not by any means a new idea – Flaubert had insisted on its importance in 1846 – but in the 1920s it became a central tenet of an influential version of modernism.

In 'Tradition and Movements' Clive distinguished between a *tradition* – 'The tradition of art begins with the first artist that ever lived, and will end with the last. Always it is being enriched or modified – never is it exhausted' – and *movements*, identified by particular works – 'a vein that is worked out'. Thus, Matisse was, in fact, part of the 'great tradition' of art, although most people did not perceive this because they had a faulty understanding of what tradition meant. The tradition, he argued, is what exists beyond individual movements, what comes to be called 'art'; each movement takes in history, archaeology, philosophy, politics, geography, fashions, religion, crime.

Several months later, Eliot's famous 'Tradition and the Individual Talent' would make clear how congruent his and Clive's thinking was. Eliot, who had forged an intimate friendship with Mary and come to appreciate her literary judgement, replied at length when she asked how he would distinguish between 'culture' and 'civilisation'. Rehearsing the arguments that would appear in the final numbers of the *Egoist* later that year, Eliot argued for the necessity of an impersonal and traditional civilisation 'which forms people unconsciously', as well as of a 'culture – which is a personal interest and curiosity in *particular things*'. 'Tradition and the Individual Talent' emphasised in its conclusion the importance of the historical sense and of order, adding that the 'emotion of art is impersonal'.

Clive's 'Tradition and Movements' inaugurated a series of articles that codified what he had spent the war years reflecting on. Their titles signalled how similar his concerns were to Eliot's: 'Standards', 'Criticism', 'Order and Authority'. Clive began to develop a view of the critic as a guide who need only point to 'good works of art' without attempting to analyse states of mind. The hermetic subjectivity of his 'aesthetic emotion' now yielded to the notion that knowledge and experience could supplement one's experience of an art object. As he would later acknowledge, *Art*'s didacticism was strategic. In a less belligerent mood, Clive now articulated a view of the critic as signpost, guiding a viewer towards worthwhile experiences by 'infecting' them with his own enthusiasm.

When the French painter André Lhote wrote in the *Athenaeum* about the reopening of the Louvre after the Armistice, Clive took the opportunity in 'Order and Authority' to comment on his perception of the tension in French culture between a 'natural taste for order' (a desirable trait that Lhote identified in the painting of Jacques-Louis David) and the individualism Clive believed was 'the breath of every artist's life'. He interpreted Lhote's paean to the seventeenth-century Nain brothers, as well as his exhortation to his peers to follow the example of David, as typical of the French acceptance of a cultural bargain whereby adherence to tradition bestowed a sophistication on its citizens for which they were willing to sacrifice individuality. Lhote's call for order was part of a broad reaction which would reverberate through Parisian intellectual circles for the next few years against what many saw as the faults of Cubism, as Clive would quickly discover when he was able to return to Paris in October 1919.

D. S. MacColl, keeper of the Wallace Collection, was a perennial antagonist of Clive's. In 1914, he had lectured at Leeds University on what he saw as the fallacies in *Art*'s aesthetic. Taking issue in May 1919 with an article about drawing in the *Burlington Magazine* by Roger Fry, MacColl mentioned that while Clive had presumably intended to be 'absurd' by saying in *Art* the 'precise opposite' of what he meant, Fry should know better. Clive replied that not only had he always deliberately used the word 'significant' rather than 'beautiful', he had reiterated his rationale for doing so in *Pot-Boilers* and would now repeat it again because MacColl apparently had either not read *Art* or was simply dull.

This spat went to the heart of an argument about aesthetics that would drag on for decades. As art historian Christopher Green has explained, the term 'significant form' had the effect of pulling together the implications of Roger's undermining of long-accepted canons of Western art; if 'beauty' was jettisoned, along with it 'was jettisoned the idea of the superiority of the European classical tradition'. MacColl allowed that Clive was a lively writer, but charged him with being too impatient to let go of an idea he should have abandoned once its contradictions became apparent. In 1919, Clive was seen as Roger's acolyte. In a small oil painting he made that year, *The Unknown God*, Henry Tonks depicted Roger preaching the post-Impressionist gospel to a disgruntled audience in which MacColl could be recognised (as well as Sickert, William Rothenstein and the art writer George Moore). At the side of the stage in Tonks' caricature stood Clive, ringing a bell and chanting 'Cézannah, Cézannah'.

As Clive's star rose and he gained an international audience with his contributions to American periodicals, he inevitably drew more detractors (Albert Barnes, for example, disparaged 'Criticism' when it appeared in the *New Republic* and had by 1919 turned vehemently against the author of *Art*, a book he had previously praised so highly). Roger had the last word in the argument with MacColl, adding a rare public distancing of himself from Clive: 'In re-stating my theories for me, Mr MacColl poses as fundamental the opposition between "significance" and "beauty" . . . I do not think I have used the word "significance" . . . the word "beauty" I try very hard to avoid . . . Whatever Mr Clive Bell may have said, I personally have never denied the existence of some amount of representation in all pictorial art.' Although Clive might have thought that the battle for acceptance of modern French painting in England was over by 1912, clearly old prejudices continued to flourish.

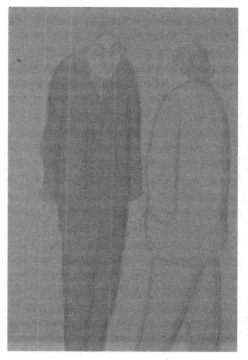

'Significant Form. Mr Clive Bell: I always think that when one feels one's been carrying a theory too far, then's the time to carry it a little further. Mr Roger Fry: A little? Good heavens, man! Are you growing old?'

The major exhibition 'Modern French Painting' came to Heal's Mansard Gallery in the summer of 1919 and Clive, writing in *The Nation*, praised Osbert and Sacheverell Sitwell for collaborating with Modigliani's dealer, Léopold Zborowski, in bringing it about. Although it was 'not exactly a third Post-Impressionist exhibition', it was a 'rich and representative' display of what Clive had missed seeing in Paris during the war. Modigliani's *Peasant Girl* hung with works by Picasso, Matisse, Derain, Friesz, Vlaminck, Survage, Soutine, Valadon, Kisling, Marcoussis, Halicka, Léger, Gabriel-Fournier, Lhote, Ortiz, Utrillo and Dufy. Clive was thrilled to see that the war had not forced French painting from the course set by Cézanne, though he would have liked to see more recent work by Picasso (such as his scenic designs for the Ballets Russes) because he understood that this was the style now being imitated by younger painters in Paris. Frankie Birrell had let Clive know that Jean Marchand was upset not to be included in the exhibition, an omission Clive noted in his review, as well as regretting the absence of anything by Braque. The show suggested to Clive that Cubism was in retreat in France. He had no time for 'the great dreary machine of Léger, or the pretty affectations of Archipenko' and did not mention the sculpture of Zadkine in his review, but Clive made clear that the Heal's exhibition was the next best thing to being in Paris.

Clive's review elicited several scornful letters in *The Nation* which revived the arguments against modern art heard before the war. A doctor named Greville MacDonald wrote from the Reform Club that he had been enticed by Clive into going to see the exhibition for himself, where he found the 'indecent distortions, the obscene colourings, the immodest subjects, were deliberate intentions to shock us out of our conventional ideas of beauty, truth, sweetness and law'. 'Philistine' wrote that he was an engineer but could not for the life of him understand what Clive was on about: 'What is it about this new art . . . that leaves the normal educated man gasping?' Osbert Sitwell defended his exhibition, dismissed 'Philistine' and scolded MacDonald for his preconceived notions of what art should be. In rebutting the views of 'Philistine', E. R. Brown of Glasgow made several points about arts education that would be debated often in the next few decades. For one thing, public institutions held hardly any modern works, with the result that 'normally educated men are totally ignorant of the traditions, and so unaware of their ignorance that they accuse the modern artist of an assault upon tradition'. Clive replied to his critics (in 'execrably bad taste' he admitted to Mary) by inviting them to 'bung down five shillings' for a copy of *Art*, but Dr MacDonald was unimpressed: this 'jazz' degeneration of art was 'repulsive' to his moral and spiritual well-being. When the correspondence had dragged on for a month, Clive wearily pointed out, again, that the battle for modern art had already been won.

21. Order and Authority

Picasso went to see the exhibition at Heal's with Clive and pleased him just before returning to Paris by asking that he write to him occasionally. When travel restrictions were lifted, Clive at once applied for a passport and let Picasso know he expected to come to Paris before the end of October. He was eager to see the exhibition of watercolours and drawings at Paul Rosenberg's gallery for which he had received one of Picasso's hand-drawn invitations. This exhibition, Michael Fitzgerald notes, 'not only recognized but celebrated Picasso's departure from Cubism', and marked his entry into the more bourgeois life Olga preferred.

Clive was almost giddy with excitement in Paris, giving Mary a daily account of his adventures. He was met at the Gare du Nord by Percy Moore Turner of the Barbazanges gallery and the next day, after collecting his luggage from the customs post, he went to see the Salon d'Automne. The Grand Palais was freezing because there were still holes in its glass roof from shells and shrapnel. It rained or snowed almost every day and the more expensive restaurants provided customers with a warm brick on which to rest their feet. But nothing could dampen Clive's spirits as he went from lunch at the Deux Magots to dinner at Lapérouse with old friends and new acquaintances.

Two days after arriving, Clive paid a visit to the Picassos on rue la Boétie. 'Picasso is one of the nicest men ever born,' he gushed to Mary, 'I'm in love with him.' When he saw the Rosenberg exhibition, Clive found Picasso's versatility 'alarming', but his powerful individuality made everything cohere. Other painters seemed to Clive to be jealous of Picasso, and he immediately understood that in the five years since he had been in France, the cultural situation he had known in 1914 had profoundly changed. Clive did not care for Cubism in general, but he recognised that Picasso was probably the most important artist working in Europe in terms of his ability to force others to re-examine their ideas about painting. He asked Othon Friesz who were the young artists to watch for, but the forty-year-old painter answered '*Nous sommes les jeunes*' because so many had been either killed or torn from their aesthetic trajectories by the war. Indeed, in contrast to Clive's experience among the COs at Garsington, nearly every artist he spent time with in Paris (with the notable exception of Picasso) had served in the conflict.

Picasso, The Artist's Salon, 1919 [left to right: Jean Cocteau, Olga Khokhlova, Erik Satie, Clive]

The French experience of the war had been entirely different from that of the English, not only because it was fought on their land but because it was seen as an opportunity to confront and put to rest the humiliation of their defeat in the Franco-Prussian war of 1870. A desire for a 'new classic age' had made itself felt by 1917, driven partly by antipathy to an aesthetic that was regarded just before the war as suspiciously foreign.

The outbreak of war had been preceded by accusations of a German assault on French culture facilitated by dealers with names like Bernheim, Basler, Kahnweiler, Wildenstein and Weill; indeed, Kahnweiler and Wilhelm Uhde had had their collections confiscated as 'enemy goods' when the war began. When Diaghilev's *Parade* premiered in Paris at the Théâtre du Châtelet on the afternoon of 18 May 1917 (a matinée due to the blackout) as a benefit for wounded soldiers, the audience was outraged by Satie's music, Picasso's set and costumes and Cocteau's 'strange little story'. The production was booed, the audience yelling a variety of coarse epithets that 'signified unpatriotic behavior'.

That year, André Salmon spoke of Cubism as only a stage on the way to a more 'ordered' art and a movement that had exhausted its usefulness. There was a gathering reaction against that very individualism that had attracted Clive to French artists before the war, exemplified by books such as *Après le cubisme* by Amédée Ozenfant and Charles-Edouard Jeanneret (the latter better known as Le Corbusier), Salmon's *L'Art vivant* and Gino Severini's *From Cubism to Classicism* (1921). Cubism still had well-respected defenders, such as the poet Pierre Reverdy, the critic Waldemar George and Paul Rosenberg's brother, Léonce.

Léonce Rosenberg mounted a series of large one-man shows at his gallery, L'Effort Moderne, in the first six months of 1919, culminating in June with a show of Picasso's work which demonstrated that Cubism had continued to develop during the war. Francis Picabia's attack on Cubism in his periodical *391* was not welcomed by its detractors, who detested Dada even more than Cubism. Picabia's break with his close friend Albert Gleizes in 1920 and his alliance with Tristan Tzara, André Breton, Philippe Soupault and Louis Aragon led to another fracture in the Parisian art world, all circumstances which Clive had to assimilate quickly if he was to feel in the swim of things. When he told Vanessa in 1920 that the French seemed to him less affected by the war than the English, it was likely because he found the café atmosphere so similar to what he had experienced on his earlier visits.

Within a week of getting to Paris, Clive had looked up Roderic O'Conor and J. W. Morrice, the painters with whom he had forged a close friendship in 1904. He took O'Conor to see Gertrude Stein's Picassos but when he ran into Richard Nevinson he declined the painter's request for an introduction to Picasso. Clive had no interest in seeing English people in Paris, although he made an exception for Frankie Birrell, of whom he was fond. André Gide, to whom Roger had introduced Clive at Durbins in 1918, took him to meet Adrienne Monnier, whose Maison des Amis du Livre sold everything modern. On the opposite side of rue l'Odéon, Sylvia Beach was opening Shakespeare & Company. Clive wanted to meet more French writers, but 'the world seems to have made up its mind that I am an art-critic'.

Clive was immensely flattered by the tributes paid him in the Paris art world. He was particularly pleased to receive invitations to see the private collections of both Léonce and Paul Rosenberg, Paul Guillaume and the critic Adolphe Basler. He was as popular as the Prince of Wales, he told Mary, who knew his 'vanity too well for me to pretend to you not to be pleased by these little attentions'. He appraised the Paris painting scene after being there a week: 'Renoir, Matisse, Picasso, Derain & Bonnard are the very big men. Then come Vlaminck, Friesz, Bracque, L'hote; then Marchand, Utrillo, and then at least a dozen excellent painters. I persist in my outrageous opinion that this is the greatest age of painting since the fifteenth century.'

By the end of the decade, Clive would decide it was 'mad' to live anywhere but Paris, but his domicile would always be English despite the pull perpetually exerted on him by France. He came to believe that he had developed two distinct selves, a French and an English. When Derain mentioned that an Englishman had referred to Clive as 'frivolous', he burst out to Mary, 'There you are! . . . There is nothing so much disliked in England as intellect-Bloomsbury.' He knew that his social success gave him a rose-tinted view of what living in Paris would be like, but he explained it simply to Vanessa: 'In a foreign country one belongs to no set and has no enemies "on principle".' With extremely rare exceptions, Clive published only in English and therefore really played no part in the aesthetic debates in France, although he became an important reporter on them for readers in England and America.

Clive especially enjoyed Derain's company, seeing him as often as he could. A day might be filled by lunch with Derain, his wife Alice and André Salmon at Moïse Kisling's studio, followed by dinner in Montmartre or an evening at the Cirque Medrano with the Picassos, ending at the Bal Tabarin, then walking through the snow to the Hotel Voltaire by the Seine. One difference from his English life that struck Clive was his preference for male company in Paris, though he may have made this observation only for Mary's benefit. Almost as soon as he had arrived, Clive implored her to join him. She could stay at the Voltaire – 'my sister as usual' – but she must hurry because rooms were hard to find, most taken by the many Parisians who had fled the German bombardments and were now waiting for their apartments to be repaired. Clive could entertain Mary lavishly because the cost of living was so low and if she came, he told her he would decline the invitations that arrived almost hourly so that they could spend time together. He assured Mary that since their last evening at the Savoy he had felt no twinge of lust but, as if to make her jealous enough to come and see for herself, Clive sometimes described encounters with young women who seemed interested in him. If it were not for Mary, he would stay in Paris for good, he said. Trying another tack, he commented on her flirting with Aldous Huxley: 'I always told you he was amusing.' He had been avoiding Valentine Tessier, but when Mary mentioned that she had seen Tom Eliot, Clive said it would serve her right if he went to bed with the Vieux Colombier actress.

While Clive was away, Vanessa and Duncan attended the London premiere of *Parade*. On the day the Picassos invited Clive to meet Cocteau and Erik Satie, he brought with him Vanessa's account of the ballet, Picasso's curtain for which had made an 'extraordinary impression' on the artists. Vanessa's letter was a great success when Clive translated it for the collaborators and he was thrilled when Picasso made a sketch of their party: 'type Ingres-Picasso', he told Mary, 'really rather remarkable'. Duncan, Clive told Vanessa, would find more friends in Paris than he expected, because many remembered his collaboration with Copeau on *La Nuit des rois*, an adaptation of Shakespeare's *Twelfth Night*. He urged Duncan and Vanessa to come to Paris as soon as possible, adding that he could pull strings if Vanessa needed a studio.

A bird's-eye view of Clive's life in the 1920s would reveal a migratory pattern at least twice a year that hardly deviated: the train from Victoria to Newhaven to catch the ferry to Dieppe and on to the Gare du Nord, where he would leave his luggage at the *douane* to collect the next day, then on to the Deux Magots or to Lipp on the boulevard St Germain to see which of his cronies might be there. After the Hotel Voltaire was made into apartments in 1922, he stayed at the Londres on rue Bonaparte, where he kept a trunk full of clothes and books. His usual band comprised the painters Jean Marchand, Othon Friesz,

André Dunoyer de Segonzac and above all his beloved Derain, who lived on rue Bonaparte and with whom, Vanessa told Maynard, Clive seemed 'really to be in love – much more than with any of the ladies'. Also at the Deux Magots he usually found the publisher and book designer François Bernouard and the writers André Salmon and Georges Duhamel. Through Duhamel (whose novel *Confession de Minuit* appeared in 1920), Clive came into contact with a monthly gathering of 'literary socialists' that included Charles Vildrac, Francis Jourdain, Charles Picart Le Doux, Léon Bazalgette and Marcel Cachin, editor of *L'humanité*. Within a short time, he became close to Georges Duthuit, the art critic who married Matisse's daughter, Marguerite, in 1923. Duthuit had been a little apprehensive when they first met in 1920 as he had just published *Le rose et le noir*, a satirical denunciation of Wilde and Pater, written under the influence of Matthew Prichard, that poked some gentle fun at the English critics Bell and Fry for always being behind the Parisian times.

Clive's closest friends in Paris were Derain and Jean Cocteau, each of whom had an eclectic circle. Like Clive, Cocteau was an ambivalent modernist, straddling the divide between the avant-garde and the return to classical values that marked French postwar art. Cocteau's 'aesthetic of ambiguity' evolved into a pluralism which gave him long-lasting influence in the Parisian cultural scene. His 'prodigiously open mind' made him seem to Clive 'the most modern of men', the 'most brilliant' man of ideas of his generation. They would meet at the Gaya (which reopened as Le Boeuf sur le Toit in 1922) for long nights of revelry, with Cocteau bashing away at drums Stravinsky had given him, accompanying Vance Lowry, a black American musician, on saxophone or banjo and Jean Wiener on piano. On other nights, Clive might join Cocteau and Georges Auric in cajoling Arthur Rubinstein into playing ragtime at a Montmartre bar.

Although he might not have heard all the details of the wartime internecine quarrels of the Parisian avant-garde, his friendship with Cocteau brought Clive into the heart of an artistic network that included the group of musicians known as Les Six – Auric, Germaine Tailleferre, Darius Milhaud, Francis Poulenc, Arthur Honegger and Louis Durey – as well as Satie, André Lhote and Blaise Cendrars. Clive's letters from Paris in the 1920s hardly ever fail to mention the musicians (he asked Mary to be nice to Tailleferre when she came to London in

Marcelle Meyer

1920). Before long, Clive was seeing home the pretty young pianist favoured by Les Six, Marcelle Meyer, or taking afternoon strolls with the classical pianist Youra Guller. In October 1920, Clive witnessed the riot that broke out at the premiere of Milhaud's Second Symphony Suite (*Protée*) due to the objections of 'disgusting great fat musical bourgeois'.

There are few extant letters from Cocteau to Clive, but all are warmly affectionate, urging him to be in touch as soon as he arrives in Paris, lamenting that he lives so far away. In 1924, Clive made sure to leave for Paris in time for the resumption of Les Six's Saturday dining club, to which Cocteau had invited him. Although André Breton's fierce hostility towards him can give the impression that Cocteau was not as daring as the Surrealists, the classicism which drew Clive to Cocteau – as it did to Derain – was mixed with a far more radical appreciation of the avant-garde than Clive possessed. As Clive noted, Cocteau really was a '*metteur en scène* of the modern movement'. Clive's appreciation of *Les Mariés de la Tour Eiffel* (1921) and of Cocteau's reimaginings of Antigone and Orpheus is genuine, but he was drawn to Cocteau as a figure who was, as he was himself, at home in the upper reaches of high society as well as in the crowded bistros of Montparnasse.

The title of Cocteau's 1926 book *Le rappel à l'ordre* (call back, or return, to order) gave its name to the mood of postwar French culture. At the heart of the collection of essays is 'Le secret professionnel', which accounted for the multiple 'isms' that defined the modernist moment and argued for the importance of a 'living classicism' exemplified by Satie in music, Picasso in painting and Raymond Radiguet in fiction. Given the 'marked preference for Antique, classical, and Latin evocations' by the end of the war, it is no wonder that Clive was thinking again of writing a book about civilisation by the time he returned to London in December 1919. Derain was among the leaders of the *rappel à l'ordre* in French painting. His diverse group of friends effectively became Clive's own circle in Paris, the regulars with whom he would spend nights drinking and debating. Vanessa and Duncan found Clive just woken up at ten one morning at his hotel: 'He had been up till 5 with Ansermet, Derain, and a lot of others, drinking and talking,' Vanessa told Roger. 'He does so nearly every night I think and seems none the worse for it.'

Such a life was alien to Vanessa, who could not understand how the artists leading it could find the time to paint, 'but they evidently do. I suppose it's very amusing . . . they never mention painting, which makes it less interesting than it might be from one's own point of view.' Derain's early experiences with the Symbolists of the Closerie des Lilas had led him to a lifelong interest in mysticism and religious doctrine, and his wide-ranging knowledge of philosophy and history was very congenial to Clive's scholarly temperament. Apollinaire had in 1916 drawn attention to the religious grandeur of Derain's paintings and, even before the war, Derain was moving towards a 'synthesis of tradition with modernity', away from Cubism. In a perverse sense, one might say that Derain was literally *avant*-garde because the *traditionisme* of his prewar work became a celebrated value after the war had 'reversed the respective values of the individual and the group'.

During the war, in which he served with resignation rather than patriotic ardour, Derain wrote to his old friend Vlaminck that the 'inexplicable', that which 'remains on the edge of our understanding', should be the painter's preoccupation, rather than 'mechanics'. When he resumed landscape painting after the war – one of several painters who exemplified the renewed importance of Corot – he became influential through what Clive termed his 'unconscious nationalism', which was to say that his expressive values fitted the spirit of the times.

Whatever his changing opinions of Derain's painting over the years, Clive maintained an intellectual sympathy with his friend, who, in an unpublished manuscript, wrote that art is a manifestation of the 'universal spirit' described in Plato's *Timaeus*. In *Art*, Clive acknowledged that 'significant form' was only a convenient term for something ineffable; he would not quarrel with anyone who preferred instead to describe 'significant relations of form' as 'rhythm'. For Derain, too, 'rhythm is the essence of the artist's work'. Reviewing an exhibition of contemporary French painting at the New Art Salon in 1920, Clive wrote that Derain 'amazes me more and more'. Neither the greatest of painters, nor with Picasso's deeper influence on European art, Derain seemed to Clive to be a reluctant 'chef d'école' who could provide a possible path for younger painters to whom Cubism had never appealed. What attracted Clive most to Derain's work immediately after the war was 'what is to-day most vital and valid in France – a passionate love of the great tradition, a longing for order and the will to win it'.

Clive knew that he could rely on seeing Derain at the Deux Magots, but Picasso had largely withdrawn from that scene. A few weeks after the lavish opening night party for the ballet *Pulcinella* (1920), for which Picasso designed the sets and drop-curtain (and for which Duncan and Vanessa came to Paris), rumours reached Clive in London that Picasso was annoyed he had not come to say goodbye. Clive was always somewhat in awe of Picasso, and wrote deferentially to explain why he had not come:

> You know, Picasso, that seeing you is a real joy for me. Speaking in all sincerity, I would gladly make the trip from London to Paris in order

to spend a few hours with you. But I know how besieged you are by tiresome people, and I would hate to be one of them.

And then, perhaps this is something you don't think about – it is a tricky thing to go bother Picasso in the morning, or the afternoon, when he might be working. Because I believe you to be a great – a very great – artist . . . well . . . to visit a great artist in the daytime really means my supposing that an hour of my chitchat is worth an hour of his work. You just cannot imagine how this intimidates me.

Picasso's endless inventiveness, his ability to produce something startlingly new just as everyone had got used to his last innovation, is a theme Clive returns to again and again in correspondence and in his relatively few articles on the artist. As he wrote in *Vogue*, 'Give him two matches and a marble and he will make a Picasso of them.' When Oliver Brown, the director of the Leicester Galleries, arranged for a Picasso exhibition at the beginning of 1921, Clive hurriedly revised for the catalogue a piece he had already published in the *Athenaeum* and the *New Republic* and had also recycled for *Arts and Decoration* (and would again for *Since Cézanne*).

'Matisse and Picasso' sets up the rival painters as emblems of the modern, a pairing as familiar as Fortnum and Mason, Shelley and Keats (or, in the catalogue version, Lenin and Trotsky). It is a tame piece that seems uncertain which aspect of Picasso's boiling creativity to emphasise, settling eventually for hailing him as the most influential painter in Europe. According to Roger, Picasso was 'rather furious' at Clive's reference to Ingres in connection with his work but, if true, this was disingenuous of Picasso. His wartime naturalism had been a 'very early foreshadowing of what was to happen in Paris postwar' when Ingres experienced a widespread revival. Clive's essay was one of the earliest instances of what became the critical commonplace that Picasso's 'restless spirit' dominated his era. Oliver Brown had worried that the English would not be receptive to the cubist works popular among Picasso's French buyers, so Clive's essay emphasised the 'intellectual' aspects of Picasso's Cubism, providing a palatable image of him as the leader of 'a return to classical forms of representation'.

Clive published seven books in the 1920s and established a reputation in America as a provocative cultural commentator. Like many of his

English contemporaries, he began to write for American periodicals that paid well – *Vogue* (which frequently reprinted in America the articles he wrote for the English version), *Vanity Fair* and the *New Republic* – as well as for more specialised periodicals such as *Arts and Decoration*. *Vogue* and *Vanity Fair* were minting 'fashion, francophilia, and modernism into the coin of international sophistication', and, in his frequent contributions to these glossies, Clive became a reliable guide for American travellers to what they should see in London and in Paris, as well as suggesting what they should think about modernism.

In 1922, he summed up the course of his postwar reflections on the function of criticism, and on several individual artists, in *Since Cézanne*, a collection of articles most of which had appeared in the *Athenaeum* and the *New Republic*. *Since Cézanne* shows the influence on Clive's thinking of the Parisian milieu into which he had plunged as soon as possible after the Armistice, as well as aligning him to some extent, despite salient differences, with the effort engaged in by Eliot, Pound, I. A. Richards and others to treat an artwork as a self-contained aesthetic object to be judged apart from any knowledge of its author or history. As Clive wrote in *Art*, the 'unholy alliance' between expertise and officialdom meant that people 'need not know whether a picture by Hals is good; they need only know it is by Hals' for them to think that it is valuable. This was relevant to an auctioneer or a wealthy person wishing to acquire cultural cachet, but as far as Clive was concerned it was extraneous to aesthetic considerations.

Since Cézanne's lengthy preface stressed the internationalism of Paris as art's capital city, where painters from all over Europe flourished. Cézanne had put painters on the track of form and Picasso – the 'animator' as Clive's friend André Salmon dubbed him – had invented Cubism as a result. However, although he still placed Cézanne at the head of the movement now entering its mature phase, like many others in Paris in the years immediately following the war, Clive drew attention for his English and American readers to the overlooked genius of Seurat. He acknowledged that *Since Cézanne* would be obsolete within a decade, its opinions rejected just as he now rejected those of Camille Mauclair, whose little book on the Impressionists had prepared him for seeing the Caillebotte collection in 1903. One of the clearest themes to emerge from *Since Cézanne* is Clive's belief that a critic is a guide whose role is to 'point and gesticulate' at what he thinks people should see because they might thus be led to experience aesthetic emotions of their own. Mauclair was one of modernist art's chief conservative antagonists, who had described Cubism as a 'bizarre conception' in his 1918 *L'Avenir de France*, but he had served a purpose for Clive at a time when he needed to be pointed towards the Luxembourg.

A critic's opinion is useful preparation whenever we go to a concert or a gallery, Clive wrote, because we always go expecting to be moved in some way, to have an aesthetic experience. If absolute beauty existed, why would we need anyone else to help us discern it? A critic simply tells us what he likes and why and, as tastes change ('did we never despise what to-day we adore?'), the critic's job is not to identify masterpieces but to express his own preferences. Clive always, throughout his life, presented his tastes as those that any 'civilised' person should share, and he did so often without a shred of humility or doubt. On the other hand, he eschewed any illusion of objectivity. The essays collected in *Since Cézanne* sound the perennial notes of his writings on art – that the anecdotal or narrative is superfluous, that form is all that matters – but they also show that he had moved beyond the deliberate polemical purity of *Art*, written at a time when the post-Impressionists were widely derided in England as lunatics and charlatans.

In 'Art and Politics', Clive reiterated the Wildean position that 'to say that a work of art is aristocratic or democratic, moral or immoral, is to say something silly and irrelevant . . . if meant to be relevant to its value as art'. Only 'artistic qualities' are essential in judging works of art. Art's flourishing does not depend upon political liberty. In the Periclean golden age, for example, the liberty of some 25,000 Athenian citizens was 'supported by the compulsory labours of some four hundred thousand slaves'. Art can flourish under any system of government because the connection between art and civilisation is not essential: an 'uncivilized' Congolese fetish maker is not inferior to the 'civilized' Mozart, if it is aesthetic value with which we are concerned. The best preparation for a career as an art critic was to write about buildings, textiles or furniture, where only 'purely aesthetic emotions' could come into play because there could be no question of 'representation'.

One of the articles Clive reprinted in *Since Cézanne* was 'Wilcoxism', which had led to a stormy exchange of letters with Wyndham Lewis when it first appeared in March 1920 in the *New Republic* and the *Athenaeum*. In her autobiography, the popular American poet Ella Wheeler Wilcox had described several of her rather undistinguished friends as literary geniuses. Such 'Wilcoxism' Clive believed to be as absurd as the notion that an English painter could be favourably compared with a French contemporary. Clive pompously stated that 'at any given moment the best painter in England is unlikely to be better than a first-rate man in the French second-class'.

The occasion for 'Wilcoxism' was a well-received exhibition of 'The Nation's War Pictures' at the Royal Academy. Clive damned with faint praise Lewis's *Battery Shelled* for its 'admirable, though somewhat negative qualities'. In keeping with his criterion that art was only that which expressed something 'permanent and universal', he disparaged the war paintings because the artists had not expressed 'what they feel for something that has moved them as artists, but, rather, what they think about something that has horrified them as men'. In Paris, a painting by Lewis 'would neither merit nor obtain from the most generous critic more than a passing word of perfunctory encouragement'. When a critic described Lewis as 'more than a match' for Matisse and Derain, this struck Clive as an example of 'Wilcoxism'.

With this provocation, battle commenced. Lewis returned the *ad hominem* attack by writing that Clive was clearly in awe of Paris, and 'when you consider the five long years he has been exiled from France it is no wonder that he should give proof of an almost ecstatic contentment at being able at last to get there again'. Perhaps it had not occurred to Clive that if he wished to become the kind of art critic he professed to be, a '*permanent* residence' in Paris was essential. Virginia thought it would be beneath Clive's dignity to reply to 'mere vulgar personal abuse', but this was the tack Clive took in his rejoinder. Lewis had misunderstood him, he wrote; his target had not been the artist himself but the critic (R. H. Wilenski) who had compared Lewis to Leonardo, but now it seemed the disease of Wilcoxism had infected the painter too. Was Lewis perhaps angry 'because someone admires him less than he admires himself'? Vanessa told Clive that she was enjoying the fight and assured him that in Paris, from where she wrote, he was 'thought to demolish Lewis completely'. But others found Clive's performance intensely distasteful.

T. S. Eliot encouraged Lewis to write again because his first letter had given 'several people considerable pleasure'. Eliot must not have been aware that Clive had given his opinion of Lewis in other places, because he told Ottoline that he was horrified by Clive's *'glaring complete indifference'* to Lewis's work and wanted to know 'what works of Lewis he has seen on which to base these opinions'. Eliot thought Clive's opinion of Lewis was based 'on vulgar spite' but Ottoline had also heard from Gertler that he believed Clive would deliver a 'knock-out blow' to Lewis. That blow came in *Since Cézanne,* where Clive added to the conclusion of 'Wilcoxism' that 'in Paris there are perhaps five hundred men and women – drawn from the four quarters of the earth – all trying to do what Mr. Lewis tries to do, and doing it better'.

In a review of *Since Cézanne* for the *Daily Herald,* Lewis wrote that 'Wilcoxism' was a 'bluff' intended to distract readers from Clive's absurd elevation of 'the little Bloomsbury fancy man'. Clive's unembarassed booming of Duncan made it unnecessary for Lewis to use his name. 'The gush, the intimately personal note, of this advocate of a certain type of modern painting, is not likely to add to his dignity . . . or to be of use even to Mr Bell's friends,' Lewis continued. It is unlikely Clive cared much for 'dignity' of the sort Lewis meant.

In the *Saturday Review,* D. S. MacColl was more blunt: 'Mr. Bell is the Mrs. Wilcox of Parisian painting, and of a tiny affiliated home circle,' though he allowed that as a critic Clive was a useful signpost. Since Lewis's very public falling out with Roger over the Omega Workshops, the antipathy between him and Bloomsbury was widely known. In *The New Witness,* Bernadette Murphy made clear that 'Bloomsbury' was already shorthand that journalists could rely on without taking any trouble to make distinctions when she described 'Wilcoxism' as devoting to Lewis 'a whole chapter of nasty little clevernesses' that she supposed was intended to finally settle 'the question which vexes Bloomsbury from time to time' as to whether he was or was not an artist.

But even those who were put off by Clive's praise of the French at the expense of the English tended to agree that he was great fun to read, especially in a field that all too often consisted of the 'half-dead drearily writing about the wholly dead'. Clive would rarely if ever let pass an opportunity to poke fun at Wyndham Lewis.

Beneath Clive's rejoinder to Lewis's outraged letter about 'Wilcoxism' was one from the art writer Ernest H. R. Collings, who argued that the 'point of view which sees foreign art as French art only is as narrow as that which sees no foreign art at all'. Collings noted that a Gallery of Modern Foreign Art had been promised for the National Gallery at Millbank, 'but no healthy growth can be looked for there unless we have a body of knowledge and critical opinion concerning modern activity in sculpture and painting.'

From as early as 1910, the issue of where to house modern foreign paintings owned by the nation had been contentious and Clive often criticised the fumbling incompetence, as he saw it, of the directors of the National Gallery.[1] When Clive mentioned that a painting by Duncan was at the Tate (his *Bathers* had hung there temporarily), he added 'who ever thought of going there to look for a work of art?' Only in 1925 when the money provided by Samuel Courtauld 'transformed' its collection did Clive relent, noting in *Vogue* that the Tate could now boast a glorious collection of modern French paintings, including Seurat's 'amazing' *Baignade*, which was 'the most important example of one of the greatest and certainly the rarest of modern masters to be found in any public gallery'. Even so, in March 1926 he complained that the Courtauld Fund pictures had been stuffed by the Tate into a 'tank with no light, pending their removal to the new Duveen Galleries, and wondered 'whether it might not be possible to appoint to the advisory committee someone or other who cares seriously for modern painting'. By 1927 he could tell Mary that the Tate was 'now the finest public collection of modern painting in the world', and yet Clive maintained an antagonistic attitude towards English public cultural institutions that time did little to alter.

There were so many artists' groups and galleries springing up in the 1920s that some complained 'there was too much art in London' but Collings was correct to say that English knowledge of European art and theory was extremely limited. Until the opening of the St George's Gallery bookshop just before the Second World War, Anton Zwemmer's art bookshop on Charing Cross Road was the only major establishment where books and magazines from abroad could be

---

[1] On the tangled and woeful history of the National Gallery at Millbank's involvement with modern foreign art see Spalding, *Tate* 38–50. Although always popularly known as Tate, after the sugar magnate who funded it, the building at Millbank was in fact not officially so named until 1932.

purchased. During the war, Roger had stocked hard-to-obtain foreign periodicals at the Omega Workshops, doing his best, Clive thought, to 'keep the flag of civilisation flying', but despite valiant efforts to sustain it, Roger had been forced to close the business in June 1919 when it ran out of money. New institutions of modernism had, however, begun to flourish, including Frankie Birrell and Bunny Garnett's bookshop on Taviton Street in Bloomsbury. As modernist writers became savvy marketers of their work, exploiting new publishing networks, Clive used his journalistic flair and witty dogmatism to promote the particular kind of painting he most enjoyed, often enraging those who championed English painters less devoted to the influence of the school of Paris.

That Duncan had emerged in 1911 as the 'most promising young artist of the English Post-Impressionists' and become the 'best English painter alive', as Clive dubbed him on the occasion of his first solo show at the Paterson-Carfax Gallery in 1920, was a matter at least for argument, even though Clive was explicit about the narrow terms by which he defined what mattered in art. Clive would say that Duncan was 'in the tradition' as the descendant of Piero della Francesca and Gainsborough and, as chief among those young British artists who had been schooled by the French, he was 'of the movement'. Eddie Marsh was converted from the 'sheeplike, soulless conventionalism' of his acquisition of Old Masters by Duncan's *Parrot Tulips*, followed shortly by his purchase of Duncan's 'resplendent' *Dancers*, but many found distasteful Clive's condescension towards anyone who did not agree with his opinion that Duncan's paintings were the 'sort of masterpieces about which there can be no further dispute among sensitive and educated people'.

22. Wives and Lovers

Clive's Paris was not the famous locale of the *années folles* celebrated by so many American writers. Although his path often crossed with the expatriates who frequented the Bal Nègre or Bricktop's, Clive usually disdained them. Americans came from a barbarous and distant land good only for its provision of dollars in exchange for his feeding them a diet of the culture they at once lacked and craved – or so he thought immediately after the war. He also resisted Thomas Wade Earp's efforts to get him to join Nancy Cunard and her 'cinema world'. The 'Corrupt Coterie' that gathered at the Eiffel Tower restaurant on Percy Street in London now frequented all the trendiest nightspots of Paris, and before long Clive's references to the 'riff-raff of the Eiffel Tower' had got back to them.[1] Clive associated Nancy and her crowd with Jack Hutchinson, suspecting him of being behind Earp's importunings about dining with them. 'Are you really coming to Paris to spend your time in that galère?' he wrote scornfully to Mary. Walking one evening after dinner with Max Jacob, Stravinsky, Ansermet, Diaghilev, Picabia and others, Clive ran into Monty Shearman, Earp, Marie Beerbohm and Cunard, who told him that Iris Tree, Curtis Moffat and Wyndham Lewis were soon to join them, as well as Jack and Mary. Knowing this, it seemed to Clive

[1]With Iris Tree, Cunard formed the 'Corrupt Coterie' whose usual members included Alvaro 'Chile' Guevara, Robert Nichols, Evan Morgan, Osbert and Sacheverell Sitwell, Edward 'Bimbo' Wyndham Tennant, and Earp; they were occasionally joined by Augustus John and Wyndham Lewis. Other friends of Cunard's who frequented the Eiffel Tower included Nina Hamnett, Marjorie Craigie, Jacob Epstein, Robert McAlmon, Curtis Moffat, Marie Beerbohm, Frank Dobson and Lytton (Gordon 27–28).

'slightly less of a privilege' to go to bed with a woman who kept such company.

Clive's affair with Mary would slowly drag itself to a bitter end by 1927, the years punctuated and followed by several liaisons with much younger women, all of which were picked apart in Vanessa and Virginia's letters. In the same period, Julian and Quentin grew from children who delighted in being taken by their father to the zoo or to tea and cakes in the Palm Court at Buzzard's, into young men who were embarrassed by his vanity and compulsive flirting. By the time Julian went up to King's College, Cambridge, in 1927, he had begun to distance himself firmly from Clive, a rift that would widen considerably in the context of 1930s politics.

Mary found it difficult when in Paris to balance her husband and her lover. Towards the end of 1920, Clive complained to Mary that their relations were becoming impossible because she spent her time 'almost entirely amongst the people who detest me most'. He felt that Jack had won by driving a wedge between them. At New Year came a *coup de foudre*. All was over between Mary and Clive, he told Vanessa, because he had fallen hopelessly in love with Juana de Gandarillas, the wealthy, estranged wife of an attaché at the Chilean Embassy in London, Tony Gandarillas (nephew of Picasso's great patron, Eugenia Errazuriz). He begged Vanessa to keep his secret from Maynard and Duncan. Secrecy in Bloomsbury was an extremely rare commodity, however, and soon Lytton told his brother James the latest gossip, that 'Clive has given up Mary and fallen madly in love with Madame Gandarillas, a female dago of the dark and passionate type – immensely rich and with the finest underclothes in Europe.' Clive invited Mary to dinner to explain that he was 'miserably in love' with someone she had probably seen but would hardly know.

Back in London, Clive's parties were soon 'all Spanish, all prostitutes, all musicians, all talking French'. The 'Fashion and Feminine Interests' column of the *Globe* found Clive at 'An Artistic Salon in Chelsea' given at the studio of the recently nominated Cervantes Reader of the University of London. But by May the great conflagration had burned itself out. Clive and Mary continued to be unhappy and Clive still occasionally took Juana to dinner or to the theatre but saw her less and less. Mary was 'obviously very much upset' to see Juana in Paris at the private view for a Picasso exhibition at Paul Rosenberg's held to coincide with Diaghilev's *Cuadro flamenco*, but Clive by then had told Vanessa

THE SISTER OF THE CHILIAN MINISTER.

THE SEÑORA DE GANDARILLAS

Juana de Gandarillas in Tatler, *3 August 1921*

that his affair with Juana was 'on its last legs'. Virginia had already noted that Juana's stupidity was only redeemed by her extraordinary beauty, and Vanessa told Roger that Juana could not 'combine' with Clive's Paris friends. No one took very seriously Clive's wild plan to tour Europe with Juana in her expensive motor car. He admitted that he knew he would soon run out of topics of conversation with her and was committed to his 'pathetic life of the intellect'.

Clive and Mary's affair struggled on and, when he took his usual trip to Paris in the autumn of 1922, she inscribed a copy of Proust's *Pastiches et Mélanges* for him to take on the journey: 'Reading this book I was put in mind of our favourites and of our conversations. I looked at my bookshelves and saw all the volumes you had given me, thought of all the hours you had made delightful. You are going away. I shall miss you. What can I give you? A ribbon? A glove? No. These would make you only remember me. Take this; if you are entertained, know that you have charmed; if you think of me, know that you are loved.' The relationship was faltering, nevertheless, because Mary had for some time shown signs of being involved with someone else. Vanessa suspected it might be Earp, but the person distracting Mary from Clive was in fact Maria Huxley, the Belgian refugee taken in by the Morrells during the war, whom Aldous had married in 1919.

On her thirtieth birthday, in 1928, Maria wrote to Mary to ask if she remembered *her* thirtieth birthday and 'that first kiss'. Mary turned thirty in 1919, so 'if these words are taken at face value,' Huxley's biographer remarks, 'the sexual relationship between Mary and Maria would have begun at around the same time she and Aldous were beginning their affair.' Clive was aware of Mary's involvement with Maria because she told him about it: 'And so you have had your way with your little tart, as I said you would: and do you know, Madame, you have written an extremely pretty account of it? Her little struggles and resistance I dare say made it all the more exciting.'

He asked for more details of Mary's escapade with the 'little Belgian goose': 'Did she make love to you as nicely as you made love to her? How many times? How long?' In 1926, Clive teased Mary about Aldous in a way that suggests he was unaware that Mary was involved sexually with both Huxleys, but a year earlier, Maria had written to Mary, 'Aldous has just come into my bed & he smelt so strongly of you still that it made one giddy.' When the Huxleys left for the long trip to India, South-East Asia and the United States that is chronicled in *Jesting Pilate* (1926), both Maria and Aldous sent passionate farewell missives to Mary and seem to have 'existed in a permanent state of sexual desire' for her while they were away.

Before the war, Molly MacCarthy tried to organise a Novel Club, hoping it would be conducive to her and Desmond's writing, but it petered out. In 1920, she began the Memoir Club, whose members were enjoined to present autobiographical papers of complete honesty. Clive read his memoir about his sexual initiation with Annie Raven-Hill to the Club in 1921. As 'Bloomsbury' came to refer to an ever-expanding cast of characters, the Memoir Club, which met for the first time in March 1920, overlapped to a large extent with those people Virginia termed 'Old Bloomsbury' in a paper of that title she read to the Club in 1928. After the war, the networks around those friends who had begun to gather in 1904 for Thoby Stephen's Thursday 'At Homes' continued to develop around Cambridge Apostles, the *Nation & Athenaeum* (the latter absorbed by the former in 1921), the squares and streets of Bloomsbury, the Hogarth Press, Charleston and, later, southern France, augmented by younger generations with a complicated spectrum of attitudes towards their elders.

Of all the friends Virginia grouped as 'Old Bloomsbury', none was as at home in the beau monde as Clive. After the war, he was a sought-after guest at the salons of London hostesses such as Sybil Colefax and Christabel Aberconway (a 'little lump of passion' with whom he had a brief affair). His eighteenth-century mannerisms flattered ladies of fashion like Lesley Jowitt, wife of the Liberal MP William Jowitt, the vestibule of whose Mayfair home contained a mosaic by Boris Anrep depicting her using the telephone in bed, mixing a cocktail and singing at a nightclub. Clive had addressed one of the poems in *Ad Familiares* to Lesley, whom he had met at Wittering through the Hutchinsons in 1915. Virginia quipped to Jacques Raverat that Clive's 'bon mots are quoted by lovely but incredibly silly ladies. Really they give parties to meet Clive Bell.' The Baroness Sackville, who had read *Art*, invited Clive to lunch in 1921 because John Singer Sargent's great friend Mary Hunter wished to meet him. The Duke and Duchess of Rutland would also be there, and perhaps her daughter, Vita, whose husband had just published a biography of Paul Verlaine.

Friendship blossomed when Vita Sackville-West and her husband, Harold Nicolson, invited Clive to stay at Long Barn, their house in Sevenoaks Weald, in 1922. Vita asked if Clive would let his sister-in-law know how much she had been thrilled by *Jacob's Room* and Clive lost no time in arranging a dinner party at Gordon Square to introduce her to Virginia. Clive admired Vita's grand lineage and style, finding also that he and Harold had much in common, such as a fascination with the life of Byron. Reviewing Harold's account of Byron's last year, Clive praised him as a brilliant pupil of the new school of biography brought about by Lytton's *Eminent Victorians*. When Harold was posted to Tehran in 1925, Clive wrote to him with gossip from London or from weekends at Sherfield Court, the country estate of Gerald and Dorothy Wellesley where he and Vita often were invited, along with Raymond Mortimer, the young critic with whom Harold had started an affair in 1924 that would lead to a lifelong friendship. Clive and Harold moved effortlessly in their correspondence among Greek, Latin and French, often sharing a tone of amused detachment from what was going on around them.

Behind Clive's affected ennui, though, lay a genuine dissatisfaction with the turn his life had taken. His weakness for the comforts and blandishments of the titled and wealthy people who liked to gather at their table the leading lights of the cultural and artistic world sometimes conflicted with Clive's need to achieve something in his work which he knew would demand a discipline he found elusive. Virginia told Raymond Mortimer that Clive's air of contentment was partly a pose, a compensation for having failed to write the 'great book' of which he imagined himself capable. In a letter to Harold from Paris, Clive alluded to his dissatisfaction with the high society life he led in London, explaining that he 'fitted better' among French intellectuals, whereas in England he was accepted only among his Bloomsbury friends or by the great hostesses like Sybil Colefax.

A perennial paradox of Clive's life was that he felt at once completely at home in Paris, but always essentially English. Unlike the Irish O'Conor or Canadian Morrice, Clive could never take the step he so often talked about in the 1920s of leaving England for good. He may have believed that being English was the least significant thing about him, 'yet were the devil to come by night and steal all that is characteristically English about me he would leave an oddly mutilated wreck'.

His appetites led Clive to swell after the war: buttons burst, rolls of fat protruded from his collar and, although he vowed to give up bread and butter, 'He says that life grows steadily more and more enchanting the fatter one gets.' When Clive gave a farewell dinner for Middleton Murry, who was leaving for France to make amends to Katherine Mansfield for his infidelity with Elizabeth Bibesco, Lytton 'whispered his horror and repulsion' to Leonard and Virginia in the hallway: '*Never* would he dine there again.' Lytton could not stand the atmosphere Clive created with his shouting bonhomie, but Virginia retained her affection for her brother-in-law, feeling often torn between the two of them. Sometimes she felt relief when Lytton left a party, the disapproval that emanated from him causing her to rein in her 'folly'. What she appreciated most in Clive was that, 'He says outright what I spend my life in concealing.' She thought Clive might outlast them all and be remembered fifty years after his death. His boundless enthusiasm and openness to every experience charmed her always, drawing her to him despite her clear-eyed awareness of his many failings and the irritation his constant praise of Mary caused both her and Leonard. She understood that 'perhaps one doesn't like the father of one's children to dissolve into pure lust & gluttony & pleasure & vainglory', yet whenever she saw him, she greedily absorbed all Clive had to tell her of the beau monde and of the younger generation's escapades. Try as she might to protect her time while writing *Jacob's Room*, Clive insisted on visiting and they talked for six hours: 'Off we go – C. & I – upon our relish for it. He enjoys *everything* – even the old hag in the doorway. There is no truth about life, he says, except what we feel. It is good if you enjoy it, & so forth.'

Like Virginia, Clive was often caught between his weakness for stimulation and his need for quiet in which to read and write. He might tell Mary that he had 'tired of the civilised world', and many times express the wish to retreat from his life of cafés and parties in Paris and London, but, unlike Virginia, Clive's spirit was most unwilling to give up the pleasures of the flesh.

Those pleasures informed Clive's perceptive essay about Virginia in the American periodical *The Dial*. He had explained to Mary that 'these old unfucked' – he had in mind women like the painter Ethel Sands – unnerved him: 'With all their culture they know nothing and so they understand nothing. And they haven't got Virginia's intelligence to give them another sort of reality . . . I can't help believing that a woman who has never really known lust, who has never felt a passionate desire to provoke it, is somehow out of place in this world of our sorrows.' A love scene in a novel by Virginia 'never put anyone in the mood for a love-affair', he wrote in *The Dial*. Even though she 'misses not one subtle, betraying gesture' between Jacob and Florinda, 'we have not been given a love scene as we understand it' because 'it was not the love affair, but the effect of the love affair, which really interested' her.

Virginia was delighted with the essay (which is a penetrating analysis of her early fiction), but teased him about her supposed lack of physical passion: 'I shall never explain to you, in words, exactly how, and for what reason, not all of them purely literary or even wholly vain, I like you to like what your affectionate sister in law writes; but perhaps as I approach a subject on which you say I have *no* knowledge, I had better be silent. Ha! ha!'

Clive took Virginia's love affair with Vita as an opportunity to indulge once more his peculiarly refracted jealousy of his sister-in-law. Just before Christmas 1925, Virginia wrote a letter '*Dictated by Clive*' to her lover from Charleston: 'It is the universal wish of the house that you should *come*'; she and Clive 'walk through the clods together talking, first one and then another, of Vita Vita Vita as the new moon rises and the lambs huddle on the downs'. At Sherfield Court one New Year's Eve, Clive suddenly asked Vita in front of everyone whether she had slept with Virginia (Vita assured Harold that her immediate firm denial had kept her secret safe). On another occasion, Vita and Clive ganged up on Virginia to tease her about a new hat that, Vita let slip, had been chosen for her by *Vogue*'s editor, Dorothy Todd (Virginia was excruciatingly self-conscious about clothes): 'Clive suddenly said, or bawled rather, what an astonishing hat you're wearing! Then he asked where I got it. I pretended a mystery, tried to change the talk, was not allowed, & they pulled me down between them, like a hare; I never felt more humiliated.'

Clive insisted that he had fallen out of love for good with Virginia in 1911 but still joked about how he would pull up her petticoats were it not for the watchful presence of Leonard. Their early intimacy gave their relations an intensity that magnified all the emotions each provoked in the other. Virginia tried to explain to Jacques Raverat how attractive she found Clive, despite her laughing behind his back or snarling to his face: 'I often wish I had married a foxhunter. It is partly the desire to share in life somehow, which is denied to us writers.' He remained 'enough of my old friend, & enough of my old lover, to make the afternoons hum'. Her suspicion that his visits to Monk's House were 'a hair shirt' from which he fled to the *luxe et volupté* Mary provided was well founded. When she and Leonard were put out that Lytton had not stayed with them on a visit to Sussex, they ascribed it to a poor review in the *Nation* of his play *A Son of Heaven*. Clive thought the more likely reason was that there was 'no bath at Monk's House, no wine, and not very nice food'. For the sybaritic Clive, the Woolfs' house was aptly named.

Leonard might not have been happy to give Clive's poem 'To V. S. with a Book' a wider audience, yet it was reprinted when the Hogarth Press published Clive's *vers de société*, as *Vanity Fair* described his *Poems* of 1921.

At the same time, the Woolfs' fledgling press was also considering work by Eliot and Roger's translations of Mallarmé, both of which were a far cry from 'To Lopokova Dancing' or 'To Gerald Shove'. *Poems* reprinted the thirteen poems that comprised *Ad Familiares* and added four new ones. The Hogarth order book shows healthy sales to its subscribers, as well as to many bookshops, including New York's Sunwise Turn and Shakespeare & Co. in Paris, but *Poems* seems to have received no reviews. Clive's reputation, nevertheless, made the publication a sound business decision, netting him a profit of just over £2 by March 1923, with £5 17s 5d for the Press.

Leonard and Virginia also published Clive's *Legend of Monte Della Sibilla* (1923), described by Tony Bradshaw as 'one of the most beautiful books' the Hogarth Press published. Designed and illustrated by Duncan and Vanessa, *The Legend* is based on Antoine de la Sale's account of his voyage to the Monts de Sibylle in 1420, entitled *Le Paradis de la Reine Sibylle*. As Clive explained in one of the rhyming footnotes he supplied for the text of his poem, he also consulted Antoine's textbook for a young prince: 'From this strange book well-named "*La Salade*"/I draw the matter of my ballad'. Dedicated to 'Polly Flinders', *The Legend* is witty, jocular and written in a fluent vernacular. Among those who had contributed to *Euphrosyne* in 1905, only Clive continued throughout his life to write poetry. Undistinguished it may have been, but the practice suited his occasionally Byronic self-image.

Early in 1920, Vanessa rented the upper floor of 50 Gordon Square from Adrian, but two years later moved back to no. 46 when Clive took over the rooms at no. 50. She would move to no. 37 in 1925. Once the lease on Charleston was secure, by the early 1920s, Vanessa set about making the house more habitable and used it for weekends and summer holidays until the outbreak of the Second World War when she made it her permanent home with Duncan and Clive. Maynard had retreated to Charleston after his resignation from the treaty negotiations in Paris to write *Economic Consequences of the Peace* and he contributed substantially to the upkeep of the household, continuing the Bloomsbury tradition of shared domestic arrangements. A letter from Vanessa to Clive in November 1921 details the way Charleston's expenses, which came to £235 for the year, were arranged – Clive paying for the boys and Vanessa for Angelica and Nellie Brittain, her nurse. Duncan paid £42 10s and Maynard £60. Of the balance, Clive contributed £30 and Vanessa £70. 'Perhaps its an expensive way of having a summer holiday,' wrote Vanessa, 'but I think if we had to take rooms or a house that would hold us all & visitors it would come to quite as much & not be nearly as nice.'

Clive seemed to Bunny a 'much nicer person' at Charleston, away from Mary, who received almost universal blame for luring Clive into the superficial beau monde. This was quite unfair, as would be plain in the 1930s when Clive found his own way to the palazzos of Venice and their rich American owners. Life at Charleston seemed the 'most peaceful domestic existence conceivable', Roger told Helen Anrep, who had left her husband, Boris, for Roger, 'there's only Clive, Vanessa and the children. It might be held up as a model of what family life ought to be.'

Having lovers stay at Charleston upset the apparent idyll. Maynard's deepening feelings for Lydia Lopokova threatened the balance of relations at Charleston and, as had occurred during the war, tensions exacerbated by Clive had to be soothed by Vanessa. The appearance of propriety demanded that Vanessa be at Charleston if Lydia were to stay while Maynard was there, and Vanessa was not sure how to integrate the ballerina into their intimate society. Matters came to a head in the summer of 1922 when Clive brought up the old wounds he had suffered when he wanted Mary to visit. Vanessa, Duncan, Maynard and Lydia all shared meals at no. 46, but the idea of Lydia moving in permanently was too much for Clive, who had retained the right to his two attic rooms but was about to move to 50 Gordon Square. Maynard wanted Lydia to come and go as she pleased and told Vanessa that it would 'be a great relief to get rid of Mary . . . We all want to have and not to have husbands and wives.' After Maynard married Lydia in 1925 and bought the nearby Tilton farmhouse, Vanessa worried continually that they would drop in at Charleston unannounced, an anxiety she alleviated by ceasing to think about them. 'And so they have ceased to exist,' Clive marvelled. 'We are all afraid that Vanessa may take it into her head to practise the same trick on us, and that we shall wake up one fine morning to find ourselves nonentities.' Vanessa's reputation for fiercely repelling invaders became legendary at Charleston.

Clive with Angelica at Cassis, ca. 1927

As it was for Vanessa, Charleston was a treasured retreat for Clive where monotony was the most pleasant aspect of life. Vanessa worked on *Clive Bell and Family* for much of 1921 (now at the New Walk Museum and Gallery, Leicester). It is an awkwardly composed painting that depicts

Clive with a large book in his lap, but gazing into the distance on his right; Julian is seated on the arm of his chair, holding a rifle and looking mournful; Quentin sits on the ground at Clive's feet, his legs tucked under him; Angelica stands between Clive's knees, staring apparently at nothing. To the outside world, and even to many of their friends, Clive and Vanessa were the parents of three children. In 1923, they spent their first Christmas together at Charleston since Angelica's birth five years earlier. Duncan was with his own family and, to all intents and purposes, Vanessa's painting of Clive as paterfamilias might have been a true representation of their circumstances, as she wryly noted in a letter to Margery Snowden: 'Here we are spending a very domestic Christmas. Really I think I shall advertise it "Mr. & Mrs. Clive Bell & family at home at Charleston. Christmas 1923. No one else admitted".'

When they were at Charleston, Clive, Vanessa, Duncan and the children laughed all day, played games, wrote letters, painted and read, gardened, went for long walks over the downs and drew close in the ease of their shared histories. Clive carried on a Stephen family tradition with his children of going out at night to catch moths. Their father 'carries on with them in wonderful style', Vanessa told Virginia. 'They listen to his stories and roar with laughter.' During the war, Vanessa and Duncan had begun to decorate furniture, fittings and surfaces throughout the house, creating a vibrant domestic aesthetic that was reflected in the many commissions they received from friends for interior design. In 1920, sixteen-year-old Grace Germany came to work for Vanessa as housemaid, providing the household with a hitherto unknown stability of care that would endure for the next fifty years, and earn her the sobriquet 'the Angel of Charleston'.

'My charms are beneath the horizon,' Virginia mused, and Vanessa's rose 'resplendent like the harvest moon'. Or so she assumed when Clive dwelled 'rapturously' on how beautiful Vanessa had looked at a party. The sisters' rivalry – Clive once referred to them as Goneril and Regan – rarely lessened, but both cherished their relationship with Clive, exasperating though he often was. When Angelica was born, Clive had not hesitated to assume the paternal role that safeguarded Vanessa's reputation, where he might so easily have taken the opportunity to leave the marriage.[2] Vanessa made her feelings about her marriage clear

[2]A point made to me by Vanessa's granddaughter Henrietta Garnett [conversation 16 July 2015].

in an angry letter to her cousin Madge Vaughan who balked at renting Charleston for a family holiday because of Vanessa's suspect living arrangements:

> What reason is there to think that I do not tell Clive everything? It is perhaps because we neither of us think much of the world's will or opinion, or that a 'conventional home' is necessarily a happy or good one, that my married life has not been full of restraints but, on the contrary, full of ease, freedom and complete confidence.

The Bells' lives were arranged to allow each a maximum of freedom in work and love, a shield against the moral codes of the time and a satisfying involvement with their children (all of which depended to a great extent upon the reliable discretion of their household servants). Clive kept Vanessa informed of Quentin and Julian's exploits when they stayed with him while she and Duncan went with Maynard to Italy in 1920. The boys enjoyed playing with their cousins Peggy and Michael, Cory's children, whose mother, Violet, took them to the zoo. Cory and Clive bought tea at Buszard's for them all to eat around the table at 46 Gordon Square. One day, a policeman knocked on the door to inform Clive that neighbours had complained the boys were dropping water bombs on passers-by.

In October 1921, Vanessa rented the Vildracs' villa, La Maison Blanche, in St Tropez, setting her on the path that would lead ultimately to her ten-year lease of La Bergère in Cassis in 1928. She regretted that Clive had missed witnessing eleven-year-old Quentin's first sight of Paris on their journey south but wrote happily of finding so many painter friends nearby, including Roger, who had for some time encouraged her to visit the area. The children took lessons with a former nun, 'La Bouvet', who assured Vanessa that she would be willing to teach them even if Vanessa did not have a husband: Vanessa encouraged Clive to write to his sons so that she could produce evidence that in fact they did have a father.

The Vildracs were due back in early January, and the boys were to be sent to stay with Clive while Vanessa and Duncan made a quick trip to Paris, but Vanessa wondered if Clive being responsible for the children might afford her a longer stay in France so that she could paint without interruption. He had been pondering an offer of $2,000 to go to America for two months as an art critic, but having decided that the fee would be swallowed up by his expenses, he told Vanessa he had set aside a week 'without one lady' to spend with the boys. He sent Angelica to Seend (with servants Blanche and Nellie), where his mother reported that she was happily playing with Lorna's children. Angelica would have gone earlier, but despite having 'five motors and two chauffeurs' the Bells could not collect her from the station until they were ready. Cleeve House continued to amaze and appal Vanessa.

23. Liberty

In a thinly veiled and almost unique passage of autobiography in one of the articles Clive reprinted in *Since Cézanne*, he explained why someone like him might choose the path he had followed:

> Any English boy born with fine sensibility, a peculiar feeling for art, or an absolutely first-rate intelligence finds himself, from the outset, at loggerheads with the world in which he is to live. For him there can be no question of accepting those conventions which express what is meanest in an unsympathetic society . . . The hearty conventions of family life . . . arouse in him nothing but a longing for escape . . . all his finer feelings will be constantly outraged; and he will live, a truculent, shame-faced misfit, with *John Bull* under his nose and *Punch* round the corner, till, at some public school, a course of compulsory games and the Arnold tradition either breaks his spirit or makes him a rebel for life.

Clive's aesthetic ideas and Francophilia appealed to the generation that would find its voice in the plays of Noël Coward and the novels of Evelyn Waugh. At Eton in the early 1920s, Harold Acton preached his own brand of aestheticism and, although for him, Brian Howard, Cyril Connolly and others, 'Bloomsbury' was associated with Roger's somewhat stringent, uplifting notions about modern art, they also recognised that they were allies against 'English obtuseness'. Acton's 'prejudice in favour of things French' resonated with the 'almost idolatrous francophilia', as Clive's granddaughter describes it, of those who sought a Bohemian experience in Paris after the war. For Acton,

Clive was the 'prophet' who made Bloomsbury into an extension of Montparnasse, writing about art 'in a language that was nearer French than English'.

The rebellious young men born in the first decade of the twentieth century who met at Oxford in the 1920s have been likened by Martin Green to the 1890s dandies epitomised by Oscar Wilde. The Oxford aesthetes staged 'another episode in a long serial conflict, which itself has no clear-cut beginning or end'. For Connolly, artists like André Gide, Jean Cocteau, Marcel Proust and Sergei Diaghilev avenged Wilde's demise 'on the bourgeoisie which had humiliated him'. In such sentiments, those who would be characterised in 1920s gossip columns as 'Bright Young People' certainly had attitudes in common with Clive, Roger, Lytton and others associated with Bloomsbury, for whom Wilde was a touchstone for the values of personal and sexual freedom they perceived as having been betrayed by the generation responsible for the war. When Lytton found at Charleston a copy of the '(almost) complete account of Oscar's trials' – probably *Oscar Wilde: Three Times Tried*, privately printed in Paris in a limited edition (c. 1915) – he remarked to Carrington that the 'history of English culture might have been quite different' had Wilde not been convicted.

Clive's credentials as an aesthete in the Wildean manner were embellished by 'The Creed of an Aesthete' in 1922, where he described a typical day, which might include reading 'the penultimate volume of Proust' after lunch, dining with a charming companion before attending the ballet, where Lopokova would dance, then going on to a 'gay supper' where Arthur Rubinstein would play the piano. After such pleasures, he would saunter up Piccadilly at dawn as the carts rumbled by on their way to the Covent Garden market. 'And tomorrow we die? So be it.' As antithesis to his creed, Clive mocked Bernard Shaw's play *Back to Methusaleh* in which the 'She-Ancient' disparages art as 'toys and dolls' and suggests that the finest things in life are worthless unless their source is divine. Clive had taken a friendly dig at Shaw in a *New Republic* forum on 'The Critic's Role' where he reiterated his position that the function of criticism was to guide and indicate rather than to instruct. 'Divine certitude,' he added breezily, should be left to 'superior beings – magistrates, for instance, and curates, and fathers of large families, and Mr Bernard Shaw.' In 'The Creed of an Aesthete', Clive returned to his long-held view that means were of no consequence to aesthetic ends; of paramount importance was to 'appreciate the beauty, the romance, the fun of life' in the moment.

Clive was 'a fathead and a voluptuary', Shaw spluttered. Tobacco and alcohol were dulling to the senses and heavenly bliss would be spent in cogitation, which was a form of passion, contrary to Clive's 'creed'. As for the idea that the moment is all, 'There is no such thing as the present,' Shaw went on, only the gateway through which we are endlessly passing from the past to the future. Between the appearance of Clive's article and of Shaw's rebuttal, Clive received a brief typed note from Shaw which concluded, 'You do not, it would appear, lead a very enviable aesthetic life; to me it seems dull.' Clive was greatly amused, telling everyone he met that poor old Shaw had evidently lost his wits. 'These vegetarians always go at the top,' he told Virginia. 'He needs Bullocks blood.' The poor old man might be ga-ga, but Clive had such affection for him that he wrote to say he was the last person in the world whom he wished to hurt. As further evidence of Shaw's senility, Clive told Lytton, the great man said he had never written to Clive in the first place. 'Clive was completely taken in by the Bernard Shaw letter!' Lytton informed Carrington, who had forged Shaw's signature on the letter as a hoax because she thought Clive had treated Shaw unfairly. Carrington 'shrieked with laughter' when she learned of the joke's success, but Virginia thought Lytton '*must* now tell Clive the truth. He is evidently making himself the laughing stock of London, and his accounts get wilder and wilder.'

His friends might laugh behind his back, but in America, where the exchange with Shaw had appeared in the *New Republic*, Clive was gaining an appreciative audience. *Vanity Fair* nominated him to its Hall of Fame that September 'because he had recently challenged George Bernard Shaw's great doctrine to the effect that all art should be utilitarian.' The same issue of the magazine included an article by Clive that drew an analogy between America's historic puritanism and the threat that lingered after the war to civil liberties in England, where the Defence of the Realm Act had used the conflict as an excuse to keep in place, and in many cases harden, antiquated restrictions. *Vanity Fair*'s subtitle for Clive's article – 'The Approaching Abolishment of the Pleasures of Sport, Art, Love, and the Table' – laid out the threat against which Clive would mount a defence in his pamphlet *On British Freedom*. When people in England did not understand art, he told his

American readers, they secretly detested it until it was old and desiccated, 'sterilized by being taken for granted'. Yet Clive also acknowledged that for the so-called 'normal man', a performance of *Le Sacre du Printemps* was probably as absurd as he would find watching animals perform unnatural tricks. The root of tolerance was the admission that 'we all dislike those pleasures that are not our own.'

In *On British Freedom*, Shaw reappeared in an entirely different role, this time as a victim of English puritanism. Clive returned to themes he had made central to his pacifist arguments in 1915, questioning the meaning of the 'freedom' and 'civilisation' for which the war had ostensibly been fought. Compared to France, especially in its immediate postwar reactionary moment of 'abominable political tyranny' (the coalition of right-wing parties comprising the *Bloc national*), England had a well-deserved reputation for liberty of *political* speech, Clive argued, but personal freedoms were curtailed by out-of-date laws that had persisted since the seventeenth and eighteenth centuries, like the Licensing Act (1737), the Gin Act (1751) and the censorship of plays. Clive compared Shaw's *Mrs Warren's Profession* to Maupassant's story 'Yvette' as an example of how restricted free expression was in England – Shaw had to make extensive cuts to his play to satisfy the Examiner of Plays in the Lord Chamberlain's office. An Englishman's home might well be his castle, but only if 'he does nothing within it that the district visitor could object to: outside, of course, all belongs to the police.'

From laws on blasphemy to gambling, drinking to sex education, England was a backwater in Europe. In *On British Freedom* Clive diagnosed as a form of tyranny the wish to impose one's will on others: 'This innate lust of dominion curses the world,' whether it took the form of telling people what they may not read or criminalising whom they may love. The modern tyrant was more likely to be found in the 'guise of a moderately successful shopkeeper' than in the historically conventional form. In a striking foreshadowing of Virginia Woolf's argument in *Three Guineas* (1938) that the personal is political, Clive saw 'all you who are incessantly interfering in our lives' as essentially the same, whether Tamerlane or Robespierre, or the 'man who hit his wife and tortured his child last Saturday'. Quentin Bell would point out thirty years after his father's death that the moral legislation against which Clive railed in *On British Freedom* did not start to be repealed until the 1960s.

24. The Lively Arts

In May 1922, Olga Picasso invited Clive to a grand dinner at the Majestic Hotel in Paris given by the wealthy patrons Violet and Sydney Schiff to celebrate the premiere of *Le Renard* by the Ballets Russes. Paris was Clive's ideal of a civilised, cosmopolitan capital where 'some people should be dancing while others are sleeping, some getting up while others are going to bed', and this now legendary dinner, stage-managed by Diaghilev, exemplified what he meant. From his seat next to Marcelle Meyer, Clive observed that James Joyce, who arrived at 2 a.m., was either too shy or too drunk to speak. Proust held court in the corner, where he had a kind word for everyone. Mingling with the dancers, musicians and painters were Coco Chanel, Daisy and Reginald Fellowes and José-Maria Sert. It 'must be confessed,' Clive told Vanessa, 'Lady Colefax was completely outdone.'

Clive already had a low opinion of Joyce and avoided him in Paris, although their paths did occasionally cross. At dinner with Darius Milhaud and François Bernouard one evening, Clive encountered Joyce with Robert McAlmon, who thrust a copy of his magazine *Contact* on him. Eliot had warned McAlmon that Clive's Paris was 'a useless one', and the writer and publisher made no more impression on Clive than most of the other Americans whose presence in Paris he usually tried to ignore. In the early 1920s, 'Paris was still yesterday', as Janet Flanner observed, and that was how Clive preferred it. His Francophilia was rooted in the classical strain evinced by the French painters he admired, not the newer world frequented by American expatriates or the Bohemia of the 'eiffel towerists'.

In America, Edmund Wilson compared Clive, Lytton, Maynard and Bertrand Russell to the eighteenth-century Encyclopaedists because they had 'concocted all the intellectual bombs which have recently been exploded in England'. Wilson singled out Clive as a 'sort of official interpreter to the Anglo-Saxon world of the great movement which has reached its maturity in France under the leadership of Matisse and Picasso'. *Vanity Fair*'s encomia were 'mere puffing', Clive told Mary: 'If this sort of thing were to get about we should be laughed at you know,' but he was pleased to have not only a larger audience for his views, but one that also paid well. While he gardened at Charleston, he considered the 'desperate cryings out for more light, for civilization, culture and a sense of what's what in their barbarous and abandoned country' emanating from America, whose young writers sent him their articles.

Symptomatic of America's barbarism in Clive's mind was one of its most popular exports, jazz. In 'Plus de Jazz', a *New Republic* article he revised for *Since Cézanne*, Clive defended a tradition of high culture against the perceived threat to its purity posed by jazz. Devoid of intellectual content, a product of mere physical passions, jazz offered the shock of novelty – a superficial pleasure that, Clive argued, could not be compared to the hard-won appreciation of 'classical concerts . . . getting Lycidas by heart . . . cricking one's neck in the Sistine Chapel.' As literary critic Michael North explains, it was 'jazzing' rather than jazz music itself to which Clive objected, the 'emphatic protest', as Clive put it, 'against the notion that one idea or emotion can be more important or significant than another'. Complicating Clive's position was that several artists he admired had already 'jazzed' traditional forms, including Stravinsky, Eliot, Cocteau and Blaise Cendrars. He had to acknowledge also that Joyce had successfully 'ragged the literary instrument' in his effort to 'break up the traditional sentence', but when Clive revised 'Plus de Jazz' for his book, he added a passage about Virginia to make clear how he thought such literary experimentation should be done. He doubted whether the gain in 'concentration' due to her 'tricks with traditional constructions' in 'An Unwritten Novel' or 'Monday or Tuesday' were worth 'the loss of those exquisite but old-fashioned qualities which make *The Mark on the Wall* a masterpiece of English prose'.

In *Art*, Clive's conservative defence of post-Impressionism had been to argue that rather than a radical break with the past, it was in fact a movement that rejoined the main European tradition from which art had deviated over centuries. Jazz was but a 'ripple' on the modernist wave and if some artists had absorbed its syncopation, its omissions of the expected, and its deformations of tradition in their work, that did not, Clive thought, detract from his point. In another passage added to the reprinted version, Clive exempted Picasso from any taint of the popular because he was utterly indifferent to what the public thought. Only inferior artists – the Futurists, for example – affront tradition deliberately to attract attention. If Picasso 'jazzed' tradition, it was just one more example of his 'prodigious inventiveness', and, in any case, Clive argued in both versions of 'Plus de Jazz', disliking a movement – Cubism, say – did not mean a critic did not recognise individual masterworks within it. He would be a fool not to acknowledge the accomplishments of a Metzinger, a Léger, a Braque or a Picasso.

Clive's articles in American periodicals in the early 1920s took a position in arguments about the aesthetic worth of popular culture that identified him with an old guard in many ways similar in its conservatism to those English critics of post-Impressionism before the war who had seen Clive as a wild-eyed rebel supporting a spurious novelty. When Clive met Gilbert Seldes in Paris in 1922, he remarked to Mary that the young American surprised him by seeming 'quite normally intelligent'. Seldes, who had just begun writing the essays he would gather in *The 7 Lively Arts*, was managing editor of *The Dial* and one of the most prominent of those making the case in America that the artefacts of popular culture demanded serious attention from critics. By 1923, Seldes and Clive had become good friends – ' "twin gilded bantams" ruling Frank Crowninshield's roost at *Vanity Fair*' – and before long Seldes had led Clive to revise his opinions about popular forms that in 1922 he saw as contaminating the purity of art.

When they met, both Seldes and Clive had articles about to appear in *Vanity Fair* which demonstrated their quite different positions in any debate about the worth of popular culture. In an American context, in particular, the argument that jazz signified 'a revolt of the passions against the intellect' carried the additional charge that it was a revolt of 'the dark race against the white'. Seldes' article in the November 1922 *Vanity Fair*, 'The Darktown Strutters on Broadway', was illustrated by a cartoon depicting the 'Horror and consternation of Mrs. Harriet Beecher Stowe, who having promoted the progress of the Negro by publishing

"Uncle Tom's Cabin", returns to earth and discovers that her protégé has become the international King of Jazz and is in full domination of the music, the dancing and the amusement of the world.' Seldes coyly reassured white theatre-goers that the pre-eminence of jazz did not mean that Americans had backed the wrong kind of 'negro'. To explain what he meant, Seldes alluded to Clive's article 'Negro Sculpture', just reprinted in *Since Cézanne*, which might have given American readers the idea that 'Europe had, in its effete way, stolen a march on' them, by treating African sculptures as 'only a little below those of the two great periods of artistic production'.

Roger and Clive had encountered African artefacts in Paul Guillaume's collection exhibited at the Chelsea Book Club in 1920. Clive's review, originally published in the *Athenaeum*, should be read in the context of debates about race in the period. As Peter Fryer has documented, racist discourse remained pervasive in the years following the First World War: the word 'nigger' was commonly used in the press, even continuing to appear as a colour category in advertisements for women's gloves and stockings several years after the end of the Second World War. But by the end of the 1920s, public comment on the word's offensiveness was increasing. A reader of Clive's 'Negro Sculpture' wrote to the *Athenaeum*, absolving him of 'any accusation of race-narrowness', but objecting to the use of 'nigger', a word that had come from the plantations, as an affront to millions of subjects of the British Empire. Clive, however, continued to use the term, referring in 'Plus de Jazz' to 'nigger music'. Marianna Torgovnick has argued that African art was viewed by Clive and Roger as of interest solely for its influence on modernism (Christopher Green's 'Expanding' gives a more nuanced view). Both denied what they termed a 'culture' to Africans, while admiring the aesthetic qualities of the carvings (Clive in fact welcomed the absence of any knowledge of the creators' names or the dates of the artefacts as there could thus be no extraneous information to distract from purely aesthetic contemplation). Yet there is another dimension to Clive's account in 'Negro Sculpture'. He mentioned that the Chelsea show had prompted people to visit the ethnographic collections of the British Museum where they could point out 'to stay-at-home cousins the relics of a civilization they helped to destroy'. His use of 'civilization' was telling: a 'savage' could produce art, even if only by instinct.

Seldes noted in *Vanity Fair* that Clive had ranked the African sculptures that influenced painters in Paris above Assyrian, Roman, Indian, true Gothic or late Renaissance art, but not as high as those 'of the supreme Chinese periods' or archaic Greek, Byzantine or Mahomedan art. While he had been doing so, 'America devoted itself and its theatres to musical shows composed and produced by the non-primitive negroes of Harlem.' Seldes' purpose was to reassure Americans who might be suffering from an inferiority complex towards Europe that a show like *Shuffle Along*, the Broadway sensation of 1921 written, produced and performed by African-Americans, was part of a distinctively American and worthwhile cultural history. This show, which launched the careers of Josephine Baker and Florence Mills, Seldes argued was part of a native artistic tradition that should be treated seriously.

In the same issue of *Vanity Fair*, Clive's 'Art and the Cinema' reaffirmed, through a convoluted argument about the recently released *Cabinet of Dr. Caligari*, his commitment to a 'pure' aesthetics. Just as photography had encroached on realist painting in the nineteenth century, while the Impressionists created new forms, now *Caligari* showed that cinema did not have to be 'hopelessly obvious and unreal' and might approach the status of art. His article offered, as its subtitle stated, 'A Prophecy that the Motion Pictures, in Exploiting Imitation Art, will Leave Real Art to the Artists'. *Caligari* was certainly better, he wrote, than the pap to which the masses flocked for trite tales set in 'common-place rooms, streets, parks and prairies', which always ended happily, and so its 'rudimentary aesthetic intention' might have salutary effects. But Clive could not let go of his concept of an aesthetic hierarchy. If *Caligari* pushed cinema a little closer to the pinnacle, the pinnacle must be defended. Clive predicted that in the distant future 'art might become . . . the preoccupation of a tiny international *élite*' capable of reacting to abstract form, though he admitted that a withdrawal to so inaccessible a stronghold would impoverish life. In 1922, he was not prepared to consider that popular forms might require an adjustment of his criteria, but his interactions with Seldes made him less rigid.

Clive took Seldes to see Picasso in his studio in 1923, talking on the way about the differences between the 'major arts' and what Seldes called the 'lively arts' of comics, movies, jazz and ragtime. They found that they had more in common than might have been supposed by readers of *Vanity Fair*. Seldes' riposte to Clive's 'Plus de Jazz' appeared in *The Dial* in August 1923, and was reprinted the following year in *The 7 Lively Arts*. In 'Toujours Jazz', Seldes explained that jazz was a characteristically American expression, recognised with a 'shudder' by the English and welcomed by the French, though they could not play it (a gentle tease of musicians like Milhaud, who had been studying jazz and ragtime in America). 'Toujours Jazz' exhibits Seldes' understanding of music, which Clive admitted he knew almost nothing about.

By the time Clive reviewed *The 7 Lively Arts*, he had changed his tune and recommended that anyone who wished to understand the postwar mind needed to read Seldes' book. Even if they were tempted to skip the 'prairies of print' about obscure 'American music-hall performers, paragraph-writers and comic illustrators', Clive urged Europeans not to because Seldes' analysis was so good. Here could be found the new ingredient that was to 'vivify Western civilization'. 'Toujours Jazz' reduced him 'to a puddle', but readers of the *Nation & Athenaeum* need not worry that the Americans were coming to storm the fortress of Culture. A certain kind of snobbery would ensure the preservation of high art, but Seldes had added to the doctrine of aesthetics an understanding of style as key to the 'lively arts'. Clive and Seldes' 'international quarrel' (as the editor put it) was concluded in *Vanity Fair* when Clive agreed that 'style consists in expressing one's self in a particular way', whether that self was Mozart or Irving Berlin. The visit to Picasso's studio had driven home for Seldes Clive's point that 'we must be on our guard lest we forget the major arts', while Seldes had changed Clive's mind about the value of the 'minor arts'. Within another two years, Clive would be observed at a 'fever pitch in defence of what he regarded as an unjustly denigrated opus of genius' when a near-riot broke out at a screening of René Clair's surrealist film *Entr'acte*.

25. Landmarks

During the General Strike of May 1926, the Woolfs' Hogarth Press hummed with activity. The industrial unrest most acutely located in the coalmines had been suspended by the war and, since the Armistice, only deferred by ineffective actions by a government confronted by widespread antagonism amongst recently demobilised soldiers. The short-lived first Labour Government of 1924 was a harbinger of social forces that would inexorably alter the political landscape in the interwar decades, splitting the Liberals and reuniting the Conservatives. Although Clive might have teased Vanessa about 'my Mr Baldwin' becoming prime minister in 1924, his political allegiances lay more with the Liberals of the wartime coalition government than with the Conservatives whose party Baldwin led and who set about enacting reforms some of the Liberals had supported. The General Strike occurred immediately after the expiration of yet another temporary manoeuvre, a government coal subsidy that ended on 30 April.

For ten days without newspapers other than the government's *British Gazette*, the radio or rumour were the sole sources of information. Maynard rang to ask if the Hogarth Press could print a skeleton edition of the *Nation & Athenaeum*. Virginia devoted her energy to obtaining signatures on a letter from the Archbishop of Canterbury seeking a resumption of negotiations between the TUC and the government. Clive heard that Winston Churchill, Chancellor of the Exchequer, wanted to settle the strike with tear-gas bombs and lamented that they did not have access to Mary Hutchinson's car so they could go and confront him directly. When the government called for special constables, Clive thought he might become a policeman, an idea Vanessa dismissed as fantastic. He told Virginia that he stood ready to serve as a negotiator if the government wanted him. After a dinner to discuss the strike, Virginia and Leonard went to 50 Gordon Square where a 'good deal was said about art'. In his autobiography, Leonard would remember the General Strike as a momentous historical event, but apart from a pervasive sense of boredom and unreality, the ten days it lasted had little effect on people in Clive's milieu. He took Mary shopping in the West End, from where there was nothing to report. When the strike ended, the Woolfs, Clive, Roger, Helen Anrep and 'other spirits' met for dinner and drank champagne to celebrate the return to normality.

In Paris a week after the strike, Clive was at the opening of Diaghilev's *Romeo and Juliet* when leaflets headed 'PROTEST' signed by Louis Aragon and André Breton were scattered from the balcony, applauded by Nancy Cunard and the American painter Eugene McCown.[1] The anarchistic Surrealists objected to Joan Miró and Max Ernst, two of their own, collaborating with the 'bourgeois capitalist' Diaghilev. The 'ridiculous row' amused Clive, though he had no sympathy for it, and the scandal only helped sell more tickets. His sensibilities were more aligned with the individualist, pacifist alternative to Breton's dadaist-surrealist aesthetics embodied in Florent Fels' short-lived *Action, Cahiers individualistes de philosophie et d'art*. As an outsider to the complicated strife of the Parisian avant-garde, Clive was ecumenical in the society he kept. Tristan Tzara might appear to him an 'arriviste', but he was well worth talking to. Clive was amused by Tzara's *Mouchoir de Nuages*, but assumed the play had no serious intent. He deemed the protest at the ballet a failure and Breton's surrealist manifesto – a 'posthumous child of Dada' – seemed to Clive nothing more than automatic writing. In 'Round About Surrealism', Clive gave his opinion that Picasso had unintentionally given birth to the movement and surely must be 'slightly abashed' at what his 'extraordinarily significant abstract art' had led to.

The Surrealists did make him laugh, however, and for that Clive was grateful. He certainly could appreciate the blasphemous wit of Max Ernst's *The Virgin Spanking the Christ Child before Three Witnesses*,

---

[1]McCown provided a portrait of Cunard as well as the cover design when the Hogarth Press published her poem *Parallax* in 1925. She returned the favour by producing the catalogue for his first show at Léonce Rosenberg's gallery that year. Clive was one of six friends whom McCown invited to provide titles for his untitled paintings in the show (Ford 273).

which he saw when Waldemar George took him to the artist's studio after an afternoon visiting galleries together. 'How witty!' he told Mary. 'Quite Voltairean in its profanity.' Clive maintained an air of slightly bemused tolerance towards the bitter cultural struggles going on in Paris, hampered from being much more than a well-informed observer both by the brevity of his visits and by the company he kept. His admiration for Segonzac, Friesz and Derain placed Clive on the more conservative wing of these conflicts, although his personal lack of interest in abstraction was never informed by the kind of political charges levelled against it by critics like Jean-Loup Forain, who accused abstract painting of being a subversive foreign invasion and praised the landscapes of Vlaminck as evidence of a desire to ' "return to the soil" to rediscover the simplicity of French culture'. This critique in any case would not have appealed to Clive who, by 1920, was finding Vlaminck's work boring.

The meaning of 'abstraction' was itself a matter of debate. Picasso was well known to hate abstraction, yet Clive's insistence that representation was not a relevant aesthetic consideration led him to refer to the 'abstraction' of Picasso's work. He ascribed the renewed popularity of Ingres to a kind of abstraction because 'like Picasso, [Ingres] empties objects of almost all significance save the purely aesthetic, and constructs works of art out of the intrinsic beauty of form.' He returned to the point when Paul Rosenberg brought an exhibition to the French Gallery on Pall Mall in 1926 that prompted Clive to remark that Ingres and Picasso – 'the beginning and end of this exhibition' – were united by 'the abstract purity of their drawing . . . by ruthless insistence on what is plastically significant'.

Clive took the opportunity to recapitulate for a general audience the narrative about modern art he had developed since 1910 when he was invited to contribute to the Encyclopaedia Britannica's two-volume *These Eventful Years* (a project with the astonishing subtitle *The Twentieth Century in the Making as Told by Many of Its Makers, Being the Dramatic Story of All that Has Happened Throughout the World During the Most Momentous Period in All History*). His article, 'Aesthetic Truth and Futurist Nonsense', first appeared in the American *Outlook* magazine, whose editors noted that in the British *Who's Who*, Clive gave his occupation as 'highly civilised loafer': they thought he had loafed to good advantage. Clive reminded this broad audience of his argument that works of art were 'beautiful' in themselves, not because they reminded us of anything else. The Fauves had followed where Cézanne had pointed and Picasso had logically invented Cubism after that, but 'Cubism proper', he announced, was now dead because it had ended up being almost a branch of mathematics. The Futurists' perversion of Cubism, as he saw it, had resulted in unhappy 'recent developments in Italian politics'. (The October 1922 march on Rome of Mussolini's National Fascist Party would lead within five years to his dictatorship.) Looking around the world, Clive saw the lessons of Matisse and Picasso most fruitfully reflected in central and eastern Europe, particularly in Germany and Russia. In his own country, Clive noted the London Group (which had emerged from Walter Sickert's Camden Town painters before the War and had, since 1919, come increasingly under Roger's influence) as a promising sign that English painters could merge their native tradition with the movement that descended from Cézanne.

Roger had formed a small offshoot of the London Group, the London Artists Association, which was largely underwritten by Maynard and counted Samuel Courtauld among its other patrons. Its first exhibition was held at the Leicester Galleries during the General Strike. In *Vogue*, Clive described the works by Roger, Duncan, Vanessa, Frederick Porter, Keith Baynes, Bernard Adeney and the sculptor Frank Dobson as 'no less than the reassertion of the existence of an English school'. He had predicted that English painting would divide into French-influenced and 'Neo-Pre-Raphaelite' schools, which he saw realised in the LAA's modernism. The painters of the LAA were 'heirs to Cézanne'. They might still be 'accused by stupid and ignorant people of being Frenchified and exotic', but they were the inheritors of the 'natural plastic tradition' of Gainsborough, Constable and Turner – a tradition that Clive repeatedly argued had been perverted by the Pre-Raphaelites. By 1927, Clive proclaimed the LAA the 'leading artistic group in England'.

Vanessa's *The Playground* illustrated Clive's review of the LAA's first show, a painting whose 'extreme severity', he wrote, was 'essentially French'. When he proclaimed Vanessa 'the best woman painter' in England in 1923, Clive likened her to Marie Laurencin because both exploited rather than concealed their 'feminine qualities'. Vanessa did 'not attempt to paint like a man, nor like anyone else', and therefore her work was 'personal – a quality rare in feminine art', a point he reiterated about Laurencin in a round-up of the 1926 Paris shows for *Vogue*. Despite the growing attention in postwar France to the work of women painters, Clive did not push very far his speculations about whether men and women painted differently. In 1919, he had added the name of Alice Halicka to a 'tiny list of distinguished female painters' when he reviewed the Sitwells' exhibition of French paintings at Heal's. A month after the publication of Virginia's *To the Lighthouse* in 1927, with its central character of a painter named Lily Briscoe, Clive asked in a review of flower paintings at Knoedler's whether there were 'still Charles Tansleys about who say "Women can't paint"? If so, let me direct their virile attention to two pictures by Berthe Morisot [*Fleurs sur une cheminée*; *Chrysanthèmes*] and one by Marie Laurencin [*Fleurs*]. Women can't paint – like men. When they paint like women they add a peculiar ingredient to the pleasure of life.'

Clive curiously foreshadowed Lily Briscoe when he said of Constantin Brancusi's sculpture that 'between conception and realization lies half the world of art'. He continued to think of all art as defined by confronting the problem of how to find a form for a personal vision, and in the 1920s began to write more about sculpture. When the LAA added six more artists for its 1927 exhibition, he devoted most of his review to Frank Dobson's *Choephora* [*Cornucopia*]. Dobson's 'artistic problem', as Clive saw it, was how to create a satisfying whole out of a series of volumes', which he had achieved by using 'poise and proportion, plane and relief', as Lipchitz would, and the 'humane rhythm of his subject' as Epstein might. As always, Clive was not interested in the subjects of the sculptures but only in how the artist had, he believed, achieved 'significant form'. Clive found Epstein's work too naturalistic, but his responses to it continued to evolve. He still believed Aristide Maillol to be the greatest living sculptor, in whose school he placed Dobson (who in turn Clive thought had influenced younger English sculptors such as Stephen Tomlin). Dobson's bust of Tallulah Bankhead might be 'frankly baroque', but since the end of the war Dobson had been creating significant form in the 'the contours, planes, and depressions' of his pieces.

When Clive visited Brancusi's studio on the Impasse Ronsin in 1925, he asked why he gave names to his works, because it gave encouragement to tittering 'oafs' who might 'suppose that the sculptor was trying to make a photographic likeness of a bird or a woman, and could get no nearer than this'. Brancusi told Clive that 'his forms express his sense of the very essence of a bird or a woman'. Clive discerned 'a beauty more mathematical than human' in Brancusi's forms and emphasised that it was 'analysis' – albeit carried on unconsciously – that led to the realisation of the artist's conception. 'The forms of the artist move us because they are exactly right, and they are exactly right because they conform to some unknown, and apparently unknowable, law of harmony which is the beginning and end of the matter.' These were the issues engaging Virginia at the time too, who told Roger as she began *To the Lighthouse* that she was 'trying to make out what I mean by form in fiction. I say it is emotion put into the right relations, and has nothing to do with form as used of painting.'

Although Clive rarely failed to take any opportunity to remind readers of the source of his fame – significant form – his critical perspectives broadened in the 1920s when he paid closer attention to the historical detail that *Art* had swept aside with polemic fervour. From 1924 to 1926 he constructed a series of carefully researched articles which would become his well-received book *Landmarks in Nineteenth-Century Painting*. He also began to give more balanced attention to developments in England, without relinquishing his conviction that the best modern painting descended from Cézanne.

When *Landmarks* was published in 1927, Clive asked Leonard (now literary editor of the *Nation & Athenaeum*) that it be sent to a literary rather than an art critic. Leonard obliged by sending it to the aviation consultant and poet Barrington Gates, who welcomed the book for giving readers a 'few biographical facts, a dash of anecdote, a compact and acute discussion of the painter's sources, affiliations and achievement, a photograph or two of one of his works, a pungent footnote or two' before implying that they should then be 'off to Paris' to see for themselves. In *Since Cézanne* Clive claimed that 'few things do more to promote and disseminate a taste for art and letters . . . than biographical and historical criticism': he knew his audience. Gates told Clive that he would have bought the book for his own enlightenment if he had not been given it to review. Most – though not all – reviewers concurred that *Landmarks* was an instructive and helpful book.

Many of the pieces in *Landmarks* had been previously published in the *New Republic* or the *Nation & Athenaeum*, but it was not entirely disingenuous for Clive to state in the Preface that he had 'made articles out of my book' rather than assembled another anthology. The 'Prolegomena' that opens the book had appeared in January 1925 in the *Criterion*, to which Clive had been invited to contribute by the assistant editor, Richard Aldington; just before *Landmarks* was published, T. S. Eliot, the *Criterion*'s editor, asked Herbert Read if he thought Clive would be a good art critic for the magazine. The heart of Clive's book was a series of six articles published in the *Nation & Athenaeum* under the general title 'Landmarks in Modern Art', which established a deliberate and scholarly approach to his subject.

In a sentence picked up in several reviews, he proposed marking out the territory between the 'Neo-Classical revival and the end of Impressionism . . . in the spirit of an old-fashioned road-map maker' – as he had many times reiterated, a critic was essentially a guide, and this was terrain he knew very well. However, *Landmarks* was a more densely historical work than his other books. Characterised by his typical subjective judgements and casual witticisms, it also drew deeply from what he had learned on many visits to the Louvre each time he was in Paris in the early years of the decade, as well as from his wide reading.

Admitting that his earlier underrating of Delacroix probably owed something to a deficiency in his own sensibilities, Clive made the modernist point that appreciating a painting involved 'collaboration, not the enjoyment of a divine gift fallen mysteriously from the skies'. The notion of 'collaboration' ran counter to the dominant critical outlook of the time, which was seeding what would ultimately flourish as the 'New Criticism' and not be significantly challenged until the role of subjective experience in evaluating an artwork was revived in the 1970s, after a long detour through Formalism. In *The Modern Movement in Art*, published in the same year as *Landmarks*, R. H. Wilenski objected to Clive's hyperbolic language and the 'hysterical way' he reacted to art, which Wilenski argued led to confusion in the public's mind between what Wilenski termed 'intrinsic' and 'acquired' value. For Wilenski, acts of perception had no bearing on the intrinsic value of any work of art, a value that was 'implicit in the attitude, motives and procedure of the man who made it and consisting in that man's perfect fulfilment of his initial purpose of enlarging his experience in the work'. For Clive, aesthetic emotion was the result of a collaboration between the viewer's unique sensibility and significant form.

Several reviewers welcomed the more sober tone of *Landmarks*, while noting that Clive had lost none of his ability to turn a phrase and could instruct and inform without boring the reader. The reviewer for *Drawing & Design* pointed out that if Clive was a highbrow then other English critics would do well to emulate the 'highbrowism' exemplified by his 'clear, witty writing, easily grasped, unflagging in interest, full of valuable fact'. Even Arnold Bennett dubbed Clive 'a considerable performer with a pen', adding that he had now outgrown Roger in his criticism. Clive made a point of deferring in *Landmarks* to Roger's greater expertise in the practice of painting: he had little curiosity about the material processes which led to the outcomes about which he wrote. Charles Marriott's complaint that Clive's discussions of art were 'too much in terms of the literary man' missed the point that Clive had no wish to challenge Roger's pre-eminence as a scholarly art critic. He consciously tried to appeal to a broad readership that simply wished to know more about 'high culture'. Throughout his life, Clive engaged graciously with autodidacts who sought his opinions or advice, from miners to sailors. In contrast to Marriott's criticism, the reviewer for *Country Life* approved of the amount of biographical material Clive included about painters in *Landmarks* because it enabled the ordinary reader to approach them more confidently. Clive would have been delighted by the *Glasgow Herald*'s saying that his 'enthusiasm' was infectious, as this was precisely what he saw as the critic's role – to send the reader back to the works with renewed interest. Astutely, the *Manchester Guardian* recognised that readers came to Clive's writing 'for his persuasive and witty advocacy of his own views rather than for finely balanced judgments'.

26. The End of the Affair

Travel between London and Paris was improved in 1926 by the introduction of the luxury boat train *Golden Arrow* linking Calais and Paris. Clive took his 'Mothersill's Travel Remedy' for the rough Channel crossing and arrived in France that October ready for his usual nights of carousing at the Deux Magots with Bernouard and Derain. His first engagement was to join Vanessa and Duncan for dinner with Julian, who was spending from autumn to summer with the family of Henri Pinault before going up to Cambridge in 1927. Pinault tutored both of Vanessa and Clive's sons at various times and, despite his communist leanings, Clive approved of his 'taste for good food, good wine and intelligent conversation . . . surpassed only by his appetite for young women'. Julian later described the profound effect this 'surrogate father' had on him. Pinault expanded his knowledge of French literature and his challenging 'Voltairean' pedagogy brought on a 'terrific intellectual-emotional crisis'. Julian's French improved so much under Pinault's tutelage that Clive asked Georges Gabory, Georges Duthuit and Waldemar George if they would invite his son out with them. 'They should be a means to interesting friends,' he told Julian, before adding some fatherly advice:

> Have you got any money? If you meet in cafes – as you probably will – insist on paying for drinks sometimes. If you are a party, insist sometimes on paying the tournée (for everyone). Ten per cent on the bill is always a sound rule for tipping . . . If you like my friends, I will write to others.

The scant remaining traces of Clive's advice to his sons are solely practical. Julian occasionally went shooting with his grandfather and seems to have acquired a reputation for recklessness, provoking a lecture from Clive about proper conduct on a shoot: 'All the pheasants in the world aren't worth a lost eye.' By the time he went up to King's College, Julian's tolerance for lectures from his father had worn thin, yet in the 'Notes for a Memoir' discovered after Julian's death, he acknowledged that 'Clive was a most admirable educator. I took his advice very largely on reading . . . he founded my French taste – with Pinault – well and solidly.'

As usual, Clive's letters to Mary documented his frenetic life in Paris as he lunched with Duthuit and Waldemar George, saw Moise Kisling, and visited museums and galleries. He spent an afternoon with Picasso gossiping about Cocteau and went to a concert with Marcelle Meyer, assuring Mary he had not flirted with her. Preparing to return to London, his appointment diary filled with dates for dinners at Boulestin's and lunches at the Ivy, as well as tennis in Gordon Square with Frances Marshall, the pretty former assistant at Birrell and Garnett's bookshop, now living with Ralph Partridge. Frances had made clear to Clive when they met that she had no interest in an affair and had become one of his closest friends. Clive and Mary had quarrelled recently and, as he set off for home he wrote, 'Darling I adore you, do let us have a charming winter together – different from and more enchanting than all the others.'

Clive spent the new year at Sherfield with the Wellesleys, where Raymond, Vita and Ethel Sands all noticed his uncharacteristically low spirits. On New Year's Day, he told Mary he could not 'bear another weekend in the cold without our charming secret'. But the winter was marred by unhappy arguments and one evening at the theatre matters came to a head when Mary finally admitted that she was in love with someone else. Cryptic letters from 50 Gordon Square began to arrive in the south of France, where Vanessa had rented the Villa Corsica for the first few months of 1927. Vanessa did not know why Clive was planning to come to Cassis, but Virginia dismissed the contretemps as yet another instance of the same old rigmarole that would end with Clive giving champagne suppers to his lover when they made up. She may have expressed annoyance that both Mary and Clive used her as interlocutor, but Virginia also enjoyed being once again embroiled in her brother-in-law's emotional drama.

As Mary and Clive's affair began to unravel, Vanessa and Virginia bore the brunt of his prevarications and misery. After Mary's admission, Virginia told her sister, Clive 'practically went mad', vowing to abandon the superficial social life he blamed Mary for having seduced him into. Mary accused Virginia of taking Clive's side, crying that she too hated the 'society they keep, longs for him to work, is often at her wits end to get out of parties, and finds him a good deal deteriorated intellectually because of his debauchery'. When Clive told Virginia that all Mary's ideas simply parroted things he had said, Virginia concurred with this low (and unfair) opinion of Mary's intelligence when she asked Vanessa, 'Don't you think its odd that he never guessed in 13 years what we could see in ten seconds?'

In a brief sketch written many years later, Mary described how Clive had nurtured her 'as though she were a favourite plant that would die without constant attention'. They shared a love of eighteenth-century French literature and took pleasure in the congruence of their aesthetic tastes, but the 'plant', to Clive's sorrow, 'grew differently to what he expected. It developed tendrils and flowers he never dreamed of, so that he became exasperated disappointed and in the end broken'. The loss of their sexual bond in 1927 devastated Clive. His letters to her had been suffused with the joy his 'enchanting little enchantress' embodied, with whom he spent so many nights in Brighton or London or Paris, waking tired from 'kissing Madame between her exquisite little legs' and he simply could not imagine a celibate relationship with her, despite everything else they shared.

In early 1927, the Huxleys pressured Mary to join them in Italy, where they were visiting D. H. Lawrence. Clive booked her a sleeper to Florence and imagined her 'enchanting little body coiled up in it'. To Lawrence, Mary appeared 'nice and gentle, very faded, poor dear – almost a little old woman. Clive Bell and Co. must be very wearing.' Clive sent Mary passionate Valentines, but at the same time was writing to both Vanessa and Virginia that he was bored with her, and just wanted time to write. Virginia had urged Clive to begin writing the long book he so often spoke of, which he planned to do in France. Shrewdly, Vanessa told Virginia she thought it would be better for Clive to 'have love affairs of a milder kind which needn't interfere with work.'

She reassured her husband that he could always depend on her, that he would not be butting in on her and Duncan if he wanted to come to Cassis to write.

Notwithstanding the force of his passion for Mary, Clive did have many affairs of a 'milder' kind. Mina Kirstein, a professor at Smith College in Massachusetts, came to London in 1924 with one of her students, a flamboyant Kentucky heiress named Henrietta Bingham. When Clive encountered Mina, who had become a friend of Bunny Garnett's on a previous summer visit, at a party given by Henrietta, a 'sizzling summer fling' ensued. Mina's memory of what transpired when she invited Clive to dinner at her house was hazy, but news of their liaison coursed quickly through the gossip networks, Carrington's husband Ralph Partridge telling Frances Marshall that Lytton had heard from Clive that Mina's underclothes were 'the best in America'.

Mina Kirstein Curtiss, ca. 1924

Ralph and Carrington had married in 1921 and lived with Lytton at Tidmarsh until all three moved to Ham Spray in Wiltshire. Ralph's discovery of Carrington's infidelity with his close friend Gerald Brenan, with whom he had served in the war, strained the marriage and by 1923 Ralph had begun an affair with Frances. The summer of 1924 was unexceptional for infidelity. While Ralph sought solace with Frances, Carrington was taken to bed by Henrietta, at whose party Alec Penrose's wife Bertha fell for Ralph Wright, a partner in the Birrell and Garnett bookshop, who was having an affair with Marjorie Joad (who worked at the Hogarth Press), who would shortly leave her husband, causing Virginia to ask Clive if he could possibly let Marjorie stay at Gordon Square for a few days.

Whether or not it was what Vanessa would describe as 'milder', Clive had been carrying on another affair since the autumn of 1925. Had Mary heard that Mrs Penrose nearly died in Cassis, he asked in September that year, adding wryly, 'that comes of drinking water instead of wine.' Bertha Penrose had been married unhappily to Alec since 1919. She had gone alone in 1924 to Cassis, where her brother-in-law, Roland, was staying, to escape her woes. She returned there in 1925, having spent some time working on Alec's production of Lytton's play *Son of Heaven*, thereby meeting Duncan, Carrington and Vanessa. Her enjoyment of the southern summer was cut short by a serious bout of typhoid. Late in her life, Bertha described how her affair with Clive had begun soon after her recovery:

> I must have caught Clive's roving eye at some London party for he was reported to me to have asked someone 'if there was any chance of success with young Mrs Alec Penrose'. . . . From the moment our eyes met we recognised each other for the rakes we were; that delicious, electric thrill foreboding pleasures ahead passed between us; we were accomplices for experiment, for gaiety, for all sorts of sins of the world, the flesh, and if you like – the devil.

Clive was forty-four, Bertha twenty-eight.

At first, assignations were easily arranged in London, but in 1926 the Penroses moved to Fenstanton in Huntingdonshire, near where Bunny lived with his wife Ray (Frances Marshall's sister). Bertha, or 'Beau', as Clive sometimes called her, began to appear often in his appointment diary, sometimes on the same day as a dinner with Mary.

Once, overhearing Clive discussing with Picasso a 'delicate mission' he needed to carry out at François Coty's *parfumerie*, Olga Picasso insisted that Coco Chanel herself had told her that Chanel's 'Gardenia' was the fashionable scent to give a lover. Henceforth, Clive and Bertha christened their rendezvous 'gardenia nights', after the perfume Clive brought back for her from Paris.

'A typical evening, the sort I loved best, started by my arrival at 50 Gordon Square, generally in a trim little tailor-made with a trim little suitcase,' Bertha wrote in her privately published memoir, *Bad Aunt Bertha*.

This would be round about six-thirty or seven. From the moment I stepped into his rich, book-lined study I was completely happy and completely at ease. Clive read every day of his life from five to seven o'clock: those were the sacred hours of his day.

I was taken to his bedroom to change – already a 'delicious intimacy' as he called it. There were a series of feminine articles on the dressing table in case of need, and there was that lovely 'O My Bath' essence. I took my bath with luxurious refreshments and anticipation.

Very groomed and slinky, I rejoined him in the study where my appearance was always commented on, for the most part favourably. One would not say Clive was handsome, nor classically proportioned, but his physical ways with one were thrilling. He knew exactly how and when to kiss me, when and how to stroke, to coax, to light one's cigarette, to tumble or ruffle one.

Clive followed a well-rehearsed pattern with his ladies; his affairs were in many respects a performance which drew on the mannered notions of that distant French past of which he was so fond. Bertha wrote to him 'sitting in a clover field on the top of a hill in the blazing sun absolutely stark naked' with her notepaper resting on a volume of Flaubert in her lap, teasing, 'what do you think of that my civilized toiletted Clive?' He liked the 'ladies I like to read the books I think they would like – the sort of books that give a civilised thrill and a delicate, but greedy, appetite for life'. Clive gave Bertha the 'sorts of books a lover would like to give his mistress because they would stimulate her sense of the pleasures of life – every sort of pleasure'.

Bertha Penrose

Mary was aware of Clive's interest in Bertha, to whom he wrote when he and Mary were together in Paris. Bertha and Clive had 'an unspoken agreement against jealousy' and, in any case, there was no question in 1926 of Bertha usurping Mary's place. Clive knew, too, that Bertha's love for Ralph Wright was deeper-rooted than her feelings for him. Even though Clive told Virginia that Bertha was a 'little bitch' with whom he must resist going to bed, their correspondence vividly makes plain the physical basis of their affair. Bertha asked Clive if the marks of her teeth were still visible on his shoulder, and worried about the difficulty of concealing a large bite-mark on the back of her neck.

By that time, Clive's relations with Mary were broken, and as 'Lalage', another nickname for Bertha, also seemed about to slip away, he encouraged her to come to France with him for an escapade. If she was worried about her husband, Bertha could tell him that she was staying at Charleston: 'Vanessa is a tower of strength, and benign to lovers.' It was a lasting regret to Bertha that she did not take up Clive's offer of a 'giro' in France, but she was confused about her feelings. 'Don't make me fall in love with you darling,' she wrote, 'I already feel far more for you than ever I meant to.' She wanted more from Clive than he would give, frustrated by how little he revealed of himself, which she used as the reason to withdraw from him. Even before they went to bed together, she had urged Clive to be more open with her about his true feelings, but by the end of 1927, his reticence annoyed her: 'You would have more success with me if you confided in me a little more instead of just amusing me.'

Clive's sojourn in Cassis, where he arrived in March 1927, was unhappy, and by April he had left for Paris, pining for Mary. By the time he returned to London, a dance had ensued which exasperated Virginia and Vanessa. Mary offered Clive a friendship without sex, but 'as I already have two sisters,' he wrote in his appointment diary, apparently drafting his reply, 'I feel no need for what you offer me.' When he heard from Georges Duthuit about an enjoyable dinner with Mary and the Huxleys, he wrote to her despairingly, 'I cannot bear not knowing where you are and what you are about.' He would arrange to see her but then immediately regret it. Virginia thought Clive had been shaken by the realisation that he was a fraud, something she feared in herself: 'It was part of my madness – that horror.' Clive said the difference between them was that she recovered after her breakdowns, 'the inference being that he was to stay mad.' Everywhere he went was associated with Mary and he could not escape the habit of wanting to tell her everything he did. He thought back to the summer of 1915 at West Wittering, regretting that, unlike Proust, he was merely a lover, not an artist with the gift of capturing memories.

The Hogarth Press that summer published *Fugitive Pieces*, a selection of Polly Flinders' articles, on the last page of which Mary wrote 'To be continued . . .', but it would be her only book. Vivienne Eliot's biographer has tied the book's 'comparative failure' to Mary's depression 'as she came to realise that the pose of decadent coolness and detachment she adopted under the influence of Aldous Huxley . . . left her simply confused and weary.' It was not until June that Vanessa and Virginia understood that Mary was seriously involved with someone else. Maria Huxley was writing love letters to Mary from Lucca in Italy: did Mary remember how Aldous 'can make your whole body quiver?' she wondered. Segonzac had once admired a blue ring given to Clive by Mary but Clive now returned it to her, because 'it was given to me by my dear mistress who is dead.' He tried to accept that he had 'a smaller part of [her] heart', but his physical longing overcame him, leading him by 1928 into a kind of sexual frenzy that alarmed and appalled not only Vanessa and Virginia, but also his sons.

Clive's affair with Bertha was waning by the end of 1927. He sadly recalled 'how you looked on the sofa – your most delicious moment – abandoned – with your little black velvet frock rucked up and your long stockings very tight on your exquisite slim legs, and your eyes closed, and your face as still and alive as the depth of a stream,' but Bertha wanted him to let her go. Clive admitted that monogamy had its charms but because he was 'in lust' with her, he would rather not see her at all. Could he not be her 'secret', just for an occasional gardenia night at the 'romantic flat at the Savoy'? 'What we shall regret when we are old,' he wrote, 'is not what we have done but what we have missed.' While at work on her memoir, Bertha one day turned up a packet of Clive's letters and became so flooded with regret and nostalgia that she had to stop writing for several weeks. Against his injunction to avoid regret, she wrote on 5 June 1975, 'Oh how true!'

Characteristically, Clive marked the end of the affair with a poem, 'Escapade', published in the *Nation & Athenaeum* on Christmas Eve 1927.

'Yes, but in six months' time', you said,
Will you . . .? And thereat prudently staid.
Admirable tact. In six months' time
Will a Brighton sea-front seem sublime?
Will the rain beat hard on the window-pane,
And we be oblivious of wind and rain?
Will your young visage smile back at mine,
Blue as the morning, merry as wine,
Or shall I appear, as alas! I can,
A cultured, intelligent, middle-aged man?
[. . .]
'Yes, but in six months' time', you say.
Darling, yes, but this is to-day.
And here you stand, slim, subtle, unique
With that ultra-mysterious curl on your cheek,
And the suit that I think looks best from behind,
And me very much like the rest of my kind.
And in six months' time if we're both alive
I shall . . . well, you will be twenty-five.

Their last letters were filled with nostalgia. When Coco Chanel took Clive shopping in Paris he felt sad whenever he saw something that would have suited Bertha. In July 1928, she spied him from the top of a bus as he walked along Wigmore Street with a woman, causing Bertha a pang of regret. Had their affair persisted, Bertha might have got more from Clive than he had been prepared to show when he was in the throes of breaking up with Mary. When he was no longer 'in lust', he wanted to see her again and tell her 'how I destroyed my own happiness by something that would have seemed to anyone else a trifle, and how – try as we will – we can't get our happiness back. A romance of twelve years standing, however, isn't destroyed by an unreality.' It would take more lovers to exorcise Mary's ghost.

Staying with Vanessa and Duncan in Cassis in April 1927, before she and Leonard went on to Sicily, Virginia found Clive 'seated at a rickety table writing on huge sheets of foolscap, which he picks out from time to time in red ink'. Despite this appearance of industry, Clive lamented that he could not concentrate at Cassis. Clive told Vanessa that Charleston was the only place he could write, which was why he could never contemplate giving it up. At the end of the month, he went to Paris, accompanied by Quentin and Julian. Quentin enjoyed his few days there before returning to England for school, especially when Clive took him to visit the Picassos. Julian, who was returning to the Pinaults, had become 'violently anti-artist' while in Cassis; Clive complained that Julian was costing him almost £200 a year.

Clive sent Mary silk stockings and garters from Paris, chattering about whom he had seen as if there was nothing amiss between them. Having apparently overcome his distaste for Nancy Cunard's Corrupt Coterie, he had been out with the painter Alvaro 'Chile' Guevara and Tommy Earp, as well as with Frankie Birrell and Raymond Mortimer. By the time he returned to London, however, it had become clear to Clive that everything had changed between him and Mary: 'I never quite believed you would break my heart with your eyes wide open,' he wrote from Gordon Square just before setting off for Seend. He had received an urgent summons from his family because his father was about to have an operation.

Cleeve House was as gloomy as ever. Dorothy and Clive sat on opposite sides of a 'large, bleak table', passing each of their deaf parents' remarks on to the other. Although at first the crisis seemed to have been a false alarm, it soon became evident that old Mr Bell was dying. Clive tried to keep as many engagements as he could, including a weekend at Sherfield where he hoped to see Vita and Harold. To more than one correspondent, he described how his brother, Cory, had burst out that he would rather be in the second battle of Ypres than face his father's sick room. The best analogy Clive could find for both his situation and his state of mind was sitting in Middlesex Hospital after Angelica and a maid had been struck by a vehicle in the spring of 1924. In the bed next to Angelica's lay a child writhing in speechless agony, to whom Clive compared himself in a letter to Mary.

W. H. Bell died on 21 June, leaving an estate worth £271,303 9s 9d. The shares Clive inherited increased his annual income by £1,200 and soon various small improvements began to be made at Charleston. That Christmas, Vanessa found no noticeable differences at Cleeve House: 'Meak the parlourmaid is unchanged, so is Ellen the housemaid, so are Ovens the chauffeur and William the ancient coachman and Eyres the gardener and many underlings whom I haven't grasped.' Virginia worried that Vanessa might not benefit from Clive's inheritance, jocularly threatening a 'round robin' complaint if he spent it all on 'some new parrokeet'. She and Clive had been sparring again since they were together in Cassis because he had gossiped about a letter of hers to her sister. Vanessa blamed Clive's 'inveterate habit of twisting anything into something slightly malicious', but Virginia knew that he also had deep-rooted feelings about her that caused him sometimes to act cruelly.

Throughout the summer Clive swung between despair at the loss of Mary and boasts about new conquests, which bored Virginia. She could sympathise with his depressed state but when he crowed about being 'Clive the undaunted lover, the Don Juan of Bloomsbury', she shuddered. One moonlit night, as they walked around the square after dining together, a despondent Clive told Virginia he admired her for having attempted suicide. Two nights later, she saw him at Raymond Mortimer's where he immediately began boasting: 'He had had an adventure. Life was changed; had met the loveliest of women.'

In common with several of his friends, Clive was besotted with the successful young actress Valerie Taylor, who had first become well known for playing Nina in Chekhov's *The Seagull* soon after she left RADA in 1920. Clive had met her at a lunch given by the director of the V&A museum, Eric Maclagan, and told Vanessa that if Quentin came to stay in Gordon Square he would find the twenty-six-year-old actress in his flat. When Vita invited Valerie to Long Barn, Clive teased her about poaching. Mary told Lytton that she had fallen in love with Valerie and heard that he had too. Speculation even began to circulate that Raymond (who was homosexual) might marry Valerie. Wise beyond her years, Valerie told Clive that she could not take too seriously all this attention in case she ended up badly hurt.

For almost twenty years, Clive had pondered writing a book about 'civilisation', and at the Villa Corsica he renewed his efforts while he tried to reconcile himself to the loss of Mary. In the autumn, he sent Virginia the first half of the manuscript she had observed him

July 23, 1927   THE ILLUSTRATED SPORTING AND DRAMATIC NEWS   145

SMALL CAST, SMALL THEATRE, BIG LAUGHS.

IN "ON APPROVAL" AT THE FORTUNE THEATRE: MISS VALERIE TAYLOR.

Into the midst of the degenerate throw-outs and weaklings of "On Approval," Mr. Frederick Lonsdale's comedy at the Fortune Theatre, steps Helen Hayle, and at once the play becomes reasonably fresh and pleasant. Miss Valerie Taylor, even more than the author, is the cause of this, and the way in which, as Helen, she purifies the air of the comedy without seeming too much out of place among her hot-house companions is really a fine achievement. There are only four characters in this play—a small cast in a little theatre. Miss Taylor recently became engaged to the artist Mr. Adrian Daintrey.

[Photograph by Dorothy Wilding.]

Valerie Taylor in Illustrated Sporting and Dramatic News, *23 July 1927*

working on that spring when she visited her sister. It was prefaced by a fulsome dedication to her dated 'Cassis, April 1927'. She praised Clive's draft and encouraged him to continue (insisting he must omit the dedication), but Clive's doubts about his work led him to question her sincerity, which infuriated her: she might lie about many things, she told him, but never about books. It seems more likely that she was dissembling as Clive suspected, because those closest to him were not kind about *Civilization* when it was published in June 1928.

Leonard found it 'very superficial'. Julian's view of his father's book can be inferred from a dissertation he wrote trying (unsuccessfully) for a fellowship at King's in which he argued that a 'belief in universal and absolute good is ... apt to lead to intolerance, interference ... and to Fascism, tyranny and reaction in politics.' Clive's promotion in his book of states of mind good in themselves were all very well for those 'more concerned to enjoy the good life than to reform the bad', Julian wrote, but these Moorean ideas were a luxury his generation felt it could not afford. Virginia's quip (according to Quentin Bell) that 'it turned out that civilization is a lunch party at No. 50 Gordon Square' has become the first thing people who have heard of the book usually think of in connection with *Civilization*.

Clive framed his book as an enquiry into what was meant by 'civilisation' because it had been in the name of that abstraction that Britain and its allies had gone to war with Germany in 1914. The Victory medals given out after the war were inscribed 'The Great War for Civilisation', but Clive was not convinced the populace had any clear notion what that meant. He began by trying to establish what civilisation is not, by means of examining 'entities universally reckoned uncivilized'. Thus, he rested his enquiry upon that error from which so many of Western master discourses have sprung, of excluding from the 'universal' anything that does not fit a preconceived notion of what belongs. Like the Victorian Matthew Arnold's 'touchstones of excellence', which he claimed were self-evidently 'excellent', Clive's 'universally accepted types' of civilised peoples depended upon the circular argument that civilisation can be discerned by examining civilised peoples. 'All the world agrees' that some societies are 'barbarous', he wrote, but presumably those so described were not part of 'all the world'.

Clive drew deeply on Edvard Westermarck's anthropological study of the *Origin and Development of the Moral Ideas* in his effort to arrive at a negative definition of civilisation – his first chapter is titled 'What Civilization Is Not' – but he parted company with Westermarck over the idea that chastity was a characteristic of civilised societies. Given his own proclivities, Clive was 'forced to conclude that chastity is not one of the distinguishing characteristics of civilization'; after all, being chaste 'was of small account in the circle of Alcibiades, the court of Hadrian, the Medici gardens, or the salons where Voltaire, Helvetius, and Diderot gave shape to a new intellectual order and preached the philosophy of pleasure'. Like *Art*, more quoted than read, *Civilization* eventually came to be treated as almost a metonym for the 'Bloomsbury Group', although it might be more accurate to see it as the product of Clive's desperate effort to distract himself from the pain of losing Mary by burying himself in a nostalgic lament for the prelapsarian world of early summer 1914 when he envisioned writing a book called 'The New Renaissance'. If *Art* marked the beginning of Mary and Clive's love affair, *Civilization* could be seen, in David Bradshaw's words, as 'at one level their epitaph'. An unusually percipient reader wrote from Venice after the Second World War that she believed Clive must have written the book when young and madly in love because it held Eros in such high regard.

Civilization became a cudgel with which to beat 'Bloomsbury', despite the fact that Leonard disdained it (offering Erasmus as his counter example of 'A Civilized Man'), and Maynard implicitly rejected its philosophy in 'My Early Beliefs'. It is a rather turgid work that displays a well-read person's learning in a high-minded, Arnoldian tone: 'It is only when there come together enough civilized individuals to form a nucleus from which light can radiate, and sweetness ooze, that a civilization becomes possible.' Clive's championing of the individual in *Civilization* was grounded in an unreformed nineteenth-century Liberalism, and his moral philosophy had advanced no farther than Moore's *Principia Ethica*. He held up the Athens of the fifth century BC as the epitome of a society arranged to produce states of mind good in themselves, but one passage of his book in particular has often been seized upon as evidence of his patrician and offensive elitism.

Clive claimed that civilisation 'requires the existence of a leisured class, and a leisured class requires the existence of slaves'. Invariably, the damning quotation is truncated, without his critics continuing to explain that by 'slaves' Clive might mean a housekeeper – the woman who tidies up the home of a middle-class writer, for example – 'people, I mean, who give some part of their surplus time and energy to the support of others.' Quentin offered a more charitable estimation of the book's turn away from democratic ideals than his brother's bitter view when he wrote that 'it was not unreasonable, after seeing the ease with which the working classes could be persuaded to forget the International and march obediently to war, for a disappointed pacifist to feel that it was wiser to rely upon the good will of those who might best bring the masses to heel,' but that perspective would obviously prove profoundly misguided within ten years of *Civilization*'s publication.

When Winifred Holtby wrote in a review of *Civilization* that it was 'hard to contemplate with rapture a Dürer engraving while one is starving, rioting, or hiding from bombs, creditors, or private enemies,' Clive would have agreed. The war had demonstrated that force and fear now ruled; in the world that emerged from the carnage of 1914–1918 it seemed to Clive that civilisation might depend entirely on the benevolence of despots who were likely to retain their power for a very long time. The leisured class he thought necessary to a civilisation did not have to be drawn from the wealthy but might even comprise 'every two-thousandth baby' in a socialist state. This idea drew scorn from the fantasy writer Ralph Fraser, who thought such a scheme would 'produce those sinuous and squeaking creatures who flourish in the faded airs of Bloomsbury and grace its intelligent parlours' (Lytton's voice was invariably described as squeaky), another familiar trope in attacks on Bloomsbury.

Cardinal Newman would have found little to disagree with in the account of education in *Civilization*: 'Liberal education teaches us to enjoy life; practical education to acquire the things that may enable us or someone else to enjoy it.' Effective liberty can flourish only if we agree that 'what we believe is not necessarily true; that what we like is not necessarily good; and that all questions are open'. *Civilization* is anti-dogmatic at the same time that it is sententious, and several reviewers complained of the coat-trailing and question-begging that marred the argument. Yet, *Civilization* appeared at a moment when the reading public was particularly receptive to such broad opinions about the state of contemporary culture and when the book was reissued in the familiar pale blue binding of a Pelican paperback in 1938, its readership continued to grow. In 1930, John Nishinori, a lecturer at Waseda University in Tokyo, who told Clive he used the book in his classes every day, published a Japanese translation.

The *Yorkshire Post* reviewed *Civilization* with Julien Benda's much more influential *La Trahison des clercs*, which had just been translated by Richard Aldington as *The Great Betrayal*. Clive and Benda both argued that reason must be the basis of civilisation, a point Raymond Mortimer reiterated in seeing Clive and Benda as kindred spirits in his review for *The Dial*. When reviews focused on Clive's classical learning, they tended to be positive, but his practical recommendations met with derision. His more progressive ideas, such as that the lot of women would not improve, despite gaining the vote, until their domestic labour was 'put on precisely the same footing as that of a mechanic or barrister' were overlooked. In publications as different as the *New Age* and the *Railway Review*, Clive was taken to task for his myopia about the cost of the civilisation he extolled, the former pointing out that the leisured class he envisioned was 'completely parasitic', the latter that he would find the civilisation he sought only in the socialism he had now rejected. During his lifetime, *Civilization* did not significantly alter the perception that Clive principally wrote about art, but through the vagaries of its publishing history, as well as the book's provision of usefully pithy quotations exemplifying supposed 'Bloomsbury' snobbery and elitism, *Civilization* gained a lop-sided prominence in his later reputation.

Throughout the autumn of 1927, Vanessa and Virginia speculated about who might be the mysterious women in Clive's life now that Mary was no longer in the picture. He had told Lytton that life was more tolerable since he had stopped pretending to be happy and when he took Fanny, as he had nicknamed her, to see the *Marriage of Figaro* at the end of November, she enjoyed his company more than she had before because he spoke of things other than love. 'He told me that at present he was in a position of perfect safety,' she wrote in her diary; 'nothing could shake him.' Clive had hinted to her that he was planning to travel with 'fascinating female companions', but inadvertently let slip that his visit to Germany in the new year would in fact be with Raymond. Shortly before Valerie Taylor saw them off to Berlin, Clive had consummated yet another flirtation, this time with someone well known to Virginia and Vanessa.

Not far from Charleston lived an old family friend of the Stephens, Beatrice Meinertzhagen, known as Bobo and married since 1912 to Robin Mayor, a civil servant. Clive would occasionally come across her walking on the downs or picnicking with her children. She had been among the young people the Stephen siblings saw frequently at parties and dances in the early years of the century. Bobo had been particularly fond of Thoby because he had seemed to take an interest in her. When she saw in the newspaper the shocking news of his death in 1906, Bobo stood outside the Stephens' house on Gordon Square for an hour, stricken with grief, staring at the curtained windows. She and her sister Betty, an aspiring actress prone to histrionics over her lack of success on the stage, had remained friendly with Virginia and Vanessa as they all moved into their married lives.

In the early 1920s, Bobo was having success as a playwright. *The Girl and the City* and *Thirty Minutes in the Street* were produced at the Kingsway Theatre, where Leonard and Virginia saw them in 1922. Bobo often tried to help her struggling sister with her career, and Virginia wondered if Betty might read the play Clive had written? *Love and Liberty*, which Clive told Vanessa he hoped would 'retrieve the fallen fortunes of our house', falls stylistically somewhere between Congreve and Wilde.[1] Although quite competently constructed, its characters' arguments about the equality of the sexes and the economic basis of matrimony repeat many of the themes from Clive's articles and correspondence of the preceding few years (with even a rehash of his diatribe against Shaw's *Back to Methuselah*). Clive had the script professionally typed, but no production is known ever to have occurred, and Betty's career continued to languish.

At first, Clive told Mary that Bobo might become a 'pest', but he was disappointed when Robin Mayor came to tea without his 'imaginative wife'. When *The Pleasure Garden*, which would be her most successful work, was accepted by the Stage Society, Clive told Eliot, with characteristic hyperbole, that it was the best play written in England in their time. Bobo began to accept Clive's invitations to lunch or dinner without her husband and by late 1927, they had begun an affair. 'Today was an enchanting day,' Clive wrote on 3 November, 'and this evening I am writing you our first love letter.'

Unusually for Clive, they took precautions to keep the affair secret. Clive prepared several typed envelopes addressed to 'Mrs R. G. Mayor'

---

[1]Vanessa asked Clive if his family would pay the £50 fee for Julian at Leighton Park school; 'unless your play brings in millions I see no hope' (VB/CB 22 December 1921 TGA).

to avoid suspicion in her household. Such caution was wise, for had Robin Mayor chanced to see a letter addressed to 'Darling slut' he would not have taken a characteristically Bloomsbury view of the situation. Clive assured Bobo that Raymond and Eddie Sackville-West, with whom he was travelling in Germany, suspected nothing, presenting as evidence that Raymond had added 'Mrs Robin Mayor' to a list of women that homosexual men found attractive (the others being Mary, Vanessa and Nancy Cunard). Bobo was, like Mary, extremely well-read and avidly interested in art. She asked Clive to find out what the Germans said of a poet named Rilke who had been the lover of her friend the Expressionist painter Lou Albert-Lasard. At the time Rilke, who had died in December 1926, was little known even in Germany.

Accompanying Clive to France in the spring would involve Bobo 'in more lying than she has stomach for', Clive ruefully told Vanessa. She was, in any case, in demand as a successful playwright and throughout their affair was nervous of writing to Clive too freely. She wrote him a love letter but dared not send it. If a letter were returned and opened, disaster might follow. She even signed one letter with her full name in case this happened, eliciting a quizzical reply from Clive. He tried often to allay her anxiety but as time went on Bobo began to tire of his sentimentality. His letters rarely mentioned her work, although he published a flattering review of 'that modern masterpiece' *The Pleasure Garden* when it was produced at the Maddermarket in Norwich.[2]

Clive's German tour began in Munich, where he dropped Quentin at the home of the Baronne von Massenbach and her three daughters. After a few nights out at dance halls, Clive lamented that his own father had not made him learn German and thus improved his ability to converse with young German women. He enjoyed the Munich Carnival, particularly impressed by a reinterpretation of *Carmen* that led him, Raymond and Eddie to discuss the 'necessity of restating and reinterpreting works of art so as to keep them alive. Which is more like a Greek play: Jean Cocteau's *Antigone* or the *Oedipus Rex* at Cambridge?' he pondered. In Berlin, *Fidelio* produced in the manner of a Russian

---

[2] This led to a correspondence with Terence Gray of the Festival Theatre in Cambridge whom he met at the Maddermarket and who wanted to enlist Clive's aid in promoting his theories about theatre as an art form rather than as mere entertainment (Cornwell 203–05).

ballet also delighted Clive, who began to understand that, despite his poor opinion of most German painters, the dynamic performance culture of Weimar Germany had opened 'up vistas of new possibilities in the matter of re-interpretation of works of art'. The companions travelled to Dresden and Prague before arriving in Berlin, where they had hoped to see Harold Nicolson, who was a Counsellor at the British Embassy, but he had returned to England because Vita's father was dying. If Munich was Paradise, Clive joked to Bobo, Dresden was Aberdeen, but he was enthralled by the art he saw in private collections and museums which reaffirmed his conviction that the fifteenth and nineteenth centuries were the great ages of painting.

In addition to the thriving Berlin art world, there were famous nightclubs to visit, such as the Eldorado, on Lutherstrasse, opposite the Scala Variety Theatre, where Clive danced with transvestites who do 'all that girls should do'. The whole journey struck him as 'rather like a German treatise on Vice and Liberty', and both Vanessa and Virginia received Clive's opinions on the legs of German women. Soon after his return, a twenty-two-year-old opera singer wrote that she had hoped to see him again before he left because she had lost her gold watch in the car on their last evening together.

On his way back to London, Clive passed through Paris to see Cory and Violet, who were taking their daughter Peggy to stay with a French family. Vanessa told Virginia that Clive seemed happy with Bobo, which Virginia confirmed when Clive told her that he could never go back to Mary because 'her friends and ways are not nearly so congenial to him as ours are.' Clive's apparent calm was deceiving; he seemed to Virginia in fact to be 'crazed', a judgement with which Vanessa concurred when she received a letter from her husband that might have been written by a 'lady of fashion', detailing his appointments at a beauty specialist from whom he received injections to promote hair growth (to no avail), his dancing lessons and his giddy life in London's haut monde. Aside from his public image as a controversialist and cultural critic, Clive now appeared frequently in gossip columns as a member of the 'Bloomsbury Set'. As 'I want to see everyone & everyone wants to see me, time does not hang heavy on my hands,' he boasted to Vanessa, which meant that his writing was suffering. She thought Clive was in an 'odd way sexually'. Vanessa was more than usually sensitive to the figure cut in

London by Clive because he, she, Duncan and Roger had all just been the target of 'an amazing piece of sourgraped rage' by the editor of *Drawing & Design*.

Although Gerald Reitlinger mentioned no names in 'A Day Trip to the Sea Coast of Bohemia', his anonymously authored attack on Bloomsbury artists was so thinly veiled that its targets were quite recognisable. In common with other antagonists, he identified them with Oscar Wilde, whose disdain for 'bourgeois morality' he said had been expressed through 'pose, sophistries and intellectual snobbery'. According to Reitlinger, Wilde was the source of an English notion that artists must be 'Bohemian', and those who had revived his legacy in an English Bohemia 'shared their lives and loves in common', living in a milieu in which 'their abstract processes of thought were discussed with the same zest as the latest cohabitation.' Vanessa thought the article libellous and was particularly upset by Reitlinger's claim that in addition to being financially secure and having control of the press, the new Bohemians had 'even surreptitiously annexed a quite charming seaside place in the South of France'. This tendentious and scathing article may well be the first in what would become the flourishing journalistic genre of what Christopher Reed has named 'Bloomsbury bashing'.

Reitlinger's attack was balanced in the same month by Raymond Mortimer's 'London Letter' in the *Dial*, where he employed the conceit of an imaginary volume of *Studies in Twentieth Century Culture* published by the Hogarth Press in 1960 to predict what might be Bloomsbury's legacy. Mortimer imagined that Clive would be celebrated as 'an apostle of contemporary art, a vigorous pamphleteer, a poet, a historian of civilization, and a psychological biographer'. Foreshadowing defences that would be made of this much-vilified group in the second half of the century, he emphasised their characteristic 'fierce mutual criticism', a point that Vanessa had often made herself.

In addition to Clive's *Civilization*, 1928 would see the publication of Virginia's *Orlando*, Lytton's *Elizabeth and Essex* and the obscenity trial of Radclyffe Hall's *Well of Loneliness*, in defence of which Morgan Forster, Virginia and Vita all stood ready to testify despite their low opinion of the novel as a work of art. By contrast, Clive noted that 'Messrs Shaw, Wells & Bennett are afraid of speaking up for poor Miss Radclyffe-Hall.' 'In a hypocritical society,' Mortimer wrote, 'these friends 'have been indecent; in a conservative society, curious; in a gentlemanly society, ruthless; and in a fighting society, pacifist.' On the other hand, they had tended 'to exalt the classical in all the arts', and already there were signs that a younger generation was in revolt against the Bloomsbury elders.

27. Insane about Females

Clive was anxious to find his niche amongst the Bright Young People whose antics were widely reported in the 1920s. He attended the notorious 'Bath and Bottle Party' in 1928, which Brenda Dean Paul recalled as something of a swansong for her generation. Elizabeth Ponsonby, 'one of the twenties' enduring symbols', whom Frances Partridge loathed (and who is assumed to be the model for Evelyn Waugh's Agatha Runcible in *Vile Bodies*) appeared frequently in Clive's appointment diary in the twenties, although he did not attend her wedding in 1929.

Virginia continued to worry that Clive was spending the inheritance that should be shared with her sister on his 'Daimler and his supper parties'. Clive admitted to Vita that he was using cocaine when he poured out his misery to her on a visit to Long Barn. She worried when he told her what Cocteau had said about his own cocaine use: 'He knows it will kill him in a few years, but he is happy in the meantime, and doesn't care how much he has to increase his dose. Clive seemed to think this a good plan.' Clive later told Mary that both he and Eliot 'drug[ged] against despair – literally and metaphorically'. When Brenda Dean Paul was charged with drug offences and could find no one to help her, Clive appeared in court to put up her bail. Nights spent dancing at the Gargoyle Club, where 'everyone congratulates me on looking young', seemed to Clive worth the risks of cocaine-induced sleeplessness.

Vanessa had taken a lease on La Bergère in 1928, a small cottage she had discovered through a Colonel Teed, who lived at Fontcreuse, a short distance from Cassis, where she had rented the Villa Corsica the year before. The environs offered none of the distractions on which Clive blamed his lack of industry, although its denizens were by no means ascetic. That spring in the company of Roger, Vanessa and Duncan, Clive would often see their close neighbours Derain, Roland Penrose, Wyndham Tryon and Jean Varda (the community satirised by Cyril Connolly in *The Rock Pool*). Newcomers included a young English painter named Tristram Hillier and his girlfriend Joan Firminger, an aspiring film actress with whom Clive at once began to flirt. 'It used to be bad enough with Mary,' Vanessa complained to Virginia, 'but its far worse now.' By the end of the year, Clive had seen Joan in London several times and was making arrangements to see her in Paris, and to accompany her and her sister Enid to Saigon. Joan, Enid and Clive made an odd quartet in Paris in early 1929 with Dick Wyndham, cousin of the Gargoyle Club's owner, David Tennant. Virginia observed how embarrassing the forty-seven-year-old Clive's behaviour was for his sons: 'Its like an old dandy fixing false whiskers – this mania to be the master of some chit . . . Its a bore, one's father being laughed at.'

Virginia and Leonard came to stay at La Bergère while Clive was there and once again the visit ended with a falling-out when Clive saw a letter in which Virginia complained that he came too often to see her, taking up too much of her time. She wanted to understand why he so often lashed out at her. Clive blamed his vehemence on their ancient history, writing with unusual self-awareness that it was due to 'some relic of the past, complicated by suppressed snobbery – I am over anxious for your good opinion.' Virginia surmised that he must have read her letters to Vanessa because he accused her of laughing at him.

It was not Virginia alone, by any means, who found Clive embarrassing in the aftermath of his break-up with Mary. Everyone ridiculed 'this perpetual description of his own ecstasies and agonies: after all this bedding or not bedding becomes a little dull; when one's out of it.' Virginia worried that Julian was already displaying signs of a similar vanity: 'He takes his poems a little too much to heart; as Clive does his derision at the hands of the great Stephen family.' When they had made up their quarrel, Clive told Virginia that he could not help his outbursts because they dated back 'to old horrors in the past'. 'Scarred and riddled with complexes' as they were, Virginia and Clive could never hope for 'a plain straightforward relationship . . . So it will go on till the daisies grow over us,' Virginia told Vanessa, although, as far as she could tell, Mary seemed to be 'under the earth for ever'.

Clive left La Bergère reluctantly to meet Bobo in Paris, by means of whose intimate company he hoped to exorcise several ghosts at the Hotel de Londres. His relations with women still seemed opaque to Vanessa and Virginia and they wondered if someone other than Bobo was affecting his mood. They would learn in time that when Bobo left Paris, Clive had an assignation in Dieppe with a young French woman named Suzanne Clément. In 1929, Vanessa and Virginia would discuss the relative merits of Clive marrying 'Susie'.

While at La Bergère, Clive wrote a long essay on Proust that would be the first monograph on the writer published in England (he had contributed 'A Foot-Note' to the collection of tributes C. K. Scott Moncrieff published shortly after Proust's death). Clive had been devotedly reading À la recherche du temps perdu since Mary had introduced it to him in 1919 and when Eliot asked for a contribution to the *Criterion*, Clive had at first thought of Proust as a subject but determined he had too much to say for a magazine article. With Virginia's encouragement, he began to re-read the entire novel shortly after the last volume, *Le temps retrouvé*, appeared posthumously in 1927. At La Bergère, where he, Duncan and Vanessa were joined by Virginia, Leonard and Raymond Mortimer, Clive found a suitable illustration for his reflections on the nature of subjectivity in Proust's narrative:

> I am living on a farm in a remote village by the Mediterranean with five of my oldest friends. We all try to work. We wear espadrilles and sweaters, wash once a day and shave twice a week. We talk as only people who have known each other twenty years can talk . . . if to-morrow the mayor of Marseille were to invite me to an official banquet . . . a nicely brushed and French-speaking Clive Bell would present himself, and would be as much me as the person who was smoking his pipe before the stove last night.

Clive dedicated *Proust* to Raymond, who recognised in it ideas from their conversations at La Bergère. Shortly before she arrived in Cassis, Virginia had finished *Orlando*, in which it is speculated that any person may have six or seven thousand different 'selves', all 'commanded and locked up by the Captain self, the Key self'. Clive's essay recounted conversations that resonated closely with what Virginia had so recently written. While he adopted different selves in different situations, Clive wrote, he also could not 'help believing that there is a self more real than any of these', one which comments upon all the others, and yet, 'it well may be, as Proust seems to have supposed, that this flattering conviction is another illusion,' albeit a necessary one. If they talked about something that had happened at Cambridge, he could see himself 'almost as if the undergraduate, Clive Bell, were another of those old friends, were someone other than my present self'. Clive borrowed an image from Leonard to illustrate the theory of personality he wished to explain in *Proust*:

> Personality he likens to a thread from which depend beads, which beads are our various selves. Some are so tightly attached to the thread that hardly can they be detached – such is the high thinking, low-living self that is slopping about the vineyards of Cassis in *espadrilles*: others – the self, for instance, that was the life and soul of a tipsy carouse last Wednesday – are so loosely attached that with the greatest ease they can be disengaged, reviewed and laughed at by the more permanent self.

Tightly attached to the thread of Clive's personality was the self who had greeted each new volume of *La Recherche* as an 'emotional event' in the *ménage à trois* formed by himself, the work and the woman who had brought Proust into his life, Mary. That self had lost its mooring since she left him.

Proust was generally well received in England, although the 'Proust-and-I air of the essay' failed to amuse the reviewer for the *Aberdeen Press and Journal*. The novelist Dorothy Richardson praised it in *The New Adelphi*, sprinkling her review with French words and phrases as if to establish her *bona fides* on the subject. Although she found its tone sometimes strained, on the whole she believed that Clive and Proust thought and felt about life in a very similar manner, even going so far as to suggest that, were he still alive, Proust 'would keep this essay at hand if only for the sake of its inclusiveness.' The reviewer with most authority to speak in England, Proust's translator C. K. Scott Moncrieff, was also positive in his (unsigned) *TLS* review, but pointed out some errors, eliciting a letter from Clive about minutiae that Moncrieff had to deal with firmly: 'Even after a luncheon party Proust would not address his friend in the French of Bloomsbury.' This was undoubtedly a blow to Clive's pride. His sons' tutor, M. Pinault, had been diplomatic about Clive's French when he commented that although it was at times more archaic than incorrect he would have liked to express himself as well in English as Clive did in French.

In London, after months of silence or apparent indifference, Clive and Mary painfully tried to find a way out of their emotional impasse. It was inevitable that their paths would cross and 'harsh untrue things' be said. Clive could not forget the agony of Mary's letters from the unhappy summer of 1927 when he was trying his best to overcome his jealousy. With the exception of Vanessa, he had not loved anyone other than Mary, and felt bitter now because he believed that if she loved him she would have fitted her new affair into their relationship, rather than the other way around. He sent her a copy of *Proust* because not doing so might have led her to think he bore her ill will but told her she need not reply. And when she did not reply, he accused Mary of holding a grudge because she had not even 'written two words of thanks'.

His life resumed a familiar pattern of lunches and dinners, tennis in Gordon Square, meetings of the Memoir Club and evenings at the theatre, occasionally interrupted by dutiful visits to his widowed mother in Seend. He went to a grand lunch given by Lesley Jowitt to celebrate the first of four mosaic floors at the National Gallery created by Boris Anrep. Paid for by Samuel Courtauld and Maud Russell, a well-connected patron of modern art, Anrep's series, which would be completed in 1952, was intended to celebrate the culture of the modern age. Clive would be the model for Bacchus on the halfway landing's *Awakening of the Muses* that Anrep made in 1933, alongside Osbert Sitwell as Apollo, surrounded in the mosaic by the nine Muses, the models for whom included two of Anrep's lovers, Maroussa Volkova and Anna Akhmatova, as well as Diana Mitford, Greta Garbo, Lydia Lopokova, Christabel Aberconway, Mary Hutchinson, Lesley Jowitt and Virginia Woolf (who represents Clio, the muse of history).

Reviewing the first installation in June 1928, Clive applauded the National Gallery's director, Charles Holmes, for having 'asserted that

Photo spread about Anrep National Gallery mosaic in Sketch, *21 June 1933*

galleries and museums were not places of instruction, to be entered out of a sense of duty or in a spirit of awe, but places of enjoyment' into which Anrep's 'lovely pattern' fitted perfectly. In the same month, he visited the London Group show, which he found so familiar as to be rather dull. It did lead him to wonder if he had overrated Frank Dobson and underrated Epstein, but he admired Vanessa's *Three Women* (sometimes known as *A Conversation*) and her portrait of Mary. The latter had been described by Roger in the catalogue 'rather stupidly', Clive thought, as a portrait of Mrs St John Hutchinson, which struck him as tactless because it was so unflattering.

Vanessa's *Portrait, M. H.* had previously been exhibited in 1917 by Roger in an exhibition he curated in Birmingham. The Tate now hypothesises that this was probably not the better known *Portrait of Mary Hutchinson*, a painting that has often been taken as evidence of

Vanessa's hostility towards Mary – 'revenge on her errant husband', in the words of one biographer. Tate's catalogue describes *Portrait, M. H.* as 'almost exactly the same design' as *Portrait of Mary Hutchinson*, 'but slightly more loosely painted'. Jeremy Hutchinson later called the Tate version an 'awful portrait' which he could not bear because he found it 'rather cruel' and not 'like her'; he never talked about it with his mother. Yet the impulse of sexual jealousy that many have ascribed to Vanessa's creation of this work is not evident anywhere in her correspondence. Spalding believes the painting shows the clash of the women's personalities, which is a more likely interpretation of any perceived hostility in it than Vanessa's feelings about the fact that Mary was Clive's lover. Probably Vanessa was simply experimenting with a style, an interpretation borne out by Duncan and Vanessa's contemporaneous portraits of Iris Tree who, in spite of being quite thin in person (as was Mary) is also rendered as huge and ungainly.

While Clive gallivanted about Europe with Joan Firminger, Virginia felt she had been left to deal with Mary's misery. Between them, Clive and Mary would claw her apart for nothing, she complained to Vita. Finding Clive 'in spats and fur coat' sitting over Vanessa's fire in Fitzroy Street one morning, marvelling at the whirlwind that was his amorous life, Virginia 'got into a fury with it all' and left abruptly. All through Joan's stormy relationship with Tristram Hillier, which staggered on until the autumn of 1930, Clive continued to see her; even in 1932, when she came to Cassis with a new young man, Clive was still appalling Vanessa by the shameless way he carried on with Joan. It recalled how he had behaved towards Sabine, an au pair Vanessa had hired to help with Angelica and her friend Judith Bagenal (Barbara and Nick's daughter) at La Bergère.

Despite finding her boring and not particularly attractive, Clive used his French to banter and flirt incessantly with Sabine, a situation exacerbated when Cory visited, inducing Clive to be even more outrageous in his attentions to the bewildered young woman. The 'most astonishing flow of male conversation' was kept up by the brothers, fuelled by copious glasses of brandy, at once horrifying and fascinating Duncan, who gained some insight into what life at Cleeve House must have been like. The shameful performance led Vanessa to agree with Julian that his father was 'insane about females'. The time had come to make Clive see what a laughing stock he had become.

Although Julian was angered and embarrassed by Clive's behaviour, Quentin was more inclined to enjoy his father's style of life. As an art student in Paris in spring 1929, Quentin spent several evenings in Clive's company, dancing at L'Ecart with Georgie Sitwell. Without a young woman at his side, Clive sometimes worried that his and Quentin's relationship might be misconstrued by other men; he also did not dare introduce Suzanne Clément to his tall son as it would make clear how much older he was than Suzanne believed. Vanessa discerned the difference in her sons' personalities – the bearded Julian content to be alone and commune with nature in the Midi, while Quentin 'paints & carries on with anyone he can find'. Julian's worry that his brother might become like their father, an 'elderly roué' who bored everyone with talk of love affairs, led Virginia to caution Quentin not to emulate Clive, who she wished would 'progress beyond love where he has been stationed these many years to the next point in the human pilgrimage'.

An intervention was ultimately performed by Christabel Aberconway, who made clear to Clive how boring everyone found his endless paeans to love. She suspected Clive was using drugs because he left the room frequently during his visit. When Virginia next saw Clive, although he did not mention the conversation with Christabel, she observed a change in his demeanour. They talked calmly about his future and the possibility that he might marry Suzanne, the young woman he had been seeing in Paris and Dieppe at the end of the 1920s.

In spite of this, it is difficult to imagine that he ever would have divorced Vanessa. It is a sign of his desperate emotional state in the years immediately following the loss of Mary that Clive could consider settling down with a woman he described to Virginia as a 'sensible peasant girl, who has good wits, great charm, and general competence'. Vanessa knew very well that Clive could not endure being alone with any of his ladies for more than a few days: even a fortnight with Mary had once made him on edge.

In the summer of 1929, Suzanne led Clive to believe she might be pregnant. He asked Vanessa to get the name of a refuge for young women 'about one month gone' from Jean Teed: 'How silly girls are – really at this time of day, with Marie Stopes and all.' But within a week she had told him it was no more than an upset stomach. By December, the affair with Suzanne was over. Years later, Clive showed Mary a poem he had written (but not sent) to Suzanne that summer, thanking her for making him forget Mary.

As 1929 drew to an end, Clive arranged to meet Frances Marshall and Ralph Partridge in Barcelona. Frances and Ralph had begun in 1926 to spend time living together at 41 Gordon Square as tenants of Alix and James Strachey, a resolution to the fraught situation at Ham Spray that eased the circumstances of the lovers, but not of Lytton and Carrington. They planned to go to the General Exposition in Barcelona on their way back from staying in Yegen with Gerald Brenan. Clive and Raymond joined them in October and, after Frances and Ralph left, Clive stayed on with the Huxleys and Georges Duthuit. Aldous was at the Expo to give lectures (there were 'conferences and seminars on topics as widely diverse as cancer and dry cleaning' given by representatives of fourteen European countries). The spectacular Art Deco lighting displays at the National Palace and the impressive illuminated fountains, for which Clive said the word *féerique* must surely have been invented, failed to make up for his disappointment at the large exhibition of Arte de España. He also disliked the paintings by Josep Maria Sert in the Vic Cathedral (which were destroyed by fire in 1936), but was enthralled by the architecture of Gaudi, describing it to Frances as 'one of the most striking manifestations of the human spirit that I have ever seen, or indeed wish to see'.

Maria Huxley wrote to Mary from Spain that her absence was keenly felt and wondered if Clive was thinking about her as intensely as she did. When he got back to London, Mary confused Clive by impulsively suggesting they go to Rome, but he retorted that she must surely understand they could never travel together simply as old friends. As Virginia reflected when she saw Clive, 'everything has been shifted by Mary; no fundament left'.

V
NOTHING WORSE
THAN WAR (1930–1939)

28. Clive Agonistes

Clive and Vanessa's correspondence could at times resemble that of any middle-class couple dealing with bills, rent, children's ailments, holiday plans and travel. When Clive needed something done at his flat while he was in Rome, or Paris, or Venice, it was usually Vanessa who arranged it. His wife might be one of those women who 'prefer to live with buggers', as he put it, but Clive and she maintained the public façade of being Mr and Mrs Clive Bell. When a brief notice in the *Daily Telegraph* about the marriage of Lord Gage, from whose Firle Estate Charleston was leased, referred to Vanessa as 'Mrs Duncan Grant', Leonard and Bunny were sure the newspaper would cough up £100 for libel. Clive urged Vanessa to sue, but they had to be satisfied with a published apology.

Maintaining the illusion of their marriage, as well as the fiction that Angelica was Clive's daughter, was as important for the sake of Hannah Taylor Bell as it was for an inquisitive public. Clive needed to keep on good terms with his mother to avoid any threat to his eventual inheritance, but he also cared about her in a way he never had for his father. After a long absence from England in 1931, he apologetically asked Vanessa to steel herself for a necessary visit to Cleeve House to make peace at Christmas time. Vanessa acknowledged their queer marriage in a letter to Julian: 'You're an odd mixture you know, my dear, like all my children perhaps and like me and Clive – I mean we're an odd mixture, aren't we?' Clive, who shared Vanessa's sceptical view of traditional marriage, had a scornful opinion of the conclusion of Lawrence's *Lady Chatterley's Lover*. 'The lovers must get married. The smug little bourgeois from Notts bobs up. Like his father & mother before him he is horrified by these irregular connexions.'

After Mary, Clive never had another such love affair but had a series of (often overlapping) liaisons and several more ephemeral sexual encounters. Rarely without female companionship, he nevertheless complained often to Vanessa that he was lonely in London and in Paris and asked continually about her plans so that he could arrange his own accordingly. Invariably, upon his return from the Continent to London, he would ask Vanessa to make sure there was a 'family dinner' in Bloomsbury with her, Duncan and whatever other old friends could be gathered. She obliged whenever she could but at the same time maintained the protective boundaries around her and Duncan's work that were an impregnable defence against Clive and others' emotional demands.

Clive managed to live and travel more or less as he wished, although he bemoaned high income tax and the poor showing of dividends on his investments. He added to his unearned income with commissions from American periodicals, royalties on his books and fees for BBC radio broadcasts, which he began doing in 1928 when he and Desmond MacCarthy discussed the relations between 'Art and Life'. When he was away for months at a time, Clive tried to rent out 50 Gordon Square. In 1929, he even looked for a tenant who would take the six-room flat for a year at a rate of £200, but usually it was occupied for shorter periods, such as when Eardley Knollys stayed there for four guineas a week in 1930.

At the start of 1930, Clive went to Paris where, although he disliked having to view the paintings by electric light, he revelled in the Cézannes loaned by Ambroise Vollard to an exhibition at the Galerie Pigalle. His social life was as crowded as ever but he was determined to get back to work after the turmoil of the previous months. Joan Firminger was there with Tristram Hillier, who was preparing for his own exhibition in Paris later that winter, and on a visit to his studio, Clive was so impressed that he bought a large painting.[1] He saw Waldemar George, whose book about French artists' drawings Clive had just reviewed,

---

[1]No record of which painting it was survives, but in 1949 Maud Russell thanked Clive for donating a Hillier to a YWCA auction (M. Russell/CB 7 May 1949 KCC).

and met Man Ray but did not have time to see his photographs before leaving for Cannes where he had rented a flat on the rue d'Antibes from Madge Garland, the fashion journalist who lived with *Vogue* editor Dorothy Todd. Vanessa and Virginia agreed that work was the only likely salvation for an 'elderly roué whose mind has gone grey and bald', and were relieved when Clive seemed to be focusing on writing rather than romance. Although Joan's considerable allure still tested his resolve, Clive had met a new companion at the end of 1929 whose independence and lack of other attachments satisfied Vanessa's hope for a milder affair than those with which he had embarrassed their sons.

As Hillier was journeying south to paint, Joan hoped that Clive might take her with him to Cannes, but accompanying him was Benita Jaeger, an aspiring film actress who had made clear her expectations: 'I never

Benita Jaeger at Le Pradet, 1933

want you to be my husband, or even my man, I want you to be my wonderful lover.' Benita had come to London from Frankfurt in 1926 with the idea of becoming either an artist (she later sculpted) or a film actor. She became the closest friend of Elsa Lanchester, the bohemian actress who co-founded the Cave of Harmony on Charlotte Street, where she and others had performed skits in the mid-twenties for an audience which included H. G. Wells, Aldous Huxley and Evelyn Waugh. Among the regulars at the Cave of Harmony was Yvonne 'Bimbo' Kapp, with whom Benita would later share a flat in Brunswick Square, beneath rooms occupied by E. M. Forster. Yvonne's ardour for Benita gave Clive's relations with his German paramour a sometimes amusing wrinkle. Elsa Lanchester became world-famous in 1935 when she starred alongside Boris Karloff as the *Bride of Frankenstein*, after moving to Hollywood with her husband, Charles Laughton; Benita's film-world gossip was of the Laughtons, Marlene Dietrich, Norma Shearer, Jean Harlow and Josef von Sternberg. She and the painter John Armstrong, whom Benita married in 1936, often stayed with Elsa at her country cottage, where the three of them made 8mm short films for their own entertainment.

Clive was adamant that Benita was no more to him than a 'type-writress' who also chauffeured him about (he never learned to drive), dealt with his correspondence and occasionally danced with him at the southern branch of Le Boeuf sur le Toit, but her uncomplicated lustiness added to the appeal of her efficiency. Benita was happy to receive whatever Clive wanted to give her, telling him she never had 'false illusions' about their relationship. 'Besides,' she said, 'if Benitas were to feel secure, they would not be Benitas.'

John Banting had recently vacated Garland's flat and moved to La Napoule nearby, where he and other Bright Young People such as Sandy Baird and Brian Howard led a louche life of drinking and rough trade which Clive found curiously relaxing. Though he had sometimes wondered whether he were bright or young enough to consort with that infamous set, Clive had enthusiastically attended David Tennant's Mozart extravaganza in April and could often be found 'Gargling at the Gargoyle Club'.[2] 'How wise was I to leave Bloomsbury and its

---

[2]'The great 1920s joke peddled by newspapers about the Bright Young People was the presence in their ranks of moonlighting middle age' (Taylor 29).

environs,' he told Frances Marshall. 'I envy the buggers – they are so passionless and peaceable – in fact I feel as if I had become a bugger almost – in fact I am sinking quietly into middle age.' When Raymond and Eddie Sackville-West visited, they found the 'constant atmosphere of intrigue and jealousy' at La Napoule depressing, but Clive enjoyed the atmosphere of the 'headquarters of Mediterranean buggery' where Benita – herself quite sexually fluid – was propositioned by more women than men. They ate well, made voyeuristic excursions to the brothels and sailors' bars of Nice, where they would sometimes see pornographic films, and on some mornings Benita drove Clive out to the hills for long walks. To Raymond, Frances, Virginia and Vanessa, Clive insisted that although there might be grounds for scandal, there was no basis for rumours of a romance between him and Benita. He ascribed his happiness to not being in love for the first time in sixteen years, and found that he could concentrate in Madge's flat. While he was there, Clive produced an appraisal of Derain for Waldemar George's magazine *Formes* (Picasso's 'Letter on Art' appeared in the same issue).

Clive somewhat inaccurately described Derain as out of fashion among young painters; some did still admire him, such as Balthus and Giacometti. In the 1930s, despite praising his old friend's continued experimentation in the effort to find a 'plastic equivalent' for the emotions provoked by a particular object, Clive remained puzzled by Derain's classically inspired landscapes. Derain was deepening his interest in myth and ritual and had abandoned the avant-garde promise of his early work. When he died in 1954, Janet Flanner commented sadly that 'what he had been painting for the past twenty-five years made it difficult to recall how great he had started to be when young'. Clive did his best to salvage Derain's reputation, pointing out in *Formes* that he was still relatively young, and that even if Derain's realist works lacked depth, he was a 'pure' painter.

In Paris that spring, after returning from Cannes, Clive led a life of 'almost Charlestonian virtue and economy' while conducting research at the Louvre for a commission he had received. It was to write a book to prepare visitors for a major exhibition of French painting at Burlington House planned by the National Art Collections Fund. Joan was still in Paris and Clive was glad when Hillier returned from the south to reclaim her. He tried to retire early from evenings spent with Duthuit and Cocteau (who was filming *Le Sang d'un poète*). 'Dragged' to tea at her sister's by Marcelle Meyer, Clive was pleased to find Larionov, Goncharova, Zadkine and Madame Tzara there, and to meet the Italian painter Valentine Prax, but he spent most of his time thinking about his *Account of French Painting*. As he had when preparing to write the articles in *Landmarks*, he supplemented the hours he spent in the Louvre with extensive reading. Benita was thrilled when he told her in June that his hard work had earned him a week's dissipation.

When she arrived in Paris, Clive noticed how much more attractive Benita seemed since she had been able to buy smart new clothes as a result of her work at Elstree with the German director Richard Eichberg. The stylish Benita fitted in easily with his Paris circle, dining at the Frieszes', and going with him to lunch with Alice Roullier of the Chicago Arts Club, to whom Clive explained that his companion had 'ceased suddenly to be a fuzzy little art-student and become an elegant and entourée cinema-actress'. A party given by Eugene McCown, attended by Nancy Cunard, Dollie Wilde and Natalie Barney, proved a little *too* dissipated for Clive when a 'party of boxers' turned up. He left with Benita, telling Vanessa 'it was no place for me'. When Benita left, Clive went to Cassis, intending to continue work on the book he was now enjoying writing as much as anything since *Art*. There, he found Quentin. Clive had recently transferred £4,000 capital to each of his sons, intending them to be responsible for living on their own investments. He drew Julian's attention to the contrast between the 'low living & high thinking' he and Quentin practised at La Bergère and Julian's spendthrift ways. Also in Cassis was Joan Firminger. She was again at odds with Hillier and wished to provoke him. Clive obliged by spending the night with her in Vanessa's bed. Quentin – 'an enchanting human being', Clive told Vanessa – managed to allay the servants' suspicions about any impropriety.

Joan's attractions proved too much for Clive; he admitted to Vanessa that he might be 'a little in love' with her, though she should not worry. His book well in hand, he and Joan set off on a tour of Italy in the autumn, starting in Venice. When he awoke one morning unable to see out of his left eye, Clive assumed the condition would quickly improve, but when it did not, he hurried back to London to see an

Joan Firminger, ca. 1927

oculist. The doctor forbade him to read – a terrible blow to one who unfailingly devoted at least two hours every day to a practice on which, as Virginia told Ethel Smyth, 'his rational life depends'. Worrying as his predicament was, more troubling to Virginia was that upon hearing this dire news, Mary Hutchinson immediately visited Clive and offered to read to him. Virginia was then summoned 'to go into the whole question of their relationship' once more.

Although she may have been irritated at being dragged yet again by Mary into picking at old wounds, Virginia was ambivalent. Not only was she fascinated by Clive's intimate life with Mary – with whom she was not averse to flirting herself – but also by his astute insights into her own sexuality. Clive told Virginia that *Orlando* was even better than *To the Lighthouse*, based on his theory that she could not 'feel sex', that she lacked the 'purple light' of physical passion, which meant that she must 'write Orlando's not Lighthouses'. Their discussion of lust led inevitably to the subject of Mary and Clive's perennial protest that 'Love is enough – or if love fails, down one goes for ever.' Virginia understood as few others could how the loss of his relationship with Mary had so profoundly affected Clive's sense of himself, unmooring him.

Clive's closeness to Thoby had always counted for a great deal with Virginia, and when he read to her some of the letters her brother had written to him, they reminded her of the young man she had first met at Cambridge: 'I always feel, how jolly, how much hunting, & talking & carousing there is in you!' she mused in her diary about Clive. 'How long we have known each other – & then Thoby's form looms behind – that queer ghost.' Mary's summons jarred an odd 'tangle of emotions' when she told Virginia that she would offer to go to bed with Clive once a fortnight if it would help him.

Although the triangular relationship between Vanessa, Clive and Virginia still underlay their emotions towards one another, at the time Clive's affliction struck, Virginia had sensed that he was trying to withdraw from intimacy with her. The sympathy she felt for him as he faced the terror of losing his sight softened her feelings of regret about his distance at the time, yet in the 1930s, as she began to focus her work more acutely on the political consequences of patriarchy, Virginia at times found Clive's wounding comments extremely painful, a situation exacerbated by her 'profound trepidation' about her appearance in the company of his smart friends. After enduring his malicious teasing at a dinner where she had 'played [her] tricks: jumped over the candlestick; & cooperated with Clive in the great business of impressing', she reflected on 'his oblique method of getting his own back . . . His own – what did I steal 20 years ago that he should never feel the debt paid?' Their difficult relations found their way into her analysis of how men treated women, informing both her novel *The Years* (1937) and her antiwar polemic *Three Guineas* (1938). She came to think of Clive as 'George, Ring the Bell & Run Away', a term 'coined in order to define those who make use of words with the desire to hurt but at the same time to escape detection'. She resolved to 'observe his method & analyse it in action' as she endured the jibes of this 'pismire' (ant).

On the other hand, she loved Clive deeply. At the end of one of the most mystical entries in her diary, in which she had tried and failed to lay her hands on a profound emptiness which haunted her, Virginia wrote, 'Its odd, now I come to think of it – I miss Clive.' When she fainted at the Ivy one evening, Clive took her home in a taxi and she felt the 'odd liberation of emotion' at being with someone she did not doubt would care for her, in contrast to Maynard and Lydia, who, when she fainted at Rodmell, had carried her into Monk's House and then left in their chauffeured car, behaviour that Clive condemned.

Word of Clive's eye trouble spread rapidly as he sought opinions from various specialists in London. Eliot recommended James Joyce's ophthalmologist, Alfred Vögt, while Aldous Huxley advised Clive to learn Braille. Clive heard from Raymond that Maria Huxley had been moved to see how worried Cocteau was about his dear friend's plight. Clive kept up a brave front but the prospect of being unable to read depressed him profoundly. Benita, who had gone to Berlin to try her luck there when film work in London had dried up, promised that his 'fun girl' would come to cheer him up as soon as she could but, as Ethel Sands shrewdly pointed out to Nan Hudson, it was Vanessa who would inevitably end up having to care for Clive were his semi-blind state to persist. By the end of the year, Clive had been referred to the Zurich clinic of the renowned Dr Vögt, who showed Clive how to monitor his condition and recommended that he return as a patient for two months in the new year.

Once settled into Vögt's 'Alpine Sing-Sing' in January 1931, Clive made the most of the situation, spending the brief outings he was allowed visiting the nearby Kunsthaus Zürich's collection of French paintings. He endured injections of cocaine into his eyes, but his fear returned when the condition spread to his right eye. Vanessa offered to come to Zurich once Angelica had returned to school at Langford Grove (from where the twelve-year-old wrote to 'Daddy' to ask if Zurich was as cold as England). Friends tried their best to keep Clive amused, but the gossip in their letters – for example, about a scandalous photograph found on a table at the Gargoyle Club of 'Mr X' entering Brenda Dean Paul from behind – could hardly be read aloud to him by the Sisters of the Red Cross. Having discussed the identity of Mr X (David Tennant) and similar matters with Raymond, Virginia professed herself bored by such gossip, but Clive ridiculed what he perceived as her jealousy of male homosexual society, especially, he told Vanessa, when 'she, Vita, Hilda Matheson e tutti quanti all huddling lesbonically together look quite as silly as any pack of buggers'. From Benita and Raymond, Clive received accounts of a large party given by Alix Strachey and Carrington at Stephen Tomlin's new studio where several of his worlds had mingled. Frankie Birrell and Raymond, Frances and Ralph, Duncan, Vanessa, Bunny and Eddie Sackville-West were there, as were Joan Firminger, Elizabeth Ponsonby and Brenda Dean Paul. It was at this party that Vanessa first encountered Benita, and admired her costume which consisted 'solely of two scarves, strategically pinned and fastened at the top of her necklace'.

29. An Account of French Painting

Hearing from Waldemar George about a ministerial hitch that might delay the French exhibition, Clive felt a slight relief from the pressure to finish his 'beginning-to-become-tiresome book', a task he had set himself to achieve at La Bergère where he went with Benita in May 1931. In a house nearby was Yvonne Kapp, whose passion for Benita Clive found amusing. Earlier that year, Benita had stayed with Charles and Marie Mauron to improve her French and now proved herself an indispensable companion, driving the Citroën Clive had bought for Vanessa to fetch supplies in Cassis and typing his letters. Quentin arrived in June and promptly crashed the car, just before Raymond joined the party.

Clive was glad to be out of England. The financial crisis which had led to the election of a Conservative-dominated National Government under Ramsay MacDonald exacerbated his worries about the high taxes on his investment income. He once again considered giving up his English domicile now that he spent so little time at Gordon Square, and suggested to Vanessa that it might help their tax situation to put Charleston in Duncan's name. It was just as easy to see his closest friends in Barcelona or Rome, or Paris, where he had noticed that although everyone cried poverty the theatres and clubs were always full.

Quentin, Yvonne and Benita seemed to Clive to be leading an ideal existence, talking incessantly in the sun as they collaborated on a psychoanalytically inflected novel. Yvonne was, in common with many people at the time, fascinated by psychoanalysis and had herself been a patient of Adrian Stephen's (who, like his wife, Karin, had become a psychoanalyst in 1926). Under the name Yvonne Cloud, she had a surprising success with her first novel, *Nobody Asked You* (published by the Willy Nilly Press, formed in Benita's name) when it was described by Gerald Gould as a work that referred 'calmly, and even lightly, to forms of depravity which, in England, are mentioned mainly in law-reports and sociological treatises'. Her outlook, like her setting, he noted, could be summed up as 'French', so it was no wonder that Clive found Yvonne an interesting addition to the local scene. Quentin – who designed the cover for the novel – recalled playing the 'part of Leporello to Clive's Don Juan' in Cassis, where Yvonne, of whom Quentin was very fond himself, vied with Clive for Benita's attentions. With the Huxleys close by at Sanary-sur-mer, Clive could enjoy the best of those worlds he most desired – rigorous intellectual discussion and the company of an attractive and intelligent woman. Talking late into the night with Raymond reminded Clive of old Cambridge days, and Quentin, he told Vanessa proudly, had acquitted himself very well. Clive and Vanessa had thought of meeting in Paris where several important exhibitions were about to open – a major Byzantine show at the Louvre, as well as a Matisse retrospective at Georges-Petit – but Vanessa could not afford to travel again to France, having just been there, and, after all, she commented dryly, 'one has seen Matisse'.

Having finished his book, Clive went to Paris with Raymond and Quentin. Despite including so many familiar works, the Matisse retrospective seemed 'magnificent' to Clive, who presented his son to the great man. A small Picasso exhibition was at Paul Rosenberg's but Picasso himself had withdrawn from Parisian circles to the Château de Boisgeloup. He answered no letters, and telephone callers were always told he was not at home. 'Thank God,' Clive told Mary, 'there's room in the world for Matisse and Picasso.'

When Raymond mentioned that Mary had joined him, Harold Nicolson and Molly MacCarthy for lunch, Clive used the information as a pretext for writing to her. Clive's eyes, having seemed cured after two months of Vögt's treatment, were troubling him again so he was coming to London to consult specialists. He hoped Mary, who was recuperating from a serious operation, would consent to meet him. He could not resist telling her that all his affairs had foundered on the same rock, which was that everyone knew he was in love with her. He tried to arouse her jealousy by telling her that he and Maria Huxley made little jokes at her expense. By the time he was back in London, having left the proofs of *An Account of French Painting* with Duthuit, to whom it was dedicated, Clive and Mary had resumed their tortured correspondence.

An Account of French Painting was published in time for autodidacts to prepare themselves for the 'Exhibition of French Art, 1200–1900', which opened at the Royal Academy in January 1932. The wide reading Clive had done to establish a solid foundation did not preclude his characteristically personal, and occasionally flippant, tone from leavening the information he provided. Duthuit could hear Clive's voice and laughter all through it, in such quips as, 'No one who generalises as much as I has a more lively mistrust of generalisations,' preceding the declaration that the 'most French thing about French art is its humanity'. Clive proposed that Rubens and Poussin were the roots of the French tradition but, in a typical rhetorical move, he claimed that he could hardly be blamed for errors because he was a 'sciolist', not a scholar. As Rebecca West noted, the book was essentially a celebration of the French culture Clive so loved: 'He hails every feature of French life and history with a cheer and a wave of the concertina as if it were one more village passed on the happy highway.'

Although not all reviewers accepted Clive's description of French painting as an expression of 'Frenchness', the *Account* was generally welcomed. Clive was amused to see his book for sale at Burlington House alongside Raymond Mortimer's contribution to the Hogarth Press's 'Letters' series. In *The French Pictures*, Raymond instructed a friend named Harriet how to get the most out of an exhibition she probably would visit only out of a sense of obligation. Clive, too, had referred to museum-goers performing 'an act of culture' by dutifully going to a similar Burlington House exhibition of Italian painting in 1930. The reason so many members of the public went to these large exhibitions appeared to Clive to be that 'everyone does'.

'The Great Age', the last chapter in *An Account*, became the core of one of the stock lectures Clive gave throughout England in the 1930s and would deliver several times in the United States in the 1950s, where he was regarded as a living monument of the European art world. Drawing also on *Landmarks in Nineteenth Century Painting*, Clive accurately identified himself as one of those who had borne the brunt of violent criticism when he championed a new art that by now had become widely accepted:

> If to-morrow, a new, unorthodox genius were to begin doing what Giotto and Raphael and Rubens and Renoir did, but doing it in an unexpected manner, in the manner neither of Cézanne nor of Matisse nor of Picasso, be sure the latest in authority would be at him almost to a man, and would be screaming 'idiots', 'perverts', 'Bolsheviks', at the handful of cranks and highbrows who recognised a new artist in unfamiliar clothes.

Roger welcomed *An Account* because it exemplified how writing about art had changed since the time when it had to be treated 'in a tone of lachrymose edification or melancholy yearning'. Praising Clive's deep understanding of the eighteenth century, Roger allowed that 'like everyone who gets into close touch with the artists through their works, he has his own special likes and dislikes,' yet the author was 'never pontifical'.

As he had in *Since Cézanne*, Clive emphasised the importance of Seurat as the 'indicated terminal' of a revolution that had begun in the nineteenth century and once again acknowledged the vital contribution of the Courtaulds in making available to the English public significant works by that painter. The Courtaulds were exempt from Clive's usual disdain for 'timid millionaires' who followed the advice of experts rather than their own aesthetic pleasure in choosing what to buy. Sam Courtauld and his wife, Lil (as Elizabeth was known), were responsible for a private collection at their house in Portman Square that had brought to England superb examples of French painting – by Boudin, Manet, Monet, Renoir, Sisley and Pissarro – that Clive ranked even higher than those bought for the nation and housed at the Tate. Luckily for the public, Courtauld had allowed Seurat's *Baignade* to go to the National Gallery.

Richard Aldington welcomed 'Clive Bell's Brilliant New Book of Art Criticism' for being a reliable guide that did not burden readers with a 'long abstract argument'. It was precisely Clive's aim to offer himself as a trustworthy cicerone who by way of his personal opinion could give the middlebrow public knowledge that would enhance their aesthetic life. Readers could have confidence in someone who enabled them to eavesdrop on famous artists – 'Odd, is it not, observed Picasso the other day, that, whereas it is thought discreditable in a child to have no discoverable father, it is thought discreditable in a painter to have any parents at all.' As the reviewer for the *Liverpool Post & Mercury* put it, Clive wrote about painting 'with gusto, as though art were as good fun as cricket'.

30. Dancing on a Volcano

In Venice with Frankie Birrell and Raymond in September 1931, Clive hobnobbed with aristocrats and took rich American ladies to Torcello to expound for them the beauties of the Byzantine mosaics at Santa Maria Assunta. 'It is terrible to think how silly we should look or how vexed we should be,' he commented wryly to Frances, 'if Mr. Lytton Strachey or Mr. Roger Fry or Mr. Paul Valery or some other unmistakable intellectual big-wig sailed into the Piazza and took the wind out of our sails.' Pompous though he might be on occasion, Clive also knew that despite being extremely well read and possessed of an acute sensibility, he had no claim to the mantle of scholar, nor did he wish to be mistaken for one. He tried to wear his deep erudition lightly.

Fittingly, his sojourn with Raymond in Venice had begun with a party hosted by an American steel magnate's wife at the Palazzo Mocenigo, from whose balcony Byron had looked over the Grand Canal in 1818. The society there was indistinguishable from the kind to be found in Chelsea at Sybil Colefax's Argyll House and, indeed, Clive told Vanessa, Sybil had invited herself for dinner. He spent the evening dancing with Mary Landon Baker, the famous 'Shy Bride' of Chicago, accounts of whose many rejected marriage proposals had filled newspaper society columns on both sides of the Atlantic from the time she left the socially prominent Alister McCormick at the altar in January 1922.

After the death in 1927 of Mary's father, president of the Chicago Stock Exchange, his widow bought the thirteenth-century Palazzo Donà della Madoneta. The Bakers were already well connected in English society, having rented an Elizabethan manor house near the Asquiths' country home, The Wharf, in the early 1920s. Mary, who was an accomplished

Mary Baker

dancer, quickly became the centre of Clive's Venetian stay, although his calendar also filled with excursions, lunches and dinners with the likes of Princesse de Polignac (the Singer sewing machines heiress), Ruby Peto, Violet Trefusis, Osbert Sitwell, Victor Cunard and Eve Fleming (whose son Ian told Clive that he was a great admirer of the poems of Julian Bell). Clive assured Vanessa he would not become over-involved with Mary, but her charms, youth, two motor cars and a speedboat, to say nothing of her palazzo, soon seduced him. *I tre signori*, as Raymond, Frankie and Clive were dubbed, were favourites with the ladies of this affluent set and when his companions left, Clive stayed on for several weeks, a fifty-year-old 'gigolo' for the thirty-year-old Mary.

Venice had other attractions for Clive, of course. He had rediscovered Giotto, perhaps the 'greatest painter of all time', and had found the names of Roger, Margery Fry and Goldie Dickinson in the guest book when he visited the Tiepolo frescoes at Villa Valmarana in Vicenza. That Mary was American did not trouble Clive unduly, though an opportunity to go sightseeing with the French fashion journalist Marie-Louise Bousquet reminded him of the pleasures of a 'completely civilised female'. 'The French!' he exclaimed: 'What would we do without them?'

Clive might have thought that the Venice he observed from Mary's balcony was essentially the same as that which Canaletto had painted, but already in 1931 Mussolini was building the architecture of a fascist city. The Riva dell'Impero was under construction and 'this city in a constant state of exhibition' would soon display the dictator's dream for Italy. Clive and Mary (and much of the world) were 'dancing on a volcano'. Clive showed little interest in the British election that October, though he took satisfaction in Oswald Mosley's New Party winning no seats. Unlike Harold Nicolson, who went with Mosley to see Mussolini in January 1932 and did not abandon him until he formed the British Union of Fascists, Clive was not swayed by Mosley's argument in the *Political Quarterly* (edited by Leonard) that Britain needed a strong new alternative to the communism by which so many young people were attracted. The national government was the lesser of two evils, as far as Clive was concerned, and he returned reluctantly to England only to see his 'aged mother' and take care of his financial affairs.

Clive began receiving letters from Mary Baker addressed 'TO MY LOVER' as soon as he was back in London. She told him that reading the books he had sent her – *Pot-Boilers*, for example – felt like chatting with him, and she enjoyed his eccentric contribution to *The New Keepsake*, a volume intended to provide 'pleasant escape' in the Victorian manner. Clive's 'A Pre-War Tragedy' was a comic short story about George Washington's honesty causing the death of his mother and the injury of his father. Among Mary's more serious reading that autumn was Nancy Cunard's searing pamphlet *Black Man and White Ladyship*, which Mary took as a personal attack on Nancy's mother, Lady Emerald, rather than a trenchant political analysis of racism. Mary herself had published two books in her twenties that she gave to Clive, both of which add to the impression that his interest in her had little to do with a meeting of the minds. *Sunshine and Gossamer* (1928) was a collection of her fairy tales illustrated by Terrell Stapp (later a Disney art director) and *Verbum Sapienti* (1920) an anthology of religious aphorisms, including, for example, 'Our existence on this earth is an episode in our Life of which death is but an incident,' and 'A soul is a bird caught in the forests of Infinity, and caged in the human frame.' No comment of Clive's has survived upon such wisdom as 'Art is a mirror in which are reflected the emotions of the soul,' or 'An artist is he who can express the nebulous ideas of a dreamer.' The book was dedicated to Mary's mother, a Christian Scientist, with whom Mary lived for most of her life. Clive was mildly interested in her tales of life in the American midwest of the previous century, but on the whole found Mrs Baker a 'nasty old bitch'.

Mary published a satirical roman à clef, *The Arcadians*, in 1934. One of her arch-enemies in Venice told Victor Cunard that Clive must have written it – an implication she knew he would not take as a compliment. 'Paaaaally', as Clive took to calling her in imitation of how she pronounced 'Polly', wanted them to be considered a couple, but she had no illusions about being the kind of silken bluestocking he preferred. Her often childish letters, usually written in pencil, filled with references to 'Japonica' and 'Myrtle', as she named her legs, or 'Pretty' and 'Charming', her dimples, invariably gossiped about parties and hairstyles more than books and ideas. She flattered what Vanessa had called the 'lady of fashion' side of Clive's character. Virginia penned a brief, penetrating sketch in her diary:

> small, pink, underbred; not a woman of the world; without distinction; nice; rich; has lived above her means, spiritually & socially; has a little edge to her mind; tells her little story . . . waspish; enamoured; C. bending over her cigarette case; fetching her coat (black: expensive): all this strained; incredible to spend weeks with her.

Vanessa had a simple explanation for what Clive saw in Mary: 'Think of the speedboat.'

Lytton's death from cancer early in 1932 finally shattered 'Bloomsbury', in Leonard's opinion. Clive left for Venice two days later and, when the news came in March that the distraught Carrington had shot herself, the miseries of his friends' lives in England seemed only half real to him. At Mary Baker's Palazzo, he led a Jane Austen-like existence of reading, writing, tea and a little dancing, but the pain of the household at Ham Spray, where Carrington's grief at losing Lytton had aroused all her old jealousy about Frances' relations with Ralph, made Clive wish a God existed so that he could hate him.

As he would for most of the early years of this dark decade, Clive distanced himself from England. 'I am pretty well used to being called unpatriotic,' he told Vanessa, explaining his lack of interest in the British elections that had failed to produce a clear majority. He would not vote for a Labour candidate, but the alternative of a national government cobbled together from Liberals and Conservatives seemed to him 'intellectually disreputable'.

Frankie Birrell and Clive had argued acrimoniously with Leonard at Charleston in 1929 over statements made at a conference in The Hague by Philip Snowden, Labour Chancellor of the Exchequer, during discussions of the Young Plan to restructure Germany's war reparations. 'The time had come when Great Britain should resume the place which her position in the world entitled her to occupy,' the *Times* reported him saying. Clive put his objections in a letter to the *Nation & Athenaeum*: 'I had thought since the year 1918 everyone had got sick of prestige and keeping national honour bright.' Julian echoed Clive's views in his transparently polemical 'Arms and the Man', published in the groundbreaking 1932 anthology *New Signatures*:

Long queues of unemployed th'Exchange besiege,
And that's all right, because of our Prestige.
O great Prestige! The helpful second cause
Of our prosperity, and fleet, and wars.
Without Prestige, how can a people live,
Their culture flourish, Arts or Letters thrive?
And National Honours, 'tis well understood
Can only be kept clean in foreign blood.

Julian and Quentin had both canvassed for the local election of Labour candidates in 1931, but Clive, suspicious of the communist influence in the party, was glad they had been unsuccessful. Still essentially a Whig, he took pleasure in what he imagined would be the discomfiture of Kingsley Martin, something of a protégé of Leonard's, who had recently become editor of the newly amalgamated *New Statesman and Nation* – the 'socialist conscience of the British Labour movement'.

In an era of increasingly obvious menace to liberty, Clive remained strikingly silent in public while intellectuals debated what was happening in Europe. Thanking him for a generous donation to the

War Resisters League, Arthur Ponsonby told Clive that former pacifists needed to speak out if war was to be averted, but it was not until after Julian's death in Spain that Clive would rise to this challenge. He had no time for the grunting Fascists of Mosley's BUF, but when right-wing leagues staged a bloody anti-government riot in Paris on 6 February 1934, Clive described only as a 'rumpus' what many intellectuals of the French left regarded as an 'attempted fascist putsch'. Remarking how differently the twenty-seven daily newspapers of Paris explained what the incident had been about, Janet Flanner commented that only *Le Matin* 'had significantly called the sixth "A Day of Civil War"'. These events, which French historians treat as one of the 'key political events' of the 1930s, led to the founding of the Comité de Vigilance des Intellectuels Antifascistes (CVIA) by François Walter (in which Roger's friend Charles Mauron was involved), one of several organisations that quickly sought alliances with like-minded people in England, including Leonard and Virginia. Clive appears to have had no involvement with any of them, later telling Mary Hutchinson that he avoided people who were 'pestering one to sign manifestos about Spain which, so far as I can make out, are based exclusively on ignorance and vulgar spite'.

Anti-appeasement was a minority position in England in the early 1930s, where memory of the First World War had turned many against militarism. Clive's insouciant attitude to the rise of dictators was therefore not remarkable at the time. The Hogarth Press published Mussolini's *Political and Social Doctrine of Fascism* in 1933 because Leonard believed the Italian dictator's historical and political ideas should be seen for the 'complete nonsense' they were. Clive's fanciful suggestion in *Civilization* that he might send his essay to Russian 'bosses', to Mussolini and to Churchill because these 'despots' could be used as a means to the end of protecting a 'leisured class, from which may spring a civilization' was merely absurd in 1928.

On the other hand, in the circles in which Clive moved in Paris, people like Waldemar George were contemplating the political implications of the cultural *rappel à l'ordre*. George had begun *Formes* to expound a neo-humanist ideology and identified Jewish painters such as Chaim Soutine, Marc Chagall and Modigliani as revolutionaries against an unduly hierarchical society. When George interviewed Mussolini in 1933, however, he began to approve of the dictator's vision as a rebuttal of the modernism produced by a 'liberal society irremediably alienated and debased by its intellectualism, atheism and materialism'.

Nazi atrocities against Jews began to be widely reported in the British press after Hitler became German Chancellor in January 1933 and at the end of that year Violet Bonham Carter spoke at a Savoy lunch to raise money for Jewish women and children who had fled Germany. In 1936, she helped found Focus in Defence of Freedom and Peace, a 'loosely organized anti-appeasement coalition under the leadership of Winston Churchill'. Violet had been very amused when the Nazi ideologue Alfred Rosenberg, expecting a warm reception, instead was dressed down by her stepmother, Margot Asquith, who told him that in England there was 'only one opinion to be heard on the horrors and stupidities emanating from the new regime in Germany', a humiliation widely reported.

In 1933, Clive thought dictators should be mocked rather than used as a pretext for war. Mary Baker agreed: 'Is it possible that the world is going mad again? Haven't they indulged enough blood lust – don't the sons have enough from surviving fathers of the barbarity of the last war to stop them fighting again at all costs? Does peace really depend on Hitler's Foreign Policies as the papers proclaim?' In Venice, even as late as a year before the influence of Hitler on Mussolini became impossible to ignore with the passage of the Manifesto on Race of 1938, the small Jewish community there was encouraged to feel safe by the Chief Rabbi of Rome.

Until at least 1935, Clive maintained the stance of a First World War pacifist. During the Abyssinian Crisis, he asked, 'Do my young friends of the Left – those who cannot remember much about the controversies of 1914 – really suppose that there were no good and honest arguments in favour of the last war?' Imposing sanctions on Italy for the invasion of the African country, he argued, would not produce peace: 'No war will ever end war.' A month after sanctions had been imposed, Mussolini decreed 18 December a national holiday when the women of Venice were asked to donate their jewellery to the nation in return for a plain steel ring. Mary sent a gold Cartier bracelet to Il Duce which, she assumed, would be melted down to assist her adopted country to conquer Abyssinia.

In England, political meetings nearly always ended in a 'vicious dispute between Communists and Pacifists' amid growing distrust of the

National Government. Leonard blamed internationalists and pacifists for the League of Nations' failure to be effective and when George Lansbury was ousted at the Labour Party conference in September 1935, it became clear that any notion of collective security of the kind promulgated by the league would have to depend on 'armaments and alliances, however distasteful this was to traditional Labour thinking'. Gerald Gould explained in 'The Pacifists' Dilemma' that conscientious objectors would 'have to develop a new technique to meet the new technique of militarism'. Clive believed that the next war would render defences obsolete because it would be fought from the air using not only bombs but also biological weapons. The best chance of surviving the coming conflagration, therefore, was to disarm so as not to pose a threat to any other nation, a unilateralist policy that would safeguard Britain because only nations which threatened other nations were likely to be bombed. As Leonard would write a few months later, 'No one knows why we re-arm except that everyone else is arming.'

31. Enjoying Pictures

Aboard the *Gripsholm* with Benita, England seemed very far away to Clive in February 1933. Benita was the perfect companion on this long cruise calling at Casablanca, Dakar, Havana, Trinidad and Jamaica. She was 'good-natured, good-looking, self-amusing, helpful, practical, utterly unpretentious, sentimental, popular, and never there when she's not wanted'. Virginia was not sure whether to believe Clive's boast about a steward being startled to find the naked Benita brushing her teeth in his cabin, but Benita had flirtatiously suggested to the young man at Thomas Cook that if only a double first-class cabin remained available, that would be acceptable.

When they travelled together to Spain in October 1934 at the height of the 'black years' of violent unrest that led to the Spanish Civil War, Clive prepared not by reading up on the political situation but by ordering from Bumpus such classics as Borrow's *The Bible in Spain* (1843), Richard Ford's *Gatherings in Spain* (1906) and F. Sánchez Cantón's life of Goya (1930). His appointment diary filled with notes on churches and museums to visit. There was talk of a rendezvous with Eric Maclagan, who would be in Madrid to attend the League of Nations' International Museum Office conference on architecture and management of museums, but staying in Spain proved too dangerous or, as Clive laconically put it, 'too difficult, too tense, too triste and too restricted – to say nothing of bullets, one of which went through Benita's window . . . about a foot above Benita's head.' John Armstrong was relieved to hear that his future wife had been helped to leave Spain with Clive by the British Ambassador, George Grahame. Unwittingly, they were in Spain just as left-wing opposition to the government

MR. CHARLES LAUGHTON, MRS. LAUGHTON (*Elsa Lanchester*), MR. JOHN ARMSTRONG, and MRS. ARMSTRONG *at the party at the Lefèvre Galleries to celebrate the opening of Mr. John Armstrong's show of surrealist pictures.*

John and Benita Armstrong with Charles & Elsa Laughton in Sketch, *7 December 1938*

erupted in a general strike in Madrid, a declaration of independence in Catalonia and a protracted violent struggle against the army by miners in Asturias. On behalf of Ambassador Grahame, Clive delivered an account of the situation to the British Embassy in Paris, from whence it was forwarded to the prime minister.

Much of Clive's writing in the 1930s was characterised by both a retrospective mood, marking the waning of an era in the reception of whose art he had played so prominent a role, and one of anticipation of new iterations of the human spirit. Out of tune with the engaged decade, he continued to see art as transcending the vagaries of time and place, an escape from the world in which politicians and generals wasted human lives in violence. *Enjoying Pictures* would be his last book, although he continued to write about art and artists in periodicals until the end of his life. In its intention to 'follow the vagaries of my mind through a tangled experience – an hour in the National Gallery', and to 'catch my reactions alive and pen them in phrases', *Enjoying Pictures* is also his most personal book, plainly stating that he has made a religion of art and that art provides 'an escape from life'. Disregarding such challenges as that presented by I. A. Richards, who had denied that aesthetic experience was of a 'fundamentally different kind' to any

other, Clive clings in *Enjoying Pictures* to his creed that there is a 'unique
aesthetic emotion' on which depended the curious experience he had
spent his life trying to understand.

Comprising three short meditations on 'personal experience controlled
carefully and honestly consulted', *Enjoying Pictures* is dedicated 'To the
colonel', Clive's foil being someone for whom the passionate enjoyment
of art is unavailable. John Squire took umbrage at the 'idiotic' notion
that all colonels were insensitive to art, but Clive certainly had his
brother, Cory – always known affectionately as 'The Colonel' – in
mind. The dedication was not mockery but an indication that the book
attempted to explain as clearly as possible experiences Clive believed
were the most profound to be had, yet remained incomprehensible to
most people. Allowing that knowledge about art might enhance and
extend such an experience, Clive yet maintained that at its core was a
peculiar sensibility which some people possessed and others did not.
He pointed to the contradiction between how art is usually ignored or
considered frivolous by the majority and the fact that masses of people –
'Joneses' – flock to what we would now call 'blockbuster' exhibitions.
'Mr. Jones' brings his family to a large show of Italian pictures at the
Royal Academy because he is convinced that something important must
be there; he is 'performing an act of culture'. The huge prices paid for
paintings support Jones' credence in this culture, but what Jones does
not know is that 'millionaires covet Rembrandts, not for their artistic
significance, but because they are the rarest kind of postage stamp on
the market'. Mr Jones will take his daughter to Florence or pay to see
an exhibition at Burlington House that is widely covered in the press,
but 'he will never give up an afternoon's golf for a visit to the National
Gallery' where on any day of the week he could see glorious works of
Italian painting for nothing.

Condescending as this is, Clive's dedication to the profound relevance
of art in a time of gathering threat could also be seen as what Virginia
in 1939 would describe as a 'little whiff of shot in the cause of freedom'.
That being said, it took a mighty effort of myopia for Clive to base his
objections to Nazism on aesthetic grounds, as he did in *Enjoying Pictures*:

> If anyone were to ask me this morning (April 12th, 1933) what
> I thought of the goings on in Germany, I should probably reply
> that I disliked them intensely but that these were early days to

condemn a movement which might well develop into something
as reasonable and efficient as Italian fascism. And then I read this
in *The Times*: Dr. Goebbels (replying to Furtwängler) said that
he realized more than the one distinction in art proposed by the
eminent conductor – the distinction between good art and bad; no
art (contends the politician) which does not emanate from the full
national life can in the end be good or mean anything to the nation
for which it is created; there must be no 'absolute' art of the kind
known to liberal democracy; besides being good, art must also be
responsible, in close touch with the people, and aggressive: which
read, I know I am anti-Hitler. Why, even in Italy, where I have had
occasion and good reason to admire the efficiency and moderation
of the régime, when I consider that an endeavour to divert art and
thought into patriotic channels has poisoned the sources of spiritual
life, and that art and thought which must be free or die being unfree
are dying, I find myself at heart a rebel. Were I an Italian peasant or
shop-keeper I should be fascist; being what I am, one of those queer
people who take art seriously, I am not.

Missing from Clive's account of the *Times* report was that the conductor
had objected to Goebbels' distinction not between bad and good art
but specifically 'between Jews and non-Jews'. The 'abominable Jewish
boycott' had begun that very month and knowledge of the full horror
of Hitler's intentions would soon become difficult to disavow.

Clive believed that a society's response to art measured its overall
liberty, that art was not an indulgence to be discarded when war
threatened. The anti-nationalist position of *Enjoying Pictures* anticipated
how Nazism would eerily echo the language that had been employed
by some critics of post-Impressionism when they compared modernist
painting to the work of lunatics, as Hitler did in his speech opening the
'Great Exhibition of German Art 1937' in Munich:

today no German or French or Japanese or Chinese art exists, but
plainly and simply only a 'modern' art . . . Every year something
new. One day Impressionism, then Futurism, Cubism, maybe even
Dadaism, etc. A further result is that even for the most insane and
inane monstrosities thousands of catchwords to label them will have
to be found, and have indeed been found.

At the concurrent exhibition of 'Degenerate Art' (*Entartete Kunst*), works by asylum inmates were mingled with those of modernist painters – a tactic the National Socialists might have learned from Dr. T. B. Hyslop, who had coined the term 'aesthetic insanity' in his lecture at the Grafton Galleries in 1911. Events of the next decade would render untenable Clive's faith in 'civilization' as a bulwark against barbarianism, but as George Steiner wrote, 'We come after. We know now that a man can read Goethe or Rilke in the evening, that he can play Bach and Schubert, and go to his day's work at Auschwitz in the morning.'

Clive's version of pacifism looked increasingly unrealistic in a world where 'people are beaten to death for holding the wrong opinions.' 'Yes,' he wrote to Frances, who shared his point of view about war, 'I take the greatest interest in Abyssinia, or rather in European peace, which I wish to possess at any price,' but he felt disengaged from the political process and disillusioned with England. The week before Clive's letter on the pacifist's dilemma appeared, Julian took part in a huge anti-war demonstration in Cambridge, although his own convictions were coming under tremendous stress. The dissertation he had written in a fruitless attempt to secure a Cambridge fellowship rejected the 'quietism' of people like Clive and Virginia in a period marked, as Julian wrote, by 'unemployment, economic crisis, nascent fascism, and approaching war'. Julian's dilemma – how to oppose both war and Hitler – was evident in his introduction to a collection of conscientious objectors' reminiscences, *We Did Not Fight* (1935). Reviewing it, Kingsley Martin argued that the rise of totalitarianism and the 'development of war in the air have made any repetition of the British 1916 situation almost impossible'.

Julian, despite the success he had enjoyed as a poet, was restless, uncertain what he wanted to do with his life. That he was leaving to teach in China startled Vanessa when he told her in summer 1935, but Clive had already asked Bertrand Russell several months earlier if he could provide any introductions for his son there (Russell informed Clive that most of the people he had known in China had been beheaded by one side or another, but that he could provide a general letter for Julian). Julian left for Wuhan at the end of August, from where he observed the deepening chaos of Europe with a growing feeling that he should

Angelica, Vanessa, Clive Bell

return and get involved. On his way to Hong Kong, he wrote Vanessa two letters to be given to her in the case of either his death or news that he had become involved in 'revolutionary activities'. In the first, he told his mother that he would 'much rather a violent finish in hot blood' than a life of passivity, and in the second that he could never be happy without experiencing action. 'I feel it in the same sort of way, with the same sort of strength, that I imagine you feel about painting,' he wrote, before concluding that he 'would rather be killed violently than die any other way'.

Most weeks while Julian was in China, Duncan and Vanessa walked with Angelica from Fitzroy Street to have dinner with Clive in Gordon Square, after which Vanessa would read aloud Julian's letters. By April 1936, Julian thought that 'it would be too tiresome to be here if war and revolution began in England.' If the League of Nations could hold together to make Hitler give up the idea of going to war, he agreed with Leonard that it should be supported. If, on the other hand, war was certain, 'then it seems to me Clive is right both from a socialist and a pacifist point of view . . . Either we could keep out of it, or if the government took us in, we could resist.' Julian was far less equivocal when he wrote to his brother: 'It's too late for democracy and reason and persuasion and writing to the *New Statesman* and Virginia signing letters saying it's all a pity. The only real choices are to submit or fight.' He was even more blunt to his friend Eddie Playfair: 'There's only one thing to be done with Fascists, and that's kill them.'

On his way back from a Greek cruise taken with Raymond, Dadie Rylands and J. T. Sheppard in late summer 1935, Clive stayed with Mary Baker in Venice, from where he reported to Virginia that the 'rich & the great' were all set on war. He intended to write to the 'parish magazine', as they called the *New Statesman*, to once more make the old argument for which Virginia liked him: 'War's so awful it cant be right anyhow.' Clive had no sympathy for communism, and took at its word Vladimir Tchernavin's *I Speak for the Silent*, an account of life in Stalin's gulags (which the communist *New Masses* denounced for its 'perverse distortion of fact' about Soviet persecution of Jews).

Julian never joined the Communist Party, although several of his Cambridge contemporaries (for example, Guy Burgess and Anthony Blunt) did, but the letter Clive wrote on 'Sanctions and War' makes clear why Julian, when he returned from China at the beginning of 1937 in the mood so movingly captured in Auden's poem 'Spain', would have found his father's views unpalatable. 'I think it desirable that the people of England should know,' Clive wrote, 'that they are being asked to smash such fragments of European civilisation as survive, and sacrifice such happiness as they may extract from their individual lives, in order (a) to gratify the reckless spite or, if you will, the righteous indignation of a group of Socialists and Radicals; (b) to stanch a wound in the pride of our Young Patriots.'

The exhibition of 'Italian Art from Cimabue to Tiepolo' at the Petit Palais in summer 1935 enthralled Clive, particularly its large display of 'primitives'. The world's political and financial crises seemed insignificant in the presence of these works of art, before which Clive performed his obeisance. It would have appalled him to think of this exhibition as in any way connected to politics and yet, as the art historian Emily Braun has argued, this display of Italy's Renaissance patrimony for a French audience was part of a conscious effort to co-opt humanism to counter the perception that Fascism was a 'regime of thugs'. As Clive and Benita lunched with his friends in Paris in early June, all seemed quiet, but Pierre Drieu La Rochelle told him that unrest was brewing.

That year, after witnessing a Nazi rally in Nuremberg, Drieu converted to the cause of National Socialism, which he believed offered the best counter to the weaknesses of liberal democracy. Drieu, whom Aldous Huxley had brought to Clive's party for the Ballets Russes in Gordon Square in 1919, was typical of many French intellectuals who deplored the inertia of the Third Republic and made the transit to Fascism in the 1930s. He had written an anti-nationalist tract, *L'Europe contre les patries*, in 1932, but in common with many of his peers disgruntled by what the parliamentary and capitalist system had wrought, as well as being anti-communist and anti-semitic, Drieu joined Jacques Doriot's nationalist Parti Populaire Français in 1936.

Clive left Paris before an International Writers' Congress took place, for which Virginia had been on the organising committee. At the last moment, she did not attend, despite being urged to do so by Morgan Forster who thought it would be among the 'last utterances of the civilized'. Aldous Huxley was disappointed by this gathering, which he believed had been 'organized by the French communist writers for their own glorification and by the Russians as a piece of Soviet propaganda'. As the political centre disappeared into extremes of right or left, Clive did his best to remain a committed, if blinkered, pacifist. Like many Liberals, he wanted nothing to do with communism in spite of its opposition to Fascism. When Virginia asked Clive to join a committee in support of an anti-fascist exhibition in which Elizabeth Bibesco, Ivor Churchill and Ralph Wright were involved, Clive got in touch with Violet Bonham Carter, Bibesco's half-sister, to find out more about it, suspecting it was communist-inspired. He then wrote 'one of his absurd pompous letters' to Lord Ivor, '& quoted Virginia Woolf inviting me to "strike a blow for freedom".' Alarmed committee members came to see Virginia, worried that Clive might publish a letter of protest; she asked him to 'leave out the quotation from me, because as you use it, nobody could see that it was meant for a joke'.

The exhibition was organised by the Cambridge Anti-War Council and it soon became clear that Clive was correct about its political leanings. Virginia had invited Bob Trevelyan to join the cause but he too had demurred, because 'to expose the evils of Fascism and Nazism, and to say nothing whatever of the similar evils of the Russian régime, is completely wrong-headed.' After Clive and Virginia discussed his 'very violent letter' to the committee, Virginia heard from Lord Ivor that he would be returning her £5 donation because the exhibition had been 'proved a Communist plot'. The Cambridge exhibition (which largely comprised a documentary history of Fascism's rise) was at 27 Soho Square, near where the Artists International Association exhibition 'Artists Against Fascism and War' was on at the same time. Clive, Vanessa and Duncan were all members of the AIA and, within two years, Quentin would become its secretary. Despite the AIA being seen 'at least from the outside' as communist, Clive's angry outburst to the committee derived 'from a prevalent attitude among AIA members' that they did not want to be perceived as communist.

Roger wrote a 'rather crusty' review of *Enjoying Pictures*, assuming Clive would want 'frank and outspoken criticism rather than a discreet evasion'. What would turn out to be Roger's last book, *Reflexions on British Painting*, was contrasted in several reviews with the 'colloquialism and affected simplicity' of *Enjoying Pictures* and Roger found embarrassing that Clive told his readers 'almost more about himself than about the pictures he discusses'. He also found 'astonishing' Clive's hasty generalisations about Tiepolo and other Venetian painters of the High Renaissance. Roger disparaged Clive's aesthetic Calvinism – 'either you have Grace or you have not' – but softened the barb by praising his chapter on Raphael's frescoes in the Vatican as 'perhaps the best piece of critical writing which he has ever done'. Lest there be any doubt of his opinion, Fry damned with faint praise the disarming frankness of Clive's subjective reactions, which could never be confused with a 'logical aesthetic system'.

Roger's concern with logic would have mattered little to Clive. *Enjoying Pictures,* after all, begins by comparing the ecstasy and happiness afforded by art with that inspired by 'embracing the beloved' and continues by pondering the differences between momentary passion and more durable happiness. Linked as they were in public consciousness as 'Bloomsbury' critics, Clive and Roger were separated by more than their fifteen-year difference in age. Roger's careful, scholarly and putatively objective writing was markedly different from the sometimes slapdash but always entertaining narratives that gave Clive his reputation as a witty guide to high culture; it would have been surprising to see Roger in the gossip and society columns of *The Sketch*, where Clive appeared frequently.

Clive was at Monk's House when news came on 9 September 1934 that Roger had died. At Charleston, Clive held Angelica close before telling her what had happened, while Vanessa 'in her bedroom howled uncontrollably'. A week after Roger's funeral, old friends gathered at Charleston for Angelica's birthday, which, as hers fell on Christmas Day, she usually celebrated on Clive's, 16 September. Virginia sentimentally recalled how they had assembled at Charleston soon after Lytton's death two years earlier, and was irritated when Clive, about to leave for Spain with Benita, said 'But you'll get over it,' as if she had overreacted to Roger's loss. Clive struck her as jealous, perhaps still angry at Roger's review of *Enjoying Pictures*. Roger was certainly sometimes bemused by what Clive got away with in his magazine columns, much as a scholar constrained by disciplinary rigour might be irritated by the glib generalisations of a journalist, but Virginia took a measured view in a letter to Julian: 'I think Clive got on Roger's nerves towards the end, and I expect he was hard on him. But it also seems to me pretty clear that Clive did pilfer a good deal without acknowledgment from Roger; and as Roger was half persecution mad – only he was far too sweet and sane to let the disease rip – he minded being pilfered far more than was reasonable.'

In a Memoir Club reminiscence in June 1939, Clive said that Roger grew less magnanimous with age. To Virginia, who was writing her biography of Roger, Clive seemed truculent, and as if he was still smarting at Roger's review of his last book. His anecdotes annoyed Vanessa, which in turn raised Clive's hackles. But these were only family squabbles. Reviewing Kenneth Clark's edition of Roger's *Last Lectures*, Clive wrote that it was a 'joy and a wonder to hear him', lamenting that Roger had not lived to write a complete history of art. With Roger dead, Clive became the standard bearer of a view of art increasingly challenged by a rising generation.

32. Art and the Public

Looking back in 1965 on the period between the two world wars, Myfanwy Piper acknowledged the pervasive influence of Roger's *Vision & Design* and *Cézanne*, and Clive's *Art* and *Since Cézanne*, but felt that those who 'blindly idolised the Ecole de Paris' had been more dangerous to young painters than the Academicians who derided modernism. When English artists separated into rival abstract and surrealist camps in the 1930s, both sides of the divide used Clive as a foil in their arguments. The artist and designer S. John Woods wrote in *Axis* that the 'abstract reviles Clive Bell but nevertheless allows no element but significant form; the surrealist places the navel in the subconscious and refutes everything else, including significant form.' For his part, Clive announced that post-Impressionism had run its course because it no longer motivated young painters. Only those painters who had been influenced by the legacy of Cézanne knew how to pick up the national tradition of Constable and Gainsborough, from whose course the Pre-Raphaelites had perverted English art. Never nationalistic, Clive was nevertheless excited to contemplate new directions in English painting. He read 'What Next in Art' to the Florentine Club at Oxford a few months before it appeared in *The Studio*, at the invitation of Vita's son Benedict, who thought it 'brilliant' but noted that in the ensuing discussion Clive came to no conclusions and 'retracted much of what he had said'.

Although he would come to be viewed as an antagonist to Clive, Herbert Read concurred that the 1930s offered for British artists a 'situation of extraordinary interest and most unforeseen possibilities'. Read was the leading light of a younger generation that had not yet decided what would replace the aesthetic doctrine associated with Clive and Roger, but knew that it would be something different. Cyril Connolly recorded the 'usual argument' going on among John Banting, Brian Howard (who at Eton had described the Omega Workshops as a 'hive of criminal aesthetics') and Eddie Gathorne-Hardy when he joined them in a café late one afternoon. Clive and Roger's ideology of the personal, private emotion, they said, was outmoded, 'Edwardian':

> 'But what is going to take the place of art criticism, Brian?'
> — 'If you read Herbert Read's article in the Listener, Eddie, you will see – I don't know – I only know it will be some thing very much more exact and very much more difficult.'

Clive continued to swat away detractors, rarely joining (in print) in the debates that so preoccupied young artists who were trying to keep up with 'an intricate, rapidly changing, and hard to grasp' art politics. Richard Nevinson had threatened a libel suit over Clive's description in *Enjoying Pictures* of his *War Scene* as a 'feeble' effort to appear up to date in 1916, but when Chatto agreed to delete the image and its accompanying description, Clive was satisfied to note that this would lead to a credit of 750 copies on his account and that Nevinson would now appear on a 'secret black list, apparently known only to publishers and editors, of people who are likely to make trouble'. Nevinson's antagonism to what he saw as Roger and Clive's pernicious influence on the London Group, or Wyndham Lewis's attacks in *Apes of God* (1930) and *Men Without Art* (1934), were of scant concern to Clive (although Virginia felt that there was 'nothing left of me in Oxford & Cambridge & places where the young read Wyndham Lewis'). The young were writing fan letters to Clive and he was content to be so closely associated with the 'first act in the history of twentieth-century painting'.

Among those fans was Hananiah Harari, a twenty-one-year-old American painter who wrote to Clive from Paris, where he had moved in 1932, about the shock he had experienced upon reading *Art*, whose every page confirmed his own aesthetic experiences. 'It is depressing to find how few people thoroughly understand your book *Art*,' he wrote, 'for after all one must live it to really understand it – it requires sensibility and intelligence.' He and his closest friend, a sculptor named

Herzl Emmanuel, both Zionists, were about to go to Palestine, full of zeal to 'create a national Hebrew art', and would gladly kill all enemies of their ideals, such as Hitler and capitalists. Harari told Clive that if he had the power, he would make him the most important man in his ideal state. A year later, the disillusioned Harari returned to America, where he continued to search for inspiration. He had read Wilenski and found him boring and wrong. 'It is strange,' he told Clive, 'how many critics are perturbed by your "ecstatic emotion" . . . Don't you think these people are hilarious?' Within a year, Harari helped found the American Abstract Artists group in New York.

What might happen in America seemed more exciting to Clive than anything that might happen in Germany or Italy. Now that Americans were too poor to survive in Paris, there was a real chance that a 'truly American school of painting and an American tradition' might develop. Stuart Preston, a student at Yale University who, within a few years, would become a friend of Raymond's and go on to a career as an art writer for the *New York Times*, told Clive that his books were the only ones that made sense to him, especially in their emphasis on the centrality of a personal response to art as in *Enjoying Pictures*.

Clive's assured pronouncements on culture could inspire confidence in readers who were far removed from the urgent debates of the London art world. A coal miner named David Morgan wrote in 1934 from Blaina in South Wales to thank Clive for the education his books had provided, which otherwise would have been unavailable to him. He wrote again in 1938 to say that he had re-read *Civilization* in the Pelican edition and had once more been profoundly enlightened by it.

Large national survey exhibitions had become increasingly common in London by the mid-1930s, welcomed by a public desirous of learning more about visual art. The Anglo-French Art and Travel Society's 1936 exhibition of 'Masters of French Nineteenth Century Painting' at the New Burlington Galleries gave Clive the opportunity to deliver in public his well-honed argument that the 'great age' of French painting was characterised by 'individualism', a point he reiterated in a brief foreword to the catalogue, reprinted in *Art News*. Clive was by this time regarded by the French government as an important cultural emissary. The news that he was to be made a member of the Légion d'Honneur in 1936 in recognition of all he had done for French art in the past twenty years came from one of his dearest friends, Roland de Margerie, first secretary at the French Embassy in London.

Roland's father had been ambassador to Germany after the First World War and Roland had become friends with Harold Nicolson in Berlin. After his posting to London in 1933, Roland was a frequent guest at small dinner parties Clive hosted at Gordon Square for a few male friends, such as Harold and Raymond, where Roland came to know a side of the English that belied their usual reputation among the French. 'I was absolutely amazed to hear these men, whom I saw in another guise in public, talk candidly about sentimental adventures that made a stark contrast to their usual stiff demeanour,' he recalled in his memoirs. Roland was also impressed by how well Clive and his guests understood French culture, once remarking that not only did Clive know Saint-Simon by heart, he also remembered the research he had conducted in diplomatic communications of the seventeenth century written by obscure Foreign Office clerks in exquisite French. Roland shared Clive's ribald humour, as well as an amateur passion for every detail of Lord Byron's life. Their amity was seasoned further by Clive's flirtation with Roland's wife, Jenny, who had advocated on behalf of Clive receiving the Légion d'Honneur. Raymond had also been pulling strings where he could in Paris since 1932 and, although Vanessa and Duncan laughed at 'The Chevalier' behind his back, Clive wore his red ribbon with pride.[1]

Clive's Francophilia and ready deprecation of any painter he thought did not follow the tradition headed by Cézanne and Seurat continued to arouse new enemies, who often followed the track that had been well worn by Wyndham Lewis. Geoffrey Grigson, for example, objected to the 'peevish pinched formalism with which art was stifled for so long in England by Roger Fry, Clive Bell and their minute protégés', among whom he named only Duncan, but his argument was with the Clive of 1914. Clive believed that implicit in any theory was the germ of its own demise, because movements typically formed in reaction to what preceded them, as had been the case with post-Impressionism.

[1] In 1954, Clive declined a CBE from Winston Churchill. Like Virginia, he was extremely discriminating when it came to such honours.

He continued to focus attention on artists working across the Channel (singling out Balthus as the 'most remarkable' painter in a Franco-Italian show that also included Maurice Brianchon and Pierre Tal-Coat), but by the early 1930s he was taking a more positive interest not only in work being done in England but in the kind of applied arts he had formerly had little time for.

The 'most interesting movement in contemporary British art' was the work of people such as Tristram Hillier and E. McKnight Kauffer, whose posters for Shell and BP Clive saw as partly the legacy of the Omega Workshops. McKnight Kauffer was famous for his London Underground posters and, with Paul Nash, John Armstrong and others, had designed striking modernist book jackets for publishers, including the Hogarth Press. Clive had never made much of a distinction among media or genres: art was art, wherever it manifested itself, and although he had in fact never expressed enthusiasm for Omega productions during the First World War, he now recognised that artists such as Rosemary and Clifford Ellis, exhibiting at Shell-Mex House, were transforming the public's perception of aesthetic value. In Clive's view, it was 'from posters and urban architecture that the man on the bus is likely to get the bulk of his aesthetic experience'.

Despite his deep-seated suspicion of committees and instititutions, Clive approved of the efforts of men like Stephen Tallents, originator of the field of public relations in England, to modernise Britain and make it a more appealing place for tourists to visit (and spend their money in). In 'An Open Letter to Any Member of the Travel Association', he revisited some of the contrasts he had drawn between England and the Continent in *On British Freedom*, pointing out that 'most people's idea of a holiday is having what most people call a "good time"', an aim stymied by England's absurd licensing laws and terrible cuisine. Raymond, Clive and Morgan Forster all joined in mocking Leonard's defence of English hotels and their cooking: 'I have never known, nor ever heard of, anyone, except Mr. Woolf, who looked forward to lunch in an English inn,' wrote Clive. Tallents, whose ideas informed the British Committee for Relations with Other Countries (which became the British Council), enlisted Clive and Kenneth Clark for a committee of the General Post Office, whose film unit he ran. When timid civil servants rejected their suggestions, Clive and Clark resigned, and Clive used the incident as a cautionary tale for anyone who still believed that the 'State is bound to be a better patron of the arts than oil or railway companies'.

Clive railed in *Enjoying Pictures* against nationalism's deleterious effects on art, concluding that its economic version would lead to the demise of Paris as a 'university of painting'. He also believed that state efforts to direct culture were a surer way of destroying it than censure, a theme he returned to in 'The Failure of State Art' when *The Listener* invited him to sum up a series of articles on the topic by authors who included Maynard, Georges Duthuit and Filippo Marinetti. The notion of 'an abstraction "State" producing an abstraction "art"' struck Clive as absurd, although he reserved judgement on Lewis Mumford's description of the American WPA's Federal Art Project because it sounded almost too good to be true. The idea that a government would provide financial support to thousands of artists and then leave them alone to do their work seemed incredible. The pernicious problem of committees was endemic to state support, for committees inevitably compromised, and were usually fearful of employing a living artist. The happy outcome of McKnight Kauffer's work for the London Underground had to be balanced against the debacle that ensued when the Cunard shipping line rejected the panels it had commissioned from Duncan for the *Queen Mary* in 1936, because, as Frances Spalding explains, the directors felt they would appeal only to a 'limited coterie interested in the development of modern painting'.

An outraged Clive thrust himself into the midst of the controversy this rejection caused. Joe Ackerley, literary editor of *The Listener*, assured Clive that BBC director John Reith would give him a free hand to comment, letting him know that Tallents, who was now Reith's deputy, had been impressed when he heard Clive was to write about the issue. Duncan had hoped that Kenneth Clark would organise a letter to the *Times* protesting against Cunard chairman Sir Percy Bates' peremptory rejection of his work, but the tempest stirred up by Clive's acerbic 'Inside the *Queen Mary*, A Businessman's Dream' led Clark to believe a letter would only make things worse. Clive's article distilled his long-held contempt for affluent people who wanted to appear sophisticated yet were always looking over their shoulder lest they offend someone. The great ocean liner was a floating testament to the 'frivolous and frightened attitude to art of rich people who are not sure of themselves', filled with a 'Teddy Bear style' of decoration that in any case did not suit Duncan's 'landmark in decorative art'.

An immediate effect was a letter ending their acquaintance from Christabel Aberconway's husband, chairman of the John Brown company that had built the *Queen Mary*. It would be several years before Christabel spoke to Clive again, but he was unmoved. 'Shall I write to the "Daily Worker",' he joked to Mary Hutchinson that summer, 'suggesting that the sister ship to the Queen Mary be called "The Mrs Simpson" or, failing that, "The Lady Aberconway".' The issue resurfaced three years later when Cunard declined the British Council's request to display Duncan's panels at the World's Fair in New York. This time, Clive wrote a measured letter of protest to the *Times*, pointing out that when they had been included in an exhibition of Duncan's recent work at Agnews, critics had almost universally praised them as masterpieces.

33. Your Schoolgirl Mistress

Two large surveys in Paris put on as part of the *Exposition Internationale des Arts et Techniques dans la Vie Moderne* in 1937 gave Clive the opportunity to write an epilogue to *Since Cézanne* placing those artists he had championed as a young man as participants in a coherent movement and acknowledging how their work had changed over the past thirty years. The Fauve work of Matisse was still 'bewilderingly beautiful', but it was instructive to look at works he had made during the war when Cubism had spurred Matisse towards a more abstract style (which Clive illustrated with *The Music Lesson* of 1917). Matisse had appreciated Clive's enthusiastic review of his black-and-white drawings exhibited at Lefevre in 1936 and was grateful that Clive seemed to understand so well what he was trying to do.

Clive left no doubt in his epilogue as to who was the dominant artist in whose wake all others in the modern movement followed:

> If Picasso is accused – and it is a plausible criticism – of repeating himself, that is not because he affects a manner or imposes on himself a formula, but because under a bottomless wardrobe of costumes he is always intensely himself . . . Having studied once again, as dispassionately as I could, fair samples of this extraordinary man's activity during more than thirty years, I understand why many intelligent people consider him not only the greatest artist alive but one of the most significant and influential figures of our time.

Protean and prolific, Picasso was enlisted in support of many different sides in the debates that consumed English artists in the 1930s. Picasso continually outpaced those whom he influenced, in Clive's view, even as artists continued to borrow form and method from him. Cubism had been a 'good servant and a bad master', damaging to painters who had not amassed sufficient experience of their own before following the paths cut by Picasso, who had by then usually moved elsewhere.

Clive had missed seeing Picasso in 1935 when the artist, despairing and depressed, had abandoned painting for poetry. This happened in the wake of his wife, Olga, moving out when she discovered that his mistress, Marie-Thérèse Walter, was pregnant. Called back to his studio in 1936 by the Spanish Civil War, Picasso was available to see Clive in March, and asked after Mary Hutchinson. His show at Zwemmer's that May was the first to offer his work for sale in London since 1921, Picasso's financial success being noted by Clive in his review. Clive also claimed for Picasso a far deeper significance than that represented by his dominance of the art world: 'He has affected our habits of seeing, still more has he affected our notions about what we see.' Like Freud, Marx and Einstein, Picasso had transformed the conditions of contemporary life.

For some years, Picasso had been collaborating with Christian Zervos, founder of the influential *Cahiers d'Art*, on a *catalogue raisonné*, the first volume of which appeared in 1932 (the last would be published in 1978). At the beginning of 1937, Clive received a formal letter from Janice Loeb, a twenty-three-year-old American art student who was assisting Zervos. Picasso had told her that Clive would know more than anyone else about collectors of 'negro' and cubist works in England and would be able to help her find documentation and photographs of his works made between 1907 and 1914. As she had been 'literally brought up' on Clive's books, Janice hoped he might have some time available to meet her.

After graduating from Vassar College, Janice had enrolled at Radcliffe to study for an MA in Fine Arts, but had left after her first year, to the consternation of her wealthy family on Manhattan's upper east side. Within days of receiving her letter, Clive told her she could usually find him any evening at the Deux Magots. A 'pneumatique' from Janice let him know that he would recognise her by her untidy red hair. 'Sincerely yours' soon changed to 'carissimo mio' as Clive and Janice began an affair sparked not only by her vivacious personality and good looks but also by her trenchant analyses of contemporary art and criticism.

Janice Loeb

Janice was precociously intelligent, very well-read, and her best friend was Daisy Barr, wife of the first director of New York's Museum of Modern Art. When she met Clive, Janice was about to part company acrimoniously with Zervos. She complained often to Daisy that he was behaving badly, spreading rumours about her and trying to control her life. Janice had recently suffered an unhappy romantic break-up in London, and had been planning to return to New York to contemplate what she might now do with her life. Meeting Clive changed all that. They went south together for ten days and she delayed her passage on the *Ile de France* until the end of March.

'He is 56 and looks it,' Janice told Daisy, 'damn funny & tubby.' Aldous Huxley had based the character of Miles Fanning in his short story 'After the Fireworks' on Clive, though in person he was 'infinitely more simpatico'. Clive was 'seriously amoureux', and although Janice was a little perturbed that he was so much older than she, his company had soon banished all the anxieties that had led to her to vow not to return to London, where he promised to show her around 'discreetly'. She swore Daisy to secrecy, and before long was regaling her with stories about meeting Virginia Woolf and staying at Ham Spray with Frances Marshall and Ralph Partridge. The night before sailing for New York, Janice was at 50 Gordon Square for dinner with Julian, Angelica, Vanessa and Duncan; Leonard joined them later. Julian told Ling Shuhua, his lover in Wuhan, that Angelica (just five years younger than Janice) had looked sweet in the dress he had brought her back from China. 'It was an amusing enough party with my father's new mistress, a red-haired American jewess,' he continued, Clive's 'old mistress' – Mary Hutchinson – being 'married and domestic'.

From East 72nd Street, Janice sent a torrent of letters, sometimes written in the pre-dawn hours. She longed for Clive to make her feel 'gay and alive' as he had between their Zervos sessions, clinging to the vision he represented of a way of life that her family could not touch 'because its put away in a box which they don't know about and which they can't get at.' She had been expected by her parents to continue on the path Radcliffe had prepared her for – 'PhD, writing a book about Picasso, etc.' – but she was fed up with it all. This 'neurotic little bitch', a 'German-Jewish American shrimp', as she described herself, conspired with the chauffeur and a maid to keep Clive's letters hidden from her family, though once her father 'accidentally' opened a telegram. Almost as soon as she landed in New York, Janice began plotting her return to Europe, an endeavour Clive assisted by writing 'business' letters that could be shown to her parents to give the impression that she had serious prospects for work. Clive and she even discussed enlisting Chatto and Windus to offer her a project that would require her being in Europe. 'What exactly is your relationship with Clive Bell?' her mother asked. This was 'Jewish family life with a vengeance', Janice explained to him. She was surrounded by people who thought she should find a suitable young man to marry, that she dressed badly and put on airs. Even Daisy Barr warned her that she was making a fool of herself.

Margaret Scolari – known as Daisy – had married Alfred Barr in 1930, a year after meeting him at the inaugural exhibition of the Museum of Modern Art. Daisy had taught Italian at Vassar and had several friends on the faculty there, including the art historians Henry-Russell Hitchcock, and Agnes Rindge, with whom Janice had studied. Daisy was closely involved with her husband's work and knew very well who Clive was; she would have known that MoMA's first president, A. Conger Goodyear, had hoped to discuss plans for the new museum with the eminent British critic. Although they were born more than a decade apart, Janice and Daisy were close, but the secretive relationship with Clive strained their friendship until they agreed they would no longer talk about him. 'Daisy Barr and I are again having a good time together,' Janice informed Clive, 'we seem to agree that you or England are never, never to be mentioned. Oh, to know the wild and passionate opinions she's burying on that subject.'

Janice had been used to 'men who would much rather you never had a head, except where it served in constructing and supporting a perpetual atmosphere of tingling eroticism, anaemic and slightly literary', but she knew that Clive respected her intellect and knowledge. He would never patronise her, despite telling Gilbert Seldes that he had been recommending his books and articles to quite the 'cleverest female child I have met for a long time'. Janice declared that she was not a feminist, but shrewdly understood that she wanted the freedom for which feminism fought: 'I'm getting what I want [therefore] do not need to be a feminist. But I'm grateful to them for all the spade work they've done + blessings they bestowed upon me – so, lazily, I take the cake and eat it & want to spend my time by your fire – looking as nice as art & nature will permit & try to seduce & enjoy being seduced & enjoy even more (because I'm sure of my freedom & that spade work that others have done) being "his woman" if he'll let me.'

Janice also wanted to educate her lover about America and enclosed articles from the *New Yorker* in letters filled with accounts of movies and exhibitions. She talked a guard into letting her into a special Renoir show at the Metropolitan Museum just before it opened and excitedly described to Clive racing through MoMA's 'Photography 1839–1937', a historical survey which ended with 'scientific shots taken at 1/100,000 second; golf ball at moment of impact; cup being crushed by hammer'. She went to the premiere of Aaron Copland's opera for schoolchildren, *The Second Hurricane*, at the Henry Street Settlement, where she enjoyed the 'lovely music + lovely children – swearing, slangy + dirty'. She told Clive she would like to take him to see Hollywood movies, not the more 'artistic' kind which Angelica recommended.

In this way, Clive gained insights into the New York cultural scene from someone who in fact was at its heart. One evening, Janice went to see Rosalind Russell and Robert Montgomery in *Night Must Fall* with a new friend named Walker Evans, 'who's really a good photographer'. She wanted to find out more about the elusive Evans, who kept disappearing into the countryside. She neglected to explain that the reason for these disappearances was his assignment with James Agee, whom she knew well, to go to Alabama for the Farm Security Administration to document rural poverty, work that would later bring them to the attention of *Fortune* magazine, whose assignment would result in the seminal record of the Depression, *Let Us Now Praise Famous Men*. Walker Evans was a protégé of Mina Kirstein's brother Lincoln, who had organised the exhibition of Evans' 'Photographs of Nineteenth Century Houses' at MoMA in 1933. Janice met Evans at the time planning was afoot for the 1938 MoMA exhibition 'Walker Evans: Photographer', and although he became a significant person in her life, Evans' friendship was not enough to compensate for her feeling adrift when she returned from London in March 1937, her American milieu not satisfying her several desires. For much of the spring Janice struggled to write a long article on Surrealism and American art criticism for Horace Gregory's magazine, *New Letters in America*, and eventually she abandoned it.

Clive's promotion of Janice as a capable writer was by no means only due to her youthful attractiveness. She had helped Daisy organise photographs by Brassaï of the Métro and worked in Paris with George Hugnet and Max Ernst on the catalogue copy for MoMA's 'Fantastic Art, Dada, Surrealism' exhibition. Janice's comprehensive analysis of Surrealism was listed in the catalogue's bibliography. This long article, published in the *Vassar Review* in February 1935, concurred in several respects with Clive's judgements about the movement but was written in the context of an American scene with which he was largely unfamiliar. In 'What Next in Art?', an article for *The Studio*, Clive had recognised Surrealism as the 'first serious deviation' from the post-Impressionist and cubist movements, but objected to its literary character and its association with Freud and Marx. Janice shared his opinion that art should be a 'self-sufficient entity', arguing that Surrealism was a 'theory dangerous to art' because 'memory and association must be brought into play to make the work interesting to us'. She considered André Breton's 1924 *Manifesto* 'romantic' in its negation of reason, but Surrealism – whose roots in Dada she traced with aplomb – depended to such an extent upon shock and disgust that the viewer would eventually become inured to it, leaving it nothing else to offer. It is not possible that either could have read the other's article, so the coincidence of Janice and Clive's views is striking and explains why Clive had such respect for her. In *The Studio*, Clive had likened Surrealism to a joke, which depends for its effect on surprise and therefore does not bear repetition. No wonder that Janice felt that a 'bit of C. B. in the evening is to the day what a cigar is to supper'.

Earlier debates about American poetry's relation to European modernism, succeeded by discussion of literary regionalism's place in an American avant-garde, were to some extent revisited in the United States in 1930s criticism of surrealist art. For those who dreamed of a 'national art with meaning and dignity', Surrealism's popularity was irritating. Janice felt that critics on both the left and right were silly to attack Surrealism on Marxist grounds (even though, at the time, for most Americans 'Marx' brought to mind Harpo and Groucho rather than Karl). Freudian ideas about the unconscious, so readily accepted in the United States, made Surrealism more palatable to American viewers. In a 1924 article, Clive had dismissed Freud's theory that art was rooted in a displacement of libido, adding that the psychoanalyst knew nothing about art.

Clive thought that Salvador Dali was 'vulgar trash' but he admitted that future critics might provide a different view of Surrealism's importance, although he would not live to see it. When Janice objected to how Dali made his outrageous personality a relevant element of his art, she echoed Clive's point of view precisely: real artists 'are experiencing something apart from their nature as human beings'.

Clive seems not to have commented in print on the sensational 'International Surrealism' exhibition at the New Burlington Galleries in June 1936, nor did he engage publicly with those adherents of the movement who so frequently used his name to sum up all that they opposed – the 'delicate, affected, sly nodding of Bell-flowers, ringing their self-peals over and over again', as Geoffrey Grigson phrased it. Clive's interest in British artists had now expanded to include Ethel Walker, Ivon Hitchens, Walter Steggles, Matthew Smith, Keith Baynes and William Coldstream. The 'next phase of English painting' for Clive was represented by the East London Group who could hold their own alongside contemporary French painters. He would come to see English painting as at a critical moment by late 1938, when his allegiances lay clearly with new forms of realism pioneered by Coldstream and those Clive dubbed the 'School of 1938', who had first come to public notice in March 1934 when Zwemmer held an 'Objective Abstraction' exhibition. Clive did not review that show, which included Coldstream, Graham Bell, Roderigo Moynihan, Geoffrey Tibble, Hitchens, Victor Pasmore and Ceri Richards, but these were the painters he believed to be developing an English version of the tradition rooted in the French masters. Coldstream, for example, had first encountered the Cézannes at the Tate, as well as Seurat's *Baignade*, in 1926 when he was a student at the Slade, which had the 'effect of a sudden assault on the sensibilities'. The artists around Coldstream and Graham Bell would become Janice's close friends when she returned to England and took up painting.

In one of the first letters she wrote him from New York, Janice had asked Clive to help her think through the article commissioned by Horace Gregory in which she intended to examine the 'Surrealism disease in London Paris New York'. She asked if there were English equivalents to 'art nationalists' like Thomas Craven, whose *Modern Art* (1934) scoffed at the school of Paris and extolled Thomas Hart Benton as the quintessential American painter, denigrating the artists associated with Alfred Stieglitz. Because she was aware of the arguments about abstraction preoccupying English artists and critics in periodicals such as *Axis* and *Circle*, she was particularly interested in whether Clive knew Herbert Read's private opinion about the 1936 surrealist exhibition. To her surprise, Clive obliged by writing to Read, who had become the butt of her crusading article (which was to be titled 'Armies and Banners'). Unfortunately, only her side of the correspondence with Clive survives, so anything Clive told Janice must be inferred from her letters to him. Her argument was that contemporary criticism was plagued by a confusion between movements and works, and furthermore between art movements and political movements. One evening she had a heated conversation about the destruction of churches in Barcelona with four friends, two of whom were Daisy and Alfred Barr: 'It was very surprising to in NY hear three of them minimize destructions in a passionate way and the other magnifying them in an even greater white heat of emotion. And after ten minutes I realized that they weren't talking pictures and buildings and sculpture at all, but politics the whole time.'

34. Today the Struggle

Through the ruse of a companionable trip with her brother's fiancée, Janice eventually got her wish and booked passage on *The American Banker*, departing New York on 9 July 1937. Taking note of the headlines from Spain, she only hoped that the 'world's last smash up' might be delayed until after she had arrived in England: 'after that – oh well'. Her mother secretly hoped that a European catastrophe would prevent her daughter from leaving. Clive had kept Janice informed about Julian's intention to join the fight against Fascism in Spain, which was something she urged on her 'sad friends' in New York because so many young people she knew were 'either gracefully or repulsively suffering from mal-de-siècle'. Like Julian, Janice believed in 'chaotic doings' to avoid the feeling of wasting one's life.

All the time he had been in China, Vanessa had worried that Julian was writing to Charles Mauron about going to Spain. Had it not been for her great anxiety, Julian would have gone straight to Spain from China, but he was persuaded to come back to England after visiting the Maurons in St-Remy, where Charles did his best to dissuade him from joining the International Brigades to fight against Franco. Throughout the spring and early summer of 1937, Julian and his mother had long discussions which led to the compromise that he would serve as an ambulance driver with Spanish Medical Aid instead of volunteering to fight.

The night before he left, Julian's immediate family met for an impromptu dinner at Clive's flat, joined later in the evening by Leonard and Virginia. Virginia saw how Julian, now twenty-nine, held his own with Leonard and Clive in a conversation about Fascism and thought that Clive was 'reining himself in with L.: being self restrained: which means there's trouble brewing' (Leonard afterwards told her this was not so). After Julian left with his mother, the others lingered to talk, Clive seeking to allay Virginia's worry by pointing out that Julian was 'very cool, like Cory'.

Julian had spent the months before he left for Spain writing various explanations of his desire for a life of action, including a letter to Morgan Forster titled 'War and Peace' in which he expressed gratitude for 'being made, as a child, to look at a stag having its throat cut' because it had given him an unsentimental view of life (in *Three Guineas*, which his aunt regarded as a posthumous argument with Julian, Virginia would adduce hunting as one source of men's tendency to be warlike). As his biographers note, Julian did not go to Spain to 'unravel the complexities of the politics but to gain military experience'.

As Julian made his way in an ambulance convoy across France to Spain, plans were in motion to raise money for Basque refugee children at the National Joint Committee for Spanish Relief's 'Spain and Culture' meeting at the Albert Hall on 24 June, where Virginia and Leonard would sit with other notable intellectuals and writers on a dais behind the speakers. Vanessa, Duncan and Quentin had visited Picasso in the spring, Quentin tasked with persuading him to participate in the event. Janice was amused to hear that Picasso 'might be sleeping on my sofa. You must tell me if he really came to help the Basque children or for a visit to London. It sounds out of character.' Picasso did not come, but designed the cover for the programme which included a reference to the agonised mother of *Guernica*, the iconic painting on which he had been working when Quentin approached him and which would first be exhibited in the Spanish Pavilion at the International Expo in Paris in July, before travelling the following year to Scandinavia and London.

Clive planned some small dinner parties at Gordon Square to welcome Janice, whose ship was due to dock on 19 July, and, with Quentin's advice, bought her a small Ford. He intended to bring her to Charleston for the August Bank Holiday weekend, immediately after which they would go on a motor tour in France. Frances Marshall, to whom Clive had told the whole story of how he had come to be involved with Janice, hoped they would visit Ham Spray again and sent Janice her love. On 20 July, the phone rang in Vanessa's Fitzroy Street studio: Julian had been killed by shrapnel from a bomb during the battle of Brunete.

Virginia and Leonard had been certain that Julian would die in Spain, preparation which may have provided Virginia the strength of mind to support her sister steadfastly in the awful aftermath of the loss. At Charleston, where she was taken nine days later, Vanessa collapsed, hardly able to leave her daybed, while Clive, 'such a pathetic, and always honest, man', cracked jokes to try to make everyone laugh. Angelica remembered Clive's 'distressing detachment at a moment when detachment was impossible'. Clive had played a far less important part in Julian's life than Vanessa had and it is impossible now to learn in any detail how he reacted to his death. Janice, just arrived and knowing no one, went at once to stay with Frances and Ralph while Clive went to Charleston. When he wrote to thank Frances for taking Janice in, Clive acknowledged that Julian's loss was worse for Vanessa than for him:

> My life is so full of things – mostly vanities – that the hole will fill up. What I mind most is not that a particular kind of family fun and good fellowship has lost an essential ingredient for ever, but that Julian will not get all the good things out of life which I think he would have got – for you know his capacity for enjoyment was large. But I doubt whether the hole in Vanessa's life will be filled up ever. However she has Duncan, and two children who are devoted to her, and painting, which is a great deal more than most people have.

It should not be thought that Clive was unaffected by Julian's death. Many friends wrote to Vanessa and Clive separately with their condolences, a quiet acknowledgment of the real circumstances of their family life, and some made clear that although he and Vanessa did not live together, Clive had suffered just as grievous a loss. 'It is cruel that you should lose your eldest son through war, you who have done everything to spare the sacrifice of young lives,' Ethel Sands wrote the day after the *Times* report of Julian's death appeared. 'Vanessa often told me of your perfect relationship with your boys, of the way in which you achieved the elder brother & friend attitude which many fathers strive for & fail to attain.'

Among the many letters was one addressed 'Dear Arthur' from his old friend Louisa Blaikie, living in Ipswich, who asked Clive to give her love to his mother and wondered if she could even take in the news at her age. Hannah Bell had learned of her first grandchild's death from Dorothy, whom Cory had rung as soon as he heard. His mother knew Quentin and Angelica would be a comfort to Clive, but also that no one could take Julian's place. Mary Hutchinson heard the news from Lesley Jowitt and wrote at once to Clive that she was thinking of Thoby (whose first name was Julian), 'the Goth you used to tell me of'.

Over the next year, plans evolved for a volume memorialising Julian. When Virginia read the 'War and Peace' letter to Forster, she heard in it 'something like Clive; shrewd & biting'. Vanessa was relieved that Clive was wholeheartedly in support of the volume, which was edited by Quentin and published by the Hogarth Press in 1938 as *Julian Bell: Essays, Poems and Letters*. Clive believed that it was appropriate to publish letters that would refer to Julian's intimate relationships, just as Vanessa had said to Julian after Lytton's death that publishing a truthful account was worth some upset feelings. Virginia, too, was glad that Clive had discussed the volume with Vanessa: 'I feel he wants to talk, only cant, unless one starts him. Its such a mistake, letting one'self become snowed under' – an indication that Clive, trained by his country's masculine norms, found it difficult to articulate his feelings. He had told Raymond he did not think Spain a cause worth dying for.

Janice and Clive set off for France in early August. Clive wrote to Picasso about Julian's death but, when they got to Paris, Clive was disappointed to find that Picasso was in the Midi. Toulouse was dirty and noisy and everyone was talking politics. Virginia acidly remarked to Vanessa that she did not envy Clive being boxed up in the little car with his 'spruce jewess' for a month. When they returned, she noted with some foreboding that Clive seemed 'a little on the bare wheels; no blown up tires' – might he have ceased to enjoy life? The tour with Janice seems to have been unremarkable, but many years later Janice would try to explain how she felt guilty for having been neurotic when she should have been happy. That Christmas, Vanessa went with Quentin and Angelica to the south of France, while Clive went on his own to Seend. Even the absence of his abrasive older sister Lorna failed to make it anything other than awful.

35. Warmongers

Virginia thought of her anti-war essay *Three Guineas* as an argument with Julian and it is possible to understand Clive's *Warmongers*, published in October 1938, three months after Virginia's pamphlet, as in some sense his anguished pacifist's reaction to Julian's death. Given that Clive finished writing *Warmongers* during the Sudetenland crisis, his deliberate insertion of specific dates signals his awareness that the situation was changing daily. The foreword is dated 21 September, just eight days before Hitler, Daladier and Chamberlain signed the Munich Agreement and one day before the British prime minister met Hitler in Godesberg. *Warmongers* is pervaded by the urgency of an unfolding crisis, yet it is at the same time ahistorical in its simple refrain that nothing is worse than war – war is always, in any situation, the worst of all possible evils. Most Europeans did not want war in 1939 and many believed the conflict 'would mean the eclipse of European civilization'. Mussolini had been widely approved of until he invaded Abyssinia – Churchill continued to praise the dictator until 1937. In 1938, public sentiment in England was very much in favour of appeasing Hitler and when Chamberlain returned to England waving his infamous slip of paper, declaring 'peace for our time', the people cheered. Most of them.

Although *Warmongers* was published by the Peace Pledge Union, it carried a disclaimer added in haste after it had been printed: 'The Peace Pledge Union does not necessarily endorse all the views expressed in this pamphlet, which is published by it as a valuable contribution to current thought.'[1] Clive was in an increasingly isolated position by September 1938 because he simply refused to adjust his First World War pacifism to new circumstances. Even in 1936, Bunny had told Mina Kirstein, with whom he had remained close since her exciting London sojourn in 1924, that Clive's 'politics have become fantastically logical & all wrong'. Bunny compared Mussolini's actions in Africa to a Dantesque hell and had no hesitation in getting a commission as an RAF officer when the war began. The transformation of former COs into jingoes was partly what led Clive to write *Warmongers*, although by 1939 he thought there was 'much to be said for being a conscientious objector when one is of military age and a soldier when one is of middle [age]'.

Warmongers oscillates between a simple plea for non-violence – never to meet force with force – and advocacy of practical actions that would have been impossible, after March 1939, to regard with anything but astonishment at their naivety. And yet there is a fascinating purity about Clive's refrain: 'The worst tyranny is better than the best war'; 'War is always the worst of all evils.' *Warmongers* begins with a reminder that its author wrote *Peace at Once* and quickly makes apparent that his thinking on war and peace has not changed. Just as he had thought in 1915 that the nationality of who paid him would make little difference to a factory worker, so in 1938 he argued that there would be 'plenty of happiness in a Nazi world'. Had not American journalist Vincent Sheean reported from Austria about the working class's satisfaction, which proved that it was 'arrant nonsense to suppose that the bulk of the population in Germany, Russia and Italy spends its days and nights groaning under a sense of tyranny'?

Jimmy Sheean, as he was known to his friends, had become a world-famous foreign correspondent since the time Raymond had arranged

---

[1]Charles Andrews observes that many PPU publications 'that took on topics potentially viewed as treasonous' carried a disclaimer, but whereas others had the notice printed on the title page, *Warmongers* had it on a paper band wrapped around it, suggesting it was 'one of the first to receive this distancing measure' (162) (other copies of the pamphlet contain the disclaimer in a pasted-on label). In 1996, the PPU historian William Hetherington told James Beechey that Bell's arguments 'were never PPU policy, and it is unclear why, despite that, the PPU saw fit to publish the pamphlet, albeit with a disclaimer. The PPU had no known obligation to Bell, who was never a member . . . and it is questionable whether the proponent of such arguments, knowing the treatment meted out at that time to Germany's own internal minorities, could legitimately be called a pacifist' (Beechey, 'Clive' 11).

for him to rent Clive's flat in 1931 while Clive was at the Zurich eye clinic.[2] Sheean's memoir, *Personal History* (1935), gained him adulation and awards for its account of his reporting on the rise of Fascism. Now based in Paris, Sheean reported from Vienna that 'terror reigns throughout the population and . . . nobody dares give a plain answer to a plain question.' Undoubtedly, the Nazis' control was supported by 'an important part of the masses', but 'Liberals, intellectuals, Communists, Jews, aristocrats and Catholics' were not faring quite so well. There were 20,000 Jews in jails or concentration camps and Austrian Nazis who were not in line with the new masters were undergoing 'party discipline' at Dachau. The 'Nazi steamroller', Sheean continued, had ground 'the swastika into the face of Vienna', which was no longer the cosmopolitan city it had been. Nevertheless, it was a 'fantastic distortion of the truth' that the Nazis ruled only through terror, because National Socialism had wide appeal among the masses. Intellectuals and cultivated people might be assumed by liberals to be 'the people', but Clive was under no illusion that he would escape being rounded up by the Nazis and even seems to have been prepared to be sacrificed if 'the masses' could continue to enjoy their simple pleasures under Nazi rule. (He was not on the Gestapo's list of those to be imprisoned after a Nazi invasion of England, but Virginia and Leonard were.) What Clive did not address in *Warmongers* was the problem of the hundreds of thousands of people of any class whom the Nazis would not *allow* to be National Socialists – Jews, homosexuals, the disabled.

In September 1938, Clive believed the best course of action, given the pressure brought to bear by warmongers, was to support the government, so he would hold his nose and vote for the Conservatives, despite having never done so before. As he saw it, the root of the current crisis was the 'Carthaginian' peace wrought by the Treaty of Versailles. Even if appeasement only afforded a delay, would that not be better than going to war without trying everything to avoid it? He advocated a 'United States of Europe' to guarantee peace and if Germany was dominant within it, that was preferable to a 'balance of power' that depended upon a constant state of readiness for war. His thinking was in line with arguments which had been made by former leftists in France

---

[2]While at the flat Sheean began an affair with Duncan (Spalding, *DG* 304–08).

(such as Alfred Fabre-Luce, the brother of Roland de Margerie's wife, Jenny) who had now moved far to the right. The argument that a plan for peace is imperfect had too often been used to deny even attempting it: 'When the town is blazing, and the one chance of avoiding total destruction lies in blowing up quickly whole blocks of buildings, you will not allow your salvage scheme to be impeded by the thought that it may come hard on some of the property owners,' Clive wrote. It was this kind of 'logic' that so infuriated people like Bunny: those 'blocks of buildings' were in reality the thousands of victims whom the Nazis had been persecuting, imprisoning, torturing and killing since 1933.

Without most of its practical suggestions (which included limiting the freedom of speech of 'warmongers' – censorship was acceptable in support of a war effort, so why not in the cause of peace?) Clive's pamphlet might stand honourably within the tradition of the literature of non-violence. It is a heartfelt and desperate rejection of the voices that lead inexorably and repeatedly to war, and war has never ended war:

> It is something that this morning, Sunday, August 14th, we are not at war. Try to imagine your state of mind at this moment, as you read these words, if Europe were at war. Imagine, or if you are old enough to recall, the feeling of miserable anxiety, futility, hopelessness and helplessness, the feeling that life had lost its savour and nothing was worth while, and then ask yourself whether any policy that assures peace for a few years even is not preferable to a policy which risks war to-morrow.

He was still 'an out-and-out pacificist', rejecting war not for any moral scruple about taking life but because 'war is the worst of all evils, and when it is a question of choosing between two evils, choose the less.'

When Clive sought advice on who might publish *Warmongers*, Harold Nicolson warned him that the left would reject it because it praised Chamberlain and the right because it was too pacifist. He recommended Clive approach George Lansbury, and provided a note of introduction. Lansbury and Clive had never met but the old campaigner respected Clive's pacifist credentials, addressing him as a 'dear comrade', and agreeing with most of what he said. Lansbury hoped that the PPU would publish the pamphlet, a suggestion that may have come from Aldous Huxley, who had become a sponsor of the PPU when his pacifism became more absolute in the 1930s. Phyllis Nichols (whose husband would become ambassador to Czechoslovakia in 1941) advocated with the PPU on Clive's behalf because she agreed with the principles in his pamphlet, but he did not sign the Pledge card she sent him. Nichols ordered fifty copies of *Warmongers*, which she thought more useful than gas masks. Several of Clive's friends proposed to 'propaganda' his argument, as Mary Baker put it, including Oliver Brett and all his children (though Brett himself thought Clive's attack on free speech was fascist). From Paris, Marie-Laure de Noailles assured Clive she would get a dozen more copies because hers had been snatched away from her as soon as it arrived. Even those who were unswayed by Clive's arguments were tolerant of his convictions, not letting their political differences damage their friendship. When Maud Russell saw Clive a month after the war had begun, she found that he was

> much the same as ever and hasn't veered away from pacifism. He says it has nothing to do with a dislike of killing and if he were ordered to go and fight he would do so at once. But he thinks war a far greater disaster, entailing far greater misery, setbacks and destruction than any arrogant and loathsome dictatorship, no matter how repugnant or how disastrous it may be to a small minority of rich or intelligent people. I can understand that, taking a long view, he may be right. But it goes against all one's instincts, feelings and ideals to stick to this, no doubt, logical view.

At the end of the war, Maud would find Clive's refusal to change with the times somehow reassuring.

The outpouring of disillusionment in plays, memoirs, novels and poetry after the First World War had burnished the appeal of pacifism for people who remembered 1914. The war talk in France of autumn 1938 seemed to Vanessa 'simply 1914 over again, only worse'. She approved of *Warmongers* because 'hardly anyone who didn't live through the last war when grown up can realise that war is always an end to reason & therefore its no good ever fighting for any given purpose at all.' Clive heard that Churchill was 'seriously annoyed' by *Warmongers* and took pleasure in the support of his housekeeper, Lottie Hope, who was an 'ardent Chamberlainite'. The 'mezzo-brows' might be enraged by appeasement, but Clive thought the 'common people' were relieved by

Chamberlain's agreement with Hitler, which struck him as a triumph for 'general common sense'. The 'stunning new fact in the world' was that two great nations had said that despite humiliation, the loss of honour and national prestige, 'by comparison with war, what does it matter'? 'Liberalism versus Totalitarianism impossible', he scribbled in his appointment diary. 'If liberal states wish to fight must become totalitarian, & then what does it matter who wins. Winston & Co. don't want the triumph of liberalism. They want the triumph of England.' When the government started to discuss reintroducing conscription, Clive argued that Baldwin was in effect saying 'if you mean to stand up to the Nazis you must adopt Nazi methods', and asked that the Labour Party make clear where it stood on the issue.

Public opinion shifted rapidly when it became clear that appeasement had been a grave error. Violet Bonham Carter, who had always understood how dictators behave, wrote angrily in her diary that the 'blind, smug inertia of Neville Chamberlain & his followers, their refusal to believe in war, to prepare for it, or even to meet it when it came is criminal.' Virginia's *Three Guineas* had been sneeringly dismissed as 'Nazi dialectic without Nazi conviction' by Q. D. Leavis in *Scrutiny*, while the political correspondent Raymond Burns excoriated Clive for the 'half-witted' and naive pronouncements of *Warmongers*. Clive told Frances he had heard that 'they say' Virginia's pamphlet was 'beneath contempt'; Virginia felt 'sent to Coventry' by her friends. Vanessa suspected that the view of *Warmongers* at Monk's House would not be sympathetic: 'What is thought of Clive's pamphlet?' she asked her sister. 'No good I expect.' Leonard would not even read it, Virginia told Quentin, though this did not prevent him from expressing his opinion (which she did not repeat). Virginia wanted to hear what Quentin – who had been irritated by *Three Guineas* – thought of his father's position before she would venture her own view. Whatever that might have been, she kept it to herself. As the war moved inexorably closer, with conscription reintroduced in April 1939, and petrol rationing in September making it more and more difficult to visit friends, Clive was one of the very few people close to Virginia whose attitude to war was uncompromising.

36. Euston Road

Clive's excursion in France with Janice after Julian's death had not been a success. Having left behind in New York a family she believed disliked her, Janice had little self-confidence and was beset by anxieties about the direction of her life. She could not explain to Clive why she felt 'underwater' after a glorious weekend together at Charleston and considered going back into psychoanalysis unless Clive thought it was 'ludicrous'. She knew that he was sceptical, 'and as I remember it, contemptuous', of what she always referred to as her 'witch-doctors', but she still began to look for an analyst in London.

She stayed for a time in Clive's flat while looking for a place of her own and soon was invited for a drink by Benita. Benita had often stayed at 50 Gordon Square while Clive travelled, taking care of his business correspondence and overseeing workmen when renovations were made. Like her, Janice loved being in Clive's luxurious environment. 'Am sitting in your bed smoking your pipe,' Janice wrote soon after they returned from France.

Janice moved into a ground-floor flat at 51 Gordon Square, becoming Adrian Stephen's tenant, and would be Clive's frequent companion in the next two years, earning the affection of many of his friends, often joining Virginia, Vanessa and Angelica for family dinners and attending Bloomsbury fancy dress parties (once in a 'great nose'). With her sharp mind and deep knowledge of art, Janice impressed even the most demanding in Clive's circle – 'At Clive's on Sunday. A good discussion of painting & music. Janice gave tongue,' Virginia wrote approvingly. Her long review of Walter Pach's translation of Delacroix's *Journal* delighted Roland de Margerie when he found that she agreed with every point of his own views. But not everyone was so taken with Janice. The Keyneses had a curious antipathy towards her, and when they refused to give Janice a lift with them to Rodmell one day, Virginia appealed to Vanessa for an explanation of the mystery but Vanessa could shed no light on it: 'Janice is really more harmless than Lydia,' she told her sister.

Some of the artists whom Clive had identified in 1935 as representing the 'next phase of English painting' were encouraged by Kenneth Clark in their plan to open a school where they could cater to those who 'wish to take up Drawing and Painting as ends in themselves', at a time when art schools were emphasising the applied arts. Graham Bell, who had assisted Clark with illustrations for Roger's *Last Lectures*, and William Coldstream drew up a prospectus for the school, which opened on 4 October 1937 at 12 Fitzroy Street. Claude Rogers had approached Helen Anrep for help and she had enlisted Vanessa and Duncan as supporters, who in turn persuaded Augustus John and John Nash to add their names to the prospectus.

By the time the school moved in spring 1938 to 314 Euston Road, it had become a 'fashionable place to visit'. Its new address enabled Clive to name the 'Euston Road school', like other celebrated artistic collectives, as a singular phenomenon in English painting. He had first drawn attention to Coldstream, Graham Bell, Victor Pasmore and Rodrigo Moynihan as the 'school of 1938' in his review of an exhibition at Wildenstein's that he thought was the first in fifteen years to escape Picasso's influence completely. When Coldstream, Pasmore, Bell, Rogers and Lawrence Gowing were among the fifteen painters who each exhibited a portrait of London at Eardley Knollys' Storran Gallery in October 1938, Clive renamed the group for the school with which it was now associated, remarking that it defined a 'critical moment for English painting, the most hopeful we have known for a hundred years'.

Among the regular students of the Euston Road school's first year were Quentin and Janice; Angelica attended in the second year. According to the school's historian, Janice 'became a hard-edged abstract painter'; she also made lasting friendships with Lawrence Gowing, Claude and Elsie Rogers, and with those sometimes called the younger generation of Bloomsbury such as Judith Stephen and Janie Bussy, some of whom would visit her in New York after the war. Painting became Janice's means of escape from psychological torments which had worsened in late 1938. She rented a studio in St John's Wood, but felt 'choked' in London and had re-entered analysis. Clive was very understanding when she could not go with him to a first night: 'my fear of "being seen" out is so great that I refused. Thank god he accepts "my oddity" at its face not its real value. We call it agrophobia & leave it at that.' She was troubled about being perceived as 'an old man's mistress' and Virginia heard from Adrian that Janice might be tiring of Clive.

Clive was fatalistic by late summer 1939, but did not want to live through another war. Sitting on the terrace at Monk's House with Virginia, their private lives as yet untouched, there was 'no feeling of patriotism', only a question of how to go on. He took some mild satisfaction at the discomfort communist friends experienced when the Russians and Germans signed a non-aggression pact, noticing that Quentin had 'stealthily' given up the *Daily Worker*. The situation in 1939 revived memories of 1914, when he had first known Mary Hutchinson. He told her in August that his life 'could not be neatly rounded off until I have known you again'. All Clive might do that seemed at all useful was try to keep the flame of civilisation burning.

Mary and Clive had forged a tolerable friendship by the mid-1930s, but he never missed an opportunity to let her know that he desired more. Once, happily surprised to find her at a party given by the Clarks, he had been pleased that she 'allowed' him to escort her home, though there had been a 'twinge of pain in it too'; an invitation to accompany him to France remained open. It was to Mary that Clive first broached the idea of doing something to 'keep civilization alive' by persuading people that they 'must go on reading books, looking at pictures, going to plays and concerts and behaving as though they were rational beings' during the war, though he was pessimistic about the prospect of success. He hoped to enlist Virginia in the cause, and was counting on Kenneth Clark. London's art treasures were moved out of the capital to safety in late August, but Clive hoped that Clark could maintain 'some remnant of a national gallery at Exeter or Bath, and a permanent show of contemporary painting in London'.

His faith in art's power to transcend such tedious concerns as war remained unshaken. Above all, he was convinced that it was worth doing anything to prevent the English becoming as barbarous as their enemies. Clive now argued in favour of 'A Ministry of Arts' to 'save the artists'. Reminding his readers that Maynard had been sent to purchase paintings from the Degas collection auctioned during the First World War, he assumed that money flowed like water in times of war. A Ministry of Arts could keep the arts alive by sponsoring theatre productions around the world, as well as concerts of British music and exhibitions of British painting. Anticipating his imminent involvement in the British Council, Clive recommended that the services of such men as Eric Maclagan, Leigh Ashton and Kenneth Clark be secured.

In the interests of promoting civilisation, Clive lectured on 'Byzantine Art and the Christian Slope' on a cruise sponsored by the Hellenic Travellers' Club in April 1939, one of a programme of speakers which included Leigh Ashton and Dean Inge. Clive's sister Dorothy had been inspired to take the cruise chiefly for the opportunity to spend time with her brother but also so that her husband, Henry Hony, could sail again through the Dardanelles, where he had served in the Gallipoli campaign of 1915 as an interpreter. With their daughter Selina, the Honys shared a table with Ashton and Clive, enjoying both his company and his knowledge of the Peloponnese whenever they disembarked. 'Dorothy, Henry & Selina were amiable and considerate,' Clive wrote to Vanessa, making a 'solid background' to the journey.

Clive had always been close to Dorothy, in stark contrast to his dislike of Lorna. Dorothy had confided in Clive about her husband's homosexuality in painfully honest letters, knowing that Clive's tolerance would guarantee a sympathetic response. On the Hellenic cruise, Clive made sure the Honys enjoyed themselves, taking them to the 'crowning meal of the trip' in Toulon – 'more hors d'oeuvres than one could believe possible & a bouillabaisse that we shall remember for the rest of our lives'. Clive's thoughtfulness was the making of the trip for his sister, just as he had thrilled her and her children in 1937 when he gave them the use of his flat during the coronation of George VI; the children had been astonished to find no decorations at 50 Gordon Square and immediately sallied forth to buy flags.

Janice thought that an America at peace would be worse than a Europe at war, but reluctantly left England in the summer of 1939, travelling via Italy and France back to New York. She told Clive he was welcome to use her studio and could dispose of any of her belongings as he wished. The day after Britain declared war, she wrote a lover's farewell:

What I want to write you is something like a condolence letter because I know how you feel about all this. It still, at times, feels as if tomorrow the newspapers would carry headlines Poisson D'Avril [April Fool]. That would make some sense at least . . . Even if I haven't looked that way I do realize, remember everything you've meant & did for me. There are things you don't know about I suppose, attitudes, emotions. But this is all silly . . . We've had an awful lot together & You've been wonderful to me.

She gave her little black Ford to Quentin, who passed it on to Leonard and Virginia. By October, Janice was back in New York from where she let Clive know that she was painting again, had been to see Frederick Ashton's new ballet, *Devil's Holiday*, and was reading Forster's *Abinger Harvest* 'with love'. They would not see one another again until 1950, by which time Janice had become a pioneering documentary film maker.

A month before the outbreak of war, Clive relinquished his Gordon Square flat. A certain kind of hectic fun could be found in the city of dreadful night for those who knew where to look, but London's 'surrealist charm' quickly wore thin. For a time he stayed at Janice's studio, but the exigencies of blackout regulations defeated him and he took a flat at the Savoy to use whenever he was in London. Air raid precautions seemed to him absurd when the lights of the Southern Railway lit the path for German bombers all the way from the coast to London. With supreme optimism he told the Chicago arts patron Bobsy Goodspeed that 1940 seemed like a good year for 'wandering'. The *Edinburgh Evening News* even announced that Clive would be 'leaving shortly on a voyage around the world. Bloomsbury will thus lose, for a time, one of her wittiest pundits and most genial hosts.' But Clive spent the war at Charleston, where his furniture was moved in August, along with Lottie Hope, his housemaid and cook. Virginia found him there wearing an 'enormous white jersey which he patted & prodded from time to time. A little testy about his room. I needn't say I've been palmed off with the worst in [the] house. Desiring sympathy, Duncan said, & admiration. All his books were put in order by the others. Rather an elderly tea party.' As Anne Olivier Bell would note dispassionately, 'Clive in fact had three of the best rooms in Charleston, and a private bathroom'.

VI

CIVILISATION'S
FLAME (1939–1949)

37. Alarm and Despondency

Clive would have no other home than Charleston after 1939, though he maintained a nomadic London life at various addresses after the war. Charleston Farmhouse had steadily undergone improvements since Molly MacCarthy, walking with Clive from Berwick railway station during the First World War, declared it the 'nearest thing she had encountered to Wuthering Heights'. For the duration of the Second World War, Charleston enabled its inhabitants to continue more or less uninterrupted lives devoted to painting, writing, reading and conversation. Major structural changes to the house had been completed just before war was declared, including the conversion of an attic room into Vanessa's studio. Her bedroom was moved to the ground floor, next to the sitting room where French windows opened onto the walled garden and a window looked out across the pond towards Tilton, where Maynard had moved in 1925 after his marriage to Lydia. It was in this garden room that in 1937, soon after Julian's death in the Spanish Civil War, Vanessa revealed to Angelica that Clive was not her father.

Vanessa and Duncan had been decorating cabinets, window frames, doors, fireplaces, tables and chairs since first moving to the house in 1916, creating the distinctive aesthetic for which Charleston is still known. The house was filled with objects that held the memories of intertwined lives, of travels, discoveries and losses. Charleston was a home, embracing family histories that reached back to Hyde Park Gate – from where Vanessa had brought a glass cabinet, and blue and white platters that had belonged to the Stephens – and to Duncan's childhood in the form of his father's piano. Pottery, pictures and plates from Italy, France, Greece and Turkey jostled with paintings by Duncan, Vanessa and many other contemporary artists. There were red and lacquer Omega chairs designed in 1913 by Roger Fry and the small Matisse painting, *Le port*, that Roger had bequeathed to Vanessa.

In 1939, much of the contents of Vanessa and Duncan's Fitzroy Street studios, as well as Clive's collection of paintings bought over the past twenty-five years, were added to an already crowded house. Roderic O'Conor's 1911 *Flowers* hung with Alice Halicka's *Couples*, inscribed to Clive, as well as drawings made for Clive by Derain and by Augustus John. A *Landscape* by Othon Friesz, inscribed for Clive 'en toute sympathie', hung with Friesz's 1920 *Pears and Apples*. Clive's Juan Gris still life, *Les Oeufs*, came from London, as did his two Vlamincks, joining the Picasso *Pots et Citron* that he and Vanessa had bought in 1911 and that had illustrated *Art* as an example of significant form. Many of these works would be sold in Clive's lifetime, or given to Quentin and Angelica. As well as the large bookcase, decorated for him by Duncan in 1925, his extensive library and six Venetian chairs, Clive even took with him the green carpeting from 50 Gordon Square, to be laid on the staircase and in his first-floor suite of rooms, which all but Clive agreed were the most luxurious in the house.

Grace Germany, who had arrived as housemaid in 1920, had married a local man, Walter Higgens, in 1934, and lived at Charleston above the kitchen, in a small apartment nicknamed High Holborn by the family. Walter maintained the garden until he joined a Local Defence Volunteer section, after which Clive, Vanessa and Duncan took it over so that its steady supply of fresh produce would not be diminished. As Clive told Mary, 'I don't exactly dig for victory but I hoe for peas & beans.' He joined Charleston's landlord, Lord Gage's shooting syndicate in 1940 and at least twice a week took an old black labrador out with him to fetch the pheasant, partridge, rabbit or hare that he shot. The household rarely lacked for wine and beer, sherry, rum and brandy, enhancing the enjoyment of lingering long over the meals Grace prepared.

The winter of 1939–40 was freezing. The Woolfs cycled from Rodmell through the fog to spend the first Christmas of the war at Charleston, Virginia's tipsy singing delighting Clive. Pipes burst at the farmhouse in January, but a visit from Adrian Stephen had everyone laughing when he and Vanessa told old family stories. The war did eventually intrude directly on Charleston; shrapnel from dogfights caused the farm labourers to stop working in the fields in 1943 and later German

Clive Bell and Virginia Woolf

flying bombs were exploded over the downs by RAF fighters. Towards
the end of the war, Clive welcomed a searchlight installation whose
Cockney operators did odd jobs around the farm, their comic banter
alleviating the boredom of watching the skies for German aeroplanes.
For the most part, Charleston appeared to be the 'earthly paradise' of
Angelica's recollection, but under its convivial surface in 1939 were
painful currents of tension caused by her affair with Bunny.

When Bunny's wife Ray succumbed to cancer in March 1940, she
had known for some time about his affair with Angelica. At twenty-
one, Duncan and Vanessa's daughter was only four years older than
the Garnetts' eldest son, Richard; Bunny himself was forty-eight.
Although to Clive it seemed 'silly' to marry someone twice her age,

he understood that Angelica was anxious to escape what had become a painful atmosphere at Charleston, where Vanessa refused to address the situation openly. Vanessa and Duncan were very angry with Bunny, their disapproval shocking Ray's sister Frances, who was beginning to form the opinion that Bloomsbury tolerance for complicated loves did not extend quite as far as she had imagined. Frances and Ralph Partridge (who had married in 1933) were witnesses at Angelica and Bunny's marriage in May 1942, but it was only when Clive later told them how coldly Vanessa and Duncan had received Bunny's announcement of his intentions that he dropped the pretence that he was Angelica's father. Frances thought Clive secretly enjoyed reminding Vanessa and Duncan of the days when they 'were always telling him what a fascinating character Bunny was'. The circle of honesty remained tightly drawn, however: even in 1947, Bunny referred to Clive as his father-in-law, an appellation the humour of which never escaped Clive.

Angelica later described her relationship with Clive as having been stunted by the fiction maintained within the family about her true paternity, as well as by an 'inherent coldness' in his personality. In her account, her mother's injunction not ever to speak with Clive about what she had been told in 1937 damaged the possibility of healthy relations between them. 'He would have understood, if he wanted to, that there was nothing to prevent him from thinking of me as his daughter, while on my side the very real affection I had for him might have been released,' she wrote in her 1984 memoir. Angelica knew that Clive liked showing off his beautiful 'daughter' and that he was pleased whenever she accompanied him on visits to Seend to see his mother, or to Ham Spray to stay with Frances and Ralph. For all intents and purposes, Clive did act as a father to Angelica, far more so than Duncan could. He settled a generous sum on her at the beginning of 1942 and later assisted her with money to buy shares in Bunny's publishing venture with Rupert Hart-Davis. When Clive revised his will in 1953, he named both Angelica and Quentin as his children, dividing his estate equally between them, with Angelica's portion in trust for her children. By 1947, Angelica had four young daughters, a circumstance Clive regretted for what seemed to him to be the curtailment of her aspirations. In Clive's opinion, looking after babies during the war was about the toughest occupation there was, apart from active service, and how anyone who understood the use of contraceptives could have so many children was a mystery.

Clive's sister Dorothy died unexpectedly in 1940, leaving Henry Hony to bring up their three young daughters alone. Although he was sorry for Henry, Clive felt that his sister's death in some way was a fortunate escape from the misery of wartime (a view she herself, a stalwart of the local Women's Institute, would almost certainly have scoffed at). Clive was most concerned about the effect on his ninety-year-old mother of the loss of Dorothy, who had been her connection to the outside world. Until his mother died in February 1942, Clive persuaded Angelica to accompany him to Seend to see her whenever he could because it also gave Henry a reason to bring his girls, who were devoted to their cousin, from his farm at nearby Hallam to Cleeve House. Such family visits were usually combined with seeing Ralph and Frances at Ham Spray, less than thirty miles from Seend. Frances welcomed Clive and Angelica because they brought 'a strong whiff of Charleston's civilisation, with its aesthetic projects and ceaseless activity'.

Preserving access to the arts became Clive's paramount aim during the war, while he never abandoned his strong desire that the conflict would be negotiated to peace. Their resolute anti-war stance created a deep bond between Frances and Clive in a climate wherein views held in peacetime could now be seen as treasonous, and not to be patriotic was no longer a harmless eccentricity but an offensively subversive act.

Ever since they had first met when she was the assistant at Birrell and Garnett's bookshop in 1923, Frances and Clive had kept up a regular correspondence that ranged widely over literature, their friends' lives and loves and their shared disgust with war. Frances was quite aware that it was her slender figure that first had attracted Clive's attention, but once she made clear she had no intention of going to bed with him, he never bothered her with 'unwanted attentions'. She came to understand his two sides, the relaxed self at Charleston where he enjoyed rural pursuits as much as the life of the mind, and the more anxious Clive she encountered at his Gordon Square dinner parties where he expected that his guests would always shine. Conversation on such occasions, or at a luncheon at the Ivy, could be too overtly manipulated by Clive's determination that the guests at his table should sparkle, but when they lunched alone, Frances found their talk so 'fast and furious' she could scarcely recall for her diary all the topics over which it ranged. Clive found her company 'extraordinarily to my taste' and their mutual commiseration about the disappearance of civilisation helped sustain them during the war.

At dinner with Virginia in February 1940, T. S. Eliot and Saxon Sydney-Turner argued that the war probably meant the triumph of barbarism over civilisation. Joining them afterwards, Clive 'pessimised', agreeing that the light of civilisation was going out, but in general he did not like to talk about the war. Two days before the 'Phony War' ended in April 1940, when Germany invaded France and the Netherlands, Clive was at Raymond's flat with Ralph and Frances. Did he still want the war to end, Raymond asked, adding, 'I'm not arguing about it, I just want to know.' Both Clive and Frances did indeed want it to end. On the day the Nazis entered Paris, Frances remarked that Clive's 'philosophy remained unshaken', but his was an ineffectual and lonely position. She was taken aback by a melancholy letter where Clive despairingly told her he could not imagine having the will to live in London, Paris or Rome after the war: 'Indeed I don't particularly want to go on living at all. But if I do life that honour, I make no doubt it will be at Charleston.' He had 'always viewed the ideas of suicide and death with horror', Frances thought, yet she understood his malaise. Clive remained vehemently opposed to war, but was no longer sure he knew what being a pacifist meant: 'I assume we and the Americans will go on making aeroplanes and tanks whether in peace or war, and I should prefer to have it done in peace,' he told Frances. He would rather go on paying his taxes with a roof over his head and both his legs intact because he remained convinced that 'whatever happens, war will never make the world a pleasanter place to live in.' This was not to say that he objected to shooting Germans. Clive joined the Local Defence Volunteers (soon to be known as the Home Guard) in June 1940, firewatching from a gamekeeper's tower on the Firle Estate with Quentin. Some historians have concluded from his donning khaki that Clive now supported the war but this is mistaken.[1] Wanting England to prevail was not the same as condoning the war.

Clive was offered a job with the Ministry of Information, but turned it down, he told Mary Hutchinson, because he had no ability to organise

---

[1]For example, Lawrence James (who erroneously claims that a quotation from *Warmongers* is from *Peace News*) writes, 'In the summer of 1940, Clive Bell was clamouring for "ceaseless war against Hitler"' (620). James misrepresents the context of these words, which appear in a letter Clive wrote about fifth columnists (discussed below).

an office, nor would he be likely to engender confidence in colleagues who knew they were better qualified than he. When Raymond went to work for the MoI, Clive assumed this was in the job he had declined. During the hiatus in his literary editorship of the *New Statesman and Nation* that this occasioned between 1940 and 1941, Raymond became chief liaison with the BBC in establishing Radio Londres, the Free French radio broadcast by which De Gaulle's government in exile rallied the French Resistance. When Clive complained that Raymond's replacement at the magazine, Cuthbert Worsley, had accepted a review by Cyril Connolly he thought contained a barely veiled dig at him ('I do not think Duncan Grant is Gainsborough'), Raymond urged Clive to come to London as often as his Home Guard duties permitted so that he could visit galleries and write reviews himself, which Clive did for the next three years.

Virginia found Clive 'sullen & effort ridden' at Charleston a week after the Vichy government had been established in France. The war mind of 1914–19 had returned with a vengeance and suspicion pervaded everyday life as the government introduced regulations to punish anyone deemed to be spreading 'alarm and despondency'. Frances wondered what a police raid on Ham Spray might take as evidence of subversion – her copy of Hugo's *German Reading Simplified*? Clive's *Warmongers*? When Gerald Brenan was suspected of signalling the enemy after careless use of his torch during a blackout, Clive sought help from Cory, who was a Wiltshire county councillor, to intercede with Brenan's Local Defence Volunteer commander. Harold Nicolson, who worried that the Ministry of Information's propaganda was being undermined by the press, warned against 'shiver-sisters' and 'chatterbugs' weakening what should be a 'solid wall of national will power'. Clive objected to those who did not support the war being termed fifth columnists, as if there were no difference between holding unpopular political opinions and genuine treason (for which he agreed execution was warranted).

In August 1940, Clive joined John Middleton Murry, Sybil Thorndike and other supporters of the Peace Pledge Union in signing what the *Daily Herald* termed a 'manifesto' calling for a statement of peace terms and a definition of what was meant by a 'free' Europe. Agreeing on such terms, in cooperation with the Americans, the signatories argued, 'might save civilisation as we know it'. Under the heading 'State Peace

Terms Now', this document was printed in the 16 August *Peace News*, the PPU's publication, above fifteen signatures, several of whom were not members of the PPU, and no more was heard of it.

Many who had been staunch pacifists throughout the First World War and the 1920s and 1930s had by now abandoned the PPU, including even Bertrand Russell. There was no parliamentary support for a pacifist position, Middleton Murry was not allowed to broadcast his views on the BBC and the government did not consider it necessary to pay much attention to conscientious objectors, most of whom were in any case willing to do some kind of war work. Clive provided a testimonial for Ralph Partridge when he went before a tribunal to claim (successfully) a conscientious objection to being conscripted into Home Guard duty in 1943, and when the painter Victor Pasmore was imprisoned in 1942 for desertion, Clive joined Kenneth Clark and Augustus John in lobbying for his release.

Soon after the *Peace News* document was published, Clive was fiercely attacked for his views at Charleston by Raymond and Desmond MacCarthy. Their visit had been enjoyable until the subject of peace terms had been raised. Clive could not understand why anyone believed that a peace achieved through war would mean that the 'whole world would live happily ever after'; to his mind, these were the stale arguments that had been made during the First World War. Raymond had goaded Ralph into a 'barking match' over the same issues, and Ralph had 'almost shouted' at Raymond that he found it hypocritical that people who were not risking their own lives insisted on how important it was for young men in the RAF to risk theirs.

When rumours circulated later that year that Hitler would offer terms, Clive again argued that they should be taken seriously and urged the government not to keep any details from the British people. In the absence of negotiations, he said, only a 'bombing match' could settle the war. Just days before he wrote this letter, Vanessa and Duncan's Fitzroy Street studios had been destroyed in the Blitz. Lawrence Gowing went to see the devastation, telling Frances that he had wept at the thought of all the paintings that were now gone for ever.

Like Clive, Frances was irritated by the propaganda that friends such as Raymond were promoting and by the normalising attitude of the *New Statesman* – Vita Sackville-West's 'Country Notes in War-Time', for example, struck her as silly (a collection of the columns was brought out in 1940 by the Hogarth Press). The atmosphere in the country had changed profoundly between October 1939 and the summer of 1940, even before the beginning of the Blitz. Virginia had recorded in her diary conversations she overheard on a train a few weeks after the declaration of war – ' "Cant think how people have time to go to war. It must be that the blokes haven't got jobs . . . I prefer a fools paradise to a real hell".'

Vita's son Benedict thought that Roger Fry and his friends had lived in a fools' paradise while Hitler consolidated his power. When Virginia's biography of Roger was published in the summer of 1940, Benedict was serving with an anti-aircraft battery in Kent, from where he wrote bitterly to Virginia that Roger had 'shut himself out from all disagreeable actualities and allowed the spirit of Nazism to grow', an indictment he made clear in a subsequent letter he intended to apply to all of those he associated with 'Bloomsbury'. Virginia's painstaking refutation of his attack exemplified what she had concluded earlier that year: 'Thinking is my fighting.' She elaborated this notion for the *New Republic* in 'Thoughts on Peace in an Air-Raid', telling a story Clive had already heard from her at Charleston, of lying in bed at Monk's House listening to bombers fly overhead. It was what Virginia termed 'thinking against the current' that underpinned Clive's opposition to the war and his desire to do what he could to protect the flame of civilisation. Benedict Nicolson complained that Roger's 'interpretation of art was too sophisticated, too private for the general public', a charge Virginia countered with the evidence of his tireless lecturing and writing. She was moved by Clive's sincere praise of *Roger Fry* as among the best of her books. Clive in fact thought that Virginia's imagination had run dry, so such works of non-fiction were just what she should be writing.

Charleston in February 1941 reminded Virginia of 1917 all over again, Clive digging a trench, Vanessa feeding the chickens, Quentin driving a tractor, and Duncan painting. She soon fell into a deep depression. Thwarted by petrol rations and bad weather from going up to London, whose bustle and society she missed, she lost faith in whether the novel she was working on (*Between the Acts*) was any good. By late March 1941, she seemed to Clive 'to be getting into one of her bad phases again', which brought back to him troubling memories of her mental state during the first war. When she disappeared on 28 March, those at Charleston hoped she might be found 'sleeping in a barn or buying biscuits in a village-shop', but once it could no longer be doubted that she must have drowned in the River Ouse, Clive worried that Vanessa would collapse, as she had when Julian was killed. In fact, Vanessa coped better than he, Duncan and Quentin expected and, by the beginning of April, they had absorbed the 'appalling loss', even though Clive knew it would be a long time before the pleasure of remembering Virginia outweighed the pain caused by her death. Clive almost envied Virginia her courage. Choosing not to live in a world ruined by war seemed to him a wise decision.

38. Art on Trial

Clive's generation would not, he thought, survive to be 'the Victorians of an Edwardian age' because the war would utterly destroy the civilisation which gave meaning to the phrase. As a self-described highbrow, Clive relished the intellectual skirmishes in which he discomfited the establishment, brushing aside the thought that he had for some time been seen as an establishment figure by the younger generation Benedict Nicolson exemplified. In the early months of the war, however, Clive managed to draw fire from several of the artistic old guard. He might have announced in the catalogue to the 'Second Post-Impressionist Exhibition' that the battle over modern art was won, but word of the victory had apparently still not reached many Royal Academicians. In December 1939, J. B. Manson and Alfred Munnings, among others, attacked *The Artist in the Witness Box*, a BBC radio series hosted by Eric Newton, for its ostensible promotion of 'ultra-modern art', which in Manson's view could never satisfy the desire for beauty of 'any normal human being'. Manson, whose drunken antics had disgraced his tenure as director of the Tate Gallery, and who once told British customs officials that a Brancusi sculpture on its way to exhibition at Peggy Guggenheim's London Gallery was 'idiotic' and 'not art', had done 'nothing but harm to modern painting' in Clive's view. Munnings, a celebrated painter of equine subjects, was a stalwart of the Royal Academy, whose president he would become in 1944. Clive had described the RA as an 'almshouse destined to become a cemetery', mocking it for exhibiting as art the dreadful daubs of Winston Churchill, the 'spurious erudition' of whose prose put Clive in mind of the paintings of Munnings.

Munnings was a spokesperson for the view that art should require no explanation, should have the 'sound, sane outlook of the great days before all this "nonsense"', as he termed modern art, appeared on the scene. At the time, an exhibition at Burlington House had brought together numerous artists' societies to raise funds for the Red Cross. An editorial in the *Times* suggested that this United Artists exhibition would afford visitors an opportunity to decide for themselves what the antagonists of 'ultra-modern art' meant by the term.

Roger Fry's *Last Lectures* had just been published, wherein he distinguished between two kinds of viewers of art – those who treated a painting as a narrative and those whom the *Times* leader writer described as approaching the plastic arts as they would a piece of music, with no concern for 'story'. The distinction had been made at least as long ago as 1919 by Clive when he tangled with D. S. MacColl in the pages of the *Burlington Magazine*, but Munnings was having none of it. Inadvertently echoing Hitler's aesthetic views, he defined the 'ultra-modern' as that which was 'painted as not seen'. He repeated that art should need no explanation but, fatally for his argument, he included among his examples of what needed no 'mystifying language from art experts' Manet's *Bar aux Folies Bergères*: a 'triumph of pictorial representation'.

Having dispatched the nonsensical modifier 'ultra' – because, after all, the 'ultra-modern' artists of today often became the old masters of tomorrow – Clive pointed out that Manet had been insulted by 'all the Munningses' of his day. Such terms of abuse as 'ultra-modern' were employed by people frightened by what they could not understand: art that unsettles the public might better be termed 'untamed', he wrote, because it usually lost its power to shock once it had been 'sterilised by usage and some years of confinement in a museum'.

As the Nazi exhibit of 'Degenerate Art' had made plain in 1937, these were not trivial issues. It was the essence of Clive's cultural politics that Munnings' exclusion from 'ordinary' life of any art he found incomprehensible was a kind of tyranny. This was the 'subconscious Hitlerism' Virginia's 'Thoughts on Peace in an Air Raid' identified in the everyday desire of ordinary people to dominate, the kind of cultural despotism Clive had satirised in *On British Freedom*. Such matters might seem negligible during a war, if the Beaverbrook press was to be believed, but, as he had in 1915, Clive again asked what it meant to fight in defence of 'civilisation' if some of its defenders were so antagonistic to liberty of thought and expression?

Clive read more voraciously than ever as he saw civilisation being extinguished in Europe, re-reading works he had always loved, such as Byron's letters and Mérimée's *Letters from an Unknown*, but also keeping up with new fiction. The prospect of Hemingway's *For Whom the Bell Tolls* (1940) depressed him, though he felt obliged to tackle it: 'You can't imagine how little appetite I have for that sort of thing,' he told Mary; 'we have all supped so full with horrors that it seems to me the bottom's rather fallen out of the tough guys, hasn't it.' More to his taste was Evelyn Waugh's *Put Out More Flags*.

As 'A Ministry of Arts' might have predicted, during the war, Clive became a dedicated, if persistently cynical, committee man, joining Eric Maclagan and Herbert Read on the fine arts advisory committee of the British Council. Clive's role with the British Council and his need to view new exhibitions to write about them for the *New Statesman and Nation* meant that he travelled up to London quite often. Mary Hutchinson's son Jeremy was serving in the Navy and for a time Clive rented his flat in Mecklenburgh Square, but it proved too expensive. He spent nights at Vanessa's studio until it was bombed and thereafter at the Savoy. Another port of call for Clive was The Camp in Ascot, a large house rented by his American former lover Mary Baker, who had decided that after her enjoyable years in Europe it would be dishonourable to flee to the United States when war broke out.

Apart from sporadic reunions with Mary Hutchinson, Clive's female companionship during the war seems to have dwindled to flirting with Land Girls in the Sussex countryside – which irritated Angelica – and occasional visits to Mary Baker, where he sometimes found himself 'pillow-fighting in the garden with young Americans from the Embassy'. Mary Baker faded from Clive's life after the war, but during it they were intimate enough for him to ask Frances for a recommendation as to where Mary could get developed 'a dozen very pretty photographs of her pretty body' by someone with the discretion not to raise objections to nudity. The Camp was a respite from London's 'inconceivable tristesse'. In the First World War, London had been exciting, danger a thrill, but the relentless destruction in the Blitzed city was quite different. Clive found Mary Hutchinson's account of an air raid 'vivid and pretty terrifying', and even the two small raids he got caught in were 'extremely worrying'. St James's and Bond Street smelled of damp charred wood, and during the blackout Clive felt the presence of ghosts from different times of his life.

Clive joined the British Council's fine arts advisory committee around the time that Britain withdrew from the Venice Biennale, the works that had been selected being instead displayed at London's Hertford House (from where the Wallace Collection had been removed to safety). Clive found that the committee's deliberations tended to leave Kenneth Clark somewhat caught between himself, Eric Maclagan and Herbert Read on one side, and Campbell Dodgson, Lawrence Haward and Major Alfred Longden on the other. Within the first two years of the war, Clark had been appointed to key positions in the Ministry of Information, from where he directed his vision of a national culture. The British Council had begun in 1935 as a direct response to fascist propaganda, but its brief absorption into the MoI in 1939 resulted in fraught relations between the two entities.

Clive used his British Council position to continue to disseminate his version of England's art history. As he wrote in his memoir *Old Friends*, during the war there were 'anxious questionings as to the future of the arts in a more or less socialist state' in which private patronage would be 'destroyed by economic egalitarianism'. It was a conversation about these issues with Maynard, who in 1942 was appointed chairman of the Council for the Encouragement of Music and the Arts (CEMA), that led to Clive's article calling for a Ministry of the Arts. Like Morgan Forster and Desmond MacCarthy, Clive saw state support of the arts in Britain as necessary to counter Nazi appropriation of culture but he maintained the antipathy for civil servants he had developed when working with Stephen Tallents on the Post Office committee in the mid-1930s. After the war, despite keeping his position with the British Council, he continued to complain about the damaging influence of civil servants who treated subsidy of the arts as a kind of social welfare programme.

Keeping the flame of civilisation burning meant occasionally lecturing for the British Council to foreign refugees at the YMCA on 'Modern British Art'. Given that his name was a 'by-word' in the press for an 'inveterate denigrator of British painting', Clive attributed the council's choice of him as a speaker to 'that excessive modesty which is said to characterise our race'. His standard talk gave a précis of the English tradition as he had outlined it in *Landmarks in Nineteenth Century Painting*, with 1910 as the dawning of a new age founded by Roger's bringing awareness of Cézanne to the English. Clive handed out to his audience a list of galleries which remained open and that would accommodate anyone who wished to follow up his account of contemporary painting in Britain by seeing examples of the work of the artists he referred to. Several major West End galleries had committed to staying open when the war began, including Agnews, the Redfern, Leicester, Reid & Lefevre, Wildenstein and Tooth's, the addresses for all of which Clive distributed at his talk. He lamented that the Tate was 'shuttered' while its director, John Rothenstein, had 'betaken himself to America', thus preventing eager students from making first-hand comparisons amongst the artists Clive mentioned. Clive made the same remark in a review of Rothenstein's father William's memoir, *Since Fifty*, and even twenty-five years later, John Rothenstein was still smarting from a slight he took as one more incident in a long-running feud he imagined had begun in 1910 when Roger and his ' "Bloomsbury" friends' had turned against his father.[1] When John Rothenstein saw Wyndham Lewis in New York early in the war, Lewis told him that Roger personified 'as much as anybody what I dislike most about the art world'.

In his British Council lecture, Clive listed Duncan, Vanessa, Matthew Smith, Paul Nash, Gertler, Frances Hodgkins, Frank Dobson and Edward Wadsworth as the 'sound middle-aged core of the contemporary movement in Great Britain'. After the First World War, these had been joined by Enslin DuPlessis (a South African who had been elected in 1929 to the London Group), Neville Lewis, Ivon Hitchens, David Jones and Henry Moore. This British school in 1940 seemed to Clive 'more complete and more promising than at any time since the death of Constable', especially after the emergence of the Euston Road artists, as well as of John Piper, Graham Sutherland, and Leila Faithfull. Clive also included Quentin in the list – evidence, were any more needed, that his bitterest adversaries were sometimes correct to question his

[1] William Rothenstein in fact wrote Clive a warmly complimentary letter upon the publication of *Art* (23 March 1914 TGA).

critical integrity. D. S. MacColl granted that Clive's uxorious praise of Vanessa was justified, but it was not as a painter that Quentin would be best known.

The war gave debates about contemporary painting a different shape, in the midst of a sudden renaissance of public interest in highbrow culture (which would precipitously wane as soon as the war ended). While Clive was lecturing to refugees, the War Artists Advisory Committee (WAAC) exhibition was on at the National Gallery. Opened in July 1940, it stayed up, and was continually added to, for the duration of the war. Under Kenneth Clark's direction, even artists whose work he otherwise supported were not invited to participate in WAAC exhibitions, several of which toured to regional centre to balance the dominance of London on the cultural scene. Clark's rationale for excluding Hitchens, Walker, Pasmore, Smith, Hodgkins and others was that they were 'pure painters who are interested solely in putting down their feelings about shapes and colours, and not in facts, drama, human emotions and life generally'. Brian Foss in his book on British art during the Second World War describes Clark's gratitude to Graham Sutherland for helping him to move away from what he understood to be Roger and Clive's insistence that an artwork should be autonomous. Owing to this, Clark 'discouraged the WAAC from acquiring work from artists who, though admirable, were unlikely to treat the war in a way that would establish close emotional connections with large audiences'. In this context, the influence of theoreticians such as Herbert Read, champion of the avant-garde, weakened. When Janice Loeb went to see 'Britain at War', an exhibition arranged by Clark for MoMA in New York, she asked Clive if it could really be true that the 'Euston Road boys' had not 'done even one portrait of one officer'. The exhibition was a 'most unholy selection of Low, Kennington, Muirhead Bone, Ravilious, Wm. Rothenstein. etc. not really out weighed by Sutherland, [Roland] Pitchforth. Maybe Sir Kenneth really couldn't help himself.'

The Fine Arts Department of the British Council was responsible for all exhibitions sent abroad, which included those of art by British children as well as various collections of contemporary art that were 'widely shown in all neutral and most Allied countries'. Clive did what he could to influence the selections, once letting Mary Hutchinson know that he had got the council to include some of the weaver and dyer Ethel Mairet's 'stuffs' in a collection being sent to North and South Africa in the autumn of 1941. He knew that Mary had a dress made of Mairet fabric, which, he told Eric Newton, he thought a match for Eugene Rodier's designs. He criticised the war pictures sent to the United States for exhibition as the 'spawn of committees', contrasting them with a show at the Redfern that was subsequently sent on to the American British Art Centre, where Clive hoped that New York viewers could see that visual art was still alive and kicking in Britain. This show included works by Ben Nicholson, Barbara Hepworth, Sutherland, Paul Nash and John Tunnard, a painter for whom Clive thought the term 'abstract' too useful to abandon, imprecise as it might be to describe his work. The Redfern show also included five of Henry Moore's drawings of wartime London scenes. Clive rarely failed to praise Moore for his extraordinary handling of detail, remarking that the 'apparition of Henry Moore as a draughtsman is the most exciting artistic event of the war'. It was in the independent galleries that Clive saw civilisation's flame burning most brightly. He praised them for not caving in to the Beaverbrook line that there was no place for culture in wartime. 'Artists of Fame and Promise' at the Leicester Galleries, where Lawrence Gowing's portrait of Julia Strachey hung alongside works by Hitchens, Pasmore and Coldstream was, to Clive, 'particularly comforting in these days of officially favoured barbarism'. Half a mile away, at the Adams Gallery, Londoners could see magnificent Bonnards and Renoirs.

Although Clark would later write that Pasmore was 'one of the two or three most talented English painters' of the twentieth century, Clive doubtless understood, without agreeing with, Clark's reason for not including him in WAAC exhibitions. Reviewing Pasmore's one-person show at Wildenstein in June 1940, where each of the thirty-four paintings signified a particular emotional experience, consituting a record of the artist's development, Clive argued that art should take us out of the current situation into a world where only aesthetic values matter.

Clive returned to this theme in a radio discussion with Herbert Read and V. S. Pritchett in October 1941, an episode of *The Living Image* series devoted to relations between art and life. Responding to Pritchett's point that surely the most worthwhile works of art had a bearing on human affairs and must support some social values against others, Clive argued that were Canaletto to paint the ruins of Bristol it would not matter to him whether those ruins were made in 1941 or two centuries earlier because the artist would paint the emotion he felt upon seeing them. Clive and Read agreed, in the discussion with Pritchett, that representation constituted only a very limited part of the history of art. They saw no difference between representational and non-representational art, with Read endorsing Clive's now well-tried notion that associations from a viewer's life were irrelevant to true art. When Pritchett protested that an artist had to be concerned with making himself intelligible to others, Clive countered that he could not understand Joyce's *Finnegans Wake*, but that did not mean it was not a good work of art.

Clive's perennial attitude of openness and tolerance has usually been obscured by the verve with which he expressed his subjective convictions, but making a forceful case for the art he loved was never intended to exclude others' different points of view. His lack of interest in abstraction was not ideological in the way that Clark's was, and Clive shared Read's perception that the 'reactionary spirit' always came to the fore in wartime.

By 1943, Read was asking if relations between himself and Clive could dispense with the persistent formality engendered by only meeting on council business, given that they often agreed about the dangers state patronage posed to artistic freedom. Discussing a possible council exhibition for Moscow, Read assumed Clive would support the view that they should choose works that best represented British art, not what 'might conceivably please Joe Stalin & his green-eyed janissaries'. Read might have described the National Gallery as a 'defiant outpost of culture right in the midst of the bombed and shattered metropolis', but he remained as wary as Clive did during and long after the war of how committees and civil servants could cramp the individuality of an artist. 'Unquestionably,' Clive wrote to Frances, civil servants were the 'most powerful, pervasive, pestilent people in England'.

In the summer of 1941, two projects got underway in Charleston's vicinity that seemed to Clive to hold promise for the sustenance of 'civilisation'. Duncan's friend Charles Reilly, a well-known architect, proposed to the Bishop of Chichester, George Bell, that the artist should undertake the decoration of St Michael and All Angels church in Berwick, about three miles from Charleston. Duncan, Vanessa and Quentin set to work in the Charleston barn on large plasterboard panels to be affixed to the church walls. Also that summer, two enterprising sisters – Frances Byng Stamper and Caroline Lucas – had an art gallery built onto the back of their house, Miller's, on the Lewes high street. The sisters were particularly fond of Duncan and enlisted his aid in borrowing paintings for their first exhibition, sponsored by the British Institute for Adult Education. Clive was from the start an enthusiastic supporter of the sisters' venture, giving their exhibition a 'great boost' in the *New Statesman*. From local friends and neighbours, including those at Charleston, a show was assembled which included works by Gris, Rouault, Matisse, Bonnard and Cézanne, and by Hitchens, Sickert, Gertler, Matthew Smith and Pasmore. 'Shamelessly', Clive drew attention to his son's 'small and ill-placed *Still Life*', but also remarked on how lucky those who visited Miller's would be to see an example of the work of 'that almost unseeable artist Gwen John'. People already came to Lewes to hear opera at Glyndebourne, so Clive saw no reason they would not also come to see paintings at Miller's.

Miller's represented to Clive an example of how art might continue to flourish in England after the war, in spite rather than because of the involvement of more formal bodies such as CEMA (which later became subsumed under the Arts Council). When the formidable sisters opened their gallery, Clive not only linked Miller's to a centuries-old local artistic tradition, he laid out a case for the importance of the 'decentralisation' of art, making it part of his argument that the 'school of Paris' had been weakened by becoming an international 'university' of painting after 1910. The importance of exhibitions such as this at Miller's was that they could inspire

local talent by showing people – young people especially – what is being done to-day; and they must be followed by exhibitions to show what has been done in the past. Above all, they should convince the inhabitants of provincial towns that art is not something that lives apart in Florence, Rome and Paris, in the National Gallery and Bond Street; but that it is a necessary part of life which takes its place, just as races and flower-shows do, in the civilisation of the district.

The Berwick church decorations (which Maynard helped finance) were completed by early 1943, having survived an attempt to stop the scheme launched by a local woman antagonistic to Bishop Bell's advocacy of a union between the church and modern art, especially carried out by such notorious characters as the denizens of Charleston. A photo spread of the church paintings in *Country Life* that summer was accompanied by Clive's praise of the three gifted artists who exemplified the medieval spirit carried into a contemporary context. Vanessa, Duncan and Quentin had used local people as models, as well as Angelica and her friend from acting school, Chattie Salaman, to populate the scenes of Duncan's *Christ in Glory*, Vanessa's *Annunciation* and *Nativity* and Quentin's *Wise and Foolish Virgins*. Clive pointed out how the models seamlessly depicted the wartime situation in the ancient genre, as Duncan's Christ was adored on one side by 'a sailor, a soldier, and an airman, all of whom have gone forth to fight for Christendom from Sussex homes'. At the dedication ceremony that October, Clive was 'deeply moved by the modesty of the service and the magnificence of the language', he told Mary, as he always was whenever he went to church – something we must assume he did solely for aesthetic reasons.

Miller's flourished throughout the war, guided by the vision of the indefatigable sisters. Morgan Forster, Desmond MacCarthy, Tancred Borenius, J. T. Sheppard, Herbert Read and Clive himself were among those who gave talks at the gallery on a variety of topics, and it continued to present well-received exhibitions. While Ivon Hitchens was showing what Clive described as a 'great leap forward' in his painting at the Leicester Galleries, his work was also on view at Miller's alongside contemporaries such as Pasmore, Coldstream, Moynihan and Claude Rogers. The ladies' art enterprise was the best in the country, Clive thought, better even than the British Council. An exceptional sculpture exhibition in 1942 included works by Rodin, Degas, Epstein, Maillol, Moore and Hepworth, and Kenneth Clark came to Lewes to open a show of French and English drawings. Under CEMA's 'Art for the People' scheme, Maynard 'ensured that Miller's received the cream of the exhibitions touring the country during the war years'.

Clive reviewed an especially forward-thinking exhibition that the sisters organised to explore the possibilities for new designs for theatres at the end of 1942. Noting that in the eighteenth century theatres were designed as much for socialising as for viewing the stage, Clive deplored the modern tendency to maximise profit that had led between the wars to 'remorselessly planned' spaces that were more like operating theatres. Duncan and Vanessa collaborated on a model theatre to which Angelica and Quentin contributed decorations. 'Designs by Various Artists for Decoration in the Theatre' attracted work by Ethel Mairet, Hitchens, DuPlessis, John Piper, Tunnard, Sutherland and two Scottish painters directly supported by the sisters, Robert Colquhoun and Robert MacBryde. Miller's became a 'centre of European civilisation' with which Clive maintained a close relationship until age forced the sisters reluctantly to retire in the 1950s. Towards the end of the war, they began a press specifically to produce lithographs, for which they enlisted the talents of Helmut Gernsheim of the Warburg Institute to photograph the medieval wall paintings of two Sussex churches – St Botolph's at Hardham and St John the Baptist's at Clayton. This project enabled Clive to travel around Sussex in 1945 using 'nationally important petrol' as he prepared to write an essay to accompany Gernsheim's photographs.

One of Clive's first letters to Mary Hutchinson in the summer of 1914 had advised her on how to gain access to the thirteenth-century paintings in the Bishop's Palace at Chichester Cathedral. There was plentiful evidence in Sussex that medieval church walls had once been adorned with colourful paintings, although by 1940 this fact had been largely forgotten by the local populace, a circumstance Clive blamed on architects of the turn of the century who stripped the buildings to the bones to reveal structural features. Kenneth Clark applauded Clive for taking issue in *Twelfth Century Paintings at Hardham & Clayton* with the decision by E. W. Tristram, Professor of Design at the Royal College of Art, to include watercolour imaginings of what such paintings might have looked like in his book *English Medieval Wall Painting* (1944). Gernsheim's photographs showed 'what actually exists' on the church walls, Clive wrote, but also showed 'rather more than the naked eye can see'. Clive's association with Gernsheim (for whom he wrote the introduction to *Julia Margaret Cameron, Her Life and Photographic Work* in 1948) led him to better appreciate photography as an art form, even joining with others in 1952 to advocate the establishment of a National Collection of Photography.

In his essay accompanying Gernsheim's photographs of the Sussex church wall paintings, Clive argued that of all English regional artistic centres, Lewes was one of the most French due to the founding of the great Cluniac (Benedictine) Lewes Priory 'which seemingly became a centre of French civilisation'. Chemical analysis of paintings was in its infancy and, although Clive acknowledged the recent research carried out by Fernand Mercier, he preferred to remain a 'stylistic' critic, relying on the 'iconographical evidence' he could see on the church walls. Although, 'to be sure, in a battered, peeled, chipped, discoloured wall-painting it is possible to mistake a bishop for a donkey or a stain for a beast of the Apocalypse', Clive discerned from Gernsheim's photogaphs a Byzantine influence at Clayton and Hardham, which he noted was pervasive in the twelfth century.[2] Continuing to write on art from the perspective that it was of inherent value, apart from any political considerations, was Clive's version of what art historian Christopher Reed has termed an 'aesthetics of conscientious objection'.

[2]Clive's supposition is confirmed by Ian Nairn and Nikolaus Pevsner in their comprehensive survey of the *Buildings of England*, where they write of the Clayton and Hardham churches that the style of their wall paintings is 'not really Cluniac' but had mixed sources, including Byzantine mosaics found in Sicily (473).

39. Collaboration

When Simon and Dorothy Bussy's daughter, Janie, tuned her radio to the BBC on the evening of 8 February 1945 in Nice, she was delighted to catch the end of Clive's broadcast about *Julius Caesar*, the play that was to be performed on the Home Service the following evening. It was not, Clive told his listeners, one of his favourites, but it was exciting and expressed Shakespeare's hatred of the mob, which politicians would do well to take heed of. Hearing Clive's voice 'magically transported' Janie to Charleston. It would still be several months before she and her parents would be able to leave France for England, but by that summer they were in London. In October, Simon Bussy, whose portrait of Lady Strachey had been loaned for the first Miller's exhibition, hung his paintings at the Lewes gallery and Janie gave a talk about their lives under German occupation.

Until communications were disrupted by the extension of the German occupation to the whole of France after November 1942, Janie's letters to Vanessa and to Quentin were a source of information about the situation of writers and artists they knew. Janie and Quentin had, in a sense, grown up together, taking lessons from a Miss Paul on Mecklenburgh Square in the early 1920s and seeing one another often in the summers, either at Charleston or at the Bussys' house, La Souco, in Roquebrune on the Bay of Monaco. Simon had been at the École des Beaux Arts with Matisse, who, Quentin remembered, would regularly visit the Bussys 'as though he were an ordinary human being'. The Bussy family spent most of the war at their apartment in Nice, or at nearby Piera Cava, staying with François and Zoum Walter. André Gide, with whom Dorothy Bussy had long been in love, stayed with the Bussys in Nice from October 1939 until May 1940, when he moved into a nearby hotel with Maria van Rysselberghe, the mother of his daughter, Catherine (born in 1923). Janie told Vanessa about Gide's 'fascinating' daughter in a letter which also brought news of Matisse's operation for cancer. It had been thought that Matisse, whose wife had left him in 1939, might go to Brazil, but he decided to stay in France, spending the war first in Nice and, after 1943, in Vence.

Clive passed on to Mary Hutchinson what he learned from Janie's letters, letting her know about Gide's involvement with the literary magazine *Nouvelle Revue Française*, which had been taken over by the fascist supporter Pierre Drieu La Rochelle. Drieu had purged the *NRF* of Jewish contributors such as Julien Benda and added Nazi sympathisers, including Alfred Fabre-Luce, but retained some of the more well-known writers, like Gide and Paul Valéry. After the fall of France in June 1940, Gide, Valéry, Proust and others were accused by Camille Mauclair of having caused the decadence that led to France's defeat. Gide had been conflicted about participating in Drieu's *NRF*, and when he left it in 1941 began subtly to articulate his opposition to the Vichy government in articles for *Le Figaro*. After he made his way to Tunis, some in Britain hoped that Gide could be brought to London to broadcast on behalf of the Free French, the government-in-exile led by Charles de Gaulle. Raymond wanted Gide to 'write for English papers about French resistance and culture' because there was no 'first-rate French writer' in England. Harold Nicolson felt sure Clive would not be annoyed that he had told Pierre Viénot – France Libre's ambassador to the British and a close friend of Roland de Margerie – to add Clive's name to a telegram stating that Gide's friends in London would welcome his presence. Gide was enthusiastic about the plan and sent a Red Cross postcard to the Bussys with a coded message letting them know that he would soon be joining Simon Bussy's in-laws – which was to say, Simon's wife Dorothy's family, the Stracheys. The British Council sponsored a 'Homage to André Gide' by Morgan Forster, but the plan was not realised and Gide remained in Algeria where he had gone in May 1943. His enemies in France, many of whom had not forgiven him for his turn against Soviet Communism in 1936, spread rumours that would complicate Gide's postwar return to his homeland.

Early in 1941, Clive heard from Jenny de Margerie, who was in New York en route to China. It would be a long time until he heard from the de Margeries again while the war in the Pacific made communication almost impossible. Jenny thanked Clive for making their years posted to the embassy in London so sweet, a sentiment echoed by Roland in a letter he managed to get to Clive a year later. It was not until 1943 that Roland was able to rely on the good offices of the neutral Swiss Legation in Beijing to carry another letter, explaining what had happened to them. While compatriots such as Viénot and René Massigli were with De Gaulle, Roland explained that he had been 'exiled out here for three years for having been the first to recommend vehemently that the French Government be moved to N. Africa'. Roland had taken minutes at the meeting in Briare on 11 June 1940 between Churchill and French government officials, when it was fast becoming clear that military resistance to Germany was going to fail. After the war, Léon Blum would testify that Roland had been sent by Paul Baudoin – who became Vichy's foreign minister – to Shanghai to get out of the way 'a man whom he knew to be fundamentally hostile to the policy of collaboration with Hitler's Germany'. Roland was made governor of the French Concession in Shanghai until Vichy ceded it in 1943, at which time he left for the French Legation in Beijing. It was from there he wrote plaintively to Clive, 'Do you recall our conversations before the war, the delicious dinners you gave us in Bloomsbury?' He could not imagine how life after the war could be anything like that past he longed to revive in Clive's company. Their nostalgia for a civilisation both felt the war had damaged irreparably remained a strong bond between Clive and Roland, who would not see one another again until 1948, in Paris.

Separating truth from rumour and gossip was extremely difficult in wartime. Janie Bussy said that Roger Martin du Gard had 'ratted to Vichy', along with 'most of the other left-wing writers', but this was inaccurate – not that it would have mattered to Clive. He had contempt for 'that little shit' Abel Bonnard, a collaborator whom Drieu brought into the *NRF*, but for the most part Clive understood those writers and artists who did what they could to avoid having their lives disrupted – or ended – by the German occupiers.

As Janie's letters dried up after the occupation spread to the Free Zone, Clive relied on Janice Loeb in New York for news of artists who had managed to escape to America. Janice was well positioned to know because, in addition to her own familiarity with the New York art world, she was now assisting Daisy and Alfred Barr in their efforts to bring artists from France to safety in America. Barr had tried to make Americans aware of the dangers posed by Hitler as early as 1933, when he had witnessed first-hand the Nazis' purging of museums and galleries of 'un-German' elements.

After the fall of Paris, MoMA had become 'a sort of life raft'. At Christmas in 1939, Janice saw H. W. Janson, one of the earliest immigrants to benefit from Barr's sponsorship. Talking with him restored her faith in *Kunstgeschichte* (art history). She told Clive whom she had seen in New York: Duchamp, Tanguy, Breton and Ernst were all there, and soon came Léger, Lipchitz and Jean Renoir. Daisy Barr let Janice know that Derain, Picasso and Braque were still in Paris early in the war, and Maillol was in the unoccupied south. Janice often prefaced her titbits with 'they say', cautioning Clive that 'no one knows for sure'. She had heard that Jean Lurçat was on good terms with Louis Hautecoeur, the head of fine arts in the Vichy government. He may well have been, but Lurçat was actually involved in the Resistance from early on in the occupation.

Janice had been too depressed to paint after returning home and had gone back into analysis in New York. She apologised often to Clive for how her neuroses had spoiled the time she spent in London before the war and let him know that her love life was not faring well. Her hopes for something more than friendship with Walker Evans were dashed when he became 'exactly the person I wanted him to be via a girl called Jane' (Jane Smith Ninas, whom Evans married in 1941). Janice missed her English friends, wanting news from Clive of the Euston Road artists, especially about Victor Pasmore's marriage to Wendy Blood, and Lawrence Gowing's relations with Julia Strachey. With the generosity that many in Clive's circle came to know well, Janice sent a cheque she hoped she had estimated accurately to be almost the full amount remaining in her English bank account and told Clive to disburse the funds to any painters in need. She asked if it would make sense to send food to her friends in England, or if Frances would welcome vitamins for her son, Burgo. Duncan had got himself into trouble with the authorities when he attempted to send food to the Bussys, but throughout the war and in the difficult years of privation that followed, Janice sent what she could from America, to the Bussys, to Charleston and to Frances at Ham Spray. After the war, Janie told Vanessa that the enormous parcels Janice sent from New York were more effective than Marshall Aid and thanked Clive for bringing her into their lives.

Duncan frequented the York Minster on Dean Street, a pub where the Free French and their supporters could often be found. After an evening there in August 1941, he let Clive know he had heard that Jacques Copeau was alive and well, and that the Vieux-Colombier actor Louis Jouvet had managed to reach New York. Not much of a pub-goer, Clive lunched regularly at the Beefsteak Club, where he would sometimes meet Harold Nicolson, Duff Cooper and Jack Hutchinson. Clive would share what he had heard from France, assuming that Jack would pass it on to Mary, but Mary was probably as well informed as Clive because she had three French refugees staying in her house and was doing what she could to support the Free French. Mary had asked Virginia a month before her suicide if she would contribute an article to *France Libre*, the magazine edited by Baroness Moura Budberg and André Labarthe, and had urged her to listen to the broadcasts of Radio Londres. 'I also feel very much for the French,' Mary wrote, 'the three in my house are so visibly spiritually wounded – so desperately anxious – and are working with passion.'

Mary had long before this moved beyond the influence on her tastes Clive had when their affair began. Although they saw one another periodically in London, Mary sometimes agreeing to spend a night or two with Clive at the Savoy, their different political views caused friction between them. Clive still adhered to the tiny minority in support of a negotiated peace as late as 1943, so for the most part he and Mary avoided discussing public events. Even Charlie Chaplin's *The Great Dictator* could not provide them common ground: 'movies bore me,' Clive told her. It had taken Clive years to accept that he really had lost Mary, but he had continued to hint that he wanted to go to bed with her, even if he invariably couched his desire in language he could say she had misunderstood were she to bristle at the suggestion. In late 1941, Jack Hutchinson fell ill and was unable to work. Clive tried to help Mary financially, suggesting to the *Times* that she write on art, and to Harold Raymond at Chatto that they give her a contract for a collection of reminiscences of Paris and London, but his efforts were unsuccessful.

When Jack died in October 1942, Clive thought it might be a 'blessing' for Mary and that she would probably remarry. For several months, his letters to her went unanswered and Clive relied on friends such as Desmond, who had delivered a eulogy at Jack's funeral, for news of Mary's whereabouts. In the spring of 1943 she relented and came to stay at Charleston. Soon afterwards, Clive was asking if they might spend a weekend together in London: 'Count to ten before you say no.' They began to see each other more often in 1943, but visits to galleries or the theatre, Clive's gifts of black market luxuries, and even Mary's occasional accession to Clive's most ardent wish – a night with him at the Savoy – could not lessen the tensions between them. Despite his claim to have had the 'unheard of luck to recapture you', Clive's hold on Mary was tenuous. He was still very much in love with her, but in many respects their relationship during and after the war resumed the old pattern that had incensed Virginia and Vanessa in the past – a frustrating dance that alternated between enjoyable escapades and bitter recriminations.

Mary's work on behalf of the Free French suggests that she would have been among those who were shocked to learn that Derain, Segonzac, Friesz and André Salmon had, as Clive told her, attended a party given by Otto Abetz, the German Ambassador to the Vichy government, for the Nazis' favourite sculptor, Arno Breker. Janice Loeb had heard from Pierre Matisse in New York that Derain was 'much beloved by the regime', but she was unsure whether Pierre's information could be trusted. Jacques Lipchitz told her that Derain was not a Vichy sympathiser, but that Marie-Laure de Noailles was a collaborator. Clive thought it likely that 'most of our friends – except Gide et Cie. – collaborate, and really its not to be wondered at.' He was sure that if he ever was to return to France 'I shall be too happy to bother much about my friends political peccadillos.' Reminiscent of Forster's famous line in 'What I Believe', that he hoped he would 'have the guts' to betray his country before betraying his friend, Clive's loyalty to collaborating friends in occupied France three years after Forster's essay was published was of a piece with his mantra in *Warmongers*, that nothing was worse than war.

Some historians have made a distinction between 'collaborationists', who joined with the Nazi regime, often inspired by anti-communism, and 'collaborators', who acted only out of self-interest. André Derain's visit to Germany in 1942 has been usually characterised as an instance of the latter. Several critics condemn Derain and the ten others, among them Segonzac, Vlaminck, van Dongen, Friesz and the sculptor Despiau, who travelled at the Nazis' invitation to Munich, Vienna, Dresden, Dusseldorf, Nuremberg and Berlin, as 'artists who willingly identified with the Germans'. Others, such as Jed Perl, acknowledge the possibility that the trip was 'made under duress, part of a deal to liberate some French prisoners of war'. When the painter Leland Bell defended Derain in 1981 against the *New York Times* critic John Russell's accusation of collaboration, he alluded to 'facts' and 'pressure' surrounding Derain's particular case that had never been made public. These circumstances were incorporated into a defence of Derain by Jane Lee after extensive research in the painter's archives. Lee pointed out that Braque (who had refused to go on the trip to Germany) 'publicly upbraided' those who, after the war, accused Derain of collaboration. The damage to the reputation of Clive's closest friend among the French painters, nonetheless, was irreparable, and Derain has since been characterised as the 'head' of the group who went to Germany, and as a 'prostitute'.

After the liberation of Paris in August 1944, Clive struck a resigned tone in a letter to Frances: 'Most of the people I care for will have been either collaborators or attentists [those who wait and see] and will presumably be murdered. There will be Janie to be sure: but one swallow does not make a summer.' Janie, who had risked her life operating a clandestine press for the Resistance, was scathing about collaborators, telling Vanessa that Segonzac, Vlaminck, Despiau and others had behaved disgracefully. Yet she made light of Marguerite Duthuit's torture by the Gestapo, quipping that it had achieved what doctors had failed to do, cure Matisse's daughter of all her neuroses. Quentin knew that although Janie had much to say about the 'comedies and tragedies' of life under occupation, her humour masked more sinister experiences.

Clive's view was that those accused of collaboration had probably 'made the best of a bad job and tried to keep out of the rumpus'. No comment of his survives on the postwar purges that swept France after the Liberation, neither the vigilantism of the *épuration sauvage* nor the codified trials of the *épuration légale* that followed. Dorothy Bussy, however, made her feelings plain to Gide when he told her that he had ignored the pleading of Robert Brasillach's mother to add his name to a petition asking that the notorious Nazi collaborationist be spared, although he did intercede on behalf of his former secretary, Lucien Combelle. Dorothy was disturbed that there was more vengeance than justice in the post-Liberation purges, and that there was no way for the public to appraise impartially any evidence brought against the suspects: 'A stroke of luck saves M. Combelle.' Brasillach was executed on 6 February 1945, despite an appeal to De Gaulle signed by, among others, Valéry, Camus and Cocteau.

Vanessa asked Janie what could really be known about the motivations of those who had collaborated. She could believe that Derain would 'do any sort of trick', but her fondness for Segonzac made her wonder if he were not 'simply an old bumbler, not really interested in anything but painting, who probably may have done what came easiest without thinking clearly what it meant'. Vanessa was unsure how she would have acted in the same circumstances. When in 1947 Segonzac's brother-in-law rented the Bussys' house in Roquebrune, Simon Bussy saw Dunoyer de Segonzac again, who charmed him. Janie let Vanessa know that it was by then agreed that 'silliness not wickedness' had caused him to travel to Germany.

40. Experts and Hoaxes

The public's interest in high culture quickly waned as the war drew to an end, the distraction provided by art exhibitions replaced by lighter entertainments. Although those bodies that sought to replace private patronage continued to expose people who lived outside London to an array of exhibitions that toured the provinces, by 1946 the poor performance of the BBC's new arts and culture-oriented Third Programme in gaining an audience and the low attendance at events sponsored by the Arts Council were signs that the public's interest in highbrow offerings had diminished. Clive continued to grumble about the British Council while he went to its Fine Arts committee meetings, to rail against the iniquity of civil servants, about the encouragement of mediocrity engendered by government subsidies for the arts, and about the absurdity of expecting to develop the next Piero by teaching urban children how to draw. When the possibility of Lawrence Gowing's appointment as head of an art school was discussed at Ham Spray, Clive sneered, 'He's just a *civil servant*! . . . Can anyone imagine Renoir giving up any of his painting time to become a civil servant?' Yet Clive contributed to the BBC ethos of approachable middlebrow talks about art when he spoke about Monet or Bonnard for Home Service programmes in the late 1940s, adding his voice to what Sam Rose has identified as the 'broad consensus that culminated in the policies of the early Arts Council'. The contradiction in Clive's attitudes is exemplified by an article he wrote commenting on a controversy involving CEMA (forerunner of the Arts Council) that erupted at the end of 1944.

A CEMA-sponsored exhibition of the collection of H. J. P. Bomford, a Swindon businessman, elicited sharp criticism when it reached

Birmingham in November 1944. Thomas Bodkin, founding director of the Barber Institute of Fine Arts, complained of three 'lamentable' paintings ascribed to Manet in CEMA's catalogue. Kenneth Clark defended the exhibition, writing that CEMA was fortunate to have such a loan at a time when many private collectors were too worried about losing their paintings to German bombs to let them travel, and adding that it was not unusual for there to be a few dubious attributions in such a collection. Critic and broadcaster Eric Newton had written the catalogue, but CEMA had accepted Bomford's descriptions of the paintings he owned, and Bodkin, shortly followed by several other correspondents, was outraged at what he argued was a waste of public money. While Sam Courtauld joined in to defend CEMA for doing noble work that should not be 'lowered in public estimation by the lengthy controversies of experts' over attribution, which was a matter of 'minor importance', the art historian Douglas Cooper, proudly describing himself as 'an expert', supported Bodkin's complaint. On one side were those who agreed with Bodkin that CEMA should not have taken Bomford's word for attributions to Manet and on the other were those who took Courtauld's view that the public 'value a picture by the merits which they find in it'. Alfred Munnings, now President of the Royal Academy, was amazed that Courtauld could take the position that these were minor issues. After two months of letters, a *Times* editorial reduced the argument to two questions: what is the value of attributions, and what responsibility for them should publicly funded exhibiting bodies assume?

Clive kept his powder dry while the correspondence went on but addressed the larger issues raised by it in an April 1945 article for the *Cornhill* magazine, now edited by his friend Peter Quennell. One might infer, Clive wrote, that the ink spilled arguing about the Bomford pictures meant that many people in England really cared about art, but this was not so. What people cared about were the labels affixed to the frames of paintings. Those rare people whose capacity for 'aesthetic enjoyment' can be completely satisfied by a single work of art do not care who made it, but the majority want something more, a 'cognitive supplement', to fully satisfy their appreciation. These additions were extraneous, but a crowd of experts stood ready to supply them, a crowd in which one might find archaeologists, historians, hagiographers, fabulists – and dealers. Clive had made a similar argument in *Art* in

1914, inaugurating his longstanding contempt for those who regarded art as a commodity by which to display their wealth, but only once their purchase had been endorsed by some kind of expert. Clive pointed out that attribution often changed in the world of Old Masters when new generations of *Kunstforschers* gave their opinion, but the works themselves remained what they had always been. (Clive once irritated Lord Gage by pronouncing the Reynolds and Gainsboroughs at Firle Place all copies.) In making 'some jokes at the expense of the experts', Clive set himself against scholars such as Douglas Cooper and Tancred Borenius (who also wrote to the *Times* in support of Bodkin) in favour of a viewer's subjective experience of a work of art, regardless of who made it. What was really at stake, he surmised, was 'national prestige', adducing the example of an outcry raised in England over the sale to America of a Rembrandt. In Clive's view, it was not love of the painting that aroused ire at the thought of it leaving the country, but possessiveness over an 'authentic' Rembrandt that bestowed prestige upon the national collection. At the heart of the issue was money. After all, if someone were suddenly to prove that twenty lines of *The Two Noble Kinsmen* were by Shakespeare rather than Fletcher 'publishers would not be a penny the better for it', but where the plastic arts were concerned enormous sums of money were often at stake.

Experts were unimpressed by Clive's essay about Renoir's *Les Parapluies*, published shortly after the famous painting was displayed at the National Gallery as April 1945's 'Picture of the Month'. When Victory in Europe was proclaimed on 8 May, the painting remained in the gallery to presage the imminent return of fifty more works from their wartime safe storage in Welsh caverns. Clive's 'Gallery Book' was another example of his involvement in the broad effort to educate the public about art that had crystallised during the war through the work of bodies such as the British Council and CEMA, and of publishers like Allen Lane, whose Pelican series of inexpensive paperbacks met the demand of middle-class readers wishing to inform themselves about a broad range of intellectual and cultural topics. The Gallery Books were intended 'to encourage the general public to look at the great masterpieces of art more closely, and thus to find in them new and more rewarding beauties', each focused on a single painting. Kenneth Clark (whose own contribution to the series was on Constable's *Hay Wain*) helped Clive secure photographs to buttress his argument that

Les Parapluies was a transitional painting which showed a number of different influences. As O. Demus pointed out in the *Burlington Magazine*, Clive accepted the now rejected date of 1879 for the painting and had built on that an erroneous argument that the work *prefigured* the change in Renoir's style effected by his visit to Italy in 1881. Benedict Nicolson, now returned after wartime service to his post as Deputy Surveyor of the King's Pictures, noted in his diary that Clive's essay was 'ludicrously inadequate', but it was generally well received as a lucid discussion of an unusual and significant painting by the public for whom it was intended.

If Clive was troubled by having it pointed out to him that in fact Renoir had worked on the painting in two stages *after* he had been to Italy, he did not say so. He repeated the dating error several years later when he wrote the introduction for Phaidon's *The French Impressionists in Full Colour*. Although Clive had based his argument on a mistaken date, his account of how the painting demonstrated Renoir's shift from Impressionism was sound enough, despite the nitpicking of experts. By the end of the year, Clive told Mary that he was 'sick to death of analysing pictures' for now.

'Picasso is still *über alles* and as if that were not enough he has joined the Communist Party,' Janie informed Vanessa in March 1945. Clive heard from his connections at the French Embassy that Picasso had not been much bothered by the Germans and had had no difficulty obtaining materials with which to work during the war. His only complaint had been about the cold. Historian Michèle Cone has commented that Picasso seemed to have 'had his own line of conduct – as if he had deconstructed the idea of resistance and of collaboration', but whatever the truth of Picasso's conduct during the war, he was treated at the Liberation as a hero. At the Salon d'Automne in 1944, seventy-four paintings and five sculptures he had made during the occupation were displayed in a room to themselves, while elsewhere in the exhibition there was evidence of a new generation of French artists, many of whom had shown together in 1941 as 'Vingt jeunes peintres de tradition française'.

Herbert Read went across the Channel to France several times after August 1944 and both John Rothenstein and Kenneth Clark obtained visas to visit the Salon that year. Raymond Mortimer, too, made haste to Paris as soon as he could, returning with tales of how a black market in luxuries such as orchids and oysters flourished, but that there was no milk, no meat, no heating and no petrol, except that sold by the Americans to black marketeers. Despite his relationships with French officials in London and the fact that he probably could have used his position with the British Council to obtain a visa, Clive did not return to his 'home from home' until 1946. Rothenstein reported that 'American influence at Allied Headquarters had been exerted to hinder British subjects visiting France,' yet it is possible that as Clive knew so many of his French friends were accused of collaboration he was reluctant to go until the situation was clearer. He heard that Segonzac, Derain, Friesz and Vlaminck had been 'put in prison for proposing a political philosophy different from that of the de facto government', though his doubts that this were true proved accurate. Clive was, in any case, kept abreast of what was happening in Paris by a counsellor at the French Embassy, Pierre Francfort, and by René Massigli, who had returned to London in 1943 to serve as De Gaulle's commissioner for foreign affairs and would become ambassador the following year.

After the war, Clive took little part in the fierce polemics around the definition of the term 'école de Paris', dwelling in his articles on those painters he had already identified as particularly important to him, and also writing more about his canon of English painters at the centre of which stood those associated with the Euston Road School. The cosmopolitanism of the School of Paris was its downfall, he argued, as the potential of pre-First World War painting had been swamped by a sea of imitations of 'one or two reigning masters'. Young British painters in the 1930s had managed to become a match for those working in Paris by forging their own paths. When the French National Committee organised a show of twentieth-century painting and sculpture at the Suffolk Street Gallery in 1943, Clive applauded the 'masters' included, such as Bonnard, Rouault, Utrillo and Modigliani, but ruefully admitted that many of the 'eagles' of his youth had turned out to be not such impressive birds after all. Friesz, Marchand, Asselin, Manguin, Lhote, Lurçat, Laurencin and even Derain and Dufy seemed dated now. He still liked their work, but viewed it only as a necessary ingredient of the soil from which had bloomed more impressive painters. Some in this exhibition did seem to Clive to have justified his early attention, however, such as Marcoussis, Brianchon and Balthus – the latter a painter he would continue to follow with interest, visiting his studio when he eventually went back to Paris.

In August 1945, Herbert Read reported on his impression of enormous activity in the Paris art world. Everyone who had not fled to other countries had continued working steadily throughout the war. Matisse, Braque and Picasso remained pre-eminent, but the struggle of artists to achieve that 'synthesis' Read valued so highly always seemed to him to take place 'within the all-embracing genius of Picasso'. A free exchange of works of culture seemed vital to Read, which was what the British Council had so successfully enabled in Paris. The council might be 'misunderstood, despised and starved of funds' in England, but in a foreign capital its work was more valuable than an embassy. Read was able to test his theory at the end of 1945 when the British Council and the French Directorate of Cultural Relations arranged an exhibition of Picasso and Matisse in London that brought to light the vexed nature of the question of a nation's identity in relation to art.

In announcing the exhibition, Leigh Ashton, who had recently succeeded Eric Maclagan as director of the Victoria and Albert Museum, acknowledged that it came from 'that country which has done so much for culture in Europe' – a phrase almost certain to offend those in the British arts establishment who still regarded modern painting as a kind of hoax. Ashton anticipated the reception this exhibition might receive, explaining that the only reason it was being held at the V&A was that the Tate, its more appropriate location, was too severely damaged and that anyone who wished to express an opinion about it should direct their letters to the British Council and not to him.

Opened on 5 December by René Massigli, the exhibition comprised a retrospective of works by Matisse made between 1896 and 1944 and those that Picasso had made during the war. These, the *Times* noted, were often dated to the day, 'as though each was a momentary impression of some critical episode of the years of war'. Matisse had 'maintained a benevolent neutrality' during the war, as Janie Bussy put it, treated at Vence by the Germans as a great man, according to Janie's mother. Matisse told his son that he did not visit the Bussys while Gide was with them in Nice because 'I cannot chat and be intimate in their circle in which one does not understand painting. They are absorbed by the war and politics and that tires me and interests me very little.' In the ensuing furore over the V&A exhibition, his canvases were generally regarded as tolerable by a public vocal in its outrage at Picasso, who in *Les lettres françaises* in 1945 had declared 'painting is not done to decorate apartments. It is an instrument of war for attack and defence against the enemy.'

Public reaction sounded little changed since the first post-Impressionist exhibition in 1910. Picasso's 'monstrosities' were a 'hoax'. D. S. MacColl and Thomas Bodkin complained of an 'invasion' of the V&A by these two foreign painters, arguing apparently seriously that schoolchildren (who had just lived through the Blitz!) should not be allowed to see the exhibition. Despite the efforts of writers such as Herman Grisewood, who would take over the BBC's Third Programme in 1947, to explain that aesthetic criteria had changed over the last thirty years, the establishment came out in force to repel the invaders. Inevitably, someone – in this case John Moore-Brabazon, Lord Brabazon of Tara – expressed his astonishment that British taxpayers were funding foreign artists. Most of the negative attention was, understandably, trained on Picasso, whose wartime oeuvre seemed to several correspondents to fit the times in its evocations of sadness, pity, sorrow and misery. To those who challenged the legitimacy of an art that did not evoke 'enjoyment', some correspondents suggested that perhaps, after the carnage and horror of the last six years, enjoyment was no longer the point. Londoners were unswayed by such arguments, and some 'climbed on chairs . . . waving rolled umbrellas and bellowing disapproval of works that seemed to make a mockery of the civilised values for which the war was fought'.

Raymond Mortimer hoped that Clive would intervene with a letter to the *Times* but he considered the row 'beneath contempt' and said nothing in print. Clive was not surprised that visitors to the museum who had never seen a Picasso could not understand his wartime work and he regarded the whole controversy as a tired rehashing of arguments which the young did not seem to realise had been settled thirty-five years before and the old seemed to have forgotten.

These ancient antagonisms continued when the Tate organised an exhibition of Paul Klee (much of which was loaned by Douglas Cooper from his own collection) in rooms made available by the National Gallery. All Clive's worst opinions about English provincialism and frantic adherence to the notion of national prestige were confirmed when MacColl once more attacked this foreign 'nonsense', casting aspersions on the Fine Arts committee of the British Council whose influence, he felt, was far less beneficial than that of the corresponding committees devoted to the promotion of music and drama. In 1941, Clive had described the works of Klee as shining 'like a good deed in a naughty world'. Cooper, assigned since 1945 to the 'Monuments Men' programme for recovering artworks stolen by the Nazis,[1] won Clive's approval when he explained to readers of the *Times* that as he travelled throughout Europe, the people with whom he spoke did not want to see only the work of Philip Wilson Steer but also that of Graham Sutherland and Henry Moore. MacColl continued to rant, singling out Herbert Read as 'our most distinguished lover of bad painting', who in turn called to his defence Roger Fry's 1922 letter in the *Burlington Magazine* headed 'The Sad Case of Mr. D. S. MacColl'. MacColl retorted that Fry had 'renounced' Picasso towards the end of his career, which Roger's sister Margery contradicted, to no avail. Not only had Fry renounced Picasso, MacColl insisted, 'there was a complete revulsion in his later writing to the meaning behind painting from the brave early days of "significant" (*i.e.*, *in*significant) "form" and Mr. Clive Bell's "still-life" by the cryptic master.'

For *Pots et Citron* to reappear in this context was a sign of how stagnant the old guard's debate had become. Read at this time was working with Douglas Cooper, Roland Penrose and others on founding a Museum of Modern Art in London, later realised as the Institute of Contemporary Arts, which Cooper described as a 'makeshift' compensation for the deficiencies of the Tate. A longstanding charge against Roger was that he had colluded with Parisian dealers to promote post-Impressionism solely to make money from gullible collectors who would be swayed by his reputation. When Thomas Bodkin seemed to allude to this in a new edition of his book *The Approach to Painting*, Clive agreed with Raymond that he should say something. His letter was curt, stating that Roger had chosen the paintings for the 1910 exhibition by himself 'in a mood of happy appreciation'. It was really time to move on.

[1]Formally, Cooper was Acting Director of British Monuments, Fine Arts and Archives for the Control Commission for Germany (monumentsmenfoundation.org).

The Picasso and Matisse exhibition had a catalytic influence on Victor Pasmore. For some months during the war he had stayed at Bryan Guinness's house, where he found writings by Cézanne, Seurat, Gauguin and van Gogh in the library, reading which led Pasmore to conclude that abstraction was the logical conclusion of post-Impressionism. The exhibition at the V&A confirmed his desire to reject 'the static and traditional position' of the Euston Road School, so he reworked several of his earlier paintings. In an essay on Pasmore for the Penguin Modern Painters series, Clive prophesied that his art would 'not stand still' but would go beyond what he had so far achieved. Clive felt that in 1940 Pasmore had not pushed his pictures to the conclusion they seemed to imply, but when he saw the retouched *Flower Barrow* at the Redfern in 1945, he sensed the artist was about to make a transformation. When Pasmore began to paint abstracts in 1947 he shocked the art world, although he continued to produce figurative work and landscapes as well. Abstract art, as Jane Rye notes, had been 'vilified by some as obscure and elitist' in the 1930s, but in 1950s Britain it was reborn as a popular form in opposition to the neo-Romanticism that had flourished during the war.

41. Retrospect

Barbara Bagenal had been compelled to listen silently, thermometer in her mouth, while her doctor denounced the Picassos and Matisses at the V&A. The old man, she told Clive, was worried that the exhibition would arouse hatred for the French. Clive and Barbara had been corresponding since they had surprised one another shortly after the end of the war by going to bed together at the Savoy. Barbara had come to Morgan Forster's lecture at Miller's in 1942 and alarmed Vanessa when she exclaimed that she had not realised how easy it was to get to Lewes from her house in Rye, intimating that she would be a frequent visitor to nearby Charleston. In common with Vanessa, Quentin and Frances, Clive found 'little' (as everyone called her) Barbara's interminable prattling and desire to ingratiate herself exasperating. She became, said Quentin, something of a family joke, albeit a not unkind one. Barbara and Nick Bagenal lived at 28 Percy Street in London, where Saxon Sydney-Turner also had a flat. Barbara looked after both men, acquiring a store of tales about Clive's old friend with which to amuse him.

Clive's opinion of Barbara had improved when she took care of Angelica's eighteen-month-old baby, Amaryllis, for two weeks while Bunny recuperated from a serious operation in October 1944. When she brought the baby for a visit to Charleston, Clive – clearly in a nostalgic mood – enjoyed reminiscing with Barbara about the old friends both had known for thirty years. He felt some sympathy for the arc of Barbara's life, which had taken her from early days of promise as a student with Carrington and Dorothy Brett at the Slade through 'marriage and babies, and the old, old story' of a woman's life. Clive, who turned sixty-four in 1945, would come to depend upon Barbara in

DG & CB

Duncan Grant & Clive Bell at Charleston, 1956 (Vanessa in background)

Barbara Bagenal

the last twenty years of his life, introducing her to a world of famous friends and high culture in exchange for her competent organisation of his practical needs and travel. Vanessa remained wary that Barbara would encroach on her carefully guarded seclusion, but was nonetheless glad that Clive had someone to care for him. When, in the spring of 1945, Vanessa began arranging in sequence Virginia's letters to her, she thought that the 'devastating wit' of her sister's descriptions would likely upset many people. Clive certainly should not see the letters, she told Angelica, but it might be possible for Angelica's daughter one day to publish them, 'as long as you don't let the Bagenal family get hold of them'.

Throughout the war, the question of whether to publish old friends' letters or memoirs had been debated often. Frances was surprised when

Clive said that if Lytton's letters were to be published 'no-one would be on speaking terms with their oldest friends'. She expected more from the 'Apostles of Truth'. Clive took an equally dim view of the possibility that Ottoline's diaries would reach the public, having determined when he had once dipped into them at Virginia's house that they contained many 'shocking lies' about him. Ottoline, who had died in 1938, was the subject of a 'grand inquest' into her character when Leonard and Desmond joined Duncan and Clive at Charleston in reminiscing about her. When Clive told Mary on New Year's Eve 1945 that he was tired of analysing pictures, his thoughts had been turning not only to what he mourned as a lost civilisation, but also to more personal remembrances of some of his old friends. A bundle of letters from Virginia, Carrington, the Shoves and others had led him to dwell on the past as 1945 drew to an end, and he began to think of writing something about Roger. An offer from Time-Life of $500 to contribute to a new magazine presented Clive with a reason to pursue this idea. The Americans' plan foundered, but Clive's article on Roger was published in the *Cornhill* and reprinted as a chapter in his own memoir, *Old Friends*.

In contrast to how Clive's feelings about Roger had usually been perceived by Virginia and Vanessa, his published references to the eminent critic during and after the war made plain the deep respect Clive had for him. There were some, like Christopher Salmon at the BBC, who saw Clive as Roger's natural successor, but Clive himself believed that Roger's mantle had more appropriately been assumed by Kenneth Clark, despite Clark's rebellion against many of Roger's judgements. Reviewing an exhibition of French paintings at the National Gallery in 1942, Clive wished Roger were still alive to explain 'in glowing but precise terms' just what he felt for Degas' *Repasseuses*. Roger 'gave us the best writing on art we have had' in Clive's opinion and whenever controversies arose which blackened Roger's good name, Clive defended him. The debacle over the Picasso and Matisse, and Klee, exhibitions depressed Clive and in the immediate aftermath of the war, his writing on art diminished sharply for a time as he found himself more often in the position of commenting on or correcting errors in accounts of his old friends' lives and influence, especially as a cottage industry devoted to the 'Bloomsbury Group' rapidly expanded in the 1950s, strung between the two poles of serious study and journalists' poorly informed generalisations.

The closest those described as 'Bloomsbury' ever came to instantiation as a group was the Memoir Club. After the war, its membership was kept up by admitting those of the younger generation whom the elder deemed least likely to cause anyone to censor their presentations. Frances was irritated by what seemed to her endless blackballing of new members – Clive exercised his veto against Julia Strachey, for example – until Leonard persuaded her that even one undesirable listener would thwart the purpose of the club, which was to speak with complete honesty about one's own life. Janie Bussy was welcomed and gave a witty account of her family's experiences with Matisse, describing his relations with Picasso as 'roughly those of one crowned head with another'. In 1944, Clive began a memoir about Lytton, trying it out on Frances and then reading it to Mary and to Dadie Rylands in Cambridge. It is uncertain whether he delivered this paper to the Memoir Club but, as he did with his piece about Roger, Clive published his reminiscences of Lytton in the *Cornhill* before revising them slightly for *Old Friends*. The Memoir Club remained very much a 'family' affair: when it met at Tilton in 1946, Lydia Keynes had to have all Molly MacCarthy's jokes explained to her. When Maynard died suddenly three months later, Clive told Mary that almost the last thing they had talked about was Maynard's wish to write something about Lytton for the Memoir Club.

Being in Clive's company seemed to Maud Russell a form of escapism, so unchanged in both his opinions and deportment was he when they met for lunch at the Ivy in January 1945. Clive still frequented the Gargoyle Club, where he danced 'rather primly', standing out in his winged collar and black tie among newer clientele such as Freddie Ayer, Benedict Nicolson, Lucian Freud and Francis Bacon. Maud noticed how Clive and Bertrand Russell were politely awkward with Cyril Connolly when they met at the Ivy soon after VE day. 'They belong to such different generations,' she wrote, 'and seem conscious of it.'

Clive was disgruntled with young and old as Britain began to adjust to the new world of Attlee's welfare state, grumbling that he might move to South Africa. He was disappointed when Peter Quennell and other young friends excoriated Evelyn Waugh for being a reactionary and a snob (which Clive agreed he was), but had nothing to say about his writing. Waugh had placed Clive's *Art* among the books in Charles Ryder's rooms in *Brideshead Revisited*, a novel Clive told its author was 'most beautiful and horribly moving' in its depiction of a world Clive knew had now gone for ever. On the evening following the discussion of Waugh, Clive was again cast down when a group of older people criticised Benjamin Britten for being a 'conchie' and said not a word about his music, which Clive admired and wished to understand better. He felt no optimism for the future in a country where even at Charleston were to be found copies of *Picture Post* and *The Listener*. In a provocative article on 'Blood Sports', Clive wrote that 'bad states of mind' could be induced by the 'crooning of crooners' and many of the 'novels, songs, and picture-papers now in vogue', adding that he also considered 'vile the state of mind of orators or publicists striving to provoke race or class or national hatred, and not much better the state of those who enjoy reading or listening to them.' He dourly complained on a *Horizon* questionnaire in 1945 about the ignorance of the rising generation, its complacency, and the general lowering of standards. Clive sounded a similar note in a contribution to Desmond Shawe-Taylor's lavish, and very short-lived, new magazine, *The Arts*, when he expressed gratitude for those few 'who by creating or caring rise a little above the brazen mediocrity of the mass'. He spent much of this essay, 'Festina Lente' ('make haste slowly'), criticising Raymond and others for preferring Duncan's early decorative work to his more recent output – a consequence, Clive charged, of not lingering long enough before paintings to observe the nuances and subtleties that a too hasty perusal overlooked. Raymond, whose essay on Duncan for the Penguin Modern Painters series Clive had damned with faint praise, was hurt that Clive had singled him out in 'Festina Lente' because, he explained, almost every painter and collector Raymond knew took a dim view of Duncan's most recent show. Raymond worried that Clive's article would lead Duncan to think he did not care for his work, which was far from the case.

The consequence of two world wars was the 'collapse of civilization: the loss of elegance and amenity: the suppressing of the first rate', Clive moaned to Frances. 'Do you realise that we live at best by B.B.C. standards?' 'Equality' became in Clive's lexicon a term of abuse for what Attlee's landslide election in July 1945 had wrought in the name of the welfare state, because equality could only mean the suppression of that unfettered individuality by which Clive had always believed civilisation is produced. Among several allies in this line of thinking, Clive had T. S. Eliot, whose *Notes Towards the Definition of Culture*, he told Frances, was 'full of good ideas'. One of Eliot's points was that 'culture has become, in some sense, a department of politics'. Clive, who complained frequently that art was in danger of becoming a form of social work in postwar England, wrote an essay in 1947 that bore many similarities to Eliot's but it remained among his unpublished drafts. (It is possible that it was the result of a long gestation since Eliot in 1930 had tried to entice Clive into giving his views on the phrase 'standard of living'.)

In that draft, 'The End of a Civilisation', Clive argued that the 'respectable ideals' of equality were 'incompatible with a civilisation based on the unjust inequality implied in the existence of a leisured and privileged élite'. Proponents of equality were, in his view, disingenuous because they never spoke about how a true equality would necessitate a general lowering of the standard of living, requiring people to give up their movies, radios and nylon stockings 'till the people of Asia have enough to eat'. Clive blamed postwar Britain's decline on the statesmen who had done nothing to prevent the First World War and then compounded their failures by creating the Treaty of Versailles. He asked, 'does anyone think in 1947 we are happier than ten years ago?'

In a letter to the *Spectator*, Clive claimed that he remained a Liberal but that only a strategic vote for the Conservatives could avert the disaster of the English spending more than they earned, a difference for the moment bridged by American charity that would at some point cease, causing a fall in the standard of living that could 'easily lead to civil war or something like it'. As David Kynaston points out in his study of the immediate postwar period, the 'much-vaunted, much-predicted, much-feared social revolution' did not occur, but resentment and envy of the United States was pervasive. At the beginning of the war, Clive had written to Frances that it was 'all to the benefit of America and Russia that we should go on ruining each other'. Clive might have agreed with the historian Tony Judt that 1941–45 was 'just an interlude in an international struggle between Western democracies and Soviet totalitarianism' which had begun in 1919, but he would have taken no comfort in it as the twentieth century's wars went on and on in the aftermath of 'victory'.

London society came out in all its glamour for the opening night of the Sadlers Wells Ballet at Covent Garden in 1946. Barbara Bagenal wore a Schiaparelli gown loaned to her by Graham Sutherland's wife, Kathleen, who had been given it by Jane Clark. Clive was accompanied by Mary, for whom he had given a Valentine's Day luncheon at the Ivy. In August they went for a few days to Paris, Clive's first venture there since 1939. The Peace Conference was underway, the black market was dwindling and the stable franc had encouraged the return of goods to the shops. However delightful a time Clive had with Mary in Paris, finding what old friends they could and seeing an exhibition at the Louvre dedicated to the Goncourt brothers, he was confused when she admonished him 'never to think of me as your mistress'. What Clive termed Mary's 'nunish' mood was unpredictable, but Clive did his best to keep the 'amitié amoureuse', which he reluctantly accepted, from becoming a platonic friendship, which, he told her, he could not.

Paris immediately after the war seemed 'sad' to Clive, 'moche' (rotten, or lousy). British travellers were restricted from spending more than £75 abroad, a regulation Clive interpreted as the government's intention to 'break cultural relations with the Continent'. As political and industrial unrest steadily increased support for the Communist Party in France, Clive commented to Frances that he was glad the French had 'dropped that odious uncivilising abstraction Egalité', with which Britain was obssessed.

By 1947, Clive had begun to make regular trips across the Channel once more to sit with his old crowd at the Deux Magots or to lunch chez Lipp, as he did with Picasso in May. Picasso's new lover, Françoise Gilot, was about to give birth to their son Claude, and the artist's studio was crowded with people. Clive thought Picasso had no idea who most of them were. There was much news to catch up on, such as that Derain now lived at Chambourcy with both his wife Alice and his model Raymonde Knaubliche with whom he had had a son in 1941, and whom Alice had welcomed into their household. Cocteau, apparently indestructible and ageless, had become wealthy and was producing new ballets, stories and films. As a particular target of the homophobic Vichy regime, Cocteau had sensed early in the occupation the danger he was in. Fascists had started a riot at the opening night of a late 1941 revival of Cocteau's play *Les Parents terribles*, with his lover Jean Marais in the leading role. After the Liberation, defended by both

Aragon and Éluard, he was completely exonerated of collaboration by the Comité National des Écrivains.

Clive kept to his old haunts, though with an eye on the rapidly changing intellectual and cultural scene, the centre of gravity of which had migrated from the Deux Magots to the Café de Flore. He reunited with Georges Duthuit, returned from New York, where he had made radio broadcasts throughout the war on behalf of the Free French. Duthuit had been working with Eugene and Marie Jolas since 1945 to revive the journal *transition* (thus also making the acquaintance of Samuel Beckett, to the study of whose work Duthuit would dedicate himself), and was about to revive interest in the Fauves with his 1949 book about them. Clive also reacquainted himself with Balthus, who took him to his studio where Clive saw his 'slightly pornographic' work. Balthus, Maurice Brianchon and Louis Marcoussis were among the painters Clive believed had successfully realised their early potential and he now began also to pay attention to Edouard Pignon, the most promising of a group termed 'young', although they were now in their forties. These French painters might have repeated what Othon Friesz supposedly said after the First World War when Clive asked who were the young artists to pay attention to: '*Nous sommes les jeunes.*'

In 1946, Clive saw the Galerie Charpentier's show of a hundred masterpieces of the School of Paris and, at L'Orangerie, an exhibition of masterworks from collections looted by the Nazis which had been recovered by the Monuments Men. Only the older generation – Chagall, Soutine, Utrillo, Matisse, Braque and Picasso – had been represented at the Charpentier show, a selection which fed the debate immediately after the Liberation about what exactly was meant by 'School of Paris'. As wide-ranging discussions about French national identity in a new European situation ensued in Paris, many critics argued that younger artists must now be included. Clive maintained that the dominant influence of Picasso was damaging because his imitators had not arrived at abstraction through an inner compulsion and therefore created 'academic' works. 'It is time for a change,' he wrote in 1949, but by then young painters who imitated Picasso had other than purely aesthetic motivations because their imitation signalled their left politics due to his prominence as a Communist Party member.

Clive read Sartre with 'grim avidity', and found the stories in *Le mur* remarkable. As a notable figure in the promotion of Anglo-French cultural relations, Clive was regularly at the embassy in London, where in 1948 he exchanged a few words with the other new star in the French literary firmament, Albert Camus, whose *L'Étranger* had impressed him enough to make him want to read *La Peste*. Clive's continuing work for the British Council led to more efforts at strengthening cultural ties between the two countries, such as the Arts Council exhibition at the Royal Scottish Academy in 1948 of paintings by Bonnard and Vuillard, for which Clive provided the catalogue with a brief introduction. That year he served with Colin Agnew on a subcommittee for the exhibition 'Huit Siècles de Vie Britannique à Paris' (Eight Centuries of British Life in Paris) at the Musée Galliera.

None of these endeavours required much more than the exercise of his memory as he was rehashing opinions he had already expressed in his writing between the wars. *Art* was still selling well, but when Harold Raymond at Chatto invited him to update and revise it, Clive decided to let the text stand. At Charleston in October 1948, he wrote a brief preface for a new edition in which, while acknowledging that he was too lazy to do what would be necessary to revise it, he described his most famous book as a 'record of what people like myself were thinking and feeling in the years before the first War'. There were, to be sure, some absurd exaggerations and errors in it, but these could be excused by the fervour of the time in which it had been written. He was 'a little envious of the adventurous young man' who had written *Art*.

Clive and Mary went to Nice in the spring of 1948, where they heard from the Bussys that Picasso was nearby at Vallauris. There Clive found an affectionate and welcoming old friend, who showed him the perfume factory he had converted into a cavernous studio, filled with startling new ceramic creations. Clive was amazed by Picasso's pottery, its extraordinarily intense colours and 'designs unlike anything one has ever seen or dreamed of'.

A few days later, Mary and Clive called on Matisse, who received them in the bed where he lay each afternoon, continuing to work on his painted paper cut-outs after spending the morning in his studio. Lydia Delectorskaya, the woman whose presence had brought about the end of the Matisses' marriage, turned the pages of *Jazz* and the *Lettres Portugaises* so that Clive and Mary could see the master's illustrations. They felt privileged to have been vouchsafed Matisse's 'profound and poetical' reflections on life and death, but less so when they saw them repeated in an interview with Matisse published in *Le Figaro* a few days later. When Mary and Clive went to Aix-en-Provence the following year, they heard from Dorothy Bussy that she hoped they would return to see the chapel at Vence Matisse was about to begin decorating (which Clive did in 1951).

While in Aix, Clive took the opportunity to look in on La Bergère, the house in Cassis that Vanessa had rented before the war from Colonel Teed. Vanessa and Clive had heard that Fontcreuse, where the Teeds lived, and La Bergère were more or less unscathed by the war, the Gestapo having used Fontcreuse as a headquarters. Although Vanessa had been to Paris with Clive, Duncan, his friend the collector Edward Le Bas and Barbara Bagenal in September 1947 (when Barbara made all their travel arrangements), it would be several years until she ventured south again, to stay at La Souco with the Bussys. Clive saw for himself how changed Cassis was since they had last seen it and let Vanessa know that she would be shocked to see the new roads and new hotels, but that the Teeds were just as they had been, and the houses looked the same.

Clive had hoped to see the de Margeries when he went to Paris with Mary in the spring of 1948, but at the last moment Roland, now Deputy Director for Political Affairs at the French Foreign Ministry and deeply involved in Robert Schuman's plans for European reconstruction, was urgently called to London. Clive, Mary and Jenny de Margerie went to a Berthe Morisot exhibition without him. Roland had looked forward to seeing Clive to enjoy 'some fruitful exchanges about the vanity and stupidity of men'. When Clive came back to Paris he would find the Luxembourg and Versailles 'flourishing. If our government worked as well as the gardeners and curators,' Roland told him, 'French affairs would go better.'

Before the war, Roland had found respite from politics at Clive's dinners in Gordon Square, where conversation was only about art and literature, or mischievous debate about their contemporaries. These intimate gatherings, where he might encounter Kenneth Clark, Eric Maclagan, Eddy Sackville-West or Raymond Mortimer, as well as those in politics such as Harold Nicolson or William Jowitt, were Roland's happiest memories from his years at the embassy in London. Looking forward to seeing Clive again, Roland recalled meeting Ottoline, about whom Clive had told him he was writing a reminiscence. 'The zoological garden of our memory is an aviary full of such old birds,' Roland mused to Clive, recalling Ottoline's often fantastic appearance. Their nostalgia for that vanished world and their mutual cynicism towards politicians strengthened the ties of a friendship which circumstances made now almost entirely epistolary.

In 1950, Roland was in New York for a conference of European foreign ministers with American Secretary of State Dean Acheson. From the Waldorf-Astoria hotel he regaled Clive with humorous behind-the-scenes anecdotes about how government officials spent their time between meetings. That year, Britain's Labour Party (which Harold Nicolson had made the 'cardinal error' of joining in 1947) rejected Schuman's proposal of a common market governed by an independent authority for coal and steel and thus excluded their country from a new European configuration of nations. Flying from New York in September, Roland looked forward to getting back to Europe where 'ancient ancestral hatreds' at least meant that people had memories. He was not, he sighed to Clive, made for the new world, despite all its 'kindness'. Although he certainly sympathised with his old friend, by then Clive had seen the new world for himself.

VII

OLD FRIENDS
(1950–1964)

42. Clive Bell Looks at American Art

Janice Loeb's letters were an abundant source of information about what was going on in the New York art world. During the war, she was able to advise Clive on whom to contact about arranging exhibitions of British painters in New York, suggesting that both Alfred Barr and Nelson Rockefeller might be interested in proposals stemming from his work on the British Council committee. She hoped Clive would come to America – New York not being, she told him, as bad as she pretended. Certainly, her stories were enticing. When Janice caught sight of Greta Garbo at MoMA, she told Clive that the legendary film star had 'an emanation of beauty quite unbelievable and strange . . . something like what comes out of Virginia, only more so'. She thought this would probably interest Angelica more than Clive, with whose tastes she was thoroughly familiar, yet Janice's New York stories began to pique his interest in American culture. When Walker Evans and James Agee brought out *Let Us Now Praise Famous Men*, Janice urged Clive to try and get hold of the 'peculiar and quite wonderful' book, despite knowing that he was unlikely to care for it.

Clive wanted to know where Janice had 'got to in life'. In recent years, Janice had been a researcher for the Project on Totalitarian Communication, funded by the Rockefeller Foundation, her name listed among the authors of *German Radio Propaganda*, published in 1944. For a time, she had assisted Frank Crowninshield, the former editor of *Vanity Fair*, with his memoirs, but found him a 'horrid guy' and did not stay long. Janice, whose portrait of Victor Pasmore hung in Clive's sitting-room at Charleston, had begun to paint again, and after the war taught introductory classes in art history at the New School in

New York. But her interests had shifted towards film, since she, James Agee and Helen Levitt had shot a short documentary in Harlem in the early 1940s. *In the Street* had garnered a *succès d'estime* from private showings and, when both her father and mother died in 1946, Janice used part of her substantial inheritance to start a production company, Film Documents, with Levitt and Levitt's brother Bill, which released *In the Street* in 1948.

This was a tumultuous year for the American art world as disagreements that had been brewing for some time came to wider attention. Alfred Barr had been ousted as director of MoMA in 1943 by trustees who disapproved of his conferral of the museum's prestige on contemporary 'naive' artists (he remained on the staff, becoming director of museum collections in 1947). The presence in the USA of so many artist refugees from Europe had created something of a crisis of faith in what was meant by an American 'national' art. Many younger artists regarded New York's Metropolitan Museum of Art as representative of a staid tradition that kept out the new and, after a huge 'Artists for Victory' exhibition there at the end of 1942, the Federation of Modern Painters, which had been founded to 'promote the welfare of true progressive artists', staged a counter-exhibit to challenge the 'socialist realist academicism' at the Metropolitan. Antagonism towards the arts establishment then crystallised in 1943 when Mark Rothko and Adolphe Gottlieb published in the *New York Times* a manifesto professing 'spiritual kinship with primitives and archaic art'. MoMA was identified with the internationalism – or globalism – that an older generation saw as a threat to American national identity. Some critics, most prominently Clement Greenberg, believed that the School of Paris was the best inspiration for the renewal of American art, or at least that was how he felt in 1946 when he published 'L'art américain au XXe siècle' in Sartre's *Les Temps modernes*. Greenberg's advocacy for abstract expressionism and MoMA's internationalism were fiercely attacked in 1948 by Lincoln Kirstein in an article for *Harper's*, which shocked and saddened Alfred Barr who considered Kirstein a friend not only of his but also of the museum, for which Kirstein had already done so much.

Kirstein's 'The State of Modern Painting' charged MoMA with promoting a deleterious French influence on young American painters. Similarly to Clive, Kirstein complained that collectors had come to be more concerned with who had painted a picture than with the quality of the picture itself, deploring also the hegemony of Matisse and Picasso over young painters who felt compelled to imitate them. Although Clive's letters to Janice Loeb have not survived, and no references to these American debates appear in his other extant correspondence, it is very likely he would have heard about them not only from Janice but also from such friends as Leigh Ashton, Georges Duthuit and Raymond Mortimer, all of whom took part in a MoMA symposium sponsored by *Life* magazine in 1948.

Clive mentioned to Vanessa that he had been surprised to hear from Raymond that Georges Duthuit represented France at this 'famous Modern Art Congress', a long, illustrated acount of which appeared in *Life*. The participants, who also included Aldous Huxley, Clement Greenberg, Kirk Askew, Meyer Schapiro and H. W. Janson, discussed paintings by Picasso, Miró, Rouault and Matisse, as well as works by 'young American extremists' such as Willem de Kooning and Jackson Pollock. *Life* summarised the conclusions of the roundtable – perhaps not surprisingly given the imminent politicising of modern art in the context of the Cold War – in a paean to the struggle of the individual to express himself in a world where he had been 'stripped' of all the absolutes that had sustained artists in the past. Raymond Mortimer echoed Clive (without mentioning him) when he spoke of the 'catastrophic' effect of the Parisian masters on young imitators who had not developed their own vision. Aldous Huxley, too, sounded a note of which Clive would have approved when he described aesthetic experience as 'an analogue of mystical experience'.

With Greenberg as what Kirstein called its 'most vocative defender', however, American Abstract Expressionism was about to become 'a cultural weapon in the Cold War', a manifestation of the individualism that Fascists and Communists had crushed. The 'highly individual attitude' of the modern artist, according to Meyer Schapiro, was an expression of that freedom which is 'one of the great assets of our civilization'. Within another ten years, modern art would be weaponised in the propaganda war against the Soviet Union and private foundations, such as Ford, would over time provide millions of dollars to support American arts organisations and individual artists.

New York was the epicentre of fierce debates during and after the war about the relation of American painting to the school of Paris, and what place in an American tradition should be occupied by contemporary experiments or movements such as abstraction. The *Magazine of Art* posed the question 'Is There an American Art?' in August 1949 and in the same month, James Thrall Soby, a trustee of MoMA, asked in the *Saturday Review*, 'Does Our Art Impress Europe?' At a time when the United States had embarked on a vast undertaking to help rebuild war-shattered countries, the terms of which exacerbated existing anti-American feeling in France and Britain, Soby noted that the charge was often brought against his rich and powerful nation that it was 'not deeply concerned with the arts or with related spiritual values'. He argued that Paris had to a great extent lost its place as 'international arbiter of fame and quality' in art, yet contemporary American artists were 'unknown or condemned' abroad. Soby called for the appointment by the government of a Secretary of Fine Arts to raise the international profile of American fine arts.

Clive had been thinking more seriously for some time about going to America. Increasingly disgruntled by an arts bureaucracy that he thought was taming art to attract government funds and sacrificing aesthetic standards in the interest of perceived social benefits, Clive wanted to see for himself the country Janice described in her letters. A visit from Lincoln Kirstein's sister, Mina, in 1947 encouraged him to consider how he might get himself there.

It had been more than twenty years since Mina had seen Clive, but she had kept in touch with Bunny. She wanted to talk with Clive about Proust, whose letters she was translating, but when they dined together in May, she was also reminded of her companion's beguiling charm. 'When you are with him you feel that you are the one woman in the world he has chosen to be with,' she wrote in her account of their evening together. She thought Clive had been unfairly stigmatised as a 'womanizer' by his friends, when in fact he simply had a 'basic attraction to women in general'. She assured Clive he could stay with her if he did come to America.

Clive's admiration of the young country's robust faith in an individual's potential 'to rise above equality' had led him to believe after the war that America might be where the embers of that civilisation he mourned in Europe could be fanned into flames. In an unpublished essay, he likened his version of America to what he imagined Elizabethan England must have been like – 'arrogant yet self-critical, self-satisfied yet sensitive'. He briefly considered an invitation from the president of

Bennington College in Vermont to join its faculty or at least to give a series of lectures there, and joked to Frances that it might turn his head to find himself in 'a land where they respect liberty and culture'.

Clive's two trips to America came about as the result of a chance meeting with a lawyer from Baltimore named Douglas Gordon. On his annual visit to England with his wife in July 1949, Gordon happened to accompany a friend to a party at Osbert Lancaster's, where he was introduced to Clive and Barbara (whom he at first took to be Clive's wife). Gordon was a pillar of Baltimore society, a passionate defender of the city's old architecture against modern encroachments and chairman of the Municipal Art Society. He was also a great Francophile and, when he discovered that Clive was about to go to Paris, invited him to look up him and his wife, Winnie, when he arrived. Clive was going with Mary to see the exhibitions of Matisse, Gauguin and Braque which had just opened. He asked Gordon if he knew of any newspaper that might pay him to come to America for the purpose of writing a series of articles but Gordon had no suggestions. The day after the Gordons got home, however, Etta Cone died, so Gordon called a meeting of the Municipal Art Society as he knew that the great collection of modern art which Etta and her sister Claribel had amassed would now go to the Baltimore Museum of Art. He persuaded the Society to offer Clive $1,200 to write an essay about the Cone Collection.

Over the next few months, Clive proposed various lecture topics to Gordon, who set about arranging a tour for his English guest that would take him from New York to Washington, Boston, Philadelphia and Baltimore. 'Foundations of the Great Age', the talk Clive had first delivered in 1936 at the Anglo-French Art and Travel Society's London exhibition of French paintings, was now a staple of his repertoire, but he suggested to Gordon that he might also speak about Lytton and about the inquiry into the visual arts sponsored by the trustees of Dartington Hall.

Published in 1946 as *The Arts Inquiry, the Visual Arts*, several of the report's recommendations had been absorbed by the Arts Council, but Clive's principal interest was in arts education. The British Council had sent some exhibitions of children's art to the United States and other countries during the war but, although Clive agreed that children could sometimes produce startling works of art, he worried that only those talents that developed in an approved manner would be encouraged. That 'intractable individualist, the independent artist' might be left devoid of support by a timid establishment that saw the arts as a form of social welfare for the betterment of mankind, and therefore within the purview of politicians and civil servants. Clive believed that the best way to educate the aesthetic sense was through teaching art history, which required looking carefully at many works of art, thus educating the eye. It would help, he said, if Oxford and Cambridge founded schools of art history.

Janice had warned Clive that if he did ever come to New York he would find her very different from when he had known her in England. She had married in 1948 and had a son, but her marriage was already foundering. Readers of the *LA Times* might have inferred as much when an article about Janice's first trip to Hollywood to attend screenings of her new film, *The Quiet One* (which would be nominated for an Oscar), ended by quoting her saying it was good for her husband that she had left him left in New York with their baby: 'He hadn't even learned to change a diaper when I left.'

Janice by now was something of a celebrity. In May 1949 she received a 'Page One Award' from the New York Newspaper Guild at an event where other recipients included Arthur Miller, Sean O'Casey, Alan Paton and Edward R. Murrow. She was thrilled to hear that Clive was at last making the transatlantic crossing, and promised to meet him at the dock in New York. She looked forward to 'endless conversation'.

Clive sailed on the *Queen Mary* on 4 January 1950, making the voyage in the company of Cecil Beaton and Leigh Ashton. Also on board were Alec Guinness and Irene Worth, on their way to appear in Eliot's *The Cocktail Party* on Broadway for most of the next year. Finding Janice 'as bright as ever and much prettier' when she helped him negotiate customs in New York, Clive was as 'excited as a schoolboy' to be in America. The Baltimore Museum of Art was to hold a reception for the opening of the Cone Collection on 13 January, at which Clive would speak briefly, after which he would lecture at the Fogg Museum at Harvard and at the Phillips Collection in Washington DC.

America impressed him. Everywhere he went he met civilised and intelligent people, and saw galleries and museums 'full of riches and surprises'. He was quite at home at the Century Club in New York, where Douglas Gordon secured him a temporary membership. He marvelled that he was not expected to pay for anything and that a car was always waiting to take him from railway station to hotel, from hotel to his lectures. In Baltimore, Clive extolled the Matisse sculptures collected by the Cones and singled out the painting *Girl in Brown Taffeta Dress* as a 'quiet, private conversation between artist and observer'. He arrived early on the day of the opening to peruse the collection, making notes at the back of his appointment diary on the superb examples of Matisse's work, as well as on a beautiful Sisley (*Poplars on a River Bank*), a group of early Marie Laurencins and the work he liked most in the collection, Renoir's *Washerwomen*. Adumbrating the essay he would write when he was back at Charleston that spring, Clive jotted down that the collection showed 'how both Matisse & Picasso moved towards simplification & abstraction'. Pierre Matisse was among the 2,000 guests gathered for the museum's gala opening and let his father know that Clive had been one of the speakers at an event which afforded Pierre the opportunity to see all together for the first time the more than forty canvases the Cones had collected since their first purchase of works by Matisse in Paris in 1906.

'Foundations of the Great Age', with its conclusion that the pre-eminence of French painting in the nineteenth century was the result of 'Individualism, Industrialism, Democracy' so apt for an American audience, was well received in Washington and Philadelphia. Those who attended the same talk at Harvard's Fogg Museum were more critical, Clive told both Vanessa and Mary, without elaborating. He felt like an impostor when he lectured.

While he was in Boston, Clive took the opportunity to see the interior designer Rowland Burdon-Muller, whom he had met the previous year in Aix-en-Provence. In New York, he lunched with Sam Lewisohn, the financier and collector of modern art who was a trustee of both MoMA and the Metropolitan Museum. Clive enjoyed the lavish hospitality of his American hosts, happily surprised to discover in New York a society comparable to London's. When he lunched at the Algonquin with Lincoln Kirstein, Frederick Ashton and Francis Poulenc, he felt obliged to walk over to greet those whom he knew at nearby tables, such as Daisy Barr, Kirk Askew and Aline Louchheim, as though he had lived there all his life. Louchheim, the *New York Times* art and architecture

critic, was an exact contemporary of Janice's at Vassar. She took Clive
to the annual exhibition of contemporary American painting at the
Whitney Museum to see what the famous British critic would think.

'Some people skirt the edges of galleries, examining each work
cautiously, with the attentive air of a furniture buyer in a merchandise
showroom,' she wrote, but Clive surprised her by swooping, 'with
the decisiveness of a seagull' certain where to find fish, directly to the
paintings that interested him, ignoring most of the others. Clive was
generous with his commentary, declaring Loren MacIver's *Venice* his
favourite in the show (MacIver had become the first woman artist
to enter MoMA's permanent collection when Barr acquired *Shack* in
1935). Of Leonid's *The Sea at Portugal*, Edward Melcarth's *Street Scene*
and Walter Stuempfig's *The Viaduct*, Clive told Louchheim that it was
'refreshing to find artists who are not afraid of representation, who
can do what they want in spite of it. I find them "modern" even so.'
Hans Hoffman's *The Red Table* he thought 'related in a strange way to
Bonnard', and before Ben Shahn's *Anatomical Man*, Clive exclaimed
emphatically, '*oh yes*'. John Sennhauser's *Synchroformic No. 4* conveyed
a sense of harmony to Clive, because 'every part of it seems necessary,
even the signature'.

The rising stars of the abstract expressionist school, on the other
hand, troubled him. Confronted with de Kooning's *Attic*, a culmination
of his experiments in black and white whose touches of red and yellow
intimated his imminent return to colour, or Rothko's *No. 19*, showing
how close the artist was getting to the colour field paintings for which
he is best known, or Pollock's *No. 14, Grey*, Clive demurred. 'Remember
I am old-fashioned,' he told Louchheim when she tried to engage
him in conversation about 'the image in motion in uncodified space'.
Expressionist works, in Clive's view, were overwhelmed by an idea rather
than by emotion. Echoing Lincoln Kirstein's complaint, Clive repeated
to Louchheim what he had already stated elsewhere: young painters
were too blindly following Picasso and thus had become 'academic'
without first learning the use of their tools. The great difference
between modern European and American painting, he opined, was that
in Europe the influence came through Picasso from Cézanne, whereas
the New York modernists derived directly from Picasso. Clive would
not in any way have agreed with Kirstein that, for example, Matisse was
'a decorator in French taste, the Boucher of his epoch', but he might

have concurred that the rising stars of American painting believed that the past fifty years were more 'instructive and worthy of imitation than the past five hundred'.

Louchheim's article brought Clive more attention in New York. He found himself in the company of art world luminaries when Blanchette Rockefeller invited him for tea at her Philip Johnson-designed guest house on East 52nd Street, which served almost as an annexe to the nearby MoMA. Lincoln Kirstein was there, as was Johnson himself, the painter Joseph Glasco, and several other architects and designers. Another guest was Edith Halpert, founder of the Downtown Gallery in Greenwich Village. As one of the most important dealers in American paintings since opening her gallery in 1926, Halpert would not have been pleased to hear Clive's more blunt private appraisal of what he had seen at the Whitney. 'American painting seems to me deplorable,' he told Vanessa, 'sham school of Paris without the talent.'

The six weeks he had spent in America, Clive told Mina Kirstein, were the 'happiest days in my post-second-war existence'. He had stayed with Mina in Washington when he was invited to lunch at Dumbarton Oaks, the estate in Georgetown which, a decade earlier, Mildred and Robert Bliss had donated to Harvard University with their collection of Byzantine and Pre-Colombian art. Despite his fulsome letters thanking Mina for all her kindnesses, the exciting young woman he had met in London a quarter of a century earlier seemed to Clive to have become a rather staid and boring widow, albeit with a heart of gold (Mina's 1926 marriage to Henry Curtiss had been ended by his untimely death a year later).

There was no such disappointment in his reunion with Janice. They had fallen at once into a 'special peculiar and profound continuity of feeling' that made conversation flow easily. Clive found Janice's films intriguing, recognising that she had discovered a métier particularly suited to her gifts. New York had been 'wildly exciting', whether shopping at Lord & Taylor for a handbag for Mary or seeing Gilbert Seldes again, with whom he ran into Rebecca West's son, Anthony. Unlike Raymond, who complained that it was not more like England or France, Clive found America enthrallingly modern.

Once back at Charleston, Clive wrote the essay on the Cone Collection which had provided the rationale (and money) for his trip. *Modern*

French Painting was published in 1951 under the auspices of Baltimore's Municipal Art Society. The Cone Collection, Clive wrote, offered juxtapositions from different stages of Matisse's career which could reveal the path he had followed in effecting the 'transformation of the conception of a picture', from objects 'regarded primarily as means to practical ends' to 'forms possessing an emotional significance of their own in a world of pure aesthetic experience'. Clive had never met the Cones, but imagined them visiting Picasso's studio on the rue de Ravignan, where in 1908 they would have seen the early works that gave evidence of how many different influences he was engaged with; after *Les Demoiselles d'Avignon*, Clive wrote, he transmuted all influences into a 'Picassonian' art.

Clive admired the Cone sisters for buying paintings because they liked them, not beholden to any particular creed. Their collection also served a pedagogic function, allowing viewers to compare a 1910 abstract to one made in 1950: 'In the former the artist has found himself a Cubist, or at any rate *cubisant*, as the result of an agonizing struggle between his sensibility and his determination to remain true to certain principles. In the latter, as often as not, he has borrowed ready-made distortions and quasi-geometrical elements, much as, a hundred years ago, prize students were borrowing the forms and mannerisms of Ingres.' Etta and Claribel Cone had begun to form their collection in the ferment of 'excitement, of experiment and of extravagant hopes' that defined modernism, but then came the war.

Soon after he had dispatched his essay to Adelyn Breeskin at the Baltimore Museum of Art, Clive and Douglas Gordon began discussing the possibility of a second lecture tour. Duncan Phillips was enthusiastic about him speaking again in Washington and Gordon suggested that were Clive to return to the United States, he should go farther afield. Clive was not sure that his essay on the Cone Collection had pleased the museum and worried, too, about repeating the lectures he had given in 1950. 'What people really want of me,' he complained, 'are reminiscences. It's not flattering; they don't care a fig for my ideas.'

It was true, but Clive gave his audiences and readers what they wanted, having little to add to the ideas by which, for forty years, he had earned his reputation as a reliable and entertaining guide to the art which had shocked London in 1910 and that art's legacy. Throughout the 1950s, his writing looked back to those artists with whom he had long been associated, his commentary on contemporaries dwindling. He contributed leading articles and reviews to the *TLS* on Manet, Gauguin, Toulouse-Lautrec and Cézanne, and summed up his views on Rouault, Utrillo and Matisse in *Apollo*. He had suggested to Gordon that one of the talks he might prepare for a second lecture tour would give his reminiscences of Matisse and the Fauves. To mark the fortieth anniversary of 'Manet and the Post-Impressionists', Clive wrote 'How England Met Modern Art' for the American *Art News*, whose editors captioned photographs of himself and of Roger as organisers of an exhibition that was to England what the Armory Show of 1913 had been to America. This article, and a talk entitled 'Recollections of Fauve and Cubist Painters', told the story of Clive's encounter with modern painting through his sojourn in Paris in 1904, his meeting with Roger, the 'howls of outrage' that greeted the first post-Impressionist exhibition and his subsequent friendships with Derain, Picasso, Cocteau and many others. As Gordon shrewdly discerned, Clive had good material for a memoir.

Alfred Barr had been shown Clive's article by the *Art News* editor, Alfred Frankfurter, who knew Barr was writing a book about Matisse. Because Barr had been corresponding with Bernard Berenson, who gave him the impression that he had long considered Matisse the most important modern painter, Barr was interested in Clive's anecdote about Berenson 'expensively' placing Matisse below René Piot. The story – in which the celebrated connoisseur realised he had made a poor judgement when he commissioned Piot rather than Matisse to decorate the library at his Florentine villa, I Tatti – is repeated in *Old Friends*, but Barr did not use it in his book. Clive was able to provide Barr with more substantive information for his comprehensive study of Matisse when he told him about Robert Dell's exhibition of French painting in Brighton the summer before the first post-Impressionist show, and supplied Barr with a copy of the catalogue from the 'Second Post-Impressionist Exhibition', at the time unobtainable anywhere in the States.

By the spring of 1951, Clive and Gordon had decided on the subjects of the lectures and Gordon had made arrangements for an extensive tour of the United States. Clive settled on talks about Matisse, Picasso and his own earliest years in Paris, as well as reminiscences of Lytton, a talk on Ingres, another on Bonnard and his old standby, 'Foundations of the

Great Age'. He sailed for New York, again on the *Queen Mary*, at the end of January 1952, catching glimpses on board of Noël Coward, whom Clive did not disturb as he seemed to be preoccupied with some young men. Clive won a prize in the ship's fine arts competition on the first day. He looked forward to seeing Janice waiting for him in New York Harbour. She had warned Clive that he must be very discreet about her lover, Bill Levitt, because if Milton Lowenstein, her husband, had any reason to believe his suspicions about her were correct it would have a terrible effect on her divorce proceedings. 'Your visit figured in the trial when I was forced to give examples of M[ilton]'s boorishness,' she told Clive. The tabloids in New York had covered the case throughout the summer of 1951 with lurid headlines over articles reporting on Lowenstein's charges that Janice's 'weird' and communist friends made her an unfit mother, or on the 'red-headed heiress' who told the court that all her husband cared about was her money. Janice explained to Clive that the communist panic gripping America made her an easy target for those who regarded 'artistic' people with suspicion.

On his second lecture tour, Clive saw much more of America than he had in 1950. He went by train to Kansas City, St Louis, Cleveland and also to Chicago, where he saw Alice Roullier of the Arts Club again, and returned to Baltimore and Washington. He had asked Duncan Phillips to send as many photographs as possible of the Bonnards in his collection and went to some trouble to overcome the challenge of obtaining slides that would fit an American projector. Clive considered himself particularly lucky to have been invited to Chicago, where the Art Institute, in collaboration with New York's Metropolitan Museum, was bringing together Cézannes from around the world. The exhibition was superb, he told Gordon, and the rest of the nineteenth- and twentieth-century collections in Chicago were 'indescribably rich'. One private collection he managed to see was that of Mary and Leigh Block, who were influential in a number of midwestern art institutions. They had purchased Van Gogh's *Self Portrait with Bandaged Ear* in 1942, the year they were married, and owned important works by Braque, Gris and Picasso. Meyer Schapiro, Theodore Rousseau (the Metropolitan Museum's curator of paintings) and Alfred Frankfurter were in Chicago for a symposium on Cézanne in connection with the exhibition, at which Clive spoke about the painter's relation to Impressionism. He reiterated some of what he had written for the Phaidon book on French

Impressionists, but added a more detailed analysis of the painter's career before concluding with the question, 'Dare I suggest that Cézanne was an Impressionist who never painted an impressionist picture?'

Clive worked harder on his talks for 1952 than he had on his previous visit. His typescripts for the lectures on Ingres and on Bonnard are heavily annotated to indicate where he wished to emphasise a word or when a particular slide should be shown, and also to ensure he kept to his allotted time, perhaps careful that his performance would reflect well on Douglas Gordon's reputation (who brought several speakers to the USA in the next few years, always measuring their success against Clive's).

From Baltimore, where he spoke about Lytton to an audience in the library at Johns Hopkins University, he went to Washington to speak again at Duncan Phillips' collection at his former home in Dupont Circle. Clive had read Thadée Natanson's just-published *Le Bonnard que je propose*, which probably led him to dwell in his talk on *L'après-midi bourgeoise ou La famille Terrasse* (A Bourgeois Afternoon or The Terrasse Family). For Natanson, this painting showed Bonnard beginning to 'find himself', but Clive, while admiring its social wit, felt that Bonnard's ability to convey a 'profound and essential significance' in ordinary objects was better shown in a painting like *Woman with Dog*, which Phillips had acquired in 1925.

After Washington, Clive travelled west for seventeen hours on a train to Kansas City and St Louis. Clive got on 'like a house on fire' with the dynamic young director of the City Art Museum of St Louis, Perry Townsend Rathbone, and was delighted when Catherine Filsinger, one of the curators, sewed a button back on his jacket that had come off in the gallery. Filsinger accompanied Clive on an expedition to find T. S. Eliot's birthplace, which, as the *St. Louis Post-Dispatch* noted, was now 'in the heart of a commercial district'. She took photographs of the house on Locust Street for him. 'Tom, you know', the *Dispatch* reported Clive saying with a twinkle in his eye, 'now out-Englishes the English with his elaborate English accent.' Clive's contribution to a *festschrift* published in honour of Eliot's sixtieth birthday in 1948 (the year he was awarded the Nobel Prize) was another piece he would republish in *Old Friends*. His remark in St Louis that he was 'about the only one left who dares tease Tom' is borne out by his comment in 'How Pleasant to Know Mr Eliot' that the renowned and serious poet became 'a sort of "family joke"' to himself and Virginia when they first got to know him. Clive thoroughly enjoyed himself in St Louis, praising the museum's large Braque, *The Blue Mandolin*, and Picasso's *Mandolin and Vase of Flowers* as 'of absolutely topmost quality',[1] and their Titian, *Ecce Homo*, as 'among the world's best'. He appreciated also the Italian 'primitives' he saw there, such as Paolo di Giovanni's *St Thomas Aquinas Confounding Averroës*.

In Kansas City, a tea was given in his honour by Clyde H. Porter and his wife Mae, with whom Clive stayed. Both were avid collectors of American Indian artefacts, as well as serious researchers into the history of immigrants to the American West. Clive found it difficult to make conversation with the Porters and their guests, grateful though he was for their kindness. Much more to his taste was Lawrence Sickman, the respected expert on Chinese art who would succeed Paul Gardner as director of the Nelson-Atkins Museum in 1953. Clive's arrival in Kansas City was announced in a newspaper article that described him as a 'consistent advocate of peace', as well as a member of a famous art and literary group, and his lecture at the Kansas City Art Institute and School, again on 'Foundations of the Great Age', was widely publicised. Clive attended a performance of O'Casey's *Juno and the Paycock* at the University of Missouri with its president, Clarence Decker, and his wife, following a dinner they gave for him, but to Douglas Gordon he confided he had not been sad to leave 'K. C.', which struck him as provincial in comparison with St Louis.

In Cleveland, where he went after his journey north to Chicago, Clive had to apologise that his 'Recollections of Fauve and Cubist Painters' had not much to do with Matisse, about whom the museum audience had been expecting him to talk because a large exhibition that had originated at MoMA had just been installed there. It was 'better arranged than I have ever seen a big Matisse collection before', Clive told Mary when he got back to New York.

Clive returned at dawn on 3 March to the snowy, silent city. There were several old friends to see, including Lewis Galantière, who had been translating Sartre's plays, and Gladwyn Jebb, serving as Britain's

---

[1] The *Dispatch* article refers only to a 'large' Picasso. My thanks to Claire Vasquez for information supporting the identification of *Mandolin and Vase of Flowers* as the painting Clive most likely intended (email 14 October 2019).

ambassador to the United Nations, as well as new American friends such as Kirk Askew, Aline Louchheim (who would shortly divorce her husband and marry the industrial designer Eero Saarinen) and Rosalind Constable of Time-Life. At MoMA, where he made sure to meet Barr, Clive probably saw an exhibition of Frank Lloyd Wright's 'Buildings for Johnson's Wax', 'Picasso: His Graphic Art', and 'Posters by Painters and Sculptors', but he made no mention of them in letters to Mary or Vanessa. He had dinner with George Bergen, whose relationship with Duncan had so upset Vanessa in 1930, and who had, in 1951, stunned them by sending a telegram announcing that he was about to get married in New York. Clive did some window shopping with Mary in mind, but decided he would have better luck in Paris, where his hoard of US travellers' cheques would go further. He saw Janice as much as he could, finding her 'happy, pretty & young' and Bill Levitt a great improvement on her husband. After spending a few days on Janice's estate in Long Island, where her little boy reminded him of Frances' son, Burgo, Clive went to Boston for another visit to Rowland Burdon-Muller in Beacon Hill.

Janice was supposed to see Clive off but made an excuse and told him not to worry about the $40 she had loaned him when he arrived. It had been 'sweet and wonderful' to see him, but at the time her divorce was still some months from being finalised. It would not be until 1957, by then married to Bill Levitt, with whom she had two children, that Janice told Clive she had not come to the dock that night because she had had an assignation with her lover. 'You probably didn't mind a pin not being seen off, but I minded very much,' she wrote. Clive and Janice would not see each other again, but Janice continued to treat Clive as a confidant for her emotions. She once made tentative efforts to see him in England when she was on her way to France in the late 1950s, but lost courage, still feeling that she had treated him badly by being so neurotic when they had first met.

As Janice began to paint seriously again, she found a close friend and mentor in Will Barnet and wanted to tell Clive all about the Art Students League. Her last extant letter to Clive excoriated the abstract expressionists, whose cultural dominance appalled her. She knew Clive would sympathise with her sense that there had once been 'a place to go, formally, spacially, in the great tradition where Picasso and Matisse (especially) leave off, where one can really do abstract painting – intuitive, formal, classical, like good painting should be'. It seems that, like Clive, Janice felt left behind by contemporary painting. His welcome in the United States in 1950 and 1952 was very much as an elder statesman of a world now only of historical interest, not as a commentator on the contemporary scene. As he said self-deprecatingly, 'my nonsense seems to suit their nonsense.'

Clive wrote nothing about such events in England as 'The Mirror and the Square', an exhibition at the New Burlington Galleries in December 1952 that showed the range from abstraction to realism in about 300 works, nor did he write anything about the developments in realism which were on display at exhibitions such as John Berger's *Looking Forward* in 1952, or David Sylvester, Robert Melville and Peter Watson's *Recent Trends in Realist Painting* or, in 1954, *New Realism in English Art*. The Dutch painter Hans van Norden was inspired by Clive's article on Picasso, 'The Shadow of the Master', to invite him to contribute an essay to the catalogue for an exhibition in Amsterdam of the 'Realisten' group of young Dutch artists who rejected abstraction (November 25–10 December 1951, Municipal Museum of Art), but nothing from Clive is found in van Norden's archives.

Just before he left for America the first time, Frances had asked Clive if he could tell her anything about a painter named Francis Bacon, whose exhibition she had gone to see because she had once met him. Bacon's *Head* paintings at the Hanover Gallery in December 1949 caused 'indescribable' shock, but if Clive had any opinion of them, it has not survived. He was certainly aware of Bacon: *Painting*, which Barr had bought for MoMA in 1946 almost before anyone else had seen it, was one of the illustrations chosen by the *Magazine of Art* to accompany Clive's article on contemporary English art critics. James Thrall Soby explained that they had had to use images of works that were available in New York.

Soby, who was pleased with Clive's article, had asked Wyndham Lewis a couple of years earlier why it was that modern English painting was not treated by critics with 'some perspective'. Never one to let a feud die down, Lewis replied that the English art world had always 'been in the hands of rich impresarios, like Roger Fry', a critic who had 'invented Duncan Grant – a little fairy-like individual who could have received no attention in any country but England'. Surprisingly, Lewis named Kenneth Clark rather than Clive as Fry's successor in this cabal dedicated to promoting Duncan and ignoring others.[2]

Since he was a young man, Clive had done his best to avoid being perceived as a 'professional' critic. So when he accepted Benedict Nicolson's invitation to become a member of the English section of a newly formed international association of art critics that met for the first time in Paris in 1948 at the UNESCO headquarters (and still exists), Clive may simply have been being agreeable, as he had always been, to Vita and Harold's son. Nicolson explained to Clive that Herbert Read had convened an exploratory meeting attended by himself, T. W. Earp, Eric Newton, Alan Clutton-Brock and Michael Middleton (art critic of the *Spectator*), but when Clive mistakenly sent his subscription to Eric Newton rather than to Nicolson, Newton told Clive that he was as mystified as Clive was about the organisation's purpose.

Clive's survey of English critics for the *Magazine of Art* mentioned Nicolson as one of the 'young men of promise', together with John Pope-Hennessy and Allan Gwynne-Jones (whose *Portrait Painters* had just been published). The article began, however, by distinguishing between the scholar – *Kunstforscher* – and those who write about art for daily or weekly newspapers. For the latter, among whom Clive implicitly placed himself, all that was necessary was to have seen something of 'the best works of the past', to love painting and to be able to write. To be a 'first-class' critic might require Douglas Cooper's 'formidable erudition', but Clive, as he had in the past, extolled the value of being a 'trustworthy signpost'. 'Critics exist not for artists but for the public,' and the public, he thought, simply needed guidance, not the theorising of a Herbert Read, or the self-interested opinion of a Wyndham Lewis who, being an artist himself, could not help looking at others' work only in regard to his own. Clive took another opportunity to lament the postwar 'age of the common man' in which the critic now 'aspires to the status of a welfare-worker' among artists who were becoming 'slightly suspect civil servants'.

---

[2]Clark's name was omitted in the published version of the letter, presumably to avoid exposure to libel because Clark was alive at the time. My thanks to Peter Corina for confirming that Lewis names Clark in the letter.

Clive never fully inhabited any of the various personae he presented to the world. He had won considerable fame writing about art, as his reception in the United States demonstrated, but he invariably presented himself as merely a 'sciolist', never a scholar. He was not a scholar, erudite though he was, but neither was Clive a dilettante. He played an important part in influencing a profound transformation of aesthetic sensibility in England and he fearlessly championed civil liberties and peace throughout his life. He was typecast by *Art*, in a sense, as someone who had rejected 'representation' in painting and then never deviated from that stance (the American artist Ben Shahn, for example, 'did his best to ring the death knell' on Clive's 'influential critical canon that representation is unimportant' in his 1956 Norton lecture at Harvard). This, too, was inaccurate.

43. Douglas Cooper

The Courtauld Institute, to which Roger Fry had bequeathed the bulk of his own collection, had become a centre for the transformation of art historical writing since the 1930s when it provided refuge for scholars from Hamburg's Warburg Institute (such as Helmut Gernsheim) after the Nazis came to power. The influence of these scholars gradually shifted English writing on art away from the belletristic and personal style favoured by Clive to the more rigorous approach he sometimes associated with a lack of 'sensibility'. When Anthony Blunt, director of the Courtauld, commissioned Douglas Cooper to catalogue its collection soon after Samuel Courtauld's death in 1947, Cooper embarked on several years of research that resulted in a 'pioneering fifty-thousand word essay on the history of exhibiting and collecting French art in Britain'. Cooper sought Clive's help to compile a list of purchases in England of Impressionist and post-Impressionist paintings between 1870 and 1920, sending him a questionnaire for the purpose.

Cooper acknowledged Clive as the 'only writer who attempted to think constructively on the subject of "modern" art', and although he repeated the view that Clive's ideas largely derived from Roger Fry, he also pointed out that Clive's vivid writing had done more than Roger's to persuade 'a great many hesitant people to look at modern French painting'. Clive never refuted the charge that he had derived ideas from Roger; the evidence of their differences spoke for itself. He assisted Benedict Nicolson with a fortieth-anniversary article on the post-Impressionist exhibitions, which Nicolson intended as a homage to Roger and for which Clive provided a photograph of his Jean Marchand *Vue de Ville*, purchased from the 1912 exhibition. Nicolson maintained that Roger's warm response to painters such as Marchand and Lhote explained why he had not appreciated the direction taken by Picasso and Braque.

Clive praised Cooper's Courtauld catalogue as a 'masterpiece of critical scholarship', but took issue with its account of the two post-Impressionist exhibitions, which Cooper said had presented a distorted view of French painting to a British public that was consequently frightened off modern art. 'The fact is,' Clive explained to Frances, 'concerning the Post-Impressionist exhibitions and the succeeding decade, I write from personal and intimate knowledge, while he depends on documents and inferences drawn therefrom.' Cooper extolled Cubism over all other tendencies in modern art and condemned Roger's preference for Vlaminck, Friesz, Lhote and Marchand – like Nicolson, seeing this as a consequence of the 'dead-end' of significant form. Clive thought Cooper misunderstood the impact of the post-Impressionist exhibitions, ascribing his view to a narrow reliance on the attitudes at the time of rich collectors, museum directors and their trustees. Younger members of the 'art-loving public', Clive countered, were 'wildly' enthusiastic about the shows. He took issue with Cooper's antipathy towards Roger (which Blunt may have tried to ameliorate) by arguing that it was Roger, not Samuel Courtauld, who had been the 'pioneer' in collecting modern French painting. When, two years later, Blunt made the point in a catalogue essay that Courtauld had not led the way in collecting post-Impressionist art, Clive regretted that Blunt had not gone further: 'if Roger Fry and a few friends' had not created the necessary enthusiasm for modern French painting, he wrote, Courtauld probably would not have collected it at all.

Clive had a wary but respectful relationship with Cooper. In his review of the Courtauld essay, Clive alluded to Cooper's reputation for 'violence' in his angry attacks on those who blasphemed against his religious feeling for art, yet Clive had himself, after all, been accused of similar excesses and extreme language in the past. Around the time that Clive had been preparing to embark on his first trip to the USA, controversy had erupted in the pages of the *Burlington Magazine* about the Tate. Benedict Nicolson, only very recently installed as the magazine's editor, compared the Tate's limitations with the 'superiority of the Museum of Modern Art in New York'. The government, he wrote, should make up for the loss of private patrons such as Duveen and Courtauld, especially 'now that the belief is gaining currency that modern art is not so much an agreeable embellishment to a sitting-room, as a burning comment on the uneasiness of the age'. The direct allusion to Picasso's well-known statement of 1945 in *Lettres Françaises* (which had appeared in English in Alfred Barr's *Picasso: Fifty Years of his Art* in 1946) spoke of a generational shift among younger critics and artists, though Picasso's turn to communism after the war was regarded very differently in England than in France.[1]

John Russell came to the Tate's defence, objecting to what he perceived as an unfair comparison with New York's privately funded and very wealthy museum, but Cooper asked why the Tate could not become 'more active and progressive' like MoMA. Among the Tate's postwar exhibitions, only the Klee had been organised in-house, the others all being arranged by either the British Council, the Arts Council or other bodies. Cooper was baffled that Tate director John Rothenstein could say that his institution's collection of late nineteenth- and early twentieth-century French painting was 'the most representative in Europe' when that statement contradicted the views of the recently concluded Massey Commission, on which Rothenstein himself had sat. The Massey report had recommended several changes in the administration of the National Gallery, the V&A and the Tate. There were many ways the Tate could become more like MoMA to realise a 'cultural and educational role in modern England', Cooper pointed out, but they would require fundamental changes in what he charged were negligent administrative practices.

The Massey report had also once more brought up the 'long-vexed question of the Chantrey Bequest'. Rothenstein's article explaining 'Why the Tate Does Not Show its Chantrey Pictures' led to an acrimonious correspondence at the same time that an exhibition at Burlington House of all the works purchased by the bequest was being savaged by the critics. In December 1953, when Cooper discovered that the Tate had sold Renoir's *Nu dans l'eau* from the Courtauld Collection,

[1]Picasso made his second visit to England in November 1950 to attend a communist-backed international peace conference in Sheffield, but it ended in a debacle when the government denied entry to many of the delegates, forcing the event to be held in Warsaw instead. Clive remarked to Gilbert Seldes that 'the government was silly; Picasso was rude and the rest of the communists behaved like communists' (CB/G. Seldes 20 November 1950 Delaware).

his alarmed letter to the *Times* initiated what came to be known as 'the Tate Affair', a controversy over Rothenstein's administration of the Tate, later described by John Richardson as 'a landmark in the British establishment's surrender to modernism'. The ensuing correspondence was bitter, but even Richardson, living at the time with Cooper in Provence at the Chateau de Castille, which Cooper had bought to house his art collection, knew that the 'intensity of his malice blinded people to the justice' of Cooper's antagonism towards Rothenstein. The incident led to questions being asked in Parliament about the Tate's administration of public funds.[2] Clive shared Cooper's disdain for Rothenstein, though his feelings had none of the aggressiveness Cooper displayed.

[2]Frances Spalding gives a detailed account of the affair in chapter 9 of her history of the Tate.

44. A Gang of Conspirators

Clive had his own reasons for disliking Rothenstein, with whom he had often sparred at British Council meetings. When the second volume of the Tate director's *Modern English Painters* appeared in 1956, Vanessa bridled at its attack on Bloomsbury as a 'gang' that employed ruthless methods 'to ruin, utterly, not only the "reactionary" figures whom they publicly denounced, but young painters and writers who showed themselves too independent to come to terms with . . . the current "party line"'. Leonard Woolf pointed out to a researcher in 1966, who had swallowed unquestioningly from *Modern Painters* the notion of a Bloomsbury 'party line', that Rothenstein was only eleven years old at the time of the first post-Impressionist exhibition. His attack on Bloomsbury continued a grudge Rothenstein carried throughout his life against Roger Fry, derived from the mistaken perception that Roger had denigrated his father's painting when they disagreed about the 'Second Post-Impressionist Exhibition'.[1] According to Rothenstein, Roger had 'communicated his rancour' about Will Rothenstein 'to a wide circle of the Bloomsbury group' which led to the 'most venomous attacks made on any artist of the time'. Vanessa was outraged by this, despite Rothenstein exempting Duncan from the 'virulent partisanship that marred the characters of some of his friends'. Clive appeared in *Modern*

[1] Rothenstein was still harping on Roger's iniquities ten years later in his autobiography, even drawing the 'still lingering influence' of Roger into his account of the long controversy over his administration of the Tate (*Brave* 248). The accuracy of Rothenstein's account of the 'Tate affair' was immediately challenged by several people (Spalding, *Tate* 297 n6) and dismissed by John Richardson as '150 pages of exculpatory whining' (*Sorcerer's* 160).

Painters as an urbane liberal with unexpectedly 'strong prejudices', representative of a Bloomsbury whose influence had waned to the extent that they were of interest now only as a kind of period piece.

John Rothenstein's name did not appear in Clive's memoir, *Old Friends*, published in the same year as *Modern Painters*, yet it was writers such as the Tate director whom Clive had in mind when he implored those who invoked the term 'Bloomsbury group' to 'state clearly whom and what they are writing about'. By the 1950s, the construction of a durable if shifting target labelled 'Bloomsbury' had been in process since at least the 1930s, when Wyndham Lewis, in *Men Without Art*, Frank Swinnerton, in *The Georgian Literary Scene*, Prince Dmitri Mirsky, in *The Intelligentsia of Great Britain*, and the Leavises in their journal *Scrutiny* had lashed out at its supposedly malevolent influence. Several reviewers pointed out the contradiction in Clive's defending something whose existence he questioned, but his plea for definition acknowledged that 'Bloomsbury' would continue to signify 'a point of view, a period, a gang of conspirators, or an infectious disease' no matter what he or any of those still alive to explain themselves might say. Letters, memoirs, autobiographies, diaries and biographies associated with Bloomsbury were first published in a postwar context shot through with anxieties about sex, class and England's place in a new Europe.

In February 1949, the *Sunday Times* began its serialisation of Osbert Sitwell's *Laughter in the Next Room*, the fourth volume of his autobiography, with an extract titled 'Bloomsbury in the 1920s'. Sitwell's description of the tones in which 'true citizens of Bloomsbury' uttered such phrases as 'ex-quisitely civilised' or 'How *simply too* extraordinary', fit snugly into the pattern established in the 1930s of Bloomsbury as a clique united in disdain for all outsiders. A few years later, class anxieties about speech were crystallised in Nancy Mitford's essay 'The English Aristocracy', which popularised discussion of 'U and non-U' vocabularies. Even so relatively sympathetic a commentator as Stephen Spender described Bloomsbury as 'almost a cult' in its perceived exclusion of those who were not aligned with its aesthetic and political views.

The 1950s saw the publication of Roy Harrod's biography of Maynard Keynes, two volumes of Bunny's memoirs, Virginia's *A Writer's Diary* and, in the same year that *Old Friends* appeared, a selection of letters between Lytton and Virginia. Bunny had brought out *Two Memoirs* by

Maynard published by Hart-Davis in 1949, one of which, 'My Early Beliefs', gave impetus to F. R. Leavis's acerbic attack on Bloomsbury in *The Common Pursuit* of 1953. The new decade seemed to Clive about to unleash a horde of 'charlatans' who were 'muscling in' on Bloomsbury, though he was willing to assist those writers he deemed serious. Clive also felt a duty to posterity and published his recollections of Roger and Lytton, and his own answer to the question 'What Was Bloomsbury?' in the first half of the decade.

Clive liked Harrod but knew that, whatever the results of his extensive research, his biography could never pass muster with Maynard's friends and made it clear he thought it was too soon for a biography. Harrod's work would serve the general public well enough, and Clive had no doubt it would treat Maynard's economic theories wisely, but it could not satisfy those who had known him intimately. After reading the first part of Harrod's work-in-progress in 1948, Clive told Frances that although there was, rightly, much in Harrod's draft about Lytton, he had got him 'ludicrously wrong'.

When Bunny read a part of his second volume of autobiography, *The Flowers of the Forest*, to Vanessa, Duncan and Clive at Charleston in 1954, Clive warned him that England's repressive sexual climate would not allow Bunny to write as freely as he wished about his own life. That year, the harsh sentences given to Michael Pitt-Rivers, Peter Wildeblood and Lord Montagu of Beaulieu for conspiracy to commit homosexual acts had inspired a movement to reform the laws that had ensnared Oscar Wilde, but they would not be repealed until 1967, following the recommendations of the Wolfenden Report. Antagonism towards 'Bloomsbury' was often couched in language whose homophobic codes could easily be deciphered. Reviewing the proofs of *Old Friends*, Clive took pains to make sure an anecdote about how André Gide had once suspected Clive of interest in a young man he had brought with him to lunch was correctly rendered. Clive did not, he told his publisher, want to be mistakenly assumed to be homosexual.

Harrod felt hamstrung by Maynard's friends and told Clive he wished he had insisted at Charleston on questioning them more, rather than just listening to delightful reminiscences. In his preface, he acknowledged that his portrait of Lytton had necessarily omitted 'a certain quality, highly individual, exciting, strangely compelling, yet elusive, which was manifested in conversation with his friends'. Only some future 'unknown writer of genius' could even attempt the task of capturing this side of one who had been such an important figure in Maynard's life. Harrod was very hurt by Bloomsbury's reaction to his book. Any biographer is a Frankenstein, assembling his creature from whatever parts are available, but Harrod faced the additional challenge of being reviewed by his subject's closest friends. Leonard offended him when he wrote in the *Listener* that the author had made 'inappropriately intimate comments and ask[ed] strings of rhetorical questions'.

Although sensitive to how the public might react to accounts of the private lives of his friends, Clive – who seems never to have discarded even a single postcard he received – also knew that in many cases those friends' lives were integral to an important part of England's cultural history. He was alarmed when Geoffrey Keynes thought the correspondence between his brother, Maynard, and Lytton should be burned, telling Mary he would do whatever he could to prevent that happening. When John Raymond used a scathing 'revaluation' of *Eminent Victorians* as the occasion for an attack on Bloomsbury in the *New Statesman and Nation*, Frances was impressed by how the surviving members of Old Bloomsbury who still attended meetings of the Memoir Club exhibited a 'really rather sublime indifference to what the world thinks of them'.

Leonard was much more concerned because he wanted to control Virginia's posthumous reputation, but Clive was dubious about his brother-in-law's handling of her legacy. When selections from her diary were published in 1953, Clive worried that they would make people angry: 'Were I a young reviewer I couldn't resist having some fun at the expense of the great novelist of the elder generation.' Virginia was, as Leonard said, 'charming, gay and affectionate', but she was also catty, jealous and spiteful. Bunny was astonished when otherwise positive reviews of his memoir and of his novel *Aspects of Love* expressed 'hatred' of the principal figures of Bloomsbury. At the time, conversations were going on with Lytton's brothers about whether his letters (apart from the anodyne ones selected by Leonard and James Strachey for *Virginia Woolf & Lytton Strachey, Letters*) could be published. The intolerance (and illegality) of homosexuality was an obvious bar, but anti-Bloomsbury sentiment was rampant, turning on its head John Rothenstein's plaintive wail that he had never known 'hatreds pursued with so much malevolence over so many years'. Leonard, whom Clive suspected of wanting to ensure that the cream was not skimmed off Virginia's valuable legacy by interlopers such as the American biographer Aileen Pippett, complained to Vita that Clive's and Bunny's memoirs had done 'considerable harm to the reputation of Bloomsbury, and therefore in particular to Virginia's'. After Leonard gave hints of what his own autobiography might contain, Clive anticipated that it would be both 'interesting and disagreeable':

> Doubtless he will sneer in his calm, disobliging way at most of us. And doubtless I shan't particularly enjoy it when he is sneering at me. But then a few pages later he will be sneering at Bertie Russell or Sydney Waterlow or Dadie or Middleton Murry, and I shall enjoy that.

When Leonard's first volume, *Sowing*, appeared in 1960, Clive thought it very good but often inaccurate, objecting in particular to Leonard's saying that he took no interest in music.

One respondent who answered Clive's call for Bloomsbury's detractors to explain what they thought he and his friends stood for was the Catholic convert Arnold Lunn, whose own memoir, *Memory to Memory*, was published shortly after *Old Friends*. Lunn was particularly offended by Bloomsbury's atheism because, as he explained in a long letter to Clive, he saw the denial of God as leading to denial of objective truth, as could be witnessed in Soviet Russia. Lunn's chapter on Bloomsbury adduced Lytton's distortion of the sources he had consulted to write 'Cardinal Manning' in *Eminent Victorians* as an example of the corrosive effect of the milieu in which the writer had flourished.[2] To Lunn, Bloomsbury's abandonment of 'objective standards' in its supposedly shared philosophy, its aesthetics, its writing of history, all could be traced to its cavalier atheism. The 'fake-objectivity' it practised resulted in loose sexual morals as well as the errors, as Lunn saw them, of leftist politics. Lunn had been a supporter of Franco in the Spanish Civil War, though he closed his chapter on Bloomsbury's pernicious effects by paying tribute to the 'splendid young men' who died for 'the Reds' in Spain, like Clive's son. Although the antagonists of Bloomsbury

[2] Holroyd discusses the articles by F. A. Simpson upon which Lunn based his criticism, as well as Lytton's reputation as a historian (423–4).

often framed their attacks in the language of aesthetics, morals or class, a fundamental political difference could usually be discerned beneath the surface.[3]

The rapidly growing interest in the work and lives of Roger, Virginia, Lytton, Morgan and Maynard, in particular, was not only producing opprobrium. Noel Annan's biography of Leslie Stephen, published in 1951, drew parallels between Bloomsbury and the Clapham Sect, a nineteenth-century circle of Evangelical philanthropists of which Virginia and Vanessa's great-grandfather James Stephen had been a member. Clive was in touch with Merle Bevington, an American professor who edited James Stephen's *Memoirs*. Bevington had hoped to bring Clive to Duke University during his 1952 American lecture tour but it could not be arranged, and they met instead when the Bevingtons came to England later that year. American students' and academics' interest in Bloomsbury, largely unaffected by the class-based tensions evident in English discussion of the group, was part of a broader Anglophilia that emerged throughout the 1950s.

For the remainder of his life, Clive fielded requests for information about not only Roger, Lytton and Virginia, but also about Gide, Cocteau and, sometimes, even about himself. He approved of the first serious treatment of his friends when *The Bloomsbury Group*, based upon J. K. Johnstone's Leeds University PhD dissertation, was published in 1954. As Frances Cornford's review in the *TLS* pointed out, this was mostly concerned with literary Bloomsbury, with Virginia, Morgan and Lytton, but Johnstone also attempted to show that G. E. Moore's philosophy was a unifying thread for all Bloomsbury's members. Clive, in the role he assumed more and more often in the 1950s of corrector of the record, argued that as Roger had been of an older generation than the others, he owed nothing to Moore and had disagreed with almost all of the conclusions of *Principia Ethica*.

'Bloomsbury' had already become a careless shorthand, as which it persists, sometimes referring to Charleston, at other times to Virginia, and invariably suggesting there were no more than negligible differences

---

[3]Sometimes it comes out into the open, as when Margaret Thatcher drew a direct line between Bloomsbury's 'rejection of Victorian virtues in their own behaviour' and the Keynesian economics which she blamed for Britain's fiscal crises in the 1970s (Hussey, 'Mrs Thatcher' 8).

among people whose views in fact were quite disparate. Clive's plea in *Old Friends* that writers specify to whom they referred usually fell on deaf ears. Thus, figures as different in their outlook as Clive and Leonard, or Maynard and Morgan, or Vanessa and Bunny could all be subsumed under the rubric of 'Bloomsbury' as a mutual admiration society. Clive succumbed to the 'sheer nonsense' of participation in the BBC's 'mosaic' of memories of Virginia broadcast on 29 August 1956 but he declined subsequent requests, referring the BBC to his memoir as his last word.

Raymond reviewed *Old Friends* in the *Sunday Times*, acknowledging his friendship with its author and several others among Clive's cast of characters. He met the charge that Bloomsbury, like 'freemasons, Jews or Jesuits' had somehow managed stealthily to bend the 'entire Press' to its service by pointing out how critical of one another Clive and his friends had been. Several reviews drew attention to Clive's occasionally negative portrayal of Maynard, whose dogmatism 'made himself ridiculous to those who did not know him well [and] to those he did annoying'. Whether they considered the Bloomsbury group's contributions to have been absorbed into the cultural mainstream, as V. S. Pritchett did, or dismissed them with good riddance, reviewers agreed that Clive's memoir was the record of a bygone era (as memoirs tend, after all, to be). Only the twenty-nine-year-old drama critic Ronald Bryden, writing in *Gemini, the Oxford and Cambridge Magazine*, suggested how Bloomsbury might be regarded from a broader historical perspective, asking what it was that appeared so hostile about 'a string of celebrated first names'. Perhaps it was 'that they make a litany; litanies imply cults; cults suggest cabals, conspiracies, priesthoods. Bloomsbury gets accused of the lot. A cult of first names: my friends before my country, and "Donald said 'Will you come with me, Guy'".'

The defection to Russia in 1951 of Guy Burgess and Donald Maclean (both Cambridge University contemporaries of Julian Bell) reverberated through the era as more details of their story emerged, attaching itself, as Bryden perceived, to suspicion of any group whose questionable moral and aesthetic tastes were taken as signs of unpatriotic betrayal. Bryden ventriloquised the prevailing attitude towards Bloomsbury: 'All those short-haired gels and long-haired fellers, livin' together in studios, paintin' meaningless Frog daubs, writin' salacious Socialist muck.'

The irony was that this English equivalent to the *Quartier Latin*, the 'first English attempt to claim, publicly, communally, as a right, the same freedom of conscience, appearance and behaviour, which artists traditionally have stolen, one by one' appeared to the youth of 1950s England as the 'epitome of respectability'.

45. Things Are Never So Bad but They Might Be Worse

Colin MacInnes, art critic for the *Observer*, wrote Clive a fan letter when *Old Friends* appeared, thanking him for *Art, Civilization* and *Since Cézanne. City of Spades*, the first of MacInnes' celebrated 'London Trilogy' of novels, would shortly be published, exploring a culture Clive knew virtually nothing about. MacInnes had wanted to tell Clive for twenty years that his books had been 'like a key', unlocking a world of modern art he had at first not been able to understand. 'Their delight in painting was so infectious & their explanations . . . an amazing feat of expressing plastic conceptions in clear verbal terms,' which, MacInnes explained, had helped him to 'see paintings in visual, i.e. non-literary terms', destroying 'a merely provincial outlook on art'.

While MacInnes treated him as a respected eminence of the art world, Clive's friend Sir Kenneth Clark was not so kind. He told Bernard Berenson not to bother with *Old Friends*, a book 'as flat as the Duke of Portland's memoirs'. Clark grumbled that Clive's review of *The Nude*, which he considered his best book, showed that he could no longer write. In an otherwise laudatory review, Clive had objected to Clark's use of the platitude 'life-enhancing' in relation to art, believing it too close to the utilitarian view of art's purpose so beloved of committees.

Clive did not dwell on the past, although he might from time to time indulge in 'the exquisite pains of nostalgia', such as were afforded by Francis Carco's book on the *belle époque*, which he reviewed in 1954. Saxon Sydney-Turner, on the other hand, seemed determined to live entirely in the past and went on offering Clive tickets to events in Cambridge that might have been the entertainments of their student years. In 1949, for example, he asked if Clive would like to accompany him to a performance of J. T. Sheppard's translation of *Oedipus Tyrannus*, with Dadie Rylands in the leading role. By 1955, it was clear that Saxon could no longer live alone, even with Barbara's help. When she and Nick had divorced in 1951, Barbara stayed on at 28 Percy Street to look after Saxon, and now moved him into what Clive described as a 'home for decayed gentlemen' (freeing his flat for Vanessa and Duncan to take). Clive's nostalgia was more often prompted by perusal of old letters, or listening to papers delivered to the Memoir Club, but he also indulged it by spending whatever time he could in the company of those works of art he had written about all his life. In March 1953, he took the Golden Arrow to Paris to see 'Le cubisme 1907–14' at the Musée d'Art Moderne, where he was pleased to find in the works by Picasso, Braque, Gris, Delaunay, Marcoussis and Lhote confirmation of his view that the movement 'had already petrified' before the First World War.

Alhough motivated by desire rather than nostalgia, Clive's efforts to recapture his previous happiness with Mary were doomed by her volatile moods. There were times he thought they should stop seeing one another altogether because he always felt on edge that she would fly into a rage if he disagreed with her opinions. Jeremy Hutchinson's recollection that his passionate mother would jump up in the middle of an argument and leave the room, slamming the door behind her, suggests that Clive's experience of Mary's temper was not exaggerated. Clive said Mary simply wanted him to be someone other than he was, and therefore turned against him whenever they began to be happy together, denigrating his 'character and talents' – an insight Mary confirmed by annotating the letter in which Clive expressed this analysis 'Quite true'. But Mary herself was frustrated when Clive withdrew into a protective shell, writing in a letter she probably did not send that she was 'maddened by the unreality' between them after they had sat stiffly together in a restaurant, talking as though they hardly knew one another.

Mary raged at Clive in order to provoke him into telling her what he really felt, angered by what she described as his 'cold Mériméeism' when he would not let her know about his plans to travel abroad. An 'escapade' in Paris in 1952, financed by the dollars Clive had earned in America that year, was a rare moment of harmony between them. Although nearly all of Mary's letters to Clive are apparently lost, interleaved with his to her are a few that might be drafts of her efforts to explain why their relations were so often unhappy. When she tried to apologise for being 'what the French call "nerveuse"', Clive punished her, she said, by 'withdrawing kindness, letters, lunches' until she had learned her lesson. She had come with Jeremy and her grandchildren on a visit to Charleston, when Clive had been so 'warm and affectionate' that his sudden announcement that he was going to Italy without 'coming to see me to give a friendly account of your plans' had enraged her. These breaches were always mended, one way or another, but the escapades gradually ceased. Mary surprised Clive in 1955 when she asked if he would try to discover where her brother was buried in Italy and lay flowers on his grave.[1] He did locate the cemetery but it was too large for him to find the grave. That he even made the attempt is an example, nonetheless, of Clive's unwavering devotion to Mary, who was still thrilling him in 1962, 'so pretty and elegant at seventy'.

The years once more assumed a familiar pattern in the 1950s. Every summer Clive spent a few sacrosanct days with his brother, Cory, watching cricket at Lords, as they had for more than thirty years. When Cory's wife, Violet, died in 1950 Clive was in America, so it was Quentin who received the news, in characteristically oblique fashion, from Cory. His wife's illness, Cory explained, had prevented him from sending some port to Charleston as he had promised. Only on the second page of his letter to Quentin did he mention, almost as an aside, that Violet had in fact died that morning. Clive often regaled his dinner guests with anecdotes about his brother, and to Roland de Margerie, Cory came to epitomise the cartoonist David Low's character Colonel Blimp, whose comic aphorisms were larded with common sense and were a reliable indicator of what 'county families' thought.

After his first trip to America, Clive introduced Douglas and Winnie Gordon to his brother when they were next in England, and from then on Cory always joined Clive to entertain them on their annual visits, Cory happily taking the American visitors on a tour of Montacute or

---

[1] Jim Barnes became a fascist apologist and Italian citizen in 1940. He broadcast and wrote anti-British propaganda during the war (see Claudia Baldoli, *A British Fascist in the Second World War* [Bloomsbury 2014]). Clive dismissed him as 'an intellectual without intellect' (CB/D. Gordon 31 October 1955 UVa).

Stourhead. He and Douglas Gordon jovially disapproved of Clive's libertinism, and in some ways the straitlaced Baltimore lawyer and The Colonel had more in common than Gordon did with Clive. Cory had not stood again for Parliament since losing his seat in 1923, preferring to devote his political energies to the county of Wiltshire, where he became Deputy Lieutenant in 1952. Even as his eyesight failed and his health deteriorated, Cory insisted on keeping his annual traditions with his brother going and when he died in 1961, Vanessa thought that probably it came as a relief to Clive, who had worried when Cory insisted on driving himself and had warned Douglas Gordon against getting into a car with him.

Clive Bell at Charleston, 1955

With his life increasingly centred on Charleston, Clive relied on a room in Barbara Bagenal's flat whenever he was in London, first on Wimpole Street, and later at 18 Percy Street (where Sonia Orwell lived upstairs). Affecting a more cloistered existence than was true, he told

Frances that Quentin and his girlfriend kept him 'in touch with the outer world'. Anne (Olivier) Popham seemed 'to know everyone and everything'. She had worked at the Ministry of Information, was a high-ranking officer in the 'Monuments Men' and, in 1947, joined the Arts Council, where she edited exhibition catalogues. Clive and Vanessa were thrilled when she and Quentin married in 1952.

Within a few years, Angelica's children were joined on visits to Charleston by Quentin and Olivier's (Julian, born in 1952, Virginia in 1955 and Cressida in 1959), Clive gruffly complaining about their noise, but taking Amaryllis Garnett or Julian Bell by the hand after lunch to walk them along the cinder path. The '3 little Bells' began to be noted on his chequebook counterfoils around Christmas time. The family that Vanessa, Duncan and Clive had created at Charleston moved naturally into the continuity embodied in this third generation.

Echoing his pre-war pattern of annual visits to Paris, Clive now travelled south every year to spend January to April on the Côte d'Azur, usually driven there by Barbara in her reliable little car. 'Little Bar' was small in stature, and also childish. 'She did caper rather a lot and once actually announced that she was a little girl of ten,' Janie Bussy told Vanessa. Barbara Bagenal's need to be over-friendly and her constant fussing irked everyone, but sometimes her kindness won over her detractors. 'I was finally even rather melted by Little B,' Janie admitted to Vanessa in 1955, when Barbara and Clive were staying in Garavan, only a few miles from La Souco, while Clive recuperated from an operation that had left him limping. Barbara took the octagenarians Dorothy Bussy and her sister Pippa Strachey on long, slow drives, sometimes across the border to Italy, and when she offered to take two heavy fur coats back to England in her car so that the Strachey women would have less to carry on the plane, Janie was won over.

Still, Barbara's annoying traits threatened often to overdraw the balance of tolerance she built up through caring for Clive. Frances, Janie, Vanessa and others saw that Clive had developed the knack of letting Barbara's endless prattle roll over him, and without her he would not have been able to go for four months every year to the south of France. 'That woman will drive me mad if I have to see much of her,' Vanessa wrote to Angelica in 1960, but Clive's technique with Barbara

of 'extreme benevolence, delicate flattery and total detachment' saved
him from a similar fate.

Picasso and Clive Bell (1950s)

John Richardson has described the atmosphere of Picasso's Cannes
villa, La Californie, in the mid-1950s, where the artist lived with Jacqueline
Roque. Sometimes, when Richardson and Douglas Cooper drove over
from Chateau de Castille, near Avignon, they 'would be summoned
upstairs to Picasso's bedroom for a Chaplinesque parody of a royal levée'
where he pondered which of his 'countless pairs of peculiar trousers' to
wear, and whether the chosen pair would 'go with the multicolored socks
knitted by Clive Bell's girlfriend, Barbara Bagenal'. 'Barbara may be a
nonentity,' Clive told Frances, but she was 'one of the nicest nonentities
in the world, as people as unexpected as Willie Maugham and Douglas
Cooper have discovered.' Staying a night or two at Cooper's villa, where
they met Richardson for the first time in 1955, became a regular stop

on Barbara and Clive's journey, either on their way to Menton or back to England each spring. In Rome in 1955, Clive found he preferred lolling outside cafés, or sightseeing with Barbara to socialising. He was disappointed to find that the streets were hectic with Vespas. Even Paris 'frightens me', he told Cooper, because it was so crowded, but in the south of France there were many old friends, and some newer ones such as Graham Sutherland and his wife Kathleen, within easy reach by car.

In the winter of 1958, Barbara drove Clive to Menton, where he was able to participate in the surrounding society of expatriates and celebrities who had either rented or bought houses on the Mediterranean. Churchill was at Coco Chanel's old villa, La Pausa, about which hordes of journalists gathered when it was learned that the great statesman had fallen ill. The Clarks were staying with Somerset Maugham at the villa he had bought in 1927, La Mauresque, on St-Jean-Cap-Ferrat, and Cocteau was close by at Santo Sospir, his friend Francine Weisweiller's villa, the walls of which he had been gradually 'tattooing' since he first stayed there in 1950. Clive was not much impressed with Cocteau's 'feeble' decorations for the wedding hall at Menton but admired the murals in the Chapelle Saint-Pierre in Villefranche on which his old friend had worked for almost two years. They made plans to see each other in Paris, where Cocteau was at work on a ballet involving 'Doudou', his adoptive son, Edouard Dermit.

To his great pleasure, Cocteau had re-entered Picasso's inner circle by the early 1950s, but it was Douglas Cooper who facilitated an invitation for Clive and Barbara to lunch with Picasso and Jacqueline in 1958. While David Douglas Duncan flitted about the restaurant taking photographs for the book he would publish that year, *The Private World of Pablo Picasso*, they heard all about Picasso's new chateau at Vauvenargues. Clive had annoyed Frances during a weekend party at Maud Russell's Mottisfont estate by boasting about how clever his friends were, about his Légion d'honneur and 'being *tutoyé* by Picasso' (that is, addressed with the familiar 'tu' rather than the more formal 'vous'), so when Clive described what had been for him a wonderful occasion, he was not sure whether Frances would want to hear 'all this about Picasso, but I have nothing else to write about'. Without doubt, seeing Picasso, by whom Clive remained somewhat starstruck, was the chief attraction of his stay in France that year. Surrounded by young people, Picasso and Clive told old Paris stories and Picasso signed a drawing for Barbara that he thought dated from around 1905 or 1906, before he had painted *Les Demoiselles d'Avignon*. 'Nous parlons des peintres de Lascaux,' Picasso quipped, knowing that for the younger members of their party, many of those whom he and Clive remembered so well would indeed seem prehistoric.

Clive and Barbara happened to be staying with Cooper the following year when Jacqueline telephoned, and so another lunch was arranged, this time in Cannes. At La Californie, which Clive could not imagine Picasso would ever actually manage to move from, given his enormous accumulation of works and material, there were 'stunning new pictures' in the studio, the effect of which Clive could not put into words for Vanessa. It is likely these were the many variations on Velazquez's *Las Meninas* that Picasso had begun in 1957, as well as new paintings with Jacqueline as their subject. An annual lunch with Picasso and Jacqueline was now something to look forward to, though in 1960, when Barbara and Clive once again were in Menton, it was spoiled by a 'pertinacious' Asian man, who could speak neither English, French nor Italian, trying to talk to Picasso. The next year, showing Raymond Mortimer the Basilica of St Michael the Archangel, Clive stumbled coming down the steps and broke his leg.

Frances was in Menton then, disoriented by her grief at Ralph Partridge's death the previous December. After his accident, Clive became consumed with self-pity, and Barbara's fussing made Frances despair, yet she also missed their company when she was alone. Raymond did what he could to help, but after he left Clive moved with Barbara to a flat belonging to the painter Humphrey Waterfield, inviting Frances to join them so that she would not be lonely. She moved instead to the Hotel des Anglais, Clive's self-pity – even after his cast had been removed and the doctor had assured him that his leg would be fine – wearing on Frances' nerves. Clive snapped at Barbara, becoming angrier than Frances had ever seen him when her chattering delayed him being helped to their flat's sunny balcony. Even before his accident, Clive at eighty seemed to Frances to have 'stepped quite a long way out of this world into the next'.

The longer one lives, the more one lives with death. Adrian Stephen died in 1948, his wife Karin, by suicide, five years later. Desmond MacCarthy died in Cambridge in 1952, days after receiving an honorary degree there, and Molly died the following year. Matisse, Simon Bussy and Derain all died in 1954. Georges Duthuit told Clive he had heard that Derain was 'jolly to the last', though this seems unlikely given it took the painter three months to die after being knocked down by a car in

Chambourcy. The Memoir Club persisted, patched with new members who included Bunny, Angelica, Frances, Molly and Desmond's son Dermod, and Janie Bussy, but it was haunted by losses, and Frances sometimes thought it should be given a decent burial. In May 1960, Vanessa wrote to her daughter-in-law, Olivier, that 'one does seem to have been involved a good deal with death lately.'

The most shocking blow was the absurd death at fifty-four of Janie Bussy, killed by fumes from a faulty water heater in the bathroom at 51 Gordon Square. The news reached Clive and Barbara in the airport at Lydd in Kent, where they had just arrived from France. Barbara collapsed in grief, Janie and she having grown surprisingly close. Janie's mother, Dorothy, died weeks later, too senile to know she had lost her daughter. Both Clive and Vanessa had for years lamented the way Janie's gifts as a painter and her potential for establishing a life of her own had been cramped and thwarted by the demands made upon her by her parents. Her death, Clive told Raymond, was a 'ghastly tragedy'.

Although he continued to travel, Clive's health had been deteriorating since the mid-1950s, an inexorable decline foreshadowed by recurring

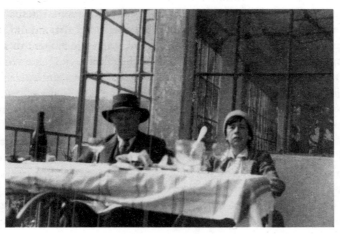

Clive Bell, Janie Bussy

dental problems. He had been 'surly' in 1953 when the Gordons had met him at the National Gallery on their annual European trip and, shortly afterwards, Saxon had told Frances he thought Clive did not look well.

Janice Loeb was considerably upset by a very sad letter from Clive, so rare was it that he ever seemed so hopeless. His usual attitude was that 'things are never so bad but they might be worse', a phrase he repeated often in his correspondence. Eventually, he told Frances, the best one can hope for is that the body be patched and repaired adequately to soldier on. His diary filled, unremarkably, with doctor and dentist appointments, with the names of medicines and lists of ingredients for the special vegetarian meals he had been prescribed.

Soon after the cast on his leg had been taken off in March 1961, Clive suddenly needed urgently to have his appendix removed. Kenneth Clark arranged for him to be flown back from the South of France to London, where he went straight into the London Clinic. It was in that depressing setting that he learned on 7 April (possibly from Quentin) that Vanessa was near death. She had been seriously ill with heart problems in 1959, worrying Clive and Duncan enough that they felt one of them should always be at Charleston with her. Now, Clive telephoned Angelica, who raced as fast as she could to Charleston, only to find that her mother had died shortly before she arrived. That it was Clive, and not Duncan, who had rung her seemed to Angelica of a piece with the deep sense of exclusion she felt throughout her life. It was Barbara who broke the dreadful news to Clive, bereft in his hospital bed. Vanessa was buried in Firle churchyard, as Grace Higgens described in her diary: 'Mr Grant, Angelica, Quentin & I went to the funeral. There was no one there, no clergyman, no flowers except what I and Angelica took, & no service.'

The next week, Clive went to stay at Barbara's house in Iden in East Sussex. At Charleston, Grace burned Vanessa's mattress, her pillows and lots of her clothes. She cleaned the ground-floor bedroom in which Vanessa had peacefully died, readying it for Clive to move into. When he arrived with Barbara on 17 April, Grace noted how frail he looked, the incision in his side still discharging. As word of Vanessa's death spread, the condolences Clive received – from Vita and Harold, Eddy Sackville-West, Julia Strachey, and many others – all remarked on how his own long winter of illness must have made the pain of losing his wife all the more difficult to bear. Frances had just sold Ham Spray, she told Clive, adding to her feeling that the world they had known and loved was now destroyed by sadness.

'Picasso 1900–1935', an exhibition at the Lefevre Gallery in 1953, prompted Bernard Denvir in the *Daily Herald* to compliment those, like Clive, who had 'got wise to Picasso before his boom started'. The journalist pointed out that an early drawing, made when Picasso was a poor student in Barcelona, was priced at £3,000, making the artist's going rate £20 a square inch. Clive and his prescient fellows had been 'on to a gilt-edged thing'. In fact, though, when *Pots et Citron* was sold at Sotheby's in 1962, it did not do as well as Bunny and Angelica Garnett hoped, only meeting the reserve price of £7,000, not the £10,000 or more that Roland Penrose believed would still have been a good investment for a buyer.

By then, Clive had given all of his paintings, with one exception, to Quentin and Angelica. Throughout the 1950s, as Charleston became more expensive to maintain, Clive and Vanessa had started to sell

Clive Bell, Henrietta Garnett, Vanessa Bell

the paintings they had acquired in the previous four decades, both to raise cash for their expenses and to provide a legacy for Quentin's and Angelica's families. The untraced *Village in Provence* by Vlaminck, bought in Paris in 1914, was sold in 1957 for 'a good little sum' of £2,600, to be divided among Clive, Vanessa and Duncan, with shares going to their children. 'Connoisseurship rewarded,' Clive thought. The following year, they sold their other Vlaminck, *Poissy-le-pont*, for £5,400. It had cost £14 at the first post-Impressionist exhibition in 1910.

Clive had agreed with Vanessa that they should hold on to the Juan Gris, *Les Oeufs*, though he worried that if a Labour government came to power in 1959 they would have to pay high capital gains tax on a future sale. He let James Thrall Soby reproduce a photograph of the painting in his catalogue for MoMA's 1958 Gris exhibition, where Soby described it as one of the artist's most important early works because it showed how he had 'worked his way through' post-Impressionism to a 'qualified, cubist definition of form' in paintings such as *Still Life with Book*. Only late in 1963, when Clive's poor health made it too difficult for him to go on living at Charleston, did he instruct the Marlborough Gallery to sell the painting, the last of the personal collection he had lived with since he and Vanessa bought Augustus John's *Childhood of Pyramus* in 1907. *Les Oeufs* netted £9,000 in February 1964 and, three months later, Clive gave notice to Lord Gage that he planned to quit Charleston, and leave Duncan as the sole tenant.

Clive had taken over the tenancy of Charleston when Vanessa died in 1961, but even then the house was in a parlous state. He and Barbara signed a lease on a flat on Great Cumberland Place in 1963 and, in November that year, Barbara bought a house in Rye, anticipating that it would be where Clive spent his final years. Clive told Duncan that merely being driven up or down the rutted lane to Charleston caused him pain from surgical wounds that had healed imperfectly and that the cold, the draughts, leaks and 'general sense of desolation' at Charleston had pushed him to the end of his tether. Requests for information about his old friends, or to speak on the radio about them, were now responded to with a printed card which read 'Mr Clive Bell regrets that, for the present, he is unable to answer letters or receive visitors.' When Grace had an accident in the spring of 1963, it brought home to Clive and Duncan that they would be done for without her. A month later,

Grace confided to her diary, 'I am so tired, I wish I could retire, but I cannot leave Mr Bell & Mr Grant, no one would look after them.'

Notwithstanding, Clive had Barbara to minister to him, and to ensure he was able still to make his annual pilgrimage to France, although a sudden illness of Barbara's in 1962 had unexpectedly thwarted their plans for the annual lunch with Picasso and Jacqueline. In any case, Clive found that the artist's Spanish hours, with lunch at three, did not suit him. Despite her grudging admiration for Barbara's care of Clive, Frances believed that she infantilised him, pulling Clive into an 'atmosphere of nursery physical intimacy' she had first experienced when they were together in Menton in 1961. After dining with Barbara and Clive at the Travellers' Club in June 1964, Frances remarked that he was as he had always been, 'courteous and gentlemanly', turning everyone's service, 'including the negro waiters . . . into an act of special and friendly kindness on their part', but Barbara destroyed the atmosphere when she reminded Clive to put on a therapeutic collar. Bunny had once written that Clive could not 'be happy if he is aware of anyone feeling unhappy in the vicinity. Thus, perhaps for selfish reasons, he does everything to create happiness about him.' But now, this most gregarious of men thought it would be best for everyone if he went into a 'home'.

As Clive entered the final weeks of his life in 1964, old friends came to Charleston to sit with him and talk. Mary came one morning in August, seeing him at Charleston for the last time. Recognising how ill he was, Barbara took Clive to London at the end of the month to see his doctor. Grace expected him back, but he was too ill to return. He entered a nursing home, Barbara coming every afternoon to read to him and prepare a meal. Frances visited and read to him from the *Times*, just as she had in 1962 when his stoicism in the face of illness had impressed her, but now her only wish for her 'dear and affectionate old friend' was that he could die quickly. His cancer was incurable, his body in that wrecked state wrought by medical interventions, and when Leonard visited on 16 September, Clive's eighty-fourth birthday, he could see that Clive was desperately ill. That evening, Clive told Barbara to go out and enjoy herself. He died the next day. Quentin came down from Leeds to see to the cremation of his father's body. There was no ceremony, no resting-place, no memorial.

Epilogue

Soon after Vanessa's death in 1961, the poet and translator Paul Roche left his wife and children in Mexico while he came to Charleston to be with Duncan. Roche, who had been Duncan's 'model, muse, friend and lover', had long studied Duncan's work and set himself the task of choosing what he considered the six best of his paintings. One day, thinking himself alone in the house, Roche was startled when Clive suddenly entered the studio.

> Clive did not move. He looked for a long time, then said: 'I have never seen any of these before. What beauties! Why haven't I seen them at a show? These are some of the best paintings Duncan has ever painted.' My elation knew no bounds. My eye, at last, it seemed, was educated. I boasted of it to Duncan when he came home – and for years afterwards.

The only way to educate the eye, Clive believed, was to look again and again and again at works of art. He could not define what he meant by 'aesthetic emotion' or 'significant form', he could only repeat where he found it, in an effort to create a community of feeling. William Bywater, an American professor of philosophy who wrote *Clive Bell's Eye*, the only monograph ever devoted to his ideas, explained that Clive was 'trying to convey a quality no idea of which is transmitted by language'. Clive, Bywater argued, understood that taste must gradually be reformed before radical aesthetic innovations can be more widely understood. That reformation was Clive Bell's mission.

Quite recently, his ideas about aesthetics have been compared to Nietzsche's Dionysian states and to Georges Bataille's 'given decisive and inexplicable state of mind', elements of which 'cannot be adequately expressed by language'. Although many critics and biographers have casually assumed that Clive often stole his ideas from Roger Fry, a more careful reading of the record reveals that, unlike Fry and very much like Virginia Woolf, Clive believed that the aesthetic emotion evoked by a work of art – any work possessing significant form, in his view – is to some extent a mystical experience which strains language beyond the bounds of what can be explained in words. Like Woolf, Clive was captivated by the ceaseless search for an ineffable 'reality' to which art seemed to give access.

Quentin Bell once described how Clive had been a familiar figure in the lanes and fields of the Firle Estate during and after the Second World War. The aesthete who had caroused with Picasso and Cocteau, who liked nothing better than to imagine himself a Byron in a Venetian palazzo, whom Isadora Duncan had pulled onto her lap at a party in Paris and whose nod of approval could increase an artist's sales at a London dealer (as Augustus John once gratefully noted), was recalled by his son returning from a day's shooting, 'tired and muddy, but content, with his gun, his dog, a brace of pheasants or in hard weather two brace of snipe for the table'.

On the morning after Clive's death, the art critic Nevile Wallis came to Charleston to interview Duncan for a *Sunday Telegraph Magazine* profile. As they talked in brilliant sunshine at the round dining table that Vanessa had decorated in 1952, Wallis sensed no sadness in the atmosphere of the house, but 'rather a zestful continuity which one can believe has marked Charleston's singular *savoir faire* ever since 1916'. The shelves in Clive's study overflowed with his books and exhibition catalogues, as they still do.

Abbreviations

L	*Letters*
Lilly	Lilly Library, Indiana University, MacCarthy Mss.
LS	Lytton Strachey
LSE	London School of Economics
LW	Leonard Woolf
Mellon	The Paul Mellon Centre for Studies in British Art, London UK, GB3010 Benedict Nicolson Archive
MH	Mary Hutchinson
MoMA	The Museum of Modern Art Archives, New York, Margaret Scolari Barr Papers
Morgan	Morgan Library and Museum, New York, Vanessa Bell collection of autograph letters
N&A	*Nation and Athenaeum*
NS&N	*New Statesman and Nation*
NGI	National Gallery of Ireland
Newberry	Newberry Library, Chicago
OM	Ottoline Morrell
Princeton	Princeton University Library, Rare Books and Special Collections,
RF	Roger Fry
Rockefeller	Rockefeller Archive Center , John D. Rockefeller 3rd Papers
Syracuse	Syracuse University Libraries, Special Collections Research Center,
Sx	University of Sussex Special Collections
TCT	The Charleston Trust
TGA	Tate Library and Archive
Trinity	Trinity College, Cambridge, Papers of Arthur Clive Heward Bell
TSE	T. S. Eliot Estate
Trotter	Bell and Hony Family Papers in possession of Graeme Trotter
UoR	University of Reading, Special Collections, Chatto & Windus Archives; Hogarth Press Archives MS 2750
UVa	Albert and Shirley Small Special Collections Library, University of Virginia, Papers of Douglas H. Gordon
VB	Vanessa Bell [used also to denote Vanessa Stephen]
VW	Virginia Woolf [used also to denote Virginia Stephen]

Unless indicated otherwise in the notes, correspondence is quoted from the following sources:

Louisa (Blaikie) Barnes/Clive Bell KCC
Clive Bell/Mary Hutchinson HRC
Clive Bell/Frances Partridge KCC
Clive Bell/Vanessa Bell Sx
Clive Bell/Virginia Woolf Sx
Vanessa Bell/Clive Bell TGA
Janice Loeb/Clive Bell KCC
J. Thoby Stephen/Clive Bell Sx (copies; originals are at the Huntington Library, CA)

Notes

6 *The encounter . . . skin*	Smith & Walasek, 27
8 *Degas . . . mistress*	Q. Bell, *Elders*, 29

2 Cambridge

9 *'like the dew . . . rough coat'*	VW, 'Sketch', 136
9 *'astonishing . . . country squire*	VW, 'Old', 187
10 *'ready to strike . . . great cities'*	TCT
10–11 *'you must manage . . . same language'; 'Never use . . . exam'*	G. M. Trevelyan/CB, nd, Sx
11 *'The all-round . . . smug'*	Hugh, 9
11 *not danced much*	?17 June 1900, VW, *L* vol. 1, 34
11 *'with a great . . .Velasquez'*	LW, *Autobiography*, vol. 1, 117
12 *'against . . . firm'*	Lubenow, 35
12 *Thoby's lack . . . him*	LW/LS, 2 January 1903, Spotts, 29
12 *'were not . . . the Society'*	Lubenow, 42
12 *'always ready . . . of talk'*	VW, 'Old', 189
12 *Edwardian rebellion*	Taddeo
12 *'beginning . . . Reason'*	LS/G. E. Moore, 11 October 1903, Levy, 17
12 *'wounded and bitter'*	Levy, *Moore*, 251
12 *'There were . . . about hunting'*	LW, *Autobiography*, vol. 1, 80
12 *favourite Apostle'*	Ibid., vol. 2, 98
12–13 *'seemed to . . . the intellectuals'*	MacCarthy, *Memories*, 175
13 *'a youth . . . cake of life'*	Ibid., 174–5
13 *Strachey . . . offender*	5 September 1901, Spotts, 19
13 *family . . . carpet*	Q. Bell, *Elders*, 34
13 *'conscientious objections'*	Hugh, 19
13 *'I know . . . intolerance'*	Stephen, 3
13–14 *'a good . . . difficulties'*	*Cambridge Review*, 30 November 1899,125–6
14 *'That in . . . interlude'*	Ibid., 4 December 1902, 121
14 *happy . . . Counsel*	T. Greg/CB, 7 January 1903, KCC

14 *One afternoon . . . Art Gallery*	Smith & Walasek, 11
15 *'Now will . . . perpetual*	*Working Men's College Journal,*
sovereign'; 'To men . . . at once'	June 1902, 314–15
16–17 *'purely pagan . . . ideal is'*	Louisa (Blaikie) Barnes/CB, 30 November?1902
17 *'almost a pro-Boer?'*	Louisa (Blaikie) Barnes/CB, 29 March?1903
17 *'rather nice'; 'lower than beasts'*	J. Thoby Stephen/CB, nd

3 A Brace of Partridges

18 *'Dear Mr Bell . . . one subject'*	10 September 1902, Marler, 8
18 *'visited . . . seen'*	Spalding, *VB*, 32
18 *'see . . . manage'*	22 April 1900, VW, *L*, vol. 1, 31
18–19 *'quite intoxicated . . . am sure'*	26 April 1900, ibid., 32
19 *'By the . . . extravagant'; 'late . . . Roman'; 'Where . . . cant'*	J. Thoby Stephen/CB, nd, Sx
19 *'religious . . . code'*	LW, *Autobiography*, vol. 1, 96
19 *'an eternal . . . hypocrites'*	J. Thoby Stephen/CB, nd, Sx
19 *'kindness and self-restraint'*	Louisa (Blaikie) Barnes/CB, 29 March 1903
19 *'converted . . . art'*	Spalding, *VB*, 37
20 *'a revolution . . . modernity'*	TCT
20 *small room . . . Caillebotte's collection*	Roe, 7
20 *'I know . . . as you do'*	Louisa (Blaikie) Barnes/CB, 15 March?1903
20 *'lofty . . . religion'*	Louisa (Blaikie) Barnes/CB, nd
20 *'made a fuss . . . allowed'*	Louisa (Blaikie) Barnes/CB, 11 February?1903, KCC
20 *'oxygen' . . . 'asphyxiated soul'*	Louisa (Blaikie) Barnes/CB, 1 March?1903
20 *'I was answering . . . explicit'*	Louisa (Blaikie) Barnes/CB, 26 April?1903
21 *'much interest . . . help'*	Louisa (Blaikie) Barnes/CB, 27 July?1902

21 *'when I'm weary . . . really love'*   Louisa (Blaikie) Barnes/CB, 26 April?1903

21 *'how the noblest . . . Holiness'*   Louisa (Blaikie) Barnes/CB, 1 March?1903

21 *'talk quite freely . . . was feeling'*   VW, 'Sketch', 139

22 *'the agonized . . . beyond recognition'*   T. Greg/CB, 13 November 1903, KCC

22 *'An ode . . . depressed'*   Ms of Exercise Book Containing Juvenilia, Trinity 4/45

22 *'The distant land . . . disappeared'*   Notebook, Trinity, Bell, II.D

22 *'You are . . . really?'*   Louisa (Blaikie) Barnes/CB, 12 June?1903

4   *Paris*

23 *'Instead . . . sights'*   'Paris 1904', Trinity, 1/8

24 *'without . . . opinion'*   Goff, 54

24 *'still the Paris . . . Naturalists'*   'Paris 1904', Trinity, 1/8

24 *In April . . . returned*   Roe, 75

25 *'The meeting . . . if it does'*   LS/LW, 18 April 1904, Levy, 28

25 *'grand meeting'*   Ibid., 29 April 1904, Levy, 28

25 *'Tintoret's . . . doubt'*   J. Thoby Stephen/CB, nd

25 *'My opinion . . . literature'*   Ibid.

25 *'incomparably . . . Titian'*   Ruskin, 11

25 *'ultimate . . . faith'*   J. Thoby Stephen/CB, nd

26 *wryly wondered . . . father*   Ibid.

26 *'These . . . abstruse'*   15 May 1900, in Holroyd, 62

26 *'a sort . . . critic'*   Holroyd, 84

26 *Bellini . . . forerunner*   Fry, *Bellini*, 30

26 *'adulation . . . But . . . master'*   J. Thoby Stephen/CB, nd

26 *'grieved . . . sculpture'*   Ibid.

26 *'rigid . . . isn't'*   LS/LW, 13 January 1904, Levy, 21

27 'Your little . . . here'   VB/M. Snowden, 2 May 1904,
                                                Marler, 16
27 'a real Bohemian . . . a piece'   ?6 May 1904, *L*, vol. 1, 140
27 'We have been . . . London   VB/CB, 11 May 1904
surroundings'
27 'one Blanche . . . uncommonly   J. Thoby Stephen/CB, May 1904
good'
27 'nugatory'   J. Thoby Stephen/CB, nd
27 'three good pictures'; 'merely   J. Thoby Stephen/CB, June 1904
filth'; 'last horror'
27 'scrag . . . Impressionism'   'Paris 1904', Trinity, 1/8
28 'contented . . . they live'   Bennett, *Journal*, 22 June 1904
28 'were anything . . . Wilde'   'Paris 1904', Trinity, 1/8
28 *In Pont-Aven . . . studio*   Spalding, *VB*, 42
28 *privilege . . . showed him*   Benington, 94
28 'bewildered . . . Vuillard'   Ibid., 92
29 'lost . . . of art'   Ibid., 96
29 'have got . . . universe';   'Paris 1904', Trinity, 1/8
'unrighteous . . . responsibility'; 'of
getting . . . complications'

<hr/>

5 Vanessa

<hr/>

30 'unique . . . England'   *Burlington Magazine*, February
                                                1905, 341
30 'general effect . . . before'   LS/LW, 16 July 1905, Levy, 49
30 'lovely . . . sea'   VW, *Passionate*, 229
30 'pompous & dull'   Ibid., 233
30 'her last . . . loyalty'   VB/CB, January 29?1905
31 'all painting . . . able to say'   VB/M. Snowden, 11 January
                                                1905, Marler, 29
32 '& we . . . one!'   VW, *Passionate*, 249
32 'He seems . . . finance it'   LS/LW, 3 April 1905, Levy, 61
32–3 'parental . . . productions'   Q. Bell, *VW*, vol. 1, 205–6

34 *'very small . . . group'* | *Cambridge Review*, 26 October 1905, 31

34 *'OXON . . . Monet'* | *Cambridge Review*, 9 November 1905, 65–6

35 *'politeness . . . neutral ground'* | VB/CB, June 1905 [my dating], Marler, 35–7

35 *'platitudinous . . . profile* | CB/LS, 20 July 1905, BL

35 *'purely Cambridge'* | LS/LW, 20 June 1905, Levy, 69

35 *'really . . . mystery'; 'he's not . . . Goth'* | LS/LW, 4 July 1905, Levy, 73

35 *'His character . . . layers'* | LS/B. Swithinbank, 1 July 1905, Levy, 71

36 *'his frightened . . . in love'* | LS/LW, 4 July 1905, Levy, 73

36 *'armfuls . . . duskiness'* | CB/LS, 20 4 July 1905, BL

36 *'small . . . lust'* | LS/LW, 4 July 1905, Levy, 73

36 *'surrender'* | CB/LS, 11 August 1905, BL

36 *'very sorry'* | VW/V. Dickinson, 27 August 1905, *L*, vol. 1, 206

36 *'unless . . . other'* | VB/M. Snowden, 13 August 1905, Marler, 34

36–7 *'horrible . . . happiness'* | VW, 'Sketch', 192

37 *'I could . . . fly'* | VB/M. Snowden, 13 August 1905, Marler, 34

37 *'Whistler incarnate'* | Louisa (Blaikie) Barnes/CB, 9 September 1905

37 *'From one . . . contempt'* | Spurling, *Unknown*, 296

37–8 *'rather well'; 'all these artists . . . degraded'* | CB/LS, 25 November 1905, BL

38 *'poitrinaire'* | LS/LW, 4 July 1905, Levy, 73

38 *'one half . . . British'* | VW/V. Dickinson, July 1905, *L*, vol. 1, 201

38 *'fiery discussion'; 'arranging . . . intellect'* | LS/LW, 2 February 1906, Levy, 98

38–9 *Taff Vale . . . members* | Dangerfield, 184

39 *'froggy doctor'* | J. Thoby Stephen/CB, February 1906

39 *Schomberg . . . State*	A. Schomberg/CB, 16 February 1906, KCC
39 *'practically . . . Forain'*	J. Thoby Stephen/CB,?February 1906
39–40 *Pollock enjoyed . . . ever read*	J. Pollock/CB, 16 February 1906, KCC
40 *'in love . . . ultimately'*	Holroyd, 133
40 *interested . . . there*	LS/DG, 20 February 1906, TGA
40 *'feel . . . much'*	DG/LS, 1 March 1906, TGA
40 *Bell returned . . . Friday Club*	VW/V. Dickinson, 27 April 1906, *L*, vol. 1, 225
40 *'It's . . . Sodom'*	LS/LW, 18 May 1906, Berg
40 *'a complete . . . French'; 'has . . . harmony'; 'When . . . endurance'*	'Strenuous Enthusiasm', *Cambridge Review*, 31 May 1906, 432–3
40–1 *'long lecture . . . art is'*	VB/M. Snowden, 15 March 1903, Marler, 10
41 *'behaved . . . possession'; 'affairs of the heart'*	VW/V. Dickinson,?June 1906, *L*, vol. 1, 227
41 *'rather . . . illiterate'; 'much . . . else'*	VB/CB, 30 July 1906, Marler, 40
41 *'to marry . . . horrible'*	Dunn, 102
41 *'drag'*	VB/CB, 18 August 1906
42 *'abominably . . . gentility'; 'true colours . . . up to date'*	LS/LW, 19 September 1906, Levy, 108
42 *'If by . . . the family!'*	Ibid.
42 *'dismantled . . . Museum'*	J. Thoby Stephen/CB, 17 September 1906
43 *Virginia read . . . her impressions*	VW, *Passionate*, 341–5
43 *'in . . . carriage'*	Ibid., 318
43 *'filthy . . . hostess'*	J. Thoby Stephen/CB, nd
43 *Vanessa wrote . . . England*	VB/CB, 24 October 1906
43 *'would . . . good'*	Spalding, *VB*, 59
43 *'I think . . . bad'*	Ibid., 60
44 *'I can't . . . business'*	VB/CB, 7 November 1906, Marler, 44

44 *'enema'*	VW/V. Dickinson, 14 November 1906, *L*, vol. 1, 244
44 *'and then . . . for you'*	VW/V. Dickinson, 16 November 1906, *L*, vol. 1, 246
44 *'love . . . unselfish nature'*	VW/V. Dickinson, 19 November 1906, *L*, vol. 1, 247
45 *'A wedding-robe . . . a bier'*; *'bringer . . . goodness'*	LS/LW, 26 November 1906, Levy, 115
45 *'has no profession . . . well off'*	Kitty Maxse/Susan Lushington, 27 November 1906
45 *unselfish . . . friend*	M. Snowden/CB, 30 November 1906, KCC
45 *'not only . . . many things'*	VW/Nelly Cecil,?2 December 1906, *L*, vol. 1, 256
45 *'dangerous'*	VW/M.Vaughan,17 December 1906, *L*, vol. 1, 265
46 *'happier . . . could be'*	VB/Madge Vaughan, 11 December 1906, Marler, 46
46 *'terrible task'*	LS/LW, 5 December 1906, Berg
46 *'rigidity'*; *'Dear . . . Clive?'*	LS/CB, 25 November 1906, Sx
46 *'Henceforth . . . conventions'*	CB, *Old*, 31

6 Virginia

51 *'absolutely . . . desolation'*; *'desire to copulate'*	Spater & Parsons, 53
51 *'wildly in love'*; *'She is . . . the Goth'*	LW/LS, 30 July 1905, Spotts, 98–9
51 *'a growing . . . relations'*	Hynes, 200
52 *'went . . . Suffrage'*	CB, *Old*, 136
52 *'universal buggery'*	LS/DG, 2 May 1907, TGA
52 *'rich . . . barbaric'*	VW/V. Dickinson, 2 January 1907, *L*, vol. 1, 274
52 *'When I . . . eyesight'*	VW/V. Dickinson,?30 December 1906, *L*, vol. 1, 273
52 *he wondered . . . if she did*	LS/LW, 6 February 1907, Berg

53 'quite dreadful . . . superior Thoby'	Edel, Henry, 392
54 'a new . . . debarred'	VW, Congenial, 38
54 'three-cornered . . . affair'	Dunn, 112
54 'turned . . . done'	VW/Gwen Raverat, 22 March 1925, L, vol. 3, 172
54 'a worshipper without'	VW/CB, February 1907, L, vol. 1, 282
54 'her left . . . crest'	VW/CB, 22 March 1907, L, vol. 1, 290
55 'come . . . Louvre'; 'What . . . Adrian'	Spalding, DG, 62
55 'various . . . paint'	VW/V. Dickinson, 12 April 1907, L, vol. 1, 291
55 favourable . . . company	CB/LS, 9 April 1907, BL
55 Raymonde . . . later	Richardson, vol. 2, 29–30
55 Géry . . . Louvre	Ibid., 20
55 At André . . . modernist art	Ibid., 21–4
55–6 'politically . . . impact'	Leighten, 610
56 'showed . . . art'	Spalding, DG, 60
56 'busily . . . Renoir'	Rutter, Art, 41
56 specialised . . . critical	Bullen, 6
56–7 Clive asked . . . idle	CB/LS, 6 May 1907, BL
57 'face . . . Friday Club'	VB/JMK, 5 December?1907, Morgan
57 'were somewhat . . . love'	LS/LW, 11 January 1907, Berg
57 'there . . . tousled'	LS/LW, 2 May 1907, Berg
57 'one important respect'	CB/LS, 30 July 1907, BL
57 Vanessa enjoyed . . . Virginia	Holroyd, 194
57 'wild sprightly couple'; 'The drawing . . . table!'	Ibid., 193
57 'all . . . scheme'	VW, 'Old', 195
58 'little . . . guessed'	VW/V. Dickinson, 2 Jan 1907, L, vol. 1, 275
58 'discussion . . . knowledge'; 'clever young man'	CB/VW, 7 August 1908
58 'seditious remarks'	VB/VW, 27 August 1909, Berg

59 *attempted . . . yellow dress*	VB/M. Snowden, 7 June 1908, TGA
59 *'conventionalities'*	VB/VW, 5 August 1907, Marler, 55
59 *'thought . . . feet'*	VB/VW, 27 December 1909, Berg
59 *'Wiltshire whore'*	CB/VW, 30 December 1910, Berg
59 *'I consulted . . . gent'*	LS/DG, 20 February 1908, TGA
60 *'the most . . . know'*	CB/VW, 11 August 1907
60 *'If only . . . perfect'*	LS/LW, 6 February 1908, Berg
60 *'Yellow & Green'*	CB/VW, 25 January 1908
61 *'laden with meaning'*	VW, *Voyage*, 326
61 *'screams all day'*	CB/VW, 13 April 1908
61 *'the pretty . . . mistake'*	Ibid.
61 *accidental . . . regiment*	Smith & Walasek, 14
61 *'advantages . . . copulation'*	VB/CB,?25 June 1910
62 *'Semen . . . good'*	VW, 'Old', 195–6
62 *more productive . . . birth*	Shone, *Portraits*, 27
62 *'made it . . . characteristic'*	VB/CB,?25 June 1910
62 *'house of all the deaths'*	Edel, *Henry*, 392
62 *speechless . . . Adam Bede*	CB/LS, 22 August 1908, BL
62 *'in the nursery'*	VB/VW, 12 August 1908, Berg
62 *'deleting . . . prose'*	H. Lee, 231
62 *'showing . . . bad'*	VW/CB, 15 April 1908, *L*, vol. 1, 325
63 *'music-halls . . . either'*	CB/VW, 18 April 1908
63 *'terrible . . . devil'*	VW/LS, 28 April 1908, *L*, vol. 1, 328
63 *'intimacy . . . life'*	CB/VW, 3 May 1908
63 *'Tormented . . . sentences'*	CB/VW, 7 May 1908
63 *'It seems . . . sex'; 'their . . . words'*	VW, 'Dialogue', 326
63 *'achieve[d] the heights'*	CB/VW, 3 May 1908
63 *'blue devils'*	VB/M. Snowden, 26 September 1908, TGA
64 *'I can't . . . if I did'; 'The robust . . . patronising tone'*	CB/VW, 11? May 1908

64 *'phantom . . . reservations'* — VW/CB, May 1908, *L*, vol. 1, 334

64 *'At lunch . . . beast would'* — VB/VW, 26 August 1908, Berg

64 *'overpowering . . . male'* — CB/VW, 27 August 1908

64 *'rarefied culture'* — VB/VW, 30 July 1908, Marler, 64–5

64–5 *'or are they too private?'* — VB/VW, 8 August 1908, Berg

65 *'one . . . epistles'* — VB/VW, 7 August 1908, Berg

65 *'into . . . mind'* — CB/VW, 7 August 1908

65 *'by sheer . . . interpreter'* — CB/VW, 3 August 1908

65 *'power . . . reality'* — Dunn, 142

65 *'the next . . . genius'* — CB/VW, 3 August 1908

65 *'splinter . . . pages'* — CB/VW, 23 August 1908

65 *'light . . . steel'* — VW, *Lighthouse*, 51

65 *'to . . . grasp'* — VW/CB, 28 August 1908, *L*, vol. 1, 362

66 *like Lytton . . . Adrian* — VB/VW, 11 August 1908, Marler, 67

66 *'I must . . . fate'* — CB/VW, August 1908

66 *'that he . . . clever'* — VW, *Passionate*, 384

66 *screamed . . . Perugia* — Q. Bell, *VW*, vol. 1, 139

66 *postcard . . . 1908* — 15 May 1935, *L*, vol. 5, 394

66 *'spent . . . line'* — CB/S. Sydney-Turner, 17 September 1908, Sx

66–7 *'enthusiasm . . . Cambio'* — Shone, *Portraits*, 27

67 *'like . . . wind-storm'* — CB/LS, 19 September 1908, BL

67 *'best . . . sex'* — CB/LS, 9 September 1908, BL

67 *'little . . . England'* — LS/LW, 8 October 1908, Spotts, 139

67 *surprised . . . married Virginia* — LS/LW, 29 October 1908, Levy, 164

67 *'They . . . remark'* — Morrell, *Study*, 120–1

67 *'gesticulating . . . approving'* — Ibid., 121

67 *'depressing . . . terrific one'* — LS/LW, 29 May 1907, Levy, 128

68 *100 guineas* — CB/LS, 3 June 1908, BL

68 *'Those . . . anarchist'* — Bullen, 49

68 *'horrid sordid'* — LS/LW, 29 May 1907, Levy 129

68 *'remarkable . . . engaged'*   VB/CB, 29 November [1908]
68 *'the baby . . . time'*   CB/VW, 30 December 1908
68 *Virginia . . . Fitzroy Square*   VW/CB, 25 December 1908, *L*,
                                         vol. 1, 37
69 *'revealed . . . association'*   Playreading Society Minute
                                         Book, KCC
69 *'I once . . . of things'*   H. Lee, 240
69 *'unsay'*   CB/LS, 19 February 1909, BL
69 *'most daring . . . present'*   MacGibbon, 64
69 *'Our views . . . I think'*   Q. Bell, *VW*, vol. 1, 209
71 *'How . . . night?'*   Ibid., 210
71 *'Your objection . . . boldness'*   VW/CB,?7 February 1909, *L*,
                                         vol. 1, 373
71 *'beautiful grey . . . nature of*   CB/VW, nd
genius'*
71 *two geniuses*   CB, *Old*, 94
72 *'cannibal'*   VW/CB, 19 February 1909, *L*,
                                         vol. 1, 386
72 *'that remarkably . . . writer'*   CB/VW, 11 April 1909
72 *'grave defect . . . facts'*   A. Clutton Brock, *Shelley: The
                                         Man and the Poet* (revised
                                         edn)*Athenaeum*, 18 December
                                         1909, 753–4
72 *'elder magazines'*   Pound, 690
72 *'staid . . . pedantic'*   R. O'Conor/CB, 5 April 1909,
                                         NGI
73 *'something . . . Cambodgian'*   R. O'Conor/CB, nd, NGI
73 *'new fangled . . . criticizes'*   R. O'Conor/CB, 30 December
                                         1910, NGI
73 *'we . . . alike'; 'no splendour . . .* CB/LS, 22 October 1909, BL
ravished'*
73 *'oppressed . . . weight'*   VB/VW, 10 April 1909, Marler,
                                         88
73 *'bundle of tempers'*   VW/CB, 13 April 1909, *L*, vol.
                                         1, 391
73–4 *Mrs Ross . . . garden was*   'Paris 1904', Trinity, 1/8
74 *'Who . . . Barnes'*   VB/LS, 30 May 1909, BL

74 *a routine . . . bedtime*	VB/M. Snowden, 11 May 1909, TGA
74 *'fat . . . invasion'*	VB/LS, 28 April 1909, Marler, 83
74 *'inclined . . . even'*	VB/M. Snowden, 18 May 1909, TGA
74 *When Walter . . . 'primitives'*	W. Lamb/CB, 15 May 1909, Sx
74–5 *'delicious'; play . . . stage*	CB/VW, 28 December 1909
75 *'To V. S. . . . Book'*	'Poetic Tribute', *Canvas*, 48 (Spring 2017), 16–17
75 *grumpily . . . infuriating Virginia*	Hall, 268, n2
75 *'They're all . . . house'*	LS/DG, 4 April 1910, TGA
76 *introduced . . . Clive's wife*	CB/S. Saxon-Turner, 2 April 1910, Sx
77 *'the savages . . . feeling'*	CB/VW, 6 June 1910
77 *'how . . . give me'*	VW/CB, 6 June 1910, *L*, vol. 1, 425
77 *'depression . . . yours'*	CB/VW, 6 June 1910
77 *'the Goat . . . considered'*	VB/CB, 23 June 1910, Marler, 93
77 *'a kind . . . lunatics'*	Q. Bell, *VW*, vol. 1, 164
78 *'meditating . . . Dolphin'*	Dunn, 123–4
78 *'strange . . . jealousies'*	CB/LS, 9 August 1908, BL
78 *'four . . . eyes'*	VB/CB,?25 June 1910
78 *'to whom . . . things'*	VW/CB, 4 September 1910, *L*, vol. 1, 434
78 *'To speculate . . . bed'*	CB/VW, 6 September 1910
79 *'get . . . all'*	VB/VW, nd, Berg
79 *'I should . . . thoughts abroad'*	CB/LS, nd [17 April 1910], Levy, 204
79 *'felt . . . gentleman'*	Hale, 124
79–80 *'Do you . . . contempt'*	CB/LS, nd [17 April 1910], Levy, 205
80 *'that . . . letter'*	VW/VB,?1 May 1910, *L*, vol. 1, 424
80 *'position . . . treatment'; 'abused'*	VW/VB, 24 June 1910, *L*, vol. 1, 429

7 Roger

81 *'terrifying . . . grasp'*	Giachero, 119
82 *'already . . . revolutionaries'*	CB, *Old*, 80
82 *'taking . . . stores'*	Spalding, *RF*, 127
82 *'ended . . . tickling'*	Diamand, 27
83 *'peculiar genius'*	Spalding, *RF*, 116
83 *'the High . . . before'*	Hoeniger, 145
83 *'Painters . . . 1970s'*	Ibid., 146
83 *'for convenience Byzantinism'*	Sutton, 300
83 *'proto-Byzantines'*	Bullen, 46
84 *'one of . . . talent'*	Ibid., 18
84 *'got rather . . . lately'*	VW, *RF*, 320
84 *'imaginative life . . . actual life'*	RF, 'An Essay', 20
84 *'ends in themselves'*	Ibid., 29
84 *'unity . . . kind'*	Ibid., 31
84 *'emotional . . . design'*	Ibid., 33
84 *'a new . . . poetry'*	RF, 'Introductory Note', Reed, 76
84 *'critic . . . tradition'*	RF, 'Oriental', 225
85 *'first . . . Indépendants'*	Wilcox, 1
85 *'were . . . London'*	Bullen, 9
85 *mayor . . . tourists*	Ibid., 11
85 *'the heresy . . . the present'*	Ibid., 80
85 *'You may . . . the artist'*	Ibid., 89
85 *'more primitive . . . realism'*	Ibid., 92
85 *'good . . . pictures'*	CB/VW, 22 August 1910
85 *discussed . . . Duncan*	CB/VW, 23 August 1910
86 *'in that . . . of art'*	VB/CB, 9 October 1910, Marler, 96
86 *25,000 people*	Altshuler, 85
86 *'a huge . . . Philistinism'*	Sutton, 337
86 *'aesthetic Bolshevism'*	VW, *RF*, 321
87 *'good . . . winner'*	MacCarthy, 'Post-Impressionists', 176
87 *'stumbled . . . situation'*	'The Grafton Gallery-I', *The Nation*, 19 November 1910, Reed, 86
87 *'reminded . . . asylum'*	MacCarthy, *Memories*, 183

87 'Their interest . . . asset'   VW, *RF*, 126
87 'a kind of freedom'   Bullen, 35, n3
87 'it was . . . be oneself'   Giachero, 130
88 'a lot . . . angry'   VW/V. Dickinson, 27 November
                                       1910, *L*, vol. 1, 440
88 'sharp . . . bed'   CB/VW, 6 September 1910
88 'fine . . . blunt'   *Athenaeum*, 3 December 1910,
                                       696
88 'nightmares . . . mad-house'   CB/VW, 25 December 1910
88 'given up . . . forms'   VW/CB, 29 December 1910, *L*,
                                       vol. 1, 446
88 'much sturdier'   VW/CB, 29 December 1910, *L*,
                                       vol. 1, 445
88 decoration . . . room   *Athenaeum*, 7 January 1911,
                                       19–20
88 'the younger . . . swampy places'   *Athenaeum*, 4 February 1911, 135
89 'dimly . . . particular'   *Athenaeum*, 8 July 1911, 51
89 'historically . . . expressed'   *Athenaeum*, 7 January 1911, 7–8
89 'sought . . . life'   *Athenaeum*, 18 February 1911,
                                       182–3
89 'Old Masters at the Grafton   *Nation*, 7 October 1911, 13–14
Galleries'
89 'blessed . . . unnecessary'   *Athenaeum*, 4 February 1911,
                                       139–40
90 Sydney . . . socialism   S. Waterlow/CB, 12 February
                                       1911, Sx
90 'New Renaissance'; 'ultimate . . . Sketchbook used as a notebook,
things'   GB 70, TGA 8010/2/413
90 Sydney . . . circles   S. Waterlow/VW, 30 March 1912,
                                       Berg
90 'in or . . . changed'   VW, 'Mr. Bennett', 320
90 'to discover . . . of sight'   'Post-Impressionism', 1 May
                                       1911, *Fortnightly Review*, Reed,
                                       100
90 'incubus . . . correspondence'   Ibid., 105
91 'little magazines'   Scholes and Wulfman, 73
91 'Art is . . . world'   Murry, 9

91 *'which . . . mysticism'*	Ibid., 10
91 *'not . . . lives'*	Ibid., 12
91 *'ideas . . . vitality'*	Carter, 36
91–2 *'men suddenly . . . at hand'*	*Athenaeum*, 7 October 1911, 428–9
92 *'ein punkt'; 'shift . . . ideas'*	D. MacCarthy/CB,?September 1912, Lilly
92 *'much worse . . . with Vanessa'*	Holroyd, 237

8 *A Hornets' Nest*

93 *'had . . . not Clive'*	H. Hony/Anne Hony, 2 March 1911, Trotter
93 *'You will . . . another name'*	H. Hony/Charles Hony, nd, Trotter
95 *'Clive gave . . . Granny'*	VB/VW, 6 April 1911, Berg
95 *'superbly Byronic'*	CB/VW,13 April 1911
95 *Kariye Camii . . . Ottomans*	Sutton, 347
95 *'very pretty . . . had happened'*	Giachero, 138
95 *'silly things'*	CB/VW, 17 April 1911
95 *'the possibility . . . intimate'*	CB/VW,?Feb/March 1911
95 *'If this . . . easy!'*	VB/RF, 15 November 1911, Reid, 127
96 *fished out of the river*	Waterlow, 20–22 March, 1912
96 *'If . . . possible'*	VB/CB, 9 October 1911
96 *'legitimate . . . Dolph'*	VB/CB, 11 October 1911
96 *'nice . . . flesh'*	VB/CB, August 1913
96 *'looked . . . a time'*	CB/VW, 12 January 1911
96 *'managed'; 'more beautiful . . . genius'*	CB/VW, 25 January 1911, Berg
96 *'little niche'*	CB/VW, 3 April 1911
96 *'blackened . . . bitterness'*	VW/VB,?25 July 1911, *L*, vol. 1, 471
97 *'perfectly absurd'*	Hall, 173
97 *Waterlow denied*	S. Waterlow/CB, 1 August 1911, Sx
97 *'seemed . . . preserve'*	Hall, 173

| 97 *'hornets' nest'* | VW/VB 21 July 1911 *L*, vol. 1, 469 |

9 *Leonard*

98 *'possibly . . . Reconciliation'*	Spalding, *DG*, 105
98 *really important*	CB/LS, 21 March 1912, C-W
99 *teasing . . . Wight*	VB/CB, 18 January 1912
99 *Molly found . . . painting*	M.MacCarthy/CB, 27 July 1912, Sx
99 *'moral'*	VB/VW, 18 September 1912, Berg
99 *'not . . . friends'; 'vital'*	Molly MacCarthy/CB, 27 July 1912, Sx
99 *'always . . . have it'*	CB/Desmond MacCarthy, nd, TGA
99 *'glad . . . in him'; 'whole . . . pattern'*	Cecil, 135
100 *'what . . . modernism'*	CB/Molly MacCarthy, 17 May 1912, Sx
100 *'very . . . woman'*	CB/Molly MacCarthy, 31 December 1912, Sx
100 *'Evidently . . . than I'*	CB/M. MacCarthy, 14 May 1912, Sx
100 *'rather . . . Jews'*	H. Lee, 316
100 *'point blank'*	VB/VW 2 June 1912 Marler 117
100 *'not . . . jealous'*	CB/VW nd
100 *'penniless Jew'*	VW/V. Dickinson 4 June 1912 *L* VI 500
100 *both were angry*	Marler 118n3
100 *believe he appreciated . . . husband could*	CB/VW Tuesday nd
101 *'what . . . lover too'*	CB/VW nd qtd. H. Lee 317
101 *'made . . . love'*	VW/CB 13 August 1912 *L* v2 1
101 *'copulating . . . home'*	VW/VB 5 March 1928 *L* v3 467
101 *'strange . . . situation'*	Q. Bell, *VW* VI 176
102 *'rather . . . place'*	VB/VW 2 September 1912 Berg
102 *'No one . . .painters'*	VB/VW 8 September 1912 Berg

102 *'retired . . . the cause'*   CB/LS 13 July 1913 C-W
102 *'Now . . . poor'*   CB, 'Tests for the Feeble-Minded',
                                          Eye-Witness, 15 August 1912, 279

103 *'too confidential'*   LS/CB 27 March 1914 Levy 238
103 *'was almost . . . with her'*   CB/LS 22 November 1913 C-W
103 *'bloody Jew'*   CB/LS 26 March 1914 C-W
103 *'excite'; 'sheer . . . God'*   CB/LS 29 April 1914 C-W
103 *Lytton . . . flowers*   CB/M. MacCarthy 7 May 1914
                                          Sx

10 Significant Form

104 *first . . . collaboration*   Shone, *Art*, 73
104 *'by unity . . . obtained';*   'The Decorations at the Borough
'always beautiful'; 'significant'   Polytechnic', *Athenaeum*, 23
                                          September 1911, 366

105 *'The battle . . . forms'*   CB, 'The English Group', 21
105 *'simplification . . . form'*   Ibid., 22
105 *'select . . . expression'*   'The London Salon at the Albert
                                          Hall', *Athenaeum*, 27 July 1912,
                                          98–9

106 *'completely Matissiste . . .*   Sutton, 348
genius'
106 *'The pictures . . . changed'*   VW, *RF*, 122
106 *'logical . . . form'; 'to be . . .* Bullen, 353
present'
106 *'the sensibility . . . at all'*   Sutton, 365
107 *'Post-Impressionist . . . Cubist*   Garafola, 473,n40
Dance'
107 *'massive . . . response'*   Bullen, 253
107 *'latest . . . Picasso'*   Ibid., 256
107 *'a muddle . . . phrases'*   Ibid., 382
107 *'free . . . beauty'*   Ibid., 376
107 *'its power . . . move us'*   'Post-Impressionism and
                                          Aesthetics', *Burlington Magazine*,
                                          22 January 1913, 226–30

108 *Barne was . . . primitive* G. H. Barne/CB, nd, Sx

108 *'The degree . . . theirs'* 'Post-Impressionism and
Aesthetics', *Burlington Magazine*,
22 January 1913, 226–30

108 *'new physiological . . .* Dickerman, 27
perceived'

108 *'It's . . . colour'* VB/VW, 19 October 1911,
Marler, 109

108 *'I would . . . painting'* VB/CB, 15 August 1912, Marler,
122

108 *'selling . . . cakes'* CB/M. MacCarthy, 9 October
1912, Sx

109 *sell . . . £5,400* *Times*, 4 December 1958

109 *'the air . . . Leonard'* VB/VW, 6 February 1913, Marler,
137

109 *'great doctrine . . . furious . . .* CB/Molly MacCarthy,?4 February
Duncan' 1913, Sx

109 *'stupid'* CB/M. MacCarthy, 17 January
1913

109 *'forms . . . We do . . . tertiary* VB/LW, 22 January 1913, Marler,
form' 133–4

109 *'to eliminate . . . forms'; 'I* CB/LW, nd, Berg
insist . . . aesthetic'

109–10 *'catalogue . . . Matisse'* 'Post-Impressionism and
Aesthetics', *Burlington Magazine*,
22 January 1913

110 *'thinking . . . don't'* CB/LW, nd, Berg

110 *'It is . . . by them'* LW/CB, 24 January 1913, Sx

110–11 *'My dear . . . I mean';* CB/M. MacCarthy, 17 January
'peace of mind'; 'stupid'; 'airs . . . 1913, Sx
writer'

111 *'When last . . . drawing'* Holroyd, 272

111 *Gertrude . . . photograph* Sutton, 365

111 *'as if . . . artist'* CB/M. MacCarthy,? February
1913, Sx

11 Omega

112 'central . . . design'; 'patches . . .	'Post-Impressionism Again', *Nation*,
scribble'	29 March 1913, 1060–1
112–13 'no one . . . of colour'	*Times*, 20 March 1914, 4
113 'fatal prettiness'	VB/RF,?21 July 1912, Marler, 120–1
113 'artists . . . form'	Reed, 'Introduction', 12
113 'loose way . . . painting'	Bullen, 461
113 'an insipid . . . modern art'	Ibid., 468
113–14 'altered . . . psychology'; 'artistic courage'	'The New Post-Impressionist Show', *Nation*, 25 October 1913, 172–3
114 'dance . . . business'	VB/RF, 6 February 1913, Marler, 135
114 *three Slade students*	Anscombe, 26
114 *reviewers . . . housewares*	Kato, 73
115 'should wrangle . . . painters'	VB/RF, 12 October 1913, Marler, 147
115 *alienation . . . Lewis*	CB/W. Lewis, Trinity, 5/4
115 'bad egg'	Q. Bell and Chaplin, 360
115 'As to . . . attention'	Ibid., 337
116 'more . . . admitted'	Spalding, *RF*, 188

12 A Complete Theory of Visual Art

117 'a little . . . soft legs'; 'bachelor . . . etc.'	VB/CB, 13 May 1914, Marler, 164–5
117 'wonderful . . . ever lived'	VB/DG, 25 March 1914, Marler, 160–1
119 'Only . . . look'	*Art*, 80–1
119 'Are you . . . subject?'	Edel, *Bloomsbury*, 193
119 'garbage'; 'poor taste'; 'life . . . conduct'	*Athenaeum*, 21 February 1914

119 'complete . . . art'   *Art*, vii
119 'a combination . . .   Ibid., 12
aesthetically'
120 'common . . . Cézanne'   Ibid., 8
120 'separated . . . life'   Reed, *Reader*, 159
120 'ultimate reality'   Ibid., 160
120 'never . . . the time'   CB, *Old*, 73
120 'any . . . habits'   *New Statesman*, 14 January 1914
120 'laboriously'   VW/CB,?20 March 1914, *L*, vol.
                                  2, 46
120 'We have . . . condemned'   LW/VW, 11 March 1914, Spotts,
                                  203
120–1 'Arthur . . . periodicals' LW, *Wise Virgins*, 86
121 'No Cambridge . . . hours'   *Art*, 280
121 'very . . . Tabley'   LS/CB, 9 November 1913, Levy,
                                  230
121 'what . . . War'   *Art*, xv
121 'the world . . . again'   Ivon Hitchens/Alan Bowness, 9
                                  October 1970, TGA 827/3

13 Mary

125 'So we are . . . peace'   Trinity, 5/5
125 'a certain . . . battleships' 'Before the War', *Cambridge
                                  Magazine*, 12 May 1917, 581–2
125–6 'Republic . . . against   'How It Struck a Contemporary',
Russia'   Trinity, 1/3
126 'desperately jingo . . . the war' Seymour, 195
126 'at a university . . . years' CB/J. Strachey, 17 September
                                  1914, BL
126 Nelly . . . noble work   Lady Cecil/CB, 29 October 1914,
                                  Sx
126 'all that . . . merry'   CB/OM,?June 1915, HRC
127 'but couldn't . . . his affairs' Spalding, *DG*, 165–6
127 'Poor old . . . a pat'   VB/CB, nd
128 'Dear Mrs . . . of art'   CB/MH, 'Wednesday night', nd
128 'Considering . . . note-paper' CB/MH, 'Sunday evening', nd

128 *'mutual enjoyment'*	M. Hutchinson, 'Playing'
129 *'very extraordinary . . . the term'*	J. Barnes, 87
129 *'difficult . . . head'*	Ibid., 89
129 *'a pagan . . . values'*	Ibid., 2
129 *'smallish . . . humour'*	Ibid., 93
129 *'Here . . . Sheba!'*	J. Hutchinson, *Desert*
129 *'documentary . . . week-end'*	CB/OM, 17 August?1915, HRC
129 *'an unlooked . . . morality'*	CB/MH, 2 March 1915
129 *'most disgusted'*	CB/MH, 11 July 1917
129 *'no little . . . existence'*	Spalding, *VB*, 139
130 *'The Hutchinsons . . . as possible'*	VB/RF,?9 May 1915, Marler, 179
130–1 *'His . . . whole of'*	Ibid., 181
131 *'to elaborate . . . civilization'*	CB/MH, 13 December 1914
131 *'Babies . . . Victorianism'*	CB/MH, 'Saturday', nd
131–2 *'You might . . . their wages'*	CB/MH, 14 January 1916
132 *'It's all . . . matter'*	CB/VB,?January 1917
132 *'in an . . . a woman'*	CB/MH, 20 January 1917
132 *'It must . . . Civilisation'*	VW/LS, 26 February 1915, *L*, vol. 2, 61
132 *'bitter . . . understand'*	CB/MH, 29 March 1915
132–3 *'all about . . . work of art'*	Ibid.
133 *'for giving . . . territorial'*	CB/MH, 9 December 1914
133 *Nietzsche's . . . discourse*	Haycock, 62
133 *'rubbishy romantic'*	CB/OM, nd, HRC
133 *'very bright'*	CB/MH, 6 February 1916
133 *'When . . . Gallery?'; 'tend the lamp'*	'Art and War', *International Journal of Ethics* 26 (October 1915), 1–10
133–4 *'I mayn't . . . about you'*	CB/MH, nd
134 *'Jack has . . . asked'*	VB/JMK, 8? August 1915, Morgan
134 *'Clive was . . . others'*	LS/OM, 4 September 1915, Levy, 256
134 *'shed tears . . . year'*	MH/LS, 3 September 1915, HRC
134 *'rather . . . sympathy'*	CB/MH, 30 March 1915

14 Peace at Once

135 *'the collapse . . . affections'*	CB/MH, 21 August 1914
135–6 *'mind of . . . passion';*	'The Silly Season', Trinity, 1/4
'seemed to . . . Belgium'; 'war . . .	
boat'; 'Their . . . destroy'	
136 *'planetary . . . honour'*	'Patriotism', Trinity, 1/6
136 *'enrolment . . . come'*	Graham, 172
136 *'exalts . . . citizens'*	Ibid., 22
136–7 *'Before . . . killed'; 'plays*	'Conscription', *The Nation*, 16
. . . England'; 'moral and	January 1915, 500–1
religious'; 'It has . . . and death'	
137 *'quacks . . . shopmen'*	CB/MH, 5 June 1915
137 *'full . . . secrets'; 'seditious*	CB/MH, 10 April 1915
pamphlet'	
137 *'little . . . tragically'*	CB/MH, 26 May 1915
137 *'crushing . . . generations';*	*Peace*, 5
'small . . . caste'; 'National . . .	
Interests'	
137 *'It is . . . composed it'*	Ibid., 20
138 *'ultimate . . . done it'*	G. Murray, 24
138 *'the men . . . feelings'*	*Peace*, 27
138 *'Would . . . corner?'*	Ibid., 21
138 *'sensible . . . people'*	Ibid., 33
138 *'drawn . . . diplomacy'*	Ibid., 36
138 *'the surest . . . someone'*	Ibid., 45
139 *'I had . . . visited'*	Skidelsky, vol. 1, 326
139 *'enough . . . agreeable'*	CB/MH, 25 April 1915
139 *'seems able . . . side'*	LS/LW, 10 July 1915, Berg
139 *'40 times as long'*	LS/CB, 11 July 1915, Sx
139 *'statesmen . . . nonsense'*	*TLS*, 15 July 1915, 8
139 *'very persuasive'*	LS/CB, 16 August 1915, Sx
139 *'sad . . . stuff'*	CB/MH, 31 July 1915
139 *'freedom'*	'Conscription', *Nation*, 26 June
	1915, 419
140 *In court . . . 1,642 copies*	Beechey, 'Clive', 8
140 *Mansion House . . . 22*	*Times*, 14 Sept 1915, 5
September	

140 *'common hangman'*   CB/OM, 23 August 1915, HRC
140 *'particularly . . . letter'; 'we . . .*   'Mr. Clive Bell's Pamphlet',
freedom'   *Nation*, 4 September 1915, 737–8
141 *'on . . . views'; 'it is . . .*   'The Suppression of a Pamphlet',
government'   *New Statesman*, 4 September
                                          1915, 515–16
141 *about-face . . . August 1914*   A. Smith, 66
141 *'thousands . . . patriotism'*   *New Statesman*, 4 September
                                          1915, 516
141 *'A nation . . . that way'*   *Nation*, 4 September 1915, 738
141 *'agreement . . . loathe'*   Ibid.
141 *'all freeborn . . . press'*   G. B. Shaw, 'In Defence of Mr.
                                          Clive Bell', *Nation*, 11 September
                                          1915, 769–70
141 *'squalid panic'*   G. K. Chesterton, 'Mr. Bernard
                                          Shaw and Mr. Bell', *Nation*, 18
                                          September 1915, 801
141 *'friendly . . . sinning'*   G. B. Shaw, 'On Sin and Death',
                                          Nation, 25 September 1915,
                                          833–4
141 *'If you . . . him on'*   CB/J. Strachey, 13? September
                                          1915, BL
141 *'Old father . . . pamphlet'*   30 September 1915, *L*, vol. 2, 65
142 *almost afraid . . . appeared*   CB/MH, 3 August 1915
142 *'No beings . . . dying for?'*   CB/OM, 4 August 1915, HRC
142 *'a handsome . . . war'*   VB/JMK, nd, Morgan
142 *'Clive . . . situation'*   DG/LS,?22 May 1915, TGA

15 Art and War

143 *'if one . . . of place'*   CB/MH, 'Sunday', nd
143 *'scented . . . table'*   CB/MH, 4 October 1915
143 *'real democratic instinct'*   CB/MH, 26 December 1915
143 *'The Life and Death of Lytton'*   Holroyd, 336
144 *'Bertie . . . don't think'*   Seymour, 249
144 *'a sentimental . . .*   CB/MH, 2 January 1916
Edwardianism'

144 *'never seen . . . Russia'* — *New Statesman*, 20 November 1915, 161

144 *'I rather . . . anybody'* — 15 November 1915, *L*, vol. 2, 435
144 *'set . . . mad'* — Rosenbaum, *Collection*, 369
144 *'all . . . piffle'* — D. H. Lawrence/S. S. Koteliansky, 21 December 1928, *Late*, 183

144 *'most . . . seen'* — Shone, 'Blast'
145 *smash . . . their due* — CB/MH, 16 July 1914
145 *'delicious . . . universe'* — CB, *Pot*, 195
145 *visitors . . . war effort* — Goebel, 172–4
145 *'I'm sure . . . else'* — LS/CB, 12 May 1916, Levy, 293
145 *avoid . . . May* — Haycock, 221
145–6 *'What traitors . . . at her'* — Carrington, 26
146 *'poseurs'* — Ibid., 25
146 *'stayed . . . Devil'* — MacDougall, 125
146 *'Yiddish Cézanne'* — Ibid., 153
146 *regretted . . . Francesca* — CB/MH, 10 June 1916
147 *'I don't know . . . my book'* — Gertler, 106
147 *'really . . . conscientious'* — CB/MH, 20 September 1917
147 *'a tremendous . . . German artists'* — Gertler, 128

147 *'Made in Germany'* — MacDougall, 122
147 *'reformation'* — CB/VB,?May 1917
147 *'splendid . . . English'* — RF/VB, 17 June 1917, Sutton, 413

147–8 *'want furniture . . . smoking-room'; 'a block . . . colours'* — 'Contemporary Art in England', *Burlington Magazine*, July 1917, 30–7
148 *'as crackpots . . . lunatics'* — Bibbings, 63
148 *'I am called . . . in Flanders'* — CB/OM, 'Friday', nd, HRC
148–9 *'some literary . . . pimp'* — 'War Notes', *New Age*, 13 January 1916

149 *'quite possibly'* — *Art*, 91
149 *'so cares . . . believe'* — Ibid.
149 *'leave . . . Daily Mail?'* — *New Age*, 20 January 1916
149 *'There is . . . survives'* — 'War Notes', *New Age*, 13 January 1916

149 *breeding bulls*	'Sport and War', *New Statesman*, 5 February 1916, 420
150 *'improper . . . the war'*	CB/MH, 21 September 1915
150 *'By passing . . . not theirs'*	'A Reign of Terror', Trinity, 1/9
150 *'riot'*	CB/MH,?15 May 1916
150 *'world . . . uneasiness'; 'all superfluous . . . rent'*	CB/VB, nd
150 *'sort of fantasia'*	CB/LS, 3 November 1917, C-W
150 *'infection'*	'Young Mr. Britling', Trinity, 1/7
151 *'impossibility . . . teeth into'*	RF/VB, 16 February 1917, TGA
151 *'most helpful'*	Albert Barnes, 'How to Judge a Painting', *Arts & Decoration*, April 1915
151 *'Who . . . book'*	Madge Jenison, *Sunwise Turn, A Human Comedy of Bookselling*, Dutton, 1923
152 *'insolent . . . public opinion'*	Petronius Arbiter, 'A Degenerate Work of Art: "The Bathers" by Cézanne', *The Art World*, January 1918, 323, 326–32
152 *'Billings case'*	Cohler, 84–5
152 *'new frankness'*	CB/MH, 18 November 1917
152 *to leave . . . war*	CB/VB,?April 1918
152 *'in so . . . intellectual books'*	CB/MH, 22 August 1918
153 *'sapphism'*	Holroyd, 336
153 *'moral . . . odour'*	*New Statesman*, 12 October 1918, 33

16 Tribunals and Tribulations

| 154 *patriotic intellectuals* | CB/G. Murray,?23 May 1916, Bodleian |
| 154 *'all as . . . against it'* | CB/G. Murray, nd, Bodleian |

155 *two letters*	' "A Grave Issue" and a Way Out', *Daily News and Leader*, 17 May 1916, 4; 'The Conscientious Objector', *Daily News and Leader*, 22 May 1916, 4
155 *'drafting . . . string-pulling'*	MH/VB, 24 May 1916, Sx
155 *At Garsington . . . Murray*	MH/VB, 25 April 1916, Sx
155 *'Adsum qui feci'*	*Times*, 17 May 1916
155 *'distinguished philosopher'*	CB/MH, 13 August 1916
155 *'physical infirmity . . . creatures'*	CB/Gilbert Murray, nd, Bodleian
155 *'subterranean . . . more'*	CB/MH, 10 October 1917
156 *'more . . . humble pie'*	CB/VB, nd
156 *Shaw declined*	G. B. Shaw/CB, 7 July 1916, Sx
156 *'a writer . . . on art'*	CB/OM, nd, HRC
156 *jail . . . land*	CB/OM, 8 April 1916, HRC
157 *'monument historique'*	CB/VB, 9 August 1916
157 *'He evidently . . . two rooms'*	JMK/VB, 25 August 1916, Skidelsky, vol. 1, 331
157 *'one of . . . for me*	VB/JMK, 29 August 1916, Morgan
157 *'dreaming . . . spies'*	CB/VB, 7 August 1917
158 *'broach . . . question'*	CB/VB, 2 February 1917
158 *'Obviously . . . bedroom'*	CB/VB, nd
159 *'oafish Finn'*	CB/MH, 19 June 1918
159 *'an ill-bred . . . boy*	CB/VB, nd
159 *'actual . . . resentment'*	Skidelsky, vol. 1, 351
159 *'to fuck . . . enough'*	Ibid.
159 *'little cracked . . . little toes'*	CB/MH, 5 October 1918
159 *'Bloomsbury-Asheham . . . that sort'*	CB/JMK, nd, Sx
159 *'who had . . . passion'*	CB/VB, nd
159 *'He means . . . difficult'*	VB/RF, 11 November 1918, Marler, 216

17 Garsington

160	'I feel . . . his sight'	CB/MH, 3 August 1916
160	'God help us all'	CB/OM, 3 August 1916, HRC
161	'immensely . . . children'	Hignett, 58
161	'traitor . . . morning'	CB/VB, nd
161	'awful . . . bodily one'	Hignett, 90–1
161	'since . . . club'	CB/VB, 7 August 1917
161	'civil . . . egoism'	CB/MH, 7 August 1917
162	' "No you . . . the other'	Darroch, 194
162	'observations . . . offensiveness'	CB/MH, 16 January 1917
162	'Lytton . . . God knows'	Lawrence, 30 May 1916, *L*, vol. 2, 612
162	'Strand . . . smutty'	CB/MH, 30 December 1916
162	'in the interests . . . scandal'	CB/MH, 27 March 1917
162	'modicum . . . power'	CB/MH, 16 October 1918
162	'O these . . . with it'	CB/MH, 21 October 1918
163	'anything interesting'	MacGibbon, 95
163	*Roger envied . . . elude*	RF/VB,? August 1916, TGA
163	'general triumph'	CB/MH, 10 April 1915
163	'homosexuality . . . Has it?'	CB/MH, 23 August 1917
163	'it didn't . . . painful'	CB/MH, 12 February 1916
163	'because . . . different sex'	Spalding, *VB*, 173
164	'had made . . . loving him'	Spalding, *DG*, 201
164	'We are . . . birthday'	CB/MH, nd
164	'being . . . his mind'	RF/VB, 12 December 1917, Sutton, 423
165	'was furious . . . Ariosto'	LS/Carrington, 26 March 1917, Levy, 349
165	'thrust on'	CB/MH, 30 August 1918
165	'I'm glad . . . instance'	CB/MH, 30–31 December 1916
165	'various . . . known'	CB/MH, 25 July 1917
165	'definitely . . . sketch'	CB/MH, 1 September 1916
165	'very . . . superior'	Morrell, *Ottoline*, 148
165–6	'wretched . . . direction'	K. Mansfield/OM, 22 May 1917, Mansfield, 308–9
166	'cut up . . . Americans'	K. Mansfield/OM,?24 June 1917, Mansfield, 312

166 'commonplace . . . fool'　　　CB/MH, 25 July 1917
166 'pretty . . . on fire'　　　CB/VW, 13 July 1918
166 'turn . . . head'　　　VW, 16 July 1918, *D*, vol. 1, 168
166 'amusing . . . view'　　　CB/MH, 14 July 1918
166 'merely . . . the Master'　　　VW/VB, 29 January 1918, *VW Miscellany* 8, Summer 1977, 2

166 'I expect . . . by Clive'　　　H. Lee, 390
167 'driving . . . wedges'　　　CB/MH, 11 July 1917
167 'She made . . . Duncan'　　　CB/MH,?20 August 1917
167 'extraordinary . . . nonage'; 'All . . . the world'　　　CB/VW, 19 July 1917
167 'Its . . . think so?'　　　VW/CB, 24 July 1917, *L*, vol. 2, 167

167 'the finest . . . cap'　　　CB/LW, 24 August 1956, Sx
168 'He is . . . his best'　　　VW, 27 October 1917, *D*, vol. 1, 67

168 'rather . . . standard'　　　VW, 23 November 1917, *D*, vol. 1, 81
168 'after . . . talking'　　　LS/Carrington, 26 March 1917, Levy, 349
168 'He's no . . . then'　　　VW, 23 Nov 1917, *D*, vol. 1, 81
168 'of course . . . to do'　　　VW, 14 January 1918, *D*, vol. 1, 105

168 'like . . . buns'　　　CB, *Old*, 121
169 'was . . . young'　　　CB/MH, 20 August 1916
169 'rows . . . old moon'　　　K. Mansfield/OM,?24 June 1917, Mansfield, 312

169 'I run . . . might say'　　　CB/MH, 5 November 1916
169 'the hundredth . . . creations'　　　CB/MH, 24 December 1916
169 'simply . . . me'　　　T. S. Eliot/MH, 2 July 1917, Eliot, *L*, vol. 1, 209

169 'the footman . . . knee'　　　CB/MH, 8 April 1917
170 'reveal . . . innocuous'　　　CB/MH, 1 April 1917
170 'Alas! . . . trash'　　　CB/MH, 17 June 1917
170 'He does . . . stuff!'　　　CB/MH,?28 June 1918
170 'about . . . Cambridge'　　　CB/MH, 30 October 1918
171 'comparing . . . pictures'　　　MH/VB, 22 October 1918, Sx

| 171 *'I can't . . . possible'* | CB/MH, 25 October 1918 |
| 171 *'very . . . old'* | CB/MH, 11 July 1918 |

18 Ad Familiares

172 *'a conspiracy . . . public'*	Brockington, 'Tending', 8
172 *'hoping . . . laughing-stocks'*	CB, *Ad*, Preface, 1–7
173 *Sydney . . . outlook*	S. Waterlow/CB, 21 December 1917, Berg
173 *kindest . . . received*	M. Hutchinson, 'Clive'
173 *'Good . . . indiscretion'*	LS/VW, 21 December 1917, Levy, 377–8
173 *'magnificent . . . bouquet'*	LS/CB, 31 December 1917, Levy, 379
173 *'enlivened . . . mind)'*	VW, 3 January 1918, *D*, vol. 1, 95
173 *'is seized . . . clutch'*	VW/LS, 28 December 1917, *L*, vol. 2, 205
174 *'Everything . . . with her'*	VW, 27 July 1918, *D*, vol. 1, 172–3
174 *'philosophical . . . sleeves'*	CB/MH, 30 August 1918
174 *'concubine'*	DG/LS, 13 October 1918, TGA
174 *'makes . . . lost'*	CB/LS, 21 May 1918, C-W
174 *'want to . . . children'*	CB/VB, nd
174–5 *'agoraphobia' . . . illness'*	CB/VB,?15 August 1917
175 *'there is . . . your own'*	MH/VB, 16 August 1917, Sx
175 *'unfortunately . . . thinking'*	MH/VB, 25 April 1916, Sx
175 *Fredegond . . . fiction*	CB/MH, 24 December 1916
175 *'Mr. Clive . . . she lay'*	Macaulay, 25
175 *'where . . . something'*	Ibid., 26
175 *'hero' . . . Bloomsbury*	CB/OM, 3 June 1916, HRC
175–6 *'a Slade . . . questions'*	Hamilton, 295–6
176 *'must be . . . the bud'*	CB/G. Whitworth, 13 February 1918, UoR
177 *'canalizing . . . Vorticism'*	'Contemporary Art in England', *Burlington Magazine*, July 1917, 30–7
177 *'There is . . . the end'*	Haycock, 290

177 *'my first . . . intellectuals'*   Haycock, 233
177 *'give . . . business'*   VW, 28 May 1918, *D*, vol. 1, 151
178 *'listening . . . ideas'*   *Tatler*, 28 August 1918
178 *narrow point of view*   *Mercure de France*, 23 October
                                1918
178 *'the Matthew . . . of 1914'*   *Egoist*, June/July 1918, 87
178 *'all . . . galleries'*   CB/MH, 5 May 1917
178 *Clive loaned*   Sutton, 413–14 for complete
                                exhibition list
178–9 *'because . . . painting';*   'The Mansard Gallery', *Pot-Boilers*,
'sense . . . art'; 'see . . . person'; 'all   199–208
. . . artist'

---

19 Angelica

---

180 *'in . . . part'*   Spalding, *VB*, 175–6
180 *'in ages . . . effective'*   CB/VB, nd
180 *Vanessa . . . two years*   CB/MH, 16 June 1918
180 *'would be . . . Bell millions'*   CB/VB,?10 June 1918
181 *'a wiser . . . child'*   CB/VB, 10 July 1918
181 *'little book . . . civilisation'*   CB/LS, 11 July 1918, C-W
181 *'write . . . respectable'*   CB/VB, nd
181 *'seem to . . . baby'*   CB/MH, 8 December 1918
181 *delighted . . . a girl*   DG/CB, 26 December 1918 TGA
182 *'seeking . . . thousand'*   CB/VB, nd
182 *'meet . . . difficulties'*   CB/VB, 'Saturday', nd
182 *'for their . . . complacency'*   VB/RF, 18 December 1913, Light,
                                144
182 *'violence . . . passion'*   CB/MH, 26 November 1916
183 *'as though . . . please Jack'*   CB/MH, 11 April 1917
183 *'I don't . . . established'*   CB/MH, 29 March 1917
183 *'If only . . . affair!'*   CB/MH, 1 April 1917
183 *'M. . . . possumus'*   LS/CB, 18 February 1918, Levy,
                                383
183 *'almost . . . respectable'*   CB/MH, 27 January 1919
183 *'that two . . . for both'*   CB/MH, 30 January 1919

---

20 *The New Ballet*

187 *'Everyone . . . merriment'*	Carrington, 101–2
187 *'played . . . head'*	Mackrell, 141
187 *Osbert . . . together*	Sitwell, *Laughter*, 22
187 *'pure . . . fantasy'*	Garafola, 13
187 *'subtle . . . emotions'*	'"Oedipus Rex" at Covent Garden', *Athenaeum*, 20 January 1912, 75–6
187 *'as the . . . Fry'*	B. Strachey, 269
188 *'disguised . . . pillow'*	Berenson, 191
188 *'attired . . . woman'*	Holroyd, 289
188 *'one . . . life'*	Garafola, 316
188 *'promoting . . . music-halls'*	Ibid., 330–1
188 *'queen . . . ballet'*	DG/VB, 23 September 1918, TGA
189 *'It's hopeless . . . together'*	CB/MH, 8 October 1918
189 *'hysterical . . . friends'*	CB/LS, 12 October 1918, C-W
189 *delighted Lydia*	L. Keynes/CB, nd, KCC
189 *charmed Lytton*	LS/CB, 28 December 1918, Levy, 423
189 *'an answer'*	RF/VB, 26 December 1918, Sutton, 442
189 *'determined . . . conversation'*	CB/MH, 12 January 1919
189 *'unseemly behaviour'*	RF/VB, nd, TGA
189 *'simply . . . it'*	J. Hutchinson, *Desert*
189 *'open . . . Bloomsbury'*	CB/LS, 12 October 1918, C-W
190 *'It must . . . style'*	CB/VB, nd
190 *He supposed . . . Ottoline*	CB/MH, 7 May 1919
190 *'last . . . defeat'; 'on account . . . Diaghilev'*	VB/JMK, 30 May 1919, Morgan
190 *'I went . . . Square'*	LS/Carrington, 22 May 1919, Levy, 435
191 *'Clive . . . gamine'*	A. Huxley/OM, 12 June 1919, Sexton, 90
191 *Vivien later . . . no one*	V. Eliot/MH, 36 September 1919, Eliot, *L*, vol. 1, 399
191 *'deep . . . liberty'*	CB/MH, ?31 January 1919

191 *'some . . . students'; 'so that . . . unison'*	CB, *Old*, 172
191 *'this . . . England'*	Richardson, vol. 3, 132
191 *interested . . . all races*	E. Ansermet/CB, nd, Sx
191 *'excitements . . . entertainments'*	CB/VB, nd
192 *'miraculous'*	'The New Ballet', *New Republic*, 30 July 1919, 414–16
192 *'white heat'*	'The Artistic Problem', *Athenaeum*, 20 June 1919, 496–7
192 *'choreographer's . . . precious'*	'The New Ballet', *New Republic*, 30 July 1919, 414–16
192 *'new way . . . design'*	Garafola, 337
192 *'foretaste . . . theatre'*	'The New Ballet', *New Republic*, 30 July 1919, 414–16
192 *'torrent'*	L. Keynes/CB, nd, KCC
193 *'The tradition . . . exhausted'; 'a vein . . . out'*	'Tradition and Movements', *Athenaeum*, 4 April 1919, 142–4
193 *'which . . . unconsciously'; 'culture . . . things'*	T. S. Eliot/MH,?11 July 1919, *L*, vol. 1, 377–9
193 *'emotion . . . impersonal'*	T. S. Eliot, 'Tradition', 22
193 *'Standards'*	'Standards', *New Republic*, 14 June 1919, 207–9
193 *'Criticism'*	'Criticism', *Athenaeum*, 26 September 1919, 953–4
193 *'Order and Authority'*	'Order and Authority', *Athenaeum*, (a) 7 November 1919, 1157–8; (b) 14 November 1919, 1191–3
194 *'absurd'; 'precise opposite'*	D. S. MacColl, 'Mr Fry and Drawing-I', *Burlington Magazine* May 1919, 204
194 *deliberately . . . dull*	'Significant Form', *Burlington Magazine*, 34 (June 1919), 257
194 *'was . . . tradition'*	C. Green, 'Expanding', 127
195 *Barnes . . . against*	A. Barnes/Forbes Watson, 8 October 1919, Barnes Foundation

195 'In re-stating . . . art'   Sutton, 454
196 'not exactly . . . representative';   'The French Pictures at Heal's',
'great . . . Archipenko'   *Nation*, 16 August 1919, 586–8
196 'indecent . . . law'; 'What is   *Nation*, 23 August 1919, 616
. . . gasping'
196 Sitwell defended . . . should be   *Nation*, 30 August 1919, 645
196–7 'normally . . . tradition'   Ibid.
197 'execrably . . . taste'   CB/MH, 3 September 1919
197 'bung . . . shillings'   'The French Pictures', *Nation*, 6
                                           September 1919, 672
197 'jazz . . . repulsive'   *Nation*, 6 September 1919
197 battle . . . won   'The French Pictures', *Nation*, 27
                                           September 1919, 766

21 Order and Authority

198 'not only . . . Cubism'   Fitzgerald, 95
198 'Picasso . . . with him'   CB/MH, 2 November 1919
198 'alarming'   CB/MH, 4 November 1919
199 'Nous . . . jeunes'   CB, *Since*, 31
199 'new . . . age'   Silver, 95
200 'enemy goods'   Ibid., 10
200 'strange . . . story' 'signified . . . Ibid., 116
behaviour'
200 'ordered'   C. Green, *Cubism*, 9
200 exemplified by books   Silver, 330
200 Cubism still . . . Léonce   C. Green, *Cubism*, 11
200 Picabia's break . . . Aragon   Ibid., 50
200 French . . . affected   CB/VB, 23 October 1920
201 'the world . . . art-critic'   CB/MH, 7 Nov 1919
201 'vanity . . . attentions'; 'Renoir   CB/MH, 8 November 1919
. . . century'
201 'mad'   CB/VB, 28 May 1929
201 'frivolous . . .   CB/MH, 30 November 1919
intellect-Bloomsbury'
201 'In a . . . principle" '   CB/VB, 27 November 1919
202 'my sister as usual'   CB/MH, 14 November 1919

202 'I always . . . amusing'   CB/MH, 18 November 1919
202 'extraordinary impression'   CB/Picasso, 18 November 1919,
                                          Musée Picasso, Paris

202 'type Ingres . . . remarkable'   CB/MH, 22 November 1919
202 He urged . . . studio   CB/VB, 27 November 1919
203 'really . . . ladies'   VB/JMK, 16 May 1922, Morgan
203 'literary socialists'   CB/MH, 4 November 1920
203 poked . . . Parisian times   Duthuit, 52
203 'aesthetic of ambiguity'   Silver, 51
203 'prodigiously . . . brilliant'   'Jean Cocteau', N&A, 5 April
                                          1924, 13–14

203 Cocteau bashing . . . piano   Arnaud, 289
204 'disgusting . . . bourgeois'   CB/MH, 25 October 1920
205 'metteur . . . movement'   'Cocteau Collected', N&A, 1
                                          May 1926, 133

205 at home . . . Montparnasse   Klüver, 81–2
205 'living classicism'   Jean Cocteau unique
205 'marked . . . evocations'   Silver, 97
205 'He had . . . point of view'   VB/RF, 16 May 1921, Marler,
                                          247

205 'synthesis . . . modernity'   J. Lee, 9
206 'reversed . . . group'   Ibid., 49
206 'inexplicable . . . mechanics'   Ibid., 53
206 'unconscious nationalism'   'The Authority of M. Derain',
                                          New Statesman, 5 March 1921,
                                          643–4

206 'universal spirit'   J. Lee, 63
206 'significant . . . rhythm'   Art, 16
206 'rhythm . . . work'   J. Lee, 63
206 'amazes . . . more'   'The New Art Salon', Athenaeum,
                                          27 February 1920, 280–1

206 'chef d'école'; 'what is . . . win   'The Authority of M. Derain',
it'   New Statesman, 5 March 1921,
                                          643–44

206–7 'You know . . . intimidates   Caws, 82 (my translation)
me'

207 'Give him . . . of them'   'To Finish the Season in Paris',
                                          Vogue, 68 (Late July 1926), 48–9

207 *'Matisse and Picasso'*   'Matisse and Picasso', *Athenaeum*
                                   14 May 1920, 643–4

207 *'rather furious'*   Sutton, 505

207 *'very . . . postwar'*   Silver, 73

207 *'restless spirit'*   Beechey, Picasso and Britain', 13

207 *'a return . . . representation'*   C. Green, 'Picassos', 22

208 *fashion . . . sophistication'*   Garafola, 370

208 *'unholy . . . by Hals'*   *Art*, 172

208 *overlooked . . . Seurat*   *Since*, 12 and see Silver, 336

209 *'bizarre conception'*   Silver, 404, n14

209 *'did we . . . adore'*   *Since*, 165

209 *'to say . . . as art'*   Ibid., 195

209 *'supported . . . slaves'*   Ibid., 198

209 *Congolese . . . Mozart*   Ibid., 200

209 *'purely . . . emotions';*   Ibid., 97
'representation'

210 *'at any . . . second-class';*   'Wilcoxism', *New Republic*, 3
'admirable . . . match'   March 1920, 21–3, revised,
                                   Athenaeum, 5 March 1920,
                                   311–12

210 *'when you . . . again';*   'Mr. Clive Bell and
'permanent *residence*'   "Wilcoxism"', *Athenaeum*, 12
                                   March 1920

210 *'mere . . . abuse'*   CB/MH, 14 March 1920

210 *'because . . . himself'*   'Wilcoxism', *Athenaeum*, 19
                                   March 1920, 379

210 *'thought . . . completely*   VB/CB, 19 March 1920

210 *'several . . . pleasure'*   T. S. Eliot/W. Lewis,?19 March
                                   1920, *L*, vol. 1, 452

211 'glaring . . . *spite*'   T. S. Eliot/OM, 21 March 1920,
                                   L, vol. 1, 453

211 *'knock-out blow'*   MacDougall, 180

211 *'in Paris . . . better'*   *Since*, 193

211 *'bluff . . . friends'*   'Modern Art and the Critics',
                                   Daily Herald, 12 April 1922

211 *'Mr Bell . . . circle'*   D. S. MacColl, 'Sequelae',
                                   Saturday Review, 4 April 1922

211 'a whole . . . to time'	'The Art of To-Day', *New Witness*, 21 April 1922
211 'half-dead . . . dead'	'Art and Mr. Clive Bell', *Outlook*, 22 April 1922
212 'point . . . painting'	*Athenaeum*, 19 March 1920
212 'who ever . . . art?'	'Duncan Grant', *Athenaeum*, 6 February 1920, 182–3
212 'transformed'	Spalding, *Tate*, 48
212 'amazing'; 'the most . . . gallery'	'See Your Own Country First', *Vogue*, 66 (Early September 1925), 50–1, 78
212 'tank'; 'whether . . . painting'	'Notes on the Courtauld Pictures', *Vogue*, 67 (Late March 1926), 64–5, 90
212 'now . . . world'	CB/MH, 5 July 1927
212 'there . . . London'	Vaux Halliday, 87
213 'keep . . . flying'	CB/VB, nd
213 'most . . . Impressionists'	Turnbaugh, 45
213 'best . . . alive'	'Duncan Grant', *Athenaeum*, 6 February 1920
213 'in the . . . movement'	'English Painting at the Moment', *Vanity Fair*, January 1923, 40, 90
213 'sheeplike . . . resplendent'	Marsh 355, 359
213 'sort . . . people'	'The Independent Gallery', *Burlington Magazine*, 38 (March 1921), 146–9

22 Wives and Lovers

214 'cinema world'	CB/MH, 4 November 1920
214 'riff-raff . . . Tower'	VB/RF, 16 May 1921, TGA
214–15 'Are you . . . galère'; 'slightly . . . privilege'	CB/MH, 9 May 1921
215 'almost . . . most'	CB/MH, nd
215 'Clive has . . . Europe'	27 January 1921, Levy, 479
215 'miserably in love'	CB/MH, nd

215 *'all Spanish . . . French'*   VW/VB, 7 January 1921, *L*, vol. 2, 453

215 *'An Artistic . . . Chelsea'*   *Globe*, 17 January 1921

215–16 *'obviously . . . upset'; 'on . . . legs'*   VB/RF, 25 May 1921, Marler, 250

216 *Juana's stupidity . . . beauty*   VW/S. Waterlow, 3 May 1921, *L*, vol. 2, 467

216 *'pathetic . . . intellect'*   Spalding, *DG*, 241

216–17 *'Reading . . . loved'*   TCT

217 *'that first . . . their affair'*   N. Murray, 214

217 *'And so . . . exciting'; 'Did she . . . long?'*   CB/MH, 20 October 1922

217 *'Aldous . . . giddy'*   N. Murray, 172, n33

217 *'existed . . . desire'*   Ibid., 175

218 *'little . . . passion'*   VW, 24 March 1922, *D*, vol. 2, 172

218 *'bon . . . Bell'*   25 August 1922, *L*, vol. 2, 544

218 *Clive praised . . . Lytton's*   'Byron's Last Year', *N&A*, 15 March 1924, 836–8, revised, 'Byron's Last Journey', *New Republic*, 28 May 1924, 25

219 *'great book'*   VW, 5 September 1923, *D*, vol. 2, 264

219 *'fitted better'*   CB/H. Nicolson, 8 June 1926, Princeton

219 *'yet . . . wreck'*   'The Reformation of the English School', *Artwork*, Summer 1926

219 *'He says . . . one gets'*   VW/B. Bagenal, 24 June 1923, *L*, vol. 3, 52

219 *'whispered . . . again'*   VW, 16 February 1921, *D*, vol. 2, 92

219 *'folly'*   VW, 28 November 1928, *D*, vol. 3, 208

219 *'He says . . . concealing'*   VW/Gerald Brenan, 1 December 1923, *L*, vol. 3, 79–80

220 *'perhaps . . . vainglory'*   VW, 13 March 1921, *D*, vol. 2, 100

220 'Off we . . . forth'   VW, 24 March 1922, *D*, vol. 2,
                                   172–3
220 'tired . . . world'   CB/MH, 23 September 1921
220 'these old . . . our sorrows' CB/MH, 17 May 1922
220 'never . . . love-affair'; 'misses 'Virginia Woolf', *Dial*, 77
not . . . interested her'   (December 1924), 451–654
220 'I shall . . . ha!'   11 September 1923, *L*, vol. 3, 70
221 'Dictated . . . downs'   23 December 1925, *L*, vol. 3, 225
221 *Vita assured . . . safe*   H. Lee, 493
221 'Clive suddenly . . .   VW, 1 July 1926, *D*, vol. 3, 91
humiliated'

221 *Clive insisted . . . 1911*   CB/MH, 27 December 1925
221 *joked . . . Leonard*   CB/VB, 15 April 1920
221 'I often . . . writers'   VW/J. Raverat, 5 February 1925,
                                   L, vol. 3, 163–4
221 'enough . . . hum'   VW, 12 March 1922, *D*, vol. 2,
                                   171
221 'hair shirt'   VW/VB, 24 October 1921, *L*,
                                   vol. 2, 487
221 'no bath . . . nice food'   CB/MH, 12 September 1925
222 *profit . . . Press*   Willis, 75
222 'one of . . . books'   T. Bradshaw, 292
222 *based on . . . Sybille*   Southworth, 151
222 'From this . . . ballad'   CB, *Legend*, 22
223 'Perhaps . . . as nice'   VB/CB, 21 November 1921
223 'much nicer person'   D. Garnett/Mina Kirstein
                                   Curtiss, 26 September 1923, Berg
223 'most peaceful . . . to be'   Sutton, 564
223 'be a . . . wives'   Skidelsky, vol. 2, 113
223 'And so . . . nonentities'   CB/MH, 12 August 1926
225 'Here we . . . admitted'   VB/M. Snowden, 25 December
                                   1923, TGA
225 'carries on . . . laughter'   VB/VW,?April 1926, Berg
225 'My charms . . . moon'   VW, 10 January 1920, *D*, vol. 2,
                                   6
225 *Goneril and Regan*   CB/MH, 29 August 1923
226 'What reason . . . confidence' VB/M. Vaughan,16 March 1920,
                                   Marler, 237

| 227 *'without one lady'* | CB/VB, 5 January 1922 |
| 227 *'five . . . chauffeurs'* | CB/VB, nd |

23 *Liberty*

228 *'Any English . . . life'*	'Order and Authority', *Athenaeum*, 14 November 1919, 1191–3
228 *'English obtuseness . . . things French'*	M. Green, 125
228 *'almost . . . francophilia'*	Nicholson, 231
228 *'prophet . . . English'*	M. Green, 254
229 *'another . . . end'*	Ibid., 20
229 *'on the . . . him'*	Connolly, 349
229 *'(almost) . . . different'*	LS/Carrington, 5 September 1921, Levy, 498
229 *'the penultimate . . . be it'*	'The Creed of an Aesthete', *New Republic*, 25 January 1922, 241–2
229 *'Divine . . . Shaw'*	'The Critic as Guide', *New Republic*, 26 October 1921, 259, 261
230 *'a fathead . . . voluptuary';* *'There . . . present'*	'Shaw's Comment on Clive Bell's Article', *New Republic*, 22 February 1922, 361–2
230 *'You do . . . dull'*	Levy, 507
230 *'These . . . blood'*	VW/LS, 23 February 1922, *L*, vol. 2, 508
230 *'Clive . . . letter!'*	LS/Carrington, 13 February 1922 Levy, 504
230 *'shrieked . . . laughter'*	Carrington, 195
230 *'must . . . wilder'*	VW/LS, 23 February 1922, *L*, vol. 2, 507–8
230 *'because . . . utilitarian'*	*Vanity Fair*, September 1922
231 *'sterilized . . . granted'* *'normal . . . our own'*	'Sport and Spoil-Sports', *Vanity Fair*, 19 (September 1922), 47
231 *'abominable . . . tyranny'*	*On British*, 7, n1
231 *cuts . . . Examiner*	Marshik, 52
231 *'he does . . . police'*	*On British*, 21

231 *'This innate . . . world'*   Ibid., 28
231 *'guise . . . shopkeeper'*   Ibid., 53
231 *'all you . . . Saturday'*   Ibid., 58
231 *Quentin . . . 1960s*   Q. Bell, *Elders*, 33

24   The Lively Arts

232 *'some people . . . bed'*   *On British*, 25
232 *stage-managed by Diaghilev*   Davenport-Hines, 5
232 *'must be . . . outdone'*   CB/VB, 22 May 1922
232 *'useless one'*   T. S. Eliot/McAlmon, 22 May 1921, *L*, vol. 1, 563
232 *'Paris . . . yesterday'*   Flanner, *Yesterday*, xxiv
233 *'concocted . . . England'; 'sort of . . . Picasso'*   'Mr. Bell, Miss Cather and Others', *Vanity Fair*, October 1922
233 *'mere . . . you know'*   CB/MH, 9 September 1922
233 *'desperate . . . country'*   CB/MH, 1 August 1922
233 *'classical . . . Chapel'*   'Plus de Jazz', *New Republic*, 21 September 1921, 92–6
233 *'jazzing'*   North, 145
233 *'emphatic . . . another'; 'ragged . . . sentence'*   'Plus de Jazz', *New Republic*, 21 September 1921, 92–6
233 *'concentration . . . prose'*   CB, *Since*, 224
234 *'prodigious inventiveness'*   Ibid., 220
234 *'quite . . . intelligent'*   CB/MH, 29 October 1922
234 *'"twin . . . Fair'*   Kammen, 52
234 *'a revolt . . . white'*   North, 144
234–5 *'Horror . . . world'*   'The Darktown Strutters on Broadway: A Reassuring Word About the Alleged Menace of the Negro Show', *Vanity Fair*, November 1922, 67, 104
235 *'Europe . . . production'*   Seldes, 146
235 *'any . . . narrowness'*   'Negro or "Nigger"', *Athenaeum*, 27 August 1922

235 *'to . . . destroy'*	'Negro Sculpture', *Athenaeum*, 20 August 1920, 247–8
236 *'America . . . Harlem'*	Seldes, 145
236 *'hopelessly . . . unreal';* *'common-place . . . intention'; 'art might . . .élite'*	'Art and the Cinema', *Vanity Fair*, 19 (November 1922), 39–40
237 *'prairies . . . illustrators'; 'vivify . . .civilization'; 'puddle'*	'The Seven Lively Arts', *New Republic*, 30 April 1924, 263–4, revised 'Arts and Art', *N&A*, 10 May 1924, 179–80
237 *'international quarrel'; 'style . . . way'*	'There is an Art in Drinking a Cup of Tea', *Vanity Fair*, July 1924
237 *'we must . . . arts'*	Seldes, 291
237 *'minor arts'*	Ibid., 292
237 *'fever . . .Entr'acte'*	Hankins, 153

25 Landmarks

238 *industrial unrest . . . soldiers*	Dangerfield, 320–8
238 *'my Mr Baldwin'*	Spalding, *DG*, 261
239 *'good . . . art'*	VW, 13 May 1926, *D*, vol. 3, 85
239 *'other spirits'*	VW/VB, 12 May 1926, *L*, vol. 3, 262
239 *'PROTEST'*	Garafola, 335
239 *'bourgeois capitalist'*	Buckle, 469
239 *'ridiculous row'*	CB/MH, 19 May 1926
239 *'arriviste'*	CB/MH, 23 May 1924
239 *amused . . . intent*	'What's On in Paris', *Vogue*, 63 (Early July 1924), 51, 74
239 *'posthumous . . . Dada'; 'slightly . . . abstract art'*	'Round about Surréalisme', *Vogue*, 68 (Early July 1926), 54–5, 80
240 *'How . . . profanity'*	CB/MH, 26 October 1926
240 *'"return . . . culture'*	Antliff, 158
240 *by 1920 . . . boring*	'The New Art Salon', *Athenaeum*, 27 February 1920, 280–1

240 *Picasso . . . hate abstraction* Bois, 40

240 *'like Picasso . . . form'* 'The Greeks and Romans', *N&A*, 1 November 1924, 182–3, revised, 'David's Contribution to Modern Art', *New Republic*, 26 November 1924, 16–18

240 *'the beginning . . . significant'* 'A Great Exhibition', *Vogue*, 67 (Early April 1926), 64–5, 90

240 *'highly civilised loafer'* 'Aesthetic Truth and Futurist Nonsense', *Outlook*, 7 May 1924, 20–3

241 *Roger's influence* Wilcox, 14

241 *'no less . . . school'* 'The Allied Artists at the Leicester Galleries', *Vogue*, 67 (Late May 1926), 64–5, 112, 114

241 *'Neo-Pre-Raphaelite'* 'English Painting at the Moment', *Vanity Fair*, January 1923, 40, 90

241 *'heirs to Cézanne'; 'accused . . . exotic'* 'A Re-Formation of the English School', *Artwork*, Summer 1926

241 *'leading . . . England'* 'Notes on Some Recent and Current Exhibitions', *Vogue*, 69 (Early March 1927), 64–5, 86

241 *'extreme . . . French'* 'The Allied Artists at the Leicester Galleries', *Vogue*, 67 (Late May 1926), 64–5, 112, 114.

241–2 *'the best . . . feminine art'* 'English Painting at the Moment', *Vanity Fair*, January 1923, 40, 90

242 *'tiny . . . painters'* 'The French Pictures at Heal's', *Nation*, 16 August 1919, 586–8

242 *'still Charles . . . of life'* 'Flowers and a Moral', *N&A*, 4 June 1927, 303–4

242 'between . . . art'   'The Art of Brancusi', *Vogue*, 66
                                 (Late December 1925), 43–5;
                                 VW, *Lighthouse*, 23

242 'to create . . . volumes'; 'poise   'Frank Dobson', *Architectural*
. . . subject'; 'frankly baroque'; 'the   *Review*, 59 (February 1926),
contours . . . depressions'   41–5

242–3 'oafs'; 'suppose . . . this'; 'his   'The Art of Brancusi', *Vogue*, 66
forms . . . the matter'   (Late December 1925), 43–5

243 'trying . . . painting'   VW/RF, 22 September 1924, *L*
                                 vol. 3, 133

243 'few . . . Paris'   'Mr. Clive Bell's French Tour',
                                 N&A, 14 May 1927

243 'few things . . . criticism'   *Since*, 178

243 Gates told . . . review   B. Gates/CB, 20 May 1927,
                                 KCC

244 'made . . . book'; 'Neo-Classical   *Landmarks*, v
. . . map-maker'

244 'one of . . . painting'   Ibid., 38

244 'collaboration . . . skies'   Ibid., 55

244 'hysterical way'   Wilenski, 170

244 'intrinsic . . . acquired'   Ibid., 171

244 'implicit . . . work'   Ibid., 172

245 'highbrowism . . . fact'   *Drawing & Design*, June 1927,
                                 191

245 'considerable . . . pen'   *Evening Standard*, 19 May 1927

245 'too much . . . man'   *TLS*, 21 April 1927

245 'enthusiasm'   *Glasgow Herald*, 21 April 1927

245 'for . . . judgments'   *Manchester Guardian*, 9 May
                                 1927

26 *The End of the Affair*

246 'taste . . . women'   Q. Bell, *Elders*, 10

246 'surrogate father'   Stansky and Abrahams, 130

246 'terrific . . . crisis'   J. Bell, 18

246 'They should . . . others'   CB/J. Bell, 5 February 1927,
                                 KCC

247 'All . . . eye'   CB/J. Bell, 17 November 1929, KCC

247 'Clive . . . solidly'   J. Bell, 16–17

247 'Darling . . . others'   CB/MH, 28 November 1926

247 'bear . . . secret'   CB/MH, 1 January 1927

248 'practically went mad'; 'society . . debauchery'   VW/VB, 2 February 1927, *L*, vol. 3, 322

248 'Don't . . . seconds'   VW/VB, 5 March 1928, *L*, vol. 3, 466

248 'as though . . . attention'; 'grew . . broken'   M. Hutchinson, 'Clive'

248 'enchanting . . . enchantress'   CB/MH, 27 June 1925

248 'kissing . . . legs'   CB/MH, 4 September 1923

248 'enchanting . . . in it'   CB/MH, 18 February 1927

248 'nice . . . wearing'   D. H. Lawrence/Dorothy Brett, 8 March 1927, *L*, vol. 4, 651

248 'have . . . with work'   VB/VW, 5 February 1927, Marler, 305

249 'sizzling . . . fling'   Bingham, 134

249 'the best . . . America'   Ibid., 122, 317n

250 'that comes . . . wine'   CB/MH, 22 September 1925

250 'I must . . . devil'   Wright, 117

251 'delicate mission'   CB/B. Penrose, 10 June 1926, KCC

251 'A typical . . . ruffle one'   Wright, 118

251 'sitting . . . toiletted Clive'   B. Penrose/CB, 3 August 1927, KCC

251 'ladies . . . life'; 'sorts . . . pleasure'   CB/B. Penrose, 7 August 1927, KCC

252 'an unspoken . . . jealousy'   Wright, 118

253 'little bitch'   VW/VB, 25 May 1927, *L*, vol. 3, 383

253 'Vanessa . . . lovers'   CB/B. Penrose, 20 August 1927, KCC

253 'Don't . . . meant to'   B. Penrose/CB, 18 September 1927, KCC

253 *'You would . . . me'*   B. Penrose/CB, 8 September 1927, KCC

253 *'as I . . . offer me'*   AD, 16 April 1927
253 *'I cannot . . . about'*   CB/MH, 30 April 1927
253 *'It was . . . stay mad'*   VW, 16 May 1927, *D*, vol. 3, 136

254 *'comparative . . . weary'*   Seymour-Jones, 500
254 *'can make . . . quiver'*   N. Murray, 212, n29
254 *'it was . . . dead'*   CB/MH, 4 July 1927
254 *'smaller . . . heart'*   CB/MH, 11 August 1927
254 *'how you . . . stream'*   CB/B. Penrose, 10 October 192?, KCC

254 *'romantic . . . Savoy'; 'What . . . missed'; 'Oh . . . true'*   CB/B. Penrose, nd, KCC

255 *'how I . . . unreality'*   CB/B. Penrose, 20 December 1928, KCC

255–6 *'seated . . . ink'*   VW/V. Sackville-West, 5 April 1927, *L*, vol. 3, 358

256 *'violently anti-artist'*   VB/VW, 23 April 1927, Marler, 312

256 *'I never . . . open'*   CB/MH, 5 May 1927
256 *'large . . . table'*   CB/VB, 15 May 1927
257 *small improvements*   Spalding, *VB*, 219–20
257 *'Meak . . . grasped'*   VB/VW and LW, 25 December 1927, Marler, 325–6

257 *'round . . . parrokeet'*   VW/VB, 5 October 1927, *L*, vol. 3, 426

257 *'inveterate . . . malicious'*   VB/VW, 4 May 1927, Berg
257 *'Clive . . . Bloomsbury'; 'He had . . . of women'*   VW, 23 July 1927, *D*, vol. 3, 148

257 *Valerie told . . . hurt*   V. Taylor/CB,?23 October 1927, KCC

259 *'very superficial'*   VW, 31 May 1928, *D*, vol. 3, 184

259 *'belief . . . politics'; 'more . . . bad'*   Stansky and Abrahams, 126

259 *'it turned . . . Square'*   Q. Bell, *Elders*, 35

259 'entities . . . types' Civilization, 15
259 'All . . . world' Ibid., 17
259–60 'forced . . . civilization' Ibid., 28
260 'was of . . . pleasure' Ibid., 24
260 'at one . . . epitaph' D. Bradshaw, 'Those', 9
260 An unusually . . . regard Laura Marchioni di Torlago/CB, 14 August 1946, KCC
260 'A Civilized Man' LW, Essays, Hogarth, 1927, 149–52
260 'My Early Beliefs' Two Memoirs, Hart-Davis, 1949
260 'It is . . . possible' Civilization, 166
260 'requires . . . slaves'; 'people . . . others' Ibid., 205
261 'it was . . . heel'; Q. Bell, Elders, 35
261 'hard . . . enemies' Holtby, 'Mr Zimmern Takes the Next Step', Time and Tide, 13 July 1928
261 'produce . . . parlours' 'Towards Bloomsbury', Observer, 19 August 1928
261 'Liberal . . . enjoy it' Civilization, 97
261 'what we . . . open' Ibid., 121
262 reason . . . civilisation 'The Rational Man', Yorkshire Post, 24 October 1928
262 'put on . . . barrister' Civilization, 238
262 'completely parasitic' James Viner, 'Views and Reviews', New Age, 22 November 1928
262 socialism . . . rejected R. B. Suthers, 'What is Civilization? Boiled Rabbit', Railway Review, 30 October 1928
262 more tolerable . . . happy CB/LS, 6 November 1927, C-W
262 'He . . . shake him'; 'fascinating . . . companions' FP, Memories, 136–7
263 'Love and Liberty' Trinity, 1/16
263 'retrieve . . . house' CB/VB, 17 December 1921
263 'pest' CB/MH, 6 August 1920

263 *'imaginative wife'*   CB/MH, 28 April 1924

263 *best play . . . time*   CB/T. S. Eliot, 25 September
                                        1927, TSE

263 *'Today . . . letter'*   CB/B. Mayor, 3 November
                                        1927, Trinity

264 *'Darling slut'*   CB/B. Mayor, 2 January 1928,
                                        Trinity

264 *Clive assured . . . attractive*   CB/B. Mayor, 25 January 1928,
                                        Trinity

264 *'in more . . . for'*   CB/VB, 2 March 1928

264 *'that modern masterpiece'*   'To visit the Maddermarket . . .',
                                        N&A, 23 June 1928, 393–4

264 *'necessity . . . Cambridge'*   CB/B. Mayor, 21 January 1928,
                                        Trinity

265 *'up vistas . . . art'*   CB/VB, 11 February 1928

265 *'all . . . do'*   CB/B. Mayor, 30 January 1928,
                                        Trinity

265 *'rather . . . Liberty'*   CB/VW, 3 February 1928

265 *Soon after . . . together*   Marion Kolb/CB, 14 February
                                        1928, KCC

265 *seemed happy*   VB/VW, 24 February 1928, Berg

265 *'her friends . . . are'*   VW/VB, 26 February 1928, *L*,
                                        vol. 3, 465

265 *'crazed'*   VW/VB, 5 March 1928, *L*, vol.
                                        3, 466

265 *'lady of fashion'*   Spalding, *VB*, 224

265 *'I want . . . my hands'*   CB/VB, 2 March 1928

265 *'odd . . . sexually'*   VB/VW, 9 March 1928,
                                        Spalding, *VB*, 224

266 *'an amazing . . . rage'*   VB/CB, 6 February 1928

266 *'bourgeois . . . snobbery'*   Reitlinger, 31

266 *'shared . . . cohabitation'; 'even*   Ibid., 32
. . . France'

266 *'an apostle . . . biographer';*   Mortimer, 'London', 242
'fierce . . . criticism'

266 *'Messrs . . . Radclyffe-Hall'*   CB/B. Mayor, 7 November
                                        1928, Trinity

266–7 *'In a . . . pacifist'*   Mortimer, 'London', 243

27 Insane about Females

268 *swansong*   Taylor, 5
268 *'one . . . symbols'*   Ibid., 13
268 *loathed . . . Runcible*   Chisholm, 124
268 *'Daimler . . . parties'*   VW/VB, 20 March 1928, *L*, vol.
                                    3, 476
268 *'He knows . . . plan'*   N. Nicolson, 199
268 *'drug[ged] . . . metaphorically'* CB/MH, 22 March 1929
268 *Clive appeared . . . bail*   Paul, 184
268 *'everyone . . . young'*   CB/VB, 20 May 1928
269 *'It used . . . worse now'*   VB/VW, 22 April 1928, Berg
269 *'Its like . . . laughed at'*   VW/V. Sackville-West, 23
                                    February 1929, *L*, vol. 4, 29
269 *'some . . . opinion'*   CB/VW, 25 April 1928
269 *'this perpetual . . . of it'; 'He* VW/VB, 29 April 1928, *L*, vol.
takes . . . family'   3, 489
269 *'to old . . . for ever'*   VW/VB, 26 May 1928, *L*, vol.
                                    3, 501
270 *'I am . . . night'*   *Proust*, 50–1
270 *'commanded . . . self'*   VW, *Orlando*, 209
271 *'help . . . illusion'*   *Proust*, 51
271 *'almost . . . self'; 'Personality* Ibid., 52
. . . self'
271 *'emotional event'*   Ibid., 8
271 *'Proust-and-I . . . essay'*   *Aberdeen Press and Journal*, 29
                                    November 1928
271 *'would . . . inclusiveness'*   *New Adelphi*, December 1928
271 *letter from Clive*   'Proust Studies', *TLS*, 28
                                    February 1929, 163
272 *'Even . . . Bloomsbury'*   'Your Reviewer', *TLS*, 21 March
                                    1929
272 *commented . . . French*   H. Pinault/CB, 11 January 1924,
                                    KCC
272 *'harsh . . . things'*   CB/MH, 14 July 1928
272 *'written . . . thanks'*   CB/MH,?17 November 1928

272–3 'asserted . . . enjoyment';   'Mr. Anrep's Mosaics in the
'lovely pattern'   National Gallery', *N&A*, 2 June
                                      1928, 296

273 'rather stupidly'   CB/VB, 20 May 1928
274 'revenge . . . husband'   Seymour-Jones, 206
274 'almost . . . painted'   'Mrs St John Hutchinson', tate.
                                      org.uk

274 'awful . . . like her'   J. Hutchinson, 'National',
274 *Spalding believes*   Spalding, *VB*, 146
274 'in spats . . . it all'   VW/V. Sackville-West, 8 January
                                      1929, *L*, vol. 4, 3

274 'most astonishing . . .   VB/VW, 10 May 1929, Berg
conversation'; 'insane about females'
 275 'paints . . . find'   VB/VW, 9 March 1929, Berg
275 'elderly roué'   VW/VB, 5 May 1929, *L*, vol. 4,
                                      52–3

275 'progress . . . pilgrimage'   VW/Q. Bell, 11 May 1929, *L*,
                                      vol. 4, 55

275 'sensible . . . competence'   VW/VB, 6 July 1929, *L*, vol. 4,
                                      73

275 *even . . . edge*   CB/FP, 20 June 1931
275 'about . . . and all'   CB/VB, 30 June 1929
275–6 *Years . . . forget Mary*   CB/MH, 4 February 1946, Sx
276 'conferences . . . cleaning'   Findling, 253
276 'one of . . . to see'   CB/FP, 29 October 1929
276 *wondered . . . she did*   M. Huxley/MH,?16 October
                                      1929, HRC

276 'everything . . . left'   VW, 26 December 1929, *D*, vol.
                                      3, 275

28 Clive Agonistes

279 'prefer . . . buggers'   CB/VB, 11 October 1932
279 'Mrs Duncan Grant'   'Farmhouse Homes', *Daily
                                      Telegraph*, 2 September 1931, 7
279 'You're an . . . aren't we'   20 May 1935, Marler, 389–90
279–80 'The lovers . . . connexions' AD, 1935

280 'Art and Life' ' "Art and Life": A Discussion between Mr. Clive Bell and Mr. Desmond MacCarthy', BBC, 2LO, 7 December 1928

281 'elderly . . . bald' VW/VB, 5 May 1929, L, vol. 4, 52–3

281–2 'I never . . . lover' B. Jaeger/CB, 27 December 1929, KCC

282 made short 8mm films Lanchester, 336
282 'false illusions'; 'Besides . . . Benitas' B. Jaeger/CB, nd, KCC

282 attended . . . extravaganza Luke, 82
282 'Gargling . . . Club' Tatler, 23 October 1929
282–3 'How wise . . . age' CB/FP,?February 1930
283 'constant . . . jealousy' Taylor, 237
283 'headquarters . . . buggery' CB/VW, 2 February 1930
283 admire . . . Giacometti J. Lee, 80
283 'plastic equivalent' 'Derain', Formes, 1 (February 1930), 5–6 (English edition)

283 'what he . . . young' Flanner, Journal, 247
283 'almost . . . economy' Spalding, DG, 300
284 'Dragged' CB/VB, 20 May 1930
284 'ceased . . . actress' CB/A. Roullier, 7 June 1930, Newberry

284 'party of boxers . . . for me' CB/VB, 9 June 1930
284 'low . . . thinking' CB/J. Bell, 19 June 1930, KCC
284 'an enchanting . . . being'; 'a little in love' CB/VB, 28 June 1930

285 'his . . . depends'; 'to go . . . relationship' VW/E. Smyth, 29 November 1930, L, vol. 4, 258–9
285–6 'feel sex . . . for ever'; 'I always . . . queer ghost' VW, 26 December 1929, D, vol. 3, 275
286 'tangle of emotions' VW/E. Smyth, 29 November 1930, L, vol. 4, 259

286 'played . . . paid' VW, 1 June 1932, D, vol. 4, 104
286 'George . . . detection' VW, D, vol. 4, 132, n5

286 'observe . . . pismire'	VW, 4 August 1934, *D*, vol. 4, 235
286 'Its odd . . . Clive'	VW, 11 October 1929, *D*, vol. 3, 260
286 'odd . . . emotion'	VW, 8 July 1932, *D*, vol. 4, 114
287 Maynard . . . condemned	CB/LS, 6 September 1930, BL
287 Eliot recommended	T. S. Eliot/J. Joyce, 11 Dec 1930, *L*, vol. 5, 426
287 Aldous . . . Braille	A. Huxley/CB, 5 January 1931, KCC
287 Clive heard . . . plight	R. Mortimer/CB, 18 February 1931, Princeton
287 'fun girl'	B. Jaeger/CB, nd, KCC
287 Ethel Sands . . . persist	E. Sands/N. Hudson, 10 December 1930, TGA
287 'Alpine Sing-Sing'	CB/VB, 13 January 1931
287 Having discussed . . . gossip	VW/CB, 7 February 1931, *L*, vol. 4, 289
287 'she . . . buggers'	CB/VB, 14 February 1931
288 'solely . . . necklace'	Spalding, *VB*, 242–4

29 An Account of French Painting

289 'beginning . . . book'	CB/VB, 17 May 1931
290 'calmly . . . treatises'; 'French'	'New Novels', *Observer*, 20 March 1932
290 'part . . . Juan'	Q. Bell, *Elders*, 11
290 Talking . . . well	CB/VB, 21 June 1931
290 'one . . . Matisse'	VB/CB, 14 June 1931, Marler, 365
290 'magnificent'	CB/VB,?29 June 1931
290 He answered . . . home	Kessler, 382
290 'Thank . . . Picasso'	CB/MH, 1 July 1931
291 'No . . . generalisations'	*Account*, 8–9
291 'most . . . humanity'	Ibid., 10
291 'He hails . . . highway'	*Daily Telegraph*, 11 October 1931

291 *Raymond . . . obligation*	Mortimer, 'French', 82
291 *'an act of culture'; 'everyone does'*	'Why do they go to the Pictures?', *Art News*, 31 May 1930, 14
292 *'If . . . clothes'*	*Account*, 148
292 *'in a . . . yearning'; 'like . . . pontifical'*	RF, *NS&N*, 14 November 1931
292 *'indicated terminal'*	*Account*, 204
292 *'timid millionaires'*	'The Private Collection of Mr and Mrs Courtauld', *Vogue*, 69 (Early February 1927), 30–1, 70
292 *'long . . . argument'*	R. Aldington, 'French Tradition in Painting, Clive Bell's Brilliant New Book of Art Criticism', *Sunday Referee*, 29 November 1931
293 *'Odd . . . at all'*	*Account*, 80
293 *'with . . . cricket'*	*Liverpool Post & Mercury*, 3 December 1931

30 Dancing on a Volcano

294 *'It is . . . sails'*	CB/FP, 16 September 1931
295 *'gigolo'*	CB/VB, 30 September 1931
295 *'greatest . . . time'*	CB/VB, 3 November 1931
296 *'completely . . . female'; 'The French . . . them?'*	CB/VB, 30 September 1931
296 *'this . . . exhibition'*	Ferris, 86
296 *'dancing . . . volcano'*	CB/VB, 21 September 1931
296 *'aged mother'*	CB/FP, 9 October 1931
296 *'pleasant escape'*	Preface, *The New Keepsake*, Cobden-Sanderson, 1931
297 *'nasty . . . bitch'*	CB/VB, 13 March 1932
297 *'small . . . her'; 'think . . . speedboat'*	VW, 18 July 1932, *D*, vol. 4, 118
297 *Leonard's opinion*	LW, *Autobiography*, vol. 2, 273
297 *half real*	CB/FP, 16 March 1932

298 *'I am . . . disreputable'*	CB/VB, 30 September 1931
298 *'The time . . . occupy'*	*Times*, 19 August 1929, 12
298 *'I . . . bright'*	'Limitation All Round', *N&A*, 24 August 1929, 676
298 *'Long queues . . . blood'*	'Arms and the Man', *New Signatures*, ed. Michael Roberts, Hogarth Press, 1932, 38–9
298 *'socialist . . . movement'*	A. Smith, 246
299 *'rumpus'*	CB/VB 17 February 1934
299 *'attempted . . . putsch'*	D. Bradshaw, 'British', 17
299 *'had . . . War"'*	Flanner, *Yesterday*, 112
299 *'key . . . events'*	Knegt, 22
299 *'pestering . . . spite'*	CB/MH, 19 October 1936
299 *'complete nonsense'*	LW, *Quack*, 56
299 *'bosses'; 'despots'; 'leisured . . . civilization'*	*Civilization*, 231
299 *neo-humanist . . . hierarchical society*	Affron, 180
299–300 *'liberal . . . materialism'*	Ibid., 184
300 *'loosely . . . Churchill'*	Bonham Carter, 187
300 *Violet . . . amused*	V. Bonham Carter/CB, 15 May 1933, KCC
300 *'only . . . Germany'*	Haas, 214
300 *'Is it . . . proclaim'*	M. Baker/CB, nd, KCC
300 *Jewish . . . Chief Rabbi*	Foscari, 161, n89
300 *'Do . . . war'*	'Sanctions', *NS&N*, 28 September 1935, 405
300 *'vicious . . . Pacifists'*	Q. Bell, *VW*, vol. 2, 187
301 *'armaments . . . thinking'*	D. Wilson, 188
301 *'have . . . militarism'*	Gould, 'The Pacifist's Dilemma', *NS&N*, 18 October 1933
301 *Clive believed . . . bombed*	CB, 'The Pacifist's Dilemma', *NS&N*, 18 November 1933, 630, letter
301 *'No . . . arming'*	D. Wilson, 189

31 Enjoying Pictures

302 'good-natured . . . wanted'	CB/VB, 25 Feb 1933
302 'too . . . head'	CB/VB, 13 October 1934
303 'follow . . . phrases'	Enjoying, 3
303 'an escape . . . life'	Ibid., 106
303 'fundamentally . . . kind'	Richards, 10
304 'unique . . . emotion'	Enjoying, 11
304 'personal . . . consulted'	Ibid., 86
304 'idiotic'	'Meditations in the Galleries', Sunday Times, 18 March 1934
304 'performing . . . culture'	Enjoying, 49
304 'millionaires . . . market'	Ibid., 50
304 'he will . . . Gallery'	Ibid., 50
304 'little . . . freedom'	VW, 6 September 1939, D, vol. 5, 235
304–5 'If . . . not'	Enjoying, 88
305 'between . . . Jews'	'German Musical Art', Times, 12 April 1933, 11
305 'abominable . . . boycott'	Kessler, 451
305 'today . . . found'	Chipp, 476
306 'aesthetic insanity'	'Post-Impressionism and Art in the Insane', VW, RF, 124
306 'We . . . morning'	Steiner, 15
306 'people . . . opinions'	Martin, 602
306 'Yes . . . price'	CB/FP, 23 September 1935
306 'unemployment . . . war'	Stansky and Abrahams, 127
306 'development . . . impossible'	Martin, 602
306 Russell . . . Julian	B. Russell/CB, 4 August 1934, KCC
307 'revolutionary activities'	J. Bell, 194
307 'much . . . blood'	Ibid., 196
307 'I feel . . . way'	Ibid., 197
307 'it would . . . England'; 'then . . . resist'	Ibid., 105
307–8 'It's . . . fight'; 'There's . . . them'	Stansky and Abraham, 235

308 *'rich & great'; 'War's . . . anyhow'*   VW, 20 September 1935, *D*, vol. 4, 343

308 *'perverse . . . fact'*   Albert Lewis, 'One Honest Report', *New Masses*, 23 July 1935, 27

308 *'I think . . . Patriots'*   'Sanctions and War', *NS&N*, 28 December 1935, 1011

308 *'regime . . . thugs'*   Braun, 174–5

309 *'last . . . civilized'*   D. Bradshaw, 'British', 7

309 *'organized . . . propaganda'*   A. Huxley/Victoria Ocampo, nd, G. Smith, 397

309 *'one of . . . freedom"'*   VW, 20 February 1935, *D*, vol. 4, 280

309 *'leave . . . joke'*   VW/CB, 19 February 1935, *L*, vol. 5, 371

309 *'to expose . . . headed'*   H. Lee, 674

309 *'very . . . letter'*   VW/Q. Bell, 27 February 1935, *L*, vol. 5, 373

310 *'proved . . . plot'*   VW/Q. Bell, 3 April 1935, *L*, vol. 5, 382

310 *'at least . . .outside'; 'from . . . members'*   Lilly, 43, n23

310 *'rather crusty'*   D. Garnett/CB, 19 April 1938, Sx

310 *'frank . . . evasion'*   RF/CB, 2 May 1934, Sx

310 *'colloquialism . . . simplicity'*   *Granta*, 25 April 1934

310 *'almost . . . discusses'; 'astonishing'; 'either . . . not'; 'perhaps . . . done'; 'logical . . . system'*   RF, 'Grace Abounding', *NS&N*, 21 April 1934

310 *'embracing . . . beloved'*   *Enjoying*, 8

311 *'in . . . uncontrollably'*   Spalding, *VB*, 267

311 *'But . . . it'*   VW, 18 September 1934, *D*, vol. 4, 244

311 *'I think . . . reasonable'*   VW/J. Bell, 11 March 1936, *L*, vol. 6, 20

311 *truculent . . . hackles*	VW/M. MacCarthy. 11 June 1939. *L*, vol. 6, 337
311 *'joy . . . him'*	'Roger Fry 's Last Lectures', *NS&N*, 21 October 1939, 564, 566

32 Art and the Public

312 *'blindly . . . Paris'*	Piper, 136
312 *'abstract . . . form'*	Woods, 19
312 *'brilliant'; 'retracted . . . said'*	B. Nicolson, *Diary*, 7 February 1935, LBN/1/6, Mellon
312 *'situation . . . possibilities'*	Read, 'English', 276
313 *'hive . . . aesthetics'*	M. Green, 143
313 *'Edwardian . . . difficult'*	Pryce-Jones, 247
313 *'an intricate . . . grasp'*	Piper, 143
313 *'secret . . . trouble'*	CB/R. Mortimer & F. Birrell, 13 March 1934, Princeton
313 *pernicious influence*	Wilcox, 191
313 *'nothing . . . Lewis'*	VW, 11 October 1934, *D*, vol. 4, 250
313 *'first . . . painting'*	'What Next in Art?', *Studio*, 109 (April 1935), 176–85
313–14 *'It is . . . intelligence'; 'create . . . art'*	H. Harari/CB, 28 March 1934, KCC
314 *'It is . . . hilarious'*	H. Harari/CB, 2 December 1935, KCC
314 *'truly . . . tradition'*	'What Next in Art?', *Studio*, 109 (April 1935), 176–85
314 *Stuart . . . Pictures*	S. Preston/CB, 8 April 1934, KCC
314 *thank Clive . . . him*	D. Morgan/CB, 3 August 1934, KCC
314 *He wrote . . . by it*	D. Morgan, 17 April 1938, KCC

314 *'great age'; 'individualism'* Foreword, *Exhibition of Masters of Modern French Painting*, 1–31 October 1936

315 *'I was . . . demeanour'* de Margerie, vol. 2, 302: 'J'étais absolument stupéfait d'entendre ces hommes, que je voyais dans le monde sous un autre aspect, parler sans fard d'aventures sentimentales qui contrastaient avec leur air habituellement gourmé'

315 *once remarking . . . exquisite French* Ibid., 303

315 *'The Chevalier'* VB/J. Bell, 5 July 1936, Marler, 414

315 *'peevish . . . protégés'* Grigson, 10

316 *'most remarkable'* 'The Franco-Italian Exhibition', *NS&N*, 6 July 1935, 14–15

316 *'most . . . art'* 'Shell-Mex and the Painters', *NS&N*, 23 June 1934, 946

316 *'from . . . experience'* 'Posters', *NS&N*, 9 July 1938, 75–6

316 *'most . . . time"'* 'At Home and Abroad', *Life and Letters*, 11 (October 1934), 106–12

316 *'I have . . . inn'* 'English Hotels', *NS&N*, 29 August 1936, 287

317 *'State . . . companies'* 'Posters', *NS&N*, 9 July 1938, 75–6

317 *'university of painting'* 'What Next in Art?', *Studio*, 109 (April 1935), 176–85

317 *'an abstraction . . . art"'* 'The Failure of State Art', *Listener*, 21 October 1936, 745–7

317 *'limited . . . painting'* Spalding, *DG*, 387

317–18 *'frivolous . . . themselves';* 'Inside the "Queen Mary": A
'Teddy . . . style'; 'landmark . . .art' Business Man's Dream', *Listener*, 8 April 1936, 658–60

| 318 *'Shall . . . Aberconway"'* | CB/MH, 21 August 1936 |
| 318 *Agnew's . . . masterpieces* | 'British Art in New York', *Times*, 21 April 1939, 12 |

33 *Your Schoolgirl Mistress*

319 *'bewilderingly beautiful'*	'Since Cézanne: Epilogue', *NS&N*, 1 January 1938, 14–15
319 *Matisse had . . . to do*	Caws, 76–7; 'Black and White', *NS&N*, 15 February 1936, 226–7
319–20 *'If Picasso . . . our time'; 'good . . . master'*	'Since Cézanne: Epilogue', *NS&N*, 8 January 1938, 47–9
320 *Called back . . . War*	Richardson, 'Portraits'
320 *'He has . . . we see'*	'Picasso', *NS&N*, 30 May 1936, 857–8
320 *'literally . . . up'*	J. Loeb/CB, 27 January 1937
321 *'He is . . . simpatico'; 'seriously amoureux'; 'discreetly'*	J. Loeb/Margaret Scolari Barr, 28 February [1938], MoMA
322 *'It was . . . domestic'*	J. Bell/Ling Shuhua, 23 March 1937, Berg
322 *'gay and alive'; 'accidentally'*	J. Loeb/CB, nd, KCC
322 *'What . . . vengeance'*	J. Loeb/CB, 15 May 1937
322 *surrounded . . . airs*	J. Loeb/CB, 16 May 1937
323 *'Daisy . . . subject'*	J. Loeb/CB, 24 April 1937
323 *'men . . . literary'*	J. Loeb/CB, 2 May [1937]
323 *'cleverest . . . time'*	CB/G. Seldes, 23 April 1937
323 *'I'm getting . . . let me'*	J. Loeb/CB, 11 April 1937
323 *'scientific . . . hammer'*	J. Loeb/CB, nd
323 *'lovely . . . dirty'*	J. Loeb/CB, 24 April 1937
323 *'who's . . . photographer'*	J. Loeb/CB, 4 June 1937
324 *'first . . . deviation'*	'What Next in Art?', *Studio*, 109 (April 1935), 176–85
324 *'self-sufficient . . . to us'*	Loeb, 6
325 *'bit of . . . supper'*	J. Loeb/CB, 19 April [1937]
325 *'national . . . dignity'*	Eggener, 31

325 *Harpo and Groucho*	Ibid., 33
325 *dismissed Freud's theory*	'Dr Freud on Art', *Athenaeum*, 26 September 1924, reprinted *Dial*, 78 (April 1925), 280–4
325 *'vulgar trash'*	'The Zwemmer Gallery', *NS&N*, 22 December 1934, 938–9
325 *future . . . importance*	'Since Cézanne: Epilogue', *NS&N*, 8 January 1938, 47–9
325 *'are . . . beings'*	Loeb, 25
325 *'delicate . . . again'*	Grigson, 10
325 *'next . . . painting'*	'What Next in Art?', *Studio*, 109 (April 1935), 176–85
325 *East London Group*	'English and French', *NS&N*, 30 January 1937, 158–9
325 *'School of 1938'*	*NS&N*, 26 March 1938
326 *'effect . . . sensibilities'*	Laughton, 30
326 *'Surrealism . . . New York'; 'art nationalists'*	J. Loeb/CB, nd
326 *'Armies and banners'*	J. Loeb/CB, 27 April 1937
326 *'It was . . . time'*	J. Loeb/CB, nd

34 *Today the Struggle*

327 *'world's . . . well'*	J. Loeb/CB, 31 May 1937
327 *'sad friends . . . chaotic doings'*	J. Loeb/CB, 17 June 1937
327 *Vanessa had worried*	VB/CB, February 1937
328 *'reining . . . brewing'; 'very cool . . . Cory'*	Q. Bell, *VW*, vol. 2, 255
328 *'being . . . cut'*	J. Bell, 364
328 *'unravel . . . experience'*	Stansky and Abrahams, 268
328 *'might be . . . character'*	J. Loeb/CB, 8 June 1937
329 *'such . . . man'*	VW/V. Sackville-West, 26 July 1937, *L*, vol. 6, 151
329 *'distressing . . . impossible'*	A. Garnett, *Deceived*, 132
329 *'My life . . . have'*	CB/FP, 30 July 1937
329 *'It is . . . attain'*	E. Sands/CB, 23 July 1937, KCC

330 'the Goth . . . of'	MH/CB, nd, KCC
330 'something . . . biting'	VW, 2 September 1937, *D*, vol. 5, 110
330 'I feel . . . under'	VW/VB, 25 June 1938, *L*, vol. 6, 245
330 'spruce jewess'	VW/VB, 5 August 1937, *L*, vol. 6, 153
330 'a little . . . tires'	VW, 1 November 1937, *D*, vol. 5, 117

35 Warmongers

331 'would . . . civilization'	Overy, 17
332 'politics . . . wrong'	D. Garnett/M Kirstein, 9 March 1936, Berg
332 Dantesque hell	Knights, 289
332 'much . . . middle'	CB/MH, 13 October 1939
332 'plenty . . . world'; 'arrant . . . tyranny'	*Warmongers*, 4
333 'terror . . . question'; 'an . . . masses'; 'Liberals . . . Catholics'; 'party discipline'; 'Nazi . . . Vienna'; 'fantastic . . . truth'	Sheean
333 'the people'; 'the masses'	*Warmongers*, 5
333 Gestapo's list	Spalding, *VW*, 157
333 'Carthaginian'	*Warmongers*, 7
333 vote . . . Conservatives	Ibid., 5
333 'United . . . Europe'	Ibid., 14
334 'balance of power'	Ibid., 11
334 'When . . . owners'	Ibid., 18
334 'It is . . . to-morrow'	Ibid.
334 'out . . . pacificist'	Ibid., 3
334 'war . . . less'	Ibid., 13
334 'dear comrade'	G. Lansbury/CB, 12 August 1938, LSE
334–5 Huxley . . . 1930s	Beechey, 'Clive', 14

335 *Nichols . . . masks*	P. Nichols/CB, 6 October 1938, KCC
335 *'much . . . view'*	E. Russell, 74
335 *'simply . . . worse'; 'hardly . . . at all'*	VB/CB, nd
335 *'seriously annoyed'*	CB/VB, 29 October 1938
335 *'ardent Chamberlainite'*	CB/VB, 22 September 1938
335 *'mezzo-brows'; 'common people'*	CB/VB, nd
336 *'general . . . matter'*	CB/VB, 3 October 1938
336 *'Liberalism . . . England'*	AD, 14 October 1938
336 *'if you . . . methods'*	'Conscription', *NS&N*, 17 December 1938, 1048
336 *'blind . . . criminal'*	Bonham Carter, 217
336 *'Nazi . . . conviction'*	Leavis, 204
336 *'half-witted'*	'Conscription – and the Pacifists', *Northern Daily Mail*, 3 June 1939, 3
336 *'they say'; 'beneath contempt'*	CB/FP, 11 November 1939
336 *'sent to Coventry'*	VW, 22 November 1938, *D*, vol. 5, 189
336 *'What . . . expect'*	VB/VW, 14 October 1938, Marler, 448
336 *Virginia told Quentin*	VW/Q. Bell, 18 October 1938, *L*, vol. 6, 293

36 Euston Road

337 *'underwater'; 'ludicrous'; 'and . . . contemptuous'; 'Am . . . pipe'*	J. Loeb/CB, nd
337 *'great nose'*	VW, 30 January 1939, *D*, vol. 5, 203
337 *'At Clive's . . . tongue'*	VW, 17 January 1939, *D*, vol. 5, 199
337 *long review*	*NS&N*, 19 March 1938
337–8 *delighted . . . views*	R. de Margerie/CB, 5 April 1938, KCC

338 *'Janice . . . Lydia'*	VB/VW, 14 October 1938, Marler, 448
338 *'next . . . painting'*	'What Next in Art?', *Studio*, 109 (April 1935), 176–85
338 *'wish . . . themselves'*	Laughton, 145
338 *'fashionable . . . visit'*	Ibid., 146
338 *'school of 1938'*	'The School of 1938', *NS&N*, 26 March 1938, 524–6
338 *'critical . . . years'*	'Present and Future', *NS&N*, 5 November 1938, 721–3
338 *'became . . . painter'*	Laughton, 170
339 *'my fear . . . at that'; 'an . . . mistress'*	J. Loeb/M. Scolari Barr, 14 September 1938, MoMA
339 *'no . . . patriotism'*	VW, 28 August 1939, *D*, vol. 5, 231
339 *'stealthily'*	CB/FP, 25 December 1939
339 *'could . . . again'*	CB/MH, 22 August 1939
339 *'allowed'; 'twinge . . . too'; 'keep . . . alive'; 'must . . . beings'*	CB/MH, 2 September 1936
339 *'some . . . London'*	CB/R. Mortimer, 14 September 1939, Princeton
339–40 *'save the artists'*	'A Ministry of Arts', *NS&N*, 14 October 1939, 518–19
340 *'Dorothy . . . background'*	CB/VB, nd
340 <u>*'crowning*</u> *. . . lives'*	D. Hony Diary, 25 April 1939, Trotter
340 *children . . . flags*	D. Hony Diary, 11 May 1937, Trotter
341 *'What . . . me'*	J. Loeb/CB, 4 September 1939
341 *'surrealist charm'*	CB/FP, 2 October 1939
341 *Air raid . . . to London*	'An Excess of Zeal?', *Times*, 16 September 1939, 6
341 *'wandering'*	CB/Bobsy Goodspeed, 7 August 1939, Newberry
341 *'leaving . . . hosts'*	*Edinburgh Evening News*, 17 July 1939

341 'enormous . . . party'	VW, 7 August 1939, *D*, vol. 5, 230
341 'Clive . . . bathroom'	VW, *D*, vol. 5, 230n

37 Alarm and Despondency

345 'nearest . . . Heights'	Shone, 'Official', 21
346 'I don't . . . beans'	CB/MH, ?May 1940
347 'earthly paradise'	A. Garnett, 'Earthly'
347 'silly'	CB/MH, 18 May 1942
348 'were always . . . was'	Partridge, *Pacifist's*, 139
348 1947 . . . father-in-law	D. Garnett/M. Kirstein Curtiss, 13 January 1947, Berg
348 'inherent coldness'; 'He would . . . released'	A. Garnett, *Deceived*, 136
348 looking after babies	CB/MH, 21 July 1943
348 contraceptives . . . mystery	CB/M. Kirstein Curtiss, 22 March 1950, Berg
349 'a strong . . . activity'	FP, *Pacifist's*, 89–90
349 'unwanted attentions'; 'fast and furious'	FP, *Everything*, 16
349 'extraordinarily . . . taste'	CB/MH, 20 June 1945
350 'pessimised'	VW, 16 February 1940, *D*, vol. 5, 268
350 'I'm not . . . to know'	FP, *Pacifist's*, 38
350 'philosophy . . . unshaken'	Ibid., 45
350 'indeed . . . Charleston'	CB/FP, 2 January 1941
350 'always . . . horror'	Partridge, *Pacifist's*, 75
350 'I assume . . . peace'; 'whatever . . . live in'	CB/FP, 2 August 1941
351 'I do . . . Gainsborough'	C. Connolly, 'Round the National Gallery', *NS&N*, 7 December 1940
351 'sullen . . . ridden'	VW, 27 June 1940, *D*, vol. 5, 299
351 'alarm and despondency'	Hansard, HC Deb, 20 June 1940, vol. 362, c223

351 *evidence of subversion*   FP, *Pacifist's*, 47–8
351 *'shiver . . . will power'*   'Shiver Sisters', *Milngavie &*
                                                Bearsden Herald, 10 August
                                                1940
351 *objected . . . warranted*   'Fifth Columnists', *NS&N*, 27
                                                July 1940, 89
351 *'manifesto . . . know it'*   *Daily Herald*, 8 August 1940
351–2 *heading . . . of it*   W. Hetherington, email, 24
                                                September 2019
352 *Pasmore . . . release*   J. Rye, 46
352 *'whole . . . after'*   CB/FP, 22 August 1940
352 *'barking . . . risk theirs*   FP, *Pacifist's*, 56
352 *'bombing match'*   'Rumours', *NS&N*, 16
                                                November 1940, 492
353 *'Cant . . . hell'*   VW, 6 October 1939, *D*, vol.
                                                5, 241
353 *'shut himself . . . grow'*   VW/B. Nicolson, 13 August
                                                1940, *L*, vol. 6, 413
353 *'Thinking . . . fighting'*   VW, 15 May 1940, *D*, vol. 5,
                                                285
353 *'thinking . . . current'*   VW, 'Thoughts', 244
353 *'interpretation . . . public'*   VW/B. Nicolson, 24 August
                                                1940, *L*, vol. 6, 420
353 *reminded Virginia . . . painting*   VW/MH, 10 February 1941,
                                                L, vol. 6, 472
353 *'to be . . . again'*   CB/MH, 25 March 1941
354 *'sleeping . . . shop'; 'appalling loss'*   CB/MH, 31 March 1941
354 *Choosing . . . decision*   CB/FP, 3 April 1941

38 Art on Trial

355 *'Victorians . . . age'*   CB/MH, 22 April 1941
355 *'ultra-modern . . . being'*   *Times*, 1 December 1939
355 *'idiotic . . . not art'*   Spalding, *Tate*, 70
355 *'nothing . . . painting'*   CB/VB, 6 March 1938
355 *'almshouse . . . cemetery';*   'The Unacademic Academy',
'spurious erudition'   *NS&N*, 21 May 1938, 870–2

356 'sound . . . "nonsense"' — *Times*, 13 December 1939

356 'painted . . . seen'; 'mystifying . . . experts'; 'triumph . . . representation' — *Times*, 21 December 1939

356 'all the Munningses'; 'untamed'; 'sterilised . . . museum' — 'Mr. Munnings and Ultra-Modern Art', *NS&N*, 6 January 1940, 10–11

357 'You can't . . . hasn't it' — CB/MH, 22 April 1941

357 enjoyable years . . . broke out — Gwen Morgan, 'Mary Landon Baker', *Chicago Tribune Magazine*, 1 April 1956

357 'pillow . . . Embassy' — FP, *Pacifist's*, 97

357 'a dozen . . . body' — CB/FP, 9 September 1940

357 'inconceivable tristesse' — CB/FP, 2 January 1941

357–8 'vivid . . . worrying' — CB/MH, 22 April 1941

358 Clark . . . vision — Foss, 173

358 begun in 1935 . . . entities — Eastment, 27–9

358 'anxious . . . state' — *Old*, 56

358 'destroyed . . . egalitarianism' — Ibid., 57

358–9 'by-word'; 'inveterate . . . painting'; 'that . . . race'; 'shuttered'; 'betaken . . . America' — 'Modern British Painting', Trinity, 4/25

359 same remark — 'Blest Pair', *NS&N*, 30 December 1939, 964

359 '"Bloomsbury" friends' — Rothenstein, *Brave*, 77

359 'as much . . . world' — Ibid., 71

359 'sound . . . Britain'; 'more . . . Constable' — 'Modern British Art', Trinity, 4/25

360 MacColl granted . . . justified — 'Blest Pair', *NS&N*, 13 Jan 1940, 43

360 'pure . . . generally' — Clark, 'War', 2

360 'discouraged . . . audiences' — Foss, 175–6

360 'done even . . . himself" — J. Loeb/CB, 5 July 1941

360 'widely . . . countries' — Eastment, 78

361 'stuffs' — CB/MH, 21 September 1941

361 'spawn of committees' — 'Pictures for America', *NS&N*, 15 November 1941, 424

361 *Tunnard . . . his work* 'Two Galleries', *NS&N*, 18 July 1942, 41

361 *'apparition . . . war'* 'Artists of Fame and Promise', *NS&N*, 26 July 1941, 82

361 *'particularly . . . barbarism'* 'Two Shows', *NS&N*, 3 August 1940, 110

361 *'one of . . . painters'* Clark, *Other*, 43

361 *Reviewing Pasmore's . . . matter* 'Victor Pasmore', *NS&N*, 15 June 1940, 746

361 *radio discussion* 'The Living Image', Discussions on the Relation Between Life and Art, I. Painting, BBC Home Service, 7 October 1941

362 *'reactionary spirit'* Foss, 188

362 *'might . . . janissaries'* H. Read/CB, 23 September 1943, Sx

362 *'defiant . . . metropolis'* Read, 'The War', 11

362 *'Unquestionably . . . England'* CB/FP, 13 October 1943

363 *'great boost'* CB/MH, 2 July 1941

363 *'Shamelessly . . . Gwen John'; 'local . . . district'* 'Miller's – The Arts in Sussex', *NS&N*, 19 July 1941, 58

364 *'a sailor . . . homes'* 'Paintings in the Berwick Church, Sussex', *Country Life*, 93 (4 June 1943), 1016–17

364 *'deeply . . . language'* CB/MH, 12 October 1943

364 *'great leap forward'* 'Three Shows', *NS&N*, 4 April 1942, 225

364 *'ensured . . . years'* Crook, 17

365 *'remorselessly planned'* 'A Positive Pleasure', *NS&N*, 12 December 1942, 388–9

365 *'centre . . . civilisation'* CB/MH, 26 December 1942

365 *'nationally . . . petrol'* CB/FP, 10 August 1945

365 *plentiful . . . populace* Spalding, *DG*, 382

365 *Clive blamed . . . features* 'Miller's – The Arts in Sussex', *NS&N*, 19 July 1941, 58

365 *'what actually . . . can see'* *Twelfth*, 9

365 *advocate . . . Photography*	'National Collection of Photography: Fostering Appreciation and Study', *Times*, 3 March 1952, 3
366 *'which . . . civilisation'*	*Twelfth*, 11
366 *'to be sure . . . Apocalypse'*	Ibid., 14
366 *'aesthetics . . . objection'*	Reed, *Rooms*, 211

39 Collaboration

367 *'magically transported'*	J. Bussy/VB, 19 February 1945, TGA
367 *'as though . . . being'*	Q. Bell, *Elders*, 156
368 *'fascinating'*	J. Bussy/VB, 18 February 1941, TGA
368 *After the fall . . . defeat*	van Tuyl, 35, n80
368 *'write for . . . culture'; 'first-rate . . . writer'*	van Tuyl, 109
369 *'exiled . . . Africa'*	R. de Margerie/CB, 18 September 1943, KCC, 'que j'ai précisement été exilé il y a trois ans pour avoir recommandé le premier et avec véhémence le transfert en Afrique du Nord du gouvernement Français'
369 *'a man . . . Germany'*	de Margerie, vol. 4, 184, 'un homme qu'il savait foncièrement hostile à la politique de collaboration avec l'Allemagne hitlérienne'
369 *'Do you . . . Bloomsbury'*	R. de Margerie/CB, 18 September 1943, KCC, 'Vous rappelez-vous nos conversations d'avant la guerre, dans les délicieux dîners que vous nous donniez à Bloomsbury?'
369 *'ratted . . . writers'*	CB/MH, 7 January 1941

369	*'that little shit'*	CB/MH, 9 October 1941
370	*'un-German'*	Anger, 151
370	*'a sort . . . raft'*	Weber, 354
370	*Lurçat . . . Resistance*	Riding, 174
370	*'exactly . . . Jane'*	J. Loeb/CB, 3 September?1940
371	*Janie told . . . their lives*	J. Bussy/VB, 1 March 1948, TGA
371	*Copeau . . . Jouvet . . . New York*	CB/MH, 24 August 1941
371	*'I also . . . passion'*	MH/VW, 2 February 1941, Sx
371	*'movies bore me'*	CB/MH, 7 January 1941
372	*'blessing'*	CB/FP, 27 November 1942
372	*'Count . . . no'*	CB/MH, 21 July 1943
372	*'unheard . . . you'*	CB/MH, 19 September 1943
372	*'much beloved . . . regime'*	J. Loeb/CB, 10 January?1941
372	*'most . . . wondered at'; 'I shall . . . peccadillos'*	CB/MH, 5 May 1942
373	*'artists . . . Germans'*	Riding, 175
373	*'made . . . war'*	Marler, 495, n5
373	*'facts'; 'pressure'*	Leland Bell, 'Contrasts in the Life and Art of André Derain', *New York Times*, 29 November 1981, letter
373	*'publicly upbraided'*	J. Lee, 87
373	*'head'*	Spurling, *Master*, 423
373	*'prostitute'*	Cone, 'Matisse'; *Artists*, 154–81
373	*'Most . . . summer'*	CB/FP, 13 September 1944
373	*telling Vanessa . . . disgracefully*	J. Bussy/VB, 6 November 1944, TGA
373	*made light . . . neuroses*	J. Bussy/VB, 19 February 1945, TGA
373	*'comedies and tragedies'*	Q. Bell, *Elders*, 160
373	*'made . . . rumpus'*	CB/FP, 17 February 1945
374	*'A stroke . . . Combelle'*	Tedeschi, 239
374	*'do . . . trick'; 'simply . . . meant'*	VB/J. Bussy, 10 April 1945, Marler, 495
374	*'silliness not wickedness'*	J. Bussy/VB, 23 April 1947, TGA

40 Experts and Hoaxes

375 'He's just . . . servant'   FP, *Everything*, 239
375 'broad . . . Council'   Rose, 610
376 'lamentable'   'A C.E.M.A. Exhibition', *Times*,
                                       23 November 1944
376 *Clark defended*   'Sir Kenneth Clark's
                                       Comment', *Times*, 25
                                       November 1944
376 'lowered . . . experts'; 'minor   'A C.E.M.A. Exhibition', *Times*,
importance'   29 November 1944
376 'an expert'   *Times*, 29 November 1944,
                                       letter
376 'aesthetic enjoyment'; 'cognitive 'Art and Expertise', *Cornhill*
supplement'   *Magazine*, 161 (April 1945),
                                       296–300
377 'some . . . experts'   CB/FP, 12 January 1945
377 'national prestige'; 'publishers   'Art and Expertise', *Cornhill*
. . . for it'   *Magazine*, 161 (April 1945),
                                       296–300
377 'to encourage . . . beauties'   CB, Introduction, *Auguste*
                                       Renoir [publisher's front matter]
378 'ludicrously inadequate'   D, 20 May 1945, LBN/1/6,
                                       Mellon
378 'sick . . . pictures'   CB/MH, 31 December 1945
378 'Picasso . . . Party'   J. Bussy/VB, 25 March 1945,
                                       TGA
378 'had . . . collaboration'   Cone, *Artists*, 153
378 *Herbert . . . 1944*   Adamson, 924, n1
378–9 *Raymond . . . marketeers*   E. Russell, 267
379 'home from home'   CB/FP, 11 August 1946
379 'American . . . France'   Rothenstein, *Brave*, 139
379 'put in . . . government'   CB/MH, 29 September 1944
379 'one or . . . masters'   'Miller's – The Arts in Sussex',
                                       NS&N, 19 July 1941, 58
379 'masters'; 'eagles'   'French Pictures in London',
                                       NS&N, 15 May 1943, 320

380 'within . . . Picasso';   'Art in Paris Now', *Listener*, 16
'misunderstood . . . funds'   Aug 1945, 188
380 'that country . . . Europe'   'Picasso and Matisse', *Times*, 4
    December 1945
380 'as though . . . of war'   'Picasso and Matisse', *Times*, 6
    December 1945
380 'maintained . . . neutrality'   J. Bussy/VB, 6 November
    1944, TGA
380 'I cannot . . . little'   Barr, 256
381 'painting . . . enemy'   Chipp, 487
381 'monstrosities'; 'hoax'; 'invasion';   'Picasso and Matisse', *Times*, 17
schoolchildren   December 1945
381 'climbed . . . fought'   Spurling, *Master*, 440–1
381 'beneath contempt'   CB/MH, 14 January 1946
381 loaned . . . collection   Richardson, *Sorcerer's*, 160
381 'nonsense'   'Picasso and Klee', *Times*, 2
    January 1946, letter
382 'like . . . world'   'Water-Colours Ancient and
    Modern', *NS&N*, 15 March
    1941, 271
382 'our most . . . painting'   'Picasso and Klee', *Times*, 4
    January 1946
382 Margery contradicted   *Times*, 15 January 1946
382 'there was . . . master'   *Times*, 18 January 1946
382 'makeshift'   'The Tate Gallery', *Burlington
    Magazine*, January 1948, 28–9
382 'in a . . . appreciation'   'Mr. Bodkin and Mr. Fry',
    NS&N, 23 February 1946, 139
383 'the static . . . position'   Laughton, 228
383 'not stand still'   CB, *Victor*, 16
383 'vilified . . . elitist'   J. Rye, 58–9

41   Retrospect

385 hatred . . . French   B Bagenal/CB, nd, Sx
385 family joke   Q. Bell, *Elders*, 41

385 *'marriage . . . story'* — CB/Sybil Colefax, 18 October 1945, KCC

387 *'devastating . . . hold of them'* — VB/A. Garnett, 6 April 1945, Marler, 490

388 *'no-one . . . friends'; 'Apostles of Truth'* — FP, *Pacifist's*, 29

388 *'shocking lies'* — CB/MH, 30 April 1943

388 *'grand inquest'* — CB/MH, 7 July 1942

388 *rebellion . . . judgements* — 'Books in General', *NS&N*, 26 November 1949, 616, 618

388 *'in glowing . . . terms'* — 'At the National Gallery', *NS&N*, 26 December 1942, 423

388 *'gave us . . . had'* — 'Contemporary Art-Criticism in England', *Magazine of Art*, 44 (May 1951), 179–83

389 *'roughly . . . another'* — Bussy, 82

389 *'rather primly'* — Luke, 192

389 *'They belong . . . of it'* — E. Russell, 288–9

390 *'most beautiful . . . moving'* — CB/E. Waugh, 12 June 1945, BL

390 *'conchie'* — CB/FP, 10 August 1945

390 *'bad . . . mind'; 'crooning . . . listening to them'* — 'Blood Sports', *NS&N*, 23 July 1949, 92–3

390 *'who . . . mass'* — 'Festina Lente', *The Arts*, 2, 1947, 13–18

390 *'collapse . . . standards'* — CB/FP, 11 August 1946

391 *'full . . . ideas'* — CB/FP, 6 December 1948

391 *'culture . . . politics'* — Eliot, *Notes*, 83

391 *'standard of living'* — T. S. Eliot/CB, 18 July 1930, *L*, vol. 5, 256

391 *'respectable ideals'; 'incompatible . . . élite'; 'till . . . eat';'does . . . ago?'* — 'The End of a Civilization', Trinity, 1/10

391 *'easily . . . like it'* — 'A Liberal's Point of View', *Spectator*, 22 October 1948, 527–8

391 *'much-vaunted . . . revolution'* — Kynaston, 173

391 *'all to . . . other'* — CB/FP, 16 October 1940
391 *'just . . . totalitarianism'* — Judt, 104
392 *black market . . . shops* — Flanner, *Journal* 67
392 *'never . . . mistress'* — CB/MH, 31 August 1946
392 *'amitié amoureuse'* — CB/MH, 4 October 1946
392 *'sad'; 'moche'* — CB/VB, 22 May 1947
392 *'break . . . Continent'* — '*Manet et ses oeuvres'*, review, *TLS*, 10 January 1948, 17

392 *'dropped . . . Egalité'* — CB/FP, 2 December 1946
392 *Cocteau . . . ageless* — Flanner, *Journal*, 61–2
392 *Fascists . . . role* — Riding, 184
393 *completely . . . Écrivains* — Arnaud, 720
393 *'slightly pornographic'* — CB/VB, 22 May 1947
393 *wide-ranging . . . included* — Kelly, 58–9
393 *'It is . . . change'* — 'The Shadow of the Master', *NS&N*, 23 April 1949, 402–3

393 *'grim avidity'* — CB/FP, 12 February 1948
394 *'record . . . War'* — *Art*, xv
394 *'a little . . . man'* — Ibid., xviii
394–5 *'designs . . . dreamed of'; 'profound and poetical'* — CB/FP, 29 April 1948

395 *'some . . . men'* — R. de Margerie/CB, 8 April 1948, KCC, 'de fructueux échanges d'histoires concernant la vanité et la sottise des hommes'

395 *'flourishing . . . better'* — R. de Margerie/CB, 13 September 1948, KCC, 'le Luxembourg, et Versailles merveilleusement fleuris. Si les gouvernements travaillaient chez nous aussi bien que les jardiniers et les conservateurs de musées, les affaires de la France en marcheraient mieux'

395 *conversation . . . contemporaries*	de Margerie, vol. 2, 302, 'je trouvais infiniment reposant de prendre part à une conversation où il s'agissait avant tout d'art et de littérature, – ou de la discussion malicieuse de nos contemporains'
395–6 *'The zoological . . . birds'*	R. de Margerie/CB, 13 September 1948, KCC, 'Le jardin zoologique de notre mémoire est une volière de ces vieux oiseaux'
396 *'cardinal error'*	H. Nicolson, 19
396 *'ancient . . . kindness'*	R. De Margerie/CB, 9 September 1950, KCC, '[les] haines ancestrales qui prouvent qu'ils ont au moins des souvenirs'; 'Je ne suis pas fait pour le Nouveau Monde, malgré toute sa gentillesse'

42 Clive Bell Looks at American Art

401 *'an emanation . . . more so'*	J. Loeb/CB, 8 February 1940
401 *'peculiar . . . book'*	J. Loeb/CB, 8 September 1941
401 *'got . . . life'*	J. Loeb/CB, 8 July 1944
401 *'horrid guy'*	J. Loeb/CB, 8 July 1944
402 *'promote . . . artists'*	www.fedart.org
402 *'socialist . . . academicism'*	Guilbaut, 69
402 *'spiritual . . . art'*	Ibid., 76
402–3 *collectors . . . imitate them*	Kirstein, 50
403 *'famous . . . Congress'*	CB/VB, 17 September 1948
403 *'young . . . extremists'; 'stripped'; 'catastrophic'; 'an analogue . . . experience'*	'Fifteen'

403 *'most . . . defender'* — Kirstein, 51

403 *'a cultural . . . War'* — Kelly, 65

403 *'highly . . . civilization'* — 'Fifteen'

404 *'not deeply . . . values'* — Soby, 147

404 *'international . . . quality'* — Ibid., 144

404 *'unknown . . . abroad'* — Ibid., 143

404 *'When . . . with'; 'basic . . . general'* — Curtiss, 111

404 *'to rise . . . equality'; 'arrogant . . . sensitive'* — 'The End of a Civilization', Trinity, 1/11

405 *'a land . . . culture'* — CB/FP, 31 January 1948

406 *'intractable . . . artist'* — 'Art Teaching', *NS&N*, 26 August 1950, 225–6

406 *best way . . . history* — 'Thoughts Provoked by Dartington', Trinity, 2/13

406 *'He hadn't . . . left'* — ' "Quiet One" Winning Fame by Accident', *LA Times*, 8 April 1949, A6

406 *'Page One'* — 'Newspaper Guild Has Page One Ball', *NY Herald Tribune*, May 21 1949

406 *'endless conversation'* — J. Loeb/CB, 23 November 1949

406 *'as bright . . . prettier'* — CB/VB, 27 January 1950, KCC

406 *'excited . . . schoolboy'* — CB/D. Gordon, 6 November 1949, UVa

406–7 *full . . . surprises* — CB/VB, 27 January 1950, KCC

407 *'quiet . . . observer'* — Catling

407 *'how . . . abstraction'* — AD, 1950, endmatter

407 *Pierre . . . all together* — P. Matisse/H. Matisse, 14 January 1950, Morgan

407 *'Individualism . . . Democracy'* — 'Foundations of the Great Age', Trinity, 4/5

407 *Fogg . . . critical* — CB/MH, 18 January 1950; CB/VB, 18 January 1950, KCC

407 *impostor* — CB/MH, 5 February 1950

408 *'Some people . . .showroom'; 'with .*   Louchheim
. . seagull'; 'refreshing . . . so'; 'related . .
. yes'; 'every . . . signature'; 'Remember .
. . fashioned'; 'the image . . . space'

408 *'a decorator . . . epoch'*   Kirstein, 51

409 *'instructive . . . hundred'*   Ibid., 50–1

409 *art world luminaries*   Tea at the Guesthouse List,
                                               February 6 1950, Rockefeller,
                                               Folder 76, Box 9

409 *'American . . . talent'*   CB/VB, 7 February 1950,
                                               KCC

409 *'happiest . . . existence'*   CB/Mina Kirstein Curtiss,
                                               22 March 1950, Berg

409 *'special . . . feeling'*   J. Loeb/CB, 20 April 1950

409 *'wildly exciting'*   CB/Mina Kirstein Curtiss,
                                               22 March 1950, Berg

410 *'transformation . . . experience'*   *Modern*, 4

410 *Picassonian*   Ibid., 7

410 *'In the . . . Ingres'*   Ibid., 11

410 *'excitement . . . hopes'*   Ibid., 14

410 *'What people . . . ideas'*   CB/D. Gordon, 18 February
                                               1951

411 *'howls of outrage'*   'Recollections of Fauve and
                                               Cubist Painters', Trinity,
                                               3/12

411 *Because Barr . . . Piot*   Alfred Barr/CB, 20 June
                                               1950, MoMA

411 *'expensively'*   'How England met Modern
                                               Art', *Art News*, October
                                               1950, 24

412 *'Your visit . . . boorishness'*   J. Loeb/CB, 10 October
                                               1951

412 *'weird'*   'Odd Pals Make Heiress
                                               Unfit Mom, Hubby Says',
                                               Daily News, 16 August 1951

412 *'red-headed heiress'* — 'He looked for Lucre, Not Love, She Says', *Daily News*, 26 September 1951

412 *'indescribably rich'* — CB/D. Gordon, 28 February 1952, UVa

413 *'Dare . . . picture?'* — 'Chicago Symposium, Cézanne and Impressionism', Trinity, 4/10

413 *'find himself'; 'profound . . . significance'* — 'Bonnard', Trinity, 4/6

413 *'like . . . fire'* — CB/D. Gordon, 25 February 1952, UVa

413 *'in . . . district'; 'Tom . . .accent'* — 'Clive Bell, British Writer, Visiting City', *St. Louis Post-Dispatch*, 25 February 1952, 38

414 *'a sort . . . joke"'* — CB, *Old*, 120; 'How Pleasant to Know Mr Eliot', *T. S. Eliot: A Symposium*, compiled by Richard March and Tambimuttu, Editions Poetry, 1948, 15

414 *'of . . . quality'; 'among . . . best'; 'primitives'* — 'Clive Bell, British Writer, Visiting City', *St. Louis Post-Dispatch*, 25 February 1952, 38

414 *'consistent . . . peace'* — 'Art Critic to Lecture', *Kansas City Star*, 25 February 1952, 29

414 *'better . . . before'* — CB/MH, 3 March 1952

415 *Bergen . . . New York* — Spalding, *DG*, 411

415 *'happy . . . young'* — CB/VB, 4 March 1952

415 *'sweet and wonderful'* — J. Loeb/CB, 2 April 1952

415 *'You . . . much'* — J. Loeb/CB, 17 January 1957

415–16 *'a place . . . should be'* — J. Loeb/CB, 4 February 1959

416 *'my . . . nonsense'* — CB/VB, 4 March 1952, KCC

416 *Dutch . . . abstraction*	H. van Norden/CB, 11 August 1951, KCC; 'The Shadow of the Master', *NS&N*, 23 April 1949, 402–3
416 *'indescribable'*	Gowing, 15
416 *which Barr . . . seen it*	Ibid., 14
416 *'some perspective'; 'been in . . . Fry'; 'invented . . . England'*	W. Rose, 412–13
417 *Nicolson explained . . . Middleton*	B. Nicolson/CB, 25 January 1949, KCC
417*Newton told . . . purpose*	E. Newton/CB, 6 May 1950, KCC
417 *'young men . . . servants'*	'Contemporary Art-Criticism in England', *Magazine of Art*, 44 (May 1951), 179–83
418 *'did . . . knell'; 'influential . . . unimportant'*	Lowell J. Rubin, 'Shahn Sees Strife in Image and Idea', *Harvard Crimson*, 21 November 1956

43 Douglas Cooper

419 *'pioneering . . . Britain'*	Calvocoressi, 187
419 *questionnaire*	reproduced in Calvocoressi, 190
419 *'only . . . art'; 'a great . . . painting'*	Cooper, *Courtauld*, 52
419 *fortieth anniversary article*	'Post-Impressionism and Roger Fry', *Burlington Magazine*, January 1951, 10–15
419 *intended . . . homage*	B. Nicolson/CB, 29 September 1950, KCC
420 *'masterpiece . . . scholarship'*	'The Courtauld Collection', *TLS*, 26 March 1954, 200
420 *'The fact . . . therefrom'*	CB/FP, 13 March 1954

420 *'dead-end'*	Cooper, *Courtauld*, 57
420 *'art-loving public'; 'wildly'*	'The Courtauld Collection', *TLS*, 26 March 1954, 200
420 *Blunt . . . ameliorate*	Calvocoressi, 188–9
420 *'if Roger . . . friends'*	'From the Courtauld Collection', *TLS*, 9 March 1956
420–1 *'superiority . . . New York'; 'now . . . age'*	'Editorial', *Burlington Magazine*, September 1947, 235
421 *objecting . . . museum*	J. Russell, 'The Tate Gallery', *Burlington Magazine*, November 1947, 320
421 *'more . . . progressive'; 'cultural . . . England'*	Cooper, 'The Tate'
421 *'long-vexed . . . Bequest'*	*Times* 28 May 1946
421 *Rothenstein's article*	*Daily Telegraph*, 20 January 1949
422 *'a landmark . . . modernism'; 'intensity . . . justice'*	Richardson, *Sorcerer's*, 158

44 A Gang of Conspirators

423 *'to ruin . . . line"'*	Rothenstein, *Modern*, 14
423 *Leonard . . . exhibition*	Spotts, 544
423 *denigrated . . . painting*	Spalding, *RF* 154–56
423 *communicated . . . of the time'*	Rothenstein, *Modern* 45
423 *'virulent . . . friends'*	ibid. 48
424 *'strong prejudices'*	ibid. 62
424 *'state . . . about'*	CB, *Old* 128
424 *'a point . . . disease'*	ibid. 126
424 *'true . . . extraordinary'*	*Sunday Times* 6 February 1949, 4
424 *'almost a cult'*	Spender 140
425 *'charlatans'; 'muscling in'*	CB/LW 5 September 1950 Sx
425 *'What Was Bloomsbury?'*	*Twentieth Century* 155 (February 1954), 153–60
425 *'ludicrously wrong'*	CB/FP 6 December 1948
425 *mistakenly . . . homosexual*	CB/Ian Parsons 21 June 1956 UoR

425–6 'a certain . . . friends';   Harrod xii
'unknown . . . genius'
426 'inappropriately . . .   Luedeking 251
questions'
426 'revaluation'   'Strachey's Eminent Victorians',
                                            NS&N 16 April 1955
426 'really . . . of them'   Chisholm 241
426 'Were I . . . generation';   CB/FP 9 November 1953
'charming . . . affectionate'
426 'hatred'   Knights 421
426 'hatreds . . . years'   Rothenstein, Modern 14
427 'considerable . . . Virginia's'   LW/V. Sackville-West 24
                                            September 1957, Spotts 503–04
427 'interesting . . . enjoy that'   CB/FP 20 November 1959
427 denial . . . Russia   A. Lunn/CB 18 January 1957
                                            KCC
427 Lunn's chapter . . . flourished   Lunn 104–05
427 'splendid . . . Reds'   Lunn 138
428 Roger . . . disagreed   'The Bloomsbury Group', TLS 27
                                            August 1954
429 'mosaic'   'Portrait of Virginia Woolf', BBC
                                            Home Service, 29 August 1956
429 'freemasons . . . Jesuits'; 'entire   'Lively Portraits: The Bloomsbury
Press'   Set from the Inside', Sunday Times,
                                            11 November 1956
429 'made himself . . . annoying'   CB, Old, 48
429 V. S. Pritchett   'Bloomsbury and the Ant-eater',
                                            NS&N, 17 November 1956
429 'a string . . . Guy"'   'The Pilgrim Bohemians', Gemini,
                                            Spring 1957, 56
429 'All those . . . muck'   Ibid., 57
430 'first English . . . one'   Ibid., 60
430 'epitome . . . respectability'   Ibid., 61

45 Things Are Never So Bad but They Might Be Worse

---

431 *'like a key'; 'Their . . . on art'*   C. MacInnes/CB, 19 November
                                            1956, KCC
431 *'as flat . . . memoirs'*   Cumming, 435
431 *best book*   Clark, *Other Half*, 87
431 *no longer write*   Cumming, 438
431 *'life-enhancing'*   *The Nude in Art*, Kenneth Clark,
                                            reviewed *TLS*, 11 January 1957,
                                            17
431 *'exquisite . . . nostalgia'*   'The Great Days', *TLS*, 17
                                            September 1954, 594
432 *'home . . . gentlemen'*   CB/VB, 7 May 1955
432 *'had . . . petrified'*   CB/VB, 15 March 1953
432 *Jeremy . . . behind her*   Hutchinson, *Desert*
432 *'character and talents'; 'Quite   CB/MH, 19 June 1948
true'*
432 *'maddened . . . Mériméeism'*   MH/CB, 13 April 1951, HRC
433 *'what the . . . your plans'*   MH/CB, 2 October 1952, HRC
433 *'so . . . seventy'*   CB/FP, 11 September 1962
433 *Roland . . . thought*   de Margerie, vol. 2, 302–3
434 *relief to Clive*   VB/A. Garnett, 7 March 1961,
                                            Marler, 552
435 *'in touch . . . world'; 'to   CB/FP, 28 December 1951
know . . . everything'*
435 *'She . . . ten'*   J. Bussy/VB, 31 March 1955,
                                            TGA
435 *'I was . . . Little B'*   J. Bussy/VB, 31 March 1955
435 *'That woman . . . of her'*   Spalding, *VB*, 359
436 *'extreme . . .detachment'*   J. Bussy/VB, 19 March 1957,
                                            TGA
436 *'would be . . . Bagenal'*   Richardson, *Sorcerer's*, 235
436 *'Barbara . . . discovered'*   CB/FP, 3 August 1955
437 *In Rome . . . socialising*   CB/VB, 1 October 1955
437 *He was . . . Vespas*   CB/D. Gordon, 31 October 1955,
                                            UVa
437 *'frightens me'*   CB/D. Cooper, 29 December
                                            1957, Getty

437 *feeble* — CB/VB, 22 February 1958

437 *'being . . . Picasso'* — FP, *Everything*, 224

437 *'all this . . . about'* — CB/FP, 12 March 1958

437 *Picasso signed* — B. Bagenal/D. Cooper, 25 February 1958, Getty

438 *'Nous . . . Lascaux'* — CB/FP, 12 March 1958

438 *'stunning new pictures'* — CB/VB, 21 February 1959

438 *'pertinacious'* — CB/FP, 14 March 1960

438 *'stepped . . . next'* — FP, *Hanging*, 23

438 *'jolly . . . last'* — CB/VB, 24 September 1954

439 *'one . . . lately'* — VB/A. O. Bell, 16 May 1960, Marler, 550

439 *'ghastly tragedy'* — CB/R. Mortimer, 3 May 1960, Princeton

439 *'surly'* — CB/D. Gordon, 25 August 1953

440 *Janice . . . hopeless* — J. Loeb/CB, 19 November 1954

440 *'things . . . worse'* — CB/FP, 2 March 1955

440 *'Mr Grant . . . service'* — G. Higgens, Diary, 12 April 1961, BL

441 *'got wise . . . started'; 'on to . . . thing'* — Bernard Denvir, 'Picasso at £20 a Square Inch', *Daily Herald*, 7 May 1953

441 *reserve price . . . investment* — D. Garnett/Mina Kirstein Curtiss, 28 July 1962, Berg

442 *untraced . . . Vlaminck* — Shone, 'Pictures', 151

442 *'good . . . sum'; 'Connoisseurship rewarded'* — CB/VB, 30 March 1957

442 *'worked . . . through'; 'qualified . . . form'* — Soby, *Juan Gris*, MoMA, 1958, 15

442 *'general . . . desolation'* — CB/DG, 23 December 1963

442 *'Mr Clive . . . visitors'* — CB/Michael Holroyd, 6 May 1963, BL

443 *'I am . . . after them'* — G. Higgens, Diary, 6 May 1963, BL

443 *'atmosphere . . . intimacy'; 'courteous . . . part'* — FP, *Other*, 63

443 *'be . . . him'* — D. Garnett, 23

443	*Frances visited . . . impressed her*	FP, *Hanging*, 132
443	*'dear . . . friend'*	FP, *Other*, 78
443	*Leonard visited*	Glendinning, 398
443	*told Barbara . . . herself*	G. Higgens, Diary, 18 September 1964, BL

Epilogue

445	*'model . . . lover'*	Clarke, 153
445	*Clive did . . . afterwards*	Roche, 6
445	*'trying . . . language'*	Bywater, 20
446	*'given . . . of mind'*	Foster Gage, 165
446	*'cannot . . . language'*	Bataille, 10
446	*Like Woolf . . . access*	Hussey, 'Case Study', 70
446	*Augustus . . . noted*	Augustus John/CB, 17 July 1945, Sx
446	*'tired . . . table'*	Q. Bell, 'Clive Bell at Charleston'
446	*'rather . . . 1916'*	Wallis, 15

Bibliography

Acton, Harold, *Memoirs of an Aesthete*, Hamish Hamilton, 1948

Adamson, Natalie, 'Herbert Read, the École de Paris and Art Criticism, c. 1946', *Art History*, September 2017, 904–927

Affron, Matthew and Mark Antliff, eds., *Fascist Visions: Art and Ideology in France And Italy*, Princeton 1997

Affron, Matthew, 'Waldemar George: A Parisian Art Critic on Modernism and Fascism', Affron and Antliff, 171–204

Altshuler, Bruce, *Exhibitions that Made Art History, Vol, 1, Salon to Biénnial*, Phaidon, 2008

Andrews, Charles, *Writing Against War, Literature, Activism, and the British Peace Movement*, Northwestern, 2017

Anger, Jenny, 'Paul Klee, Anni and Josef Albers, and Robert Rauschenberg: Weaving and the Grid at Black Mountain College', *Klee and America*, ed. Josef Helfenstein and Elizabeth Hutton Turner, Hatje Cantz, 2006, 238–53. Exh. cat.

Anscombe, Isabelle, *Omega and After, Bloomsbury and the Decorative Arts*, Thames & Hudson, 1981

Antliff, Mark '*La Cité Française*: Georges Valois, Le Corbusier, and Fascist Theories of Urbanism', Affron and Antliff, 134–70

Arnaud, Claude, *Jean Cocteau, A Life*, trans. Lauren Elkin and Charlotte Mandell, Yale, 2016

Baker, Mary Landon, *The Arcadians, A Satire*, Golden Shield, 1934

—, *Sunshine and Gossamer*, Chicago, privately printed, 1928

—, *Verbum Sapienti*, Chicago, Ralph Fletcher Seymour, 1920

Barnes, James Strachey, *Half a Life*, Coward McCann, 1934

Barr, Alfred H. Jr, *Matisse: His Art and His Public*, MoMA, 1951

Bataille, George, 'The Language of Flowers', *Visions of Excess, Selected Writings 1927–1939*, ed. Allan Sokal, U of Minnesota P, 1985, 10–14

Beechey, James, 'Clive Bell: Pacifism and Politics', *Charleston Magazine* 14 (Autumn/Winter 1996), 5–13

—, 'Picasso and Britain', *Picasso & Modern British Art*, Tate, 2012, Exh. cat.

Bell, Clive, *An Account of French Painting*, Harcourt, 1932

—, *Ad Familiares*, Pelican Press, 1917

—, *Art*, ed. J. B. Bullen, Oxford, 1987

—, Introduction, *Auguste Renoir, Les Parapluies in the National Gallery, London*, Lund Humphries, 1945

—, *Civilization, An Essay*, Chatto, 1928

—, 'The English Group', *Second Post-Impressionist Exhibition*, Second Edition, Grafton Galleries, Ballantyne & Co, 1912, 21–24, Exh. cat.

—, *Enjoying Pictures*, Harcourt, 1934

—, et al., *Euphrosyne*, Elijah Johnson, 1905

—, Introduction, *The French Impressionists in Full Colour*, Phaidon, 1952

—, [1927] *Landmarks in Nineteenth-Century Painting*, Books for Libraries, 1967

—, *The Legend of Monte della Sibilla*, Hogarth, 1923

—, *Modern French Painting: The Cone Collection*, Johns Hopkins, 1951

—, [1956] *Old Friends*, Harcourt 1957

—, *On British Freedom*, Harcourt, 1923

—, *Peace at Once*, National Labour Press, 1915

—, *Poems*, Hogarth, 1921

—, *Pot-Boilers*, Chatto, 1918

—, *Proust*, Hogarth, 1928

—, *Since Cézanne*, Chatto, 1922

—, *Twelfth Century Paintings at Hardham and Clayton*, Miller's, 1947

—, *Victor Pasmore*, Penguin, 1945

—, *Warmongers*, Peace Pledge Union, 1938

Bell, Julian, *Essays, Poems and Letters*, ed. Quentin Bell, Hogarth, 1938

Bell, Quentin, 'Clive Bell at Charleston', *Clive Bell at Charleston*, Gallery Edward Harvane, 24 May– 30 June 1972, exh. cat.

—, *Elders and Betters*, John Murray, 1995

—, and Stephen Chaplin, 'The Ideal Home Rumpus', *The Bloomsbury Group*, ed. S. P. Rosenbaum, U of Toronto P, 1975, 335–361

—, *Virginia Woolf, A Biography*, vi *Virginia Stephen, 1882–1912*; v2 *Mrs Woolf 1912–1941*, Hogarth, 1973

Benington, Jonathan, *Roderic O'Conor, A Biography with a Catalogue of His Work*, Irish Academic P, 1992

Bennett, Arnold *The Journal of Arnold Bennett, 1896–1910*, Book League of America, 1932

Berenson, Mary, *A Self-Portrait from Her Diary and Letters*, ed. Barbara
   Strachey and Jayne Samuels, W.W. Norton, 1983,

Berkowitz, Elizabeth Sarah, 'Bloomsbury's Byzantium and the Writing of
   Modern Art', PhD dissertation, Graduate Center of the City University
   of New York, 2018

Bibbings, Lois, *Telling Tales About Men: Conscientious Objectors to Military
   Service During the First World War*, Manchester U P, 2009

Bingham, Emily, *Irrepressible: The Jazz Age Life of Henrietta Bingham*, Farrar
   Straus Giroux, 2015

Bois, Yves-Alain, 'Pablo Picasso: The Cadaqués Experiment', in Dickerman,
   40–45

Bonham Carter, Violet, *Champion Redoubtable, The Diaries and Letters
   of Violet Bonham Carter 1914–1945*, ed. Mark Pottle, Weidenfeld &
   Nicolson, 1998

Bradshaw, David, ' "Those Extraordinary Parakeets": Clive Bell and Mary
   Hutchinson', Part One *Charleston Magazine* 16 (Autumn/Winter 1997),
   5–12; Part Two, *Charleston Magazine* 17 (Spring/Summer 1998), 5–11

—, 'British Writers and Anti-Fascism in the 1930s, Part One: The Bray and
   Drone of Tortured Voices', *Woolf Studies Annual* 3, 1997, 3–27

Bradshaw, Tony, 'Virginia Woolf and Book Design', *The Edinburgh
   Companion to Virginia Wolf and the Arts*, ed. Maggie Humm, Edinburgh
   U P, 2010, 280–97

Braun, Emily, 'Leonardo's Smile', *Donatello Among the Blackshirts: History
   and Modernity in the Visual Culture of Fascist Italy*, ed. Claudia Lazzaro
   and Robert J. Crum, Cornell, 2004

Brockington, Grace, 'The Omega and the End of Civilisation: Pacifism,
   Publishing and Performance in the First World War', in Gerstein, 61–70

—, ' "Tending the lamp" or "minding their own business"? Bloomsbury Art
   and Pacifism in World War One', *Immediations* 1, 2004, 7-19

Brown, Oliver, *Exhibition, The Memoirs of Oliver Brown*, Evelyn, Adams &
   Mackay, 1968

Buchanan, Donald W., *James Wilson Morrice, A Biography*, Ryerson Press,
   1936

Buckle, Richard, *Diaghilev*, Atheneum, 1979

Bullen, J. B., ed., *Post-Impressionists in England: The Critical Reception*,
   Routledge, 1988

Bussy, Jane Simone, 'A Great Man', *Burlington Magazine*, February 1986,
   80-85

Bywater, William G., *Clive Bell's Eye*, Wayne State U P, 1975

Calvocoressi, Richard, 'Douglas Cooper and His Catalogue of the Courtauld Collection', *Burlington Magazine*, March 2012, 187–90

Carrington [Dora], *Carrington's Letters*, ed. Anne Chisholm, Chatto & Windus, 2017

Carter, Huntly, 'Art & Drama', *New Age*, 9 November 1911, 36

Catling, Patrick Skene, 'Critic Finds "The Finest" ', *Baltimore Sun*, 13 January 1950, 12

Caws, Mary Ann and Sarah Bird Wright, *Bloomsbury in France: Art and Friends*, Oxford, 2000

Cecil, Hugh and Mirabel Cecil, *Clever Hearts, Desmond and Molly MacCarthy, A Biography*, Victor Gollancz, 1990

Chipp, Herschel B., *Theories of Modern Art*, U of California P, 1968

Chisholm, Anne, *Frances Partridge, The Biography*, Weidenfeld & Nicolson, 2009

Clark, Kenneth, *The Other Half: A Self-Portrait*, Harper & Row, 1977

—, 'War Artists at the National Gallery', *The Studio*, January 1942, 1–3

Clarke, Darren, 'Duncan Grant and Charleston's Queer Arcadia', *Queer Bloomsbury*, eds. Brenda Helt and Madelyn Detloff, Edinburgh U P, 2016, 152–71

Cohler, Deborah, 'Sapphism and Sedition: Homosexuality in Great War Britain', *Journal of the History of Sexuality* 16.1 (2007), 68–94

Cone, Michèle C., 'Matisse and the Nationalism of Vichy, 1940-1944' *artnet Magazine*, 19 December 2015, available at www.artnet.com/magazineus/books/cone/cone12-19-05.asp

—, *Artists Under Vichy, A Case of Prejudice and Persecution*, Princeton, 1992

Cooper, Douglas, *The Courtauld Collection, A Catalogue and Introduction*, Athlone, 1954

—, 'The Tate Gallery', *Burlington Magazine*, January 1948, 28-29

Cork, Richard, *Vorticism and Abstract Art in the First Machine Age. Vol 1. Origins and Development*, U of California, 1976

Cornwell, Paul, *Only By Failure: The Many Faces of the Impossible Life of Terence Gray*, Salt, 2004

Crook, Diana, 'The Ladies of Miller's' *Charleston Newsletter* 18, April 1987, 16-23

Cumming, Robert, ed., *My Dear BB: The Letters of Bernard Berenson and Kenneth Clark, 1925–1959*, Yale, 2015

Curtiss, Mina Kirstein, *Other People's Letters, A Memoir*, Houghton Mifflin, 1978

Dangerfield, George, *The Strange Death of Liberal England* [1935], Stanford U P, 1997

Darroch, Sandra Jobson, *Ottoline, The Life of Lady Ottoline Morrell*, Chatto & Windus, 1976

Davenport-Hines, Richard, *A Night at the Majestic: Proust and the Great Modernist Dinner Party of 1922*, Faber 2006

Demus, O. 'The Literature of Art', *Burlington Magazine*, October 1945, 258–59

Diamand, Pamela, 'Durbins', *Charleston Newsletter* 10, 21–29

Dickerman, Leah, *Inventing Abstraction 1910–1925, How a Radical Idea Changed Modern Art*, Museum of Modern Art, New York, 2012, exh. cat.

Dunn, Jane, *A Very Close Conspiracy*, Little, Brown, 1991

Duthuit, Georges, *Le rose et le noir, de Walter Pater à Oscar Wilde*, La Renaissance du Livre, undated

Eastment, Diana Jane, 'The Policies and Position of the British Council from the Outbreak of War to 1950', PhD dissertation, U of Leeds, 1982

Edel, Leon, *Bloomsbury: A House of Lions*, Lippincott, 1979

—, *Henry James: The Master: 1901–1916*, Avon, 1953

Eggener, Keith L., ' "An Amusing Lack of Logic": Surrealism and Popular Entertainment', *American Art* vol. 7, No. 4, 1993, 30–45

Eliot, T. S. *The Letters of T. S. Eliot, Vol. 1 1898–1922*, eds. Valerie Eliot and John Haffenden [Revised edition], Yale, 2011

—, *The Letters of T. S. Eliot, Vol. 5 1930–1931*, eds. Valerie Eliot and John Haffenden, Yale, 2015

—, [1948] *Notes towards the Definition of Culture*, Faber, 1972

—, 'Tradition and the Individual Talent', *Selected Essays*, Faber, 1932

Ferris, Kate, *Everyday Life in Fascist Venice, 1929–40*, Palgrave Macmillan, 2012

'Fifteen Distinguished Critics and Connoisseurs Undertake to Clarify the Strange Art of To-Day', *Life*, 11 October 1948, 56+

Findling, John E. and Kimberly D. Pelle, eds., *Encyclopedia of Worlds Fairs and Expositions*, McFarland, 2008

Fitzgerald, Michael C., *Making Modernism: Picasso and the Creation of the Market for Twentieth-Century Art*, U of California P, 1996

Flanner, Janet [Genêt], *Paris Was Yesterday 1925–1939*, Viking, 1972

—, *Paris Journal 1944–1965*, ed. Wallace Shawn, Atheneum, 1965

Ford, Hugh, *Published in Paris: American and British Writers, Printers, and Publishers in Paris, 1920–1939*, Macmillan, 1975

Foscari, Antonio, *Tumult and Order: Malcontenta 1924–1939*, Lars Müller, 2012

Foss, Brian, *War Paint: Art, War, State and Identity in Britain, 1939–1945*, Yale, 2007

Foster Gage, Mark, *Aesthetic Theory: Essential Texts for Architecture and Design*, Norton, 2011

Four Americans in Paris, The Collections of Gertrude Stein and Her Family, MoMA, 1970, exh. cat.

Fry, Roger, 'An Essay in Aesthetics', *Vision and Design*, Chatto & Windus, 1928, 16–38

—, [1899] *Giovanni Bellini*, Longmans Green, 1901

—, 'Oriental Art', *Quarterly Review*, January 1910, 225–39

Fryer, Peter, *Staying Power: The History of Black People in Britain*, Pluto, 1984

Garafola, Lynn, *Diaghilev's Ballets Russes*, Oxford, 1989

Garnett, Angelica, *Deceived with Kindness, A Bloomsbury Childhood*, Oxford, 1984

—, 'The Earthly Paradise', *Charleston Past and Present*, ed. Quentin Bell et al., Harcourt, 1987

Garnett, David, *The Flowers of the Forest*, Chatto, 1955

Gerstein, Alexandra, ed., *Beyond Bloomsbury, Designs of the Omega Workshops 1913–19*, Courtauld Gallery, 2009

Gertler, Mark, *Selected Letters*, ed. Noel Carrington, Hart-Davis, 1965

Giachero, Lia, ed., *Vanessa Bell, Sketches in Pen and Ink*, Pimlico, 1998

Gill, Gillian, *Virginia Woolf and the Women Who Shaped Her World*, Houghton Mifflin Harcourt, 2019

Gillespie, Diane Filby, ed., *The Multiple Muses of Virginia Woolf*, U of Missouri P, 1993

Glendinning, Victoria, *Leonard Woolf, A Biography*, Free Press, 2006

Goebel, Stefan 'Exhibitions', in Jay Winter, ed., *Capital Cities at War: Paris, London, Berlin 1914–1919*, Cambridge, 2007

Goff, Jennifer, *Eileen Gray: Her Work and Her World*, National Museum of Ireland, 2015

Gordon, Lois, *Nancy Cunard: Heiress, Muse, Political Idealist*, Columbia U P, 2007

Gowing, Lawrence, 'Francis Bacon: The Human Presence', *Francis Bacon*, Hirshhorn Museum and Sculpture Garden, Thames & Hudson, 1989, exh. cat.

Graham, John W., *Conscription and Conscience: A History 1916–1919*, George Allen & Unwin, 1922

Green, Christopher, *Art Made Modern: Roger Fry's Vision of Art*, Merrell Hoberton/Courtauld Gallery, 1999, exh. cat.

—, 'Expanding the Canon: Roger Fry's Evaluations of the "Civilised" and the "Savage"', *Art Made Modern*, 119–30

—, *Cubism and Its Enemies: Modern Movements and Reaction in French Art, 1916–1928*, Yale, 1987

—, 'The Picassos of British Criticism c.1910–1945' in *Picasso & Modern British Art*, Tate 2012, exh. cat.

Green, Martin, *Children of the Sun: A Narrative of "Decadence" in England After 1918*, Basic, 1976

Grigson, Geoffrey, 'Comment on England', *Axis* 1, 1935, 8–10

Gruetzner Robins, Anna, *Modern Art in Britain 1910–1914*, Merrell Holberton, 1997, exh. cat.

—, ' "Manet and the Post-Impressionists": a checklist of exhibits', *Burlington Magazine*, December 2010, 782–93

Guilbaut, Serge, *How New York Stole the Idea of Modern Art: Abstract Expressionism, Freedom, and the Cold War*, trans. Arthur Goldhammer, U of Chicago P, 1983

Haas, Michael, *Forbidden Music: The Jewish Composers Banned by the Nazis*, Yale, 2013

Hale, Keith, ed., *Friends and Apostles, The Correspondence of Rupert Brooke and James Strachey*, Yale, 1998

Hall, Sarah M., *Before Leonard: The Early Suitors of Virginia Woolf*, Peter Owen, 2006

Hamilton, Agnes, *Dead Yesterday*, Doran, 1916

Hankins, Leslie Kathleen, ' "Across the Screen of My Brain": Virginia Woolf's "The Cinema" and Film Forums of the Twenties', in Gillespie, 148–79

Harrod, R. F., *The Life of John Maynard Keynes*, Harcourt, 1951

Haycock, David Boyd, *A Crisis of Brilliance: Five Young British Artists and the Great War*, Street, 2009

Hignett, Sean, *Brett: From Bloomsbury to New Mexico, A Biography*, Franklin Watts, 1983

Hoeniger, Cathleen, 'The Restoration of the Early Italian "Primitives" during the 20th Century: Valuing Art and Its Consequences', *Journal of the American Institute for Conservation* 38, 2 (Summer 1999), 144–61

Holroyd, Michael, *Lytton Strachey, The New Biography*, Farrar Straus Giroux, 1994

Hugh, Evans, *The Freshman at Cambridge*, Cambridge, 1899

Hussey, Mark, 'Case Study: Legacies of "significant form" ', *Handbook to the Bloomsbury Group*, eds. Derek Ryan and Stephen Ross, Bloomsbury Academic, 2018, 60–73

—, 'Clive Bell, "a fathead and a voluptuary": Conscientious Objection and British Masculinity', *Queer Bloomsbury*, eds. Brenda Helt and Madelyn Detloff, Edinburgh U P, 2016, 240–57

—, 'Mrs Thatcher and Mrs Woolf', *Modern Fiction Studies*, Spring 2004, 8–30

Hutchinson, Jeremy, *Desert Island Discs*, BBC Radio 4, 25 October 2013

—, 'National Life Stories: Artist's Lives', oral history, British Library, 1994 sounds.bl.uk/Oral-history/Art

Hutchinson, Mary, 'Playing the Game', *Nation & Athenaeum*, 17 November 1928, 261–62

—, 'Clive Bell', typescript memoir, undated, HRC

Hynes, Samuel, *The Edwardian Turn of Mind*, Princeton, 1968

James, Henry, *The Art of the Novel*, Scribners, 1934

James, Lawrence, *Warrior Race, The British Experience of War from Roman Times to the Present*, Little, Brown, 2001

Jean Cocteau unique et multiple, cocteau.biu-montpellier.fr

Judt, Tony, *Postwar, A History of Europe since 1945*, Penguin, 2005

Kammen, Michael, *The Lively Arts, Gilbert Seldes and the Transformation of Cultural Criticism in the United States*, Oxford, 1997

Kapp, Yvonne, *Time Will Tell*, Verso, 2003

Kato, Akiko, 'The Omega Workshops: Roger Fry's Search for Community', in Gerstein, 71–77

Kelly, Debra, 'Loss and Recuperation, Order and Subversion: Post-War Painting in France 1945–51', *French Cultural Studies* 8, 22 (1997), 53–66

Kessler, Count Harry, *Berlin in Lights, The Diaries of Count Harry Kessler (1918–1937)*, trans. and ed. Charles Kessler, Grove, 1999

Kirstein, Lincoln, 'The State of Modern Painting', *Harper's*, October 1948, 47–52

Klüver, Billy, *A Day with Picasso, Twenty-four photographs by Jean Cocteau*, MIT, 1997

Knegt, Daniel, *Fascism, Liberalism and Europeanism in the Thought of Bertrand de Jouvenel and Alfred Fabre-Luce*, Amsterdam U P, 2017

Knights, Sarah, *Bloomsbury's Outsider*, Bloomsbury, 2015

Kynaston, David, *Austerity Britain, 1945–51*, Walker, 2008

Lambirth, Andrew, *John Armstrong, The Paintings*, Philip Wilson, 2009

Lanchester, Elsa, 'From Hollywood to Paris', *Atlantic Monthly* 161, March 1938, 332–339

Laughton, Bruce, *The Euston Road School: A Study in Objective Painting*, Scolar, 1986

Lawrence, D. H., *Late Essays and Articles*, v2, ed. James T. Boulton, Cambridge, 2004

—, *Letters of D. H. Lawrence, v2, June 1913–October 1916*, ed. George J. Zytaruk and James T. Boulton, Cambridge, 1981

—, *Letters of D. H. Lawrence, v4 March 1924–March 1927*, ed. James T. Boulton and Lindeth Vasey, Cambridge, 1989

Leavis, Q. D., 'Caterpillars of the World Unite!' *Scrutiny*, September 1938, 203–14

Lee, Hermione, *Virginia Woolf*, Knopf, 1997

Lee, Jane, *Derain*, Phaidon, 1990, exh. cat.

Leighten, Patricia, 'The White Peril and *L'Art nègre*: Picasso, Primitivism, and Anticolonialism', *The Art Bulletin* 72, 4 (December 1990), 609–30

Levy, Paul, ed., *The Letters of Lytton Strachey*, Farrar Straus & Giroux, 2005

—, *Moore: G. E. Moore and the Cambridge Apostles*, Holt, Rinehart & Winston, 1979

Light, Alison, *Mrs Woolf and the Servants*, Penguin/Fig Tree, 2007

Lilly, Amy M., '*Three Guineas*, Two Exhibits: Woolf's Politics of Display', *Woolf Studies Annual* 9, 2003, 29–54

Loeb, Janice, 'Surrealism', *Vassar Review*, February 1935, 5–12, 22–25

Louchheim, Aline B., 'Clive Bell Looks at American Art', *New York Times*, 29 January 1950

Lubenow, W. C. *The Cambridge Apostles, 1820–1914: Liberalism, Imagination and Friendship in British Intellectual and Professional Life*, Cambridge, 1998

Luedeking, Leila and Michael Edmonds, *Leonard Woolf, A Bibliography*, Oak Knoll, 1992

Lunn, Arnold, *Memory to Memory*, Hollis & Carter, 1956

Luke, Michael, *David Tennant and the Gargoyle Years*, Weidenfeld & Nicolson, 1991

Macaulay, Rose, *Non-Combatants and Others*, Hodder & Stoughton, 1916

MacCarthy, Desmond, *Memories*, MacGibbon & Kee, 1953

—, 'The Post-Impressionists', *Modernism, an Anthology of Sources and Documents*, ed. Vassiliki Kolocotroni et al., Edinburgh U P, 1998, 174–78

MacDougall, Sarah, *Mark Gertler*, John Murray, 2002

MacGibbon, Jean, *There's the Lighthouse, A Biography of Adrian Stephen*, James & James, 1997

Mackrell, Judith, *Bloomsbury Ballerina*, Weidenfeld & Nicolson, 2008

Mansfield, Katherine, *The Collected Letters of Katherine Mansfield, Vol. 1 1903–1917*, ed. Vincent O'Sullivan and Margaret Scott, OUP/Clarendon, 1984

Margerie, Roland de, *Tous mes Adieux sont Faits,* Mémoires inédits de Roland de Margerie, Edition en 5 volumes préparée par Laure de Margerie-Meslay, McNally-Jackson, 2013

Marler, Regina, ed. *Selected Letters of Vanessa Bell*, Pantheon, 1993

Marsh, Edward, *A Number of People*, Harper, 1939

Marshik, Celia, *British Modernism and Censorship*, Cambridge, 2006

Martin, Kingsley, 'Conchies All', review of *We Did Not Fight, New Statesman & Nation*, 26 October 1935, 602, 604

Mayor, Beatrice, 'Resume of Recorded Talk with Beatrice Mayor, Tuesday September 12, 1967', University of Sussex, SxMs-18/4/23/1/5

McNeillie, Andrew, 'Bloomsbury', *The Cambridge Companion to Virginia Woolf*, ed. Susan Sellers, 2nd edition, Cambridge, 2010, 1–28

Morrell, Lady Ottoline, *Memoirs of Lady Ottoline Morrell, A Study in Friendship 1873–1915*, ed. Robert Gathorne-Hardy, Knopf, 1964

—, *Ottoline at Garsington, Memoirs of Lady Ottoline Morrell 1915–1918*, ed. Robert Gathorne-Hardy, Knopf, 1975

Mortimer, Raymond, 'London Letter', *The Dial*, February 1928, 238–40 repr. S. P. Rosenbaum, ed. *The Bloomsbury Group*, U of Toronto P, 1975, 241–45

—, 'The French Pictures, A Letter to Harriet', *The Hogarth Letters*, introduction by Hermione Lee, U of Georgia P, 1996

Murray, Gilbert, *How Can War Ever Be Right?*, Oxford, 1914

Murray, Nicholas, *Aldous Huxley: An English Intellectual*, Little, Brown, 2002

Murry, John Middleton, 'Art and Philosophy', *Rhythm* 1, Summer 1911, 9–12, available at modjourn.org

Nairn, Ian, and Nikolaus Pevsner, *Sussex, The Buildings of England*, Penguin, 1965

Nicholson, Virginia, *Among the Bohemians, Experiments in Living 1900–1939*, Penguin, 2003

Nicolson, Harold, *The Later Years, 1945–1962, Diaries and Letters*, ed. Nigel Nicolson, Athenaeum, 1968

Nicolson, Nigel, ed., *Vita and Harold, The Letters of Vita Sackville-West and Harold Nicolson*, Putnam's, 1992

North, Michael, *Reading 1922: A Return to the Scene of the Modern*, Oxford, 1999

Overy, Richard, *1939: Countdown to War*, Penguin, 2009

Partridge, Frances, *Hanging On, Diaries 1960–1963*, Flamingo, 1994

—, *Everything to Lose, Diaries 1945–1960*, Little, Brown, 1985

—, *Memories*, Gollancz, 1981

—, *Other People, Diaries September 1963–December 1966*, HarperCollins, 1993

—, *A Pacifist's War*, Hogarth, 1978

Paul, Brenda Dean, *My First Life*, John Long, 1935

Pery, Jenny, *Painter Pilgrim, The Art and Life of Tristram Hillier*, Royal Academy of Arts, 2008

Perry, Gill, 'Women Painting Women: Gender, Modernism and "Feminine" Art c.1910–c.1930', *Rethinking Art Between the Wars: New Perspectives in Art History*, ed. Hans Dam Christensen, Øystein Hjort and Niels Marup Jensen, Museum Tusculanum, 2000, 47–72

Piper, Myfanwy, 'Back in the Thirties', *Art and Literature* 7, 1965, 136–57

Pound, Ezra, 'Small Magazines', *The English Journal* 19.9 (1930), 689–704

Pryce-Jones, David, ed., *Cyril Connolly, Journal and Memoir*, Collins, 1983

Read, Herbert, 'Clive Bell', *The British Journal of Aesthetics* 5, 2, 1965, 107–110

—, 'English Art', *Burlington Magazine*, December 1933, 242+

—, 'The War as Seen by British Artists', *Britain at War*, ed. Monroe Wheeler, MoMA, 1941, 11–12, Exh. cat.

Reed, Christopher, 'Introduction', in Gerstein, 11-15

—, ed., *The Roger Fry Reader*, Chicago, 1996

—, 'Bloomsbury Bashing: Homophobia and the Politics of Criticism in the Eighties', in *Queer Bloomsbury*, edited by Brenda Helt and Madelyn Detloff, Edinburgh U P, 2016, 36–63

—, *Bloomsbury Rooms, Modernism, Subculture, and Domesticity*, Yale, 2004

Reid, Panthea, *Art and Affection, a Life of Virginia Woolf*, Oxford, 1996

[Reitlinger, Gerald] 'A Day Trip to the Sea Coast of Bohemia', *Drawing & Design*, February 1928

Richards, I. A., *Principles of Literary Criticism*, 1924, Routledge and Kegan Paul, 1976

Richardson, John, *A Life of Picasso, Vol. II, The Painter of Modern Life, 1907–1917*, Random House, 1996

—, *A Life of Picasso, Vol. III, The Triumphant Years, 1917–1932*, Knopf, 2007

—, *The Sorcerer's Apprentice, Picasso, Provence, and Douglas Cooper*, Knopf, 1999

—, 'Portraits of a Marriage', *Vanity Fair*, December 2007. Available at www.vanityfair.com/news/2007/12/picassos-wife-200712

Riding, Alan, *And the Show Went On: Cultural Life in Nazi-Occupied Paris*, Duckworth, 2011

Roche, Paul, *With Duncan Grant in Southern Turkey*, Honeyglen, 1982

Roe, Sue, *In Montmartre: Picasso, Matisse and Modernism in Paris 1900–1910*, Penguin, 2016

Rose, Sam, 'The Visual Arts in the BBC's "The Listener"', *Burlington Magazine*, September 2013, 606–611

Rose, William Kent, ed., *Letters of Wyndham Lewis*, Methuen, 1963

Rosenbaum, S. P., ed., *The Bloomsbury Group, A Collection of Memoirs, Commentary and Criticism*, Toronto, 1975

—, 'The First Book of Bloomsbury', *Twentieth Century Literature* 30, 4, Winter 1984, 388–403

Rothenstein, John, *Modern English Painters: Lewis to Moore*, Macmillan, 1956

—, *Brave Day, Hideous Night, Autobiography 1939–1965*, Holt, Rinehart & Winston, 1966

Ruskin, John, *The Stones of Venice* VI (1851), Cosimo Classics, 2007

Russell, Emily, ed., *A Constant Heart, The War Diaries of Maud Russell 1938–1945*, Dovecote, 2017

Russell, John, 'Clive Bell', *Encounter*, December 1949, 48–49

Rutter, Frank, *Art in My Time*, Rich & Cowan, 1933

—, *Revolution in Art*, Art News, 1910

Rye, Jane, *Adrian Heath*, Lund Humphries, 2012

Scholes, Robert, and Clifford Wulfman, *Modernism in the Magazines, An Introduction*, Yale, 2010

Seldes, Gilbert, [1924] *The 7 Lively Arts*, Sagamore, 1957

Sexton, James, *Selected Letters of Aldous Huxley*, Ivan R. Dee, 2007

Seymour, Miranda, *Ottoline Morrell, Life on the Grand Scale*, Hodder & Stoughton, 1992

Seymour-Jones, Carole, *Painted Shadow*, Doubleday, 2002

Sheean, Vincent, '50,000 Jailed in Austria in 3½ Months of Terror Leaving Nazis Supreme', *New York Herald Tribune*, 5 July 1938, 1, 7

Shone, Richard, 'Blast from the past: the vorticist moment', *Guardian*, 5 June 2015

—, *Bloomsbury Portraits*, Phaidon, 1993

—, *The Art of Bloomsbury: Roger Fry, Vanessa Bell and Duncan Grant*, Princeton, 1999, exh. cat.

—, 'Official Guide to the House and Garden', *Charleston Past and Present*, ed. Quentin Bell et al., Harcourt, 1987

—, 'Pictures at Charleston: Past and Present', *A Cézanne in the Hedge and Other Memories of Bloomsbury and Charleston*, ed. Hugh Lee, Chicago, 1993, 150–54

Silver, Kenneth E., *Esprit de Corps: The Art of the Parisian Avant-Garde and the First World War, 1914–1925*, Princeton, 1989

Sitwell, Osbert, *Laughter in the Next Room*, Little, Brown, 1948

Skidelsky, Robert, *John Maynard Keynes, Vol. 1 Hopes Betrayed, 1883–1920*, Viking Penguin, 1983

—, *John Maynard Keynes, Vol. 2 The Economist as Savior 1920–1937*, Viking Penguin, 1992

Smith, Adrian, *The* New Statesman: *Portrait of a Political Weekly, 1913–1931*, Frank Cass, 1996

Smith, Grover, ed., *Letters of Aldous Huxley*, Harper & Row, 1969

Smith, Martin Ferguson and Helen Walasek, 'Clive Bell's Memoir of Annie Raven Hill', *English Studies*, 2019, 1–33

Soby, James Thrall, 'Does Our Art Impress Europe?', *Saturday Review*, 6 August 1949, 142–48

Southworth, Helen, 'The Bloomsbury Group and the Book Arts', *The Cambridge Companion to the Bloomsbury Group*, ed. Victoria Rosner, Cambridge, 2014, 144–61

Spalding, Frances, *Roger Fry, Art and Life*, U of California P, 1980

—, *Vanessa Bell*, Ticknor & Fields, 1983

—, *Duncan Grant*, Chatto, 1997

—, *The Tate, A History*, Tate, 1998

—, *Virginia Woolf, Art, Life and Vision*, National Portrait Gallery, 2014, exh. cat.

Spater, George and Ian Parsons, *A Marriage of True Minds*, Harcourt, 1977

Spender, Stephen, *World within World, The Autobiography of Stephen Spender*, U of California P, 1966

Spotts, Frederic, ed., *Letters of Leonard Woolf*, Harcourt, 1989

Spurling, Hilary, *The Unknown Matisse, A Life of Henri Matisse: The Early Years, 1869–1908*, Knopf, 2000,

—, *Matisse the Master, A Life of Henri Matisse, The Conquest of Colour, 1909–1954*, Knopf, 2005

Stansky, Peter, *On or About December 1910, Early Bloomsbury and Its Intimate World*, Harvard, 1996

Stansky, Peter and William Abrahams, *Julian Bell: From Bloomsbury to the Spanish Civil War*, Stanford U P, 2012

Steiner, George, *Language and Silence, Essays 1958–1966*, Penguin, 1969

[Stephen, Julian Thoby], *Compulsory Chapel*, 1904

Strachey, Barbara, *Remarkable Relations: The Story of the Pearsall Smith Family*, Gollancz, 1981

Sutton, Denys, ed., *Letters of Roger Fry*, Random House, 1972

Taddeo, Julie, 'Plato's Apostles: Edwardian Cambridge and the "New Style of Love"', *Journal of the History of Sexuality* 8, 2, 1997, 196–228

Taylor, D. J. *Bright Young People: The Lost Generation of London's Jazz Age*, Farrar Straus, 2007

Tedeschi, Richard, ed., *Selected Letters of André Gide and Dorothy Bussy*, Oxford, 1983

Tickner, Lisa, 'The Popular Culture of *Kermesse*: Lewis, Painting, and Performance 1912–13', *Modernism/modernity* 4, 2, 1997, 67–120

Torgovnick, Marianna, *Gone Primitive: Savage Intellects, Modern Lives*, Chicago, 1990

Trombley, Stephen, *'All that Summer She was Mad'*, *Virginia Woolf: Female Victim of Male Medicine*, Continuum, 1982

Turnbaugh, Douglas Blair, *Duncan Grant and the Bloomsbury Group*, Bloomsbury, 1987

Van Tuyl, Jocelyn, *André Gide and the Second World War: A Novelist's Occupation*, SUNY, 2006

Vaux Halliday, Nigel, *More than a Bookshop: Zwemmer's and Art in the 20th century*, Philip Wilson, 1991

Wallis, Nevile, 'Clive Bell', *Spectator*, 25 September 1964, 15

Waterlow, Sydney, Holograph Diary April 1907–April 1912, Berg

Weber, Nicholas Fox, *Patron Saints: Five Rebels who Opened America to a New Art 1928–1943*, Knopf, 1992

Wilcox, Denys, *The London Group 1913–1939*, Scolar, 1995

Wilenski, R. H. *The Modern Movement in Art*, Faber & Gwyer, 1927

Willis, J. H. *Leonard and Virginia Woolf as Publishers, The Hogarth Press 1917–1941*, U P of Virginia, 1992

Wilson, Duncan, *Leonard Woolf, A Political Biography*, St. Martin's, 1978

Woods, S. John, 'Time to forget ourselves', *Axis* 6, Summer 1936, 19–21

Woolf, Leonard, *An Autobiography* vol. 1 1880–1911 (*Sowing, Growing*); vol. 2 1911–1969 (*Beginning Again*; *Downhill All the Way*, *The Journey Not the Arrival Matters*), Oxford, 1980

—, *Quack, Quack!*, Hogarth, 1935

—, [1914] *The Wise Virgins, A Story of Words, Opinions and a Few Emotions*, Hogarth, 1979

Woolf, Virginia, 'Dialogue upon a Hill', *The Complete Shorter Fiction*, ed. Susan K. Dick, Harcourt, 1989

—, *Congenial Spirits, The Selected Letters of Virginia Woolf*, ed. Joanne Trautmann Banks, Harcourt, 1989

—, *The Diary of Virginia Woolf*, ed. Anne Olivier Bell, 5 volumes, Hogarth, 1977–84

—, *The Letters of Virginia Woolf*, ed. Nigel Nicolson and Joanne Trautmann Banks, 6 volumes, Hogarth, 1975–1980

—, 'Mr. Bennett and Mrs. Brown', *Collected Essays* 1, Harcourt, 1967, 319–37

—, 'Old Bloomsbury', *Moments of Being*, Harcourt, 1985, 181–201

—, *Orlando, A Biography* (1928), Harcourt, 1956

—, *A Passionate Apprentice: The Early Journals 1897–1909*, ed. Mitchell A. Leaska, Harcourt, 1990

—, 'Reminiscences', *Moments of Being*, Harcourt, 1985, 28–59

—, [1941] *Roger Fry*, ed. Diane F. Gillespie, Blackwell/Shakespeare Head, 1995

—, 'A Sketch of the Past', *Moments of Being*, Harcourt, 1985, 64–159

—, 'Thoughts on Peace in an Air Raid', *The Death of the Moth and Other Essays*, Hogarth, 1942, 154–57

—, *Three Guineas* (1938), Hogarth, 1952

—, *To the Lighthouse* (1927), Harcourt, 2005

—, *The Voyage Out* (1915), Harcourt, 1948

Wright, Bertha, *Bad Aunt Bertha, The Memoirs of Bertha Wright*, Biograph, 2010

Archives and Collections

BBC BBC Written Archives Centre

Berg The Henry W. and Albert A. Berg Collection of English and American Literature, The New York Public Library, Astor, Lenox and Tilden Foundations

Bodleian Gilbert Murray Papers, Bodleian Libraries

BL British Library

C-W CB/LS correspondence in the Collection of Annette Campbell-White (Copies in BL)

Delaware MS99 Clive Bell Letters to Gilbert Seldes, Special Collections, University of Delaware Library, Newark, Delaware

Getty Douglas Cooper Papers, Getty Research Institute

HRC Harry Ransom Center, University of Texas at Austin

KCC Modern Archives Centre, King's College, Cambridge Charleston Papers; Papers of Frances Catherine Partridge

Lilly Lilly Library, Indiana University MacCarthy Mss.

LSE London School of Economics

Mellon GB3010 Benedict Nicolson Archive, The Paul Mellon Centre for Studies in British Art, London UK

MoMA The Museum of Modern Art Archives, New York Margaret Scolari Barr Papers

Morgan Morgan Library and Museum, New York Vanessa Bell collection of autograph letters

NGI National Gallery of Ireland

Newberry	Newberry Library, Chicago
Princeton	Rare Books and Special Collections, Princeton University Library
Rockefeller	John D. Rockefeller 3rd Papers, Rockefeller Archive Center
Syracuse	Special Collections Research Center, Syracuse University Libraries
Sx	University of Sussex Special Collections
TCT	The Charleston Trust
TGA	Tate Library and Archive
Trinity	Trinity College, Cambridge
	Papers of Arthur Clive Heward Bell
TSE	T. S. Eliot Estate
Trotter	Bell and Hony Family Papers in possession of Graeme Trotter
UoR	University of Reading, Special Collections
	Chatto & Windus Archives
	Hogarth Press Archives MS 2750
UVa	Albert and Shirley Small Special Collections Library, University of Virginia
	Papers of Douglas H. Gordon

Index

Acknowledgements

This project began with occasional glances during the past twenty or so years towards the shelves in my office, where I noted that among my far too many books on Virginia Woolf and Bloomsbury there was, oddly, no biography of Clive Bell. One announced early in the new century as forthcoming never came forth. A conversation in 2013 with Frances Spalding led to my meeting Anne Olivier Bell, who encouraged me to write her father-in-law's biography. I am deeply grateful to the late Mrs Bell, whose generosity and hospitality first gave me the confidence to attempt this book. Her son, Julian Bell, has been a stalwart and patient interlocutor throughout the years it has taken to get to this point, and I owe him a great deal. I am also grateful to Julian's two sisters, Virginia Nicholson and Cressida Bell, for their encouragement of my work on their grandfather and in particular to Virginia for providing photographs from her mother's albums. My thanks, too, to Richard Shone for an important early meeting, and for his friendly and helpful responses to all my queries.

Henrietta Garnett gave me encouragement at a crucial stage, and continued to provide wise advice in witty letters and emails. I am sad that she did not live to read this book. I am deeply grateful to her daughter, Sophie Partridge, for granting me permission to quote from unpublished letters of her great-grandparents, Vanessa Bell and Duncan Grant.

I thank Andrew McNeillie for a critical lunch on Charlotte Street as I was pondering how to approach Bell, and for his continued advice and friendship. He, Frances Spalding, Christopher Reed, and Peter

Stansky have continually encouraged my efforts, provided invaluable advice, feedback, and recommendation letters, as well as friendship. Jane Garrity has willingly shared her scholarship on Mary Hutchinson, and I am grateful for her friendship and generosity.

In its earliest stages, this book benefited from the counsel of Brenda S. Helt, who gave me plentiful excellent advice. I am very grateful for all she did.

Faye Hammill and Beth Rigel Daugherty both took the time to read an early draft, providing me with insights and recommendations which ensure the remaining faults are entirely my own.

Claire Davison graciously tried to save me from embarrassing errors in translations from the French, and provided valuable insights along the way. My thanks also to Laure Meslay for performing a similar service with respect to the writings of her grandfather, Roland de Margerie, and for her permission to quote from his letters and memoirs.

My thanks to Rosa Bozhkov, who gave me time-saving assistance when gathering Clive Bell's writings.

Annette Campbell-White gave permission to the British Library for me to read copies of letters from Clive Bell to Lytton Strachey in her possession, for which I am most grateful. My thanks to Paul Levy for alerting me to them, and for his friendly facilitating of permissions. I also wish to thank Sarah Baxter at the Society of Authors for her assistance with permissions and her efforts to explain the arcana of UK copyright law to me.

Graeme Trotter, Clive Bell's great-nephew, and his wife, Anne, opened their home to me in Edinburgh, and generously allowed me to peruse the Bell family photograph albums, the letters of Henry Hony, and the diary of Dorothy (Bell) Hony in their possession. For this, and also for their willingness to allow me to reproduce some of the photographs and to quote from the letters and diary, I am deeply grateful. My thanks, also, to Graeme's mother, Henrietta Trotter, and to her sister Dinah Hony, Bell's nieces, for sharing their memories and responding to questions. I am particularly grateful to Henrietta Trotter for showing me the copies of his books which Clive Bell inscribed to her.

Nicholas Hutchinson, Mary Hutchinson's grandson, has been unfailingly generous and helpful, and I am very grateful for his permission to quote from his grandmother's letters and to reproduce a photograph of her. My thanks, also, to his late father, Jeremy, Lord Hutchinson, who gave me encouragement at an early stage.

Cassie Dippo patiently answered an excessive number of emails asking about her mother, Janice Loeb. I am deeply grateful for her generosity in allowing me to quote from her mother's letters and for providing a photograph of her.

I wish particularly to thank the following archivists and librarians who provided the indispensable assistance that is the hallmark of their profession:

Patricia McGuire, Modern Archives Centre of King's College, Cambridge, especially for her amused tolerance of my interminable badgering about photography, as well as for her thoughtfulness in providing materials; Peter Monteith at KCC, for his friendly patience at the desk; Charlotte Brunskill at Mellon for so willingly providing what I could not travel to London to see for myself; Fiona Courage, Karen Watson, and Rose Lock at The Keep for making the transition from the familiar University of Sussex environment to the Monks House Papers' new home so painless; Jonathan Smith at the Wren Library, Trinity College, Cambridge, whose chance question led to my reading the letters from Beatrice Mayor to Clive Bell; Darren Clarke, Rausing Head of Collections, Research and Exhibitions, The Charleston Trust, who allowed me to spend two absorbing days in Clive Bell's Library at Charleston Farmhouse; Dean M. Rogers, Special Collections, Vassar College, for whom no request ever seemed too much trouble; Cynthia Cathcart at the Condé Nast archive, who not only helped me track down some of Clive Bell's publications, but allowed me to use the library at One World Trade, as well as putting me in touch with her counterparts in London.

My heartfelt thanks to Michael Fishwick and Lauren Whybrow at Bloomsbury for making this book happen.

For their invaluable and cheerful assistance throughout this project, I thank the staff of the Birnbaum and Mortola Libraries at Pace University, especially Amernel Denton, Eloise Flood, Xiaohong (Sheila) Hu (who always went above and beyond what was asked), Alicia Joseph-Marino, Greg Murphy, Brian A. Moses, and Chloe Pinera.

I am very grateful to the staff at Pace University who facilitated and supported this project administratively: Dean Nira Herrmann; Arlene M. Bocskocsky; Dominick Bumbaco; Diane Bynum; Clarissa Cyclich;

Diane DeMeo; Sally Dickerson; Katherine Disher; Maria Iacullo-Bird; Inita Mix; Cathy Pagano; Jessica Paredes; Matt Renna; Uday Sukhatme; Adelia Williams.

I also wish to thank my colleagues in the English Department at Pace University for their companionship and support, especially the chair, Erica Johnson.

My thanks to the National Endowment for the Humanities for a 2017 Fellowship enabling me to take a semester away from teaching responsibilities.

My mother, Shirley Lord, has supported this project from the beginning, for which I am deeply grateful. My thanks, too, to my friends Gerry Bunyan, Helane Levine-Keating, Alexandra Truitt, Jerry Marshall, Susanna and Daniel Bozhkov, Fred and Nancy Weber, Nancy Sall and David Brogno, each of whom reminded me there is a world beyond the book. Louise Tucker's London flat provided a home away from home during several research trips, and I am grateful, too, for her friendship and advice.

The time necessary for archival research and for writing has made me absent from my family far more than I would have wished, and I cannot sufficiently thank my children, Xavier and Miranda, and my wife, Evelyn (who also read the draft), for always making it possible for me to do the work. I dedicate this book to them, with great love.

My profound thanks to all who responded so generously to my queries and requests:

Judith Allen; Jonathan Anderson; Charles Andrews; Elaine Andrews (Morley College); Sophie Annoepel-Cabrignac (Picasso Archives); Ria Banerjee; Ariane Bankes; Stephen Barkway; Deborah Bauder (Syracuse U Libraries); Barbara Anne Beaucar (Barnes Foundation); Salvatore Bellavia (King's College London Archives); Elizabeth Berkowitz; Shelagh Bevan (Morgan Library); Lesley Blume; Tony Bradshaw; David Bradshaw; Ramses van Bragt (Library & Archives, RKD– Netherlands Institute for Art History); Peter Brown; Sarah Funke Butler; Mary Ann Caws; Delphine Chabaille; Emma Chambers (Tate); Anna Chovanec (Special Collections Research Center, Syracuse U Libraries); Jonathan Clark; Stuart N. Clarke; Lisa Cole (Tate); Patrick Collier; Danni Corfield (UoR); Peter Corina (Kroch Library, Cornell U); Judith Curthoys; Kristin Czarnecki; Mary Jo Darrah; Marjorie

Delabarre (IMEC); Marysa Demoor; David Eberly; Diana Edkins (Art Resource); Stephanie Fletcher (Art Inst. of Chicago); M. Flynn (London Metropolitan Archives); Nancy Fulford (T. S. Eliot Estate); Sandra Inskeep-Fox; Ilda François (Paul Rosenberg Archives); Gretchen Holbrook Gerzina; Isaac Gewirtz (Berg); Samantha Gilchrist (U of Glasgow); Adrian Glew (Tate); Beverly Glover; Georgia Glover (David Higham Associates); Diane F. Gillespie; Jane Goldman; Alice Gregory; Christopher Griffin (Tate); Cheryl Gunselman (Washington State U Libraries); Sarah M. Hall; Leslie K. Hankins; Colin Harris (Bodleian); Charles Harrowell (Senate House Library, U of London); Mark William Cory Hassall; Jean Hayes; William Hetherington (Honorary Archivist, Peace Pledge Union); Anna-Claire Hillier; Marvin Hoshino; Oliver House (Bodleian Libraries); Alison Huftalen (Toledo Museum of Art); Yuko Ito; Jackie Jones; Rachel Klingberg; Emily Kopley; Andrea Kouklanakis (Bard High School Early College); Karen V. Kukil (Smith College); David Kuzma (Rutgers U Library); Michael Lackey; Gaby Laing (U of Glasgow Archive Services); Andrew Lambirth; Bjorn Larsson; Joanna Lee (Curtis Brown); Karen Levenback; Sarah Lindberg (Bonhams); Gill Lowe; Hannah Lowery (Special Collections, U of Bristol); Donal Maguire (NGI); Celia Marshik; Sir Michael St John-McAlister (British Library); Josh McKeon (Berg); Eleanor McNees; Hayley Mercer (Schlesinger Library, Radcliffe College); Frieda Midgley (Kettles Yard); Sarah McElroy Mitchell (Lilly Library); Sarah McMahon (Penguin Random House); Louise Morgan (NGI); Al Morley (Cambridge Arts Theatre); Vara Neverow; Vanessa Nicolson; Liesl Olsen (Newberry Library); Sophie Orpen (Henry Moore Fdn); Laura Payne (Bennington College); Jenny Pery; Julian Pooley (Surrey History Centre); Emily Rafferty (Cone Archives, Baltimore Museum of Art); Chris Rawlings (British Library); Simon Rendall; Jon Richardson; Stéphanie Rivoire (Pompidou Ctr); Carl Rollyson; Victoria Rosner; Clare Russell (Marlborough College Archives); Emily Russell; Sonita Sarker; Mike Saunders (National Library of Scotland); Witold Szczyglowski (Working Men's College); Ruth Seager; Susan Sellers; Curtis Small (U of Delaware); Martin Ferguson Smith; Carmen Königsreuther Socknat (Victoria U Libraries); Helen Southworth; Alice Staveley; Libby Stubbs (Westminster School); David Taylor; Elisabeth Thomas (MoMA); Anna Towlson (LSE); Caroline Trotter; Alkestius Tsilika (National Trust); Claire Vasquez (St. Louis Art Museum); Melinda Wallington (River

Campus Libraries, U of Rochester); Rick Watson (HRC); Christian White; Penny White (Small Library, U of Virginia); Cherry Dunham Williams (Lilly Library); Harriet Wilson (Condé Nast Publications); Rishona Zimring.

My thanks also to the staffs of the Art & Architecture Room, NYPL, the Frick Art Reference Library, and the Thomas J. Watson Library, Metropolitan Museum of Art, New York.

Permissions for unpublished writings

Julian Bell, and the Society of Authors as Representatives of the Estate of Clive Bell

Julian Bell, and the Society of Authors as Representatives of the Estate of Julian Heward Bell

Charles Hillman for Louisa Blaikie Barnes

Amy Jenkins for Jane Bussy

Rachel Cole for Roger Fry

Michael Harari for Hananiah Harari

Jonathan Clark for Ivon Hitchens

The Estate of Jeremy Hutchinson for Mary Hutchinson

Curtis Brown for Colin MacInnes © Colin MacInnes 1956

Richard Armstrong for Benita Jaeger

London School of Economics for George Lansbury

Charles MacCarthy for Desmond and Molly MacCarthy

The Surrey History Centre for Kitty Maxse to Susan Lushington (SHC ref. 7854/4/4/)

Laure de Margerie-Meslay for Roland de Margerie

Angela Derville for Bertha Penrose

Image Credits

Page 295 © New York Times
Page 321 © Cassie Dippo
Pages 386, 434, 441 © Estate of Anne Olivier Bell
Page 399 © Baltimore Sun
Page 436 © Barbara Bagenal/Tate

A Note on the Type

The text of this book is set Adobe Garamond. It is one of several versions of Garamond based on the designs of Claude Garamond. It is thought that Garamond based his font on Bembo, cut in 1495 by Francesco Griffo in collaboration with the Italian printer Aldus Manutius. Garamond types were first used in books printed in Paris around 1532. Many of the present-day versions of this type are based on the *Typi Academiae* of Jean Jannon cut in Sedan in 1615.

Claude Garamond was born in Paris in 1480. He learned how to cut type from his father and by the age of fifteen he was able to fashion steel punches the size of a pica with great precision. At the age of sixty he was commissioned by King Francis I to design a Greek alphabet, and for this he was given the honourable title of royal type founder. He died in 1561.